The Data Warehouse Lifecycle Toolkit

Second Edition

The Data Warehouse
Lifecycle Toolkit

Second Edition

Ralph Kimball
Margy Ross
Warren Thornthwaite
Joy Mundy
Bob Becker

Wiley Publishing, Inc.

The Data Warehouse Lifecycle Toolkit, Second Edition

Published by
Wiley Publishing, Inc.
10475 Crosspoint Boulevard
Indianapolis, IN 46256
www.wiley.com

Copyright © 2008 by Ralph Kimball, Margy Ross, Warren Thornthwaite, Joy Mundy and Bob Becker

Published by Wiley Publishing, Inc., Indianapolis, Indiana

Published simultaneously in Canada

ISBN: 978-0-470-14977-5

Manufactured in the United States of America

10 9 8 7

For general information on our other products and services or to obtain technical support, please contact our Customer Care Department within the U.S. at (800) 762-2974, outside the U.S. at (317) 572-3993 or fax (317) 572-4002.

Library of Congress Cataloging-in-Publication Data:

The data warehouse lifecycle toolkit / Ralph Kimball... [et al.]. -- 2nd ed.
  p. cm.
 Includes index.
 ISBN 978-0-470-14977-5 (paper/website)
1. Data warehousing. I. Kimball, Ralph.
 QA76.9.D37D38 2007
 005.74--dc22

                    2007040691

About the Authors

The authors' professional careers have followed remarkably similar paths. Each author has focused on data warehousing and business intelligence (DW/BI) consulting and education for more than fifteen years. Most worked together at Metaphor Computer Systems, a pioneering decision support vendor, in the 1980s. All the authors are members of the Kimball Group and teach for Kimball University. They contribute regularly to *Intelligent Enterprise* magazine and other industry publications; most have previously written books in the *Toolkit* series.

Ralph Kimball founded the Kimball Group. Since the mid 1980s, he has been the DW/BI industry's thought leader on the dimensional approach and trained more than 10,000 IT professionals. Ralph has his Ph.D. in Electrical Engineering from Stanford University.

Margy Ross is President of the Kimball Group. She has focused exclusively on DW/BI since 1982 with an emphasis on business requirements analysis and dimensional modeling. Margy graduated with a BS in Industrial Engineering from Northwestern University.

Warren Thornthwaite began his DW/BI career in 1980. After managing Metaphor's consulting organization, he worked for Stanford University and WebTV. Warren holds a BA in Communications Studies from the University of Michigan and an MBA from the University of Pennsylvania's Wharton School.

Joy Mundy has focused on DW/BI systems since 1992 with stints at Stanford, Web TV, and Microsoft's SQL Server product development organization. Joy graduated from Tufts University with a BA in Economics, and from Stanford University with an MS in Engineering Economic Systems.

Bob Becker has helped clients across a variety of industries with their DW/BI challenges and solutions since 1989, including extensive work with health care organizations. Bob has a BSB in Marketing from the University of Minnesota's School of Business.

Credits

Executive Editor
Robert Elliott

Development Editor
Sara Shlaer

Production Editor
Debra Banninger

Copy Editor
Kim Cofer

Editorial Manager
Mary Beth Wakefield

Production Manager
Tim Tate

Vice President and Executive Group Publisher
Richard Swadley

Vice President and Executive Publisher
Joseph B. Wikert

Project Coordinator, Cover
Lynsey Osborn

Proofreader
Nancy Carrasco

Indexer
Melanie Belkin

Anniversary Logo Design
Richard Pacifico

Cover Image
© Steve Allen/Getty Images

Acknowledgments

First, thanks to our students, clients, readers, and former colleagues for supporting, teaching, and influencing us. One of the authors recently received a fortune cookie that read, "You learn most when teaching others." We couldn't agree more. Our Kimball University students have pushed us to provide precise, specific guidance and kept us on our toes with their questions. Similarly, the challenges faced by our Kimball Group consulting clients have become our challenges, and have kept us grounded in reality. Finally, ex-colleagues have contributed to our thinking about the concepts in this book, including Laura Reeves who participated as a co-author of the first edition of the *Lifecycle Toolkit*. Beginning with our associates from the early days at Metaphor, through Red Brick, Stanford University, DecisionWorks Consulting, InfoDynamics, and Microsoft, we've learned lots from each of you.

Thanks to the Wiley team for making this book a reality. Bob Elliott's subtle, yet persistent prodding got the project off the ground. Sara Shlaer did a wonderful job editing our text with an incredible amount of patience, tenacity, and attention to detail. Deb Banninger and the behind-the-scenes folks worked tirelessly to deliver a quality product. We've enjoyed working with all of you.

Finally, thanks to our spouses, partners, and children for putting up with the demands of our careers, while supporting us unconditionally. You've suffered through late nights and missed vacations alongside us. Thanks to Julie Kimball, Sara Kimball Smith, and Brian Kimball, Scott and Katie Ross, Elizabeth Wright, Tony Navarrete, and Pam, Elisa, and Jenna Becker. We couldn't have done it without you!

Contents at a Glance

Contents

Introduction

Remarkable transformations have occurred in the nine years since the first edition of *The Data Warehouse Lifecycle Toolkit* was published. The data warehouse industry has reached full maturity and acceptance across the business world. Hardware and software have made mind boggling advances in these nine years. We have replaced "gigabytes" with "terabytes" in all our conversations. Yet somehow the data warehousing task has remained fundamentally unchanged.

Many of you have thousands of data warehouse users in your organizations. You have welcomed operational decision makers to the ranks of data warehouse users to accompany the original cadres of marketing and finance users. In fact, operational urgencies are the hottest aspects of data warehousing, with everybody insisting that they need the data in "real time." As our data warehouses have become more important and more visible, we have been hammered by privacy, security, and compliance requirements that are non-negotiable. Business users are waking up to the value of high quality data in much the same way that conventional manufacturing has embraced the management of quality. Finally, and perhaps most important, we have a new name for what we do that reflects our true purpose. It is *business intelligence*. To emphasize that point, in most places in this book we refer to the overall system you are building as the *DW/BI system*.

The shift to business intelligence puts initiative in the hands of business users, not IT. But at the same time this shift puts into perfect focus the mission of the data warehouse: It is the necessary platform for business intelligence. The data warehouse does the hard work of wrangling the data out of the source systems, cleaning it, and organizing it so that normal business users can understand it. Of course we strive for world class business intelligence, but world class business intelligence is only possible if you have a world class data warehouse. And conversely, a data warehouse without business intelligence will fail spectacularly.

This book is a relentlessly practical field guide for designers, managers, and owners of the DW/BI system. We have tried to distinguish this book from other DW/BI books by making the content very concrete and actionable. It's okay to be dazzled by the landscape but we want you to make it all the way to the finish line. This book describes a coherent framework that goes all the way from the original scoping of an overall enterprise DW/BI system, through the detailed steps of developing and deploying, to the final steps of planning the next phases.

There are tens of thousands of functioning data warehouse installations across the world. Many DW/BI owners have developed a complete lifecycle perspective. Probably the biggest insight that comes from this perspective is that each DW/BI system is continuously evolving and dynamic. It cannot be static. It never stops transforming. New business requirements arise. New managers and executives place unexpected demands on the system. New data sources become available. At the very least, the DW/BI system needs to evolve as fast as the surrounding organization evolves. Stable organizations will place modest demands on the system to evolve. Dynamic, turbulent organizations will make the task more challenging.

Given this churning, evolving nature of the DW/BI system, we need design techniques that are flexible and adaptable. We need to be half DBA and half MBA. We need to opportunistically hook together little pieces from individual business processes into larger pieces, making enterprise data warehouses. And we need our changes to the system always to be graceful. A graceful change is one that doesn't invalidate previous data or previous applications.

How this Book is Organized

This book has two deep underlying themes. The first is the Kimball Lifecycle approach. You might ask "What makes the Kimball Lifecycle different from any other methodology?" The shortest answer is that we build DW/BI systems by starting with the business users and figuring out what they need to do their jobs. Then, with those results in mind, we systematically work backward through the reports, applications, databases, and software, finally arriving at the most physical layers of the implementation. This contrasts strongly with technology driven approaches, which proceed in the opposite direction. In the early days of the 1990s, some IT shops didn't know what to make of our business and user oriented approach. But as we publish this book in 2008, the very name "business intelligence" says it all. The user and the business drive the data warehouse.

The second theme is the "bus architecture." We will show you how to build a succession of individual business process iterations that will, in time, create an enterprise DW/BI system. In this book, you will see a heavy reliance on dimensional modeling as a way to present data to business users. We recommend this approach for only one reason: It is demonstrably the best organization of data to meet the business user's desires for simplicity and high query performance. We thank you in advance for following the dimensional approach that is developed in this book. In the end, you are free to present data to users in any way you think appropriate. But we urge you to constantly revisit the fundamental goal of user satisfaction. We have learned to be humble in the presence of business users. It's not our opinion that matters; it's theirs.

This book captures these perspectives. We will give you actionable skills and actionable tools for getting your job done. Along the way, we hope to give you the perspective and judgment we have accumulated in building DW/BI systems since 1982.

Who Should Read this Book

The primary reader of this book should be a designer or a manager who really needs to get about the business of building and managing a "data warehouse that is a platform for business intelligence applications." Because that is quite a mouthful, we have consistently referred to this overall system with the name "DW/BI" to drive home the point that you are responsible for getting the data all the way from the original source systems to the business users' screens.

Although the book contains some introductory material, we think the book will be of most use to an IT professional who has already had some exposure to data warehousing. An appropriate next book, which would concentrate more deeply on dimensional modeling, would be *The Data Warehouse Toolkit, Second Edition*, by Ralph Kimball and Margy Ross, published in 2002.

You may have developed your experience and formed your opinions by designing and delivering a real data warehouse. That is the best background of all! There is no substitute for having had the responsibility of delivering an effective DW/BI system. We the authors have all had the humbling experience of presenting our "baby" to a crowd of demanding business users. It is sometimes hard to accept the reality that most users have real jobs that don't involve technology. They may not even like technology particularly. But business users will use our technology if it is easy to use and provides obvious value.

This book is rather technical. The discussion of design techniques and architectures will undoubtedly introduce terminology that you have not encountered. We have combed this book carefully to make sure that the more technical topics are ones we think you must understand. We have tried not to get bogged down in detail for its own sake. There is a glossary of DW/BI terms at the back of the book that will briefly explain the most insidious terms that we all have to live with.

Although we hope you read this book in its entirety to understand the complete Kimball Lifecycle, we highlight the target audience at the start of each chapter, so you can best judge what to read carefully, and what to skim. Hopefully, your experiences and opinions will give you your own personal framework on which to hang all these ideas. After reading Chapter 1, you will see that there are three parallel threads that must be pursued in building a DW/BI system: the technology, the data, and the business intelligence applications. We even show these three threads in the "You Are Here" diagrams at the beginning of each chapter. Although these threads clearly affect each other, they should be developed in parallel and asynchronously.

However, because a book is necessarily a linear thing, we have had to present the steps in the Kimball Lifecycle as if they occur in just one fixed order. Hopefully as you work through the book, you will visualize the more realistic and complex real world relationships among the various steps. After reading this book, please return eventually to each individual chapter and re-read it very carefully when your project gets to that particular phase. That is why we called it the *Lifecycle Toolkit*.

How this Book Differs from the First Edition

This second edition of the *Lifecycle Toolkit* is significantly updated and reorganized compared to the first edition. The first three chapters set you up for understanding the complete Kimball Lifecycle process and for making sure your effort has satisfied the requirements for moving forward. We then worked very hard to make the complex discussion of architectures more actionable and more obviously tied to the sequence of the Kimball Lifecycle. In Chapter 4 we carefully describe the complete technical architecture of the DW/BI system, from original data extraction to the final painting of results on the business users' screens. In Chapter 5 we show you how to create specific plans for this technical architecture and select products. Then in Chapters 6 through 12 we systematically expand the three main deliverables (database designs, ETL system, and BI applications) by first describing each one conceptually and then physically. Finally, in the last two chapters we show you how to deploy this amazing edifice into real operational environments and how to think about expanding and growing your DW/BI system beyond the first implementation.

We hope our enthusiasm for data warehousing and business intelligence shows through in this book. The DW/BI challenge is a fascinating and worthy one. Undoubtedly, the labels will change over the years as vendors position their products to be new things that will remove all the old objections. But our mission has remained constant: Bring the data and analyses to the business users so they can make better business decisions.

CHAPTER 1

Introducing the Kimball Lifecycle

Before delving into the specifics of data warehouse/business intelligence (DW/BI) design, development, and deployment, we want to first introduce the Kimball Lifecycle methodology. The Kimball Lifecycle provides the overall framework that ties together the various activities of a DW/BI implementation. The Lifecycle also ties together the content of this book, setting the stage and providing context for the detailed information that unfolds in the subsequent chapters.

This chapter begins with a historical perspective on the origination and evolution of the Kimball Lifecycle. We introduce the Lifecycle roadmap, describing the major tasks and general guidelines for effectively using the Lifecycle throughout your project. Finally, we review the core vocabulary used in the book.

We recommend that all readers take the time to peruse this brief introductory chapter, even if you are involved in only one facet of the DW/BI project. We believe it is beneficial for the entire team to understand and visualize the big picture and overall game plan. This chapter focuses on the forest; each remaining chapter will turn its attention to the individual trees.

Lifecycle History Lesson

The Kimball Lifecycle methodology first took root at Metaphor Computer Systems in the 1980s. Metaphor was a pioneering decision support vendor; its hardware/software product offering was based on LAN technology with a relational database server and graphical user interface client built on a 32-bit operating system. Nearly a quarter century ago, analysts in large corporations were using Metaphor to build queries and download results into spreadsheets and graphs. Sounds familiar, doesn't it?

Most of this book's authors worked together to implement decision support solutions during the early days at Metaphor. At the time, there were no industry best practices or formal methodologies. But the sequential steps of decision support were as obvious then as they are now; our 1984 training manual described them as *extract, query, analysis,* and *presentation.*

The authors and other Metaphor colleagues began honing techniques and approaches to deal with the idiosyncrasies of decision support. We had been groomed in traditional development methodologies, but we modified and enhanced those practices to address the unique challenges of providing data access and analytics to business users, while considering growth and extensibility for the long haul.

Over the years, the authors have been involved with literally hundreds of DW/BI projects in a variety of capacities, including vendor, consultant, IT project team member, and business user. Many of these projects have been wildly successful, some have merely met expectations, and a few have failed in spectacular ways. Each project taught us a lesson. In addition, we have all had the opportunity to learn from many talented individuals and organizations over the years. Our approaches and techniques have been refined over time — and distilled into *The Data Warehouse Lifecycle Toolkit.*

When we first published this book in 1998, we struggled with the appropriate name for our methodology. Someone suggested calling it the Kimball Lifecycle, but Ralph modestly resisted because he felt that many others, in addition to him, contributed to the overall approach.

We eventually determined that the official name would be the Business Dimensional Lifecycle because this moniker reinforced the unique core tenets of our methods. We felt very strongly that successful data warehousing depends on three fundamental concepts:

- Focus on the business.
- Dimensionally structure the data that's delivered to the business via ad hoc queries or reports.
- Iteratively develop the overall data warehouse environment in manageable lifecycle increments rather than attempting a galactic Big Bang.

Rewinding back to the 1990s, we were one of the few organizations emphasizing these core principles at the time, so the Business Dimensional Lifecycle name also differentiated our methods from others in the marketplace. Fast forwarding to today, we still firmly believe in these core concepts; however the industry has evolved since the first edition of the *Lifecycle Toolkit* was published. Now nearly everyone else touts these same principles; they've become mainstream best practices. Vocabulary from our approach including dimension tables, fact tables, and slowly changing dimensions have been embedded in the interfaces of many DW/BI tools. While it's both thrilling and affirming that the concepts have been woven into the fiber of our industry, they're no longer differentiators of our approach. Second, despite our thoughtful naming of the Business Dimensional Lifecycle, the result was a mouthful, so most people in the industry simply refer to our methods as the Kimball approach, anyhow. Therefore, we're officially adopting the Kimball Lifecycle nomenclature going forward.

In spite of dramatic advancements in technology and understanding during the last couple of decades, the basic constructs of the Kimball Lifecycle have remained strikingly constant. Our approach to designing, developing, and deploying DW/BI solutions is tried and true. It has been tested with projects across virtually every industry, business function, and platform. The Kimball Lifecycle approach has proven to work again and again. In fact, that's the reasoning behind the Kimball Group's "practical techniques, proven results" motto.

Lifecycle Milestones

The overall Kimball Lifecycle approach to DW/BI initiatives is illustrated in Figure 1-1. Successful implementation of a DW/BI system depends on the appropriate integration of numerous tasks and components. It is not enough to have the perfect data model or best-of-breed technology. You need to coordinate the many facets of a DW/BI project, much like a conductor must unify the many instruments in an orchestra. A soloist cannot carry a full orchestra. Likewise, the DW/BI implementation effort needs to demonstrate strength across all aspects of the project for success. The Kimball Lifecycle is

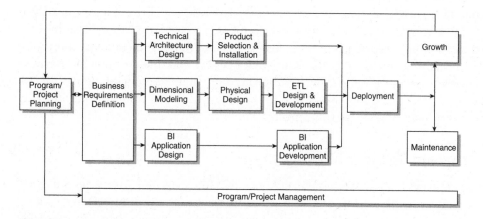

Figure 1-1 The Kimball Lifecycle diagram.

similar to the conductor's score. It ensures that the project pieces are brought together in the right order and at the right time.

The Lifecycle diagram depicts the sequence of high level tasks required for effective DW/BI design, development, and deployment. The diagram shows the overall roadmap, while each box serves as a guidepost or mile/kilometer marker. We'll briefly describe the milestones, as well as provide references to the corresponding chapters in this book for more specific driving instructions.

Program/Project Planning

The Lifecycle begins with program and project planning, as one would expect. Throughout this book, *project* refers to a single iteration of the Kimball Lifecycle from launch through deployment; projects have a finite start and end. On the other hand, *program* refers to the broader, ongoing coordination of resources, infrastructure, timelines, and communication across multiple projects; a program is an overall umbrella encompassing more than one project. It should continuously renew itself and should rarely have an abrupt end.

Which comes first, the program or the project? Much like the classic chicken and egg conundrum, it's not always obvious which comes first. In some organizations, executive agreement is reached to launch a DW/BI program and then it's a matter of prioritizing to identify the initial project. In other situations, funding is provided for a single project or two, and then the need for program coordination is subsequently realized. There's no single right approach or sequence.

There's much greater consistency around project planning, beginning with the scoping of the DW/BI project. Obviously, you must have a basic understanding of the business's requirements to make appropriate scope decisions; the bi-directional arrow between the project planning and business requirements boxes in Figure 1-1 shows this dependency. Project planning then turns to resource staffing, coupled with project task identification, assignment, duration, and sequencing. The resulting integrated project plan identifies all tasks associated with the Kimball Lifecycle and the responsible parties. It serves as the cornerstone for the ongoing management of your DW/BI project. Chapter 2 details these launch activities, in addition to the ongoing management of the program/project.

Program/Project Management

Program/project management ensures that the Kimball Lifecycle activities remain on track and in sync. Program/project management activities focus on monitoring project status, issue tracking, and change control to preserve scope boundaries. Ongoing management also includes the development of a comprehensive communication plan that addresses both the business and information technology (IT) constituencies. Continuing communication is critical to managing expectations; managing expectations is critical to achieving your DW/BI goals.

Business Requirements Definition

A DW/BI initiative's likelihood of success is greatly increased by a sound understanding of the business users and their requirements. Without this understanding, DW/BI often becomes a technical exercise in futility for the project team.

Our approach for gathering knowledge workers' analytic requirements differs significantly from more traditional, data-driven requirements analysis. DW/BI analysts must understand the key factors driving the business in order to successfully translate the business requirements into design considerations. An effective business requirements definition is crucial as it establishes the foundation for all downstream Lifecycle activities. Chapter 3 provides a comprehensive discussion of tips and techniques for gathering business requirements.

Technology Track

Following the business requirements definition, there are three concurrent tracks focusing on technology, data, and business intelligence applications, respectively. While the arrows in the Figure 1-1 Lifecycle diagram designate the activity workflow along each of the parallel tracks, there are also implied dependencies between the tasks, as illustrated by the vertical alignment of the task boxes.

The technology track is covered in Chapters 4 and 5. Chapter 4 introduces overall technical architecture concepts, and Chapter 5 focuses on the process of designing your architecture and then selecting products to instantiate it. You can think of these two companion chapters as delivering the "what," followed by the "how."

Technical Architecture Design

DW/BI environments require the integration of numerous technologies. The technical architecture design establishes the overall architectural framework and vision. Three factors — the business requirements, current technical environment, and planned strategic technical directions — must be considered simultaneously to establish the appropriate DW/BI technical architecture design. You should resist the natural tendency to begin by focusing on technology in isolation.

Product Selection and Installation

Using your technical architecture plan as a virtual shopping list of needed capabilities, specific architectural components such as the hardware platform, database management system, extract-transformation-load (ETL) tool, or data access query and reporting tool must be evaluated and selected. Once the products have been selected, they are then installed and tested to ensure appropriate end-to-end integration within your DW/BI environment.

Data Track

The second parallel set of activities following the business requirements definition is the data track, from the design of the target dimensional model, to the physical instantiation of the model, and finally the "heavy lifting" where source data is extracted, transformed, and loaded into the target models.

Dimensional Modeling

During the gathering of business requirements, the organization's data needs are determined and documented in a preliminary *enterprise data warehouse bus matrix* representing the organization's key business processes and their associated dimensionality. This matrix serves as a data architecture blueprint to ensure that the DW/BI data can be integrated and extended across the organization over time.

Designing dimensional models to support the business's reporting and analytic needs requires a different approach than that used for transaction processing design. Following a more detailed data analysis of a single business process matrix row, modelers identify the fact table granularity, associated dimensions and attributes, and numeric facts.

These dimensional modeling concepts are discussed in Chapters 6 and 7. Similar to our handling of the technology track, Chapter 6 introduces dimensional modeling concepts, and Chapter 7 describes the recommended approach and process for developing a dimensional model.

Physical Design

Physical database design focuses on defining the physical structures, including setting up the database environment and instituting appropriate security. Although the physical data model in the relational database will be virtually identical to the dimensional model, there are additional issues to address, such as preliminary performance tuning strategies, from indexing to partitioning and aggregations. If appropriate, OLAP databases are also designed during this process. Physical design topics are discussed in Chapter 8.

ETL Design and Development

Design and development of the extract, transformation, and load (ETL) system remains one of the most vexing challenges confronted by a DW/BI project team; even when all the other tasks have been well planned and executed, 70% of the risk and effort in the DW/BI project comes from this step.

Chapter 9 discusses the overall architecture of the ETL system and provides a comprehensive review of the 34 subsystem building blocks that are needed in nearly every data warehouse back room to provide extraction, cleansing and conforming, and delivery and management capabilities. Chapter 10 then converts the subsystem discussion into reality with specific details of the ETL design and development process and associated tasks, including both historical data loads and incremental processing and automation.

Business Intelligence Application Track

The final concurrent activity track focuses on the business intelligence (BI) applications. General concepts and rationale are presented in Chapter 11, and design and development best practices are covered in Chapter 12.

BI Application Design

Immediately following the business requirements definition, while some DW/BI team members are working on the technical architecture and dimensional models, others should be working with the business to identify the candidate BI applications, along with appropriate navigation interfaces to address the users' needs and capabilities. For most business users, parameter-driven BI applications are as ad hoc as they want or need. BI applications are the vehicle for delivering business value from the DW/BI solution, rather than just delivering the data.

BI Application Development

Following BI application specification, application development tasks include configuring the business metadata and tool infrastructure, and then constructing and validating the specified analytic and operational BI applications, along with the navigational portal.

Deployment

The three parallel tracks, focused on technology, data, and BI applications, converge at deployment. Extensive planning is required to ensure that these puzzle pieces are tested and fit together properly, in conjunction with the appropriate education and support infrastructure. As emphasized in Chapter 13, it is critical that deployment be well orchestrated; deployment should be deferred if all the pieces, such as training, documentation, and validated data, are not ready for prime time release.

Maintenance

Once the DW/BI system is in production, technical operational tasks are necessary to keep the system performing optimally, including usage monitoring, performance tuning, index maintenance, and system backup. You must also continue focusing on the business users with ongoing support, education, and communication. These maintenance issues and associated tasks are discussed in Chapter 13.

Growth

If you have done your job well, the DW/BI system is bound to expand and evolve to deliver more value to the business. Unlike traditional systems development initiatives, change should be viewed as a sign of success, not failure. Prioritization processes must be established to deal with the ongoing business demand. We then go back to the beginning of the Lifecycle, leveraging and building upon the foundation that has already been established, while turning our attention to the new requirements. Chapter 14 details recommendations to address the long-term health and growth of your DW/BI environment.

Using the Lifecycle Roadmap

The Kimball Lifecycle diagram in Figure 1-1 illustrates the general flow of a DW/BI implementation. It identifies task sequencing and highlights the activities that should happen concurrently throughout the technology, data, and BI application tracks.

The Lifecycle diagram, however, does not attempt to reflect an absolute project timeline. Each box in Figure 1-1 is the same width, with the exception of program/project management. If you have any experience with data warehousing and business intelligence, you know that the resources and time required for each Lifecycle box are *not* equal. Clearly, the reader should not lay a ruler along the bottom of the diagram and divide the tasks into timeline months; focus on sequencing and concurrency, not absolute timelines.

As with most approaches, you may need to customize the Kimball Lifecycle to address the unique needs of your organization. If this is the case, we applaud your adoption of the framework, as well as your creativity. Truth be told, we usually tailor the specific Lifecycle tasks for each new project. Throughout this book, we attempt to describe nearly everything you need to think about during the design, development, and deployment of a DW/BI solution. Don't let the volume of material overwhelm you. Not every detail of every Lifecycle task will be performed on every project.

Finally, as we'll further describe in Chapter 2, the Kimball Lifecycle is most effective when used to implement projects of manageable, yet meaningful scope. It is nearly impossible to tackle everything at once, so don't let your business users, fellow team members, or management force that approach.

Lifecycle Navigation Aids

Not surprisingly, the book is riddled with references to the Kimball Lifecycle. For starters, each chapter title page includes a miniature graphic of the Lifecycle diagram, highlighting where you are within the overall framework. You should view this as your Lifecycle mile marker. Be forewarned that there is not always a one-to-one relationship between mile markers and book chapters. In some cases, a single chapter addresses multiple markers, as in Chapter 2, which covers both program/project planning and management. In other cases, multiple chapters cover a single mile marker, such as Chapters 6 and 7, which discuss dimensional modeling, or Chapters 9 and 10, which provide detailed coverage of ETL design and development.

In addition to the "you are here" mile markers, there's a "blueprint for action" at the end of each process-oriented chapter that includes the following guidance and recommendations:

- Managing the effort and reducing risk.
- Assuring quality.
- Key project team roles involved in the process.
- Key deliverables.
- Estimating guidelines.
- Templates and other resources available on the companion book website at www.kimballgroup.com.
- Detailed listing of project tasks.

Lifecycle Vocabulary Primer

You are inevitably anxious to jump into the details and move ahead with your DW/BI program/project, but we first want to define several terms that are used throughout this book. We'll also note core vocabulary changes since the first edition of this publication.

Unfortunately, the DW/BI industry is plagued with terminology that's used imprecisely or in contradictory ways. Some of the long-standing debates in our industry are fueled as much from misunderstandings about what others mean by a term, as from true differences in philosophy. Though we can't settle the debates in this forum, we will try to be clear and consistent throughout this text.

Data Warehouse versus Business Intelligence

As an industry, we can't seem to reach consensus about what to call ourselves. Traditionally, the Kimball Group has referred to the overall process of providing information to support business decision making as *data warehousing*. Delivering the entire end-to-end solution, from the source extracts to the queries and applications that the business users interact with, has always been one of our fundamental principles; we would never consider building data warehouse databases without delivering the presentation and access capabilities. This terminology is strongly tied to our legacy of books, articles, and design tips. In fact, nearly all our *Toolkit* books include references to the data warehouse in their titles.

The term *business intelligence* initially emerged in the 1990s to refer to the reporting and analysis of data stored in the warehouse. When it first appeared on the industry's radar, several of this book's authors were dumbfounded about the hoopla it was generating because we'd been advocating the practices for years. It wasn't until we dug a little deeper that we discovered many organizations had built data warehouses as if they were archival librarians, without any regard to getting the data out and delivered to the business users in a useful manner. No wonder earlier data warehouses had failed and people were excited about BI as a vehicle to deliver on the promise of business value!

Some folks in our industry continue to refer to data warehousing as the overall umbrella term, with the data warehouse databases and BI layers as subset deliverables within that context. Alternatively, others refer to business intelligence as the overarching term, with the data warehouse relegated to describe the central data store foundation of the overall business intelligence environment.

Because the industry has not reached agreement, we consistently use the phrase "data warehouse/business intelligence" (DW/BI) to mean the complete end-to-end system. Though some would argue that you can theoretically deliver BI without a data warehouse, and vice versa, that is ill-advised from our perspective. Linking the two together in the DW/BI acronym further reinforces their dependency.

Independently, we refer to the queryable data in your DW/BI system as the *enterprise data warehouse*, and value-add analytics as *BI applications*. In other words, the *data warehouse is the foundation for business intelligence*. We disagree with others who insist that the data warehouse is a highly normalized data store whose primary purpose is not query support, but to serve as a source for the transformation and loading of data into summarized dimensional structures.

ETL System

We often refer to the extract, transformation, and load (ETL) system as the back room kitchen of the DW/BI environment. In a commercial restaurant's kitchen, raw materials are dropped off at the back door and then transformed into a delectable meal for the restaurant patrons by talented chefs. Long before a commercial kitchen is put into productive use, a significant amount of planning goes into the workspace and components' blueprint.

The restaurant's kitchen is designed for efficiency, while at the same time ensuring high quality and integrity. Kitchen throughput is critical when the restaurant is packed with patrons, but the establishment is doomed if the meals coming out of the kitchen are inconsistent, fail to meet expectations, or worse, cause food poisoning. Chefs strive to procure high quality products and reject those that don't meet their standards.

Skilled kitchen professionals wield the tools of their trade. Due to the sharp knives and hot surfaces in the kitchen, restaurant patrons aren't invited behind the scenes to check out the food preparation or taste the sauce before ordering an entree. It's just not safe, plus there's a variety of "processing" in the kitchen that patrons just shouldn't be privy to.

Much the same holds true for the DW/BI kitchen. Raw data is extracted from the operational source systems and dumped into the kitchen where it is transformed into meaningful information for the business. The ETL area must be laid out and architected long before any data is extracted from the source. The ETL system strives to deliver high throughput, as well as high quality output. Incoming data is checked for reasonable quality; data quality conditions are continuously monitored.

Skilled ETL architects and developers wield the tools of their trade in the DW/BI kitchen; business users and BI applications are barred from entering the ETL system and querying the associated work-in-process files before the data is quality assured and ready for business consumption. ETL professionals and the system throughput shouldn't be compromised by unpredictable inquiries. Once the data is verified and ready for business consumption, it is appropriately arranged "on the plate" and brought through the door into the DW/BI front room.

In this edition of *Lifecycle Toolkit*, we have greatly expanded our coverage of ETL architecture best practices, largely because we observed so many DW/BI teams taking a haphazard approach to designing and developing their kitchen.

The introduction of 34 subsystems provides a formidable checklist for anyone constructing or remodeling an ETL kitchen.

For readers who are familiar with the first edition, we have abandoned the *data staging* terminology due to several developments. When the book was originally written, ETL had not been established as an industry standard acronym. And while we consistently used data staging to refer to all the cleansing and data preparation processing that occurred between the source extraction and loading into target databases, others used the term to merely mean the initial dumping of raw source data into a work zone.

Business Process Dimensional Model

Now let's turn our attention to the restaurant's dining room where the focus shifts to the patrons' overall dining experience. Patrons want quality food, appealing décor, prompt service, and reasonable cost. The dining room is designed and managed based on the preferences expressed by the restaurant's patrons, not the kitchen staff.

Similarly, the DW/BI system's front room must be designed and managed with the business users' needs first and foremost at all times. Dimensional models are a fundamental front room deliverable. Dimensional modeling is a design discipline optimized to deliver on the twin goals of business users' ease of use and BI query performance. Dimensional models contain the same data content and relationships as models normalized into third normal form; they're just structured differently. Normalized models are optimized for high volume, single row inserts and updates as typified by transaction processing systems, but they fail to deliver the understandability and query performance required by DW/BI.

The two primary constructs of a dimensional model are fact tables and dimension tables. Fact tables contain the metrics resulting from a business process or measurement event, such as the sales ordering process or service call event. While it may appear as a subtlety for the casual reader, our business process orientation has widespread ramifications throughout the Lifecycle. We put a deep stake in the ground about the importance of structuring dimensional models around business processes and their associated data sources, instead of taking a business department/function or analytic reporting perspective advocated by others in the industry. This allows us to design identical, consistent views of data for all observers, regardless of which department they belong to, which goes a long way toward eliminating misunderstandings at business meetings!

We also feel strongly about the need for precise declaration of the fact table's grain at the lowest, most atomic level captured by the business process for maximum flexibility and extensibility. Atomic data lets business users ask constantly changing, free-ranging, and very precise questions. It is unacceptable to have this robust data locked in normalized schemas where it is unable to quickly and easily respond to business queries.

Dimension tables contain the descriptive attributes and characteristics associated with specific, tangible measurement events, such as the customer, product, or sales representative associated with an order being placed. Dimension attributes are used for constraining, grouping, or labeling in a query. Hierarchical many-to-one relationships are denormalized into single dimension tables. *Conformed dimensions* are the master data of the DW/BI environment, managed once in the kitchen and then shared by multiple dimensional models to enable enterprise integration and ensure consistency.

Dimensional models may be physically instantiated in a relational database, in which case they're often referred to as *star schema*. Alternatively, dimensional models can also be stored in an online analytic processing (OLAP) database where they're commonly referred to as *cubes*. We recommend that the OLAP cubes be populated from the relational atomic dimensional models for operational reasons.

In the first edition of *Lifecycle Toolkit*, we used the term *data mart* extensively instead of *business process dimensional models*. While data mart wins the brevity competition, the term has been marginalized by others to mean summarized departmental, independent non-architected datasets.

Business Intelligence Applications

It's not enough to just deliver dimensional data to the DW/BI system's front dining room. While some business users are interested in and capable of formulating ad hoc queries on the spur of the moment, the majority of the business community will be more satisfied with the ability to execute predefined applications that query, analyze, and present information from the dimensional model. There is a broad spectrum of *BI application* capabilities, ranging in complexity from a set of canned static reports to analytic applications that directly interact with the operational transaction systems. In all cases, the goal is to deliver capabilities that are accepted by the business to support and enhance their decision making. Clearly, the BI applications in your dining room must address the patron's needs, be organized to their liking, and deliver results in an acceptable timeframe. While you're at it, you'll also want to provide a "menu" to describe what's available; fortunately, metadata should come to the rescue on this front.

There's one final nomenclature change that we want to make you aware of. In the first edition, we referred to these templates and applications as *end user applications*, instead of the more current BI application terminology.

Conclusion

The Kimball Lifecycle provides the framework to organize the numerous tasks required to implement a successful DW/BI system. It has evolved through years of hands-on experience and is firmly grounded in the realities you face today. Now with the Lifecycle framework in mind, let's get started!

CHAPTER 2

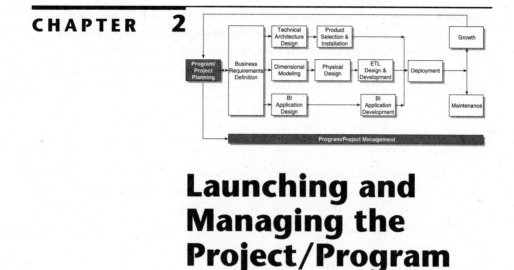

Launching and Managing the Project/Program

Now that you have a high level understanding of the Kimball Lifecycle approach and core vocabulary, it is time to dig in and get started. This chapter explores the project and program planning and management boxes of the Lifecycle diagram.

The chapter is organized into four major sections. The first section focuses on defining your initial data warehouse/business intelligence (DW/BI) project. It provides advice and guidelines for getting started with your initiative, from assessing readiness through scoping and justification for funding. The second section concentrates on detailed project planning activities, including staffing and project plan development. From there, we discuss considerations for keeping your DW/BI project on track. Last, we describe best practices for managing the overall DW/BI program and coordinating across projects.

This chapter is geared toward people responsible for the DW/BI project or program, regardless of whether they are part of the information technology (IT) or functional business organization. Because a successful DW/BI effort depends on a profound IT and business partnership, management from both groups should peruse this chapter to better understand the overall project/program landscape and their essential roles. Other project team members would also benefit from a common understanding of these planning and management challenges and recommendations, but it is not required that they read this chapter in depth.

NOTE This chapter is not intended to be an exhaustive guide to general project management best practices. Numerous resources are available to professional project managers, including *A Guide to the Project Management Body of Knowledge* [Project Management Institute (PMI), 2004]. We're focused on the application of general practices to the unique nuances of the DW/BI project lifecycle.

Define the Project

So you have been asked to spearhead the DW/BI project at your company. What does that mean and where do you start? We suggest you take a moment to assess your organization's readiness for a DW/BI system before proceeding full steam ahead with the project.

Assess Your Readiness for DW/BI

Based on our experience, three key factors must be in place to ensure DW/BI success. If you are unable to confidently give your organization a passing grade on the combined readiness factors, we strongly suggest slowing down and reconsidering. Readiness shortfalls represent project risks; the shortfalls will not correct themselves over time. It is far better to pull the plug on the project before significant investments have been made than it is to continue marching down a path filled with hazards and obstacles.

Strong Senior Business Management Sponsor(s)

Strong support and sponsorship from senior business management is the most critical factor when assessing DW/BI readiness. Effective business sponsors share several key characteristics. First, they have a vision for the potential impact of a DW/BI solution. They can visualize how improved access to information will result in incremental value to the business. Strong sponsors possess a personal conviction about their vision, which is generally demonstrated by their willingness to be accountable for it.

Strong business sponsors are influential leaders within the organization. Typically, they have demonstrated a solid track record of success and are well respected by others. In other words, they have organizational clout. Strong business sponsors are typically politically astute and well connected. Although we have seen newcomers to an organization perform effectively as DW/BI sponsors, this is a riskier proposition given their lack of knowledge about the culture, players, politics, and processes.

The ideal business sponsor is demanding, but realistic and supportive. It helps if they have a basic understanding of DW/BI concepts, including the iterative development cycle, to avoid unrealistic expectations. Effective sponsors are able to deal with short-term problems and setbacks because they are focused on the long-term success of the project. Realistic sponsors are willing to compromise. They are also able to make the tough decisions and live with the consequences.

Successful DW/BI teams typically cultivate several strong business sponsors within their organization; they don't put all their eggs in one basket. It is not uncommon for a DW/BI initiative to stall in the wake of the departure of a sole business sponsor.

Compelling Business Motivation

From our vantage point, DW/BI systems are successful if they've been accepted by the business folks to support their decision making. Organizations that successfully implement DW/BI solutions typically have a powerful sense of urgency for improved access to information caused by one or more compelling business motivations. Sometimes competition and changes in the external landscape are the motivators. Elsewhere, internal crisis has motivated organizations, particularly if growth through acquisition creates compelling demand for an integrated environment to gauge performance across the organization. In other cases, the strategic vision of a potential marketplace opportunity is the overpowering motivator. In each case, there is strong demand coming from the business community to address their requirements.

DW/BI systems that align with strategic business motivations and initiatives stand a good chance of succeeding. Likewise, business justification becomes nearly a non-issue if the DW/BI system is poised to support a compelling business motivation. In these situations, the organization likely also has the economic willpower to continue investing in the DW/BI environment for the long haul.

Feasibility

Feasibility commonly refers exclusively to technical feasibility. However, our primary feasibility concern regarding DW/BI readiness relates to the data itself. If the data required to support the compelling business motivation is too filthy, overly complex for the initial effort, or not even collected, you have a significant feasibility issue on your hands. Unfortunately, there's no short-term fix to address serious data feasibility issues.

Data profiling is the technical analysis of data to describe its content, consistency, and structure. In some sense, any SELECT DISTINCT investigative query on a database field could be considered data profiling, but today there are purpose-built tools to facilitate the task. As you're evaluating your readiness to proceed with a candidate data source, a quick data profiling assessment should be done as an early qualification or disqualification. More in-depth data profiling will be conducted during the requirements analysis, data modeling, and ETL design activities of the Lifecycle.

Factors Not Considered Readiness Deal Breakers

Some readers might be surprised that technology is not included in our list of critical readiness factors, but at this stage of the game, technology is a non-issue that doesn't yet warrant your attention or energy.

In the first edition of this book, we also identified the relationship between IT and the business, as well as the organization's current analytic culture, as lesser readiness factors. Although a healthy relationship and partnership between the business and IT makes for a smoother implementation, the lack of a positive relationship is not a deal breaker, as long as the other readiness factors, including business sponsorship and motivation, are present.

Since we authored the last edition, organizations of all sizes, shapes, and forms have embraced fact-based analysis and decision making. Today, most knowledge workers believe instinctively that data is a crucial requirement for them to function in their jobs. Cultural issues surrounding analytics have largely become non-issues. However, if your organization still operates on gut intuition rather than analysis, there's no reason not to move ahead with a DW/BI project, although you'll need to be prepared for the additional burden of shifting the cultural mindset.

Address Shortfalls and Determine Next Steps

As we indicated earlier, the three readiness factors are not equally weighted in importance. Strong business management sponsorship bears a disproportionate share of the overall importance, with compelling business motivation and feasibility splitting the remainder.

Business sponsorship is critically important for a number of reasons. Strong sponsors formulate and articulate the necessary vision and its impact on the organization. DW/BI systems tend to be expensive, with support and growth costs that never end. Strong sponsorship, coupled with a solid financial return, is needed to obtain and sustain funding. A strong sponsor is also able to command the appropriate resources even when competing with other mission-critical projects. Finally, DW/BI systems are sometimes the catalyst for cultural change; a strong sponsor will embrace and facilitate this change.

Strong business sponsorship can cover a multitude of shortcomings elsewhere on the project. Conversely, if your project has everything going for it but lacks a strong business sponsor, you have a very steep hill to climb. Even the most elegantly designed DW/BI solution cannot overcome a lack of business sponsorship.

At this point, you need to evaluate your combined readiness. Risk reduction strategies and contingency plans should be developed to address any shortfalls. We describe several common scenarios and recommended action plans for moving forward.

Strong Sponsor, Compelling Business Need, and Quality Data

Congratulations! You have all the key readiness factors in place. You can bypass the remainder of this shortfalls section and proceed directly to developing the preliminary project scope and charter.

Poor Quality Data

Even with a strong sponsor and a compelling business need, without quality data the project inevitably evolves into mission impossible. If the right data is not collected, or not collected at the right level of detail, or not collected with any regard to data quality, it becomes very challenging to construct a DW/BI system on this shaky foundation. Rather than proceeding with this type of project, it would be wiser to identify another high value requirement for this business sponsor with fewer data feasibility obstacles. In the meantime, other IT resources not associated with the DW/BI initiative should identify appropriate actions to address the data challenges for the deferred opportunity.

Weak Business Sponsor or IT-Only Sponsor

If your preliminary business sponsor lacks organizational clout, doesn't envision what a DW/BI system could do for the organization, or isn't engaged, then you have some work to do. The same holds true if the CIO is the only person leading the charge for a DW/BI solution.

If your candidate business sponsor is either missing-in-action or doesn't exemplify the traits described earlier, you need to start fishing for potential business sponsors in the organization. The most effective technique for locating an appropriate business sponsor is to conduct a high level business requirements analysis.

Chapter 3 spells out detailed tactics and techniques for gathering business requirements. Many of the same techniques apply in this situation with a few minor adjustments. For now, we want to focus on high level business issues and business value impact; we don't need to drop down to 500 feet to gather gory details for designing the dimensional data model. In general, you will want to uncover the following during a high level requirements analysis with business management:

- Understand their strategic business initiatives.

- Identify the key performance indicators or success metrics for each core business process they monitor and want to impact.

- Determine the potential impact on their performance metrics with better access to improved information.

If your sponsor has many of the requisite qualities, but lacks a clear vision for the potential business value, then some education may be called for. This may be as straightforward as a conversation to help paint a picture of the possibilities. Some DW/BI teams are quick to jump into proof-of-concept development to demonstrate the potential impact to the business community. Though we're not fundamentally opposed to this idea, we have observed some potential drawbacks with this approach.

Developing a proof-of-concept should not be an excuse to avoid direct interaction with the functional business departments. You shouldn't build a proof-of-concept purely because it allows you to experiment with new gadgets rather than overcoming your fear of meeting face-to-face with business representatives. Obviously, if the proof-of-concept is to demonstrate potential value, then development should focus on the compelling business motivations discussed earlier.

At this point in the project lifecycle, the proof-of-concept is purely a demonstration tool. Expectations must be appropriately managed so the demonstration held together by baling twine and duct tape isn't suddenly transformed into a production system; it should be positioned as completely disposable.

> **NOTE** Proof-of-concepts often undermine rational expectation setting. The proof-of-concept is built in a matter of days or weeks, and then management has a hard time comprehending why it's going to take months to deliver the production DW/BI system.

Too Much Demand from Multiple Business Sponsors

In this scenario, multiple potential business sponsors are clamoring for improved access to better information. It's wonderful that there's so much organizational enthusiasm to move forward with a DW/BI initiative. The problem with demand from multiple corners of the organization is that you can't effectively tackle it all at once, especially if there's no technical, data, or BI application architectural foundation in place. You must work with the business community to prioritize the demand.

In Chapter 3, we describe a facilitation-based process for prioritizing business requirements based on a combined assessment of their potential business value, along with feasibility. Business and IT leaders work with a two-by-two grid where the vertical Y axis represents business impact and the horizontal X axis conveys feasibility, both valued from low to high. Each opportunity is placed relative to the others on the two-by-two grid. Inevitably, the group reaches consensus on the opportunity with the highest business impact and greatest feasibility — the optimal place to start rather than pursuing projects with either lower impact or feasibility. The attendees leave the session with buy-in and a sense of ownership for the charted outcome, which is far preferable to having IT or the business dictate a course of action in isolation.

Well Meaning, But Overly Aggressive Business Sponsor

DW/BI efforts get off on the wrong foot when the business sponsor is so enthused about the 360 degree view of the business that they insist the project immediately integrate data coming from numerous major source systems. This is worse than scope creep; perhaps we should call it scope gallop. Because the aggressive sponsor is likely a member of the executive staff, they often outrank the IT personnel involved and repeatedly expand scope without effective push-back. At some point, IT needs to gently lay down the following guideline: *Each new major data source adds six months to the development time of the DW/BI effort*. This will help focus the discussion on the right topics!

Legacy of Underperforming, Isolated Data Silos

Many organizations have already built a data warehouse or data mart. In fact, perhaps many warehouses or marts, so that the organization's performance metrics are redundantly stored in multiple places with similar-but-different business rules without any overarching framework or architecture. This data quagmire is the bane of many CIOs due to the inherent inconsistencies and inefficiencies. The business might also be frustrated by the chaotic mess.

Even in this situation, the business's requirements need to drive the DW/BI initiative. Funding for a pure infrastructure project is hard to come by in most organizations. You still need to locate a viable opportunity with strong business sponsorship and motivation to proceed with confidence; establishing the appropriate architecture and infrastructure will be a side benefit of delivering the business value.

Develop the Preliminary Scope and Charter

By now, you should be comfortable with your organization's overall readiness to proceed with a DW/BI system. You need to begin putting a fence around the project's scope and getting it justified. In reality, scope and justification go hand-in-hand — it is nearly impossible to complete one without the other, so teams often loop between the two activities. For clarity, we present the concepts separately in the next two sections, but these activities will probably be intermixed on your project.

NOTE Project scope should be driven by the business's requirements. In the Lifecycle diagram, this influence is designated by the bi-directional arrow between the Program/Project Planning and Business Requirements Definition boxes.

Before we get started with specifics, it is important to first discuss *what* you are scoping. Once again, this varies widely. Are you scoping and requesting funding to cover the short-term requirements definition and design phases? Or the first delivery of information and analyses to the business community? Or the three-year grand plan? It is almost certain that the further you try to see, the worse your vision becomes. Consequently, defining the scope and building the justification becomes more perilous the further you need to predict into the future. Project managers are most frequently asked at this stage to put together a scope and justification for the initial delivery to business users, so we will proceed under this premise.

Focus on a Single Business Process

DW/BI projects deliver the key performance metrics resulting from the organization's core business processes, such as the sales ordering or billing processes. One of the most critical scope boundaries, especially in the early stages of your DW/BI program, is to focus on a single business process. Centering on a single process helps ensure a more manageably sized design and development iteration because a single business process is typically supported by a single major source system module. It is much more reasonable to extract and transform data from a single source in the early formative stages rather than initially attempting to extract and integrate information from multiple processes generated by multiple source systems.

NOTE Each early iteration of your DW/BI program should be limited in scope to the data resulting from a single business process. The extract, transformation, and load effort grows exponentially when consolidating metrics from multiple business processes in a single implementation cycle. Stay clear of projects focused on profitability or satisfaction initially because they inherently require data from multiple major source systems.

Here are additional guidelines for developing the preliminary DW/BI project scope:

- The DW/BI project scope should be meaningful, yet manageable. *Meaningful* translates into perceived business value. Your initial target business process must deliver enough value to warrant the investment; otherwise, you may need to pursue an alternative process or bundle multiple development iterations into a single user deployment. *Manageable* means doable. In other words, start small. The Kimball Lifecycle methods are intended to support iterative development of your DW/BI environment. We encourage launching smaller, quicker-to-market projects rather than tackling the monolithic multiyear effort in one big gulp. Again, the key variable to consider in terms of satisfying our "small" recommendation is the number of source systems.

- Defining scope is an exercise performed jointly by IT and business representatives. Neither party should attempt to establish scope on their own.

- Scope is occasionally driven by a target delivery date, and then the deliverable is managed to meet the delivery date. Of course, if this riskier route is pursued, the DW/BI deliverable must still deliver business value.

- Begin establishing success criteria for the project while scope is being defined. It is extremely important to understand what business management expects from the DW/BI project. More details are described in Chapter 3 about establishing specific, measurable project success criteria.

THE DANGER OF DASHBOARDS Given the interest in dashboards and scorecards, we want to discuss their potential implications on project scope. With a recognizable, graphically appealing user interface, senior management is often enthused about a dashboard because it closely aligns with the way they operate. However, there's a dark side to dashboard projects given their vulnerability to runaway expectations. Dashboards typically consist of key performance indicators from a multitude of business processes. If you have an existing data warehouse that's populated with the requisite detailed, integrated data, you can tackle the proposed dashboard development with gusto. Dashboards are a great way to deliver business value. On the other hand, if there's no existing foundation to be leveraged, signing up to deliver the dashboard as your first DW/BI initiative is likely a career-limiting move. Because there's inevitably insufficient time to deliver the required detailed data from multiple processes, teams often resort to a semi-manual collection of pre-aggregated, stand-alone subsets of data that is unsustainable in the long run. And it's not enough to just deliver the summarized results to senior executives; their managers and analysts need the ability to dive into the details where the true causal factors affecting performance are lurking. While perhaps less politically attractive at first, a more sustainable approach would be to deliver the detailed data, one business process at a time. As the underlying details become available, embellish the dashboard with additional information. Though this approach doesn't deliver the immediate "wow" factor and requires executive patience, you can typically convert them to this steadier, more sustainable approach by describing the inevitable rework that could result from taking the alternative shortcut.

The Role of Rapid Application Development

Given the lengthy project timeframes associated with complex software development projects combined with the realities of relatively high rates of under-delivery, there's been much interest in the rapid application development movement, known by a variety of names such as Agile, Extreme Programming, and others. Though there are variations on the theme, most share a common focus on iterative development and risk minimization by delivering new functionality in short timeframes, often measured in weeks. These approaches were initially referred to as "lightweight methodologies" in contrast to more regimented, documentation-intensive traditional methods.

There are many principals or tenets of rapid application development that resonate and tightly align with the Kimball method's standard techniques:

- Focus on the primary objective of delivering business value. This has been our mantra for decades.

- Value collaboration between the development team and stakeholders, especially business representatives. Like the agile camp, we strongly encourage a close relationship and partnership with the business.

- Stress the importance of ongoing face-to-face communication, feedback, and prioritization with the business stakeholders. Though the Kimball Lifecycle approach encourages some written documentation, we don't want the burden to be onerous or pointless.

- Adapt quickly to evolving requirements. Change is inevitable.

- Tackle development of reusable software in an iterative, incremental manner with concurrent, overlapping tasks. But don't get sidetracked trying to evangelize an enterprise reusable software strategy. Your job is to build a DW/BI system, not redo the plumbing of your organization.

NOTE Standardizing on the "agile" nomenclature was a marketing triumph; wouldn't you rather be agile than spiraling or stuck in a waterfall methodology?

So what's the bottom line? In reality, one size seldom fits all, despite what the label claims. From our vantage point, there's a time and place for agile techniques when creating a DW/BI system. They seem to most naturally fit with the BI application layer. Designing and developing the analytic reports and analyses involve unpredictable, rapidly changing requirements. The developers often have strong business acumen and curiosity, allowing them to communicate effectively with the business users. In fact, we suggest that BI team members work in close proximity to the business so they're readily available and responsive; this in turn encourages more business involvement. And it's reasonable to release incremental BI functionality in a matter of weeks. At the other end of the spectrum, the real-world wrangling of the data during the extract, transform, and load is inherently more complex and dependent on structure and order.

One final word of caution: Some development teams have naturally fallen into the trap of creating analytic or reporting solutions in a vacuum. In most of these situations, the team worked with a small set of users to extract a limited set of source data and make it available to solve their unique problems. The outcome is often a stand-alone data stovepipe that can't be leveraged by others or worse yet, delivers data that doesn't tie to the organization's other analytic information. We encourage agility, when appropriate; however, building isolated datasets must be avoided. As with most things in life, moderation and balance between extremes is almost always prudent.

NOTE Releasing functionality on a more frequent basis still must be done within the context of an overall architecture and master plan.

Document the Scope/Charter

Once IT and business management have agreed on the project's scope, it should be documented; writing it down ensures everyone involved has a consistent understanding. Often referred to as a *project charter*, the document explains the project's focus and motivating business requirements, objectives, approach, anticipated data and target users, involved parties and stakeholders, success criteria, assumptions and risks. It may also be appropriate to explicitly list data and analyses that will not be addressed with the initial project; by identifying what is outside of the scope, you are demonstrating that you heard the users' requests and are not just ignoring them. Figure 2-1 shows an excerpt from a sample project scope/charter document. Although the project manager is responsible for creating this document, its contents are determined in collaboration with the business.

NOTE The sooner proper project boundaries are established and documented, the less you will need to deal with misperceptions. You can gain as much clarity and respect by saying what you will not do, as for saying what you will do.

PROJECT NAME
Scope Document

Background

BigCo wants to maximize its return on promotion investments. It currently spends approximately $40 million annually in promotional efforts. BigCo's goal is to reduce promotion spending by 25 percent in three years.

The next phase of BigCo's data warehouse and business intelligence system will focus on promotion information, complementing the earlier project focused on sales information. Brand teams, sales operations, and marketing research will have access to both the sales and promotion information to enable more effective promotion spending to improve BigCo's return on promotion investments.

Project Scope

This phase of the overall DW/BI program is defined as follows:
- o Three years of historical internal promotion detail information.
- o Maximum of 25 initial users, with roll-out plans for 150 ultimate users in brands, sales operations, and marketing research.
- o Technical architecture for this project will be based on . . .
- o Current project timeline calls for initial production deployment by the end of second quarter.
- o ...

Exclusions From Scope

The following items are specifically excluded from the project's scope:
- o External data such as competitive sales and promotion information.
- o Support for non-domestic promotion programs.
- o ...

Success Criteria

Several key success criteria have been designated for the promotion data project:
- o Provide a single source to support promotions-related analysis.
- o Reduce the time required to perform a promotions-related analysis.
- o Increase the effectiveness of promotion programs by 5 percent due to improved allocation decisions based on insights from the promotion data.
- o ...

Risks and Risk Reduction Action Plan

This phase poses the following risks:
- o ...

Figure 2-1 Sample project scope/charter excerpt.

The scope of your DW/BI project will inevitably evolve before the initial business users access the final deliverable. This is to be expected because the scope becomes more clearly defined and more clearly negotiated with each step toward delivery. The project scope statement should not sit on a shelf; it should be reviewed frequently, revised as needed, and republished. Finally, it is important to recognize that scope refinement is different from scope creep. The goal of scope refinement is to retain the same sized box, although the contents may change; in the case of scope creep, the dimensions of the box expand.

Build the Business Case and Justification

Once the preliminary scope has been established with the business and IT sponsors and management, the project's business justification needs to be built. Justification is another joint activity that depends on a strong IT/business partnership. IT cannot develop the DW/BI justification alone; you need the business to also step up to the plate.

Building the justification simply means that you are identifying the anticipated costs and benefits associated with the project over time. You shouldn't let terms like return on investment (ROI) intimidate you. Basically you are comparing the predicted financial return or business benefits against the predicted investment or costs to determine the business value of the project. Other traditional financial performance measurements such as net present value (NPV) or internal rate of return (IRR) are variations on the theme. If you are unfamiliar or uncomfortable with these concepts, enlist the help of others in your organization who are seasoned veterans of this process.

We begin by reviewing the investment or cost side of the equation, followed by the more elusive financial return or benefits. Finally, we pull the two components together to create the justification and business case. Most organizations have a standardized financial model for consistently analyzing project justifications; we focus on deriving or estimating the numbers to input into that model.

Determine the Financial Investments and Costs

People often view the cost estimation as simpler than the benefits calculation, but at this early stage, even the costs can present challenges given all the inherent uncertainties surrounding the project. At this point, you're just trying to determine ballpark figures; they will need to be revisited following product selection. Typically cost components to be considered include the following:

- **Hardware costs.**   You should account for all hardware components and/or upgrades, including database and application servers, data storage, and network and communication. However, be sure to consider if the existing infrastructure can be leveraged to avoid lost credibility from gross cost overestimations.

- **Software costs.**   On the software side, consider the cost of purchasing or upgrading software for data profiling, ETL, BI query, reporting and analysis (including potentially data mining and packaged analytics), and metadata management, as well as platform operating system and database management system software.

- **Internal staffing.**   Staffing is a major cost component depending on the magnitude of your project. We detail all the requisite project roles and responsibilities later in this chapter.

- **External resources.** Are you planning to leverage external consulting and vendor services? If so, what role do you anticipate them playing in your project? It's wise to budget at a minimum for vendor technical support, as well as external education.

You also need to consider ongoing costs, depending on your organization's planning horizon and culture. Are you trying to estimate the cost of building the DW/BI environment or the ongoing cost of owning it? Unlike some IT development efforts, the ongoing costs of operating and supporting the DW/BI environment are quite significant. In addition to maintaining the current state, there will also inevitably be demand for enhancements and growth assuming the project was successful. Here are some other costs to add into the equation:

- **Ongoing maintenance expenses.** Most hardware and software purchases will be accompanied by ongoing maintenance charges. Be certain to determine whether these maintenance charges are based on the list price or negotiated discount price.

- **Ongoing support.** The existing user help desk will not suffice for DW/BI support. Also, unlike many systems, business user support will not decline over time. As business usage evolves, the DW/BI system will need ongoing monitoring and performance tuning.

- **Expenses to support growth.** You may need to consider ongoing expenses to support changing business requirements, expanded user populations, new release upgrades, and technology to support higher performance demands.

Determine the Financial Returns and Benefits

Now that the costs have been estimated, we turn our attention to the more intimidating business benefits or financial returns. Business folks typically struggle to provide specific business impact numbers. They will state the potential benefit as something like "better access to better information." Unfortunately, this frequently heard benefit does not translate immediately into bottom-line business impact.

DW/BI benefits typically fall into either tangible or intangible categories. Tangible benefits are more critical than intangibles because they're quantifiable, such as the following list of potential impacts on profitability resulting from either revenue generation or cost reduction:

- Increased revenue from new sales to new customers

- Increase revenue from up-selling more expensive products or cross-selling additional products to existing customers

- Increased response rate to mailings through improved targeting

- Increased average sale per mailing through improved assortment planning
- Elimination of low-margin products
- Decreased raw material costs due to improved supplier management and negotiation
- Reduced promotional spending or direct marketing costs with more timely midcourse adjustments during the campaign
- Reduced fraudulent claim expense
- Reduced customer churn or turnover
- Reduced defect rates
- Increased closure rate on first contact
- Reduced inventory carrying costs or manufacturing overproduction
- Reduced time to market for new products
- Improved pricing policies based on more complete revenue and cost information
- Eliminated cost of producing legacy reports
- Reduced time to collect data and produce analysis (although headcount savings are typically redeployed rather than eliminated)

Intangible or "soft" benefits, such as the following examples, are also worth noting because they provide value to the organization, but don't readily convert into a financial metric that easily translates into bottom line impact and fits neatly in the ROI model:

- More timely access to information
- Improved decision making based on facts rather than flying blind
- Greater information standardization and consistency across the organization
- Greater confidence in the data with fewer debates about accuracy and reduced data reconciliation effort
- Eliminate inefficiencies by providing one version of the data
- Faster response to changing conditions
- Enhanced ability to analyze alternatives
- Improved employee satisfaction and morale
- Improved customer satisfaction
- DW/BI is a strategic necessity to remain competitive

The key to ferreting out tangible business benefits is to keep asking probing questions. The layers of the onion need to be peeled back to understand the why, what if, and how much is associated with seemingly innocent benefit statements. What would it mean to the business if you had ...? Would you be able to ...? How much is ... worth? You need to continue questioning and searching for the component numbers that can be extrapolated into business benefits.

For example, assume the direct marketing manager said that better targeted mailings would allow them to increase response rates by 10 percent. There is not enough information in that statement alone to derive the financial impact. You need to ask follow-up questions to bring that high level impact prediction down into dollars and cents. Asking "What's the average revenue generated by a direct mail campaign?" and "How many campaigns do you run each year?" delivers the data needed to derive the financial impact from the 10 percent response rate increase. Take the $600,000 average revenue per campaign times 15 campaigns per year times 10 percent increased response rate to come up with $900,000 in annual incremental revenue attributed to the response rate improvement.

Combine the Investments and Returns to Calculate ROI

At this point, the investments and returns figures are typically entered into a financial model to calculate the return on investment. The resulting ROI percentage tends to be very large. It's often so large that even taking a fraction of the predicted return will probably be satisfactory to provide adequate justification and obtain funding approval.

You can also look at the financial justification in terms of the "opportunity cost" of doing nothing. There's a lost opportunity cost to the business when they're unable to make decisions due to insufficient information. For example, if the projected business benefit of the DW/BI system is $100,000 in incremental revenue per month, then you could argue that it costs the organization $100,000 in lost opportunity each month the project is delayed.

CAUTION If you are struggling with the financial justification for your DW/BI project, then you are probably still in search of the right sponsor and right compelling business problem.

Some organizations are more rigorous about the justification process than others. As a division president at a multi-billion dollar company explained, in his mind, justification was merely a test to ensure that the people in his organization were committed to making the initiative work. The raw numbers weren't particularly important; he viewed the justification as a measure of organizational commitment. Other organizations examine costs and benefits rounded to the nearest whole dollar.

NOTE In addition to ROI, sometimes outside pressures like competitive activity or changing market conditions are also weighed in the justification process.

Project teams are most often asked to predict the return on investment before the DW/BI system is built. Of course, it is easier and more believable to retroactively assess the return on investment after the solution is implemented. Even if a pre-project estimated ROI is required, we strongly encourage post-implementation monitoring of ROI as a great tool for proactively documenting the ongoing business benefits of the DW/BI environment.

Clearly, improved business decisions depend on people and processes, but the DW/BI system is an enabler. As better decisions are made based on DW/BI information and analyses, the project should take credit for at least a portion of the financial impact of those decisions. But don't get greedy; it's not necessary. We have found that consistently taking only 10 percent of the credit for bottom line improvements eventually yields an enormous number that you can "take to the bank." For example, if the credit department decides to grant more liberal credit to a group of customers after using the DW/BI system, the financial implications of this decision should be claimed. Likewise the decision should be claimed if the store operations group decides to merchandise the stores differently as a result of using the DW/BI system. Once these kinds of decisions are claimed, calculating the ROI is relatively straightforward. The DW/BI project/program manager needs to be on alert for decisions that can be legitimately claimed as enabled or impacted by the project. Finally, if over time you've been putting the DW/BI system's contributions "in the bank," you'll gradually create a culture that understands the need for strategic investments to support business decision making.

Plan the Project

Bravo, you have defined the initial project and gained approval and funding to move forward! What next? You are now ready to do detailed project planning.

In this section, we describe key considerations for getting the project staffed and building the overall project plan. But first, we deal with the project's identity crisis.

Establish the Project Identity

Your project needs a name. The name should be distinctive and memorable. Like most systems initiatives, the name you select is often reduced to an acronym, such as PAM for the Pricing Analysis for Marketing project; luckily it wasn't called the Strategic Pricing Analysis for Marketing project instead.

In any case, this task requires creativity, so it is a good time to collaborate with your business cohorts.

Some organizations create DW/BI system logos, which then appear on presentations, deliverables, T-shirts, and coffee mugs. As anyone who has been to the vendor booths at a conference knows, one can never have too many T-shirts or coffee mugs. As we describe in Chapter 12, include the logo on all predefined reports that are published and approved by the DW/BI team; the logo becomes identified with the high quality results from the system.

Staff the Project

A DW/BI project requires a number of different roles and skills from both the business and IT communities during its lifecycle. The various project roles are analogous to those in a professional sports team. The team starts with a front office of owners and general managers; in the DW/BI world, these are the sponsors and drivers who set the direction and foot the bill. The front office relies on the coaching staff to establish a regular starting lineup and provide day-to-day leadership; in our parlance, the project manager and business project lead are the coaches who manage the core project team charged with developing the DW/BI system. Along the way, specialty players are added to the team roster. Finally, the professional sports team wouldn't last long if it weren't for the fans; if we do our job right, the business users are analogous to these fans, enthusiastically cheering for their team.

In this section, we review the major roles involved in the DW/BI implementation, including the front office, coaches, regular lineup, and special teams. Most of the roles are project-centric, but several are often elevated to program-level responsibilities, as we discuss later in this chapter. We briefly describe the tasks each role is responsible for; these are illustrated in greater detail in the project task lists located at the end of appropriate chapters, as well as on the companion website.

Before we get started, remember that there is seldom a one-to-one relationship between roles and individuals. Although there are many roles in a DW/BI project, individual staff members often wear several hats at once. Like the regular lineup running back on the football team who also returns kickoffs, the same player may fill multiple roles on the DW/BI project. The relationship between project roles and actual headcount varies by organization. We have worked with DW/BI teams as small as one person who did it all. At the other end of the spectrum, it's not unusual to see project teams with more than 50 members in mature DW/BI shops. When you're first getting started, the project team is often more manageably sized with around three to seven full time members, along with access to others as required.

Front Office: Sponsors and Drivers

Folks in the front office aren't involved on a daily basis, but they have a significant influence on the rest of the team.

Business Sponsor/Business Driver

As we described earlier in this chapter, business sponsors play an extremely critical role on the DW/BI team. They are the business owners of the project and often have financial responsibility. Business sponsors help determine and then support prioritization and scope decisions. In addition, they fill both high level cheerleader and enforcer roles for the project. As cheerleaders, their enthusiasm encourages others to envision the potential impact of improved information access. At the other end of the spectrum, their reinforcement causes apprehensive or doubting users to jump on the bandwagon. Sponsors should be visionary, resourceful, and reasonable.

In some cases, a steering committee composed of senior business executives fills the sponsorship role. We further elaborate on the executive steering committee later in this chapter when we discuss ongoing program management.

Often the business sponsor is not readily available to the project team due to his stature in an organization, so a business driver is designated to tactically serve in his place. The business driver should be accessible, engaged, and empowered to resolve issues. Business drivers should have a solid understanding of the business and be well-respected by others in the business community. The best business drivers exemplify all the same characteristics of the best business sponsors; they're just more readily accessible.

CAUTION Sometimes folks are designated as business drivers because they have spare time on their hands. These are NOT the people you want to fill this role.

DW/BI Director/Program Manager

Complementing the business sponsorship role, the IT organization's DW/BI director works closely with the business sponsor to ensure a joint success. This person is the primary liaison between the business sponsors and DW/BI teams, heavily involved in developing and selling the business case and then maintaining funding. They must be effective communicators to influence both senior business and IT management and often become the DW/BI evangelist to the rest of the organization.

The DW/BI director is responsible for the overall leadership and direction of the initiative and environment, greatly influencing the overall strategy and architecture while overseeing the underlying programs/projects. Depending on the organizational structure, this role is sometimes referred to as the *program manager*, emphasizing its distinct cross-project responsibilities.

Although this role most often reports into the CIO, we have also seen it report to a business function such as the chief operating officer or chief financial officer to further reinforce that DW/BI needs to focus more on the business than technology.

Coaches: Project Managers and Leads

In professional sports, the team has several coaches directing day-to-day activities with a slightly different focus; the same is true for a DW/BI project. Collectively, the coaches want their team to be a winner, reflecting well on both the coaching staff and front office.

Project Manager

The project manager is the head coach, responsible for detailed management of project tasks and activities, including resource coordination, status tracking, and communication of project progress and issues, in conjunction with the business project lead. Project managers, typically staffed from among the best and the brightest in the IT organization, need to be knowledgeable about, and respected by, both the IT and business organizations. They must have strong written and oral communication skills, as well as listening skills. Ideally, they are also adept at navigating the political waters of the organization.

Project managers often have an uncanny ability to identify, react to, and resolve issues before they escalate into serious problems. Project managers need strong organizational and leadership skills to keep everyone involved moving in the same direction. Finally, they must have a good sense of balancing the mechanics of project management without becoming a slave to its tools.

This is a dedicated position — it just doesn't work to have a part-time DW/BI project manager. However, sometimes the project manager is a player/coach who both leads the charge and plays other lesser roles on the project team.

Business Project Lead

This business community representative works with the project manager on a day-to-day basis, jointly monitoring project progress and communicating to the rest of the organization. The business project lead should have a solid understanding of the business requirements and be well respected by the business community. This is typically a part-time role, but the business project lead is expected to attend status meetings and be extremely accessible to the team, just as every coach would attend team meetings. Depending on the size of the organization, the business driver and business project lead may be the same person.

Regular Lineup: Core Project Team

The core team bears the bulk of the responsibility for designing and developing the DW/BI system. We will introduce the players in approximately the order that they come onto the scene.

Some team members are assigned to the project full time; others are involved on a part-time or sporadic basis. It is common for the DW/BI team to take on both development and operational duties given the highly iterative nature of the DW/BI project development cycle. Obviously, this is not the norm for typical technology project teams.

In several areas, we've identified both an architect role with oversight and coordination responsibilities, as well as developer roles. Obviously, on smaller projects, both roles would be satisfied by a single individual. At the other end of the spectrum, sometimes there's a chief architect on larger teams who oversees the other architects.

Business Analyst

The business analyst is responsible for leading the business requirements definition activities and then representing those requirements as the technical architecture, dimensional model, and BI applications are specified. The business analyst role is often filled by an IT resource that is extremely user-centric and knowledgeable about the business. Alternatively, it may be staffed with a resource currently residing in the business organization, but with a solid technical foundation. Business analysts sometimes suffer from multiple personality disorder because they're constantly straddling the boundaries between the business and IT worlds, bridging the two. On smaller projects, the project manager or business project lead may fill this position. The business analyst must have strong communication skills; it is certainly beneficial if they are respected by the business community because the business analyst, along with the business project lead, will be representing their requirements to the rest of the team.

Data Steward/Quality Assurance Analyst

The data steward is responsible for driving organizational agreement on definitions, business rules, and permissible domain values for the warehouse data, and then publishing and reinforcing these definitions and rules. Historically, this role was referred to as data administration, a function within the IT organization. However, it's much better if the data steward role is staffed by the subject matter experts from the business community.

Clearly, this is a politically challenging role. Stewards must be well respected leaders, committed to working through the inevitable cross-functional issues, and supported by senior management, especially when organizational compromise is required.

Sometimes the data stewards work in conjunction with quality assurance (QA) analysts who ensure that the data loaded into the warehouse is accurate and complete. They identify potential data errors and drive them to resolution. The QA analyst is sometimes also responsible for verifying the business integrity of the BI applications. This role is typically staffed from within the business community, often with resources who straddle the business and IT organizations. Once a data error has been identified by the QA analyst, the error must be corrected at the source, fixed in the ETL, or tagged and passed through the ETL. Remember, data quality errors are indicators of broken business processes and often require executive support to correct; relatively few can be fixed in the data warehouse.

The QA analyst has a significant workload during the initial data load to ensure that the ETL system is working properly. And given the need for ongoing data verification, the QA analyst role does not end once the warehouse is put into production.

Data Architect/Data Modeler/Database Administrator

The data architect is responsible for developing the overall data architecture strategy of the DW/BI system, ensuring reusability, integration, and optimization.

The data modeler is responsible for performing detailed data analysis and developing the dimensional data model. Although not the most prominent person on the project's org chart, the data modeler wields undue influence on the success of the project; well designed models delight the business users and are easier to implement, whereas poorly designed models can drag down the whole DW/BI effort. Knowledge about existing corporate data models and business rules is certainly valuable. Strong data modeling experience is beneficial, but the individual must be willing to break away from traditional normalized design practices and embrace dimensional design techniques. This person often designs both the detailed dimensional model in the relational platform, as well as the OLAP databases in conjunction with the BI application developer. The data modeler often participates in the requirements definition activities in a secondary role. They should instinctively understand that their goal is to design the data platform for BI applications that users agree is simple and fast.

The database administrator (DBA) translates the dimensional model into physical table structures. In many cases, they are involved in the dimensional modeling process; at a minimum, this person should be familiar with these design techniques. The DBA is responsible for the overall physical design including disk layout, partitioning, and the initial indexing plan. The DBA is often responsible for the day-to-day operational support of the database, ensuring data integrity, availability, and performance. In larger organizations, this role is sometimes divided into separate design and operational production DBA roles.

Metadata Manager

Metadata is located in so many nooks and crannies of the DW/BI system that it's necessary for someone to take responsibility for coordinating the metadata. This person is not responsible for inputting all the metadata, but rather is a watchdog to ensure that everyone is contributing their relevant piece, from the original sources all the way through the ETL system to the final BI applications. This person has the final word on what metadata is collected, where it is kept, and how it's published to the business community.

ETL Architect/ETL Developer

The ETL architect is responsible for the end-to-end design of the production process to extract, transform, and load the data. While many aspects of DW/BI differ from traditional development, ETL system development requires strong modular system design skills. Too often this role is not identified, and developers just begin coding.

Returning to our restaurant analogy, the ETL architect shouldn't be stuck in the kitchen, isolated from the overall DW/BI system design process. They are the chefs who carefully plate the food that's delivered from the kitchen to please the patrons. The architect should be involved in the requirements gathering and have a significant working relationship with the BI application team, because after all, the BI application team lives and dies with the platform created by the ETL system.

ETL developers construct, unit test, and automate the extract, transformation, and load processes under the direction of the ETL architect. Optimally, this resource has an intimate knowledge of the source systems to aid in the mapping, as well as a basic understanding of the target dimensional models. This person must be highly conversant in the ETL tool's capabilities.

BI Architect/BI Application Developer/BI Portal Developer

The BI architect has overall responsibility for the front room of the DW/BI system, ensuring that the BI environment is optimized to address the business's requirements. The architect establishes the framework and enforces the standards that are used by the BI application developers.

The BI application developer creates and maintains the BI applications, typically using off-the-shelf query and reporting software. The BI application developer is also responsible for configuring the BI tool's semantic layer. This role requires moderate database and PC knowledge, and possibly programming skills, along with a deep interest and understanding of the business, its requirements, and the underlying data. Like the business analysts, this role may be filled from either the IT or business organizations; resources that currently reside in the business organization, but behave as systems professionals by developing databases and creating ad hoc reports, are prime candidates for this role. The business analyst may handle the BI application development responsibility on smaller projects.

The BI portal developer manages the BI portal, working with other team members to determine the portal's content and format, and then ensuring that it remains updated.

> **NOTE** Some organizations have divided their core team resources into separate DW and BI teams. While we sympathize with span of control issues and appreciate the benefits of specialization, overly compartmentalized DW and BI teams are risky because neither can be successful on their own. If the resources are divided, joint collaboration and communication is absolutely critical.

Special Teams

These team members contribute to the project on a specialized, limited basis. As we mentioned earlier, these special roles may be assumed by resources who are already members of the core team.

Technical Architect/Technical Support Specialist

The technical architect is responsible for the design of the technical architecture and infrastructure for the DW/BI environment. The person in this role does not need to be an expert in all the technologies, but provides the overall cohesiveness to ensure that the components fit together. They develop the plan that identifies the required technical functionality and then help evaluate and select products on the basis of this overall architecture.

Depending on your environment, there may be platform specialists who get involved in early stages of the design to perform resource and capacity planning. During product selection, they ensure compatibility with the existing technical environment. Once technology has been selected, they are involved in the installation and configuration of the new components and often provide ongoing production support.

Security Manager

The DW/BI system has multiple security exposures ranging from the initial source system extracts all the way to the final screens displayed to business users. But we often remark that the only place in the enterprise where the sensitivity of the data can be balanced against the need to know or manipulate the data is the DW/BI team. Security for the data warehouse absolutely cannot be "liaised" to another group within IT. The DW/BI team must have a security manager who is responsible for all back room security, front room security, and possibly external security if the DW/BI system supports external web services available to the public.

Lead Tester

This role is important during the testing and deployment phases of the project. The lead tester develops test methodologies, and confirms that the tests cover the span of the data, processes, and systems. This person may be borrowed from a corporate testing team, and should be brought on board early enough to understand the unique challenges of testing a DW/BI system. The responsibility for running tests is often shared with other team members.

Data Mining/Statistical Specialist

This optional analyst role develops data mining models and works with the BI application developers to design operational applications that use mining capabilities. They should be very familiar with the business and often have a background in statistics. In some environments with a heavy commitment to data mining, there may be a whole team of specialists. We often regard data mining folks and their applications as sophisticated clients of the data warehouse, fitting architecturally after the data warehouse, but before business intelligence.

Educator

Users of the DW/BI system must be educated on the data content, BI applications, and ad hoc data access tool capabilities in some cases. The educator must have in-depth knowledge in each of these areas. This role typically develops the initial education materials, as well as delivers the education on an ongoing basis. Responsibility for education may be delegated to other team members; for example, the data steward may cover data content and business rules, while the BI application developer may handle the BI applications and data access tool training.

Free Agents

In professional sports, a free agent is a player whose contract with a team has expired so they're able to contract with another. In the world of DW/BI, we refer to these folks as consultants. Admittedly, the authors of this book are free agents as we offer DW/BI consulting services. Skilled consultants can fill critical skill gaps on your project team, accelerate development, and ensure you're on the right track before large expenditures are made. However, putting our biases aside, you should be aware of several considerations before enlisting consultants.

Like most systems development projects, you obviously want to work with experienced people. However, the unending nature of a DW/BI project and its business orientation warrants additional requirements of external consultants:

- Don't let consultants fill all the key leadership roles on your core project team. You should retain ownership of the project and not let an external organization build it entirely for you.

- Demand extensive knowledge transfer and mentoring from your consultants.

- Require written deliverables so the process and knowledge don't walk out your door when the consultants do.

- Clearly understand if you are buying a consultant with specialized skills or whether you are merely augmenting your regular staff with someone who is learning on the job.

- Don't let a consultant talk you into a data- or technology-centric development approach, even if it feels more comfortable to both you and your consultants. In other words, don't start exclusively with data and/or technology without a major grounding in the business analyses needs.

Convert Individual Talent into a Team

Once the DW/BI team is staffed, the coaches need to turn their attention to team cohesiveness and development. Team building activities are important to ensure that the team gels. Personality issues can quickly undermine a talented roster. In terms of player development, chances are that some team members lack the first-hand experience necessary to build a successful DW/BI. You need to acknowledge that DW/BI demands new techniques and skills, and then allocate the time and money to get your team up to speed on general concepts and methodologies, dimensional modeling, ETL, and technology-specific topics through specialized courses.

NOTE It is far cheaper to invest in education than it is to fund rework due to lack of knowledge.

Develop the Project Plan

The DW/BI project needs a detailed, integrated project plan given its complexity, both in terms of tasks and players. Unfortunately, teams often have multiple project plans that don't tie together; there may be a plan for the modeling tasks, another for the ETL system development, and perhaps yet another for defining the technical architecture. Without a single integrated plan, the likelihood that appropriate tasks are completed in the same timeframe plummets.

The level of detail tracked is a common problem with DW/BI project plans. A single task called "Develop the ETL system" is not sufficient given the many underlying subtasks required. The goal is to provide enough detail to track progress on key tasks and identify issues or delays as soon as possible. If a single task requires more than two weeks, subtasks should be identified.

Many organizations have already established methodologies and supporting software for internal systems development projects. We encourage you to use the resources available to you. However, we want to remind you that the best project management software package will be worthless unless the time is invested to input and maintain the project plan, including detailed dependencies. Too often, significant time is spent developing the initial plan, but then it is not updated and used throughout the Lifecycle. The key to effective project management is to employ tools that you and the team will actually use, even if that means resorting to a spreadsheet for project task tracking.

Figure 2-2 illustrates an excerpt from a project plan. We recommend tracking the following information for each task:

- **Resources:**   Individuals responsible for completing this task. There should be only one person with primary responsibility for each task.

- **Original estimated effort:**   Original estimated number of days to complete task. This number should never be revised.

- **Original estimated start date:**   Date task is estimated to begin.

- **Original estimated completion date:**   Original date when task is to be completed. Again, this date should never be revised.

- **Status:**   Current status label (such as future task, in process, or done).

- **Updated start date:**   Current estimated start date reflecting a change from the original.

- **Updated completion date:**   Current estimated completion date reflecting a change from the original.

- **Effort to finish:**   Currently estimated number of work days required to complete task.

- **Late days:**   Calculation between the estimated completion date and current date to identify tasks behind schedule.

- **% Completed:**   Current status as a percentage of the total effort required based on current estimated effort to finish.

- **Dependencies:**   Identification of other tasks that must be completed prior to this task.

On the book's companion website at www.kimballgroup.com, there's a sample project plan task list that outlines high level tasks and each role's responsibilities. Specific project task lists are described in the subsequent chapters,

	Task Name	Resources	Original estimated effort	Original estimated start date	Original estimated completion date	Status	Updated start date	Updated completion date	Effort to finish	Late days	% Completed	Dependencies
1	Project planning		15 days	Tue 1/1/08	Tue 1/22/08	Future Task	NA	NA	15 days	0 days	0%	
2	Establish project identity	PM/Proj Lead	0.5 days	Tue 1/1/08	Tue 1/1/08	Future Task	NA	NA	0.5 days	0 days	0%	
3	Identify project resources		3 days	Wed 1/2/08	Fri 1/4/08	Future Task	NA	NA	3 days	0 days	0%	2
4	Determine required roles	PM	0.5 days	Wed 1/2/08	Wed 1/2/08	Future Task	NA	NA	0.5 days	0 days	0%	2
5	Determine resources	PM/Proj Lead	2 days	Wed 1/2/08	Fri 1/4/08	Future Task	NA	NA	2 days	0 days	0%	4
6	Assign roles to resources	PM	0.5 days	Fri 1/4/08	Fri 1/4/08	Future Task	NA	NA	0.5 days	0 days	0%	5
7	Develop project communication plan	PM	1 day	Mon 1/7/08	Mon 1/7/08	Future Task	NA	NA	1 day	0 days	0%	6
8	Prepare draft skeleton project plan	PM	3 days	Tue 1/8/08	Thu 1/10/08	Future Task	NA	NA	3 days	0 days	0%	7
9	Establish project management procedures		1.5 days	Fri 1/11/08	Mon 1/14/08	Future Task	NA	NA	1.5 days	0 days	0%	8
10	Establish change management process	PM	0.5 days	Fri 1/11/08	Fri 1/11/08	Future Task	NA	NA	0.5 days	0 days	0%	10
11	Create issue resolution process	PM	0.5 days	Fri 1/11/08	Fri 1/11/08	Future Task	NA	NA	0.5 days	0 days	0%	11
12	Establish enhancement tracking process	PM	0.5 days	Mon 1/14/08	Mon 1/14/08	Future Task	NA	NA	0.5 days	0 days	0%	11
13	Conduct project team kick-off	PM	1 day	Mon 1/14/08	Tue 1/15/08	Future Task	NA	NA	1 day	0 days	0%	9
14	Revise project plan	PM/Team	5 days	Tue 1/15/08	Tue 1/22/08	Future Task	NA	NA	5 days	0 days	0%	13

Figure 2-2 Sample project plan excerpt.

if applicable, along with estimating guidelines and considerations. In general, there is no single variable that drives the amount of time required to build a DW/BI system. The number of business users is an estimating variable that drives the time spent collecting requirements and deploying the DW/BI system. However, the business user count has virtually no impact on the effort required to design and develop the ETL process because that effort is the same for one or one hundred users.

We suggest identifying all the tasks associated with the entire project lifecycle. The task should be included even if you do not yet precisely know the timing, resources, or effort required. You can estimate approximate dates, but they should be flagged as estimates. Otherwise, you can just list the tasks, but only complete the other pertinent information as you develop greater visibility with project progress.

As you are building the project plan, remember to appropriately inflate estimates for unknowns. Due to the unexpected data realities hidden in most source data, ETL system design and development has a well-earned reputation of being difficult to estimate and deliver on time. Also don't forget that ETL development is a classic software development task with five distinct phases: development, unit testing, system testing, acceptance testing, and final rollout with documentation. Inexperienced project managers may focus most of their attention on what turns out to be only the first of the five steps.

You may also need to inflate estimates due to cultural issues. We worked with one organization where it often took three weeks lead time to get several managers in the same room at the same time. They needed to incorporate this cultural reality into their project plan.

The project manager typically develops a skeleton project plan and then meets with key representatives from each major lifecycle activity for their input on tasks. These representatives are responsible for developing the estimated effort and preliminary schedule for their activities. Their participation in this up-front planning encourages buy-in from the people who will actually be doing the work.

More often than not, we witness a lack of project planning and management on DW/BI projects, but have also seen the opposite extreme. Don't delay the start of the project for six weeks while the project manager develops an overly detailed project plan. Project plans need to be defined and tracked, but not just for the sake of project management.

Develop the Communication Plan

DW/BI project managers should establish a communication plan to address the needs of their various audiences or constituencies. Regular, ongoing communication allows the project manager to consistently establish and manage expectations; expectation management is an absolute key to success for a DW/BI project.

The overall communication plan should outline general message content, medium, and frequency for communicating with each constituency group, as illustrated in Figure 2-3. Documenting a communication plan forces the project manager to proactively consider the organization's communication requirements. Otherwise, communication either slips between the cracks or occurs reactively.

NOTE Today's world of easy electronic communication tends to encourage indiscriminate over-communication. Bombarding your constituents with too much information is no better than not sharing enough. We strongly encourage you to tailor the message to the audience. You can always provide a link to more detailed information for those who are interested.

This section reviews communication recommendations for the typical DW/BI constituency groups.

Project Team

Naturally, most project managers tend to focus on communication within the project team, much as a sports team's coach reviews the play book and game plan with the team regularly. Many of the tools described in this chapter, such as the project scope document, status meetings, status reports, and project plans, facilitate communication within the team. These communication vehicles should be shared with both the core team and specialty players as appropriate, but they are not an effective means for communicating far beyond the team.

PROJECT NAME Communication Plan			
Constituency	**Frequency**	**Forum**	**Key Messages**
Project team	Weekly	Status meeting	Task level progress, issue identification and resolution
Business sponsors	Monthly	Face-to-face briefing	Issue resolution, overall progress, major issues and resolution, expectation management, funding
Business community	Monthly	BI portal	Requisite involvement, overall progress, expectation management, critical dates
IT colleagues	Bimonthly	Existing IT staff meeting	System progress, expectation management, resource needs

Figure 2-3 Sample communication plan.

Sponsor and Driver Briefings

Obviously, you need to keep the business and IT sponsors and drivers in the loop. Face-to-face communication is much more effective than merely copying them on project documents. Everyone in the front office has access to the coach's playbook, but most aren't interested in that level of detail. Clearly, these communication briefings need to be well planned, focusing on progress to date and any issues requiring higher-level assistance. Project managers should schedule sponsor briefings approximately every four to six weeks. The briefings should be concise, allowing about 15 minutes of presentation and 15 minutes of discussion and issue resolution. Meetings with the business driver will be more frequent and lengthier.

NOTE Communicate face to face with your sponsors. Do not rely on project status meeting notes and other standard project management documentation.

We believe it is imperative that you develop a "no surprises" communication strategy with the sponsors and drivers, especially when you're stalled. Honesty is the best policy because it fosters trust and respect. The problem or issue you are trying to ignore or mask will surface eventually, so you should tell all early; who knows, your sponsors and drivers might even have the wherewithal to make the problem go away.

Business User Community

Communication is critical to ensuring that the business users' perception of the DW/BI system matches reality. In addition, communication with the business helps maintain their involvement with the project; greater involvement typically translates into a greater likelihood of acceptance and usage.

The first formal communication with the business users involved in the project, the user kickoff meeting, is described in Chapter 3. It is important that you follow up this launch meeting with regular, ongoing communication. As with communication to the sponsor and driver constituency, we discourage you from merely distributing the status reports to the business community. Chances are slim that they will take the time to read a status report; the chances are greater that they will be confused if they do.

NOTE Business users should be reading the front page of the sports section, not the detailed game plan.

User communication should focus on what's in it for them in terms of capabilities, exclusions, and timeframes. It should also detail the team's expectations regarding the users' involvement and feedback checkpoints. Finally, business users should be reminded every so often about the iterative nature of DW/BI development. Let them know that it's going to evolve, just as their business does.

Business user communication is broadcast in a variety of formats — one-page monthly emails, newsletters, or a regularly updated web page. Regardless of the communication medium, the message should be brief, pointed, and free of any technical vocabulary. Involved business users should also receive the project scope document as it is updated and republished. Finally, in addition to written communication, the business driver and project lead should routinely communicate informally with the business community.

Communication with Other Interested Parties

In addition to the key communication constituencies just described, several other audiences should be kept in the loop.

General Executive Management

The organization's executive team is typically briefed on high visibility initiatives, such as the DW/BI project. The joint business and IT sponsors typically spearhead this briefing. You will need high level DW/BI acceptance across the organization if it is to grow and thrive — these briefings are a start.

IT Staff Not Involved in DW/BI

Naturally, other IT professionals in the organization will be interested in what's happening with DW/BI. The program/project manager often provides a monthly status briefing to other IT managers. This communication helps ensure that the DW/BI system is integrated with other development activities. Also, it seems that DW/BI often becomes the answer to everyone else's reporting problems in an IT organization, so you need to manage expectations appropriately.

Business Community at Large

Finally, there are others within your business community who are interested in DW/BI. Many people hear about it through non-technical publications and other business contacts. Again, a short newsletter or web page can publicize DW/BI news to the rest of the organization, conveying a consistent message across the organization rather than letting the corporate rumor mill serve as the primary source of information.

Manage the Project

In this section, we discuss techniques for keeping your DW/BI project on track as it begins to unfold, starting with the team kickoff, through monitoring status and managing scope, and finally, managing expectations and recognizing warning signs. Many of these concepts are rooted in basic project management techniques. However, DW/BI projects have a few unique characteristics that cause some of these concepts to warrant additional discussion:

- **Cross-functional implementation team.**   The sheer number of players with varying responsibilities in a DW/BI project drives the need to monitor status closely.

- **Iterative development cycle.**   Development of the DW/BI environment never ends. This causes a greater need for communication to keep everyone in sync, issue/change tracking for future enhancements, and detailed project documentation to support an evolving team.

- **Inevitable data issues.**   DW/BI projects are extremely vulnerable to unexpected data issues which wreak havoc on anyone's best laid project plans. This is why we will repeatedly hammer on the theme of data profiling as early as possible in the design of each data pipeline from a candidate data source.

- **Elevated visibility.**   Organizational expectations of a DW/BI system typically run high, so proactive communication is required to keep them in check.

We assume you are generally familiar with basic project management concepts; however, the basics are often forgotten or ignored. We review key activities at a high level, focusing on the unique aspects of managing a DW/BI project whenever possible.

Conduct the Project Team Kickoff Meeting

The DW/BI project officially begins with a project team kickoff meeting. The purpose is to get the entire project team on the same page in terms of where the project stands and where it plans to go. Attendees should include the coaches, members of the core project team, and all specialty players if possible. A separate launch meeting, described in Chapter 3, will be held for the business community.

As illustrated in the sample agenda in Figure 2-4, the meeting begins with a brief introduction by the business sponsor, who describes the overall goals for the project and its business relevance. From there, the project manager assumes responsibility for the remainder of the meeting. Project team roles and responsibilities are discussed. The project plan is presented at a very high level, probably without estimated effort and due dates, and general project management expectations are reviewed. Finally, the next steps are identified.

The project manager typically compiles a project kickoff packet for distribution at the meeting, including copies of the project scope document, project

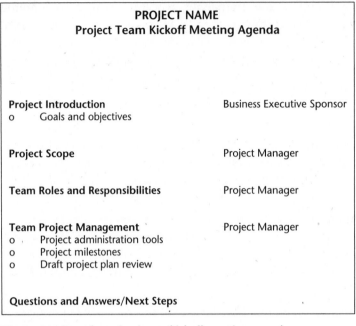

Figure 2-4 Sample project team kickoff meeting agenda.

team contact list with responsibilities, initial project plan, and sample status meeting agenda, status report, issue log, and change control documents.

Monitor Project Status

Like all systems development projects, the project status must be regularly monitored. The DW/BI project lifecycle requires the integration of numerous resources and tasks that must be brought together at the right time to achieve success. Monitoring project status is key to achieving this coordination.

We have observed many teams that initially have fine intentions concerning status monitoring, but then status-related activities take a back seat once the project is in crunch mode. Unfortunately, that is when status should be monitored most closely.

Project Status Meetings

We recommend regular status meetings for the core project team, typically scheduled for a one-hour time slot at the same time and place each week. As illustrated on the sample status meeting agenda in Figure 2-5, the status meeting should focus on accomplishments and current task progress, particularly

```
┌──────────────────────────────────────────────────────────────────────┐
│                            PROJECT NAME                                │
│                        Status Meeting Agenda                           │
│                                                                        │
│  Review Project Plan                                                   │
│                                                                        │
│     o   Review completed tasks or tasks scheduled for completion       │
│                                                                        │
│     o   Review milestones completed and pending                        │
│                                                                        │
│     o   Review major deliverables status                               │
│                                                                        │
│     o   Task assignments for the next week                             │
│                                                                        │
│  Review Issues and Follow-up                                           │
│                                                                        │
│     o   Review issues resolved since last meeting (resolution, who, when, move to closed) │
│                                                                        │
│     o   Review new issues (determine steps to resolve, ownership, priority, date to be resolved) │
│                                                                        │
│     o   Review open issues and determine if a change in status is needed │
│                                                                        │
│  Review Change Requests                                                │
│                                                                        │
│     o   Review change requests closed since last meeting               │
│                                                                        │
│     o   Review new change requests (determine ownership, impact analysis, priority) │
│                                                                        │
│     o   Review open change requests to determine if a change in status is needed │
│                                                                        │
│  Announcements/General Comments/Questions and Answers                  │
└──────────────────────────────────────────────────────────────────────┘
```

Figure 2-5 Sample status meeting agenda.

critical path tasks that are past due. In addition to reviewing the project plan, the status meeting is a forum to identify concerns and issues.

The project manager plays an important role in setting the tone of the status meeting and running an efficient meeting without numerous discussion tangents. Attendance will eventually suffer if you allow the meeting to overrun or stray off course. In addition, the project manager should create an atmosphere of openness within the team. It is far better to know about task overruns sooner rather than later.

Project Status Reports

Status reports provide a high level snapshot of project progress, going hand-in-hand with the regularly scheduled status meetings. The status report documents key accomplishments, significant decisions, planned activities for the next period, and major issues. The status report should not be overly detailed; keep it relatively brief so that people will actually read it. Status reports should be distributed to the entire project team, the business project lead, and DW/BI program/project leadership.

Maintain the Project Plan

The integrated project plan should be updated weekly to accurately reflect progress and then shared with the core project team. The project plan should reflect reality, whether it is good, bad, or ugly. Early flagging of project plan problems allows the team to develop strategies to adjust, as well as minimize downstream ripple effects.

Like most system projects, you need to understand and evaluate your options if your project falls behind on critical path tasks that impact the schedule. Working with your business sponsor, you may be able to reduce the project scope. Alternatively, you may need to obtain an extension on the project deliverable date. Finally, you could obtain more funding to supplement the project team with additional resources, although as any experienced project manager knows, adding more resources can create additional challenges.

Regardless of the alternative selected, the important thing is to have the courage to acknowledge to your management and sponsors that you are behind. It is only worse if expectations continue gaining speed with hopes that the team will make up the schedule shortfall during the two weeks before the target deliverable date. It won't happen. Pretending that it will and continuing to go through the motions with user education and deployment is typically a fatal mistake.

Consolidate the Project Documentation

The unending nature of a DW/BI program generates the need for consolidated project documentation. In addition, the project team is bound to evolve; additional players will come on board and others will head for greener pastures now that they have DW/BI on their resumes. Robust documentation will help ease the burden of getting the new team members up to speed. Documenting project assumptions and decision points is also helpful in the event that the deliverable does not meet expectations.

Unfortunately, documentation is no one's favorite task. When time pressures mount, the first item that gets eliminated is typically formal documentation. Try to avoid falling into this trap.

Project documentation, with dated copies of all project communication and major deliverables, is often stored in a set of official project binders, as well as in electronic format with a section corresponding to each major activity or box in the Lifecycle.

Manage the Scope

There is only one guarantee for any DW/BI project and that is that there will be change! The project manager has the unenviable job of managing scope changes. Out of one side of our mouths, we encourage you to focus on the business users and their requirements, while the other side is reminding you to stay on track. In general, the project manager has several options when facing a previously unidentified user request:

- Just say no.

- Adjust scope assuming a zero-sum. In other words, the overall effort remains the same, but what is in and out of scope is modified.

- Expand the scope. In this case, the fence around the project grows. It is then mandatory to expand the timeline and/or budget appropriately.

The right choice depends on the specific situation. Regardless of the situation, it is certain that the project manager should not make scope decisions in a vacuum. We have observed that numerous DW/BI project managers ignore this warning — and their solo decisions regarding scope changes were inevitably second guessed. Don't bear the burden of adjusting scope alone. A strong IT and business partnership is invaluable when evaluating scope alternatives.

In the following sections, we discuss techniques to track issues and change requests. Many organizations have already adopted issue tracking or change management methodologies and software. Obviously, you should use the resources available to you and that you are expected to use.

Track Issues

DW/BI project issue tracking is no different from other systems projects. The integration of numerous resources, data, and technologies in a DW/BI project tends to generate plenty of issues.

Issue tracking is critical to ensure that nothing slips between the cracks, that everyone's concerns have been heard, and that the rationale used to resolve issues has been captured for future reference. Identifying issues or roadblocks is the first step toward resolving them. The project manager should establish a team mindset that having numerous issues is allowed and preferable to simply pretending they don't exist.

There are two classes of issues — project issues that impact the overall project and task-related issues that must be resolved to complete a major task but may have no impact on the overall project budget and/or schedule.

A simple log format can be used to track at either level. It doesn't matter if the issues are tracked in a document, spreadsheet, database, or special purpose tool, as long as they are tracked somewhere. Details you'll likely want to capture for each issue include the following:

- Issue # and description

- Date identified

- Reported by
- Owner
- Status
- Priority
- Date to be resolved by
- Date closed

The project issue log should be reviewed at each status meeting. The task issues should be reviewed at major design or working sessions. It is helpful to shade closed issues to maintain group focus on open issues in these forums.

Control Changes

Formal acknowledgment of project changes is critical to successfully managing a project. Any issue resolution that impacts the project schedule, budget, or scope should be considered a change.

Organizations and project managers often have mechanisms in place to handle requests for major changes, which are scrutinized and then a collective decision is made. But the changes that often cause the biggest impact on a project are the little ones, cumulatively applied. Individually, the minor requests might be quite simple to implement. However, problems develop if there are too many small requests.

Similar to the issue log just described, the project manager often manages a change control log if there's not a more formal tracking mechanism in place. Information tracked in a change request control log includes:

- Change request control # and description
- Date requested
- Requested by
- Priority (in terms of business impact)
- Owner
- Estimated effort (workdays)
- Estimated cost
- Status
- Date closed

The change control log can also be leveraged to document enhancement requests for future releases. In this case, it's beneficial to also identify the enhancement's business value to facilitate future prioritization.

Manage Expectations

Executing the communications plan is the primary method for managing expectations about the DW/BI initiative throughout the organization.

Another technique for managing the expectations of business users is to maintain their involvement throughout the Lifecycle. The DW/BI team must interact with the business representatives during the requirements definition process, but the team should also seek out opportunities to keep them actively involved via BI application specifications, data model design reviews, stewardship, and potentially the BI tool evaluation.

NOTE The project plan should include business user acceptance tasks following each major deliverable on the Lifecycle.

Managing the expectations of the project team is often overlooked. Due to the iterative nature of DW/BI development, frustrations can mount on the team. In a traditional systems development effort, rework is a sign of poor design or execution, but in the DW/BI world, rework is a fact of life to address changing business conditions and growth. The team needs to be reminded of this necessary mindset shift.

Recognize Project Trouble Signs

This book is loaded with practical advice and guidance for designing, developing, and deploying a DW/BI solution. Obviously, we can't synthesize all those nuggets in one list; however we did want to identify common project warning signs while we're on the topic of project management. Unfortunately, numerous project teams have fallen into these pitfalls or traps in the past.

- Fail to recruit an influential visionary from the senior ranks of the business community.

- Assume the project's resources can learn everything they need to know on the job.

- Tackle too much at once rather than pursuing a more manageable iterative development effort focused on a single business process.

- Become enamored of technology rather than focusing on alignment with the business's goals and needs.

- Assume you can develop a DW/BI project without involvement from the business throughout the project's lifecycle, from requirements analysis to data and BI application design and stewardship.

- Commit to moving forward with a project, even though the source data is known to be of poor quality, or worse, has not even been vetted yet to see if it can support your mission.

- Believe the DW/BI databases should be designed like normalized transaction processing databases or only loaded with summary information.

- Underestimate the data cleansing and quality assurance workload.

- Pay more attention to ETL operational performance and ease of development rather than BI query performance and ease of use. On the other hand, the pendulum can swing too far in the other direction where including every analytic bell-and-whistle puts so much burden on the ETL that nothing ever comes out of the data kitchen.

- Be oblivious to the need for BI applications to empower the business community.

- Last, but certainly not least, fail to acknowledge that DW/BI success is tied directly to user acceptance. If the business community hasn't accepted the DW/BI system as a foundation for improved decision making, your efforts have been exercises in futility.

Manage the Program

In this final section, we explore DW/BI program management concepts. Until this point, we have focused on the needs of an individual project iteration of the Lifecycle because this is commonly where organizations begin. However, once the initial project is deployed successfully, demand will increase rapidly, creating the need and opportunity for coordination and management across individual projects.

Program management elevates awareness above the individual release or project effort. While the DW/BI environment will continue to expand in small manageable chunks on a project-by-project basis, the program looks across those discrete iterations, leveraging learning and development from one project to others. While we focus on delivering business value with each and every project, the potential organizational impact begins to grow exponentially when we focus on synchronization at the program level.

When we described team responsibilities earlier in this chapter, we were already introducing the program perspective, especially with the front office DW/BI director or program manager roles. In addition, the architects and data stewards often operate at a program capacity. Players with program-level responsibilities need to focus on the following activities.

Establish Governance Responsibility and Processes

Although the solo senior business sponsor may be perfectly adequate for the first iteration of your DW/BI environment, the program manager will want to establish a more permanent and broader governance structure, typically in the form of an executive level steering committee or advisory board. Composed of representatives from various business units, the governance steering committee meets regularly, typically quarterly or semi-annually, to set goals, establish priorities, and allocate funds. Strong, effective governance committees share the following characteristics:

- **Visionary leadership.**   Just as with individual business sponsors, members of the governance committee need to both visualize and verbalize the potential impact of improved information on the organization's key initiatives. They need to be passionate about the cause or step aside, because they'll be asked to rally others up, down, and across the organization. As the business and its initiatives evolve, the vision for DW/BI must also evolve.

- **Prioritize based on enterprise-level needs.**   The governance committee must resist the urge to lobby for their own special interest group. Members need to focus on the good of the greater whole, even if that means their departmental desires end up on the back burner. The prioritization technique that we mentioned earlier in this chapter and elaborate on in Chapter 3 is a powerful technique to institutionalize with the group for ongoing prioritization exercises. Often members of the DW/BI governance committee also participate in the organization's annual planning process to establish key business goals and objectives, which is excellent input to the DW/BI prioritization activity.

- **Support enterprise data integration.**   Consistent, integrated data sounds like an IT concern, but the executive governance committee must be equally concerned. They must clearly understand the business benefits of integration and show their support. Enterprise data integration faces far more political challenges than technical obstacles. Without executive commitment, integration will remain an IT pipe dream.

- **Prepare to spend money for the long haul.**   Unfortunately, establishing an environment to support business analysis doesn't come cheap and the maintenance costs don't go away. Of course, just as you can choose to drive an economy or luxury car, the same holds true for DW/BI implementations. The executive governance board needs to provide ongoing financial support for the foreseeable future. DW/BI programs collapse without adequate funding. On the other hand, it is also possible to overspend; although a big budget provides short-term euphoria for the team, nothing is sustainable if the costs exceed the benefits.

- **Ensure IT and the business remains aligned.**   Though the DW/BI program/project often starts out well-intentioned with initially tight alignment between the business and IT, it's easy to drift back to historical comfort zones. The governance committee needs to relentlessly reinforce the focus on business acceptance as the key ongoing success metric for the initiative. It may also need to remind the business community that successful DW/BI environments are built incrementally, requiring some organizational patience, which is often in short supply.

Beneath this executive governance structure, there are often working committees focused on more tactical issues influencing the overall program, such as data stewardship or technical upgrade planning.

Elevate Data Stewardship to Enterprise Level

A common approach to managing the enterprise's data assets is avoidance. In this scenario, data is managed and deployed departmentally rather than at the enterprise level. Each department or function builds its own private databases, data marts, or repository, but there's no overall enterprise view. It's initially appealing because everyone gets exactly what they want without contending with organizational consensus. Numerous existing DW/BI systems have been constructed on this basis, including prepackaged analytics bundled with transaction systems.

However, because each department uses slightly different definitions and interpretations, no one's data ties to anyone else's and the result is anarchy. You lose the ability to look across the enterprise, missing opportunities for cross-functional sharing. Likewise, this mayhem produces significant organizational waste. Nearly redundant departmental databases translate into nearly redundant data development, administration, and storage expenses. Even more wasteful are the resources devoted to understanding and/or reconciling the inconsistently defined data.

These data silos are a curse to many mature DW/BI environments. Tackling data architecture for the enterprise is one of the most important items to focus on at the program level. You can bring order to the chaos, but you need the political clout, financial means, and inclination to challenge the status quo. Rather than letting everyone build independent, department-centric databases, corporate information assets need to be proactively managed. Many CIOs are stepping up to their fiduciary responsibility. The executive governance committee also needs to commit resources and clout given the inevitable geo-political landmines. The DW/BI team needs to assess the enterprise's level of commitment to integration. If senior executives want integrated information systems, you can rely on their support when tough compromises need to be made. But if the vision of integration does not exist, the DW/BI team can rarely wake up an entire enterprise.

We discussed the role of data stewards earlier in this chapter. At the program level, it is critical that this function transcend individual projects.

The data stewards should be establishing common definitions and transformation business rules for all information that's of cross-organizational interest in the enterprise. The descriptive master data of the organization should be managed centrally and then shared with any project that needs it. This common shared reference data serves as the foundation for integration, as we further explore in Chapter 6. The ability to ask questions and integrate performance metrics based on common reference data elevates the DW/BI environment to new heights in terms of potential business value.

Likewise, core performance metrics should be extracted from the source once and shared, rather than redundantly extracting the information for each department that's interested. We strongly encourage a process-centric perspective to delivering analytic information, thereby eradicating the departmental bias that permeates much of the existing DW/BI literature.

Leverage Methods and Architectural Best Practices

With its cross-project vantage point, program management should take responsibility for defining, documenting, and promoting best practices. Often referred to as *competency centers* or *centers of excellence*, these program level resources provide central coordination to leverage the organization's DW/BI assets and encourage collaboration for optimal usage. They determine what's worked, and what hasn't, across projects to disseminate expertise and consistent best practices around proven methods, deliverables, standards, and training. They sometimes serve a role akin to in-house consultants to leverage experience, avoid recreating the wheel, and ultimately reduce the time to deliver consistent, quality solutions. Competency center resources often provide specialized services, focusing on areas such as data modeling, ETL, metadata management, BI application development, or technology planning. Obviously, one size doesn't fit all in terms of the organizational reporting structure of these resources; however, the function performed is critical for optimization at the program level. Roles and responsibilities need to be clearly defined to avoid confusion and potential conflict with other enterprise functions and/or project-level resources.

Conduct Periodic Assessments

Given program management's concern with ongoing funding, it's critical that assessments are regularly conducted to ensure that the DW/BI deliverables are satisfying the needs of the business. Rather than assuming that no news is good news, we encourage program management to proactively assess the health of the environment. This entails going out and speaking with representatives from the business. Our natural tendency is to speak with the experts and liaisons to the DW/BI program in the business units, but you need to also speak with the real business folks themselves. They're the ones who should be leveraging the information and analyses to make better decisions, so they should be the ones telling us how we're doing. Identify and prioritize action items to address any shortcomings uncovered during the check up.

Communicate, Communicate, Communicate

Finally, program management is constantly communicating or facilitating communication among others. Whether it's selling upward, evangelizing outward, or coordinating downward, the program manager's communication job is never done.

Conclusion

The upfront definition of your DW/BI initiative plants numerous stakes in the ground that have downstream implications on your ultimate success. We encourage you to assess your overall readiness, paying extra attention to the requisite business sponsorship.

Once the initiative is funded, the project manager needs to focus on resource staffing and detailed project task and timeline planning. Ongoing management of a DW/BI project is similar to more traditional system development efforts, but the realities of a cross-functional project team working on a highly visible initiative imposes additional demands on status monitoring, documentation, scope control, and, most importantly, communication.

Finally, coordination of sponsorship, stewardship, and best practices at the program level is crucial to maximize the potential business return from your DW/BI investment.

BLUEPRINT FOR ACTION

Managing the Effort and Reducing Risk

Because this chapter focused specifically on program/project management, we won't reiterate all our previously discussed management recommendations and guidelines.

Risk is reduced by first assessing whether your organization is ready for a DW/BI initiative. An honest appraisal of the business sponsorship, problem set, skilled resource availability, and underlying data feasibility gets the project on

(continued)

stable footing from the beginning. From there, risk is mitigated by biting off small, manageable chunks of effort, while still ensuring business alignment.

Regular, frequent monitoring of progress and proactive communication and involvement with the business boosts the likelihood of an on-time delivery of capabilities that the business is clamoring for. Each major Lifecycle box or milestone should conclude with a business acceptance task.

Assuring Quality

Getting the right resources on the team goes a long way to assuring quality. Of course, seasoned veterans with track records of success are optimal. If your team is young and green, be prepared to spend money on education and/or guidance from skilled resources at key decision points.

Key Roles

Key roles for program/project planning and management include:

◆ The project manager and business project lead drive the project definition activities, with heavy involvement from both the business and IT sponsors.

◆ Project planning is also guided by the project manager and business project lead, with active participation and input from all other team members.

◆ Ongoing project management responsibilities rest primarily on the shoulders of the project manager, again with assistance from the business project lead.

◆ Ongoing program management is typically handled by the DW/BI director or program manager, working in conjunction with the executive governance steering committee.

◆ Though the business sponsor(s) is not responsible for any major project tasks, their involvement is critical throughout the program/project planning and management activities, especially when it comes to prioritization, issue resolution, and organizational culture changes. Departure of the business sponsor is the most common cause for DW/BI program/project stagnation.

Key Deliverables

Key deliverables for program/project planning and management include:

◆ Program/project scope and charter
◆ Program/project business justification

(continued)

BLUEPRINT FOR ACTION *(continued)*

- ◆ Program/project communication plan
- ◆ Program/project plan and task list
- ◆ Program/project status meeting agenda and meeting notes
- ◆ Program/project progress presentations for business sponsors and the executive governance committee, IT peers and management, and the business community at large
- ◆ Program/project issue and change control logs

Estimating Considerations

The effort required to define your DW/BI project is highly dependent on your readiness and situation. At one end of the spectrum, it may require only a few weeks to establish scope and build the justification. However, if you identify a significant readiness shortfall, it may require several months of effort to conduct a high level business requirements analysis, construct a proof-of-concept, and recruit a well-qualified sponsor before you can proceed.

The initial project plan should be developed in less than two weeks. This plan will continue to be revised every step of the way.

The effort to manage the project is directly related to its size and scope. The DW/BI project manager should be assigned full time to the initiative, although they may also perform non-project management tasks depending on their availability and skill set.

Finally, ongoing program management is just as it sounds — ongoing in perpetuity.

Website Resources

The following template for program/project planning and management is available on the book's website at www.kimballgroup.com :

- ◆ Project plan task list

Task List

PROJECT/PROGRAM PLANNING & MANAGEMENT

Legend:
- ● Primary responsibility
- ○ Involved
- ◆ Provides input
- ▢ Informed of results

Task	Fans	Front Office		Coaches		Regular Line-Up							Special Teams			
	Business Users	Business Sponsor / Business Driver	DW/BI Director / Program Manager	Project Manager	Business Project Lead	Business Analyst	Data Steward / QA Analyst	Data Architect / Data Modeler / DBA	Metadata Manager	ETL Architect / ETL Developer	BI Architect / App Developer / Portal Developer	Technical Architect / Tech Support Specialist	Security Manager	Lead Tester	Data Mining / Stats Specialist	Educator
PROJECT DEFINITION																
1 Assess DW/BI readiness		○	○	●	●	◆		◆		◆	◆	◆				
2 Develop preliminary project scope/charter		○	○	●	●	◆		◆		◆	◆	◆				
3 Build business justification	◆	○	◆	●	●	◆		◆								
PROJECT PLANNING & MANAGEMENT																
1 Establish project identity		◆	◆	●	●											
2 Identify project resources		◆	◆	●	●											
3 Prepare project plan		▢	▢	●	●	○	○	○	○	○	○	○	○	○	○	○
4 Develop project communication plan		◆	◆	●	●											
5 Conduct project team kick-off & planning		◆	◆	●	●	○	○	○	○	○	○	○	○	○	○	○
6 Develop process to manage scope/control changes		◆	◆	●	●											
7 Develop process to measure success			◆	●	●											
8 User acceptance/project review	▢	○	○	○	○	○	○	○	○	○	○	○	○	○	○	○
9 Ongoing project management	▢	▢	▢	○	○	▢	▢	▢	▢	▢	▢	▢	▢	▢	▢	▢
PROGRAM PLANNING & MANAGEMENT																
1 Establish governance responsibility/process	▢	○	●	○	○	▢		▢	▢	▢	▢	▢	▢	▢	▢	▢
2 Establish program communication plan		○	●	○	○											
3 Establish enterprise data stewardship		▢	●	○	○	○	○	○	○	○	○	○	○	○	○	○
4 Establish program best practices			●	○	○	○	○	○	○	○	○	○	○	○	○	○
5 Conduct periodic program assessments	◆	○	●	○	○	○	○	○	○	○	○	○	○	○	○	○
6 Ongoing program management	▢	▢	●			▢	▢	▢	▢	▢	▢	▢	▢	▢	▢	▢

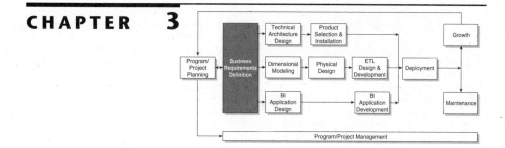

CHAPTER 3

Collecting the Requirements

Business users and their requirements impact nearly every decision made throughout the design and implementation of a DW/BI system. From our perspective, business requirements sit at the center of the universe, as illustrated in Figure 3-1, because they are so critical to successful data warehousing. Your understanding of the requirements influence most Lifecycle choices, from establishing the right scope, modeling the right data, picking the right tools, applying the right transformation rules, building the right analyses, and providing the right deployment support.

Business requirements analysis occurs at two distinct levels. At the more macro level, you need to understand the business's needs and priorities relative to a program perspective. This may be as broad as the entire enterprise, or simply across multiple projects. On the micro level, you delve into the users' needs and desires in the context of a single, relatively narrowly defined project.

For your first DW/BI initiative, you'll likely make two passes, gathering higher level program requirements to survey the landscape and set direction with senior executives, followed by a more detailed, grounded effort focused on project-specific requirements. In subsequent Lifecycle iterations, you'll probably delve directly into the lower level project requirements, unless it's time to expand or reprioritize the program.

As you might imagine, the general process and our recommended best practices for gathering business requirements are quite similar regardless of whether you're focused on the program or project. All requirements gathering

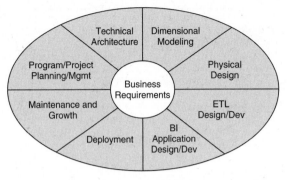

Figure 3-1 Business requirements impact virtually every aspect of the project.

initiatives begin with a preparation phase, followed by interactive face-to-face elicitation meetings with the business, and are then brought to an orderly conclusion with documentation and determination of next steps. Where the activities differ, depending on whether you're operating at the macro or micro level, include the participant selection, breadth and depth of the information collected, resulting documentation, and techniques for finalizing next steps. Table 3.1 highlights these distinctions.

In this chapter, we begin with tips and techniques that cover the entire appetizer-to-dessert requirements definition process at the macro program level. We then circle back through the activities to highlight recommended modifications for project requirements. Don't be daunted that we're circling back; it mirrors what you should do to establish the overall DW/BI program strategy and roadmap and then dive into the details.

This chapter is a must-read for program/project managers and business analysts who are leading requirements definition activities. Even if you're focused on a specific project instead of the overall program, you need to read this entire chapter because there are helpful hints sprinkled throughout. Likewise, other team members participating in the requirements process, such as the dimensional modeler, should become familiar with the techniques and guidelines outlined in this chapter. Business and IT project sponsors should also peruse this material to help manage organizational expectations appropriately.

Overall Approach to Requirements Definition

To better understand the business's requirements, begin by talking to the business users. What a novel concept! Although this may sound obvious, we have seen many organizations try alternative approaches. Gathering business requirements is often outside an IT person's comfort zone; it's easier and less threatening to look at operational source data layouts, talk with DBAs

Table 3-1 Differences Between Program and Project Requirements Definition Efforts

	PROGRAM REQUIREMENTS	PROJECT REQUIREMENTS
Preparation	Broader organizational research	Focus preparation around single business process
Participants	Cross functional horizontal representation; more heavily weighted to senior business management	Potential users/beneficiaries of improved access to single business process (not necessarily single business department); more heavily weighted to middle management and analysts
Business Questioning	High level understanding of business goals, opportunities, and key supporting processes	More detailed information and analysis requirements; more inclusion of existing reports and analyses
Data Audit	Preliminary feasibility assessment of multiple potential data sources	Preliminary data profiling of single primary data source
Documentation	Narrative on each process-centric requirement; include preliminary data warehouse bus matrix	Detailed findings related to three impact areas: data model, BI reports/analytics, and technical architecture
Next Steps	Prioritization with senior management, loop back to Lifecycle project planning, and prepare for detailed project requirements	Business acceptance of findings; updated project scope, if appropriate; move ahead with next Lifecycle tasks

and source system experts, or review existing reports. On the other hand, business users can be intimidating and demanding. And they speak a language unfamiliar to the typical IT person; business is a second language for most of us. Regardless of the intimidation factor, you need to begin with the business users. Remember, they sit at the center of your DW/BI universe; you must learn to see the world from their perspective.

You can't just ask users what data they want in the data warehouse. Instead, you need to talk to them about their jobs, their objectives, and their challenges. You need to better understand what they do and how they make decisions, both today and in the future, to ensure that the DW/BI system addresses their needs.

As you gather requirements from the business users, you should intersperse some data reality into the process by interviewing key IT personnel. You must consider the business's needs in tandem with the availability of data to support these requirements. It's a balancing act, but failure is inevitable if you consider one without the other. The data audit interviews help you understand whether the data is there to support what the business is asking for and whether the data is complete and reliable. They also uncover the land mines hidden in the data, such as indicator fields that were never populated or were labeled one thing but then used for something completely different.

Interviews versus Facilitated Sessions

Face-to-face sessions with the business stakeholders are critical to accurately understand their requirements. In addition, the interactive meetings with the business people deliver another benefit. They help build positive working relationships and more tightly bond the business representatives to the program/project initiative, which greatly influences their ultimate acceptance of the deliverables.

There are two basic interactive techniques for gathering requirements: interviews and facilitated sessions. Interviews are conducted either with individuals or small groups. One advantage of this approach is that you need to schedule a relatively limited amount of time on the interviewees' calendars; you don't need to try to coordinate ten people for a full all-day meeting. Interviews also encourage a high degree of participation from the interviewees, which generates tremendous detail data. There is no way an interviewee can just listen without participating in one of these meetings. Interviews ensure that every voice is heard.

> **NOTE** DW/BI teams will often tell us that they fully understand the business, only to be amazed after sitting through an interview by all that was uncovered and learned.

The alternative approach is to schedule larger group sessions led by a facilitator. Facilitated sessions can be used to encourage creative brainstorming. Although they require a greater time commitment from each participant, facilitated sessions can actually reduce the total time required to gather information, assuming you can schedule a meeting with ten to twelve people within a reasonable time period. Based on our experience, facilitation is more appropriate after you have gathered enough baseline information to generally understand the business and its vocabulary.

In addition to interviews and facilitated sessions, there is a third face-to-face technique. It involves immersing the business analyst into the user community so they practically morph into a business user. There's no better way to understand the business, but this immersion technique occurs infrequently due to the commitment and skill sets required.

We don't believe one technique is necessarily always better than the other. We recommend using the technique that is most appropriate given your organization's expertise, challenges, and what you have already subjected your business users to. No two organizations are identical; so there is no right approach. It's worth noting that most of our recommendations throughout this chapter will be applicable regardless of the technique chosen.

Having acknowledged that different approaches should be used in different situations, we are going to describe the approach that seems to fit most often. It is actually a hybrid of the two techniques. Interviews are used to gather the gory details, and then facilitated sessions are used to agree on priorities and next steps. We believe the "interview first" approach ensures effective, productive facilitated group sessions.

Methods to Avoid for Collecting Requirements

We have seen organizations attempt to gather requirements using methods other than the face-to-face approaches just described. Non-interactive alternatives may seem easier or less demanding for the requirements team, but the results are also less complete and conclusive. This is a time when the adage, "you get what you pay for," holds true. We'll briefly discuss these non-recommended methods, along with the inherent risks and challenges.

Sending out surveys or questionnaires is not an effective requirements gathering technique for several reasons. First of all, only a limited self-selected subset of business users will respond. Respondents typically come from the individual contributor or power user ranks, as opposed to middle or senior management. Also, the pre-canned survey questions are static so there's no opportunity to drill down into more detail based on their responses.

In an attempt to gather business requirements, project teams sometimes procure the largest binder they can locate and fill it with samples of the business's existing reports. It's a fast and easy way to gather requirements, right? Wrong! While there is some value in analyzing existing reports, doing so in the absence of a face-to-face session with the business to understand *what* and *why* behind every report may be misleading. Organizations may have been producing a large portfolio of reports for years, but only a fraction are actually used. Inventorying reports is an equalizing activity; it's easy to lose sight of the forest from the trees. Finally, remember that you're building an analytic environment to answer today's business questions, as well as tomorrow's concerns. You're not just re-platforming the current reporting capabilities.

Another supposed requirements gathering technique is to distribute a list of data elements to the business so they can easily indicate whether each element should be included in the data warehouse. Of course, a business user who's asked this question has only one logical response: "I need all the data elements." While this data-centric approach may make life easier for the modeler, it's a terribly ineffective way to solicit business requirements. You'll learn virtually nothing about what the business is trying to accomplish. And your chances of successfully deploying a DW/BI solution based on requirements gathered via this method are exceedingly slim.

Prepare for the Interview

The prerequisite setup activities prior to gathering business requirements are often overlooked. We want to review these techniques because they position you for success by eliminating as many unknowns during the requirements gathering process as possible. These are all commonsense activities, but are frequently forgotten.

Identify the Interview Team

First, you need to establish roles and responsibilities within the interview team. We strive to have the same team conduct both the business user requirements and IT data audit meetings for continuity. The team is typically structured with the following team members.

Lead Interviewer

The primary responsibility of the lead interviewer is to direct the questioning. A key candidate for this role is the business analyst described in Chapter 2. Desirable characteristics include basic business knowledge and good verbal communication skills. It helps if the lead interviewer has a genuine interest and curiosity about the business. The best lead interviewers are quick studies who can think on their feet and are nimble enough to go with the flow.

This is a high profile role. Not everyone is cut out to be a lead interviewer. We caution against coercing potential candidates into working beyond their personally deemed competence levels. The lead interviewer's relationship with interviewees and the business community should also be taken into consideration. The requirements analysis process depends on open, honest communication between the lead interviewer and interviewees.

> **NOTE** If you opt to engage a consulting organization because you don't have the internal expertise to lead requirements gathering sessions with senior executives, make sure internal project resources participate in the effort for skills transfer and project continuity.

Scribe

The scribe's primary responsibility is to take copious notes during the interview, capturing as much interview content detail as possible, regardless of whether it is news to them. These notes serve as the documentation base for the entire DW/BI team, many of whom may not be as familiar with the subject matter. The scribe also asks for clarification if disconnects or misunderstandings between the lead interviewer and interviewee occur. The scribe is the safety net that catches any points missed by the lead interviewer and can intervene if the interviewee is becoming frustrated with the process.

Although it sounds like a relatively easy role to fill, again, not everyone is destined to be an effective scribe. Good scribes must be willing and able to capture excruciating details. Also, the scribe typically develops the initial draft of deliverables from the requirements definition activities, so solid written communication skills are necessary. Finally, some people may find the scribe's naturally passive role frustrating and be tempted to barge onto the lead interviewer's turf and establish themselves as the expert. Potential conflicts like these between the lead interviewer and scribe should be avoided because they are distracting to everyone in the interview.

We are sometimes asked about using a tape recorder instead of a human scribe, but we generally discourage this practice for several reasons. First of all, tape recorders change the dynamics of the meeting. Users are often uncomfortable with the notion of being taped. They might want segments of the meeting to be off the record, which makes for awkward transitions. Second, the lead interviewer's written notes will inevitably not capture the full content of the interview. Someone will need to listen to the tape recordings and take supplemental notes from them. This process is somewhat like watching a television rerun; it is not very interesting but consumes large chunks of time. We believe it is better to have two people with two brains and two sets of eyes and ears actively engaged in the session rather than using a tape recorder as your partner.

Tape recorders may be used to supplement the scribe, depending on their experience and comfort level with physical note taking. You will not want to listen to the whole tape, but it can be useful as a backup. If an interviewee is really on a roll, the recorder may be helpful to ensure that the complete content is captured without slowing down the interviewee. If you choose to use a tape recorder, you should inform the interviewee during the meeting introduction that the tape will only be used by the interview team; the tape is not part of the permanent project files and will be erased once the interview has been documented.

NOTE While we generally discourage the use of tape recorders during the requirements gathering, we're more open to the use of laptops to immediately capture the business person's input electronically.

Over the past few years, some scribes have abandoned pen and paper to immediately capture notes in electronic form on a laptop during the interview. Of course, electronic capture from the start aids the post-interview documentation development process. While many people can type more rapidly than they write, using the laptop as a data capture tool has some downsides. Users don't typically communicate in a structured outline format. Handwritten interview notes are often riddled with arrows to reference earlier comments, which can present challenges when using a laptop. Some interviewees are quick to jump to a whiteboard to visually diagram their organization or processes; capturing these evolving diagrams is easier done on paper than electronically. Finally, sitting behind a laptop screen creates a physical barrier that may distance the scribe from the proceedings. Clearly, we don't want the lead interviewer using a laptop during the interview. As for the scribe, there are both advantages and disadvantages to working with a laptop. In the end, you need to decide if the benefits outweigh the costs in your environment.

Observers

Observers are an optional part of the interview team. Other data warehouse team members, such as data modelers, DBAs, BI application developers, or technical support specialists involved in tool evaluations, are often interested in sitting in on interviews. We frequently have observers during our interviews because we are transferring interviewing skills to our clients' DW/BI teams. Optimally, there should be no more than two observers during an interview. Finally, remember that the role of observers is to observe — they are spectators.

Research the Organization

It is important to do your homework before starting the requirements gathering process. Start by reading your company's annual report. This is especially true when gathering requirements at the enterprise/program level. The annual report's letter from senior management provides clues about strategic corporate initiatives. You should also read the narrative review of business operations. You can usually skip the detailed financial statements because the important financial highlights have probably already been presented elsewhere in the report. Finally, the last couple of pages of the annual report may provide insight regarding organizational structure and reporting hierarchies.

If it is available, get a copy of the resulting documentation from the latest internal business/IT strategy and planning meeting. This session often begins with a list of objectives that the DW/BI solution will need to dovetail with. Also, try to track down any other pertinent internal strategy documents. You are inevitably going to discuss the details during the interviews, so you might as well read them ahead of time.

The interview team should also go online and look at your organization's website to understand the public messages your company is projecting. Also, use the Internet to research your key competitors and learn what others are saying about your company and its industry.

NOTE In preparation for requirements gathering sessions, learn as much as you can about your business, customers, and competitive marketplace, but always expect to learn more directly from the business participants.

The saying "those who forget the past are condemned to repeat it" certainly applies to data warehousing initiatives. Earlier efforts may not have been called data warehouse or business intelligence; it might have been the marketing information system or some cleverly constructed acronym for a business-oriented reporting and analysis system. It is in your best interest to find out what worked, what didn't, and why. Most importantly, you need to determine who was involved in these prior initiatives. You may want to use a different approach when dealing with any interviewees who were involved in a recent unsuccessful data warehouse attempt.

Select the Interviewees

Work with your business and IT management sponsors to determine who should be interviewed. It is inefficient, not to mention impossible, to speak with everyone, so you need to select a cross section of representatives. Reviewing a documented organization chart with your sponsors or a trusted coach can be very helpful. It is important that you understand the formal organization structure as well as the more informal, undocumented organization. You need to know who is highly influential, who is considered a visionary, who is the departmental mover and shaker, who is a supporter, and finally, who is a naysayer when it comes to information-based decision making. You also need to consider the political ramifications of not interviewing someone. It may be easier to conduct an extraneous interview for political reasons than to risk alienating someone.

Business Interviewees

At the enterprise program level, you obviously need to gather requirements horizontally across the organization. This cross-functional perspective allows the team to understand the organization's requirements at a macro level so that an overall DW/BI roadmap can be established. Understanding the key performance business processes and common descriptive information allows you to create a blueprint for extensibility across the program. The enterprise data warehouse bus architecture matrix, as we describe in more detail in Chapter 6, provides the enterprise-wide plan. It helps ensure that you can integrate data in the warehouse over time and avoid building those dreaded data islands or stovepipes.

NOTE The enterprise data warehouse bus architecture and associated matrix serves multiple purposes, including architecture planning, data integration coordination, and organizational communication. Stay tuned for more details in Chapter 6.

With program requirements gathering, we typically meet with nearly everyone at the senior executive level. Depending on your organization and scope of the effort, you may opt to exclude some executives. For example, in some organizations, there would be no reason to involve the legal general counsel, whereas their involvement may be absolutely critical in other situations.

In addition to the executive coverage, it's also beneficial to dip into the middle management ranks for further representation and additional details. You'll want to meet with the go-to folks in the organization, aptly named because they're the ones whom people turn to when they need analyses. Middle management interviews also bring more reality into the picture. They understand how those high level executive strategies are translated into business tactics. They also have a realistic perspective of where they'd like to be going with information and analysis versus where they are today. With program requirements, you won't spend much time with individual analysts, with the exception of the best and the brightest who are called upon to support the executive's needs.

IT and Compliance/Security Interviewees

The IT data audit interviews have a distinctively different flavor than the business user interviews. With broader program level requirements, you're not getting your hands dirty by doing detailed profiling of the data. You're merely trying to assess the feasibility of the underlying operational source systems to support the requirements emerging from the business side of the house. To assess preliminary feasibility, you typically speak with the key IT people who know the data and underlying systems inside and out. You may also get a sense of the feasibility by meeting with the IT liaisons to the user community.

In addition, we often meet with senior IT management during the interviewing process. IT management sometimes offers a vision for the potential use of information for competitive advantage. In other cases, these interviews offer guidance regarding overall plans for information dissemination throughout the organization. Although senior IT management may have already approved funding for the DW/BI initiative, depending on the size of the organization and communication channels, the DW/BI team may not fully understand IT management's vision or perspective on the project. It is important that the team allocate time to meet with these players to ensure they are in sync with general direction and strategies related to data warehousing and business intelligence.

Because these program requirements impact the overall DW/BI strategy, it's often helpful to include the compliance or security officers, as appropriate, to gain visibility to their requirements or constraints at this formative stage.

Develop the Interview Questionnaires

The lead interviewer must develop an interview questionnaire before interviewing begins. Actually, multiple questionnaires should be developed because the questioning will vary by job function and level. You are not going to ask a marketing executive the same questions you would a financial analyst. Also, the questionnaires for the data audit sessions will differ from business requirements questionnaires. Though data audit meetings are more within our comfort zone, it is still important that the lead interviewer generate a more systems and data-oriented list of questions prior to sitting down with the IT gurus.

The interview questionnaires should be structured to align with your intended interview flow. It should fit on one page so you are not flipping through pages if the interview comes to a lull. It is important that the lead interviewer view the questionnaire as a fallback device, not a rigid script. The questionnaire helps organize your thoughts before the interview, but don't follow it like a recipe during the interview. The lead interviewer needs to be mentally prepared for on-the-fly questioning to be successful. Figure 3-2 provides a sample questionnaire for a business manager.

Schedule the Interviews

When it is time to schedule the interviews, we strongly suggest you get an administrative assistant to help. Scheduling and rescheduling can become a nightmare. Also, don't be surprised by the lead time that is sometimes required. Especially with rigorous travel schedules, it might be two to three weeks before you can conduct an interview with a key player.

Sequence the Interviews

Begin the requirements definition process by first meeting with your business sponsorship. Optimally, you would interview the business driver, followed by a meeting with the business sponsor. You should understand the playing field from their perspective.

From there, our preference is to initially interview in the middle of the organizational hierarchy, rather than leading off at the top or bottom. The bottom is a disastrous place to begin because you have no idea where you are headed. The top is a great place for overall vision, but you need the business background, confidence, and credibility to converse at those levels. If you are not adequately prepared with in-depth business familiarity, the safest route is to begin in the middle of the organization.

A. INTRODUCTION (5 minutes)

Discuss DW/BI project objectives and overall status.

Discuss interview goals (e.g., focus on business requirements, talk about what you do, what you want to be doing, and why) and flow.

Introduce interview team and roles and confirm time available.

B. RESPONSIBILITIES

Describe your organization and its relationship to the rest of the company.

What are your primary responsibilities?

C. BUSINESS OBJECTIVES AND ISSUES

What are the objectives of your organization? What are you trying to accomplish? What are your top priority business goals?

How do you know you're doing well? What are your success metrics? How often do you monitor key success factors?

What are the key business issues you face today? What prevents you from meeting your business objectives? What's the impact on the organization?

How do you identify problems/exceptions or know you're headed for trouble?

Describe your products (or other key business dimension such as customer or vendor). How do you distinguish between products? Is there a natural way you categorize products? How would you narrow a list of thousands of products?

How often do these categorizations change? What should happen with your business analysis following a change?

D. ANALYSIS REQUIREMENTS

What type of routine analysis do you currently perform? What data is used? How do you currently get the data? What do you do with the information once you get it?

What analysis would you like to perform? Are there potential improvements to your current method/process?

What type of on-the-fly, ad hoc analysis do you typically perform?

What do you do with the analysis? Do you have time to ask the follow-up questions?

Which reports do you currently use? What data on the report is important? How do you use the information? If the report were dynamic, what would the report do differently?

How much historical information is required?

E. WRAP-UP

Summarize findings heard.

What opportunities exist to dramatically improve your business based on improved access to information? What's the financial impact?

What must this project accomplish to be deemed successful? Criteria should be measurable.

Thank participants.

Describe next steps (e.g., draft interview write-ups available within week) and upcoming opportunities for business involvement.

Figure 3-2 Sample interview questionnaire for a business manager or analyst.

With program level requirements gathering, you are typically interviewing representatives from multiple organizations, such as marketing, finance, field sales, and IT. You should scramble the interviews so that you don't complete one group or functional area before speaking with another. It is common to hear certain themes from one group and then get quite a different perspective from another. If you have completed all your interviews with the first functional area, it is difficult to return to these people and try to resolve the discrepancies you subsequently uncovered.

Establish the Interview Time and Place

As for logistics, we suggest scheduling executives for private interviews. They can handle being a lone interviewee with a two- or three-person interview team. If an executive insists on bringing anyone else to the interview, their lieutenant will either participate sparingly or monopolize the interview. If they do contribute, it probably won't be at the level of detail you need, so it is better to interview them separately. Executives should be interviewed in their own offices or an adjacent conference room.

NOTE It is always best to conduct requirements sessions on the users' turf. This minimizes delays and allows users to fetch supporting documentation at the end of the interview.

The remaining interviews should either be scheduled in candidates' offices, assuming there is adequate space for the interview team, or in a conference room in their department. We have been asked to conduct interviews in an IT conference room that was a 15-minute drive from the business community. It may have been an easy room for the administrator to reserve, but users struggled to locate it. We wasted valuable interview time waiting for, or searching for, lost interviewees. When they finally found the room, they didn't have ready access to key resources, like their binder of performance reports.

You should make sure the interview space is large enough to accommodate the interviewees and interview team, including the observers. No one wants to be shoved together like sardines. If you do meet in an office, make sure disruptions such as phone calls are minimized.

Interviews with non-executive business users may be set up as individual interviews or small group sessions. Middle management can handle an interview team, but the team may overwhelm a lone individual contributor. If you are scheduling small groups, the groups must be homogenous. The fact that all the interviewees come from marketing is not homogeneous enough; you want the interview group to come from the same function and/or job focus.

In small group interviews, no more than four people should be interviewed at once, representing no more than two organizational levels. Having their boss's boss in the same meeting is enough to squelch most users' candor. Sometimes even two levels of organizational hierarchy in the same interview are too much, depending on the working relationship between them. It's difficult to have a productive session when there are too many people with varying agendas.

Executive interviews typically require about thirty minutes. However, we suggest you schedule an hour because executives notoriously run late; your half hour session could turn into fifteen minutes if they're behind schedule. You should allow a minimum of an hour for individual interviewees and one and a half hours for small groups. Last but not least, you need to reserve at least thirty minutes between interviews. You need this break to debrief, begin to fill in your meeting notes, and deal with biological requirements. Interviewing can be an extremely painful process otherwise.

> **CAUTION** Business requirements and data audit interviewing is exhausting. It requires intense concentration to listen, take notes, and formulate the next brilliant question. You shouldn't schedule more than three or four interviews in a day.

Although you can't schedule eight interviews a day, try to schedule the interviews in a relatively short period of time, remembering to allow adequate time for interview absorption, analysis, and documentation. As you saw in Figure 3-1, the requirements impact every aspect of the implementation. Because you can't immerse yourself in dimensional data modeling or technical architecture design until completion of the interviews, you don't want to drag out the entire process. Interviewing is a critical path. Get it scheduled and finished in a reasonable period of time so that you can move on to the next step of the DW/BI implementation.

Prepare the Interviewees

Even before you start scheduling interviews, it is important that the interviewees are appropriately briefed and prepared to participate. With program level requirements, it is typically unrealistic to conduct a kickoff meeting for the participants; convening high-ranking officials from across the enterprise for an informational meeting is likely mission impossible. Sometimes the executive team receives a high level briefing at one of their regularly scheduled team gatherings.

At a minimum, a letter should be emailed to all the interview participants to inform them about the process and the importance of their participation and contribution. You will waste valuable minutes at the beginning of every interview explaining this general information if it is not communicated up front.

The briefing letter, such as the sample illustrated in Figure 3-3, should let the interviewee know what to expect during the interview. Explain that the goal is to understand their job responsibilities and business objectives, which then translate into the information and analyses required to get their job done. The interviewees may be asked to bring copies of frequently used reports or spreadsheet analyses. Finally, remind them of the interview time, duration, and location. A variation of the pre-interview letter should also be sent to the IT interviewees.

This letter should be signed by a high ranking sponsor, perhaps the head of the steering committee or CIO. The project manager can draft the communication, but it should be sent by someone well-respected by the interviewees.

Dear ATTENDEE,

Thank you for participating in business user meetings for the PROJECT NAME data warehouse/business intelligence project. As a reminder, the PROJECT NAME initiative is focused on . . .

The objective of the meeting is to better understand your area's business goals and priorities which translate into data and analyses needs. Your insight during these meetings is crucial to defining the requirements for PROJECT NAME.

Specifically, project team members intend to discuss the following topics during their meeting with you:

* **Responsibilities**
  Individual and departmental responsibilities

* **Business Objectives and Issues**
  Business metrics, industry and competitive trends, opportunities and obstacles

* **Analyses and Data Requirements**
  Key reports and analyses, frequencies, and current limitations

* **Project Success Criteria**

Please **bring copies of the analyses** you are currently performing and/or requesting.

ATTENDEE, thanks in advance for your participation. The project team looks forward to meeting you on DATE at TIME in MEETING ROOM. Please let me know if you have any questions in the meantime.

Sincerely,

Executive Sponsor

Figure 3-3 Sample pre-interview briefing letter.

NOTE If you have outsourced the requirements definition to an outside consulting organization, make sure the briefing letter is signed by a high level internal person instead of the lead consultant because most consultants lack the internal credibility and influence to rally the troops and ensure a high degree of participation.

We typically advise against attaching a list of the fifty questions you might ask in hopes that the interviewees will come prepared with answers. It is nearly inevitable that they won't take the time to prepare responses to your list. Some interviewees might cancel because they've been overly intimidated by the volume of your questions. Finally, a few might answer your questions on paper and then feel no need to show up for the interview itself.

Review Interviewing Ground Rules

Before we delve into the actual interview, we want to review some general interviewing ground rules.

Remember Your Interview Role

The first ground rule for effective interviewing is to abide by your designated roles on the interview team. The lead interviewer is supposed to ask unbiased questions; the user is to answer; the scribe should take notes and everyone else should listen. The entire interview team should be absorbing like a sponge. Unfortunately, people seem to often forget their job assignments.

We have witnessed interviewers ask very leading questions of the user rather than the classic, open-ended why, how, what-if, and what-then questions. We have seen scribes get so caught up in the conversation that they forget to take notes. We have seen observers answering the questions rather than letting the user respond, or defending the current systems in response to criticism. We've observed interview team members debating and arguing with one another, while the interviewee watched the ping pong match from the sidelines.

Good interviewers should be seen, but not heard (at least not heard too much). Strong active listening skills are required. Use physical body language and verbal clues to encourage the interviewees and show your interest. Interviewees often understand what information you're looking for during the requirements process. With a little prodding and lots of subtle encouragement, some will essentially interview themselves.

Assume You Will Learn

Before sitting down for an interview, you need to make sure you're approaching the session with the right mindset. You can't presume that you already know it all. If that's your attitude, then the interviews will be a waste of time for everyone involved. Skilled interviewers are curious and want to learn more.

We have occasionally observed too-smart interviewers. In an effort to demonstrate what they know, their questions tend to be long-winded, often eliciting blank stares or responses like "What was the question again?" Interviewers who try to impress others are missing the point. Ask simple, straightforward questions and you'll have a better chance of understanding complex concepts.

Verify Communications

During the interview, make sure you comprehend what the interviewee is saying. Paraphrasing what you heard is one technique to ensure comprehension. It is also critical that you address any confusion during the interview; you shouldn't wait until the interview is over to confide to your team members that you didn't understand what the interviewee was referring to during a fifteen minute segment. The lead interviewer and scribe should have the courage to acknowledge that they are lost and resolve any miscommunications during the meeting.

As you are conducting interviews, it is also important that vocabulary not be taken for granted. In many organizations, the same word has multiple meanings and different words are used to mean the same thing. For example, business users might want better access to customer revenue, but it's unclear whether they're referring to the customer's gross or net revenue. Vocabulary standardization issues become especially apparent with program requirements as you conduct interviews horizontally across the organization. You should be identifying and noting vocabulary inconsistencies during the interviews, but don't attempt to resolve them in the interview forum. You have just sent up a red flag that more work awaits you down the road as you attempt to define common vocabulary. This type of issue is best resolved by a facilitated session with cross-department empowered data stewards.

Be Conversational

It can be intimidating to conduct an interview with executive management. After all, we are mere mortals, and they are division presidents. If possible, the interview team should try to ignore those hierarchical differences and assume equality. It helps the flow of the interview if you are able to establish a peer relationship with the interviewee. A key to establishing this type of rapport is to use the interviewees' vocabulary. It is also helpful to demonstrate general business acumen, especially when you are trying to get the interviewees to think outside of the box. You may integrate general learning from earlier interviews, while remembering that the interview is all about them talking and you listening. Finally, the lead interviewer's attitude and demeanor is also important. Within the same day, they may need to demonstrate the confidence to converse with an executive without being condescending to analysts.

Maintain Interview Schedule Flexibility

During the interview process, the number of interviews typically grows from 10 to 20 percent. It is fairly common for an interviewee to suggest meeting with someone else in the organization. The interview team should anticipate these additional interviewees and view them as a bonus rather than a burden. Based on our experience, these additional interviewees frequently have keen insights to add.

Having just suggested that the interview team stay flexible about adding interviews to the schedule, remember that user interviewing is draining. You will probably be exhausted and uncertain what you asked whom by the third or fourth interview in a day. It is a waste of everyone's time to attempt to conduct thirty interviews in a week due to the diminishing returns. Depending on the players involved, you may want to rotate the lead interviewer and scribe responsibilities.

> **NOTE** You will know the interview process is nearly complete when you begin to hear significant repetition during the interviews, although you may still need to conduct some interviews for political or organizational reasons. Hearing the same answers repetitively is good news. It means that you have encircled the organization's business requirements.

Manage Expectations Continuously

The final interview ground rule is to manage user expectations during the course of the interviews. DW/BI projects are typically high visibility initiatives. Throughout the interview, as appropriate, the initiative should be presented positively, without overselling and making promises that can't be delivered on. Business interviewees should be informed that the DW/BI system will evolve. They are probably used to a more traditional, one-time requirements gathering process followed by frozen specifications and a lengthy enhancement queue. Now is the time to set the expectation that data warehousing requires an iterative design and development effort. There will be an ongoing process for gathering requirements and releasing functionality in the DW/BI environment. This leaves the door open for a return visit to gather more requirements for the next phase.

Conduct the Interview

You're now ready to begin interviewing. Every interview starts with brief introductions to remind the interviewee who you are and why you're there. Depending on the interview team composition, the project manager or business project lead may convey this high level project information; otherwise, the lead interviewer takes responsibility for this part of the interview. The important thing is that responsibility for the introduction has been assigned in advance. The project and interview objectives should be reviewed. It is also appropriate to introduce the team players in attendance and explain their roles during the interview; otherwise, the interviewees may wonder why the scribe isn't asking any questions.

The overall requirements process should also be communicated during the introduction. Let the interviewee know that you will be documenting the interview, providing documentation to them for review and feedback, and then publishing the consolidated findings. Finally, it is always wise to reconfirm the time available for the interview.

The first couple of minutes of the interview are critical because they set the tone for the rest of the meeting. We strongly suggest you use organized notes or a pseudo script for this segment of the meeting and rehearse what you are going to say in advance. You must convey a crisp and clean message.

You want the users to feel at ease and comfortable talking with you openly. At the same time, you want them to understand the importance of the requirements gathering activity. In part, you convey this importance by being organized and prepared for the meeting; this is not the time or place to wing it. Use the interviewee's vocabulary during the introduction. You should tell them that this will not be a technical meeting. Unfortunately, we have been on teams where the interview introductions were rambling dialogues, littered with techno babble including hardware model numbers, database versions, and network protocols. These comments were totally inappropriate and did not set a productive tone for the business user interview.

NOTE You send a clear message to the interviewee that they're respected and important to the process by arriving to the interview on time and well prepared. Putting your phone and pager on mute is another sign of your respect.

Following the introduction, the lead interviewer jumps into the substance of the meeting by getting participants to talk about what they do and why. The initial questions should focus on their jobs and where they fit. These are lob balls that interviewees respond to easily because they're simple, non-threatening questions that don't require the interviewee to think very hard from the start. Although you may already know their official title from the organization charts, it is always useful to hear them describe their key job responsibilities.

With program requirements analysis, the questioning tends to hover in the treetops rather than diving into the gory details. This is typically a comfortable level of questioning for executives; however, you may be tempted to dive into more detail with the analysts in the business. The objective at this point is to obtain an understanding of the lay of the land. Once an initial project or area of focus has been identified, you'll circle back for more detailed project requirements analysis with middle management and individual analysts.

Although you aren't delving into the specifics required to design the dimensional model, technical architecture, or BI application specs, you should still strive to peel back the layers of the onion by asking high level questions and then following the interviewee's lead. The ability to ask appropriate follow-up questions distinguishes a mediocre interviewer from an outstanding one. In doing so, you build credibility by demonstrating that you are listening and absorbing what they're saying. Also, it's a very comfortable flow for the interviewee because it's conversational. People typically don't mind taking the time to tell you what they do. However, it is not much fun to be pelted with questions from a five page questionnaire whether or not they make sense to ask at this time. Come prepared with sample questions, but every interview flows differently. Don't expect to ask all of these questions or to ask them in a particular order; you need to go with the flow.

NOTE The lead interviewer should have primary responsibility for steering the session. You don't want the interview to turn into a free-for-all, bounding randomly from one interviewer to another.

Program Business Interviews

The objective of these interviews is to get an overall understanding of the organization, where it is headed, and the associated information and analytic needs. High level questions you might ask of an executive include the following:

What are the objectives of your organization? What are you trying to accomplish?

These questions provide insight into the key business initiatives and underlying processes that the business monitors and attempts to impact, such as increasing sales or decreasing direct mail expenses.

How do you measure success? How do you know you are doing well? How often do you measure yourselves?

It is absolutely critical that you understand the organization's success metrics because they are the core data elements that must be tracked in the DW/BI system. Depending on the situation, this data might be sales volume, market share, response rate, profit, on-time delivery, or length of stay. The response to "How often do you measure yourself" has implications on the data latency and update strategy for the data warehouse.

What are the key business issues you face today? What are you doing to address them? What is the impact on the organization?

This is the classic "What keeps you awake at night?" question, which may be a challenge for some interviewers to pose to their senior executives.

How do you identify problems or know when you might be headed for trouble? How do you spot exceptions in your business? What opportunities exist to dramatically impact your business based on improved access to information? What is the financial impact? If you could . . . , what would it mean to your business?

These are important questions, especially if you still need to financially justify the DW/BI initiative. Even if quantified business impact isn't a current project concern, ask the questions anyway because the answers will be helpful at some point down the road.

What is your vision to better leverage information within your organization? How do you anticipate that your staff will interact directly with information?

With this question, you are getting an understanding of their vision, and assessing whether they have the political willpower to encourage and reinforce fact-based decision making instead of the more prevalent gut-based process. You will also understand expectations regarding their staff's interaction with data. Sometimes IT folks insist on delivering the ultimate data slicing-and-dicing machine, while the business merely wants their analyses delivered on a silver platter with a bow tied around it.

Program IT Interviews

The goal of the program data audit interviews is to assess whether the data exists to support the themes you are hearing from the business interviews. These IT interviews are intended to provide a reality check. At this point in time, you should view these data audit meetings as surface scratchers because you're trying to assess feasibility across a variety of business processes. There will be subsequent meetings to dive into the details once a specific project has been selected. In the meantime, you're looking for an overview of the key operational source systems, including their update frequency and availability of historical data. You're also trying to uncover any gotchas, caveats, or known quality issues in the data.

Program Compliance/Security Interviews

It is important to understand if your organization has any security, privacy, and compliance issues that impact the DW/BI program. A first step is finding out whether anyone in the organization claims to be in charge of security, privacy, and/or compliance.

Does the organization have clear guidelines, standards, or regulatory mandates that you have to know about? If the chief compliance officer states that the operational source systems are solely responsible for compliance, then you should carefully ask that person if the profitability results computed by the data warehouse and reported to shareholders are also subject to compliance. You could ask if internal division profitability numbers could be subject to unexpected due diligence in the event that the enterprise decides to sell the division in the future. You might also ask about data retention requirements and whether the mandate to purge certain kinds of data on a scheduled basis conflicts with the need to retain data for legal or intellectual property reasons. We can say candidly that this kind of interview is tricky because the last thing you want to do is alarm a corporate lawyer who decides the best thing to do is not expose any business data to anyone. But at the same time, you need to establish whether there is a corporate executive who will run interference for you when you have to make decisions about data security, privacy, and/or compliance.

Wrap Up the Interview

The final step of the interview is its closure. The lead interviewer should watch the time and allocate at least five minutes at the end of the session to bring the interview to an orderly conclusion. The wrap-up should begin with a summarization of what was discussed during the session.

Determine the Success Criteria

This is the time to ask about success criteria. You have established rapport during the meeting; now is the perfect opportunity to better understand their attitudes and expectations. The lead interviewer should ask, "What is the number one thing this program must accomplish to be deemed successful?" You should try to get them to articulate measurable, quantifiable success criteria. *Easy to use* and *fast* are not adequate success criteria because they mean something different to everyone. This success criteria question sometimes makes members of the interview team uncomfortable; they worry that users will want sub-second response time to deem the initiative successful. If users' success criteria are unrealistic, it is better to know it now when you still have time to react and reset their expectations, rather than learn of their expectations as you are about to deploy the warehouse. At the program level, success metrics tend to focus on higher level factors, such as business acceptance based on usage measures like the number of queries issued or active user counts, rather than more detailed operational metrics like database/server downtime. Some interviewees will identify success criteria based on the availability of specific data, the training required to access the data, or the timeliness of the updates.

NOTE Listen carefully if a senior manager's success criteria includes "everyone working from the same numbers," or "a single version of information," or even simply "integrated data." Knowing that data integration is an organizational challenge, this is a great time to delve a little deeper to better understand management's commitment.

Business impact metrics include the financial impact associated with cost savings or incremental revenue generation. This financial impact can then be used to calculate a return on investment. These are typically the most important success metrics for a DW/BI system, although they are difficult to capture. Even if your numbers aren't absolutely precise, you should strive to capture and calculate these business impact metrics.

Finally, the success metrics may focus on performance against a pre-DW/BI baseline. For example, you may hear that it took a week to perform a given analysis prior to the data warehouse; following the implementation of the DW/BI system, the same analysis could be completed in less than an hour.

These before-and-after examples are typically useful and impressive, although they presume the availability of a pre-baseline measurement for comparative purposes.

Say Thanks and See You Later

As you're wrapping up the interviews, you should thank interviewees for their participation and valuable insights. It's a good idea to request their permission for future contact to clarify any key points.

You should also let them know what to expect in terms of deliverables and opportunities for feedback. As we stated in Chapter 2, communication with your users is extremely important, but too often forgotten. Rather than leaving them in the dark, take advantage of every opportunity to let them know what to expect next. Tell them they will receive a documented interview write-up by a certain date and that you will need their review and comments returned by another specific date. Of course, it is then important that you meet the deadline established because you are building credibility with the users at every point of contact.

Finally, you should include a general disclaimer at the end of each interview, reminding the interviewee there is no firm commitment that what was discussed will be delivered in the initial release. This is especially true with broad-brush program requirements gathering. Again, let the interviewee know about the process and general timeframes for prioritizing requirements.

Review the Interview Results

Just because the interview is over doesn't mean your requirements definition work is done. The team should informally debrief with each other right after the interview. It is helpful to confirm that everyone is on the same page regarding common, repetitive business requirements themes. You should also identify areas where there is any misunderstanding so these points can be clarified in subsequent interviews. The lead interviewer should keep a running list of unresolved questions or open issues.

If any team member has experience with the source operational systems, they should share their thoughts regarding the feasibility of the requirements being heard. There is no sense letting these requirements gain momentum if they can't be supported by data captured in the current operational systems.

As soon as possible following each interview, review your interview notes and complete any partial remarks. Inevitably, your notes will be littered with dangling thoughts or stubs, such as "key metric for monitoring performance...," followed by white space as you jumped to capture the interviewee's next point. Comb through your notes and highlight key findings. We often supplement our notes with margin tags to identify business issues/initiatives, business processes and the associated information and analytic requirements, and success criteria. These documentation review activities should occur immediately following the debriefing, if possible. Your interview notes will become an indistinguishable blob after even one full day of interviews.

As the requirements collection process begins to wind down, you need to synthesize the data by essentially gathering everything you've heard into RAM in your brain to identify the common themes across interviewees.

Synthesize Around Business Processes

To synthesize what you've heard, try clustering the requirements findings around the organization's core business processes. Business processes are the fundamental building blocks of your DW/BI system because they typically represent a manageably sized implementation of data and analyses.

A business process is the lowest level event or activity that the business performs, such as taking orders, shipping, invoicing, receiving payments, handling service calls, and processing claims. When identifying business processes, common characteristics and patterns emerge:

- Business processes are frequently expressed as action verbs because they represent activities that the business performs.

- Business processes are typically supported by an operational system or module, such as the billing or purchasing systems.

- Business processes generate or capture key performance metrics. Sometimes the metrics are a direct result of the business process; other times, the measurements are derivations. Regardless, the business process delivers performance metrics used by a variety of analytic processes. Analysts invariably want to scrutinize and evaluate these metrics by a seemingly limitless combination of filters and constraints. For example, the ordering process supports numerous reports and analyses, such as customer sales analysis or rep performance analysis.

- It's also worth noting what a business process is not. It does not refer to a business department, organization, or function. Likewise, it shouldn't refer to a single report or analysis.

Often the business will speak about *strategic business initiatives* instead of business processes. These initiatives are typically enterprise plans, championed by executive leadership, to deliver financial or competitive advantage to the organization. The DW/BI initiative should align with strategic business initiatives to ensure that the program/project is delivering something of value or relevance to the business community.

To tie a business initiative, which is where senior executives may focus, to a business process, which represents a project-sized unit of work to the DW/BI team, you need to break down or decompose the business initiative into the underlying business processes. This means digging a bit deeper to understand the data and operational systems that support the initiative's analytic requirements. For example, assume that one of the strategic business initiatives for a consumer package goods company is to focus on sales and market share growth for their largest brands. In this situation, you'd need to deliver the data captured by the following business processes: customer shipments, promotion spending, and syndicated consumer sales data or point-of-sale activity from key accounts for competitive market share tracking.

As discussed in Chapter 2, a single business process typically corresponds to a Lifecycle project iteration. And we'll certainly talk more about business processes when we embark on dimensional modeling in Chapter 6. The bottom line is that the sooner the business and IT have a common understanding of the organization's key business processes, along with the associated performance metrics and the business initiatives and analytics they support, the better.

> **NOTE** Reviewing your requirements meeting notes to identify key business processes provides an organizing framework for synthesizing your findings. Depending on the breadth of interviews, we sometimes use a spreadsheet to consolidate information across interviews, which allows you to track frequencies and more easily categorize or group the interview findings.

Prepare and Publish Requirements Deliverables

Formal documentation seems to be everyone's least favorite activity, so it is consequently the most frequently skipped task. We strongly recommend that you develop formal documentation from the requirements analysis process.

It is essential to write down the information gathered for several reasons. First, documentation becomes the encyclopedia of reference material as resources are added to the DW/BI team. Likewise, critical information will be lost if people roll off the team without documenting their findings. You won't have the opportunity to send the replacement resources back for a tour of the users' world because of team attrition. Secondly, documentation helps the team crystallize and better understand the interview content. It is one thing to listen passively to an interviewee, but another to actively document what was said. Finally, documentation allows you to validate the findings with users. It closes the loop with the users by confirming that you accurately heard and documented what they said. This checkpoint further reinforces the business users' role as the driver for the entire DW/BI effort.

Interview Write-Ups

As the first level of documentation, write up each interview as soon as possible following the interview session. This is not meant to be a verbatim transcript; the write-up needs to be well organized and should make sense to someone who wasn't in the interview. The write-ups are typically organized with the following sections:

- Interviewees' job responsibilities, along with background on their business and objectives.
- Key business processes and associated performance metrics. Include the following details, as available:
  - Narrative description of the requirement for better access to the metrics generated by this business process
  - Current analytic obstacles
  - Sample questions
  - Specific data or analytic needs
  - Potential business impact
- Preliminary success criteria

Validate this document with the interviewee and get their sign-off before publishing it for others' consumption.

Program Requirements Findings Document

In addition to the individual interview write-ups, consolidate and synthesize the data from all the interviews into an overall requirements findings document. This document is organized similarly to the interview write-ups to facilitate its creation:

- Executive overview
- Project overview, including requirements definition approach and participants
- Business requirements, organized by business process
  - Narrative description of the requirement for better access to the metrics generated by this business process, along with the potential business and current analytical obstacles, as illustrated in Figure 3-4
  - Typical questions that could be addressed via improved availability and access
  - Initial assessment of data feasibility
- High level enterprise data warehouse bus matrix
- Preliminary success criteria

Sales Analysis

Business users in the Sales Division want to leverage existing sales order information to better understand customer, product, and sales channel performance. They need to see the impact of pricing changes or promotional trade offerings on sales volumes and sales mix by product or customer grouping. Users currently receive summary monthly sales performance reports, but are unable to drill into the detail information. They also need to see sales trends over time, rather than just viewing a single month's activity compared to last year. Due to the lack of timely, actionable information, sales business users may be unaware of customer opportunities and problem situations. They need access to sales information on a daily basis in order to react to performance problems or opportunities *before* the close of the current month.

Typical analytic questions that could be answered with access to more timely sales order information include:

- How much volume have we done with a specific customer or group of customers over the last 6 months?
- Has my customer participated yet in a promotion which ends in two weeks?
- What is the sales mix by market and customer? Is there an opportunity to up-sell or cross-sell? Has that mix changed over the last 12 months?
- How does the sales mix for a given store compare with similar stores in the chain?
- What other products are frequently ordered with lower-productivity SKUs — are they dragging along sales and creating a larger "market basket"?

Data Feasibility:

This data is captured by the orders module of the new ERP system. No historical data was converted when this system went into production on 7/1/2007. The module's customer and product data are synchronized with the enterprise master reference hub.

Figure 3-4 Sample requirements findings excerpt.

NOTE The business requirements findings document is immensely important because it establishes the relevance and credibility of the DW/BI project. It also is probably the first time anyone has tied the business requirements to the realistic availability of data.

As you're organizing the interview findings by business process, most of the requirements will fall into neatly contained single-process buckets. However, don't be surprised if you're confronted with requirements for things like customer profiling, product profitability, or a vendor scorecard. These examples require metrics from multiple business processes and should only be tackled as a secondary effort after the core process-centric building blocks have been delivered. These dependencies should also be noted as a warning factor impacting feasibility.

As indicated in the outline of the findings document, include a high level enterprise data warehouse bus matrix. We explore this tool in detail in Chapter 6; however, here's a sneak peak. As illustrated in Figure 3-5, the rows of the matrix correspond to business processes. Essentially, each business process detailed in the findings document becomes a matrix row. The columns of the matrix correspond to natural groupings of standardized descriptive

Common Dimensions

Business Process / Event	Date	Policyholder	Coverage	Covered Item	Agent	Policy	Claim	Claimant	Payee
Underwriting Transactions	X	X	X	X	X	X			
Policy Premium Billing	X	X	X	X	X	X			
Agents' Commissions	X	X	X	X	X	X			
Claims Transactions	X	X	X	X	X	X	X	X	X

Figure 3-5 Sample high level enterprise data warehouse bus matrix.

reference data, or *conformed dimensions* in Kimball parlance. They represent the "by" words heard during the interviews, as in "we need to look at claim payments by policyholder, agent, and coverage." Matrix cells are shaded to indicate which dimensions are related to each business process. At this stage of the game, the matrix is a preliminary draft because you have not done a detailed analysis of each business process row. You merely want to focus on the key descriptive nouns and process verbs to visually present the integration opportunities and challenges to senior management.

Sometimes the bus matrix is supplemented with an opportunity matrix, as illustrated in Figure 3-6. The rows of the opportunity matrix are identical to the bus matrix rows, but the columns now reflect major organizations or workgroups involved in the requirements process. Each shaded cell in the matrix indicates which groups are interested in the metrics associated with the business process rows. In this manner, the opportunity matrix captures

Organization/Workgroup

Business Process / Event	Underwriting & Actuarial	Marketing & Sales	Customer Service	Finance
Underwriting Transactions	X	X	X	
Policy Premium Billing	X	X	X	X
Agents' Commissions		X		X
Claims Transactions	X	X	X	X

Figure 3-6 Sample opportunity matrix.

shared data needs and interests across the organization. Keep in mind, however, that focusing on the most frequently requested business process and its metrics doesn't necessarily translate into the top organizational priority.

It is important that you communicate both the requirements and realities back to the business users in this consolidated document. A draft of the requirements findings should be reviewed with the joint IT and business project leads and sponsors prior to the disclosure to a broader audience.

Prioritize and Agree on Next Steps

At this point, you have listened to business users' program-centric requirements and conducted a high level investigation of likely source systems. You have a sense of what users want and what it is going to take to deliver against those requirements. Of course, by their very nature, program requirements are broader than what can reasonably be delivered in a single Lifecycle design and development iteration. The logical next step is to replay your findings and then reach consensus on scope and priorities going forward.

Culminate with a Review and Prioritization Meeting

As we mentioned in Chapter 2, one of our favorite techniques for prioritizing individual projects within the overall program is the prioritization grid. In this setting, you need to gather approximately 10–12 executive representatives, preferably from among those who have participated in the requirements process thus far, along with DW/BI and IT leadership.

The review and prioritization meeting begins with a presentation of the business requirements findings. Along the lines of the consolidated findings document, several slides are allocated to an overview of the initiative, including a sense of the participants involved, which will add credibility to the results.

From there, the requirements are presented with a slide or two for each business process, describing what it refers to, core metrics, perceived business value and/or support for key initiatives, and a relative assessment of feasibility. This is often an eye-opener for senior management because they're unaware of the common information needs across the organization, not to mention the redundant resources and organizational waste associated with the existing isolated departmental solutions.

You should then paint the long-term picture of integrated analytic data across the enterprise. Rather than showing a complex diagram with numerous boxes and arrows representing various data sources, present a simplified version of the data warehouse bus architecture matrix to the participants. It's a wonderful tool to establish a common vision and understanding without getting mired in the technical details. It might also be helpful to show the opportunity matrix to further reinforce the commonality of needs.

Once everyone is on the same page regarding the organization's program requirements, it's time to pull out the two-by-two prioritization grid, as illustrated in Figure 3-7.

The vertical Y axis of the prioritization grid captures relative business value or impact, while the horizontal X axis focuses on relative feasibility. Each business process requirement, corresponding to a row in the bus matrix, is placed on the grid, as indicated by the shaded boxes in Figure 3-7. The DW/BI team has already assessed feasibility, so the approximate horizontal placement of each business process opportunity is known, but the business representatives need to determine the vertical placement based on business value and impact. Use self-stick paper for each business process so it can be easily relocated during the meeting based on its relative placement to the other opportunities.

Once each business process-focused opportunity is placed on the grid, it's visually obvious where you should begin. The upper right hand quadrant is the sweet spot of high impact and highly feasible projects. You should start with the project closest to the top right hand corner.

Projects in the top left quadrant are often where the business wants to begin. Rather than tackling these riskier projects, focus on the sweet spot first, and get non-DW/BI resources assigned to investigate and address the feasibility issues with these upper left projects. Meanwhile, you clearly don't want to begin with projects in the bottom quadrants because they're relatively low value to the business. Low value/low feasibility projects in the lower left quadrant are particularly career limiting.

TIP You can further embellish the two-by-two prioritization process by using differently sized circles, such as small, medium, and large, to indicate the relative magnitude of the effort required for each project.

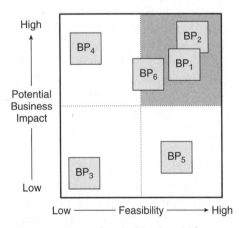

Figure 3-7 Sample prioritization grid.

This capstone event is an excellent way to culminate the requirements definition process because the benefits to both the business and DW/BI team are so significant. By the conclusion of the meeting, there's cross-organizational understanding of the present state of the data, a vision for the ultimate long-term enterprise/program plan, and an agreed-upon roadmap for addressing the gap that's been prioritized by both the business and IT. What more could you ask for?

NOTE Business people typically respond very favorably to the two-by-two prioritization grid because it's a classic MBA tool taught in business school. The technique was popularized in the early 1970s by the Boston Consulting Group. We've just taken the liberty of adapting it to DW/BI.

Close the Loop

Once the business executives and DW/BI team have established priorities for a short-term roadmap, supplement the findings document with this additional information.

Schedule a session with the other interviewees to review the findings and agreed upon next step outcomes. This presentation would utilize the same slides as the executive prioritization session, along with another slide or two with the final prioritization grid.

At this point, it's time to loop back to the first box in the Lifecycle, Project Planning, to update the scope document and proceed to a secondary round of interviews, further delving into the analytic requirements and data realities for the designated initial project.

Adjustments for Project Level Requirements

As we mentioned at the beginning of this chapter, requirements gathering typically occurs at two different levels: high level program and detailed project. We just walked through the process of gathering program requirements; in this section, we discuss the nuances related to the deeper dive into project level requirements.

We've assumed that your program requirements effort cast a wide net across the enterprise. The organization reached consensus on the first project based on a single business process, so you can now hone in on this focused area.

Project Level Approach

Nearly everything we advised earlier in this chapter about launching the requirements gathering effort holds true regardless of whether we're focused on program or project level requirements. Interactive face-to-face sessions with the business are just as important with project level requirements analysis as they are at the program level. Likewise, sending canned surveys or merely reviewing existing reports are just as inappropriate.

As we mentioned earlier, both interviews and facilitated sessions are well-accepted techniques for gathering requirements. People often consider facilitation and interviewing to be dramatically different approaches, but as you can see from the following task list, the two approaches share many core elements. Much of what we described earlier is relevant to facilitation, if you decide to use this technique instead of interviews.

- Identify the facilitation team and roles. The facilitator needs to be strong to keep the session on track.
- Prepare the facilitation team with background information and pre-workshop briefings. It is critical that you have a solid understanding of the business and its vocabulary in advance of a facilitated session.
- Determine workshop participants.
- Determine workshop schedule and coordinate logistics.
- Develop workshop materials.
- Prepare the participants with a pre-workshop packet sent by the workshop sponsor, outlining the project and workshop objectives and their roles to manage participant expectations.
- Conduct the workshop, beginning with a structured introduction, followed by interaction driven largely by the facilitator's style, skills, and prior experience, and concluding with a session wrap-up.
- Document the workshop results.
- Distribute results to the participants for validation.

For the remainder of this chapter, we'll continue to refer to interviews for continuity and clarity, but feel free to substitute "facilitated session" instead.

Prepare for the Project Requirements Interview

Preparing for project level requirements is similar to the preparation recommended at the program level. You need to identify and prepare the interview team. The pre-interview preparation and homework is more narrowly focused on a specific project. Of course, any work done for the program requirements gathering should be leveraged for an individual project. In other words, be sure to read the consolidated program requirements findings document.

Select the Interviewees

When it comes to selecting interviewees for the project requirements, you'll spend more time in the middle management and individual contributor ranks, and less time in executive row.

In our experience, the performance metrics resulting from key business processes (especially those that are early high priority projects) are used by multiple departments across the organization. So don't get lulled into thinking that being focused on a single business process translates into a focus on a single business area or department. For example, if the sales order business process is identified as your first project, you'll obviously want to speak with folks in the sales department, but you'll likely also want to meet with representatives from the marketing, logistics, customer service, and finance functions because they're also typically interested in the same performance metrics.

With project level requirements analysis, we tend to have greater vertical representation in the interviews. Executive business management is critical for understanding strategy and overall vision at the program level. However, if the project requirements activity is a direct follow on from the enterprise program initiative, then there's likely no need to revisit the targeted executives; if more than six months has lapsed between the requirements gathering efforts, then it's worth doing a follow up.

Plan to spend lots of time with middle management because they have one foot in vision and the other grounded in reality. You'll inevitably spend more time with individual analysts than you did with the program requirements gathering. These individuals will have great insight into existing information usage. Naturally, we are all attracted to the best and brightest analysts, but you should meet with a cross-section of business analyst representatives to understand the needs of the masses, not just the empowered, privileged few.

On the IT data audit side, because you're focused on a single business process, you will want to speak with the people who are responsible for the core operational system, as well as the key database administrator and data modeler. You will need to do much more detailed analysis and data profiling of the underlying source data. Reviewing existing documentation about the operational system will be important preparation for the interview team.

Prepare the Interviewees

With project level requirements, it's likely more feasible to conduct a business user kickoff meeting to disseminate a consistent message to all the interviewees. This meeting is similar to the DW/BI team kickoff meeting described in Chapter 2, but the focus and emphasis is shifted.

Figure 3-8 Sample user kickoff meeting agenda.

A sample agenda for the user kickoff meeting is shown in Figure 3-8. We suggest the business sponsor start the meeting by communicating the *why* behind the DW/BI project. Everyone at the meeting needs to understand the importance of this initiative and the high level commitment behind it. The joint IT and business project leads should then discuss the *hows* and *whens* of the project to help everyone understand the general approach without getting bogged down in minutia. You need to make sure the business users understand what's in it for them.

This meeting is an important tool for managing business users' expectations. Everyone should get a consistent message regarding the preliminary scope and general timeframes. It is also an opportunity to set expectations regarding the amount of user time required during this project for interviews, requirements validation, checkpoint reviews on the data model or application specifications, and education. One of the indirect benefits of this meeting is to communicate that this is a joint user/IT project, not a technology-driven IT initiative. The DW/BI system is driven by business requirements. Everyone should walk away from the kickoff meeting with a sense of ownership and commitment to make the project successful.

The kickoff meeting is not a substitute for the pre-interview letter as illustrated in Figure 3-3. The letter is another opportunity to reiterate the overall project objectives and let the interviewees know what to expect during the requirements process.

Conduct the Interviews

The same general ground rules hold true whether you're gathering program or project requirements. Even though you'll be spending more time in the lower ranks of the organization, you still need to be impeccably prepared for the sessions.

One bit of caution with more detailed project requirements: Be careful not to dive too deeply too quickly. We still suggest that you begin with higher level questioning and gradually get into the details instead of immediately doing a nosedive. And as we insisted earlier, this still isn't the time or place to gather requirements by pulling out a list of available source data elements.

The content of project-focused interviews conducted with business executives will be very similar to the flow we described earlier. The business manager or analyst interview is similar, but the lead interviewer asks more detailed questions. Following introductions, we ask questions about departmental objectives and goals, exactly as detailed earlier with the program interviews, and then dive into more focused project-specific questions:

> *Describe your products. How do you distinguish between products? Is there a natural way to categorize your products? How often do these major categorizations change? Assuming you can't physically look at a list of all your thousands of products, how would you narrow the list to find the one you are looking for?*

Users' responses to these questions provide insight into how they describe key aspects of their business. The data warehouse must support slicing-and-dicing on these descriptive characteristics. The example questions assume you are interviewing someone focused on a product-based business. You could just as easily be asking about customers, vendors, patients, or whatever nouns are important in your business.

The team should also try to understand the relationship between key attributes. For example, "Is there only one broker associated with an account?" or "Can a rep cover more than one territory?" The team needs to pay close attention to the exceptional relationships. A red flag should go up if the answer to questions like these is "Not usually."

Following these higher level business objectives and overview questions, we typically move onto analysis requirements with questions such as the following:

> *What types of routine analysis do you currently perform? What data is used? How do you currently get that data? What do you do with the information once you get it?*

> *Which reports do you currently use? Which data on the report is important? How do you use the information? If the report were dynamic, what would it do differently?*

Unfortunately, there is an abundance of data on current standard reports that is never looked at. The lead interviewer should try to identify opportunities for improving current reports.

> *What analysis would you like to perform? Are there potential improvements to your current methods/process?*
>
> *Currently, what on-the-fly analysis do you typically perform? Who requests these ad hoc analyses? What do they do with the analyses? How long does it typically take? Do you have the time to ask follow-on questions?*
>
> *How much historical information is required? How frequently must the data be updated to reflect what's captured operationally? How long does it need to be retained? Are there any special security, compliance, or auditing needs you are aware of?*
>
> *What opportunities exist to dramatically improve your business based on improved access to information? What is the financial impact? If you had the capability just described, what would it mean to your business?*

These are key questions that should be asked regardless of whether quantified business impact is a current project concern.

Review Existing Reports and Analyses

Sometimes it is easier for users, especially analysts, to describe their existing key reports and analyses, rather than respond to more freeform questioning. Instead of simply collecting copies of their current standard reports and spreadsheets, you should ask for details about how they currently use these documents. Inevitably, they rekey data into a spreadsheet program, where they are then building their personal data warehouse.

NOTE Don't forget to ask for key reports at the end of each interview. You will be amazed at what you will receive after a positive interview. Mark each received report with the provider's name and the date received.

As you analyze their current reports and analyses, remember that you are designing an analytic DW/BI environment, not just a reporting system. The interview team needs to resist the temptation to focus only on the top ten reports or questions. You need to understand the larger picture so you can construct an analytic platform that will allow users to build today's top reports without running into a brick wall three months from now when they want a different set of top reports.

Wrap Up the Interview

Because the interviews have been more focused, the associated project success criteria also tend to be more narrowly defined. There is often more discussion of service level metrics, such as:

- Availability based on database and BI server down time.

- Data quality based on the number of errors (e.g., completeness or adherence to transformation business rules) per million quality checks. To achieve the Six Sigma quality standard, a process must not produce more than 3.4 defects or measured errors per million error checks.

- Data timeliness based on the amount of time between the operational data capture and when the data is available in the data warehouse.

- Data warehouse responsiveness based on the average response time to a standard set of queries and applications.

- Support responsiveness based on the average response time to service requests or average time to resolve service requests. Both these measures are extremely cumbersome to track.

Even though the interview theoretically focused on a single business process, there's still no guarantee that everything discussed can reasonably be delivered in the initial release. Remember to include a general disclaimer at the end of each interview and thank the participants for their brilliant insights.

Dig into the Data

Once you're focused on a single business process, you should dig more deeply into the relevant primary source data. Remember, you're still gathering requirements instead of doing design work, but a solid understanding of the underlying source data allows you to more realistically manage user expectations.

There are specialized data profiling tools in the market to facilitate this data exploration. This is the first point in the Lifecycle where data profiling should occur. More detailed data investigation will happen during the dimensional modeling and ETL design activities.

At this stage, the requirements team should conduct data audit interviews and profile the data until they are confident that source data exists to support the business requirements. You don't need to understand every nuance of the data, but you must be comfortable with the availability of data to address the requirements. This may require more data digging than initially imagined. Resist being overly hasty with your data audit interviews and profiling. It's far better to disqualify a data source at this juncture, even if the consequence is major disappointment for your business sponsor and users, rather than coming to this realization during the ETL development effort.

Review the Interview Results

The synthesis of project interview results is not as complex or challenging as the effort required at the broader program level. It's still beneficial to review and highlight your interview notes shortly after the session has ended. At this point, the margin tags should designate insights as data, BI report/analytic, or technical architecture requirements and implications.

Review the key reports and analyses gathered following the interviews because they typically provide a rough translation into your dimensional data model. As illustrated in Figure 3-9 and further described in Chapter 6, dimension tables will supply the values for the report headings and row or super column headings. The reported numeric measures are represented as facts. It is often helpful to review the gathered reports offline for further insight on the business's dimensionality and users' analytic requirements. Sometimes you will see dimensions or attributes in these reports that never came up in interviews. Deeper granularity or more dimensionality should then be discussed in follow-up conversations with business users.

Prepare and Publish Project Deliverables

Once again, we suggest both individual interview write-ups and a consolidated findings document. In the spirit of full disclosure, we don't always produce

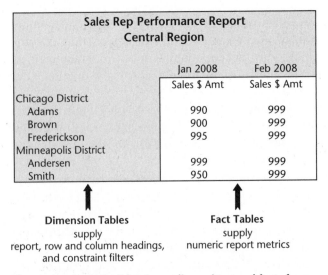

Figure 3-9 Analysis of business dimensions and facts from users' key reports.

individual interview summaries because of the time required, but that's obviously taking a shortcut.

The consolidated document at the project level takes on a different format than the program document. Because the project requirements interviews were more narrowly focused, but deeper, the document begins with the standard executive and project/process overview, but then focuses on findings as they relate to three areas: data model, BI reports/analytics, and technical architecture.

Agree on Next Steps and Close the Loop

Bringing the project requirements definition effort to an orderly conclusion is often just a discussion (or perhaps negotiation) and sign-off between the DW/BI project manager and the business project lead. Of course, you should then also close the loop with the business sponsor and the other participants in the business community to ensure everyone is in sync.

Deal with Challenging Interviewees

Finally, there are several common interviewing obstacles that you might run into as you gather business requirements at either the program or project level. We've described each of these challenges and techniques for contending with them in the following sections.

Abused User

This is an uncooperative business representative who claims, "we already told IT what we want." These users have been interviewed repeatedly in the past, but have yet to see anything result from their efforts. They are frustrated by the historical false starts and may refuse to meet with an interview team again.

You should proactively determine who was involved and interviewed in earlier attempts at data warehousing and business intelligence. Review any requirements documentation from the prior project. Unfortunately, documentation is seldom sufficient to take the place of a face-to-face meeting with the user again. When scheduling meetings with these abused users, it is helpful to acknowledge their participation in previous efforts and let them know that you have already reviewed the resulting documentation. The new session can be presented as a validation, rather than as another back-to-the-beginning interview. Naturally, users will resist rehashing previously covered territory, but may be more willing to meet if you are focused on understanding current priorities. Finally, this is probably a good time to select an alternative forum for gathering requirements. If interviews were conducted previously, use the earlier requirements documentation as a baseline and grounding for a facilitated session to gather details on changes within their business.

Overbooked/Substitute User

These disengaged business users are simply too busy to meet anytime soon. They may agree to a scheduled interview time, but then subsequently not show or send a substitute in their place. Often an email from the program sponsor to all the participants about their importance to the initiative nips this disorder in the bud. However, if this is a contagious malady and executive management is unwilling or unable to address the condition, we suggest you stop now before expending more effort on this initiative. It is a safe bet that business users who don't have time to meet and share their requirements won't have time to attend education and incorporate new information and analyses into their daily jobs. This results in a never-ending uphill struggle for the DW/BI team. We strongly recommend that you get off this slippery slope now before any further damage is done. You may be able to find a more cooperative business partner elsewhere within your organization.

Comatose User

These business users respond to your classic, open-ended questions with monosyllabic, one word responses. Fortunately, this is a relatively rare syndrome. Most often, their apathetic responses are due to external causes totally unrelated to the DW/BI project. It is sometimes effective to ask these people questions from a more negative perspective. For example, rather than trying to get them to envision life outside the box, they sometimes find it easier to tell you what is wrong inside the box. You can try to pry information out of interviewees like this, but it is senseless to prolong everyone's pain because these interviews are no fun for anyone involved. We suggest you make a valiant attempt, but if it is still not working, stop the interview and schedule a replacement representative if this user is in a critical function or position.

Overzealous User

Overzealous users are at the opposite end of the spectrum. You think you are interviewing two business users, but seven people arrive in the designated conference room instead; the users are excited and want to be heard directly by the DW/BI team. It is great news that the users are so engaged and enthused. However, that won't last long if you try to interview seven people in a one hour meeting. We suggest you quickly assess the homogeneity of the crowd.

Are they all doing the same job and could build off of one another's ideas, or do they represent various jobs and functions? It is almost always the latter, so you should break them into smaller groups and give them separate slots on the interview schedule. This ensures that adequate time is allocated for each meeting to gather the details you need.

Know-It-All User

Folks in this category often sit between IT and the real ultimate business users. Know-it-all users sometimes act as gatekeepers, rationalizing that there's no need to bother the other business folks for their requirements when they already have a thorough understanding and can represent their needs. Sometimes the know-it-all does know it all, but other times, their perspective is skewed. Even if their understanding is spot-on accurate, bypassing opportunities to bond with the rest of the business community via requirements sessions is difficult to recover from. We suggest engaging the know-it-alls and even elevating their perceived role and importance, but don't fall into the trap of overdependence. This potential political quagmire may require some finessing and feather smoothing on the part of the business sponsor.

As an aside, be aware that know-it-all users are sometimes IT wannabes. In addition to limiting access to the rest of the business community, they sometimes also want to perform IT's design duties by thoroughly specifying the data layouts for their proposed system solution. In their defense, IT wannabes have sometimes been forced into this role because IT has traditionally underperformed and underdelivered.

Clueless User

Do you have users that just don't get it? You feel it's a worthless exercise in futility to schedule requirements interviews with them because they don't have any requirements? From our vantage point, 99.9 percent of the time, clueless users are a figment of an IT professional's imagination. Users may not be able to articulate precisely which data elements in which source systems interest them, but nearly all the time, they can clearly describe what they do, why, and what they want to be doing in the future. It is then IT's job to translate this information into data and functional specifications for the DW/BI system. Asking the right questions is critical to obtaining relevant, useful guidance.

Nonexistent User

The final obstacle is typically fatal to a DW/BI initiative. This condition results when members of the IT organization say they know what the business users need, "in fact, we know it better than they do." These are the IT organizations that attempt to model their data warehouse based on source data layouts exclusively and then don't understand why business users aren't clamoring to use the data warehouse. The good news is that this obstacle is totally within the ability of the IT organization to overcome.

Conclusion

The Kimball Lifecycle approach is anchored in a fundamental belief that data warehouses and business intelligence systems *must* focus on the business and its requirements. This chapter provided specific tips and techniques to establish that focus with your business community; you need to be prepared, focus on listening, document what you heard, and then close the loop. The business requirements gathered using the tools described in this chapter will be invaluable as your DW/BI design and development effort unfolds.

BLUEPRINT FOR ACTION

Managing the Effort and Reducing Risk

The greatest risk surrounding requirements definition is skipping the process. Perhaps the team doesn't want to take the time or thinks they already know what the business needs, but building a DW/BI system without a solid foundation of business requirements is risky business.

We've outlined many best practices for effectively executing requirements interviews. From a management perspective, it is critical that the requirements process has a finite start and stop. Requirements are a critical part of the path because they impact so many downstream decisions. We're not suggesting that the design and development team is prohibited from further clarification with the business community about their needs; rather, we recommend that the requirements process not extend interminably.

The prioritization activity is also critical to managing the requirements definition effort. The DW/BI team needs clear direction about which requirements are critical versus those that are nice-to-have. Reaching business and IT consensus on an appropriately sized project and broadly communicating the decisions to the rest of the organization will be extremely beneficial as you move forward in the Lifecycle.

(continued)

BLUEPRINT FOR ACTION *(continued)*

Assuring Quality

Interviewing the right people is critical to ensuring a high quality result from the requirements definition process. The effort must encompass both horizontal and vertical business representation. Ignoring the vertical span leaves the DW/BI team vulnerable to here-and-now myopia, while potentially failing to grasp the organization's direction and likely future needs. Likewise, bypassing the horizontal perspective leaves the team vulnerable to isolated, departmental development that's likely inextensible and inefficient.

Validating the individual interview results with the interviewees, reviewing the consolidated findings with the business, and collaborating on next step decisions also help guarantee a quality result.

Key Roles

Key roles for collecting the requirements include:

◆ The business analyst drives the process to gather and document requirements.

◆ The project manager, business project lead, data modeler, and BI application developer may assist with requirements definition activities. It is especially useful to involve the data modeler and BI application developer with project level requirements analysis.

◆ Representative business users and management are actively involved in the interviews and prioritization activities. IT resources knowledgeable about the source systems also participate as data audit interviewees.

Key Deliverables

Key deliverables for collecting the requirements include:

◆ Interview questionnaires

◆ Business user kickoff meeting agenda

◆ Pre-interview briefing letter for the interviewees

◆ Program and/or project interview write-ups

◆ Program requirements findings document, including the preliminary enterprise data warehouse bus matrix and agreed-upon prioritization grid

◆ Project requirements findings document

(continued)

Estimating Considerations

The effort needed to collect the requirements is obviously impacted by the project magnitude and scope. In general, we try to complete the requirements definition tasks within a three to four week window. Dependencies include:

◆ **Number of requirements sessions.** Assume a maximum of three or four interviews per day. Each session will last 60 to 90 minutes, plus 30 minutes for debriefing and recovery.

◆ **Ability to get on interviewees' schedules.** If possible, try to avoid conducting requirements definition interviews or facilitated sessions during the busy season, while the annual planning process is taking place, or in the midst of some other time consuming corporate initiative. These competing activities will have an impact on your ability to schedule the requirements sessions and on the quality of the sessions given the inevitable distractions.

◆ **Number of source systems involved.** The number of IT data audit sessions will be impacted by the number of source systems.

◆ **Level of documentation produced.** Allocate approximately four hours per session to produce an interview write-up, including the review and update process. Also, be sure to allocate time in the project plan for the analysis of the interview findings and development of the overall findings document.

◆ **Ability to schedule a facilitated session for prioritization and consensus.** You should begin lining up calendars for the wrap-up facilitated session well before the completion of your overall findings document. Travel schedules can severely impact the timeliness of this meeting. Also, don't forget to allow time to prepare materials for this meeting.

Website Resources

The following templates and resources for collecting business requirements are available on the book's website at `www.kimballgroup.com`:

◆ **Requirements questionnaire for business manager or analyst**

◆ **Example pre-interview letter to brief interviewees**

◆ **Example business user kickoff meeting agenda**

Task List

BUSINESS REQUIREMENTS DEFINITION

	Fans	Front Office		Coaches			Regular Line-Up					Special Teams				
	Business Users	Business Sponsor / Business Driver	DW/BI Director / Program Manager	Project Manager	Business Project Lead	Business Analyst	Data Steward / QA Analyst	Data Architect / Data Modeler / DBA	Metadata Manager	ETL Architect / ETL Developer	BI Architect / App Developer / Portal Developer	Technical Architect / Tech Support Specialist	Security Manager	Lead Tester	Data Mining / Stats Specialist	Educator
1 Identify and prepare interview team	○			●	○	○										
2 Select interviewees	○	◆	◆	●	●	○	◆	◆			◆					
3 Schedule interviews				●	●	●										
4 Prepare interview questionnaires			○	○	○	●	◆	◆		◆	◆	◆			◆	
5 Conduct user kick-off & prepare interviewees			○	○	○	○	◆			◆	◆	◆				
6 Conduct business user interviews				○	○	●	○	○		○	○				○	
7 Conduct IT data audit interviews				○		●		○		○	○				○	
8 Publish interview write-ups and incorporate feedback	□			○	□	●		□		□	□					
9 Analyze interview findings				○	○	●	○	○		○	○					
10 Document findings and review		◆	◆	○	○	●										
11 Publish requirements deliverables	□	□	□	○	○	○	□	□	□	□	□	□	□	□	□	□
12 Prioritize and revise project scope	◆	○	○	●	●	○		◆			◆	◆				
13 User acceptance/project review	□	○	○	●	●	○		□		□	□	□	□	□	□	□

LEGEND:

- ● Primary responsibility
- ○ Involved
- ◆ Provides input
- □ Informed of results

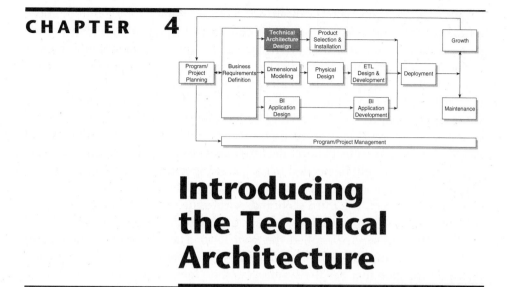

CHAPTER 4

Introducing the Technical Architecture

Most of us wouldn't think of building a $1,000,000 custom home without a set of blueprints. Yet, it's quite common for people to dive right into a DW/BI system program costing 10 times as much without any clear idea of what they're actually building. The most common example we see is the data warehouse project that starts with an RDBMS running on a leftover server from another project's recent upgrade. It's like saying, "Hey, I've got some wood and some concrete; let's build a house!" The point is you have to have a plan before you get started.

The analogy of architectural blueprints for a custom home is helpful to show the purpose and value of a technical architecture. In the custom home example, the architect first meets with the future homeowners several times to learn what's important to them in terms of space, flow, area usage, access, and light; in other words, their requirements. Next, the architect creates a set of blueprints to describe the desired results and help communicate these results and the nature of the construction effort to the customer. Before the first shovel digs into the dirt, a good contractor can examine the blueprints and determine the resources required, dependencies, timing, and costs of the project. The subcontractors can also work from the blueprints to understand their roles in the project — one worries about the plumbing, another about the electrical systems, and another about the finished carpentry. Finally, the team can get to work and build the structure described in the blueprints. Note that the blueprints must accurately capture the requirements of the homeowner because some implementers might not have firsthand knowledge of those requirements. And down the road, a good set of blueprints, like any good documentation, helps the homeowner when it is time to remodel or add on.

The next two chapters are dedicated to the technology track of the Kimball Lifecycle. This chapter describes all of the functional components found in a typical DW/BI technical architecture. We begin with a short sermon on the value of creating an explicit architecture along with a high level overview of the DW/BI architecture. We then dive into the details, describing what happens in each area of the architecture and listing specific examples of the capabilities that might be needed in each area. Specifically, the second section of this chapter zooms in on the data acquisition, or ETL, side of the architecture, called the *back room*. The third section describes the presentation server where the queryable data is stored, and the fourth section concentrates on the BI applications and services, called the *front room*. The fifth section digs down to the infrastructure that underpins the DW/BI system, and the sixth section describes the glue that ties the system together: metadata. Finally, we discuss security relative to the DW/BI system. Once you have all these concepts in place, Chapter 5 presents the practical steps for creating an architecture and selecting products based on your specific business requirements.

Chapters 4 and 5 are targeted primarily at the technical architects and technical support specialists on the team. These people need an in-depth understanding of this material to create the DW/BI technical architecture. Team members responsible for back room tasks, the ETL team and database administrator, should also read these chapters to better understand the major components they will be working with and how they fit together. The BI architects and application developers benefit from understanding how their tools fit into the overall DW/BI system. The project manager must become familiar enough with this material to be able to identify landmines and steer the team around them. Although these chapters are optional reading for non-technical team members, we encourage everyone to at least skim them to appreciate the complexity and magnitude of the DW/BI system's technologies. The more you understand, the more you can help guide the design toward solving real business problems.

The Value of Architecture

As we've mentioned, in the information systems world, an architecture adds value in much the same way as blueprints for a construction project. The benefits of a sound DW/BI technical architecture include:

- **Greater likelihood of satisfying business requirements.**   As you'll see in Chapter 5, business requirements are the primary determinant of system functionality. Though almost all DW/BI systems have the same basic architecture, they differ radically in terms of their specific functionality and capabilities because of the specific business requirements they must address.

■ **Communication.**   The architecture plan is an excellent communications tool at several levels. Within the team and with other IT groups, the architecture provides participants with a sense of where they fit in the process and what they must accomplish.

The architecture plan also helps communicate upwards, educating management about the magnitude and complexity of the DW/BI system program and projects. If management does not understand the complexity of the DW/BI system, they may assume it's easy and wonder why it costs so much and takes so long. Using the architecture plan to educate can help you get support and resources when you need them.

■ **Planning.**   The architecture provides a crosscheck for the project plan. Many architectural details end up scattered throughout, buried in the depths of the project plan. The architecture collects them in one place and prescribes how they fit together. The architecture plan also typically uncovers technical requirements and dependencies that do not come out during the planning process for a specific project. For example, suddenly realizing while you are attempting to install the software that the data access tool you picked requires a separate server can be distressing. Unexpectedly having to ask for more money (or time) can be even more distressing.

■ **Flexibility, productivity, and maintenance.**   Creating an architecture is about anticipating as many potential issues as possible and building a system that can handle those issues as a matter of course, rather than having to stop and rework after the problems surface. The architecture described in this chapter relies heavily on metadata, adding a *semantic layer* to the warehouse. This layer defines and describes the warehouse contents and processes and is used in those processes to create, navigate, and maintain the warehouse. Practically speaking, this means the data warehouse is more flexible and easier to maintain.

Productivity is improved because the architecture helps you choose tools to automate parts of the warehouse process, rather than building layers and layers of custom code by hand. Because the warehouse processes and database contents are more readily understood, it becomes easier for a developer to reuse existing modules than to build from scratch. Adding a new business process dimensional model is easier if you can work from existing design patterns.

The data models and metadata allow you to analyze the impact of a major change, like the conversion to a new transaction system, and potentially provide a single point of change to support that conversion.

▪ **Learning.**   The architecture plays an important documentation role. It helps new team members get up to speed more quickly on the components, contents, and connections. The alternative is to turn new people loose to build their own mental maps through trial, error, and folklore. People working from their own mental maps are not going to be as productive as they would be if they had accurate, complete documentation.

Technical Architecture Overview

Where the business requirements answer the question "What do we need to do?" the architecture answers the question "How will we do it?" The technical architecture is the overall plan for what you want the DW/BI system to be when it's ready for serious use. It describes the flow of data from the source systems to the decision makers and the transformations and data stores that data goes through along the way. It also specifies the tools, techniques, utilities, and platforms needed to make that flow happen.

Technical architecture consists of three major pieces: data architecture, which we discuss in Chapter 6, application architecture, which we spend the bulk of this chapter describing, and infrastructure, which is described later in this chapter.

The core functions of the DW/BI system are to get the data out of the source systems, clean, align, and conform it, transport it to the presentation servers, and then make it available to use in an effective manner by the ultimate business user clients. Your architecture must describe these functions as they will exist in your environment with your sources and uses.

The approach described in Chapter 5 for developing your DW/BI architecture starts with business requirements. Whereas the high level DW/BI functions and processes tend to be similar, the deliverable from your technical architecture effort will be the customized set of technical models and functional specifications specifically designed to meet your organization's requirements and resources.

This chapter is a starting point for your own customized technical architecture. Because each organization's requirements and resources differ, so will each organization's specific architecture.

NOTE Remember that the business requirements are your primary guide to the contents and priorities of your architecture.

At the risk of stating the obvious, technology is constantly changing. Consolidation has been a major trend in our industry for the past several years, with a few major players buying companies and adding components to their product lines with the goal of offering full, end-to-end DW/BI systems. A second trend is the growing number of ways to leverage the data in DW/BI systems. Organizations are constantly expanding the reach of BI with vendors upgrading products and delivering new tools to bring BI to new audiences and applications.

Figure 4-1 provides the high level elements of the DW/BI technical architecture. This figure is our roadmap for this chapter. We will use it to discuss each element of the architecture, including some of the underlying components, like security and infrastructure. In this section, we describe the overall flow of the DW/BI system architecture and discuss the natural separation between the internal workings of the warehouse — the back room — and its public business intelligence face — the front room. This separation provides a useful organizing framework because different roles, and often different people, focus on these two areas.

It is important to note that Figure 4-1 is a logical model. The actual physical servers and what runs on them will vary depending on many factors, including the maturity of the warehouse, its size, and the products you choose. We talk a bit about server considerations in the infrastructure section.

Flow from Source System to User Screen

From a high level view, the back room on the left side of Figure 4-1 shows how data moves from the source systems through the ETL process using the capabilities provided by the ETL services layer. This flow is driven by metadata that describes the locations and definitions of the sources and targets, data transformations, timings, and dependencies. Once the data is cleaned and aligned in the ETL process, the ETL system selects, aggregates, and restructures the data into business process dimensional models as defined in Chapter 6. These datasets are loaded onto the presentation server platforms in Figure 4-1 and tied together via the conformed dimensions and conformed facts specified in the enterprise bus architecture. Remember that we define all data accessed in any way by a business user, query tool, report writer, or software application as belonging to one or more business process dimensional models. In any case, it helps to separate the issues of ETL from data presentation because they have very different dynamics. ETL is mostly load oriented, whereas BI applications are business query driven.

NOTE The back room does not provide business user query services. Only the presentation servers support query services by storing and presenting the data in a dimensional format.

The front room on the right side of Figure 4-1 shows how users access the data in the presentation servers through various BI tools and applications.

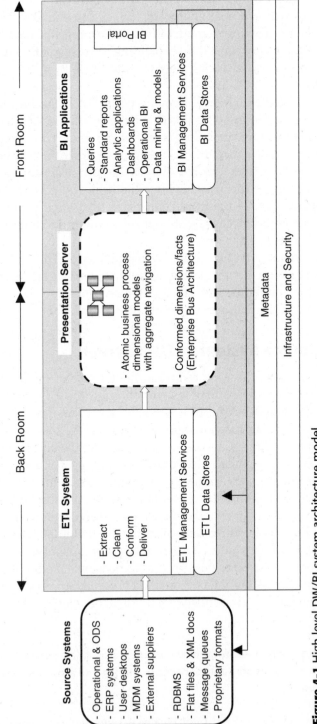

Figure 4-1 High level DW/BI system architecture model.

Different BI applications need different tools, so the architecture usually includes a combination of off-the-shelf tools and custom front ends created in an application development environment. These tools take advantage of query management services to help manage the logon, locate the appropriate data, and collect information about the usage and performance of the system. Most of these services are defined by metadata that describes the location and contents of the warehouse, business descriptions and groupings, user access rights and data processes like aggregate navigation. The major BI tool suites include their own query management services; stand-alone tools may rely on externally provided services, like a report library function, or simply go without.

We describe logical data flows, but haven't yet dealt with which function is provided by which piece of software running on which machine. Certainly, the presentation server is the first place where logical and physical concepts tend to get mixed up. You might store detail level data in a relational database and use an online analytical processing (OLAP) engine for managing aggregate data and providing more complex analytic capabilities. However, from the user's point of view, there should only be one place to go for information. They shouldn't need to worry about detail versus summary, or relational versus OLAP. The dotted line around the presentation server in Figure 4-1 represents this single logical view of the world; all business process dimensional models are directly accessible to the user community. This result can be created in many ways; the most common starting point is to physically locate the data together in the same platform. If that isn't possible, other approaches such as middleware, application servers, metadata, physical tables, views, or some combination can provide this insulating layer to the users.

Common Architecture Features

Several features of the technical architecture apply across the board, regardless of whether you're focused on the back room or front room.

Metadata Driven

Metadata is an amazing topic in the DW/BI system world. Considering that we don't know exactly what it is or where it is, we spend more time talking about it, more time worrying about it, and more time feeling guilty we aren't doing anything about it than any other topic. Saying that "metadata is any data about data" isn't very helpful because it doesn't paint a clear picture in our minds as to what exactly this darn stuff is. Fortunately, this fuzzy view has gradually clarified.

We think about metadata as *all the information that defines and describes the structures, operations, and contents of the DW/BI system.* The DW/BI industry often refers to two main categories of metadata: *technical* and *business*. We've added a third category: *process metadata*. As you'll see in the descriptions of these categories that follow, technical metadata is primarily definitional, while business and process metadata are primarily descriptive. Be careful with these categories because there is some overlap. It's best to not get too dogmatic when you are dealing with metadata.

- **Technical metadata** defines the objects and processes that make up the DW/BI system from a technical perspective. This includes the system metadata that defines the data structures themselves, like tables, fields, data types, indexes, and partitions in the relational engine, and databases, dimensions, measures, and data mining models. In the ETL process, technical metadata defines the sources and targets for a particular task, the transformations (including business rules and data quality screens), and their frequency. Technical metadata does the same kinds of things in the front room. It defines the data model and how it is to be displayed to the users, along with the reports, schedules, distribution lists, and user security rights.

  Some technical metadata elements are useful for the business users, like tables and column names; others, like the definition of a table partition function, are of no interest.

- **Business metadata** describes the contents of the data warehouse in more user accessible terms. It tells you what data you have, where it comes from, what it means, and what its relationship is to other data in the warehouse. The display name and content description fields are basic examples of business metadata. Business metadata often serves as documentation for the DW/BI system. As such, it may include additional layers of categorization that simplify the user's view by subsetting tables into business process oriented groups, or by grouping related columns within a dimension. The metadata models used by the major BI tools provide these kinds of groupings. When users browse the metadata to see what's in the warehouse, they are primarily viewing business metadata.

- **Process metadata** describes the results of various operations in the warehouse. In the ETL process, each task logs key data about its execution, such as start time, end time, CPU seconds used, disk reads, disk writes, and rows processed. Similar process metadata is generated when users query the warehouse. This data is initially valuable for troubleshooting the ETL or query process. After people begin using the system, this data is a critical input to the performance monitoring and improvement process. It can also be valuable to monitor user access both as a demonstration of the popularity of the warehouse and for security and compliance purposes.

Process metadata is event measurement data for the processes of building and using the DW/BI system. If this is your organization's core
business — an information provider who collects sales data for an industry and sells access to that data to many customers, for example — then
what we would normally call process metadata becomes the business
process data for the fact and dimension tables in your data warehouse.
Business folks at an information provider would be interested in analyzing this process data because it tells them who is using their products,
what products they're using, and what service level they are receiving.

Metadata is the DNA of the data warehouse, defining its elements and how
they work together. Metadata drives the warehouse and provides flexibility by
buffering the various components of the system from each other. For example,
when a source migrates to a new operational system, substituting in the new
data can be relatively easy. Because the metadata repository holds the source
data definition, the ETL developer can redefine the source to point to the new
system. Unless the underlying data definitions change, the target dimensional
model does not need to change. People will continue to access the old target
without necessarily realizing the source has changed. Of course, to the extent
that the new source collects additional data, the ETL developer and DBA can
add that data as needed.

NOTE Metadata plays such a critical role in the architecture that it makes sense
to describe the architecture as being *metadata driven*. Metadata provides
parameters and information that allow the applications to perform their tasks — a
set of control information about the warehouse, its contents, the source systems,
its load processes, and its usage.

The holy grail of data warehousing is to have a single integrated metadata
repository shared by all services across the DW/BI system. In that case,
a single change made in the metadata repository is reflected throughout the
architecture and available to all services at once. Unfortunately, most tools want
to manage their own metadata and are reluctant to share it with others. Given
this kind of parochial mentality, it's not practical to bring all the information
into a single place. Therefore, metadata lives in various repositories created by
the tools, programs, and utilities that make the DW/BI system work. We talk
more about metadata throughout this chapter.

Flexible Services Layers

We define a service as an elemental function or task. It might be as simple as
creating a table in a database or returning results to a BI application request.
How you deliver a service depends on your business requirements, resources,

and priorities. It is becoming increasingly common for vendors to expose their tool's functions via web services. This service oriented architecture (SOA) approach provides greater flexibility for incorporating those functions in your DW/BI system; they are no longer locked inside a specific tool.

At the time of this writing, the SOA movement is gathering momentum in many IT organizations as a way to provide reusable services and technology independent integration across complex organizations. The DW/BI world can learn from the SOA movement as SOA practitioners develop enterprise-level experience planning and specifying:

- Service interface definitions
- Quality of service characteristics
- Repositories for business policies
- Governance of services
- Lifecycle management, including development to test to production
- Models of IT-to-business cooperation

But it is also true that, as of this writing, significant issues such as providing acceptable security have not been solved in general SOA environments. Thus we regard SOA as a promising but immature approach that bears watching over the next several years.

The ETL services and BI application services provide a level of indirection that adds to the flexibility of the architecture. For example, when a user issues a query, it is submitted to a query service that uses metadata to resolve the location and nature of the request. There are several points in the services layers that can redirect the query, starting with the BI tool and its metadata layer, to any middle tier application server, to the network and DNS server, all the way to the database via the optimizer, views, or external data providers. Centralized services, like user authentication, allow you to leverage a single resource rather than having to repeat the functionality in each tool.

Evolution of Your DW/BI Architecture

Your DW/BI architecture plan will evolve. Business requirements change, new data becomes available, and new technologies emerge in the marketplace. In fact, the DW/BI system itself causes many of these changes. You will know you are successful if the business users are pressuring you to make significant changes. Your initial DW/BI system implementation will cover only a small section of your ultimate architecture. As products, platforms, and designs improve over time, the physical implementation you choose will evolve to more closely resemble the logical model. The architecture will also evolve over time as you learn more about the business and technology from your own experience and the experiences of others.

The techniques in this book are intended to be resilient in the face of a changing architecture. For instance, we always are more comfortable with granular data expressed at the lowest possible level. Premature aggregation of data is one of the biggest enemies of flexibility. Atomic level data is highly resilient in the face of changing business requirements and the availability of more powerful technology. Perhaps the other important perspective we teach in this book that insulates against architectural changes is the dimensional modeling approach. As we argue at the beginning of Chapter 6, the dimensional modeling approach is so symmetrical that each user request, even one we have never seen before, follows the same pattern and is not surprising. That is what we mean when we say our designs are resilient when faced with changes in the environment. Once you have defined the bus architecture, you can be assured that your business process dimensional models will connect together to create a true enterprise information resource.

For the rest of this chapter, Figure 4-1 is your guide. The next several sections deal with the major areas of the DW/BI system architecture in more detail. The tour starts behind the scenes, in the back room, moves to the presentation server, then out to the front room and the business use of the data. Subsequent sections cover infrastructure, metadata, and security issues from an architectural perspective.

Back Room Architecture

The back room is where the ETL processing occurs. The primary concern of the ETL architects, developers, and DBAs in the back room is getting the right data from point A to point B with the appropriate transformations at the appropriate time. Today's ETL tools can speed development and automate the process itself to a large degree, but it is still a complex, temperamental system.

This section examines the back room's architecture. We start with a brief list of general ETL requirements, then follow the standard ETL flow, starting with a cataloging of the major source systems. Next we look at the four major components of the ETL process: extracting, cleaning and conforming, delivering, and managing. Within these components, there are 34 subsystems required in the ETL process, which are described in detail in Chapter 9. We finish with discussions on ETL data stores and back room metadata. The goal of this section is to communicate the range of functions and data stores typically found in the back room architecture, and get you thinking about your own back room.

General ETL Requirements

Before we start listing detailed ETL capabilities, it's helpful to consider a set of overall ETL system requirements:

■ **Productivity support.** Any ETL system needs to provide basic development environment capabilities, like code library management check in/check out, version control, and production and development system builds.

■ **Usability.** The ETL system must be as usable as possible given the underlying complexity of the task. In contrast to scripting languages, most ETL tools employ a graphical user interface to define an ETL task. A good interface can reduce learning time, speed development, and be self-documenting (to a degree). Of course, a bad GUI can reduce productivity instead of improving it.

System documentation is another part of usability. The ETL system must allow developers to easily capture information about the processes they are creating. This metadata should be easily accessible to the team and the users via reports and queries. System documentation is also a key contributor to compliance because one of the first questions a compliance auditor will ask is "What did you do with the data in your custody?"

■ **Metadata driven.** One of the most important characteristics of the services that support the ETL process is that they should be metadata driven. By this, we mean they should draw from a repository of information about the tables, columns, mappings, transformations, data quality screens, jobs, and other components rather than embed this information in the ETL tool or SQL code where it is almost impossible to find and change.

Build versus Buy

Most of the services described in this section are available as off-the-shelf tools specifically designed for the DW/BI system. The tools are constantly improving and becoming less expensive as the data warehouse market matures. ETL tools can improve productivity immensely, but don't expect to see the payback on day one. In our experience, these tools do not improve productivity *in the first iteration* of a data warehouse program. In most cases, it takes as much time to set them up and learn how to use them as they save in the first round. After that, as new business processes are added and the initial schema is embellished, the productivity gains become clear and significant.

We wouldn't want to build a serious warehouse without an ETL tool. However, a high-end stand-alone ETL tool may not be cost effective for a small warehouse effort. These projects should start with whatever tools come bundled with the DBMS or BI tool suite and then add on missing functionality needed to meet their requirements.

That said, let's take a look at the functionality needed to develop and manage the ETL process flow.

Back Room ETL Flow

In the back room, data moves from the source systems through the ETL process and into the presentation servers. Back room services, or ETL services, are the tools and techniques employed to support the ETL process. Our focus in this section is to describe the typical ETL flow, including common sources and the major services we've seen to be valuable in various warehouse environments. The list of services ties to the 34 subsystems that are common to most ETL systems, described in detail in Chapter 9. Your warehouse will not include all these sources or need all of these services, at least not all at once, and you will most likely need some custom services we have not described here.

Figure 4-2 shows the more detailed architecture model of the back room from Figure 4-1.

The ETL process flow involves four major operations: *extracting* the data from the sources, running it through a set of *cleansing and conforming* transformation processes, *delivering* it to the presentation server, and *managing* the ETL process and back room environment.

NOTE As a rule of thumb, 70 percent of the warehouse development hours are spent on the ETL process. If you are building a new extract system, plan on at least six work months of total ETL development time for each business process dimensional model. Remember that total development time includes understanding source data formats, data profiling, data cleaning, unit testing, system testing, placing into production, and documentation.

The source systems are the starting point for almost every ETL job. We describe a few of the common source systems, followed by the main extract services.

Source Systems

It is a rare data warehouse, especially at the enterprise level, that does not pull data from multiple sources. In most cases, data must come from multiple systems built with multiple data stores hosted on multiple platforms. Usually, the initial business need is for access to the core operational systems of the business, including order entry, production, shipping, customer service, and the accounting systems. Other high value sources may be external to the business, like customer demographic information, target customer lists, commercial business segments, and competitive sales data. In some cases, especially in large organizations, you may not have direct access to the source systems so the source systems group needs to provide the appropriate data on a regular basis. This often means generating an extract file and handing it off to the warehouse.

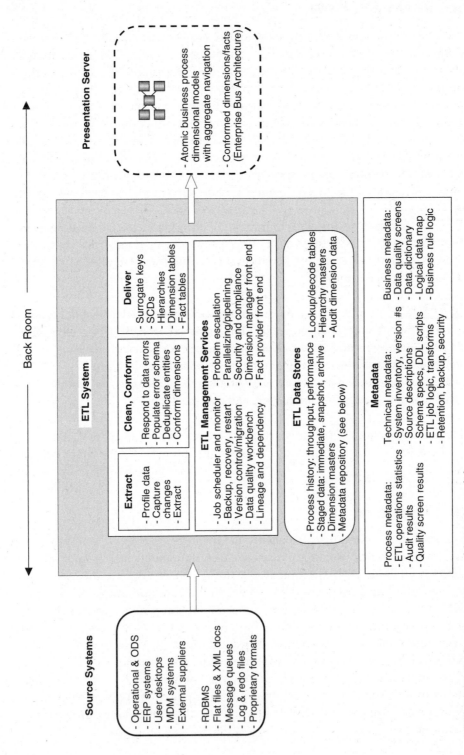

Figure 4-2 Back room system architecture model.

Make sure the ETL tools you are considering work with your key source systems, or that you are willing and able to generate the extract code needed to get the data into a neutral format like a flat file. A few specific source systems merit additional discussion, including client/server ERP systems, operational data store (ODS) systems, master data management (MDM) systems, and XML files.

Enterprise Resource Planning Systems

A few major companies have won the battle to provide the client/server generation of operational systems. These *enterprise resource planning* (ERP) systems are typically made up of dozens of modules that cover major functional areas of the business, such as order entry, human resources, purchasing, and manufacturing. These systems were originally created to address the problem of stovepipe transaction applications.

We pay two major penalties for this wonderful integration from the data warehouse point of view. First, there are often literally thousands of tables in these ERP source systems, and in some cases, they may be named in a language foreign to you. Figuring out which tables hold the interesting data for the warehouse and how they interconnect can be a nightmare for an ETL developer. Second, these systems typically cannot support a significant analytic query load. This should come as no surprise because it has long been known that systems designed for transaction processing have trouble with wide-ranging analytic queries — that is a major justification for building DW/BI systems in the first place. These systems have to manage a much more complex distributed process; they rarely have the cycles left for analytic support.

The ERP vendors recognize this gap and offer complete canned DW/BI systems as part of their product lines. ETL tool providers and other third parties also provide pre-built extract modules designed for standard ERP systems.

Although the ERP data warehouse modules can be helpful, many companies do not have all their data in the ERP system. It can be a challenge to bring external data into the vendor-provided DW/BI system. On the other hand, it can be just as big a challenge getting the data out. We've seen several companies that use the vendor supplied DW/BI system as the first stage of their ETL process, leveraging its built-in knowledge of the source system to extract the data and put it into a more understandable form. Then they extract from the ERP-provided DW/BI system and integrate the output with other data to create the final enterprise conformed DW/BI system.

Even if you have all your data in the ERP system, and your organization has done no customization, using a vendor-supplied, canned data warehouse does not mean you can forget about business requirements, design, and architecture. You must make sure the ERP warehouse product can address the business requirements and will most likely still need standard DW/BI system tools and processes to load data kept in systems other than the ERP.

Operational Data Stores

The term operational data store (ODS) has been used to describe many different functional components over the years, causing significant confusion. In the early days of data warehousing, it was often necessary to create a decision support-oriented ODS separate from the main data warehouse because it was based on "operational" data, meaning detailed transaction-level data. Conventional wisdom used to say that the data warehouse was almost always somewhat summarized and frequently delayed by days or even weeks. Because the warehouse was a complete historical record, we didn't dare store this operational transaction data in the data warehouse as a complete history — we couldn't afford to.

However, the hardware and software technology that supports warehousing has advanced, and we can now embrace the lowest level transaction data as a multiyear historical time series. We have also figured out how to extract and clean data rapidly, and how to model it for user comprehension and extreme query performance. We are no longer willing to accept the original ODS assumption that you cannot store the individual transactions of a large business in a historical time series.

Let us take this opportunity to tighten and restrict the definition of the ODS. We view the decision support–oriented ODS simply as the "front edge" of the data warehouse, no longer warranting a separate designation or environment. Thus, the only free-standing ODS we should expect to encounter is supporting operational needs with integrated transaction data. One of the major operational needs we've seen for an ODS is to offload operational reporting needs from the transaction system. We call this a *reporting ODS* and describe it in the next section.

There are also operational transaction system data stores described as ODSs. In fact, one of the original references to an ODS was the automated teller machine (ATM) transaction system in banking. The ATM ODS brought the business keys from disparate checking and savings systems together to support real time ATM transactions. Such a transaction ODS is part of the transaction system, responding to transaction requests and meeting transaction service levels. It is not part of the DW/BI system, but serves as an excellent potential source system.

If you already have something that you believe is an ODS, examine it carefully to determine its purpose. If it is meant to play an operational, real time role, then it is truly an operational data store and should have its own place in your systems environment. On the other hand, if it is meant to provide reporting or decision support capabilities, it should be integrated into the warehouse at the atomic level, conforming to the enterprise bus architecture. Ultimately, most reporting-related uses of an ODS can be migrated to the DW/BI system as you begin to load data more frequently.

Reporting Operational Data Stores

Some organizations with client/server based transaction systems or resource-constrained legacy systems create a separate copy of the operational database to serve as the reporting environment for the operational systems. This comes about because the operational systems do not have enough horsepower to support both transaction processing and standard reporting, let alone ad hoc decision support queries. The reporting ODS supports reporting against operational data on a less than 24-hour load cycle without directly querying the transaction system. This is usually accomplished via some form of copy of the transaction system, such as a snapshot or disk copy, which is made several times a day, or replication, which can keep the ODS current with the transaction system.

The reporting ODS is useful because it supports the operational reports designed to run against the transaction system data model. On the other hand, it's not so good because it doesn't have the data cleansing, change tracking, historical data, enterprise conformed dimensions, performance tuning, and usable dimensional model that the DW/BI system has. This means the organization will have two versions of the truth. The reporting ODS can be a legitimate way to meet operational reporting requirements, but expect to migrate it to the DW/BI system at some point.

NOTE If you need a reporting ODS, it should be managed as a core component of the operational system with appropriate service levels, monitoring, tuning, and planning. It is another data source from the warehouse point of view.

Master Data Management

Master data management (MDM) systems are centralized facilities designed to hold master copies of key entities, such as customers or products. These systems have been built in response to the proliferation of tables that often have the same customer or product represented multiple times with multiple keys. MDM systems are meant to support transaction systems and usually have some means to reconcile different sources for the same attribute, like CustomerName. They provide a bridging mechanism to move from the old transaction silos to a single source for customer or product information.

As of this writing, we are beginning to see adoption of master data management systems as part of the transaction system environment. This is a great thing for the DW/BI system because a lot of the work in the cleansing and conforming stage of the ETL system centers on creating exactly this single conformed version of customer or product. In fact, the quality experts have been telling us for decades that quality problems must be fixed at the source. Master data management systems help us move the data integration problem back to the source systems that created it. If you have a serious customer or product integration problem, you should start lobbying for a master data management system rather than continuously fixing the problem in the data warehouse ETL system.

Looking to the future, we predict that many master data management implementations will be based on web services (SOA) architectures because it would be ideal to have distributed clients all over large organizations access single versions of the truth about the key entities. But as we remarked earlier, it is premature at this time to rush to an SOA approach until SOA-based MDM systems are more mature.

XML Sources

One of the most common default formats for incoming source data has been the flat file. Over the past few years, data provided in an XML schema has been making more of an appearance. This is good for the ETL process because the XML file is much more self-documenting than the old flat files. Even though XML can have a greater processing and storage overhead, you have a much better chance of actually getting the XML file correctly loaded on a consistent basis.

XML files are most often used for exchanging data across organizational boundaries and to provide independence from specific computer implementations. In fact, many industries have created standard XML schemas. For example, the insurance industry has standard XML schemas defined for the components of a claim. Governments are also working on XML standards for many of the datasets they require from companies, states, and even individuals. See www.xml.org for links to example XML schemas in different industries.

Message Queues, Log Files, and Redo Files

As data warehouses move to more operational, real time applications, ETL architects have had to look beyond the conventional batch file download to more rapid methods of accessing source data. One alternative is to attach the data warehouse to an enterprise application integration (EAI) message bus. This message bus contains real time operational transactions being exchanged by the primary operational systems. The best way to describe this option is "drinking from the fire hose." The tradeoffs of using message queues as a data warehouse source are described in the real time ETL discussion in Chapter 9.

Another alternative is to read transaction log files (or "redo files" in Oracle parlance). Like message queue traffic, these log files contain the raw inputs to operational transaction systems and are subject to many of the same tradeoffs.

Proprietary Formats

The operational world is replete with dozens, if not hundreds, of proprietary source formats. Some, such as older IBM database systems like IMS and IDMS, and the Model 204 database, are well documented and have commercially available source adapters that allow reading the data. Many older mainframe applications have up-to-date COBOL copybook metadata that can be used to perform the extraction. In some cases, the ETL team has to discover the data formats and business rules, and implement the extraction routines by hand.

Extract

Most often, the challenge in the extract process is determining what data to extract and what kinds of filters to apply. We all have stories about fields that have multiple uses, values that can't possibly exist, payments being made from accounts that haven't been created, and other horror stories. From an architecture point of view, you need to understand the requirements of the extract process so you can determine what kinds of services will be needed.

In the following listings of ETL subsystems, the numbers in parentheses relate to specific subsystems described in Chapter 9. The extract-related ETL functions include:

- Data profiling (1)
- Change data capture (2)
- Extract system (3)

Clean and Conform

Once the data is extracted from the source system, we move to the cleaning and conforming step in Figure 4-2. Cleaning and conforming services are the core of the data quality work that takes place in the ETL process. In this step, a range of transformations are performed to convert the data into something valuable and presentable to the business. In one example, we had to run customer service data through more than 20 transformation steps to get it into a usable state. This involved steps like remapping the old activity codes into the new codes, cleaning up the freeform entry fields, and populating a dummy customer ID for pre-sales inquiries.

There are five major services in the cleaning and conforming step:

- Data cleansing system (4)
- Error event tracking (5)
- Audit dimension creation (6)
- Deduplicating (7)
- Conforming (8)

Deliver

Once the data is properly cleaned and aligned, the next step in the ETL process involves preparing the data for user consumption and delivering it to the presentation servers. Chapter 9 describes 13 functional subsystems in this step. If your ETL tool doesn't provide these functions, you will need to build them yourself.

The delivery subsystems in the ETL back room consist of:

- Slowly changing dimension (SCD) manager (9)
- Surrogate key generator (10)
- Hierarchy manager (11)
- Special dimensions manager (12)
- Fact table builders (13)
- Surrogate key pipeline (14)
- Multi-valued bridge table builder (15)
- Late arriving data handler (16)
- Dimension manager system (17)
- Fact table provider system (18)
- Aggregate builder (19)
- OLAP cube builder (20)
- Data propagation manager (21)

ETL Management Services

The final set of ETL modules described in Chapter 9 includes 13 management services, some of which are actively involved in the ETL flow, like the job scheduler, and some of which are part of the general development environment, like security. These services include:

- Job scheduler (22)
- Backup system (23)
- Recovery and restart (24)
- Version control (25)
- Version migration (26)
- Workflow monitor (27)
- Sorting (28)
- Lineage and dependency (29)
- Problem escalation (30)
- Paralleling and pipelining (31)
- Compliance manager (32)

- Security (33)
- Metadata repository (34)

Additional Back Room Services and Trends

Because your architecture is determined by your business requirements, you may find a need for some unusual functionality in your ETL system. Here are a few we expect to see more often.

Data Service Providers

Certain businesses, like large retailers, often provide data to their vendors. Historically, retailers and other data providers used different, custom data structures to deliver this data. Web services, under a service oriented architecture (SOA), are beginning to provide this kind of external access to data warehouse data. This loosely coupled self-describing approach gives the customer better structured data, more information about their data, and greater control around the process of accessing the data. This kind of web service can also apply to internal operational processes that need a specific data context from the warehouse to support the transaction process or operational BI, as we describe with ETL subsystem 21, the data propagation manager.

Functional Service Providers

We've seen some DW/BI systems offer ETL and reporting capabilities to other parts of the IT organization via web services. One example was a company that was doing name and address cleanup every night as part of the ETL process. An ETL developer packaged the function as a web service and showed it to the source system developer, who immediately saw the value and embedded it in the source system data capture component where it should have been all along. They ultimately had to move the service into the transaction environment, but at least they got things started.

Data Delivery Services

The adoption of data buses or message queues at the backbone of ERP transaction systems is enabling interesting ways for the DW/BI system to capture data. In this scenario, the ETL system monitors the message queue for transactions against specific datasets. These incremental transactions can feed directly into the ETL process, essentially providing the change data capture function. Given their near real time nature, they can be fed directly into a real time version of the data warehouse. Again, more on this in Chapter 9.

ETL Data Stores

Data stores are the temporary or permanent landing places for data across the DW/BI system. Deciding to store data has obvious implications for the DW/BI system architecture — you need a place to put it. The data stores described here are based on the technical architecture shown in Figure 4-2. The actual data stores you need depend on your business requirements, the stability of your source systems, and the complexity of your extract and transformation processes.

ETL System Data Stores

There is always some local storage needed by the ETL process. We typically keep supporting tables, such as the dimension master copies, lookup tables that we've created, and user-managed data, permanently stored. These tables usually live in a database for easy access, maintenance, and backup. We also keep copies of the incrementally extracted fact and dimension datasets around for some period of time. These datasets often live in flat files, or files based on a proprietary structure from the ETL system that supports fast reads and writes. Note that the term "period of time" is flexible. In some cases, we'll keep the dataset only until we are sure the load ran properly and the results are correct. This could be as long as seven days or more. In other cases, if the source system overwrites data and we will never be able to accurately recreate the data set, we may keep it for years, using the archive system to move it off to cheaper storage if needed.

Staging the incremental extract data in a relational database is common, and although it has advantages, it may not be as efficient as a streaming process. The relational system imposes a lot of overhead to load, index, sort, and otherwise manipulate the data. The programming languages built into RDBMSs are relatively slow as well. On the other hand, one advantage of a relational platform is its broad accessibility. Many of the ETL tools are designed to work with relational databases. Also, you can choose from a wide range of query tools to examine the contents of the ETL data stores at any point in time.

Lookup and Decode Tables

We often create lookup tables that don't exist in the source systems to support the ETL process, as shown in the ETL data stores box in Figure 4-2. A simple lookup table to translate gender codes in the source system to more meaningful full descriptions is a good example. These descriptions make the BI reports and analyses easier to read and understand. This means the ETL process has to be aware of missing entries, add default values, and notify the responsible user that a new entry is required.

We also often host similar lookup tables or hierarchies for the business users. It's pretty common to find an organizational or product hierarchy that doesn't exist in the source system that business users work with all the time. If you choose to include these attributes, which can add significant business value, you should negotiate ownership responsibility for managing these tables with the users. Ideally, you would create a simple web front end that allows users to edit entries and add new ones. This front end is represented as the dimension manager front end in Figure 4-2.

Data Quality Data Stores

If you have significant data quality problems and will address those in the ETL flow, you will need several data stores to help manage that process. We describe the metadata tables in the data cleansing step in Chapter 9. You may also want to store before and after copies of the data itself for audit and data validation purposes. One function of the data quality workbench in Figure 4-2 is to help the data steward compare these two end points to verify the successful application of the data quality screens.

NOTE Remember, the ETL area is not for meant for user access. You can do whatever you need to in order to make the ETL process work efficiently and effectively.

ETL Metadata

We remarked earlier that 70 percent of the data warehouse development time is in the back room. Not surprisingly, 70 percent of the metadata is there, too. ETL metadata assets can be grouped into three categories: process, technical, and business metadata.

PROCESS METADATA

- **ETL operations statistics** including start times, end times, CPU seconds used, disk reads, disk writes, and row counts.
- **Audit results** including checksums and other measures of quality and completeness.
- **Quality screen results** describing the error conditions, frequencies of occurrence, and ETL system actions taken (if any) for all quality screening findings.

TECHNICAL METADATA

- **System inventory including version numbers** describing all the software required to assemble the complete ETL system.

- **Source descriptions** of all data sources, including record layouts, column definitions, and business rules.

- **Source access methods** including rights, privileges, and legal limitations.

- **ETL data store specifications and DDL scripts** for all ETL tables, including normalized schemas, dimensional schemas, aggregates, stand-alone relational tables, persistent XML files, and flat files.

- **ETL data store policies and procedures** including retention, backup, archive, recovery, ownership, and security settings.

- **ETL job logic, extract and transforms** including all data flow logic embedded in the ETL tools, as well as the sources for all scripts and code modules. These data flows define lineage and dependency relationships.

- **Exception handling logic** to determine what happens when a data quality screen detects an error.

- **Processing schedules** that control ETL job sequencing and dependencies.

- **Current maximum surrogate key values** for all dimensions.

- **Batch parameters** that identify the current active source and target tables for all ETL jobs.

BUSINESS METADATA

- **Data quality screen specifications** including the code for data quality tests, severity score of the potential error, and action to be taken when the error occurs.

- **Data dictionary** describing the business content of all columns and tables across the data warehouse.

- **Logical data map** showing the overall data flow from source tables and fields through the ETL system to target tables and columns.

- **Business rule logic** describing all business rules that are either explicitly checked or implemented in the data warehouse, including slowly changing dimension policies and null handling.

Back Room Summary

The ETL process is conceptually straightforward, even if the details and complexities of building an ETL system can be overwhelming. Some of the difficulty stems from the fact that the steps in the ETL process tend to overlap.

Don't get locked into a rigid worldview of the ETL process. This section outlined a list of functional subsystems and dependencies. But the flow itself can change. Sometimes it's ETL, sometimes it's ELT, or ELTL, or TETL. You get the idea.

We return to this topic in Chapter 9 for a detailed description of the ETL subsystems and Chapter 10 for a step-by-step description of the ETL design and development process. The list of ETL services in this section should be enough to get you started on your own list. The end point of the ETL process is the presentation area and the servers found therein. In the next section, we look at some of the architectural alternatives for the presentation server layer.

Presentation Server Architecture

Presentation servers are the target platforms where the data is stored for direct querying by business users, reporting systems, and other BI applications. The presentation server architecture described here is conceptually similar to the architecture we described a decade ago, but it is has a few radically different underlying principles. Solid improvements in relational, aggregate, and OLAP technologies, amazing advances in server hardware platforms and disk subsystems, and drastic reductions in cost have all aligned to help simplify the DW/BI presentation server component.

Before we discuss the details of the presentation server architecture, it's helpful to consider how the business requirements for information help define the appropriate approach.

Business Requirements for Information

Business intelligence users in almost all organizations have requirements for:

- **Access to data from all major business processes,** or everyone wants to see everything. Everyone wants to see orders data, only from different perspectives. The sales people are interested in orders by customer. Marketing is interested in orders by product. Logistics is interested in orders by distribution center. In a similar vein, everyone wants to see customer care data. Sales can measure customer satisfaction, marketing can measure churn indicators, logistics can model product returns, and manufacturing can track product quality, all from the same business process dimensional model. Management wants to see all key performance indicators across all business processes.

- **Access to both summary and atomic data,** or everyone wants to see the big picture and all the detail behind it. Once marketing has product level data, they will insist that you add customer detail so they can create some customer segmentation models. The same is true for the sales people, and logistics. Management wants to drill down to the detail on any given performance indicator.

- **Single source for analytic data.**   The goal is to focus management discussions on decision making rather than on who has the right numbers. We strongly discourage so called departmental data marts because these often end up with different business rules, transformation logic, and column names and definitions, ultimately undermining the enterprise decision making process.

> **NOTE** These common requirements sound a warning for departmental data marts. Given that everyone wants a consistent source for data from all major business processes at the detail level, delivering data in departmental data marts ends up mushrooming into a data management nightmare. As a result, we are no longer using the term *data mart* in our presentation server architecture because it generally evokes the image of a summary level, departmental dataset, usually detached from the data warehouse. This is certainly not the direction we want you to go.

Detail Atomic Data

The short version of these three core requirements is that analytic queries are unpredictable, come from all corners of the organization, and require detail or summary data at a moment's notice. This leads to the presentation server architecture model shown in Figure 4-3. The foundation of the presentation server is based on *atomic level business process dimensional models*. As we describe in Chapter 6, your starting point should always be the lowest level of detail available. This is the primary determinate of flexibility. These atomic-level datasets are built with the conformed dimensions as defined in the enterprise bus matrix, and are generally stored in a relational database rather than an OLAP engine. This is primarily because of the data management capabilities, flexibility, and broad accessibility that relational databases provide.

If you have small datasets, or big hardware, all you need is this atomic layer. The database engine could summarize data on the fly to any level requested by the business user. Analyses that cross business processes could do so easily via drill across fact table queries that share conformed dimensions.

Aggregates

Unfortunately, most organizations have fairly large datasets; at least large enough so users would have to wait a relatively long time for any summary level query to return. In order to improve performance at summary levels, we add the second element of the presentation server layer: *aggregates*. Pre-aggregating data during the load process is one of the primary tools available to improve performance for analytic queries. These aggregates occupy a separate logical layer, but they could be implemented in the relational database, in an OLAP server, or on a separate application server.

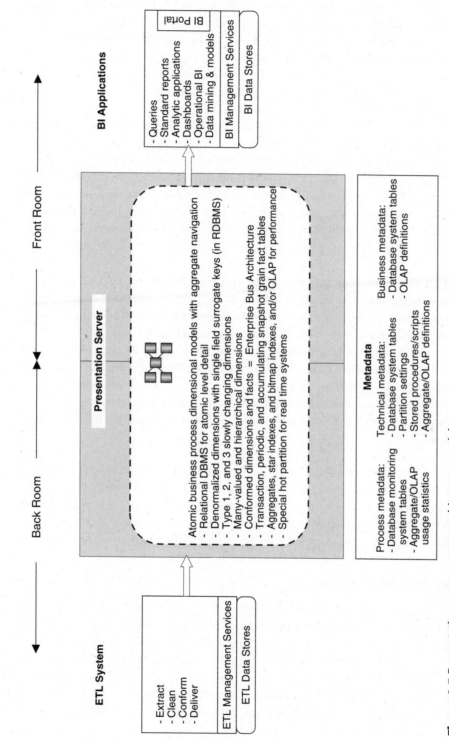

Figure 4-3 Presentation server system architecture model.

Aggregates are like indexes. They will be built and rebuilt on a daily basis; the choice of aggregates will change over time based on analysis of actual query usage. Your architecture will need to include functionality to track aggregate usage to support this. Ideally, the aggregate navigation system will do this for you, and automatically adjust the aggregates it creates. We call this *usage based optimization*. This is also why it's a good idea to have your atomic data stored in a solid, reliable, flexible relational database.

Although we refer to this layer as aggregates, the actual data structures may also include detail level data for performance purposes. Some OLAP engines, for example, perform much faster when retrieving data from the OLAP database rather than drilling through to the relational engine. In this case, if the OLAP engine can hold the detail, it makes sense to put it in the OLAP database along with the aggregates. This flagrant data redundancy may offend the database design sensibilities of some readers. We encourage you to think of the aggregate layer as essentially a fat index.

NOTE This description defines a fundamentally different architectural role for aggregates and OLAP engines. Historically, aggregates and OLAP engines were considered part of the BI area, owned by the business users outside of the core data warehouse platform. They were the platform of choice for the departmental data mart. In this book, we clarify the contents of the aggregate component to be a part of a single seamless business process from detail through summary data, built in the back room by IT. We are re-emphasizing that the focus must switch from department to enterprise to eliminate the dreaded departmental data silo. If sales and marketing want to see orders by customer, the same aggregate will serve them both well.

These aggregate datasets should follow the same dimensional structure of the data in the atomic layer. The basic dimensionality of the data is the same, but its presentation may include additional business rules and contain additional derived facts. Some of the dimensions may be shrunken or omitted altogether as you ascend to higher levels of summarization.

Aggregate Navigation

Having aggregates and atomic data increases the complexity of the data environment. Therefore, you must provide a way to insulate the users from this complexity. As we said earlier, aggregates are like indexes; they are a tool to improve performance, and they should be transparent to user queries and BI application developers. This leads us to the third essential component of the presentation server: the *aggregate navigator*. Presuming you create aggregates for performance, your architecture must include aggregate navigation functionality.

The aggregate navigator receives a user query based on the atomic level dimensional model. It examines the query to see if it can be answered using a smaller, aggregate table. If so, the query is rewritten to work against the aggregate table and submitted to the database engine. The results are returned to the user, who is happy with such fast performance and unaware of the magic it took to deliver it.

At the implementation level, there are a range of technologies to provide aggregate navigation functionality, including:

- OLAP engines
- Materialized views in the relational database with optimizer-based navigation
- Relational OLAP (ROLAP) services
- BI application servers or query tools

Many of these technologies include functionality to build and host the aggregates. In the case of an OLAP engine, these aggregates are typically kept in a separate server, often running on a separate machine.

The combination of these three components — atomic level business process dimensional models, performance aggregates, and an aggregate navigator — as shown in Figure 4-3 allow users from any part of the business to transparently query the data at any level of detail for any available business process, without any awareness of the existence of aggregates, and receive the results in a reasonable timeframe.

ATOMIC LEVEL DATA MODEL Based on the name *atomic level business process dimensional model*, it should be clear that we recommend that atomic data be stored in a dimensional model, not a normalized model. Whenever someone insists that the atomic data be kept in third normal form, the argument usually stems from a difference in definitions, not a true difference of opinion.

Ask three questions to clarify the issue: (1) What is the preferred model to support user access, taking into consideration how your database optimizer works for BI queries and what model your BI tool works best with? (2) Will users need or want to access the detail? and (3) Will you be tracking attribute changes over time?

Almost everyone we've talked to agrees that the dimensional model is the best user access model. Everyone also agrees that users will want to access the detail at some point. Because the atomic data contains the lowest level of detail and users will want to access it, it should be kept in the same dimensional structure. It makes no sense to carry the overhead of a complex mapping layer to give users the simplified, dimensional view of the business they need but from a normalized source, unless, of course, your hardware requires it for best performance.

Finally, if you are using the type 2 method to track changes in your dimensions, as we describe in Chapter 6, you will find it is much easier to manage in a dimensional model. And because everyone will need to track at least some attribute changes using the type 2 method, everyone should be working with dimensional models at the atomic level.

Design Disciplines within the Presentation Server

The presentation server in the technical architecture we are describing is not a general purpose database environment. Rather it is specifically engineered to meet the needs of delivering dimensional models to BI applications. As a result, the contents of the presentation server are subject to very specific design disciplines and restrictions that we develop in Chapters 6 and 7. We simply list these design disciplines here to begin setting the reader's expectations for the full design logic of the dimensional approach to data warehousing. The contents of the presentation server will characteristically include:

- Denormalized dimension tables with single field surrogate keys
- Type 1, 2, and 3 slowly changing dimensions
- Many-valued and hierarchical dimensions
- Conformed dimensions and facts based on the enterprise bus architecture
- Transaction, periodic snapshot, and accumulating snapshot fact tables
- Aggregates, star indexes, bitmap indexes, and/or OLAP for performance
- Optional special hot partitions for real time BI applications, as we describe in Chapter 9

Adjusting the Presentation Server Architecture

Scale is one of the biggest technical challenges for most large organizations. If you have more data than can fit in a single database on a single server and still perform reasonably well, you will need to make adjustments to the physical implementation of the core presentation server architecture. Typical adjustments include partitioning the warehouse onto multiple servers, either vertically, horizontally, or both. *Vertical partitioning* means breaking up the components of the presentation server architecture into separate platforms, typically running on separate servers. In this case you could have a server for the atomic level data, a server for the aggregate data (which may also include atomic level data for performance reasons), and a server for aggregate management and navigation. Often this last server has its own caching capabilities, acting as an additional data layer. You may also have separate servers for background ETL processing.

Horizontal partitioning means distributing the load based on datasets. In this case, you may have separate presentation servers (or sets of vertically partitioned servers) dedicated to hosting specific business process dimensional models. For example, you may put your two largest datasets on two separate servers, each of which holds atomic level and aggregate data. You will need functionality somewhere between the user and data to support analyses that query data from both business processes. Fortunately, this is fairly easy because you used the same conformed dimensions on both servers, right?

If this does not meet your performance requirements, you may need to consider platform products that have been developed specifically for the data warehouse market. We talk more about this in the infrastructure section later in this chapter.

Organizational Considerations

In an ideal world, the central DW/BI team would build the presentation layer as an enterprise resource with atomic data from across the enterprise bus matrix and aggregates to meet every query need. In the real world, it rarely works this way, especially in larger organizations where the complexity of the business processes and the quality of the data can greatly lengthen the time it takes to build the presentation layer. This is compounded by the fact that lines of business and large departments often have their own IT-like resources and are unwilling to wait for the central DW/BI team to get to their data priorities. We typically see the DW/BI system fragment in two ways: by data source and by business group.

A *data source split* usually happens when there are few organizational overlaps, like two separate lines of business that don't share conformed dimensions. In this case, it may make sense to have parallel, dedicated DW/BI systems. Where they do share dimensions, they must agree to work together to use the same conformed dimension tables.

A *business group split* usually happens when a group has a BI application opportunity that needs certain data, calculations, or aggregations and the central DW/BI team is too busy to respond. When this happens, local analytic data stores may be built and managed independently by IT resources that are dedicated to the business group, or even by power users with desktop database tools. In our opinion, this approach is a slippery slope that often leads to stovepipe data marts that are incompatible with the rest of the enterprise.

From an enterprise point of view, the goal is to encourage all aggregate data projects to leverage the work that has already been done and to source their internal data through the atomic presentation layer, and occasionally directly from the ETL data storage area (in the case of external data, for example). The warehouse team can accomplish this by making the value added in the ETL process so great that alternative sources aren't even considered. This will cause future aggregate datasets to be based on the same standard sources and use the same dimensions. As a result, they will be consistent with each other. They will also be able to take advantage of shared data management tools and access services to speed development and improve maintenance. In larger organizations, the role of the central warehouse team evolves to being responsible for the master conformed dimension tables, warehouse tools, and data integration.

Presentation Server Metadata

In our technical architecture, the ETL metadata contains all the processes and declarations necessary to populate the presentation server. At the other end, the BI applications' metadata contains all the processes and declarations necessary to fetch data from the presentation server on behalf of the BI environment. That leaves relatively little metadata uniquely owned by the presentation server.

PROCESS METADATA

- **Database monitoring system tables** containing information about the use of tables throughout the presentation server.
- **Aggregate usage statistics** including OLAP usage.

TECHNICAL METADATA

- **Database system tables** containing standard RDBMS table, column, view, index, and security information.
- **Partition settings** including partition definitions and logic for managing them over time.
- **Stored procedures and SQL scripts** for creating partitions, indexes, and aggregates, as well as security management.
- **Aggregate definitions** containing the definitions of system entities such as materialized views, as well as other information necessary for the query re-write facility of the aggregate navigator.
- **OLAP system definitions** containing system information specific to OLAP databases.
- **Target data policies and procedures** including retention, backup, archive, recovery, ownership, and security settings.

BUSINESS METADATA

Business metadata regarding the presentation server is provided by the BI applications' semantic layer, the OLAP definitions, or the database system table and column definitions directly.

Presentation Server Summary

The presentation server layer must have functionality to handle the unpredictable nature of wide ranging analytic queries. The logical architecture described in this section includes a set of atomic business process dimensional models that feed aggregates designed for performance. An aggregate navigator insulates the user from this complexity by rewriting queries to take advantage of aggregates on the fly. There are literally dozens of ways to implement this functionality at the physical level; how you build it will depend on your business requirements and organizational resources.

The next stop on our tour of the overall architecture model from Figure 4-1 is the front room, where we examine the major data stores and services that support user access.

Front Room Architecture

The front room is the public face of the warehouse. It's what the business users see and work with day-to-day. In fact, for most folks, the user interface *is* the data warehouse. They don't know (or care) about all the time, energy, and resources behind it — they just want answers. Unfortunately, the data they want to access is complex. The dimensional model helps reduce the complexity, but businesses are rife with rules and exceptions that must be included in the warehouse so business people can analyze them and understand their impact. This complexity only gets worse as you grow your DW/BI system and add more business process rows from the enterprise bus matrix into the mix.

One of the primary goals of any DW/BI system is to make information as accessible as possible — to help people get the information they need in the form and format they require. To accomplish this, you need to build a BI applications layer between the users and the information that will hide some of the complexities and help them find what they are looking for. You also need to provide functionality that delivers results in the desired form and format. Figure 4-4 shows the major stores and services found in the front room to help you achieve these goals.

In this section, we begin by reviewing the various types of BI applications and services needed in the front room to deliver information to the users and manage the environment. We discuss the front room's underlying data stores, and finish this section with a brief description of the core BI metadata. We leave the discussion of detailed BI tool functional capabilities for Chapter 11.

BI Application Types

The role of the data warehouse is to be the platform for business intelligence. This is seen most clearly as we look at the range of BI applications that demand

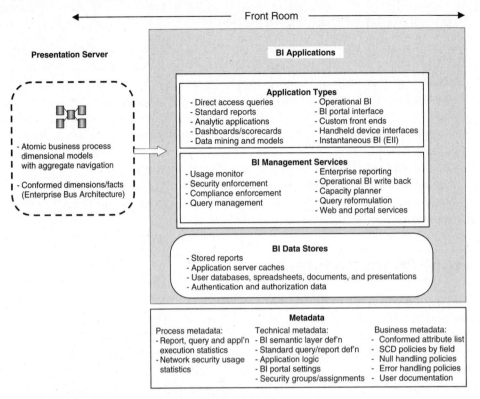

Figure 4-4 Front room technical architecture model.

data from the presentation server. This very broad range of applications makes it clear why the presentation server must be designed in a flexible, symmetric, scalable way to support many different kinds of requests simultaneously.

The most important BI application types include the following:

- **Direct access queries:** the classic ad hoc requests initiated by business users from desktop query tool applications.

- **Standard reports:** regularly scheduled reports typically delivered via the BI portal or as spreadsheets or PDFs to an online library.

- **Analytic applications:** applications containing powerful analysis algorithms in addition to normal database queries. Pre-built analytic applications packages include budgeting, forecasting, and business activity monitoring (BAM).

- **Dashboards and scorecards:** multi-subject user interfaces showing key performance indicators (KPIs) textually and graphically.

- **Data mining and models:** exploratory analysis of large "observation sets" usually downloaded from the data warehouse to data mining software. Data mining is also used to create the underlying models used by some analytic and operational BI applications.

- **Operational BI:** real time or near real time queries of operational status, often accompanied by transaction write-back interfaces.

These BI applications are delivered to the business users through a variety of application interface options, including:

- **BI portals and custom front ends:** special purpose user interfaces to provide easy access to web based BI applications or for specific complex queries and screen results.

- **Handheld device interfaces:** special versions of BI applications engineered for handheld screens and input devices.

- **Instantaneous BI (EII):** an extreme form of real time data warehouse architecture with a direct connection from the source transaction system to the user's screen.

We provide a detailed description of these BI application types and application interfaces, especially the BI portal, in Chapter 11.

BI Management Services

Three major forces have been dragging the data access services off the desktop and into the applications tier over the past ten years. First, the buying power of the DW/BI market is providing an incentive for database vendors to improve their products specifically to support data warehousing. Second, the demand for thin client tools has caused BI tool vendors to slim down their desktop clients and move much of the shared functionality to an application server. Third, there has been a recent push in the IT industry to move to a service oriented architecture (SOA). In the best of all possible DW/BI systems, the data access services would be true services. That is, they would be independent of specific tools, available to all, and add as much value to the data access process as the data management services do in the back room.

BI management services run the gamut from shared services that typically reside between the presentation server and the user to desktop services that are typically presented at the user level and mostly pertain to report definition and results display.

Shared Services

Shared services include metadata services, security services, usage monitoring, query management, enterprise reporting, and web and portal services. These are listed in the management services box in Figure 4-4.

Metadata Services

It should come as no surprise to hear that metadata defines the front end world. Most of the major BI tools work with a metadata model that describes the structure of the data warehouse for the tool's benefit, and simplifies and enhances it for the user's understanding. These models attempt to shield the user from the complexities of the data by limiting the user's view to subsets of the tables and columns, predefining join rules (including columns, types, and path preferences), predefining computed values and standard filters, and offering additional descriptive elements and organizing categories. Content simplification metadata is usually specific to the BI tool rather than a generally available service. This simplification metadata is usually stored in the BI tool's metadata repository.

If a BI tool is metadata driven, the vendor usually provides an administrative interface to create and manage the metadata. You may want additional metadata elements, in which case you will need to build functionality to create, manage, and store these elements yourself.

Metadata reporting leverages this metadata repository to support the users in their efforts to find and access the information they need. Ideally, a user who needs business information should have an interactive report to peruse the DW/BI system metadata, looking for the subject area, table, column, report, or any other element of interest.

> **NOTE** The interactive metadata report should dynamically link to the metadata repository to display currently available subject areas and the associated data elements. It should pull in the definitions and derivations of the various data elements and show a set of standard reports that include those elements. Once the user finds the item of interest, the browser should provide a link to the appropriate resource: a standard report, query tool, report scheduler, or list of BI applications.

Metadata reporting sounds like a lot of work, but the payback is a self-sufficient user community. Most BI tools provide this browsing capability within the tool environment; you could also use the tool to build some simple reports against the metadata repository. We've also seen homegrown systems using web-based tools provide much of this functionality. We discuss this further in the metadata section later in this chapter and Chapter 5.

Security Services

Security services facilitate a user's connection to the database. This can be a major design and management challenge. We talk more about security later in this chapter and in Chapter 5, so our goal here is merely to present an overview of how access and security fit into the front room architecture.

Security services include authorization and authentication services through which the user is identified and access rights are determined or access is refused. For our purposes, *authentication* means some method of verifying that you are who you say you are. There are several levels of authentication, and how far you go depends on how sensitive the data is. A simple, static password is the first level, followed by a system-enforced password pattern and periodically required changes. Beyond the password, it is also possible to require some physical or biometric evidence of identity, like a magnetic card or thumbprint. There are hardware- and network-based schemes that work from a pre-assigned IP address, particularly on dial-in connections. Authentication is one of those enterprise infrastructure services that the DW/BI system should be able to count on.

Authorization is a method for determining what specific content a user is allowed to access. Once you've identified someone to your satisfaction, you need to determine what they are authorized to see. Authorization is a much more complex problem in the DW/BI system than authentication because limiting access can have significant maintenance and computational overhead, especially in a relational environment. We discuss this further in the security section in Chapter 5.

Usage Monitoring

Usage monitoring involves capturing information about the use of the data warehouse. There are at least five excellent reasons to include usage monitoring capabilities in your front room architecture:

- **Performance.**   Leverage usage information to effectively tune the DW/BI system.

- **User support.**   Monitor query activity occasionally throughout the day to intervene on poorly formed queries and learn who needs help in constructing more efficient queries.

- **Marketing.**   Publish simple usage statistics to inform management of how their investment is being used. A nice growth curve is a wonderful marketing tool; a flat or decreasing curve is a call to action for the DW/BI team.

- **Planning.**   Analyze usage growth, average query time, concurrent user counts, database sizes, and load times to quantify the need and timing for capacity increases.

- **Compliance.**   In some industries, like health care, or for certain kinds of data, like human resources or financial data, you may need to provide an audit trail of all user query activity.

Like many of the services we've discussed, you can build a rudimentary version of a usage monitor yourself or buy a more full-featured package. Some of the BI tools offer their own usage monitoring support as well. Chapter 13 has additional information on usage monitoring.

Query Management

Query management services are the capabilities that manage the translation of the user's specification of the query on the screen into the query syntax submitted to the server, the execution of the query on the database, and the return of the result set to the desktop. The following bullets describe the major query management services you will likely want in your architecture. Each item has a corresponding business requirement. We explore some of these capabilities further when we discuss BI application requirements in Chapter 11. Note that many of these services are metadata driven.

- **Query reformulation.** The basic problem is that most interesting business questions require a lot of data manipulation. Even simple sounding questions like "How much did we grow last year?" or "Which accounts grew by more than 100 percent?" can be a challenge to the BI tool. The query reformulation service needs to parse an incoming query and figure out how it can best be resolved. Query retargeting, as described in the next section, is the simplest form of reformulation. Beyond that, a query reformulation service should be able to generate complex queries in the language of your target presentation server. Many of these queries require multiple passes to retrieve separate subsets required for the final query or report. In some cases, the results of the first query are part of the formulation of the second query.

- **Query retargeting and drill across.** The query retargeting service parses the incoming query, looks up the elements in the metadata to see where they actually exist, and then redirects the query or its components as appropriate. This includes simple redirects, heterogeneous joins, and set functions such as union and minus. This capability makes it possible to host separate fact tables on separate hardware platforms. Drill across allows users to query data from two fact tables, like manufacturing costs and customer sales, potentially on two different servers, and seamlessly integrate the results into a customer contribution report. The major BI tools provide this functionality at some level, or you can use one of the enterprise information integration (EII) services.

- **Aggregate navigation.** Aggregate navigation is a special case of query retargeting where the service recognizes that a query can be satisfied by an available aggregate table rather than summing up detail records on the fly. We described aggregate navigation and management functions as part of the presentation server. Though this presentation server approach makes the functionality available to all queries, there is an argument for moving this capability to an application server. An intermediate location allows the aggregate navigator to create queries that cross platforms and even technologies. The major BI tools also support aggregate awareness in their metadata models.

- **Query governing and prioritization.** It's relatively easy to create a query that can slow the data warehouse to a crawl, especially a large database. Obviously, you'd like to stop these before they happen. After good design and good training, the next line of defense against these runaway queries is a query governing service.

  The simplest version of a query governing service lets you place a limit on the number of minutes a query can run or the number of rows it can return. The problem with these limits is that they are imposed after the fact. If you let a query run for an hour before you kill it, an hour of processing time is lost. And the user who submitted it probably suspects it would have finished in the next minute or two if you hadn't killed it. To govern queries effectively, the service needs to estimate the effort of executing a query before it is actually run. This can be accomplished in some cases by getting the query plan from the database optimizer and using its estimate. A sophisticated query manager can check if the user has permission to run such a long query, ask if the user wants to schedule it for later execution, or just tell the user to reformulate it.

  You will also want a way to prioritize specific users and queries. The account that executes the standard reports may need a high priority so those queries complete as quickly as possible. The CEO's user ID may also need a high priority for obvious reasons. Many of these functions make most sense at the database level, where the best guess can be made about how much work a query will take.

Enterprise Reporting Services

Enterprise reporting provides the ability to create and deliver production style pre-defined reports that have some level of user interaction, a broad audience, and regular execution schedules. Standard reports, as described in Chapter 11, are one type of BI application that leverages enterprise reporting services.

NOTE At the formal end of the spectrum, large enterprise reporting systems tend to surface when the ERP system cannot handle the workload of operational transactions and reporting. Be careful not to take this responsibility casually. Full-scale enterprise reporting is a big job that involves its own set of requirements, services, and service levels. If you do take this on, you should set up an enterprise reporting project or subgroup solely dedicated to managing this effort.

Most of the query activity in many DW/BI systems today comes from what could be considered enterprise reporting. In some ways, this idea of running production reports in a user environment seems inappropriate, but it is actually a natural evolution. Often analyses that are developed in an ad hoc fashion become standard reports. The ability to put these into a managed reporting environment is an obvious requirement. They will need to be run on a regular basis and made available to a broad base of consumers either on a push or pull basis, such as via an email or web posting. Most BI tool vendors include some form of this reporting capability in their products. Functional requirements for enterprise reporting tools include:

- **Report development environment.**   This should include most of the ad hoc tool functionality and usability.

- **Flexible report definitions.**   These should include compound document layout, such as dashboards with graphs and tables on the same page, and full pivot capabilities for tables. The tool also needs to support exact formatting control for both display and print. People get very picky about how these standard reports look.

- **Report execution server.**   The report execution server is a central resource for running reports and staging them for delivery, either as finished reports in a file system or a custom report cache.

- **Parameter- or variable-driven capabilities.**   For example, you can change the region name parameter and have an entire set of reports run based on that new parameter value.

- **Time- and event-based scheduling of report execution.**   A report can be scheduled to run at a particular time of day or based on a system event, such as the completion of an ETL process.

- **Iterative execution or separation of results.**   If you provide a list of regions, for example, the server will create a copy of the report for each region. Each report could then be a separate file emailed to each regional manager. This is similar to the concept of a report section or page break, where every time a new value of a given column is encountered, the report starts over on a new page with new subtotals, except in this case, separate files are created. We used to call this *bursting* when the printed reports were actually physically separated at the section break. The idea is to speed up the process by running the whole report once and breaking up the results in the report server for separate distribution.

- **Flexible report delivery.**   Reports can be provided via multiple delivery methods (email, web, network directory, desktop directory, printer, or automatic fax). In addition, they can be provided in multiple result types (data access tool file, html, PDF, database table, or spreadsheet).

- **User accessible publish-and-subscribe capabilities.**   Users should be able to make reports they've created available to their departments or the whole company. Likewise, they should be able to subscribe to reports others have made and receive copies or notification whenever the report is refreshed or improved. This could include the concept of a "My Reports" section for each user in the BI portal.

- **Report linking.** This is a simple method for providing drilldown. If you have pre-run reports for all the departments in a division, you should be able to click on a department name in the division summary report and have the department detail report show up.

- **Report library with browsing capability.** This is a kind of metadata reference that describes each report in the library, its content, and when it was last run. A user interface allows the user to search the library using different criteria.

- **Mass distribution.** Simple, cheap access tools for mass distribution and viewing by users across the organization and potentially to customers, suppliers, and other third parties via the Internet.

- **Report environment administration tools.** The administrator should be able to schedule, monitor, and troubleshoot report problems from the administrator's module. This also includes the ability to monitor usage and weed out unused reports.

- **User access security.** The report service needs to authenticate users and determine if they have access rights to view a given report.

Web Access

Your front room architecture needs to provide users with web browser-based data access services. This is harder than it sounds. The service must act as the intermediary among the thin client, query management services, and presentation servers. At the low end of the spectrum, many tools can create HTML documents. These static documents could be put in a directory and made available to the business community through a series of standard links on a web page. On the other hand, most of the dynamic, web-based data access alternatives provide users with a reasonable level of query and reporting flexibility.

In addition to internal access, many businesses utilize the Internet to provide customers or suppliers with direct access to specific information. This usually happens through tightly controlled access applications, similar to the lookup services provided by express package delivery companies today. For example, a credit card company might provide significant value to its corporate customers by allowing them to analyze their employees' spending patterns directly without staging the data in-house. Or a manufacturer or service provider might provide customers with monthly summaries of their purchases, sliced in various interesting ways. If you must provide external access, the security, maintenance, and infrastructure issues are significant, but the business value might be significant as well.

Note that this functionality might be considered part of a product your customers would actually pay for, thus putting the DW/BI system in the position of generating real revenue.

Portal Services

Portal tools usually leverage the web server to provide a more general user interface for accessing organizational, communications, and presentation services. The standard reports, dashboards, and other BI applications can be accessed through the BI portal, along with metadata reports, documentation, tutorials, and other supporting information. We describe the BI portal functionality in greater detail in Chapter 11.

Operational BI Write Back

Although transaction processing tools are not normally considered part of the BI environment, this newly important class of operational BI applications often requires the front room developer to include a way for the decision maker to post transactions to the source system. This capability must be integrated into the operational BI application, with appropriate security and usage safeguards.

Vendor Specific Architectural Choices

Most major BI tool vendors have created their own three-tier architecture and located many of their services on application servers between the desktop front end and database. Architecturally, this works well because it allows the client to take advantage of a shared resource. The client can concentrate on presenting the query formulation and report creation environment, without the burden of additional data access services. Unfortunately, few standards for these application servers exist, so they are relatively proprietary and can't be leveraged by other BI tools. There are also stand-alone middleware products that provide many of these same data access services.

Database vendors are moving to include some of these services into the core database engine as well. This is significantly better than having them trapped in a single BI tool because all BI applications can then take advantage of the service. On the other hand, it is a little more limiting than the application-server approach because it makes it difficult to support cross-machine or cross-database awareness.

As you gain experience with these services, you'll better understand what value they bring and where they belong in your architecture. We encourage you to explore the marketplace and communicate your requirements for these kinds of services to your BI tool and database vendors.

BI Data Stores

In theory, there shouldn't be any data stores in the front room. The data lives in the presentation server and is retrieved when it's needed for an analysis or report. Once again, theory and reality seldom match up. In the real world, when the answer set to a specific data request leaves the presentation server, it usually ends up in the user's browser and may be saved locally as part of the report file. Alternatively, the result set can be fed into a local analytic store, like an OLAP engine, Access, or even Excel, or it might end up in a BI application or downstream system. This section looks at the architecture issues around BI-related data stores downstream from the warehouse.

Stored Reports

As data moves into the front room and closer to the user, it becomes more diffused. Users can generate hundreds of ad hoc queries and reports in a day. These are typically centered on specific questions, investigations of anomalies, or tracking the impact of a program or event. Most individual queries yield result sets with fewer than 10,000 rows — a large percentage have fewer than 1,000 rows. These result sets are stored in the BI tool, at least temporarily. Much of the time, the results are actually transferred into a spreadsheet and analyzed further.

Some data access tools work with their own intermediate application server, which adds another component and layer to your front room architecture. In some cases, this server provides an additional data store to cache the results of user queries and standard reports. This cache provides much faster response time when it receives a request for a previously retrieved result set.

Application Server Caches

There are several data-oriented services in the front room. Figure 4-4 shows services for operational BI, analytic applications, and enterprise reporting, all of which may have their own data stores. This is usually in the form of a local cache for application logic or to provide lightning fast response time.

Local User Databases

The idea of a local or departmental data store is as old as the personal computer. What is new is that industrial-strength database tools have made it to the desktop and the desktop machine is the new server. The merchant database vendors all have desktop versions that are essentially full-strength, no-compromise relational databases and there are open source databases that can run on the desktop. There are also products on the market that take advantage of data compression, indexing techniques, and in-memory structures to give amazing capacity and performance on a desktop computer.

We talked about local data stores in the presentation server section when we described the dangerous practice of a business group implementing its own portion of the data warehouse. The reality is local data stores are difficult to outlaw because they are driven by urgent analysis needs identified by the business community. Architecturally, you should plan for this reality and make it easy for local data store developers to take advantage of standard warehouse tools and processes (like conformed dimensions, ETL capabilities, metadata, job scheduling, event notification, and BI application tools). Local data stores may require a replication framework to ensure they are always in synch with the data warehouse. If it is at all possible, work to migrate these local data stores back into the enterprise dimensional warehouse.

Organizationally, you should push back on the development of local data stores. Try and understand the need for any long term local data store. Ask why these departments can't get the information they need straight out of the DW/BI system. There may be legitimate reasons, like the data is not available, but in many cases it's more about politics than practicality. If the reason is practical, like missing data, it's often better from the enterprise perspective to apply the resources to the task of getting the data into the DW/BI system for all to use rather than pipe it directly into a limited use local data store.

Disposable Analytic Data Stores

The disposable data store is a set of data created to support a specific short-lived business situation. It is similar to the local data store, but it is intended to have a limited life span. For example, a company may be launching a significant promotion or new product and want to set up a special launch control room.

Theoretically, the business needs for the disposable data store can be met from the DW/BI system. In practice, it may make sense to create a separate data store. There may be a temporary need for external data sources or internal sources that are not yet in the warehouse. There may be security reasons for creating a separate environment, as when a company is evaluating a merger or acquisition candidate. The disposable data store also allows the data to be designed specifically for the analytic requirements, applying business rules and filters to create a simple sandbox for the analysts to play in.

Results from Analytic Applications

From a data store point of view, the analytic processes usually sit on a separate machine (or at least a separate processor) and work with their own data drawn from the data warehouse. Often, it makes sense to feed the results from an analytic application or data mining process back into the warehouse as attributes in a dimension. Credit rating and churn scores are good examples of analytic application output that would be valuable in the context of the rest of the data in the warehouse. We return to data mining in Chapter 11.

Downstream Systems

As the DW/BI system becomes the authoritative data source for analysis and reporting, the developers of other downstream systems are drawn to it. Their basic need is still reporting, but they tend to fall closer to the operational edge of the spectrum.

Though these systems are typically transaction-oriented, they gain significant value by leveraging the data cleansing, integration, and historical depth found in the warehouse. Good examples are budgeting systems that pull some of their input from the warehouse (e.g., monthly average phone charges by office for the last three years) and forecasting systems that draw on as many years of history as possible and incorporate whatever causal data might be available.

The whole area of customer relationship management (CRM) is a great example of systems that leverage the data in the DW/BI system. Full scale CRM systems include all the major customer touch points, like promotions, email solicitations, sales force interactions, and customer support. The sales force automation module pulls in as much information as it can about a company's relationship with its customers. The same is true on the customer support side. When the phone rings in the call center, it is extremely helpful to have the customer's order history, aligned with payments, credits, and open orders pop up on the same screen. In most cases, these applications draw from data in the data warehouse, but are enabled in separate environments. Sales reps for CRM vendors may try to convince you that you don't need a DW/BI system to implement their CRM product. Though this is technically true, you are better off building the enterprise DW/BI platform and feeding the CRM system rather than hard-coding the CRM feeds and losing the potential value of providing that data to the rest of the enterprise.

The implication is you need to include support for these downstream systems in your architecture. Specifically, you need to make sure you can meet their service levels for availability and response time. There are also implications for acceptable data latency and access methods. Some downstream systems will prefer bulk extracts; others may want you to provide an SOA service that gives them exactly the information they need. This may be a big effort, but it can also provide significant business value.

Data Store Security

All this data dispersion inevitably raises questions of security and compliance. Depending on your security requirements, you may need functionality that can track and control access even out to the spreadsheet. We talk about a range of security issues at the end of this chapter. We offer a set of security strategies and tactics in Chapter 5, and describe systems to support compliance in Chapter 9.

Desktop Tool Architecture Approaches

Only a few functions actually live, or are at least executed, on the desktop, but they are some of the most important services in the warehouse. These services are found in the BI tools that provide users with access to the data in the warehouse. Much of the quality of the user's overall experience with the warehouse will be determined by how well these tools meet their needs. To the users, the rest of the warehouse is plumbing — they just want it to work (and things get messy if it doesn't).

As detailed in Chapter 11, these business intelligence tools range from simple pushbutton access applications to standard reports to capabilities for extensive data mining. Different vendors have implemented different subsets of these data access functions in different ways. At the simple end of the market, there are desktop tools that connect directly to the database. They are useful for quick queries, but generally do not scale to the enterprise level because they do not have shared services or metadata. Most mainstream BI tools have a server component that provisions the browser-based front end and the metadata repository. The larger BI suites offer the full range of services and front end options, from simple client viewers to power user and administrator workbenches. Most of these vendors can query relational or OLAP sources directly. Some vendors offer an application server component for aggregate management and navigation along with multi-pass query rewrite functionality. Generally called relational OLAP (ROLAP), these tools provide the functionality and flexibility of OLAP engines in a relational environment. It's a good idea to research the vendor architectural approaches when planning your presentation server layer and BI tool strategy. The architecture of the BI tool will impact your overall DW/BI system architecture.

BI Metadata

Front room BI metadata includes the elements detailed in the following sections.

PROCESS METADATA

- **Report and query execution statistics** including user, column, table, and application usage tracking, run times, and result set row counts.
- **Network security usage statistics**, including logon attempts, access attempts, and user ID by location.

TECHNICAL METADATA

- **BI semantic layer definition** including business names for all tables and columns mapped to appropriate presentation server objects, join paths, computed columns, and business groupings. May also include aggregate navigation and drill across functionality.

- **Standard query and report definitions** including query logic, execution schedules, and delivery specifications.

- **Application logic** for the detailed processing steps for complex BI applications.

- **BI portal settings** including default settings and user-specified customization and parameters.

- **Security groups and user assignments** linked to or part of network-based directory services. May also include external user assignments.

BUSINESS METADATA

Obviously, the BI semantic layer definition contains robust business-oriented metadata. Additional BI business metadata includes the following:

- **Conformed attribute and fact definitions and business rules** including slowly changing dimension policies, null handling, and error handling for each column.

- **User documentation and training materials** including the complete library of online and printed documentation available to business users.

Front Room Summary

The front room is certainly the richest part of the warehouse as far as the availability, variety, and functionality of the tools is concerned. In fact, this very wealth of choices makes BI tool selection difficult, as we discuss in Chapter 5.

Providing the best functionality possible is vital in the front room because it's the part of the warehouse that your business users see and use. Most users don't care about the database or the difficulties of architecture and implementation. To them, what they see on the desktop is the beginning and end of the DW/BI system.

Your warehouse will serve a broad user community with diverse needs, and you must architect the front room to support that spectrum. As always, the business needs determine the functionality required.

The front room services consist of metadata, security, monitoring, reporting, administration, and — by far most important — querying and other desktop services. These desktop services that support the wide variety of business user requirements will most affect your front room architecture.

Infrastructure

Infrastructure provides the underlying foundation for all of the architectural elements we've described thus far in this chapter. Infrastructure for the DW/BI system includes the hardware, network, and lower-level functions, such as security, that the higher-level components take for granted. In the first part of this section, we look at the general factors impacting the back room and presentation server infrastructure. Then we review specific considerations for hardware, operating systems, and DBMS platforms, including some basic definitions. Next, we take a similar look at the front room's infrastructure. Finally, to tie it all together, we briefly discuss connectivity and networking considerations.

Many factors combine to determine the appropriate infrastructure for a given implementation, and many of them are not necessarily technical. Let us be clear right up front that the DW/BI system should not attempt to define and build all the primary infrastructure across the organization. In many areas, the DW/BI system should be an important client of the infrastructure providers elsewhere in the IT organization. Our goal in this section is to identify and define the major infrastructure components involved in a typical DW/BI system.

Infrastructure Drivers

Even in the deepest technical layers of the warehouse, business requirements are still the primary determinant of what you need to provide. For example, the business needs determine the appropriate level of detail and amount of historical data in the warehouse, which has data volume infrastructure implications. Business requirements determine how often you need to load data and the complexity of the transformation business rules. These in turn help you estimate how much computing horsepower you need to make it all happen.

Technical and systems issues often drive infrastructure choices. In some cases, the extract process's performance drain on the operational systems is too great and can even necessitate an investment in a separate mirrored hardware environment. The specific skills and experience of the data warehouse implementers also impact infrastructure decisions. Back room teams with mostly mainframe experience tend to develop mainframe-based warehouses. The same holds true for the database platform. If the DBAs have invested significant time and energy learning a specific DBMS, getting them to switch will be nontrivial.

Policy and other organizational issues also play a role in determining the infrastructure. Often, there are "temporary" limits on capital spending, which means you will need to secure infrastructure through more creative means. Also, IT policies often dictate certain platform decisions. Standardizing on a single platform allows a company to negotiate significant discounts, establish core expertise, and ultimately, develop applications that are relatively easy to move from one system to another as the application grows. It might also mean you get a platform that is not optimal for your DW/BI system needs.

Finally, your infrastructure choices will be impacted by the expected growth rates. DW/BI systems grow quickly in the first 24 months, both in terms of data and usage. At the small end of the spectrum, we've seen real DW/BI systems successfully implemented on a single box. However, even small systems should expect to have an application server to support web-based data access. As your warehouse increases in size, it is common to split out the ETL server from the presentation server. Many companies start out at this level because they plan to grow and want to avoid the effort of migrating too soon. Moving up the scale, a large, enterprise-level warehouse is often implemented across several separate servers. Obviously, there is plenty of room for variation, but the message is that the number of servers can grow significantly.

Back Room and Presentation Server Infrastructure Factors

The major factors in determining infrastructure requirements for the back room and presentation servers include the following:

- **Data size.** Data volumes are driven by the business problems you are trying to solve. If the business goal is to develop one-to-one customer relationships, you need customer-level transaction detail. In an increasingly online world, customer-level transactions can include tracking every visit, page view, and mouse click.

- **Volatility.** Volatility measures the dynamic nature of the database. It includes how often the database will be updated, how much data changes or is replaced each time, and how long the load window is. Again, look to the business requirements for clues to the volatility of the warehouse. Customer churn rates can tell you how much your customer dimension changes over time. The answers to these questions have a direct impact on the size and speed of the hardware platform. Data warehouses bear the full brunt of both the business and technology curves. That is, business and technology are changing rapidly, and the data warehouse has to adjust to both.

- **Number of users.** Obviously, the number of users, how active they are, how many are active concurrently, and any periodic peaks in their activity (such as month end) are all important factors in selecting a platform. For most organizations, the initial DW/BI system efforts usually start out with 25 to 50 active users. Within 12 months or so, this number grows to between 100 and 200, and in 2 years, there can be thousands of users, especially if the warehouse is used for both ad hoc purposes and standard reporting in a large organization.

- **Number of business processes.**   The number of distinct business processes, and hence data sources, supported in the warehouse increases the complexity significantly. If the data volumes are large enough or the business justification strong enough, it may make sense to have separate hardware platforms for some business processes. Note that you may still need a large, centralized server if consolidated data is critical to senior management and middleware methods of providing virtual consolidation are not viable.

- **Nature of use.**   The nature of the front end BI tool and its usage has implications on platform selection. Even a few active ad hoc users can put a significant strain on the presentation server. It is difficult to optimize for this kind of use because good analysts are all over the map, looking for opportunities by generating unpredictable ad hoc queries. On the other hand, a system that mostly generates standard reports can be optimized around those reports. (Note that if you are providing only structured access to the data through standard reports with limited flexibility, you will probably not get full value out of your DW/BI system investment.) Many reporting tools on the market provide for canned report scheduling so they run in the early morning hours after the load is complete but before people arrive for work. This helps balance the load by shifting many of the standard reports into the off-peak hours. Large scale data mining also puts a massive demand on the hardware platform, both in terms of data size and I/O scalability. These beasts take in huge amounts of data, comb through it with the teeth of a good mining tool, and stream the results back out to support further analysis and downstream business uses. Ad hoc query, reporting, and data mining have different query demand profiles and may do better on different platforms.

- **Service level agreements.**   Performance and availability requirements both affect the size and quantity of hardware needed. If your users expect sub-second response times for on-the-fly aggregations, you will need a bigger box (as long as they are willing to pay for it). If you have users around the world, 24×7 availability is a likely requirement. In this case, if the operational systems are centralized, the warehouse would probably be centralized, too, but the hardware would need to support parallel or trickle load processes that allow it to be constantly available. If the operational systems are decentralized, it may make sense to have decentralized presentation server components as well.

- **Technical readiness.**   From an administrative perspective, the server environment is similar to the mainframe environment at a conceptual level, but it is very different at the implementation level. Do not think you can simply install a UNIX server or even a large Windows system without an experienced, professional technical support resource as part of the back room team. Servers have a range of support requirements, including basic hardware and system software administration, connectivity (both to the desktop and back to the source systems), database administration, and backup and recovery. There is a category of DW/BI presentation server platforms known as data warehouse appliances that come preconfigured with hardware, operating system, and database; this makes the initial setup easier, but you still have to manage it. The quantity, quality, and experience of the IT support resources you can muster may have a significant impact on your platform decision.

- **Software availability.**   Often, the requirements analysis will indicate a need for a certain capability, like a geographic information system for displaying warehouse data on a map. The software selection process may reveal that the best geographic mapping software for your particular requirements only runs on a certain high-end, graphics-based platform. Obviously, your decision is easy in a case like this. The business requirement simplifies the platform decision significantly.

- **Financial resources.**   The amount of money spent on a project is usually a function of the project's expected value. With the DW/BI system, this can be a chicken-and-egg problem. The better you understand the business requirements and target the DW/BI system at solving the high value, relatively easy requirements, the easier it will be to get the money you need. In terms of hardware, get the biggest server you can afford.

Parallel Processing Hardware Architectures

The hardware industry pioneered the creative use of acronyms and continues to turn out new ones at a rapid pace. There are three basic parallel processing hardware architectures in the server market: symmetric multiprocessing (SMP), massively parallel processing (MPP), and non-uniform memory architecture (NUMA), as shown in Figure 4-5. These architectures differ in the way the processors work with disk, memory, and each other. Over time, the defining edges of these architectures are getting fuzzy as the hardware, database, operating system, and networking technologies improve. The next section summarizes how these hardware options apply to the DW/BI system.

Symmetric Multiprocessing (SMP)

The SMP architecture is a single machine with multiple processors, all managed by one operating system and all accessing the same disk and memory area.

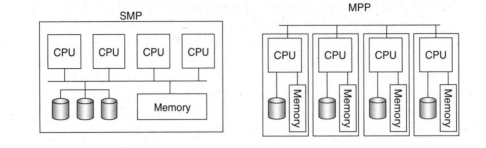

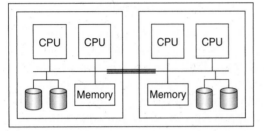

Figure 4-5 Basic parallel processing hardware architectures.

An SMP machine with 8 to 32 processors, a parallel database, large memory (at least 4 GB plus 1 GB per CPU core), a sufficient number of disks to handle the projected I/O requirements, and a good database design should perform well with a medium-sized warehouse. The major database products are capable of running query and load processes in parallel. You need to make sure other data warehouse processes are also designed to take advantage of parallel capabilities.

> **NOTE** SMP machines are well suited for ad hoc queries. Most cost-based optimizers work best in an SMP environment. For ad hoc queries, the shared, centralized nature of the SMP architecture gives the system the ability to allocate processing power across the entire database.

Although the processors in an SMP environment can access shared resources (memory and disk) very quickly, the use of a single shared communications channel to communicate between CPU, memory, and I/O can become a bottleneck to system performance as the number of CPUs and their clock speeds increase. In addition, because an SMP machine is a single entity, it also has the weakness of being a single point of failure in the warehouse. This single point of failure can be eliminated by the use of high availability clustering, which we describe later in this section.

Massively Parallel Processing (MPP)

MPP systems are basically a string of relatively independent computers, each with its own operating system, memory, and disk, all coordinated by passing messages back and forth. The strength of MPP is the ability to connect hundreds of machine nodes together and apply them to a problem using a brute-force approach. For example, if you need to do a full table scan of a large table, spreading that table across a 100-node MPP system and letting each node scan its $1/100^{th}$ of the table should be relatively fast. It's the computer equivalent of "many hands make light work." The challenge comes when the problem is difficult to split into clean, well-segmented pieces. For example, joining two large tables together can be a problem, if both are spread across the 100 nodes. Any given record in one table may have matching records in the other table that are located on any (or all!) of the other 99 nodes. In this case, the coordination task among nodes can get overloaded. Of course, developers of MPP-based systems have designed workarounds for this and other parallelization issues.

MPP systems are typically found in larger scale, multi-terabyte data warehouses. They can be configured for high availability by mirroring data on multiple nodes. MPP machines work best when the data access paths are predefined and the data can be spread across nodes and disks accordingly.

NOTE MPP systems tend to support canned query or standard reporting environments, or store the atomic data that feeds aggregate data stores in the presentation layer. MPP is considered to be more expensive and more difficult to tune and manage. Again, the database needs to be designed to take advantage of this hardware structure — the optimal physical data model for MPP can be significantly different than for SMP or NUMA machines.

Non-Uniform Memory Architecture (NUMA)

NUMA is essentially a hybrid of SMP and MPP, combining the shared disk flexibility of SMP with the parallel speed of MPP. NUMA is conceptually similar to clustering SMP machines, but with tighter connections, more bandwidth, and greater coordination among nodes. If you can segment your warehouse into relatively independent usage groups and place each group on its own node, the NUMA architecture may be effective for you.

Clusters

It is possible to connect several computers together in a cluster that acts like a single server. There are two major uses for clusters: high availability and extending server capacity, called *scale out*.

In high availability environments, two or more systems are connected together, typically with shared storage in a master-slave configuration with one system running the primary database with automated fail-over capabilities. As the DW/BI system becomes more mission critical this type of installation is becoming more prevalent.

The term *scale out* means expanding your server capacity by adding more boxes, as opposed to *scale up*, which means adding capacity by getting a bigger machine. The goal of a scale out cluster is to provide an environment where multiple systems can concurrently access the same data. The big challenge with clustering is what happens when a query on one node needs data stored on another node. The overhead of cross system communication that's required to resolve this can be very high. Different database and operating system combinations approach this problem in different ways, including shared cache, federated data, and replicated data.

- **Shared cache.** When storage is shared among all the machines in a cluster environment, the system must keep track of uncommitted transactions. This requires distributed lock management capabilities to allow coordination of resources between cooperating nodes.

- **Federated data.** The federated data environment requires that data is split or *federated* across multiple nodes and that queries are satisfied by collecting data from multiple nodes and joining the data to satisfy the queries.

- **Replicated data.** The data replication environment requires that data be replicated to different nodes and that queries are satisfied by the local relational engine. Each node has access to its own copy of the data and doesn't have to manage coordination problems.

Advances in operating systems, databases, and communications technology are dramatically impacting this area. We are reaching the point where a cluster of several relatively cheap computers connected to a high performance disk subsystem will look much like a NUMA machine, but at a lower price point.

Warehouse Appliances

The high end of the data warehouse platform market has opened up to niche players because the major relational database products are not specifically designed to handle the mixed workload of the DW/BI system with vast quantities of data. Several companies have appeared in recent years offering pre-configured hardware and database platforms designed specifically for data warehousing. The newer versions of these products are based on off-the-shelf technology and open source databases. They offer the convenience of a single source provider, with some degree of customization to support large scale data warehousing at a fairly aggressive price. This pre-packaging concept, known as a data warehouse or information appliance, has been co-opted by the major database vendors who are working with hardware partners to provide their own appliance offerings.

Partitioning Hardware

In most cases, it is possible to logically or physically partition a large server into smaller servers that have their own operating system and resources. On a single 16 processor machine, you could create a 4 processor partition for the ETL process, an 8 processor partition for the relational database, and a 4 processor partition for the reporting service. If you decide this allocation of resources isn't quite right, you can reconfigure it relatively easily.

Considerations Common to All Parallel Architectures

As with all platforms, it pays to ask specific questions about software availability and system administration complexities. In particular, be sure to consider what type and version of the operating system it runs on. Also, you need to determine the applications, utilities, and drivers available on this version of the operating system. If the vendor of the software you want has not ported its package to your operating system, it just won't work. In particular, you want to know if it runs the most current version of your RDBMS, ETL tool, development environment, data warehouse utilities, and application servers.

Hardware Performance Boosters

Disk speed and memory are especially important for data warehouses because the queries can be data intensive. A transaction system request typically retrieves a single record from a table optimized to already have that record in cache. A data warehouse query may require a scan or aggregation of millions of records across several tables.

Disk Issues

Disk drives can have a major impact on the performance, flexibility, and scalability of the warehouse platform. The cost per gigabyte for server storage can easily vary by an order of magnitude depending on the I/O capacity of the controller/disk combination and the aggregate throughput of the storage subsystem. For typical data warehouse environments, the limiting factor is the bandwidth of the I/O subsystem, especially for larger transactions, like data loads or full scan queries. This is the opposite of OLTP workloads, where a lot of small transactions mean the number of I/Os per second is the key measure.

At the high end, the drives are essentially built into a stand-alone computer or disk subsystem called a storage area network (SAN) that manages disk access. These drive systems are fast, easily expandable (especially important for growth) and portable (meaning they can be moved across servers and operating systems). They can also be set up with redundant storage for fault tolerance (RAID 1 or 5) to give the warehouse greater availability and with striping (RAID 0) to distribute the read/write workload across multiple disk drives and controllers. Fault tolerant drive systems can be configured to be hot swappable to minimize downtime when there is a problem. Fault tolerance and hot swapping are important because disk drives are the most likely components to fail, and large data warehouses tend to have hundreds of drives. Note that databases need large temporary storage spaces where sorts, joins, and aggregations are performed. This space needs to be on high-performance drives and controllers, but it does not need to be mirrored — a cost savings.

Disk drive subsystems are more expensive, but represent a good value over time. Start with enough disk for the next year or two, and expand as needed and as prices drop. Most large organizations have a person or group who is responsible for managing the disk subsystem; work closely with that group to make sure you have the optimal storage space, I/O capacity, and configuration.

Memory

When it comes to memory, more is better across the DW/BI system. Again, this is another difference between business intelligence and transaction processing. Transaction requests are small and typically don't need as much memory. Business intelligence queries are much larger and often involve several passes through large tables. If the table is already in memory, performance can theoretically improve by one to two orders of magnitude, or 10 to 100 times. The database isn't the only memory hog; all of the major components of the DW/BI system are memory intensive. This is one of the big advantages of 64-bit platforms. For example, 32-bit systems are limited to less than 4 GB of memory, but 64-bit chips can address a much larger memory space (depending on the hardware manufacturer). You should plan for your major servers to be 64 bit. Note that for a 64-bit chip to be effective, the machine, operating system, and database all must be based on 64-bit code.

NOTE The idea of preferring memory to disk has been around for decades — the speed difference is irresistible. In round numbers, the access time for a disk drive is about 10 milliseconds compared to about 0.1 millisecond for memory, making memory about 100 times faster than disk. Of course, the effective improvement of doing database processing with data already in memory instead of on disk is less than 100 times due to lots of intervening factors (like disk read-aheads and memory cache on the controller or in the operating system). Nonetheless, we've seen improvements in data warehouse performance of 10 to 30 times simply by adding a lot more memory to the database configuration.

CPUs

In general, more is better and faster is better. Dual core and quad core CPUs can provide greater processing power at a much lower overall price, depending on the pricing models of your various software vendors.

Secondary Storage

Make sure your configuration includes resources to support backup and archiving. If at all possible, try to get a backup system that is fast enough to do the job during the load window. We've reached the point where it is economically feasible to do disk-to-disk backups. Although it is possible to back up a warehouse while it is online, doing so can add significant overhead, which will compete with the business users' queries for CPU cycles.

Database Platform Factors

In the data warehouse world, the choice of database platform is as incendiary as religion or politics. In addition to the major relational database products, there are more than a dozen alternative database platforms, each with examples of successful data warehouse implementations and each with its own pack of supporting (and opposing) zealots. Many of the factors that drive the hardware platform decision also apply to the database decision. In our experience, what's right for you depends on considerations specific to your situation.

The database platform decision has changed dramatically in some ways and very little in other ways. The major relational database vendors are still the platforms of choice, covering about 80 percent of the DW/BI database market. The rest is made up of high end data warehouse appliance vendors and specialized database products designed for data warehouse workloads. For most DW/BI systems, this decision can be an easy one. Unless you are at the large end of the data scale, the decision will probably center on what your organization is comfortable with in terms of licensing and skill sets.

One major factor that plays in the database platform decision is aggregate management and navigation. The major database vendors have chosen different architectural strategies to provide aggregate functionality. You will need to decide which of these approaches will be more effective in your environment.

Characteristics of Relational Engines

Most major relational database vendors continue to invest in data warehouse specific improvements and provide reasonably good performance. The major RDBMS vendors have added capabilities like dimensional model support, star join optimization, bit-mapped indexes, data compression, and improved cost-based optimizers. These advances and the advent of technologies like aggregate management and navigation have improved data warehouse performance significantly. Relational databases have the advantage of being able to hold much more data at a detailed level. Of course, systems that are designed to solve specific problems must have advantages over general-purpose systems in order to survive in the marketplace.

> **NOTE** If you're building your warehouse on a relational platform, it makes little sense to consider anything other than the mainstream RDBMS alternatives for most small-to-medium efforts.

If your warehouse is going to be a big one, in the double-digit terabyte range, it's a good idea to do a little research before you buy. We provide some guidance in the product selection section in Chapter 5.

Characteristics of OLAP Engines

Multidimensional database management systems, also known as OLAP engines, are proprietary database management systems designed to provide highly specialized support for analysis. OLAP engines serve two purposes: They improve query performance primarily by pre-aggregating data and support complex analyses through a more analytically oriented query language.

OLAP engines have made huge advances in the past decade. They now limit the pre-aggregation process to a subset of aggregates, thus avoiding the data explosion of earlier versions. They also can handle more and larger dimensions, and much more data overall. In the first edition of the *Lifecycle Toolkit*, we spoke of practical limits like 5GB of input data and about 300,000 rows in the largest dimension. At this writing, we know of OLAP engine implementations that take in more than a terabyte of input data and have dimensions with several million rows. This is more than enough headroom for most DW/BI systems.

One of the advances in OLAP technology is that some leading products are now truly dimensional. This means that the relational dimensions can translate directly into the OLAP layer on a one-to-one basis. You used to have to split a single dimension, like customer, into several sub-dimensions, like demographics, geography, customer type, and sales group. In fact, if you ever needed to compare any two attributes, like age range and gender, they had to be in separate dimensions.

What we used to consider a platform for local use has grown up to become a core part of the enterprise data warehouse's presentation server. Today's market leading OLAP engines can be an excellent complement to the relational platform, handling aggregate management and navigation and providing enhanced analytic capabilities.

On the other hand, if you have aggregate management and navigation in your relational database, and your BI tool supports complex analyses directly against the database, you have no need for an OLAP engine.

The evaluation of multidimensional engines cannot be uncoupled from the BI data access tool evaluation, described in detail in Chapter 5. The major BI tools claim to support both OLAP and relational sources. The best tools for querying OLAP engines were designed to generate the underlying language from the start. Including an OLAP engine in your architecture could limit your choice of BI tools.

Lightweight desktop-based OLAP solutions could be attractive in the short term, but they will likely end up creating more work than value. The DW/BI team needs to assess the product's size limitations and functionality carefully.

The interesting twist in this decision is that all the major database vendors have some version of OLAP capabilities as part of their product base. Their dedication to these products varies greatly, and their willingness to explore how to merge the best of their relational and OLAP engines has been weak. We expect them to continue improving the integration of these functional components.

Front Room Infrastructure Factors

Infrastructure requirements for the front room are more diverse than those for the back room because they are more business and tool dependent and there are many more alternatives to chose from. Let's look at some of the high level considerations that affect the front room.

Application Server Considerations

Servers are proliferating in the front room like mad. There are servers to handle data access from the web, query management, enterprise reporting, authentication, metadata databases, and more. It's difficult to give any meaningful information or advice on these devices because there are so many and they are so different. The best tactic you can take is to ask your vendors for detailed configuration information and search the Internet for user reported problems. In particular, ask about the following:

- **Memory.**   How much memory does the system require? How much does it take to perform well? As we said earlier, more is always better.
- **Disk.**   What determines disk usage? How much do you typically need? How fast does it usually grow?
- **Platform sharing.**   Is it okay to run multiple services on the same hardware platform? What are the performance impacts? What are the trade-offs? Are there any products that have poor compatibility?

■ **Bottlenecks.** What creates hot spots in the system? What slows it down? Is it truly multithreaded? Can it spawn independent processes and let them run to completion? What difference will multiple processors or additional memory make? How many simultaneous users can it handle?

Desktop Considerations

Most desktop machines in business today are powerful enough to support most BI applications. Here are a couple of desktop-related challenges to watch out for:

■ **Cross-platform support.** Some organizations use Macintosh computers, and others use UNIX workstations. Supporting multiple desktop platforms means much more work for the front end team. Installation and support issues vary from platform to platform, requiring the team to have expertise in all platforms. And the problems don't end once the software is successfully installed. Often reports will need to be created on each platform, potentially doubling the development and maintenance effort. Few front end vendors still support platforms other than Windows/Intel. A requirement to support multiple desktop platforms will simplify the data access tool selection process.

■ **Desktop operating system and software.** Even if everyone is on the same desktop hardware platform, they still may not be able to support the client software because they are not on the right version of the desktop operating system, they don't have the current version of your office productivity suite, or their browser version is old. Find out which versions of which software components your BI tools and applications require and take a survey to make sure it matches reality.

■ **Memory.** It should come as no surprise that memory can make a big difference in performance on the desktop machine. You can spend a lot of time and energy researching what appears to be a network issue, only to discover that the performance bottleneck is the desktop machines paging data and programs in and out of virtual memory. Once again, more memory is better.

Our recommendation is to determine the minimum desktop configuration that will support your BI tool set in a responsive, effective way. Then consider a second, more powerful, recommended configuration especially for power users, because these folks are fewer in number but larger in impact. Finally, include a large monitor, or two, in the recommended configuration for your power users and developers. They will thank you for this.

Connectivity and Networking Factors

Connectivity and networking provide the links between the back room and front room. In general, connectivity is a straightforward component of the infrastructure. Because this is a prerequisite to implementing any kind of client/server application, the groundwork is usually already in place. Most organizations have established communications networks, along with a group dedicated to keeping them working. Connectivity issues that are likely to come up include:

- **Bandwidth.**   Often it helps to locate the database and application servers on a dedicated high speed LAN along with the source systems if possible. This provides the needed bandwidth to transfer large blocks of data from the sources to the presentation servers as quickly as possible. Bandwidth to the disk subsystem is a critical link in the chain, both for data loading and query performance.

- **Remote access.**   If you have users in remote locations, they will obviously need access to the warehouse in much the same fashion as local users. This means you need a reliable, high bandwidth connection between their LAN and the LAN where the database and application servers are located.

   Bandwidth to the desktop is becoming more important because the BI tools are changing their approach. Some tools are now providing the ability to specify an interesting analytic set of the data, retrieve it, and slice and dice it locally. This means a fairly large chunk of data is coming down the pipe. In some cases, this data is stored with the report. If the report is on the server, it can take several minutes for the report to open on the remote desktop. Once you have a sense of what the reporting requirements are, work with the networking folks who can help you determine if the connection has enough bandwidth and when it's available.

- **File transfer.**   There are many file transfer protocols out there, along with programs that implement them. Certainly chief among them is File Transfer Protocol (FTP), which is a universal data transfer utility. FTP has been around as long as the Internet, and it provides file transfer services among the various and sundry computers on the Internet. It provides a base-level capability for establishing connectivity between two machines and moving files across that connection. Secured Sockets Layer (SSL) has the advantage of providing encryption built into the process so someone tapping into your network won't get the senior executive sales summary before the senior executives do. SSL is widely implemented in the UNIX server world because it is used to conduct secure transactions between web browsers and servers.

- **Database connectivity.** Most database, ETL, and BI tool vendors include drivers that provide connectivity to databases from other vendors and legacy data sources. Most vendors provide a range of connection alternatives, including the proprietary protocol native to each database product. Third party drivers are also available and can be faster and more robust than the default drivers. Third party middleware products provide this connectivity as well and include the ability to combine data from multiple sources. These products tend to be marketed under the enterprise information integration category.

- **Directory services.** Your networking infrastructure needs some form of directory server to provide a single point of logon and administration. Most network-based directory services exist in the form of X.500 or Lightweight Directory Access Protocol (LDAP) directories. These directories contain much richer information than simple IP addresses. They can incorporate many types of directories, including name and address, email addresses, telephone lists, and hardware directories (like printers and computers) — just about anything you might want to look up. These directories can be used to list the locations of servers, user directories for data delivery, and email lists for distributing standard reports.

Infrastructure Summary

As you've seen, there are a lot of components in the DW/BI system infrastructure covering hardware platforms, database platforms, connectivity and networking, and the desktop. For each of these major areas, you will need to understand the implications of the business requirements and the pivotal decision points in your environment. Fortunately, the responsibility for infrastructure extends well beyond the DW/BI system. Most operational systems have very similar infrastructure requirements, so in most cases, the DW/BI system can simply rely on existing infrastructure.

Infrastructure provides the foundation upon which you build the DW/BI system. Under-powered or insufficient infrastructure will weaken the entire system. It is like a snake in the grass — it will rise up and bite you if you are not careful, and you won't realize you've been bitten until it's too late.

Metadata

Earlier in this chapter, we described many instances of metadata in the DW/BI system. In this section, we try to step back from those details to give some perspective about integrating this messy but important resource. Metadata is a bit more ethereal than other infrastructure components, but it provides the same kind of enabling base layer for DW/BI system tools, users, and processes.

The reality is that most tools create and manage their own metadata and keep it in a local physical storage location called a *repository*. This means you will have several metadata repositories scattered around the DW/BI system, often using different storage types ranging from relational tables to XML files. It also means they will have overlapping content. For example, the ETL tool will keep a definition of each target table, as will the BI tool, and of course the database itself. It's this combination of multiple repositories and overlapping content that causes problems.

Value of Metadata Integration

A single integrated repository for DW/BI system metadata would be valuable in several ways, if it were possible to build. Chief among these are impact analysis, audit and documentation, and metadata quality management.

Impact Analysis

First, an integrated repository could help you identify the impact of making a change to the DW/BI system. We describe impact and lineage analysis in the ETL management subsystems in Chapter 9, but these concepts really apply across the DW/BI system. A change to the source system data model would impact the ETL process, and may cause a change to the target data model, which would then impact any database definitions based on that element, like indexes, partitions, and aggregates. It would also impact any reports that include that element. If all the metadata is in one place, or at least connected by common keys and IDs, then it would be fairly easy to understand the impact of this change.

Audit and Documentation

In Chapter 9, we describe lineage analysis as the reverse of impact analysis. Rather than starting at one point and looking at what depends on a given element, lineage analysis picks an element and determines where it came from and what went into its creation. This is particularly important for understanding the contents and source of a given column, table, or other object in the DW/BI system; it is essentially system generated documentation. In its most rigorous form, lineage analysis can use the audit metadata to determine the origin of any given fact or dimension row. In some compliance scenarios, this is required information.

Metadata Quality and Management

Multiple copies of metadata elements kept in different systems will invariably get out of sync. For the DW/BI system structures and processes, this kind of error is self-identifying because the next time a process runs or the structure is referenced, the action will fail. The DW/BI developer could have spotted this ahead of time with an impact analysis report if one were available. Errors in descriptive or business metadata synchronization are not so obvious. For example, if the data steward updates the description of a customer dimension attribute in the data model, it may not be updated in any of the other half dozen or so repositories around the DW/BI system that hold copies of this description. A user will still see the old description in the BI tool metadata. The query will still work, but the user's understanding of the result may be incorrect. A single repository would have one entry for the description of this field, which is then referred to wherever it is needed. A change in the single entry automatically means everyone will see the new value.

Options for Metadata Integration

Most DW/BI systems are based on products from multiple vendors. Getting products from multiple vendors to work together sounds like an ideal opportunity for standards. The good news is, we have a standard called the Common Warehouse Metamodel (CWM), along with XMI, which is an XML based metadata interchange standard, and the MetaObject Facility (MOF), which is the underlying storage facility for CWM. These standards are managed by the Object Management Group. The bad news is that vendor support for working with a standard metadata repository is slow in coming, to put it kindly. Without support from the vendors, this single standard repository is an unlikely outcome in a multi-vendor environment, and trying to build and maintain it yourself is more work than it's worth. Nonetheless, there are a few options for achieving some level of metadata integration.

Single Source DW/BI System Vendors

The major database, ERP, and BI tool vendors are all pushing hard to build complete, credible DW/BI system technology stacks to offer what they call end-to-end BI. As they build, or rebuild, their products, they are including metadata management as part of their toolsets, and designing their tools to share a central metadata repository and play nice together. In a case like this, the vendor has no excuse for avoiding a single repository. It will be proprietary, because they don't want you to simply copy all that metadata into another toolset, but at least it will be integrated and support some of the uses we described. Single source DW/BI technology providers are probably your best hope of getting a single, integrated metadata repository.

Core Vendor Product

If you work in a large organization, you will probably have to support multiple vendors in your DW/BI system. In this case, look and see what you already have as a starting point. Some of the ETL and BI tool vendors are working hard to become the metadata repository supplier by offering metadata management and repository tools that support their tools and include other tools as well. If your current vendors don't have any offerings, there are metadata management systems, some of which are based on the CWM, that offer a central metadata repository and modules for reading from and writing to most of the major DW/BI tool vendor metadata repositories.

Do It Yourself

It is not an unreasonable approach to pick certain metadata elements to manage and let the rest manage itself. If you think about it, the preceding metadata quality and management discussion tells you that you should focus on business metadata because technical metadata has to be right or the system breaks. In other words, as the builder and manager of the DW/BI system you are responsible for making sure the technical metadata is right. No one is responsible for the business metadata. You need to change that one way or another. We describe a comprehensive practical approach to managing your metadata in Chapter 5.

Metadata Summary

Metadata is an amorphous subject if you focus separately on each little parcel of metadata because it is spread so widely across the DW/BI system. We have tried to leave you with a few unifying principles:

- Inventory all of your metadata so you know what you have.
- Subject your metadata to standard software library practices including version control, version migration, and reliable backup and recovery.
- Document your metadata. This is known as metametadatadata.
- Appreciate the value of your metadata assets.

Security

The DW/BI system must publish data to those who need to see it, while simultaneously protecting that data. On the one hand, the DW/BI team is judged by how easily a business user can access the data. On the other hand, the team is blamed if sensitive data gets into the wrong hands or if data is lost. The loss of data warehouse data to hostile parties can have extremely serious legal, financial, and competitive impacts on an organization. In most cases today, DW/BI system security is largely about recognizing legitimate users and giving them very specific rights to look at some but not all of the data.

This is alarmingly short sighted. The Internet has completely altered the way systems are architected. Security is a complex area, intertwined with the networking infrastructure. There are various hardware, database, and application components of the DW/BI system distributed across the enterprise, and even beyond its boundaries. This means you face an equivalently distributed security problem. We recommend you identify someone on the DW/BI team to be the security manager; the security manager's first action should be calling a meeting with your organization's security team.

In this section we identify the major vulnerabilities in the DW/BI system architecture, primarily to motivate you to take this risk seriously. Chapter 5 provides more specifics on the architecture and tools to implement your security strategy and address these vulnerabilities.

Security Vulnerabilities

For this section, please try to think like a good security analyst instead of a DW/BI team member — that is, be a pessimist. We present various types of vulnerabilities in a modern networked DW/BI system. For each type of vulnerability, we invite you to imagine how the activities of a DW/BI system could be specifically impacted if the vulnerability were exploited, and how a responsible security manager could reduce or eliminate the vulnerability while keeping the data flowing.

The security problem is surprisingly large and underappreciated. A report published in 2007 from the IT Policy Compliance Group reports that one-fifth of organizations are hit with 22 or more sensitive data losses per year. The report goes on to say that notifying customers and restoring data costs $73 per customer record, and companies see an 8 percent drop in revenue and customers when the loss is reported publicly.

The sources of vulnerability are very diverse, including threats from internal sources, not just "hackers on the Internet." We describe the major areas of vulnerability that the DW/BI security manager should be aware of in the following sections, framed in terms of the implications on the system architecture. Chapter 5 addresses the implementation and security strategy in more detail.

Threats to Physical Assets

Physical assets are the obvious ones, including mainframes and servers, desktop workstations, and laptops. Physical assets also include communications equipment, wires and fiber optics, buildings, file drawers, and offline media. The main vulnerabilities of physical assets include theft, intentional or accidental destruction, natural forces such as electrical and magnetic disturbances, technological obsolescence or neglect, and hijacking control of an asset by inside or outside forces.

To mitigate the danger from these risks, all servers should be located in a secure, limited access environment. Most organizations working on a DW/BI system are likely to have such an environment. This environment protects the servers from many of the physical vulnerabilities listed earlier, including physical damage or theft, temperature, electrical, and dust and dirt. This centralization also makes it easier to control the software and information assets as well.

Threats to Information and Software Assets

Information assets include nearly everything of value that isn't a physical asset and isn't software that you obtain from outsiders. These assets include all of the metadata categories, as well as all the "real" data in documents, spreadsheets, email, graphics systems, and databases of all kinds. Information assets also include all derivative forms of electronic information, including printouts, photocopies, and the information carried in people's heads.

Our software assets are also vulnerable. We distinguish these vulnerabilities from physical asset and other information asset vulnerabilities, although clearly they overlap with each other. Software vulnerabilities include theft of object or source code, and infiltration via hijacking, compromised certification, or viruses.

Theft or violation of information assets can lead to a range of troubles, beginning with unwanted disclosure of confidential or sensitive information, business plans, or code. It can result in theft of financial or service assets, loss of privacy, or identity theft. Malicious parties may gain access to your information through various means, including opportunistic snatching, inadvertent broadcasting, eavesdropping, physical theft of data storage assets, impersonation, use of trapdoors, or the more old-fashioned routes of bribery, robbery, or extortion.

To protect against loss of information assets, the centralized server facility should provide the core information asset protection functionality, such as the capability to back up and restore to secure local media and to a secure remote facility for disaster recovery.

Server software should be under the control of the group that manages the servers. It is often kept in the machine room, under lock and key. Upgrades and other maintenance must be carefully tested and coordinated with the DW/BI team.

Your organization will need to have an information security policy in place, along with regular and widespread education. Sensitive data should either be left out of the DW/BI system, encrypted, or masked using security components in the database and reporting environment. You must monitor system usage to identify unusual events, like downloads of large datasets or attempts to query sensitive data without permission, and then investigate them. It does no good to simply monitor the events.

Threats to Business Continuance

Other vulnerabilities may affect your ability to conduct your business mission, including:

- **Denial of service attack.** Your information system is compromised specifically for the purpose of halting or bottlenecking one or more critical components. For example, your servers may be deluged with millions of false requests.

- **Inability to reconstruct consistent software snapshot.** Through deliberate sabotage, accidental loss, or simple oversight, you may not be able to reconstruct a consistent snapshot of your systems.

- **Terrorism.** A very serious kind of denial of service attack is one intended to cause major public infrastructure to fail. One might imagine a public utility such as a telephone company or a power utility subject to a denial of service attack through an information systems security breach. This form of terrorism could only be a password away. Fortunately, most organizations do not have the kind of broadly used, high profile systems that would make enticing terrorist targets, like the stock exchange or the air traffic control system. Even in those high profile organizations, the DW/BI system is usually not on the front line. However, as the DW/BI system takes on more operational activities, it becomes a more attractive target for terrorist activities.

Each of these vulnerabilities has its own defense techniques. Denial of service attacks are handled in the network layer, which we discuss next and in Chapter 5. Consistent snapshots are part of a detailed backup strategy that includes file system objects, metadata stores, and perhaps even system images in addition to the usual database backups. Most of the security responses described in this section and in Chapter 5 help limit the possibility of a terrorist attack.

Network Threats

The popularity of the Internet has driven nearly all of us to rely on the Internet's communication scheme to implement wide area networks. The good news is that the Internet has become a common highway that connects all of us together, but the bad news is that the Internet was never designed to protect privacy or commerce. The range of network threats is only limited by the creativity of the various people who want to compromise our networks. These are not just hackers; the list of would be network attackers includes disgruntled employees, customers or other amateur hackers, career criminals seeking financial gain, competitors, information brokers, and system crackers intent on proving their skill or wreaking havoc. The common types of threats include:

- **Denial of service (DOS) attacks:** overwhelming a host with too many connection requests that are left incomplete, forcing the host to keep them open until they timeout.

- **Viruses, worms, and Trojan horses:** programs that execute on a computer and can cause a range of dysfunctions.

- **Hijacking:** taking over a user session or program by eavesdropping to obtain authentication tokens, or by inserting code into the application.

- **Spoofing:** impersonating a user or computer to gain access to the network.

- **Phishing:** impersonating a legitimate enterprise to obtain user IDs, passwords, and other information.

- **Backdoors or trapdoors:** an undocumented way of gaining access to a program, service, or computer system.

The core components that make up your organization's communications backbone also provide your primary defense mechanisms against network threats. In addition to the routers and firewalls that manage Internet traffic and limit access, there are security-specific network devices that monitor for specific malware behaviors and mitigate their effects. We talk more about using these tools in Chapter 5.

REFERENCES If you have taken on the role of the DW/BI security manager, you will most likely need to obtain the involvement of the IT security professionals in your organization. You might also want to study up on the topic a bit more. One place to start is Charles Pfleeger and Shari Pfleeger's book, *Security in Computing, 4th Edition* (Prentice Hall PTR, 2006).

Security Summary

Security is a big, esoteric, and complex topic. It's also the kind of responsibility you might get away with ignoring for the most part. But if you do have a problem, it is likely to be a big one. In this section, we described a range of potential problems you might encounter. In Chapter 5, we review some of the major tools and techniques you can use to avoid many of those problems, or at least limit their impact. We also describe approaches for controlling access and authorization to the information assets; the one security job that is the exclusive responsibility of the DW/BI security manager.

Conclusion

Probably the only reader left standing at this point is the DW/BI technical architect, and that's mostly due to a paralyzing sense of fear and overwhelm. True, there are a lot of issues to consider when you are designing a DW/BI system. Let's review the major topics we covered in this chapter:

- Back room architecture, including the ETL process, source system, and ETL data stores.

- Presentation server layer, including atomic and aggregate data, and aggregate navigation functionality.

- Front room architecture, encompassing a range of data access services including metadata, security, administration, enterprise reporting, modeling, planning and performance management, web and portal services, and operational BI, not to mention BI application functionality covering query and reporting.

- Infrastructure, including hardware and database platforms, and networking and desktop issues.

- Metadata, including a discussion of the value of an integrated metadata repository.

- Security, including the major areas of vulnerability for the DW/BI system.

Though each of the major sections in this chapter warrants its own book, the good news is you don't have to be a certified professional in every associated technology to create a viable DW/BI technical architecture. In the next chapter, we present a step-by-step process for creating the architecture. We also review recommendations for approaching the product selection process to help avoid some pain and suffering.

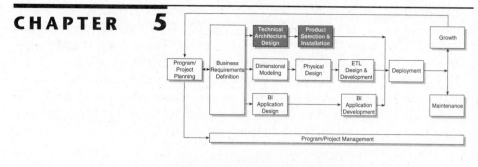

CHAPTER 5

Creating the Architecture Plan and Selecting Products

In this chapter, we switch from the theoretical details of architectural components and services to the practical matters of how to actually design your architecture, select products to support it, manage the associated metadata, and establish the initial access security system. The first part of this chapter concentrates on the architecture design process. The architecture plan is the technical translation of the business requirements. It says, "these are the capabilities we must provide to meet the information needs of the business." Once the plan is in place, you turn your attention to product selection — the process of comparing products to your functional requirements reveals who shines and who fades. The architecture and product selection are both critical inputs to the infrastructure map that we discuss toward the end of the chapter. Finally, once you have selected and installed the products, you must turn your attention to the initial metadata management and security tasks.

Your job in creating the architecture plan is to identify the capabilities that are most important to your organization. Start with the highest priority business opportunity and determine what functionality you need to address that opportunity. Once you have this list of functional requirements, you can identify the vendors who provide these capabilities, and determine which is the best fit for your situation. If you start doing product selection before you understand the business requirements, you are doing it wrong and you are much less likely to succeed. Is this a clear and direct enough statement?

The truth is, 90 percent of the time, the choice of products isn't a key determinant of overall DW/BI success. You can pick the best product, but if you use it to solve the wrong problem, nobody cares. Or you can pick a mediocre product, solve a high value problem, and be the hero.

Though the primary audience for this chapter is technical architects, other DW/BI team members should review it as well because they often participate in the product selection process. The entire team must be familiar with your architecture design and their role in bringing it to life.

Create the Architecture

If you are an IT systems architect, you are familiar with at least a few of the rigorous, comprehensive approaches to architecture development such as the Cap Gemini Ernst and Young Integrated Architecture Framework or the Zachman Framework for Enterprise Architecture. Many of these approaches deal with overall IT issues, and thus fall outside of the DW/BI system span of control. A straight application of these enterprise IT architecture approaches is probably more than you need for all but the largest DW/BI systems.

The approach we use to develop the architecture is based on the 80–20 rule; that is, we spend 20 percent of the effort to get 80 percent of the benefit. This is not to say that more wouldn't be better, but in our experience, most organizations can barely muster the resources for this 20 percent. Of course, this approach is an iterative process, much like the DW/BI system overall. Get the big picture in place, determine the priorities, and split the implementation into phases. As you move forward, you will uncover new information that will cause you to revise significant parts of the architecture. Celebrate these changes — they mean your map of the world is getting more accurate (and your chances of falling off the edge are decreasing).

Architecture Development Process

Creating an architecture is a top-down process. You start with an understanding of the business requirements, create a high level model that describes the solution from a big picture perspective, and then break it down into subsystems and their specifications, then select products, then implement. Figure 5-1 shows this top-down process from the DW/BI system application architecture perspective.

At the top of Figure 5-1, the business requirements set the boundaries and baselines for the application architecture; at the other end, the implementation is its realization. The two rows in the middle make up the core of the application architecture itself. The back room and front room have parallel tracks because

LEVEL OF DETAIL	BACK ROOM	FRONT ROOM
Business Requirements and Data Audit	How will we get the data needed to address our major business opportunities, transform it, and make it available to users? How is this done today?	What are our major business opportunities? How do we want to measure, track, analyze, and enable them?
Architecture Implications and Models	What are the functions and components needed to get the data into a usable form in the desired locations at the appropriate time? What are the major data stores and services and where should they be located? What is our metadata strategy?	What do users need to get the information out in a usable form? What types of BI applications are needed and what are the priorities? What is our BI portal strategy? What is our metadata strategy?
Detailed Models and Specs	What is the specific content of each data store, and what are the specific capabilities of each service?	What do our standard BI templates and reports look like, including rows, columns, graphic elements, sections, filters, and headers? How will we deliver them? To whom? What is the design of our BI Portal?
Product Selection and Implementation	What products provide the needed capabilities and how will we hook them together? Write the ETL system, manage the process, and document the results.	What products provide the needed capabilities and how will we hook them together? Implement the BI applications, build the initial report set, provide ad hoc access, train users, manage the process, and document.

Figure 5-1 DW/BI system's application architecture top-down approach.

they both have their own set of application requirements. The questions in the cells at each of the four levels of detail give you a sense for the issues you need to address at that level.

The application architecture is a component of the overall DW/BI architecture. Figure 5-2 shows the major interactions between the data architecture, application architecture, and infrastructure from a process flow perspective as you progress down from the business requirements to the ultimate implementation.

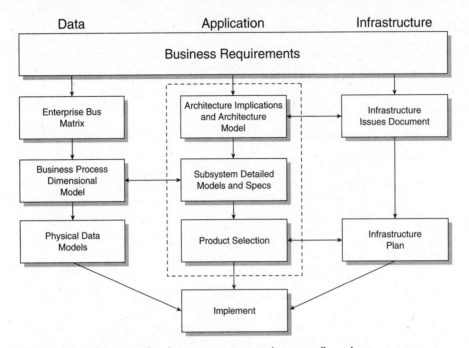

Data　　　　　　　　Application　　　　　　Infrastructure

Figure 5-2 Architecture development context and process flow chart.

In this section, we develop the application architecture shown in the dashed-line box in the center of Figure 5-2, specifically focusing on the back room ETL and front room BI application architectures. We discuss the infrastructure efforts later in this chapter.

Your primary deliverables from the application architecture development process will be the application architecture plan. The application architecture plan is usually 50 or more pages long, and it describes your vision for the future structure of the DW/BI system. This may sound like a daunting task, but we'll help you get through it.

There is a spectrum of approaches for creating an architecture, ranging from a few scribbles on the back of an envelope, to a full-blown, multi-person, multiyear struggle. In general, where your project falls on the spectrum depends on the overall size and scope of the DW/BI system and on the level of detail desired. The approach we advocate is somewhere in the middle, usually requiring a month or two of elapsed time, concurrent with other activities as illustrated on the Lifecycle diagram, and resulting in a practical, usable blueprint for the DW/BI system. Figure 5-3 shows a matrix of the major drivers of an architecture effort.

The closer you can get to the lower left quadrant, the better. The upper left quadrant has both organizational and technical issues. Even if the current iteration is technically simple, broader organizational scope almost always

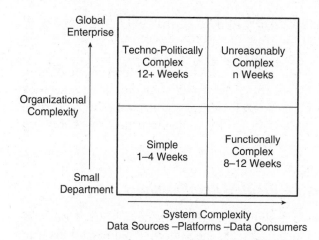

Figure 5-3 Architecture development estimated effort.

means additional source systems, platforms, and data consumers. In other words, as you move up, you often get dragged to the right at the same time. The upper right quadrant ends up being an enterprise architecture project and inevitably gets tangled up in a complex web of challenges. Try to avoid this if possible by narrowing your scope, or reducing the number of organizational entities involved.

Develop the Application Architecture Plan

The DW/BI application architecture design process, which culminates in the creation of the architecture plan document, unfolds in a series of eight steps, which we describe in the following sections.

Step 1 – Form an Architecture Task Force

The task force is an ad hoc group brought together specifically to create the DW/BI architecture. The task force is led by the DW/BI technical architect. If the technical architect has not been through a DW/BI implementation before, it's a good idea to hold off on the architecture development until after the requirements have been identified and initial dimensional models designed. This deferment is valuable because it is difficult to begin creating an architecture for a DW/BI system without having already seen one up close. Of course, postponing the architecture development will extend the duration of the project, so if you cannot afford to extend the project an extra month or two, plan to bring in an experienced DW/BI architect early on.

The architecture task force should include someone with back room experience and someone with front room experience. The size of the task force depends on the magnitude of the project. In general, a small group of two to four people is better than a larger group. Even for a small DW/BI system, where one person might create the architecture (in her spare time), it helps to include another participant to provide an additional viewpoint. Identify the team early on, before the requirements get underway, so they know they will be responsible for the architecture and keep it in mind during the early stages. The group should begin by reviewing their tasks, timing, roles, and deliverables.

Step 2 – Gather Architecture-Related Requirements

Most of what you must know to design the architecture comes out of the business requirements. It's a good idea to discuss the interview plans with the lead interviewer ahead of time to make sure they include questions addressing architectural topics, such as user counts, response time expectations, and analytic functionality. Then attend the business user interviews and listen carefully for architecture-related issues, without sidetracking the process. If you need more information, conduct a few follow-up interviews.

You also need to understand the existing technical environment to identify elements you can leverage and any limitations or boundaries the environment may impose. In particular, there are probably some IT development and infrastructure folks who didn't make the business interview list. Figure 5-4 shows a set of sample questions targeted at IT people, not business users. While you're talking to the technical folks, keep an eye out for existing architectural "standards" and directions.

Step 3 – Create a Draft Architectural Implications Document

This document lists the business requirements that have architectural implications along with a list of the implications. It is created by reviewing and summarizing the requirements documentation, but from an architectural view. Look for business requirements that imply a need for some capability or service or that set boundaries and baselines. A good way to approach this is to use a tabular format like the example shown in Figure 5-5.

List the major requirements and opportunities in the first column; then, list the functional implications of each opportunity in the second column. Each opportunity often has several implications. What functions and tools will you need to deliver on this business requirement? Are there any service level implications for performance, availability, or data latency? Are there any scale implications in terms of simultaneous users or data volumes? It is also beneficial to include business priority or ranking information in this document, if it's available.

A. IT BUSINESS ROLE

How important is business or data analysis in support of management decision making at the company?

What role does IT play in the management decision making process?

Is this changing (due to the competitive environment, organizational restructuring, etc.)?

Who is responsible for operational reporting? How is that serviced today, and how is it changing?

B. TECHNOLOGY DIRECTION

What is the company's general approach to information technology over the next few years (e.g., SOA, ERP conversion)? Is there a general direction or plan to address the related software infrastructure requirements (network-based security, enterprise service bus, etc.)?

What are your system plans and priorities for the foreseeable future?

What infrastructure initiatives or plans will have an impact on information access (data movement, task scheduling, directory servers, security, software distribution, etc.)?

Is there a specific role for metadata? How will it be managed?

What are the company's product standards today? What platforms, system software, DBMS, client software, and utilities do you think are going to be strategic over the next few years?

What are the biggest bottlenecks or issues in the infrastructure area?

Is there a group responsible for architecture, or are any documents or guidelines available?

C. INFRASTRUCTURE PROCESS

What groups are involved in acquiring, installing, and supporting new infrastructure (e.g., servers, utility software, connectivity)? What is the process for securing required infrastructure?

Is there a centralized data and systems security function in the organization? How do they work with other groups?

What kinds of timeframes are typically involved in these activities?

Figure 5-4 Example architecture-related interview questions.

Step 4 – Create the Architecture Model

It's time to sequester the architecture task force in a conference room with lots of wall space for two days to hash out the architecture model. Because the architecture must be requirements-driven, begin with Step 3's architecture implications document to make sure you include all the necessary components and capabilities. The goal here is to use the wall space to create a large version of the DW/BI architecture model, similar to Figure 4-1, but customized for your organization.

Take every item from the Architectural/Functional Implications column in Figure 5-5 and put it in its appropriate section of your model. Group them together in terms of how you plan to use them, which should match the Functional Areas column. These groups of functions will become input to the product selection process. Carefully go through the flow of your DW/BI system model from end to end, simulating the working DW/BI system in your mind, reviewing each step to verify the needed functionality, overall flow, and management. Take lots of notes; you will use these as the starting point for

Business Requirement / Opportunity	Architectural / Functional Implications	Functional Areas	Business Value / Priority
- Improve response rates to special offers by enabling a cross-sell capability	- Customer integration tool to match customers from currently independent product lines	ETL	H / 8
	- Create cross-sell lists and do basic monitoring with standard BI tools	BI Apps	H / 8
	- NOTE: CRM system must process offers and track responses to enable monitoring	BI Apps / Source	N/A
- Improve email campaign response rates by providing analysts with tools to generate target email lists and submit them to CRM system	- Analytic application (build vs. buy)	BI Apps / Data Mining	H / 7
- Increase accuracy of the sales forecast with better sales history and sales pipeline information, and better analytics	- Analytic applications, including time series forecasting with seasonality (build vs. buy)	BI Apps / Data Mining	H / 8
	- Extract connectors to outsourced sales tracking database system	ETL	H / 8

Figure 5-5 Architectural implications document sample.

Step 6. At the end of Step 4, you should be able to look at the model you've created and feel confident that it meets the business requirements. You can take a peek ahead at Figure 5-7 for an example of what this model might look like. Remember, your model will be based on your business requirements and will not contain many of the specific elements in Figure 5-7.

Step 5 – Determine the Architecture Implementation Phases

Generally, your architectural phases correspond to iterations of the Lifecycle. You must identify clear functional requirements and deliverables for each phase of the architecture. First, review the priorities for the major components of the architecture and the estimated personnel and monetary resources needed to implement them. Look at the architecture model from Step 4 and see what functionality is required to support the top priority business requirement. You might highlight these in one color, the next priority in a different color, and so on as far out as you can see. If you draw the model in a drawing tool, consider one that supports layers. Put each phase on a layer to show how the architecture will evolve. This will help you set timing expectations for spending on additional tools or development efforts.

Step 6 – Design and Specify the Subsystems

A large percentage of the functionality you need to deliver will be met by the standard offerings of the major tool providers, but there are almost always a few subsystems that are not commonly found in the off-the-shelf tools. Examples include some of the more advanced data quality screening described in Chapter 9, or a specific data extract, integration, or BI application problem. These are often unique to your organization and its internal data systems. You need to define each of these subsystems in enough detail so either someone can build it for you, or so you can evaluate products against your needs.

Step 7 – Create the Application Architecture Plan Document

The results from the previous steps are now rolled into a master plan document. The application architecture plan describes the form and function of the DW/BI system, both for the initial phase and across its expected life span. The architecture plan often spans 50 or more pages with detailed descriptions of the required components and functions, business rules, definitions where appropriate, priorities, resources, and implementation timeframes. Write the document with the expectation that a wide variety of people in your IT organization will read it; do not assume the readers have significant knowledge of data warehousing and business intelligence.

Begin with a summary of the DW/BI business requirements, focusing on how those requirements affect the architecture. Describe the types of users and different access requirements. Discuss significant data issues. For example, if you must develop a service to identify and integrate unique individuals from multiple systems, you should introduce that concept here. Describe the business requirements for integrated data and the associated value. Set expectations now for the resources needed to support a successful DW/BI system, including user support, education, training, and documentation.

NOTE The architecture plan typically does not include specific products. In fact, you will find that products may not exist to satisfy all your requirements. It's particularly important to have an architecture plan so you can build the modular components and plan for new products and services to "snap into" the existing framework.

Step 8 – Review the Draft

Review the draft plan with the DW/BI team in a design review session. Expect changes. You will get lots of good feedback and buy in, if you listen well and remain flexible. Incorporate the feedback into a final architecture plan document, then create a presentation to review the finalized architecture with key management and technical stakeholders. Don't make it too fancy. The purpose is to help people across the organization understand the nature and complexity of the DW/BI system. If people don't understand the effort that goes into the ETL process, or the BI application delivery, they will assume it's easy. The goal here is more education than input, although you will get some additional feedback.

Example Application Architecture Plan Outline and Model

To make these eight steps more tangible, here's a fictitious case study based on a regional retail grocery chain that decided to implement a club card program for its frequent shoppers. Analyzing and leveraging the club card program's data is the high value business need for the initial DW/BI effort. The ETL system will draw retail point of sale data from two primary source systems: the legacy point of sale (POS) system still in place for 20 percent of the stores that were acquired as part of a subsidiary, and the new primary POS system that runs most of the stores. The ETL system will also need to pull from a source system built to track and manage the club card member information. Fortunately, both POS systems are able to capture the club card member ID at the point of sale.

There are a few other ETL extracts needed to complete the dimensional model. The system has to pull employee data from the human resources module of the ERP system, and historical store attributes for the subsidiary stores from a separate archive. Finally, the DW/BI system must integrate demographic information from a third party source via an Internet based lookup service.

This example includes the table of contents from an architecture plan document, shown in Figure 5-6, and an application architecture model shown in Figure 5-7. In describing the architectural elements, remember that you are depicting your vision for the future. Describe the required services, such as ETL and BI applications, in enough detail so that the architecture plan document can help guide the product selection process, or development, if necessary.

The model shown in Figure 5-7 follows the basic layout we first saw in Figure 4-1. The sources and ETL system are on the left, the presentation server layer is in the middle, and the data access services and the BI applications are on the right. The metadata and security services provide centralized support for the back and front rooms.

Figure 5-7 does not include every eventual data source, ETL function, or data access service, mainly because we didn't have room on the diagram.

```
Application Architecture Document
A. EXECUTIVE SUMMARY
      Business Understanding
      Project Focus
B. METHODOLOGY
      Business Requirements
      High-Level Architecture Development
      Standards & Products
      Ongoing Refinement
C. BUSINESS REQUIREMENTS AND ARCHITECTURAL IMPLICATIONS
      CRM (Campaign Management & Target Marketing)
      Sales Forecasting
      Inventory Planning
      Sales Performance
      Additional Business Issues
            Data Quality
            Common Data Elements and Business Definitions
D. ARCHITECTURE OVERVIEW
      High Level Model
      Metadata Driven
      Flexible Services Layers
E. MAJOR ARCHITECTURAL ELEMENTS
      Services and Functions
            ETL Services
                  Customer Data Integration
                  External Demographics
            Data Access Services
                  BI Applications (CRM/Campaign Mgmt; Forecasting)
                  Sales Management Dashboard
                  Ad Hoc Query and Standard Reporting
            Metadata Maintenance
            User Maintained Data System
      Data Stores
            Sources and Reference Data
            ETL Data Staging and Data Quality Support
            Presentation Servers
            Business Metadata Repository
      Infrastructure and Utilities
      Metadata Strategy
F. ARCHITECTURE DEVELOPMENT PROCESS
      Architecture Development Phases
      Architecture Proof of Concept
      Standards and Product Selection
      High Level Enterprise Bus Matrix
APPENDIX A—ARCHITECTURE MODELS
```

Figure 5-6 Application architecture plan document sample table of contents.

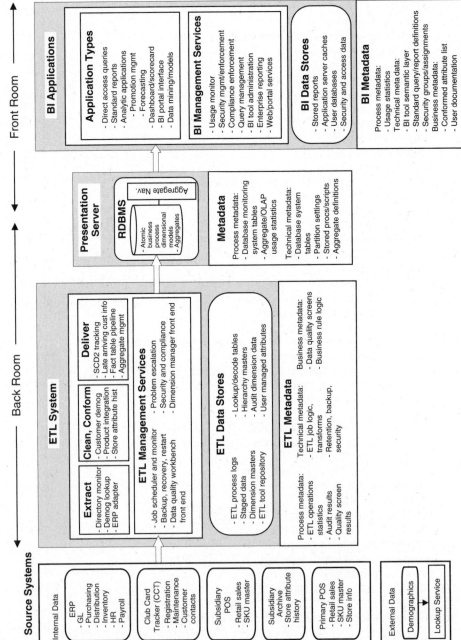

Figure 5-7 Application architecture model sample.

Your architecture model should include functionality needed to deliver at least the top three business opportunities. You can list future sources, functions, and services to keep them in mind and avoid making implementation decisions that will limit the ability to include them down the road. But to manage expectations, make sure you identify them as *future* phases — you might even consider graying them out on the model or not including them on the phase one version.

The model in Figure 5-7 is only an example — one possible approach to a single situation — not the answer. Your model will be very different. Also, this example is only the tip of the iceberg with respect to the DW/BI architecture for a mid-sized or larger warehouse.

NOTE Don't let the complexity of the architecture development process paralyze you. If you start from the business requirements and take it step by step, the architecture model and plan will fall neatly into place.

Select Products

Once the DW/BI architecture is in place, you have the two key components that drive the product selection process: business and functional requirements.

In this section we discuss the major product evaluation areas for a DW/BI system. Next, we walk through a general evaluation process. Finally, we review details specific to each of the major evaluation areas.

Keep a Business Focus

Before getting started, remember that the business needs should drive the evaluation process. This is our standard liturgy: How can you rationally select a tool if you don't know what you need to do with that tool? It may seem absurd to select tools without the slightest idea of the requirements. Unfortunately, we have seen this happen all too often. The speech usually goes like this: "We're just getting started, but we have the database and hardware up and running." As we said earlier, in case you skipped it, if you select products before understanding the business requirements and priorities, you are doing it wrong.

The timing of the technical product evaluation is critical. If you do it too early, without an understanding of the requirements, you will end up testing product features without any way to compare their relative merits. If you do it too late, you will slow down the project and may end up redesigning and rebuilding to support product and platform-specific considerations.

Major DW/BI Evaluation Areas

There are four major purchase areas for the typical DW/BI system, and each can include multiple tools in a technical evaluation process:

- **Hardware platform(s).**   There may be multiple hardware platforms in the data warehouse, including different servers/platforms for the ETL system, presentation servers, and application servers. Most hardware testing is about scale, throughput, and capacity.

- **DBMS platform(s).**   In most DW/BI systems, the atomic level warehouse DBMS is a relational engine. Often the DBMS choice is a corporate standard, and any deviation requires a serious justification effort. The OLAP database is also a DBMS platform, and its evaluation is tightly linked to the relational engine. The OLAP databases are less of a commodity than the relational engines; at the time of this writing, there are significant differences among the OLAP engines.

- **ETL tool.**   A stand-alone ETL tool can be a major cost for the DW/BI system. There are relatively low cost alternatives, but they may not deliver the functionality needed. The ETL tool decision is also an early one, but it doesn't have to be completed until after the dimensional model is done.

- **BI tools.**   Most DW/BI systems end up with more than one tool to support different kinds of data access and BI application requirements. Even if you buy from a single vendor, you are probably buying multiple tools. The sheer number of tool alternatives makes this evaluation area a particularly difficult one.

The thought of evaluating products in each of these areas is a little daunting. The good news is that at least at the hardware and database platform level, the choices are relatively equal. For most small to medium sized warehouses, the mainstream BI tool vendors and database vendors all have reasonable platforms. On the other hand, if you expect your warehouse to be large, you must evaluate all the areas more carefully. Note that most of the large vendors have product lines that cover most of the DW/BI functional stack. Having a single-source provider might simplify contract negotiation and support. Then again, it might not.

Evaluate Options and Choose a Product

There are several basic steps in the evaluation process that are common regardless of the evaluation area. This section outlines those steps; the following sections describe the twists, additions, and deletions specific to each area.

If you want a meaningful and thorough product evaluation process, you must have sufficient resources assigned to this effort. The timeline must also be reasonable. You need to allow enough time to conduct testing and involve users. You also need time to work with your vendors so they can properly respond to your requests. On the other hand, don't take too long. A major new release can completely alter the relative appeal of a given product.

For now, let's turn our attention to the eight steps in the product selection process.

Step 1 – Understand the Purchasing Process

The first thing you need is a good sense of how big ticket items are purchased in your organization. Work with your business sponsor and key IT contacts to understand the major steps, players, and documentation required. In a large organization, you may need to get approval from several levels of senior business and IT management. A big server or new program may also need approval from an investment committee of some sort. You may need to provide a detailed business plan with cost justifications and return on investment (ROI) calculations.

The purchasing process is one of the many places in the Lifecycle where your emphasis on business value pays off. If you prioritized the business opportunities with senior management, they already have a clear picture of the value and associated ROI. The purchasing process is a good litmus test. If you are getting resistance on the spending, it means you have not identified a high value business opportunity and associated business sponsor. Go back to Chapter 2 and start again.

Step 2 – Develop the Product Evaluation Matrix

At this point, your architecture plan should paint a pretty clear picture of what you need in your DW/BI system. Pull the lists of required functions directly out of the detail sections of your architecture plan for the areas you are evaluating and list them down the left side of the matrix. This list will likely expand as you do market research and learn more about useful functionality you hadn't thought of yourself.

All of the functional product requirements should be prioritized. At a minimum, the requirements should be flagged as "must have" or "nice to have." Prioritization allows you to apply different weighting factors to different requirements. We typically use a 0–100 scale, and adjust the relative weightings as we add each new requirement. Once you start to fill in the product assessments, assign a numeric value, typically between 1 and 5, to indicate how well each requirement is handled by each product. These values can then be combined with the weightings to generate an overall score for each product.

Any evaluation matrix included here will be misleading for two reasons. First, the market is different as you read this book than it was when we wrote it. Second, your situation and requirements are different from any generic situation we could imagine. On the other hand, there is value in seeing how someone else approached a problem. Figure 5-8 shows a simplified version of an evaluation matrix for ETL tools. Only the first three sections have been expanded, the rest only show totals. The complete version of Figure 5-8 can be found on the book's website at www.kimballgroup.com. Remember that your matrix will be different because you have different business requirements and priorities.

Step 3 – Conduct Market Research

The goal of this market research is for you to become a more informed consumer. The variety of DW/BI products can be overwhelming, especially

ETL Tool Product Evaluation Worksheet Example	Project Weight	Vendor One	Vendor Two	Vendor Three	Vendor Four	Vendor Five
Core Functionality						
Ease of installation and maintenance	40					
Support for key sources (e.g. DB2, Oracle, SQL Server, ERP)	30					
Support for key targets (e.g. SQL Server, MOLAP engine)	10					
Full featured scripting language	10					
Extensible	10					
Execute steps across platforms	10					
Uses fast load facilities on target	10					
Core Functionality	**120**					
Transformation Functionality						
Slowly changing dimension mgmt (Type 2)	40					
Data quality screen management	40					
Fact table pipeline key substitution	30					
Late arriving dimension handling	30					
Lookups/validation against large tables	20					
Surrogate key management	20					
Late arriving fact handling	20					
Complex joins; outer joins	20					
Change data capture & propagation	20					
Built-in knowledge of ERP system internals	15					
Aggregation build and management	10					
Complex calculations	10					
Exception/error row handling	10					
Source filtering & validation	10					
Transformation Functionality	**295**					
Performance						
Test scores (standard platform and ETL script)	50					
Support for parallel execution	50					
Scalability options (add CPUs, clusters, distributed, etc.)	40					
Database drivers tuned for performance	30					
Performance management and monitoring	30					
Performance	**200**					
Productivity (specific functionality hidden)	**170**					
Operations and Job Control (specific functionality hidden)	**105**					
Metadata (specific functionality hidden)	**145**					
Vendor Info (specific vendor requirements hidden)	**190**					
TOTAL	**6125 (Max)**					

Figure 5-8 Sample ETL tool product evaluation matrix.

because many products profess to solve all of your problems. Basic information about products can be collected using the following techniques:

- **Search the Internet.** Look for product information, blogs, discussion groups, forums, and user groups. This initial research can also help identify candidate products. Vendor websites often have lots of information, but of course they have a bias. Look at the support information on the vendor's website.

- **Network.** Attend DW/BI courses, conferences, and seminars. Look for people in class who are working with the tools you are evaluating. Ask them about their experiences. Get their contact information. Also, use your personal network and contacts from other folks on the DW/BI team. Talk to anyone you can find who has hands-on experience with the products you are evaluating.

- **Read trade publications.** Every so often, there are good product evaluation articles. More often, they are paid promotional pieces, so be careful.

- **Seek opinions from industry analysts.** Most IT organizations have contracts with one or more major information technology consulting firms. Some of these firms actually do product comparisons, although you need to recognize they also receive a large percentage of their income from the vendors. Ask your corporate library or IT research folks.

As you collect and distill this information, use what you are learning to fill in your product evaluation matrix.

While you're evaluating products, you also need to evaluate the vendors who sell them. You will have a relationship with this vendor for as long as you own the tool, so part of determining capabilities for the tool involves determining required capabilities for the vendor as well. These concerns relate to the nature and extent of support you can expect from the vendor and the technical community. This is where market share counts. The larger the installed base of the tool, the more likely it is that you will be able to find someone who can help when problems surface.

- **Vendor support.** What resources do they provide to help you be successful? Many companies make their documentation, support knowledgebase, and even tutorials available to the public on their websites. In particular, look for the following:

  - *Documentation.* You should expect a range of well-written materials targeted at specific readers: business users, power users, developers, and administrators. The materials should be available online in a form that's easy to search and browse.

  - *Training.* Local training facilities are useful if you will not be setting up your own training facility. Training materials need to be extremely hands-on. Classes should be set up with one student per computer. The company should offer customized training or materials you can customize yourself.

- *Technical support*. This one is hard to gauge in advance. Ask the references about their experience with the vendor's technical support services. In addition to pure technical expertise, you want the support organization to have the right attitude: a real willingness to help figure out solutions to the inevitable problems.

- *Consulting*. The company should have an organization of consultants who are experts in the tool. They should also have a list of consulting organizations in the area that have been trained and are experienced.

- **External support.**   Beyond what the company can give you, look for external support structures as well. This includes an active online technical support forum, local consultants who are certified in the product, and a local user group for the product. How easy is it to hire people skilled with this vendor's products?

- **Vendor relationship.**   How will this company be to work with? The representatives should be reasonable, rational people. The company should offer flexible pricing and a fair upgrade policy. It should be financially stable with a good growth record. In particular, check into the company's background. How long have they been in business? How many developers are on staff? Research the firm's revenue, profitability, growth, and product release history.

Step 4 – Narrow Your Options to a Short List

Once you've made your best guess at how well each product delivers against the selection criteria, take a look at the scores. More often than not, there is a fairly clear winner. Occasionally, we have seen multiple products end up with relatively equal scores. In these cases, the first thing to do is honestly reassess the priority weighting factors. Because you know more at this point, you will often change the weightings, which may break the tie. Don't do this just because your favorite product is losing.

The goal is to select only a few products for detailed evaluation. Though eliminating products from the list of candidates seems a bit arbitrary at first, you will find that the results of your market research can help quickly narrow the list of products that meet your combined business, technical, and organizational criteria. You should select no more than three products that you believe may be able to meet your overall requirements. In many cases, you may find that only two or even a single product needs to be scrutinized in more detail.

Involve key stakeholders in the decision to eliminate products from the list. You do not want to reach the end of the evaluation process and find out that you cut the CIO's favorite product in Step 4.

This may sound obvious, but it's a good idea to make sure you are evaluating comparable products. Too often, we see organizations attempting to compare apples and oranges. If you do not feel that you are equipped to make these decisions, get more help. There are sessions on selecting technologies at most of the trade shows. Seek the advice of other professionals with one caveat: Make sure that you understand clearly the formal and informal relationships between your advisor and any vendors.

WHY REQUESTS FOR INFORMATION ARE PROBLEMATIC

An age old practice in product selection is to create a formal Request for Information (RFI) or Request for Proposal (RFP). This is a compilation of the questions and features you think are important. Each of the vendors that respond will do what they can to respond positively to each of your questions. They are vying for the opportunity to compete. In our experience, the responses don't tell you much more than who has a better marketing or proposal generating organization. You don't really learn more about the product's functionality or what is required to deliver that functionality. It requires a lot of time to put together a comprehensive request, and a lot of time to review the responses. Don't do this unless you have to.

Some high quality vendors do not routinely respond to RFIs because they recognize the beauty contest nature of the process.

If your organization's standard mode of operation requires an RFI, provide each vendor on the short list with the same business case study to solve. This case study should be small, but it should contain well defined examples of your key requirements. Ask each vendor to respond with a working demonstration that solves the business problem. You will often find several vendors graciously bowing out of the competition. Of those who remain, you have a firsthand view of what the solution looks like.

Step 5 – Evaluate the Candidates

Once you have the short list, you need to evaluate the candidates in more detail. There are two major components to the evaluation step: in-depth research and hands-on evaluations.

In-Depth Research

We usually avoid direct contact with the vendors until this point because once their sales reps know you have budget money, they won't let go until the money is spent. Set up meetings with each candidate vendor; we call these *grill sessions* to make it clear that you must control the agenda. If you don't, they will give you the standard pitch, which usually doesn't provide the information you need. Give them a list of your requirements, concerns, and what you are trying to accomplish ahead of time. During the meeting, do the following:

- Listen to their presentation. Allow them to highlight their strengths, but make sure they address the issues you specifically requested.

- Ask pointed questions that address any of your requirements they missed.

- Ask each competitor to discuss *how* they would deliver key functionality.

- Include plenty of time for a detailed, live demo and ask them to show you how they accomplish specific problems, like type 2 change tracking in the ETL system, or including facts from two different fact tables in the BI tool. If you share the list of capabilities you'd like to see ahead of time, make sure to ask if they had to do any extra work to demonstrate them.

- Use the evaluation matrix as a guide during these sessions. Fill it in as you get answers to each issue. Actually, you might want to wait until the sales folk have left.

You may want to have more than one meeting with each vendor. This allows you to pursue issues you have learned from meeting with their competitors. You should also insist that they bring a technical person from their staff; someone who has implemented a real DW/BI system similar to yours with their product and can speak to your concerns. If you are evaluating BI tools, it is also helpful to include the key business people who will be using the tool in these sessions.

CHECK REFERENCES Checking references can be useful, because it's only from actual users of the product that you will get reliable information about how the product works in the real world. Ideally, you'll want to talk to a customer that is "just like you," which practically speaking means that you'll need to talk to a handful of references and synthesize the results. Just because the product works with a "30-terabyte warehouse" doesn't mean their implementation is anything like yours. Make sure that the references have implemented a dimensional warehouse. Talk to them without the vendor present; you're more likely to get the full story. And take everything you hear from vendor supplied references with a grain of salt because it's safe to assume the references are handpicked to give positive feedback.

Hands-On Evaluations

In many cases, you can only get the information you need by actually trying the product first hand. This is especially true for BI tools, as we discuss later in this section. You may be able to bring the tool onsite for a period of time, or you may need to go to the vendor's sales office, test center, or training facility.

An onsite evaluation is often harder to arrange because the sales rep needs to get copies of the software and install keys. If this is a big deal, try to get hands-on access some other way because you will be asking for a trial later in the process.

As a result of these vendor sessions and evaluations, you should be able to decide which product you believe is most likely to meet your requirements; but don't tell anyone. Before making a final commitment, you should bring the product in for a trial period to make sure that everything works as advertised. If you have narrowed the selection to two vendors, but are unable to decide between the two, it can be helpful to develop a prototype for each.

Product Comparison Prototypes, if Necessary

If you are faced with two or more tool options that are too close to call, you may consider developing a formal product comparison prototype. This involves putting both products through the same set of tests, often with vendor involvement. These guidelines will help you manage a comparison prototype:

- Define your prototype scope, including completion criteria.
- Avoid tackling too much at once.
- Use a meaningful but small subset of data.
- Provide only a quick and dirty data load process for a BI tool comparison exercise. Consider hard coding the ETL process using SQL scripts rather than an ETL tool. This will make it more difficult to convert your prototype into a weak, unstable production system at a later time.
- Use a data profiling tool to learn as much as possible about source system data problems during prototype development.
- Learn as much as possible about hardware and software capabilities during prototype development. Take notes about configurations, settings, and other tricks you see along the way.
- Learn as much as possible about support requirements during prototype development.
- Get business user feedback when evaluating BI tools. Don't just put the tool on their desk and ask them what they think after a week or two. Work side by side with them for several short sessions.
- Get references and call them. You'll be amazed at what you learn, and you may end up with another resource to call on when you need some experienced guidance.
- Do not allow a prototype to be put into production!
- Keep a close handle on expectations. Do not allow them to spiral out of control.

Most importantly, be honest about what you see and learn while developing a prototype. Celebrate the positives and explore the negatives to determine what can be done to resolve or minimize the impact on the project. An objective analysis here can save a lot of time and money down the road.

Evaluation Shortcuts

It is rare for a DW/BI project to go through detailed evaluations for all four of the major areas listed earlier. Usually, one of several factors intervenes to make the evaluation process irrelevant, such as:

- **Existing IT product standards.**   In other words, "We only buy our servers from _____ (fill in the blank for your organization)."

- **Existing resources.**   This usually means spare boxes or software licenses. Often these are cast-offs resulting from transaction system upgrades. If your company has a site license for a certain database product, it will take some strong evidence to justify additional spending for a different product.

- **Team experience.**   Often, if someone on the team has had a successful experience with a DW/BI product, that product becomes the leading candidate. This internal experience with a known quantity is extremely valuable to the team. The opposite case is also valuable. A negative experience will eliminate a product early on. Make sure this referral comes from a competent source.

- **Political factors.**   We know it's shocking to hear, but practical decisions like product selection often get made based on political factors. We see this all the time. In one example, a state government department was told to build a DW/BI system using tools from a certain vendor who just happened to be the largest software company in the state. Several times we've witnessed the heartbreak of a team going through a full evaluation process only to be told at the end that the CEO had reached an agreement with another vendor, whose CEO happens to be a golf buddy.

Note that product selection by decree doesn't necessarily mean failure, but it does mean you need to perform a gap analysis, reviewing your requirements against the imposed system and immediately reporting any reduction in scope or capability caused by this decision. For example, you may not be able to update all the data every night, or the system might not be physically able to store the level of detail or amount of history desired. This trade-off should be a business decision; present the alternatives to business management and work with them to reach a decision.

Step 6 — Recommend a Product

You should include everyone who is significantly affected by a product selection in the decision making process. For the ETL tool, this is a relatively small group, but for the BI tool, this could involve a fairly large number of people. Hold a meeting where you work through the matrix, research results, reference checks, vendor information, and hands-on evaluation feedback with the group. Discuss the pros and cons of the leading candidate and listen to any concerns the group has. If you can reach a general agreement, you are done with this step. If not, assess the concerns and figure out how to deal with them. Some concerns may be legitimate issues with the product. Others are personal preferences. Either may be a big enough reason to reconsider the decision.

The final product recommendation should be presented in a report summarizing what was learned and the rationale for the team's recommendations. The recommendation typically must be approved by a variety of people or committees as we discussed in Step 1 of the product selection process. Once the recommendation is approved, you are not done yet.

Whatever product choices you make, keep in mind that the DW/BI market is changing rapidly, especially in the BI and ETL tool areas. You should expect to reevaluate your choices in two or three years and migrate to new tools if the benefits support it.

Step 7 — Trial

Be warned that no matter how good a job you do on product evaluation, even if you do a prototype comparison, it's never good enough. You just cannot know about all the quirks of a product until you are deep in the details of your implementation, at which point it's often too late. Our advice, which the vendor community will hate, is to follow the thorough evaluation process that we've described, make your best choice, and tell your vendor that you want a 90-day trial period or longer if possible. Implement the product as if you had already bought it, but keep careful track of any problems you discover. At the end of the 90 days you will have a list of significant issues to discuss with the vendor (We promise you will!). You will be in a good position — before the contract has been signed — to negotiate resolution of these issues. Or you may have found problems that are serious enough that you need to back down from your first choice and try an alternative product.

Step 8 — Contract Negotiations

Once the recommendation has been accepted and you are nearing the end of your trial period, the contract negotiation can begin. Different vendors price based on different measures, such as concurrent users, named users, number of connections, number of servers, number of CPUs (sockets or cores), site, enterprise, and so on. Watch out for maintenance, services, support, and other add-on costs. Make sure you include the ancillary items, such as:

- Development and test system licenses, especially for server-based products
- Consulting services
- Training classes
- Training and documentation materials
- Premium support levels

It's helpful to get an expert involved on your side; someone who has done major IT purchases in the past and has a good track record. Often you can negotiate many of these items at a lower price, or free as part of the initial contract. If you ask later, they will be more expensive. By the way, the amount of leverage you have depends on how big your check is. Twenty-five thousand dollars is not a big deal, $250,000 is better, and $2.5 million is serious leverage. Good timing can also give you more leverage. If you have all your approvals in place and can get the check issued before month end, you will have significant leverage, especially if it's before the end of the quarter or fiscal year.

Especially for a large DW/BI system, it's a good idea to negotiate acceptance criteria based on minimum performance levels determined during the evaluation process.

Considerations for the Back Room and Presentation Server

While following the general process just described, there are characteristics that are unique to each specific area of evaluation. In the back room and presentation server areas, this includes hardware, database, and ETL tool evaluations.

Hardware Platform

If you are building a small to medium sized DW/BI system, a full blown hardware, software, and data test probably isn't necessary. Your vendor should have DW/BI reference platform configurations based on expected data size, simultaneous query load, query workload profile, and service levels that provide a good starting point. Identify references with similar warehouse projects through your own network or from your vendor. Meet with them to carefully review their experiences with the platform. You should also try to do a few tests on a live system that is similar to the one you are planning to use, just to make sure it will meet the need.

If you do an in-depth test, take advantage of vendor facilities and resources as much as possible. Your test suites should include both front room and back room activities, along with multi-user stress tests based on your data. You'll want to do similar tests in-house if you will be using a cast-off server to verify that it has the capacity to handle your needs. A hardware test typically goes through the following steps:

1. Determine the configuration based on architecture, requirements, and database testing. See Chapter 4 for more information on hardware architectures. Key components include:

   - *Memory*. Data warehouses are memory hogs, and performance is often greatly improved by having a lot of memory. The 64-bit architecture allows very large memory configurations.

   - *CPUs*. Start with at least two dual-core CPUs, even for small implementations.

   - *Disk*. See the discussion in Chapter 8 about fault tolerance and storage area network considerations.

   - *Database optimizer*. Verify the database is configured to support data warehouse specific features.

2. Design and implement routines to collect test results.

3. Design the physical database (disk, indexes, and aggregations).

4. Load test data.

5. Code and implement the test suite, including ETL and query scenarios, and results collection process.

6. Run baseline tests.

7. Tune.

8. Run final tests.

DBMS Platform

There are two types of DBMS platforms to consider in your architecture: the relational engine and the OLAP engine. First, the relational engine. Unless your data warehouse is large, with tens of terabytes of data, any major relational database can do an adequate job of loading and managing a dimensional data warehouse. This is good news because often the choice of relational platform is dictated by your corporate policy. The relational engine differences are greater when it comes to querying and it is here that things get complicated because we can add OLAP to the picture.

The OLAP engine is also a DBMS platform, but the OLAP products are more diverse than the relational engines. OLAP products differ notably in their scalability, performance, and ease of use. Most OLAP engines can build their cubes from a variety of relational platforms, though there are some minor feature differences that could be important to your evaluation.

If you are planning to use OLAP as the primary user access presentation server, focus your evaluation efforts on choosing the best OLAP server for your needs. In this case, the choice of RDBMS is less critical. If you are planning on a relational-only architecture, or are relegating OLAP to smaller datasets, you must pay serious attention to the features of your relational choices that most affect query performance, including star join optimization, bit-mapped indexes, aggregate management, and other features designed especially for data warehouse systems.

If your system is very large, your choice of RDBMS platform is vital because you may not be able to service all queries from OLAP. At the high end of the scale, the database and hardware vendors will work hard to convince you that their technologies are best. Insist on a realistic official test as we described for the hardware platform evaluation.

ETL Tool

If you don't have ETL tool experience, you'll find that they work a little differently from most other IT development tools. Count on one to three weeks of training before you can start testing.

An easy starting point for ETL functional testing is to draw from the list of 34 subsystems we provided in Chapter 4 and elaborate on in Chapter 9. For example, can the tools generate surrogate keys and do key lookups? How do they handle slowly changing dimensions? Can they create aggregations?

Create a set of tests that cover the range of load and transformation scenarios — more than the initial warehouse set. Certainly you should test dimension management and fact table updates, including slowly changing dimension type 2 tracking described in Chapter 6. You should also test the tool's ability to recover from a failed load.

Your DW/BI project may also need scheduling, source code management, bug tracking, connectivity, and web server software. Typically, these tool choices have already been made for you, which is fine because the DW/BI system's requirements for these tools are very similar to other projects' requirements.

If the candidate ETL tool does not include embedded data profiling capabilities, you should create a separate task for evaluating a stand-alone data profiling tool. You should test the tool's ease of use for quickly investigating column and structure rules, as well as the tool's integration with the rest of your ETL architecture. For instance, when you identify a data anomaly that is likely to appear in the source data extract, you want to be able to build a pluggable ETL module testing for this condition immediately and insert it into your ETL data flow.

Considerations for the Front Room

There are many different tool options in the front room. You can avoid feeling overwhelmed by focusing on the tools and functions needed to meet the top business priority. The most common starting points in the front room are ad hoc analysis and standard reporting. Hardware must be selected here, too, but it is often an easy choice based upon the BI tool and presentation server platform.

The BI tool market space has consolidated significantly over the past 10 years, but that doesn't make the choice any easier. The problem is that the leading BI tool vendors can meet almost all of your BI tool functional requirements one way or another. Certainly, all of the vendors give beautiful demonstrations of their solutions. It then becomes your job to sort out fact from fiction and begin to understand how the different tools work from both a functional and architectural perspective.

Selecting a BI tool is an exasperating process. Vendors have taken different approaches with different strengths and weaknesses, but none ever seems to solve the problem completely. Often they have different components that were developed by different groups, sometimes by different companies. Every piece has an incremental cost, and may not quite fit with the other pieces. As we describe in Chapter 11, there is often more than one problem to solve. In fairness, some of the leading vendors are completely reworking their code base to create more integrated, coherent product lines.

BEWARE OF THE "NO PROBLEM" SALES PITCH Even the best intentioned sales organization must also make quota every quarter. Many vendors have developed product offerings, standard schemas and templates, or approaches to help shorten the sales cycle for their sales reps. Many are designed to appeal to you by promising to shorten the Lifecycle process. Though they may be helpful, we have yet to see an organization that has been able to drastically reduce the time it takes to build a robust enterprise DW/BI system by using one of these products. You might be able to throw up a few data marts (pun intended) and get a positive short term response. But you will be digging yourself, or your successor, into a deeper hole by building even more stovepipe systems. Carefully examine these offerings in light of your business requirements and data realities.

Tool selection becomes more challenging when you don't understand and accept that there is a range of access needs, and that one tool might not meet all of them. You naturally want all the capabilities from all the BI functional application categories described in Chapter 4 in a single, excellent tool. For example, once you build a query and validate it in the ad hoc environment, it may make sense to schedule that query and run it as a standard report. Next, you'll want to include the resulting report in a dashboard along with several other reports and graphs all linked to the same time period parameter.

This all-in-one desire has made the tool choice problem more difficult. Most tool vendors have their roots in one category, but they've been pushed to include some or all of the remaining features. They all can safely say they provide many of the requested functions. Your challenge will be to determine if they do it in a way that effectively meets your requirements.

NOTE Additional questions for BI tool evaluation are not only *how* they perform the functions, but how well do the tools scale, how much administration do the tools require, and what is the payoff for that level of administration.

The BI tool evaluation is probably the one evaluation area almost every warehouse project goes through at some point. BI tool selection is not a completely rational process. People feel very strongly about their personal preferences. If you want to ensure user acceptance, you must have significant user participation. Although the general product selection process described earlier in this chapter still applies, the nuances of the BI tools warrant additional clarification and recommendations:

- Be very specific about the requirements. Compile a comprehensive list of the calculations that the tool will need to support (such as this year/last year, regression, time period comparisons, share, and drilling across multiple fact tables). Include other critical functionality, like web-based access, complex formatting, and report scheduling.

- Educate yourself and the evaluation team on the basics so that the vendors cannot pull the wool over your eyes. Conduct literature searches for product information. Obtain industry analyst reports on BI tool comparisons. Contact anyone you know who may have some direct experience.

- Review the data access tool features in Chapter 11 to make sure you haven't omitted important features.

- Identify product candidates and rank based on priorities.

- Develop a business case that represents a reasonable scenario. Look to your own BI application specifications as described in Chapter 12. They typically include a range of metrics, calculations, layouts, and delivery formats. These, tied together with a scaled-down dimensional model, will be very helpful.

- Install and test top candidates. Involve key power users in this process. If you are evaluating onsite, set up a lab and specific times to work through the tutorials and build some sample reports. It's a good idea to have several people work together under your guidance. You can help them if they get lost or confused, and you can influence their experience. This means you need to stay at least a lesson ahead of them in the tutorials.

- Conduct user review sessions. User involvement is invaluable for two reasons: to understand their perspective and get their support for the final choice.

- Follow up with references. You are looking for sites with similar business problems, similar technical environments, and similar data and user volumes. Of course, all these characteristics will probably never be shared by the same reference; so you need to talk to or visit several sites.

- Collect and organize test results and user feedback.

- Expect to be surprised when you actually select and install the tool in your own environment. No matter how good your tool selection process, there will always be surprises.

Manage the Metadata

As we discussed in Chapter 4, metadata is a critical component of your overall DW/BI architecture. Hopefully, the definitions and metadata lists provided in Chapter 4 gave you some perspective on metadata. But with this perspective, do you really need to keep track of all this? Yes, in our opinion. The metadata lists from Chapter 4 are the essential framework of your data warehouse.

This brings us to the question you've all been asking: What do you do about metadata to support your DW/BI system? It's easy to get trapped in the metadata morass. It's a major effort to figure out what metadata to capture, where to capture it, how to integrate it, how it should be used in the warehouse processes, and how to keep it synchronized and maintained. Vendors have been building metadata repositories and maintenance utilities for decades, and some companies have been trying to use these tools, or tools of their own creation, to tame the metadata beast for just as long. Even so, there are very few examples of large scale, robust, successful metadata systems. It's a hard problem.

Appoint the Metadata Manager

You need to appoint someone on the team to the role of metadata manager because if no one owns the problem, it will not be addressed. The metadata manager is responsible for creating and implementing the metadata strategy. The ideal candidate has to know everything! If one person has to do the whole thing, he or she will need to have SQL and DBA skills. The metadata manager will need to know how to program in your development environment, how to create and publish reports, and will need to understand the business at a detailed level. Okay, so the metadata manager doesn't need to know everything. If you also have one or more data stewards, a security manager and data modeler, they can help, too.

Create the Metadata Strategy

The following approach is a good compromise between having little or no managed metadata and building an enterprise metadata system. Our main recommendation is to concentrate on business metadata first. Make sure it is correct, complete, and maintained. Also, make sure it is accessible to the business users. Once that's done, provide a way to view the other major metadata stores. We often see a tendency to over-engineer metadata. The key to making this strategy work is to not overdo it. Here's the assignment list for the metadata manager:

1. Know what's out there. Survey the landscape to identify the various locations, formats, and uses of metadata across your DW/BI system. The lists from Chapter 4 give you a starting point. Use whatever metadata tools you have to explore the system for metadata. Where there aren't tools, you will need to create query or programmatic access to the other sources so you can explore and track them. Create a list of the metadata elements you find, including where they are, where they came from, who owns them, how you view and change them, and where and how they are used. This list is your metadata *catalog*. The catalog is not the repository itself; rather, it is a logical mapping of what could be the integrated repository.

2. Work with your data steward to educate the DW/BI team and key business users about the importance of metadata and the metadata strategy. Involve them in the initial creation of metadata content. Assign metadata creation and updating responsibilities.

3. Identify and/or define metadata that needs to be captured and managed. This is a subset of the elements from step 1 that you will use more broadly and therefore need to keep updated and distributed throughout the system. What you need to manage depends on a lot of factors: your organizational predisposition to actively manage metadata, the level of support for actively managing metadata on the DW/BI team, and the resources available to address the problem. At the very least, you must manage a basic level of business metadata. (See step 5 below.)

4. While you're at it, decide on the definitive location and version identification for each metadata element to be managed. This is the location where the element will be stored and edited. It is the source for any copies that are needed by other parts of the system. It might be in the relational database for some elements, in the ETL or BI tool for others, and so on. For some elements, you might decide to keep it in a third-party tool, like a modeling tool, or even your organization's repository tool.

5. Create systems to capture any business or process metadata that does not have a home. Try to use all available pre-existing metadata structures

like description fields in your BI tool, before you add your own metadata tables. However, you will likely identify many fields that need a place to live; comment fields or long descriptions from the data model are good examples of this. If data stewards from the business are the owners of these elements, they should be responsible for maintaining them. Many of our clients have created a separate database that holds these metadata tables along with any value-added content tables that are maintained by the business. It's not too difficult to create a simple web front end to let them manage the contents of these tables.

6. Create programs or tools to share and synchronize metadata as needed. This primarily involves copying the metadata from its master location to whatever subsystem needs it. This may include creating a relationship table in your repository that ties metadata fields together from the various tool repositories. You may have to learn the APIs and object models for your tools to get at their metadata. By the way, you might be able to use this relationship table to provide rudimentary impact and lineage analysis.

   Make sure you populate the description fields, source fields, and business name fields in all the tables, extended properties, and object models from the initial database all the way out to the front end tools. If these are populated from the start as part of the design and development process, they will be easier to maintain on an ongoing basis. You will also be able to more easily see what elements appear in the browsers and front end tools as you move through the process. Note that moving data from one location to another sounds like an ideal task for your ETL tool.

7. Design and implement the delivery approach for getting business metadata to the user community. Start with your BI tool's metadata layer and see what it can support. If that's not good enough, you may need to create your own metadata access reporting application. Often you need to create a simple metadata repository for business metadata and provide users with a way to browse the repository to find what's available in the DW/BI system. Though you may actually use several reporting tools to provide access to the metadata, this should appear as seamless as possible to the users. The different metadata access tools can be linked to from a single page in the documentation section of the BI portal. You can find the schema for a simple business metadata repository on the book's web page at www.kimballgroup.com.

8. Manage the metadata and monitor usage and compliance. Make sure people know the information is out there and are able to use it. Make sure the metadata is complete, current, and correct. A large part of the

baseline metadata effort is spent building reports and browsers to provide access to the metadata. Then monitoring involves looking at those reports on a regular basis.

Even though this is the balanced strategy between nothing and too much, it is still a fair amount of work. Make sure you include tasks and time in your project plan to capture and manage metadata during each major Lifecycle activity.

Secure the System

Once you have products identified, you can design and implement your DW/BI security strategy. The security tools and techniques described in this section help you avoid the vulnerabilities identified in Chapter 4, and establish a system to allow users access to the data they need without opening up the system to abuse.

The first step in managing the security for the DW/BI system is to identify a security manager who must develop and document a security plan and work with management to get buy-in on any new policies. The security manager should be involved in the architecture design and verify the actual setup and use of the DW/BI system. Every new component, upgrade, user group, indeed any system change, needs to be examined from a security perspective to make sure it doesn't compromise the system. Many organizations require a mandatory sign-off by the security manager as part of the deployment process.

The tasks of defining and implementing security span the Lifecycle. During business requirements gathering, document the real business needs for security. It's important to get senior management's view, but also talk to analysts and other potential users about the kinds of information they need to do their jobs effectively. You may need to push back to senior management, helping them understand the costs of restricting access to data. From there, designing and implementing security occurs throughout the Lifecycle's architecture, data, and BI application tracks. And the cost of deploying and maintaining security never goes away.

Before slamming the security doors shut, you must remember that a DW/BI system is valuable only if people can access it. The more information that's broadly available, the more valuable your system will be. Careful stewardship of data requires that you protect the information that's truly confidential and broadly publish the rest. Some organizations' executive teams and culture are opposed to a culture of open access, but it's worth arguing and pushing. Hopefully, your executive sponsor can carry this battle forward.

Of course, you need to ensure that only authorized users can access the DW/BI system, and limit everyone's view of data as appropriate. There are as many ways to do this as there are possible configurations for your DW/BI system. This section discusses various means of implementing your security policy. We end the section with a brief discussion of usage monitoring.

Secure the Hardware and Operating System

The most direct way to access the valuable information in the DW/BI system is to gain physical access to the computers on which the system is running. All test and production servers must be kept in a data center: a locked room with restricted access. Your IT organization's standards for protecting other production servers should be assigned to the DW/BI system's servers as well.

The second most direct way to access the DW/BI system is by way of the operating system. You should implement the following procedures for all the servers in your development, test, and production systems:

- Restrict login access. Only system administrators need to log in to the server running the DW/BI components; others can access services across the network.

- Restrict network access.

- Ensure data directories are secure, including database files.

- Keep up to date with security patches for the operating system.

Secure the Development Environment

Many teams have loose standards — or no standards at all — for managing the development environment. The development environment and servers should be managed professionally, though usually not to the same standards as the test and production systems. The data on development servers is often sensitive because it's drawn from the production source systems. Secure the hardware and operating system as we've just described, within reason. Strictly control access to development servers to anyone outside the development portion of the organization.

To ease deployment, make the development machines' security environment similar to the production systems'. However, you don't want to lock down the systems so tightly that developers will have problems getting their work done.

Secure the Network

The Internet is a largely UNIX-oriented system that was designed in the 1960s as a way for universities and researchers to communicate informally. The Internet uses the Transmission Control Protocol/Internet Protocol (TCP/IP). TCP governs how two machines establish and maintain a connection and requires a back-and-forth conversation. A denial of service attack can be generated when a machine initiates many connections but never completes them. The receiving machine can become clogged with incomplete sessions that must slowly time out before being dropped.

The IP portion of the protocol governs how machines on the Internet find each other. It can be thought of as the envelope, the intended address, and the return address, but not the enclosed greeting or message. IP is in some sense unreliable; by itself it does not guarantee that a message is delivered or that the message is in any way legitimate. IP simply provides the addresses and the envelope. Messages have to be viewed with a certain level of suspicion; an IP source address can be "spoofed" by anyone with a physical connection to the Internet backbone. In other words, you have no real guarantee that a communication is from a known host just by looking at the IP source address. Similarly, a communication packet from a legitimate source can be diverted to any destination by copying the packet and replacing the destination IP address. Although this all sounds threatening, it is important not to get side-tracked by the weaknesses of IP. You can achieve all the reliability and security you need using TCP/IP, but you do so by ensuring the proper network components are in place, and by protecting the *contents* of the envelope via encryption, not by tinkering with the addresses on the outside.

Network Components

Most intranets inside organizations use the same TCP/IP protocol as the Internet. Most networks have a complex set of devices and functions that help manage the flow of packets around the organization and out to the Internet, and limit unauthorized access to the intranet and internal information assets. These devices and functions include routers, firewalls, and the directory server.

Routers and Firewalls

Every place one network connects to another must have a device called a *router* that transmits packets between the two networks. The router listens to every TCP/IP packet on each net and looks at the destination addresses. If a packet on one network is addressed to a computer on the other network, then the job of the router is to pass that packet through. If nothing else, routers do a useful job of isolating the "local" traffic on each network. If this didn't happen, there would be far too much unnecessary noise on remote networks. Routers also know what to do if they see a packet addressed to an outside network.

Obviously, because a router looks at every destination address in every packet, it can also look at the source address. In this way, a router can serve as a *packet filter*. A packet-filtering router, also called a packet-filtering firewall, can provide the following useful functions:

▪ Reject connection attempts from unknown hosts.

- Reject attempts from the outside that are spoofing as insiders.
- Accept only traffic that comes from a single machine.
- Halt pollution and sniffing.

NOTE Packet-filtering firewalls are one of the basic elements of security. The data warehouse technical architect and security manager should develop a specific plan for isolating and protecting key pieces of the technical architecture.

A good overall security configuration for an Internet-connected DW/BI environment is the so-called *screened subnet firewall configuration*. The screened subnet firewall actually has two packet filters. The first filter acts as a primary firewall and sends nearly all incoming network traffic to a special internal host called the *bastion server*. The bastion server acts as a powerful, controlling bottleneck for all communications coming to the organization from the outside. Except for certain specially qualified outsiders, all communications must go through "proxy" applications running on the bastion server. However, the packet-filtering firewall can carefully allow selected external hosts to bypass the bastion server and directly access other internal servers. These "trusted packets" do not need a proxy server; they are allowed to talk to the real server. If this configuration is coupled with a powerful authentication and encryption system provided by the directory server, an organization can get the best of both worlds. Powerful remote applications from trusted and authenticated clients get full access to internal resources, whereas ordinary access attempts must run the gantlet of the bastion server.

Directory Server

The directory server is a kind of data warehouse of resources available on the associated network. Resources include database machines, individual databases, document repositories, transaction systems, file storage areas, printers, and people. The people descriptions include names and addresses, organization roles, email addresses, and more. The directory server reveals selected items of information to legitimate, authenticated requesters. It is meant to be the useful, centralized, controlling resource for finding out how to communicate on the associated network.

Many vendors have agreed on the LDAP standard for communicating with a directory server, and thus, implicitly for implementing a directory server. The term *lightweight* (the "L" in the acronym) is a reaction to a more comprehensive directory standard previously proposed, known as X.500, that was regarded as too complicated and cumbersome to implement fully. LDAP is a derivative of X.500.

NOTE The directory server is very important to the DW/BI security manager. It must be the single, central point for authenticating and authorizing all users of

the data warehouse, regardless of whether they are connected to the internal network or coming in from the Internet.

The directory server has the following characteristics:

- **Single point of access.** All access comes through a single point of control. Consistent and complete administration and auditing are possible with this approach. The single point of access allows a single metadata description of security privileges and security use.

- **Single point of authorization.** Everyone must run the same authorization gantlet regardless of how they connect to a DW/BI resource.

- **Single point of administration.** Perhaps most important, the directory server is a single administrative console where access policies are defined and enforced just once. Lacking such an approach, the DBA may try to race from machine to machine, setting up low-level SQL GRANTS and REVOKES to implement security. This approach invites disaster and defeats flexibility.

The DW/BI security manager will need to work with the enterprise network security people to implement the appropriate user groups and user assignments on the directory server. Ideally, you should obtain access rights to administer these groups. You will also need to make sure your BI tools, database, and any other services can obtain authentication and authorization information from your directory service. We talk more about this process later in this chapter.

Encryption

In the preceding sections we tried to whittle down the security nightmare somewhat by erecting multiple layer firewalls and concentrating all data warehouse access attempts onto a single directory server. So far, so good. But all along we have been warning that the real protection has to apply to the contents of the communications, not just the mechanisms for delivering the communications. Fortunately, encryption is a powerful technology that, if used correctly, can largely protect the contents of our communications.

Encryption in the broadest sense is altering a message with a secret code so that it can be read only by people who know the code. In a sense, that is all the DW/BI security manager has to know about encryption. There is an unfortunate tendency for encryption enthusiasts to describe the mathematical underpinning of the coding schemes. The mathematics of encryption, as appealing as it is to us techies, is basically irrelevant to the issue of using encryption. DW/BI security managers need to understand the uses of a half dozen forms of encryption. No one encryption scheme will solve every security problem. Encryption schemes range from being automatic and anonymous and of almost no concern to the DW/BI security manager to being highly visible to all users of the data warehouse and potentially an onerous burden if implemented incorrectly.

NOTE If you really need to protect your communications, you must protect the contents, not the addressing scheme. If you continue to insist on sending everything via postcards, with the messages in effect being written for everyone to see; then you get what you deserve.

As the DW/BI system security manager, you will need to know about the following elements that encrypt communications at some level:

- Private and public key encryption
- Trusted certificate authorities
- Signed software certificates
- Secured sockets layer (SSL)
- Virtual private networks (VPN)
- Kerberos authentication

Authenticate the Users

Most DW/BI systems use a two-part security mechanism. The first piece is to authenticate users — to confirm users are who they say they are and allow them into the system. Authentication services are either part of the network and tied to the operating system or a low-level service such as Kerberos. Within the authentication system, you set up users and groups, and assign users to one or more groups. Your system administrators should have the expertise to set up and manage the authentication components.

The second element of the security architecture is to secure the data. This task usually falls to the BI team, because it faces the business users and implements functionality of the data access tools and databases.

Secure the Data

Now we come to the most interesting part of the security plan: securing the data while making it available for users to query. The primary concern for DW/BI system security is querying. Any writing activities, such as developing forecasts and budgets, should be securely managed by an application.

Provide Open Access for Internal Users

We strongly encourage you to develop a data access policy that is fairly open for corporate users. The best way to think about it is to start from the position that all data should be available to internal users; any exceptions should be justified. The more information you hide, the less valuable your DW/BI system is going to be. The ideal situation is to minimize the truly sensitive information in the data warehouse. If you must include sensitive information, document it as an exception to the general rule of data availability.

In order for an open access policy to work, you must:

- Gain executive sponsorship for the approach and the list of sensitive data elements.

- Develop a system use policy statement, which users must sign before gaining access.

- Publish the detailed security policy, including the list of sensitive data elements.

- Monitor usage.

Itemize Sensitive Data

Whether you approach the problem from a mindset of "most data is available" or "most data is sensitive," you must develop a matrix of what data are protected (or available), and from or for whom. As you're developing your data sensitivity matrix, remember that the vast majority of system use is at aggregated levels, where sensitivity is usually significantly less. The data sensitivity matrix must specify the level at which aggregated information becomes available. For example, most people can't see sales by salesperson, but any authenticated user can see aggregated sales at the district, region, or corporate levels. Thus, the sales portion of a data sensitivity matrix might look like Figure 5-9.

Minimize or Mask Sensitive Data

The most secure DW/BI system is one with no data in it. That would be foolish, but each time you itemize a sensitive data element, you should ask yourself

---

SALES

    Sales data is captured at the transaction line item level. For each sale, we know the customer, product, salesperson, and channel.

    * Restricted Access: None

    * Open Access: Atomic and aggregated sales data, including any base measure and any calculation involving only sales data

    * External Access: None. In the future, we may modify this policy to open access at an aggregate level to reseller partners.

Figure 5-9 Sales section of a sample data sensitivity matrix.

(and business users) if it's really required in the data warehouse. Most often the answer is yes, but you must safeguard the privacy of your employees and customers.

A national ID number, such as a social security number in the United States, is an appealing unique identifier for a person. However, national ID numbers really should be held in confidence. You may mask the ID number during the ETL process by generating a meaningless key to identify a person.

Tightly control access to highly sensitive information, such as employee compensation or customer credit card numbers. If you can't avoid adding these attributes to your DW/BI system, encrypt them. Most database engines can encrypt the data in a column.

Secure the Data Access

The more restricted data you have, the more difficult it is to provide ad hoc access to the DW/BI system. Look back at the data sensitivity matrix example and think about how to implement open access at aggregate levels and restricted access at detailed levels. The easiest way to do that is through a BI application such as a report; define aggregate-level reports that everyone can see, and limit access to reports that contain sensitive information.

If you allow ad hoc access to the underlying data, you may need to apply complex access rules in the database. This is difficult in the relational database because the relational engine on its own doesn't have enough metadata to create multi-level security roles. The more ad hoc access your users require to data that is partially restricted, the more compelling is a sophisticated BI-oriented presentation server such as an OLAP database.

Most client access tools contain some security features. Carefully examine the security features of any client tool before you decide to rely on those capabilities. If a user has login privileges to the underlying database, the security must be applied to the database objects. Otherwise, users could simply use Excel or any other client tool to create an ad hoc connection, log on, and browse restricted data.

Many BI tools can — or even must — be configured with a single administrative ID for access to the database server. If your BI tool manages individual user logins and uses a single administrative ID for server access, then all user access must be limited to that tool (unless you also secure the users in the database, as we describe under ad hoc access later in this section). And you must be exceptionally careful not to compromise that administrative ID.

Most implementations have a variety of security requirements. Some reports are available for anyone in the company, some have limited access to the complete report, and some reports return a different result depending on who runs the report. Beyond reporting, you'll need to support ad hoc access as well.

Unrestricted Reports

An unrestricted report is a predefined report that's accessible to everyone who can access the reporting portal. The only security on an unrestricted report is authentication into the BI portal. Users who access the report do not need login privileges into the underlying database; the report's query runs under the reporting service account, not under the user's account.

Restricted Reports

As the name implies, access to restricted reports is limited to some subset of the organization. Restricted reports are also predefined, so the report looks the same to everyone who is allowed to access it. For example, anyone at the executive level can access all corporate financial data. Restricted reports are a good security model for all but the most sensitive data. Most reporting tools offer easy-to-use functionality to manage restricted report security in the reporting portal. Restricted reports don't require a security layer within the underlying databases. You will probably run the reports under the reporting service account rather than have business users authenticate to the database.

Filtered Reports

A filtered report is a predefined report that returns a different result set depending on who runs the report. Filtered reports usually are also restricted and are appropriate for the most sensitive data in your organization. The classic example is a budget variance report, generated monthly for each department within the company.

In order to implement a filtered report, you'll need some way to connect the user's name to the list of departments, columns, and other data elements that she's allowed to see. If the report is run on demand by the user, it must be executed dynamically using the user's credentials; the report can't be cached. In this case, the query underlying the report needs to return the filtered result set. The most common way to do this is to have the source query be a stored procedure that takes the user's identification as an input parameter, or to use row level security in the database. Alternatively, there are some reporting tools that can filter reports at the report server level.

If you have only a handful of filtered reports, you can create a separate report for each department, and grant access only to the appropriate version. This approach has obvious scalability and management problems, and isn't recommended except as a stopgap measure or for a very small organization.

Filtered reports are expensive to develop and maintain. You need to develop a security infrastructure, and maintain the list of what elements each user is privileged to access. You may need to write a simple application to help manage these processes.

Ad Hoc Access

Ad hoc access means the user is allowed to leave the boundaries of predefined reports to create new queries, reports, and analyses. Up to this point, it's been possible to avoid giving database login privileges to users because the report server or BI applications do the authentication and authorization. But users who need ad hoc access obviously need login privileges. In a database containing sensitive information, that means handling authorization at the database level.

Within the relational database, it's easy to define permissions to tables, views, and columns within a table or view, but defining row-level security involves creating additional views or row level security policies. For example, the common approach to limiting a user's access to one or more departments is to create a separate table that has at least two columns: the business user's ID and a list of keys, such as department_ID, that the user is permitted to see. Using the view method, you create a view that joins the fact table to the security table on the key column, filtering on the user ID. Each business user who queries this view sees only rows for the keys listed for them in the security table. The row level security policy is defined in a similar way, but it is appended to the WHERE clause of every query against the fact table.

The problem with this approach is that it's difficult to secure access to detailed data, yet provide open access to aggregated data. For rich yet secured ad hoc access, most DW/BI systems implement an analytic server. The additional security information these tools can manage is a significant piece of their value in an environment that supports secure ad hoc access.

External Reports

An external report is a BI report that's available to people outside your organization. For example, you may let your suppliers see inventory levels of their products or see how well their products are selling.

The easiest way to meet the security requirements for standard external reporting is to use a push model: email reports to your partners. If you will support external reports, make sure the product evaluation matrix for your BI technology places a high priority on data-driven subscription functionality.

Data-driven subscriptions don't meet all external access requirements. You probably don't want to send a daily email to millions of customers about their account status. We're tempted to call this operational reporting, and wash our hands of the problem. Indeed, you should think seriously about whether you want external users accessing the same system that your employees are using to run the business. Most often you'll decide to spin out a separate database, and associated reporting portal, dedicated to this application. You'll need to figure out how to authenticate those external users to allow them into the portal. External users will typically access only filtered reports, using the same techniques we've already discussed. Again, some of the BI tools are better at supporting external access than others.

It's unusual for a company to provide ad hoc access to external people. Those who do are generally in the information provider business. Most external access can be met through predefined reports, especially if your reporting tool lets you define reports with drilldown capabilities.

Monitor Usage and Ensure Compliance

Even with an open door policy, it's important to monitor system usage. Some industries have legal or ethical obligations to ensure appropriate usage. For example, in the U.S. healthcare industry, each view of a patient's records must be recorded and available for audit.

There are several events that every DW/BI system should monitor:

- User connections, including login and logout date/time.
- Users' failed attempts to connect.
- User report executions, including report name and version and any user-supplied parameters.
- User ad hoc query activity, usually captured as query start and end date/time.
- Processing activities such as database transactions.
- Development activities such as publishing a new report.

It's extremely valuable to capture ad hoc query text as well. This information is vital for periodic performance tuning, and might also be necessary to ensure regulatory compliance. However, query text will consume more space in the logging database than all other logging combined. Even if you're not required to capture query text, you might choose to do so for a subset of queries. It's still a good idea to have the ability to capture all query texts on an as needed basis. You may want to keep a random subset of this data in a structured form. Or create an application that runs through the detailed query strings, parsing out key elements, like table and column names, and WHERE clause contents.

Once you've captured information about who's using the system and how, you should generate and publish reports on that usage. The security manager should evaluate the reports for unusual and suspicious behaviors. Senior management often finds the usage reports extremely interesting and valuable as well.

Plan for Backup and Recovery

A solid backup and recovery system is a key element of any security plan. At least one of the security vulnerabilities listed in Chapter 4 will manifest at some point, even if it is no more malicious than a power surge that smokes a disk drive. When that happens, you have two options: Re-extract the appropriate source data subset and re-apply the ETL process, or restore the lost data from a backup. In most cases, re-extracting simply isn't possible. The data has been overwritten or is no longer available. To avoid this potential disaster, you must create and implement a backup plan. Start by listing all the tables by category in the presentation server and ETL area. Then, go through and estimate the effort and time it would take to re-create these tables and files. This exercise often provides enough motivation to start a backup program immediately. Frequently, this process uncovers tables that contain history that essentially could not be re-created. If you lose this data, you will need to start collecting it all over again from scratch. Chapter 13 offers more specifics about creating your backup and recovery system.

Create the Infrastructure Map

The infrastructure map describes the nuts and bolts of the DW/BI system: the servers, network, and desktops. We use it primarily to communicate with the IT operations folks who will help support the system to provide a clear and early warning of what the DW/BI system entails. We have found that it's easy to forget about operations, and simply assume they will support the DW/BI system as they would any system. Generally they are quite willing to do so, but they do need to be told what the requirements are and, like the rest of us, don't like to be surprised.

Without spending time thinking about infrastructure — and communicating those thoughts to the people chartered with delivering that infrastructure — you run a high risk of delaying the project for no good reason. For example, the machine room does not have enough floor space, electricity, or air conditioning to host the ETL and presentation servers; the disk subsystem isn't configured properly; user desktop computers are underpowered; or a security shell does not permit data transfer between operational systems and the ETL server. All of these problems are easy enough to solve, but they all require time, money, and management attention.

Determining your infrastructure requirements is a chicken-or-egg problem. You can't tell how big your presentation server needs to be until you try loading some data or doing a complex query to see how long it takes. But you can't do that testing without a server. You will not be able to determine all your infrastructure requirements up front.

Figure 5-10 illustrates an infrastructure map for the same regional grocery chain as the architecture model back in Figure 5-7. Your map may not start out as complex as this one, but it probably won't take long. You should also create a page or two of text to document any additional information that might

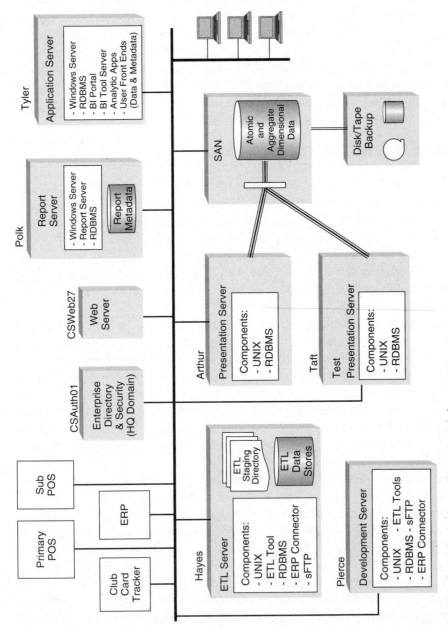

Figure 5-10 Example DW/BI system infrastructure map.

be useful, like server names, database names, disk sizes, types and configurations, operating system versions, and memory sizes.

Because one goal of the infrastructure map is to communicate requirements to the IT operations groups, it's best to structure the plan so that each group's requirements are in a separate section. Work with the operational groups to finalize the plan. There are five main areas to cover in the infrastructure map: server hardware, disk subsystems, network, security, and desktop.

- **Server hardware.** At this point in the project, you should be putting final stakes in the ground regarding your server hardware. Determine your main warehouse platform (hardware and operating system) based on business requirements and initial sizing estimates. Decide whether your ETL process will live on the source system, on its own server, or be co-hosted with the warehouse, and what its size requirements are. You may need to specify your servers in phases as you make product decisions. It's harder to specify the number of smaller application servers you will need until the BI tools have been chosen, but you can warn the server group about the kinds of requirements you will have and when you expect to know the details.

  You should also think about your development, test, and production servers. What you do in this area depends on the size of your DW/BI system and the required service levels. The infrastructure map in Figure 5-10 shows a single development server for both ETL and the presentation layer. It has a separate test server for the presentation server layer, but the plan is to use the ETL server as the test server during the day, when the server is mostly idle.

  There are significant operational advantages to using virtualization, including less hardware to manage and easier system backups. We have seen virtual servers used for development, functional testing, and application server support. However, the extra I/O abstraction layer slows database activities, like loads and queries, so the production presentation servers are not usually virtual machines. This may change as the hardware, operating systems, and virtualization products improve. Note that in many cases you have to pay license fees to run extra copies of software on virtual servers, even on the same hardware.

- **Disk systems.** Storage area networks (SANs) are common in most IT environments, even in smaller companies. The flexibility, management, and performance are compelling enough to overcome the additional price compared to direct attached disk. The group responsible for server hardware may also be the one you work with to arrange for shared storage.

- **Network.** There are two parts of the network to consider. You need a big pipe between the source systems, ETL area, and presentation servers, and good throughput between the presentation servers and user desktops. Broadly specify the volumes and frequencies that data will be moving between different systems. Document how the security systems will affect data flow, and outline the solution for moving data through different security protocols.

- **Security.**   Meet with the security people to make sure they understand your plans and can help you understand the security implications. Functionality like providing external customer access might require a separate server located outside the corporate intranet, for example. You will also need to understand your organization's network-based authentication and authorization services, and how you can work with them to define users, groups, and other attributes needed in the DW/BI system.

- **Desktop.**   Decide what kind of data access applications the DW/BI system will support. Generally, the BI tools require a fairly powerful PC to run well. Specify the desktop operating systems the project will support, and any other standard components, like the Internet browser. Determine what local components you may need, like database drivers or other connectivity files, even for "thin" clients.

You should continue to keep the infrastructure document up-to-date as the warehouse evolves over time. What starts as a description of hardware, operating systems, and software for the operations group will turn into documentation for an increasingly complex system. That documentation comes in handy when you have to troubleshoot a problem, and is extremely helpful when a new person joins the group.

Install the Hardware and Software

Installation issues are very different among software products, and obviously different between software and hardware. Your best bet to ensure a successful installation is to pay close attention and take careful notes during the evaluation process. In most cases, you should have an expert in the product involved in the installation. Certain configuration parameters set during installation can have a major impact on the performance of each system component. The following major steps should help you ask the right questions:

- **Site preparation.**   Make sure you have a place to put the component, whether it is hardware or software. There's more to installing a large server than just plugging it in. You need a controlled environment with clean power and space. Servers have proliferated over the last few years, and in many cases, space is at a premium. Make sure you work with the operations folks to find out where the box is going before it shows up on the loading dock.

■ **Training.**   Hopefully, the operations group has experience with the components you are bringing in. The DW/BI team will need to know how it works as well, so include appropriate training in your install plan, including hardware and operating system administration training. There is nothing more frustrating than for an uninitiated team member to be stumbling around in a UNIX environment, trying to figure it out by trial and error.

■ **Installation, checkout, and test.**   Many products are getting easier to install. The wizards are actually helpful, and the default configurations are not bad in many cases. However, each product has its own idiosyncrasies, and not knowing them can result in needless pain and suffering. For example, where you put the temp space for your database and how big you initially define it can make a big difference in query performance. And it's not just the database that needs careful installation; we've worked with enterprise report servers that really hammered their metadata databases. Although the default install put the report server and metadata database on the same machine, it was clear that for a certain size machine, you could get 30 percent better throughput by moving the metadata database to another machine.

Hopefully you took good notes when you did your evaluations and trials during the product selection process. Take them out now and work through them with the operations people who will be responsible for running the servers. If neither of you have significant experience with the product, and it is a core component that will impact people's experience, bring in an expert. Include some consulting time from the vendor when you negotiate the contract. Keep an eye out when there are vendor folks on site to see who is most competent, and ask for them when it comes time to install.

After the product is installed, test it to make sure there are no obvious problems. If your organization has a testing tool, use it to generate queries or report requests. If it's an ETL process, create a few load modules yourself and see if they run as expected. How many rows per minute are you getting? If it's a database, create a few scripts that start several representative queries and write the response times out to a table. Create another script that calls each of those scripts to get them running at the same time. Finally, create a report based on the output table that shows query counts per minute and rows per minute, along with any additional measures that make sense in your environment. Chapter 9 describes the ETL audit system, which is a good source for ETL test data, and Chapter 13 describes monitoring and reporting for the major DW/BI system components.

Conclusion

Trying to build a DW/BI system without an architecture plan is like using a 14th century map of the world to plan a trip. Once you step outside the narrowly defined known world, the terrain is gray and uncharted. Without an accurate map, you are doomed to wander aimlessly around the systems landscape. If you're lucky, you'll discover the new world. More likely, you'll sail off the edge of the earth or get eaten by dragons. In our experience, there are plenty of dragons in the DW/BI system implementation process.

In this chapter, we reviewed the processes used to create and implement the DW/BI architecture. First we reviewed creation of your architecture, focusing on the main deliverable: the application architecture plan. Then we described how to select products to make your architecture real. Once the products were in place, we offered a set of recommendations for dealing with metadata and securing the DW/BI system and its contents. Finally, we discussed the infrastructure map and briefly reviewed general considerations for product installation.

Creating a DW/BI architecture can be overwhelming. If this is your first time, we encourage you to include someone else in your organization who has created a system architecture before. Even if you are on your own, this chapter gives you enough guidance to get started. As you move through the steps in the process, your understanding and confidence will build. Be sure to consult the project plan task list at the end of this chapter for a summary of the tasks and responsibilities for creating the architecture plan, selecting products, managing the metadata, and implementing security.

BLUEPRINT FOR ACTION

Managing the Effort and Reducing Risk

There are several common high risk behavior patterns you should watch for during architecture planning:

- ◆ Not enough effort — teams that don't think through their architecture. This almost always leads to rework, missed deadlines, and additional funding requests.

- ◆ Too much effort — teams that get wrapped up in the architecture process. These groups often emerge months or years later with the grand architecture plan, only to find that the world has moved on.

- ◆ Independent effort — teams that work in isolation from the rest of the organization. There are lots of interested parties who control, manage, or in

(continued)

some way interface with the DW/BI architecture. Often they know more than you about their area of expertise. You must involve them early on; don't wait until implementation time to inform them of your plan.

The big risks in product selection are under-testing the hardware, database and ETL tools, especially for larger systems, and not including the business people who will use the BI tool. A secondary risk is accepting externally imposed product choices without assessing their ability to meet your requirements.

The greatest danger in the metadata area is not appointing someone to the role of metadata manager. Metadata, especially business metadata, will become meaningless or misleading without direct, hands-on management. A similar risk applies to security, although it is a lesser risk because of external organizational pressures and a broader understanding of the need for security.

Assuring Quality

Involvement of expert IT resources outside the team is one of the best ways of creating a quality architecture plan. Directly involve domain experts in creating architecture plans for their specific subsystems. It is also a great idea to involve these architecture contributors and the DW/BI system team in incremental reviews and a full review prior to delivering the architecture plan document.

Following a thorough product selection process is critical to obtaining a good result. In particular, the more input you get from trusted individuals who have direct experience with the tool in question, the more likely you are to make the right choice for your organization.

Getting IT and business leadership to emphasize the importance of capturing and maintaining accurate, descriptive metadata will help inspire the individuals who have to do the work.

Solid testing and, in some cases, bringing in an independent security expert is critical to ensuring a quality security implementation.

Key Roles

Key roles for creating the architecture plan, selecting products, and addressing metadata and security issues include:

◆ The DW/BI technical architect must work closely with special teams who play a central role in creating the architecture. The DW/BI architecture must be an extension of the existing corporate IT architecture, thus requiring participation from source systems, server management, networking, and security specialists.

◆ The DW/BI security manager must take a lead role in the battle for a secure environment, from educating the organization through ensuring that proper

(continued)

measures are implemented and maintained. Although the security manager will not be the one to implement these measures in most cases, he needs to take responsibility; otherwise it will slip through the cracks.

◆ The DW/BI metadata manager has the challenge of mapping out the complex web of metadata across the DW/BI system, creating an overall strategy for dealing with metadata, and encouraging the metadata owners to enter and maintain the metadata.

◆ Specific technical specialists need to implement any changes to the technical environment based upon the tactical and strategic plans.

◆ The product selection process requires involvement from the technical specialists, as well as from the key team members who are the primary users of that component. For example, the ETL team plays a critical role in selection of extract, cleansing, and transformation products.

◆ Installation again requires a joint effort between the core DW/BI team and the technical specialists who have the necessary skills to install each component properly.

Key Deliverables

Key deliverables for creating the architecture plan, selecting products, and establishing the metadata and security strategies include:

◆ Architecture plan

◆ Product evaluation matrices and recommendations

◆ Metadata strategy

◆ Metadata inventory

◆ Metadata capture and synchronization tools

◆ Security policies and data sensitivities

◆ Security monitoring and compliance system

◆ Infrastructure map

Estimating Considerations

Creating the Architecture Plan

If the high priority business requirements have been identified, you should be able to create an architecture plan that covers the first two to three years in a

(continued)

reasonable amount of time. Count on 1 to 2 weeks for a small system, 2 to 6 weeks for a medium sized system, and 2 to 3 months for a larger system. This does not include product selection, or metadata and security efforts.

Selecting Products

If you go through a full product selection process, count on two work months of effort for each major area. Allow more time for larger DW/BI systems because of the larger data volumes and broader user communities.

Metadata

The metadata inventory could take 1 to 2 weeks for a medium sized DW/BI system, and more than twice that for a larger system. Building a system to capture and manage key metadata elements could take 2 to 4 weeks. Any synchronization systems could also take 2 to 4 weeks to build, assuming they are relatively simple. Ongoing metadata management can take a day a week. Remember, managing metadata can mushroom into a massive task. Concentrate on the important 20 percent.

Security

There are too many cultural and site-specific factors to estimate how long it will take to establish a secure environment. Building awareness may take months. The actual implementation of these security measures may also take an extended period of time. More optimistically, little additional effort may be required of the DW/BI team if your organization is already tackling these issues.

Website Resources

The following templates and resources for creating the architecture plan, selecting products, and managing metadata are available on the book's website at www.kimballgroup.com:

- ◆ Example application architecture plan document
- ◆ Example product evaluation matrix
- ◆ Business metadata repository schema

Task List

TECHNICAL ARCHITECTURE, PRODUCT SELECTION & INSTALLATION

	Fans	Front Office		Coaches		Regular Line-Up						Special Teams				
	Business Users	Business Sponsor / Business Driver	DW/BI Director / Program Manager	Project Manager	Business Project Lead	Business Analyst	Data Steward / QA Analyst	Data Architect / Data Modeler / DBA	Metadata Manager	ETL Architect / ETL Developer	BI Architect / App Developer / Portal Developer	Technical Architect / Tech Support Specialist	Security Manager	Lead Tester	Data Mining / Stats Specialist	Educator
APPLICATION ARCHITECTURE DESIGN																
1 Create architecture task force				○	○							●				
2 Gather & document technical requirements				○		○		○		○	○	●				
3 Review current technical environment						○		○		○	○	●				
4 Develop architecture implications document						◆		○		○	○	●				
5 Create architecture model												●				
6 Determine phased implementation approach				○	○			○		○	○	●				
7 Define and specify subsystems								◆		◆	◆	●				
8 Create the architecture plan								◆		◆	◆	●				
9 Develop configuration recommendations												●				
10 User acceptance/project review	□	□	□	○	○	□	□		□	□	□	○	□	□	□	□
PRODUCT SELECTION																
(Repeat for each selection area)																
1 Develop evaluation matrix				●	●	○		○		○	○	●				
2 Research candidate products				○		○		○		○	○	●				
3 Develop product short list				○	○	○		○		○	○	●				
4 Evaluate product options	◆			○		○		○				●				
5 Optional prototype (may repeat for multi products)												○				
Select business process / data for evaluation				●	●	○		○								
Define completion criteria				●	●	○										
Acquire resources (internal/vendor)				●	○	○										
Determine test configuration				○												
Install evaluation prerequisites & components	○			●				○		○	○	●				
Train the evaluation team				●				○		○	○	○			○	○
Develop & tune prototype	◆			◆	◆	◆		●		●	●	●				
Conduct tests	◆			●	◆	◆		●		●	●	●				◆
Analyze & document results					○			◆			◆	●				

(Continued)

TECHNICAL ARCHITECTURE, PRODUCT SELECTION & INSTALLATION

	Fans	Front Office		Coaches		Regular Line-Up							Special Teams				
	Business Users	Business Sponsor / Business Driver	DW/BI Director / Program Manager	Project Manager	Business Project Lead	Business Analyst	Data Steward / QA Analyst	Data Architect / Data Modeler / DBA	Metadata Manager	ETL Architect / ETL Developer	BI Architect / App Developer / Portal Developer	Technical Architect / Tech Support Specialist	Security Manager	Lead Tester	Data Mining / Stats Specialist	Educator
PRODUCT SELECTION																
6 Determine product recommendation	◆	□	□	●	●	○		○			○	●	○			
7 Present findings/results to management		□	□	●	●	◆		○		○	○	○	○		○	○
8 Enter trial phase	○	○	○	●		○				○	○	○			○	
9 Negotiate contract		○	○	●							○	○				○
10 User acceptance/project review	□	□	□	○	○	○	□	□	□	□	□	○	□	□	□	○
MANAGE METADATA																
1 Inventory metadata elements, locations, and relationships	○	○		○	○	○	○	○	●	○	○	○	○		○	○
2 Educate team on metadata situation and responsibilities	○			○	○	○	○	○	●	○	○	○	○		○	○
3 Identify key elements to manage					○		○	○	●		○					
4 Create systems to capture additional metadata								○	●		○					
5 Create tools to synchronize metadata									●		○					
6 Design and implement metadata delivery system									●		○					
7 Document metadata strategy				○					●							
8 Ongoing metadata management and monitoring				●				○	●			○				
9 User acceptance/project review	□	□	□	○	○	□	□	□	●	□	□	○	□	□	□	□
IMPLEMENT TACTICAL SECURITY MEASURES																
1 Develop tactical security plan				○	○							○	●			
2 Secure physical environment				○								●	○			
3 Secure access into environment				○								●	●			
4 Secure access out of environment				○								●	●			
5 Implement rigorous password scheme				○								●	●			
6 Implement controls for software installation				○	○							●	●			
7 Audit security violations				○	○							○	○			
8 Monitor security privileges by individual				●	○							□	□			
9 User acceptance/project review	□	□	□	○	○	□	□	□	□	□	□	○	○	□	□	□

(Continued)

Task List (continued)

TECHNICAL ARCHITECTURE, PRODUCT SELECTION & INSTALLATION

Task	Fans	Front Office		Coaches		Regular Line-Up						Special Teams				
	Business Users	Business Sponsor / Business Driver	DW/BI Director / Program Manager	Project Manager	Business Project Lead	Business Analyst	Data Steward / QA Analyst	Data Architect / Data Modeler / DBA	Metadata Manager	ETL Architect / ETL Developer	BI Architect / App Developer / Portal Developer	Technical Architect / Tech Support Specialist	Security Manager	Lead Tester	Data Mining / Stats Specialist	Educator
DEVELOP STRATEGIC SECURITY PLAN																
1 Design security architecture				○								○	●			
2 Implement access services				○								○	●			
3 Implement authentication services				○								○	●			
4 Implement external access services				○								○	●			
5 Centralize authentication and access control				○								○	●			
6 Implement security monitoring and compliance sys				○								○	●			
7 User acceptance/project review	□	□	□	●	○	□	□	□	□	□	□	○	□	□	□	□
CREATE INFRASTRUCTURE PLAN																
1 Create draft infrastructure model and plan				○								●				
2 Review/update plan with key IT groups				○								●				
3 Create final version of initial plan				○								●				
4 Monitor and update plan				○								●				
5 User acceptance/project review	○	□	□	●	○	□	□	□	□	□	□	○	□	□	□	□
PRODUCT INSTALLATION																
(Repeat for each product)																
1 Installation planning				●								●				
2 Meet prerequisites												●				
3 Install hardware / software												●				
4 Test hardware / software												●				
5 User acceptance/project review	○	□	□	○	○	○	○	○	○	○	○	○	□	□	□	□

LEGEND:
- ● Primary responsibility
- ○ Involved
- ♦ Provides input
- □ Informed of results

CHAPTER 6

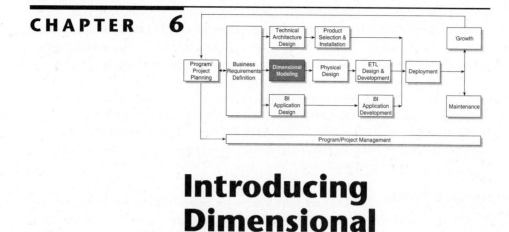

Introducing Dimensional Modeling

B eginning with this chapter, you embark on the data track of the Kimball Lifecycle. The majority of the effort required to build the data warehouse/business intelligence (DW/BI) system is expended in this track of activities, so it's critical that you get started on the right foot with a properly designed data model that addresses the business requirements.

The authors of this book have spent most of their careers, going back to the early 1980s, designing and using databases that support the business's decision making process. From this collective experience, we have concluded that dimensional modeling is the most viable technique to deliver data for business intelligence because it addresses the twin non-negotiable goals of business understandability and fast query performance. Fortunately, many others in our industry have been similarly convinced over the years so we're no longer repeatedly debating this fundamental matter as we did in the 1990s.

This chapter begins with a brief discussion comparing dimensional models to normalized models. We then provide a primer of core dimensional modeling concepts, followed by a discussion of the enterprise data warehouse bus architecture for ensuring consistency and integrating your organization's dimensional models. We then delve deeper into the common patterns you'll likely encounter in your source data and the corresponding dimensional response. Finally, we describe misleading myths and misperceptions about dimensional modeling that unfortunately continue to circulate in the industry. Chapter 6 provides the conceptual foundation of core dimensional modeling techniques, which is subsequently leveraged in Chapter 7 with its discussion of the dimensional modeling design process and associated tasks.

This introduction to dimensional modeling is a must-read for the DW/BI team's data architects and dimensional modelers. Given the critical role played by the dimensional model, other team members such as the business analysts, ETL architects and developers, and BI application architects and developers should minimally read the first half of this chapter through the bus architecture discussion.

REFERENCE Obviously, we can't synthesize everything there is to know about dimensional modeling into a single chapter. We strongly suggest that the modeling team has access to *The Data Warehouse Toolkit, Second Edition* (Wiley Publishing, 2002) by Ralph Kimball and Margy Ross as a reference. That book includes more detailed guidance using examples from a variety of industries, such as retail, financial services, telecommunications, education, and healthcare/insurance, as well as diverse business functions, including inventory, procurement, customer relationship management, accounting, and human resources. It's everything you wanted to know about dimensional modeling, but were afraid to ask.

You can also search the articles and Design Tips available on our website at `www.kimballgroup.com` for additional dimensional modeling recommendations.

Making the Case for Dimensional Modeling

Before diving into specific guidance for designing dimensional models, we begin with a comparison to the normalized models typically encountered in the transaction source systems.

What Is Dimensional Modeling?

Dimensional modeling is a logical design technique for structuring data so that it's intuitive to business users and delivers fast query performance.

Dimensional modeling is widely accepted as the preferred approach for DW/BI presentation. Practitioners and pundits alike have recognized that the data presented to the business intelligence tools must be grounded in simplicity to stand any chance of success. Simplicity is a fundamental requirement because it ensures that users can easily understand databases, as well as allows software to efficiently navigate databases. In case after case, IT organizations, consultants, users, and vendors have gravitated to a simple dimensional structure to match the basic human need for simplicity.

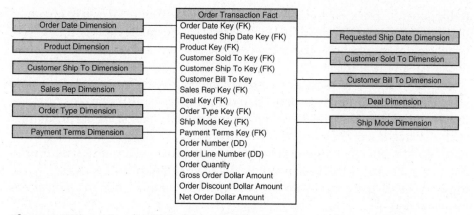

Figure 6-1 Dimensional model of the orders business process for a manufacturer.

NOTE It is probably accurate to say that the dimensional approach was not invented by any single person. It is an irresistible force in the design of databases that always surfaces when designers place understandability and performance as the highest goals.

Dimensional modeling divides the world into *measurements* and *context*. Measurements are captured by the organization's business processes and their supporting operational source systems. Measurements are usually numeric values; we refer to them as *facts*.

Facts are surrounded by largely textual context that is true at the moment the fact is recorded. This context is intuitively divided into independent logical clumps called *dimensions*. Dimensions describe the "who, what, when, where, why, and how" context of the measurement.

Each of the organization's business processes can be represented by a dimensional model that consists of a fact table containing the numeric measurements surrounded by a halo of dimension tables containing the textual context, as illustrated in Figure 6-1. This characteristic star-like structure is often called a *star join*, a term dating back to the earliest days of relational databases.

Dimensional models stored in a relational database platform are typically referred to as *star schemas*; dimensional models stored in multidimensional online analytical processing (OLAP) structures are called *cubes*. In Chapter 8, we recommend that OLAP cubes be populated from dimensional star schemas in almost all cases.

What about Normalized Modeling?

Third normal form (3NF) modeling is quite different from dimensional modeling. 3NF modeling is a design technique that seeks to eliminate data redundancies. Data is divided into many discrete entities, each of which becomes a table in the relational database. This normalization is immensely beneficial for transaction processing because it makes transaction loading and updating simple and fast.

Because normalized modeling captures the micro-relationships among data elements, even the simple orders business process results in dozens of tables that are linked together by a bewildering spider web of joins. We are all familiar with the oversized charts on the walls of database designers' cubicles. The normalized model for the enterprise has hundreds of logical entities. Enterprise resource planning (ERP) systems typically have thousands of entities. Each of these entities usually turns into a separate physical table when the database is implemented.

> **NOTE** Dimensional and normalized models look strikingly different. Some designers react to this by saying that there must be less information in the dimensional model. It's the same information and the same data relationships; it's just structured differently.

The industry sometimes refers to 3NF models as *ER models*. ER is an acronym for entity-relationship. Entity-relationship diagrams (ER diagrams or ERDs) are drawings of boxes and lines to communicate the relationships between database tables. Both 3NF and dimensional models can be represented in entity-relationship diagrams because both consist of joined relational tables; the key difference between 3NF and dimensional models is the degree of normalization. Because both model types can be presented as ERDs, we'll refrain from referring to 3NF models as ER models; instead, we'll call them normalized models to minimize confusion.

> **NOTE** This already murky vocabulary is further muddied by people who use the term "relational modeling" to describe 3NF data models. Of course, dimensional modeling and 3NF modeling both result in physical tables substantiated in a relational database system. The resulting table structures differ, but all have the same relational database properties, regardless of the modeling technique.

It's worth noting that converting from normalized structures to dimensional models is relatively straightforward. The first step is to designate the many-to-many relationships in the normalized model containing numeric and additive non-key metrics as fact tables; fact tables are typically normalized to 3NF in a dimensional model because the related context is removed to dimension tables. The second step is to denormalize the remaining tables into flat dimension tables with single-part keys that connect directly to the fact table; dimension tables most often resemble second normal form tables with many low cardinality descriptors.

NOTE Interestingly, the dimensional modeling approach may predate normalized modeling. As best we can determine, in the late 1960s, a joint research project conducted by General Mills and Dartmouth University developed vocabulary consisting of "facts" and "dimensions." We believe this allowed Nielsen Marketing Research to carry these techniques forward with grocery and drug store audit data in the 1970s and later with scanner data in the 1980s. Several of this book's authors first became aware of these ideas from Nielsen in 1984.

Benefits of Dimensional Modeling

Understandability is one of the primary reasons that dimensional modeling is the widely accepted best practice for structuring the data presented to the business intelligence layer. Albert Einstein captured the design principles behind dimensional modeling when he said, "Make everything as simple as possible, but not simpler." The dimensional model is easier for a business user to understand than the typical source system normalized model because information is grouped into coherent business categories or dimensions that make sense to business people. The business categories help users navigate the model because entire categories can be disregarded if they aren't relevant to a particular analysis. But "as simple as possible" does not mean the model is simplistic. The dimensional model must reflect the complexities of the business. If you oversimplify, the model loses valuable information that's critical to understanding the business and its performance.

Query performance is the second dominant driver for dimensional modeling. Denormalizing dimension hierarchies and decode lookups can have a significant impact on query performance. Most relational database optimizers are tuned for star joins. The predictable framework of a dimensional model allows the database to make strong assumptions about the data that aid in performance. The database engine leverages the star join by first constraining the dimension tables and gathering the keys satisfying the query filters, and then querying the fact table with the Cartesian product of the relevant dimension keys. That's a far cry from trying to optimize the querying of hundreds of interrelated tables in a large normalized model. And even though the overall suite of dimensional models in an enterprise is complex, the query processing remains predictable; performance is managed by querying each fact table separately.

Beyond ease-of-use and query performance, there are a number of additional benefits associated with dimensional modeling. One subtle advantage is that each dimension is an equivalent entry point into the fact table. This symmetry allows the dimensional model to withstand unexpected changes in query patterns. There is no predictable pattern to the blizzard of queries coming from every possible angle during an ad hoc attack. The dimensional model's symmetrical structure allows it to effectively handle whatever is thrown at it.

In technical terms, this means that query optimization for star join databases is simple, predictable, and controllable.

Best-of-breed ETL and BI tool vendors have incorporated dimensional intelligence into their products, such as pre-built ETL wizards to facilitate standard dimensional capabilities like the handling of slowly changing dimensions. Most BI tools prefer an underlying dimensional model to best showcase their capabilities.

Finally, dimensional models are gracefully extensible to accommodate unexpected new data. Existing tables can be changed in place either by simply adding new data rows in the table or executing an SQL ALTER TABLE command; data should not have to be reloaded. Graceful extensibility means that that no query or BI application needs to be reprogrammed to accommodate the change. And finally, graceful extensibility means that all old queries and applications continue to run without yielding different results.

> **NOTE** Periodically, there's distracting noise in the industry about the feasibility of bypassing dimensional modeling and data warehouse databases to simply query and analyze operational data directly. Vendors promise magical middleware that hides the complexity of the source system so that business users can theoretically query the operational systems of record, eliminating the costly and time consuming extract, transformation, and load processing. Though middleware may be able to mask the underlying data structures, it doesn't address the inherent problems surrounding the performance conflicts of interest. You don't want open-ended queries contending for the same resources that are attempting to quickly capture the transactions of the business. You may find middleware solutions are only capable of relatively light on-the-fly data transformations, leaving your data integration requirements dangling. Also, middleware does nothing to address the realities of relatively short-term data retention in the operational source systems. Finally, it cannot support the tracking of dimension attribute changes over time.

Dimensional Modeling Primer

Having made the case for dimensional modeling, let us further explore the standard vocabulary of this modeling discipline. As we mentioned earlier, dimensional modeling distinguishes between measurements and context, or facts and dimensions in the parlance of a dimensional modeler.

Fact Tables

Fact tables store the performance measurements generated by the organization's business activities or events. The term *fact* refers to each performance measure. You typically don't know the value of a fact in advance because it's variable; the fact's valuation occurs at the time of the measurement event, such as when an order is received, a shipment is sent, or a service problem is logged. You can imagine standing on the loading dock to observe the shipments process; each movement of product onto an outbound truck generates performance measures or facts, such as the shipment quantity. Facts are typically continuously valued, meaning they can take on virtually any value within a broad range.

NOTE Fact tables naturally correspond to business process measurement events. Some pundits insist that fact tables should be designed around common business questions and reports, but we strongly disagree.

Nearly every fact is numeric. The most useful facts are both numeric and additive. Additivity is important because BI applications seldom retrieve a single fact table row; queries typically select hundreds or thousands of fact rows at a time, and the only useful thing to do with so many rows is to add them up. Most metrics are fully additive. However, numerical point-in-time measures of intensity, such as account balances or inventory levels, are semi-additive because they can't be summed across time periods. Some numeric measures are completely non-additive, such as a unit price or a temperature, because these facts can't be added across any dimension. Since most textual context is drawn from a discrete list of domain values, such context should be stored in dimension tables, rather than as text facts.

While much attention is focused on conformed dimensions, facts also conform if their definitions are identical. Conformed facts are allowed to have the same standardized name in separate tables. If facts do not conform, then the different interpretations much be given different names.

NOTE Not every numeric value belongs in the fact table. For example, the square footage of a facility is a static descriptor that should be stored in the facility dimension, not the fact table. A good rule of thumb is to ask whether the attribute is discretely valued and used for filtering or labeling, in which case it belongs in the dimension table. If the attribute takes on lots of values and is used in calculations, then it should be handled as a fact. This rule of thumb addresses 99 percent of all numeric values you will encounter. The remaining percent can be modeled either as facts, or dimension attributes, or as both simultaneously.

Fact tables are huge, with millions or billions of rows, but they're efficient. Because fact tables often store more than 90 percent of the data in a dimensional model, we're careful to minimize redundant data in a fact table. Also, we strive to store the measurements resulting from a business process in a single fact table that's shared across the organization. Because measurement data is the most voluminous data, we purposely avoid duplicating the detailed metrics in multiple fact tables around the enterprise, as we further describe with the enterprise data warehouse bus architecture.

Fact Table Keys

Fact tables are characterized by a multipart key made up of foreign keys from the intersecting dimension tables involved in a business process. The multipart key means that fact tables always express a many-to-many relationship.

Every foreign key in the fact table must match to a unique primary key in the corresponding dimension table. This implies that the fact table's foreign keys should never be null because this would violate referential integrity. Sometimes a dimension value is missing from a perfectly legitimate measurement event, such as a purchase made by someone without a frequent shopper loyalty card. In this case, the fact table row should reference a special key in the customer dimension representing "Not a Frequent Shopper" to establish a proper foreign key-primary key relationship.

The primary key of the fact table is typically a subset of the dimension foreign keys. Sometimes the primary key uniquely identifying a row in the fact table consists of degenerate dimensions, as we discuss later in this chapter.

Fact Table Granularity

The fact table's *grain* is the business definition of the measurement event that produces the fact row. Declaring the grain means saying exactly what a fact table row represents by filling in the blank in the following phrase: A fact row is created when _____ occurs. While the grain determines the fact table's primary key, granularity itself is always expressed in business terms, in advance of looking at the foreign keys that may be present.

All the rows in a fact table should have a single uniform grain. The grain is determined by the physical realities of the data's source; its declaration becomes clear when you visualize the measurement process. Once the grain is established, the design can proceed by determining the dimensions that decorate the measurements at that level of detail. This logical sequence of first declaring the grain and then assembling the dimensional context is immensely helpful, and is a key characteristic of the dimensional design process. The grain is your anchor: you must include enough dimensional context in your design to implement the grain, and you must exclude dimensional context that violates the grain.

Fact tables should contain the lowest, most detailed atomic grain captured by a business process. There is tremendous power, flexibility, and resiliency in granular atomic fact data. It allows queries to ask the most precise questions possible. Even if users don't care about the particulars of a single transaction or transaction line, their "question of the moment" requires summarizing these details in unpredictable ways. Atomic data withstand assaults from unpredictable ad hoc queries because the details can be grouped "any which way." Granular atomic fact tables are also more impervious to changes; they can be gracefully extended by adding newly sourced facts, newly sourced dimension attributes, and by adding entirely new dimensions (assuming the grain is not altered by the new dimension).

NOTE Architect Mies van der Rohe is credited with saying, "God is in the details." Delivering dimensional models populated with the most detailed data possible ensures maximum flexibility and extensibility. Delivering anything less in your dimensional models undermines the foundation necessary for robust business intelligence.

Dimension Tables

In contrast to the stark and sleek qualities of fact tables consisting of just keys and numeric measurements, dimension tables are anything but stark and sleek; they're filled with big and bulky descriptive fields. The attributes in a dimension table serve two critical purposes: query constraining/filtering and query result set labeling. In many ways, the power of the data warehouse is proportional to the quality and depth of the dimension attributes; robust dimensions translate into robust querying and analysis capabilities.

NOTE You can listen for dimensions or their attributes as the "by" words (by year, by product, by region) that are used by business people when they're requesting a query or report.

Dimension attributes are typically textual fields, or they are discrete numbers that behave like text. The beauty of the dimensional model is that all the attributes are equivalent candidates to become filters or labels. Dimension attributes should be:

- Verbose (labels consisting of full words)
- Descriptive
- Complete (no missing values)
- Discretely valued (take on only one value for each row in the dimension table)
- Quality assured (no misspellings, impossible values, obsolete or orphaned values, or cosmetically different versions of the same attribute).

TIP Null values in dimension attribute columns can be confusing to business users and cause rude behavior in an SQL query, so we generally recommend a descriptive string, such as "Unknown" or "Not applicable" instead.

It's not uncommon for a dimension table to have dozens of attributes, although that's not always the case. Codes and abbreviations can be stored as dimension attributes; however it's advisable to include a corresponding descriptive field. In most instances, designers who insist that the business users prefer codes over textual fields haven't spent much time with the users. Many business intelligence tools can perform decoding within their semantic meta-data layer; however we encourage you to store the descriptive decodes in the database rather than relying on the BI tool because often more than one tool is used by an organization. Broader consistency is ensured when the description is maintained once by the ETL system and physically stored in the table.

NOTE Operational codes stored as dimension attributes often have embedded meaning. For example, the first two characters might indicate a line of business, while the next two designate a region, and so on. In this case, you should establish separate verbose dimension attributes for each embedded component so they're readily available for filtering and labeling.

Almost inevitably, dimension tables represent hierarchical relationships. It's not at all unusual to resolve several many-to-one hierarchies within a single dimension. This is a natural consequence of denormalization. For example, if products roll up into brands and brands roll into categories, we would represent this hierarchical relationship within a single product dimension table that included attributes for the corresponding brand and category descriptions. We understand that this results in redundant storage of the brand and category description on each product row. Though we could save space by storing the brand and category decodes in separate dimensions, doing so would hinder both understandability and query performance. We further explore this argument later in this chapter when we discuss snowflaking.

Dimension tables consist of highly correlated clumps of attributes grouped to represent the key objects of a business, such as its products, customers, employees, or facilities. You can think of them as the nouns of the data warehouse. There is some degree of designer judgment and intuition about the decision to create separate or combined dimensions. For example, in a retail schema, you could attempt to combine the product dimension with the store dimension and make a single monolithic product-store dimension. Assume you have 1,000 products and 100 stores. If there was no meaningful correlation between product and store, and every product was sold in every store, then your combined product-store dimension would be the Cartesian product of the two original dimensions with 100,000 product-stores. Although this new combined dimension would contain exactly the same information as separate store and product dimensions, you would undoubtedly reject this design because the larger combined dimension would be unwieldy, potentially present performance problems, deliver no user interface advantages, and likely not seem logical to the business users.

Most dimensional models end up with somewhere between 8 and 15 dimension tables. Fact tables that store transactional details end up being the most dimensional, and those that capture period snapshots invariably have a fewer number of dimensions. Some industries, such as health care, are notoriously complicated with numerous many-to-many relationships that can't be resolved within a dimension table. In these cases, the fact table may have upwards of twenty dimension foreign keys; however, this should be the exception at the high end of the spectrum rather than the rule.

Dimension Table Keys

Whereas fact tables have a multipart key, dimension rows are uniquely identified by a single key field. We strongly suggest that the dimension tables' primary keys are simple integers assigned in sequence starting with 1, meaning that when we create a key for a new dimension record, we simply add 1 to the last value we have used. These surrogate keys are meaningless; they merely serve as join fields between the fact and dimension tables.

In most cases, a 4-byte integer makes a great surrogate key because it can represent 2^{32} values, or more than two billion positive integers, starting with 1. Two billion is enough for just about any reasonable dimension, including customer.

There are several advantages of using surrogate dimension keys instead of merely referencing the operational natural keys:

- **Performance.** Surrogate integer keys are tight and efficient, especially compared to the sometimes bulky alphanumeric natural keys used by the operational transaction systems. Compact surrogate keys translate into better performance due to more efficient joins, smaller indices, and more fact rows per block. A single field surrogate key allows much more efficient join processing than a multi-field key containing original source system values.

- **Buffer from operational key management practices.** In the operational systems, data is often retained for relatively short periods of time, such as 30 to 60 days. Due to their limited retention needs, operational keys may be reused or reassigned after a period of dormancy. Although this is not problematic for the transaction processing systems, it would wreak havoc in the data warehouse where data is retained for years. If you relied on the operational natural key in the warehouse, previously obsolete products or deceased customers might reappear as miraculously resurrected when their natural keys are reassigned in the future by the operational system.

▪ **Mapping to integrate disparate sources.** In some operational environments, the same entity is assigned different natural keys by different source systems. These disparate natural keys can be matched and then associated with a neutral surrogate via a mapping table in the ETL system to uniquely identify the linked natural keys.

▪ **Handle unknown or not applicable conditions.** As we mentioned earlier, the fact table's foreign keys should never be null. Using a surrogate key instead of the operational natural key allows us to easily assign a surrogate key value to a row representing these null conditions.

▪ **Track changes in dimension attribute values.** Although dimension tables are much more static than fact tables, they are still subject to change. As we discuss later in this chapter when we cover type 2 slowly changing dimensions, one of the most popular and compliant ways to capture dimension changes is to create a new dimension row representing the new attribute profile, and then assign the next available surrogate as its primary key.

Since we've focused on the benefits, it's only fair to acknowledge that there's also a cost to using surrogate keys. Assigning and managing dimension table surrogate keys and appropriately substituting them for the operational natural keys in fact rows puts a burden on the ETL system. Fortunately, the pipeline processing is virtually identical across dimension and fact tables, so it can be built once and then reused. Also, many ETL tool vendors deliver built-in capabilities to facilitate the surrogate key processing.

Conformed Dimensions

Standardized *conformed dimensions* are the goal for any well-architected data warehouse. Sometimes referred to as master dimensions or common reference dimensions, conformed dimensions are shared across the enterprise's data warehouse environment, joining to multiple fact tables representing various business processes.

Conformed dimensions come in two flavors. With the basic flavor, two conformed dimensions are absolutely identical, with the same keys, attribute names, attribute definitions, and domain values regardless of the fact table that they join to. For example, the product dimension referenced by the sales order fact table is identical to the product dimension joined to the inventory facts. This dimension table delivers the same content, interpretation, and presentation regardless of the business process involved.

Alternatively, dimensions conform when one dimension is a perfect subset of a more detailed, granular dimension table. In this case, the attributes that are common to both the detailed and shrunken subset dimension have the same attribute names, definitions, and domain values. For example, as illustrated

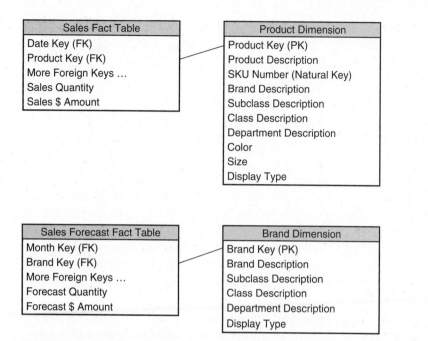

Figure 6-2 Conformed detailed and shrunken dimension tables corresponding to fact tables at different granularity.

in Figure 6-2, the sales fact table joins to a dimension table at the individual product level. But sales forecast facts are captured at the granularity of a brand rather than an individual product, so you need a shrunken brand dimension that conforms to the product dimension. Attributes that are common to both the detailed product dimension and shrunken brand dimension should be labeled, defined, and valued identically in both tables, even though the entire tables are not identical.

> **NOTE** Shrunken conformed dimension tables are created to describe fact tables that either naturally capture measurements at a higher level of detail, or facts that have been aggregated to a less granular, rolled up level for performance reasons.

Conformed dimensions are enormously important to the enterprise nature of the DW/BI system because they deliver the following benefits:

- **Consistency.** Conformed dimensions ensure that every fact table is filtered consistently and the resulting query answer sets are labeled consistently.

- **Integration.** Strict adherence to conformed dimensions allows the DW/BI environment to operate as an integrated whole. Conformed dimensions allow queries to drill across fact tables representing different processes by issuing separate queries of each individual fact table, and then joining the result sets on common dimension attributes.

- **Reduced development time to market.** While there's an organizational investment required to define and manage conformed dimensions, once built, they can dramatically reduce the development time for a project because the common dimensions are available without recreating the wheel over and over again.

Recently, there's lots of industry interest in master data management. Conformed dimensions are the descriptive master data for the DW/BI environment. We elaborate on the role of data stewards for establishing these all-important conformed dimensions in Chapter 7; they play a critical role as organizational agreement on conformed dimensions faces more geo-political challenges than technical hurdles. And while conformed dimensions may be replicated either logically or physically throughout the enterprise, they should be built once by the ETL system as we further describe in Chapter 9.

NOTE Even in a highly diversified conglomerate business, there are typically a handful of core product or customer attributes that should be conformed across the enterprise, although it would be foolhardy to attempt to get folks in the disparate lines of business to agree on all the attributes describing their businesses. The procedures we describe for building and managing conformed dimensions give you the flexibility needed to reap the value of commonly defined attributes, without forcing the enterprise to give up "private" attributes.

Four-Step Dimensional Design Process

With this understanding of key vocabulary and core concepts, now it's important to describe our approach for bringing together the fact and dimension puzzle pieces. The logical design of a dimensional model is driven by four key decisions, as we further explore in Chapter 7.

Step 1 – Choose the Business Process

The first step in the design process is to determine the business process or measurement event to be modeled. As we briefly described in Chapter 3 and elaborate on in the next section, each row of the enterprise data warehouse bus matrix corresponds to a candidate business process identified while gathering the business requirements. This selection step likely occurred during the prioritization activity with senior business management.

Step 2 – Declare the Grain

Once the business process has been identified, the design team must declare the grain of the fact table. It is crucial to crisply define exactly what a fact table row is in the proposed business process dimensional model. Without agreement on the grain of the fact table, the design process cannot successfully move forward.

> **NOTE** Be very precise when defining the fact table grain in business terms. Do not skip this step. The grain is the business answer to the question "What is a fact row, exactly?"

Generally, the fact table grain is chosen to be as atomic or finely grained as possible. Fact tables designed with the most granular data produce the most robust design. Atomic data is far better at responding to both unexpected new queries and unanticipated new data elements than higher levels of granularity.

Step 3 – Identify the Dimensions

Once the grain of the fact table is firmly established, the choice of dimensions is fairly straightforward. It is at this point you can start thinking about foreign keys. The grain itself will often determine a primary or minimal set of dimensions. From there, the design is embellished with additional dimensions that take on a unique value at the declared grain of the fact table.

Step 4 – Identify the Facts

The final step in the four-step design process is to carefully select the facts or metrics that are applicable to the business process. The facts may be physically captured by the measurement event or derived from these measurements. Each fact must be true to the grain of the fact table; do not mix facts from other time periods or other levels of detail that do not match the crisply declared grain.

As illustrated in Figure 6-3, before you drive stakes in the ground for each of these four decision points, it's important that you have a solid understanding

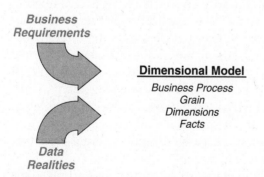

Figure 6-3 Business requirements and data realities drive the decisions made during the four-step process.

of the needs of the business, along with an understanding of the realities of the available source data.

Enterprise Data Warehouse Bus Architecture

Planning the construction of your overall DW/BI environment is a critical activity. Historically, the debate has focused on the alternatives of building the entire enterprise data warehouse from a centralized, planned perspective or building smaller, independent solutions for specific business units. Of course, neither of these approaches is effective. The galactic approach results in development efforts that take far too long to deliver business value, and thus lose business enthusiasm and ultimately falter. On the other hand, building independent departmental systems may lead to quick results, but will soon erode due to the proliferation of stovepipe, non-integrated, stand-alone solutions that fail to meet overall enterprise objectives.

> **NOTE** Departmental, stand-alone solutions are often referred to as *data marts*. When we first started using the data mart terminology in the 1990s, we were describing process-centric detailed databases that represented a subset of the enterprise's overall data architecture — a far cry from a stand-alone point solution. However, the term was hijacked to refer to independent, non-architected, departmental databases. Given the disparity in definitions and lack of consistent understanding, we've migrated away from the data mart nomenclature.

Planning Crisis

The task of planning the enterprise DW/BI data architecture is daunting. The newly appointed program manager of the DW/BI effort in a large enterprise is faced with two huge and seemingly unrelated challenges. On the one hand, the manager is supposed to understand the content and location of the most complicated asset owned by the enterprise: the source data. Somehow the DW/BI manager is supposed to become an authority on exactly what is contained in all those legacy mainframe, ERP, web server, application server, and other business systems. Every data element in every system must be understood. The DW/BI manager must be able to retrieve any requested element of data and, if necessary, clean it up and correct it. On the other hand, the DW/BI manager is supposed to understand exactly what keeps management awake at night. The DW/BI system is expected to contain exactly the data needed to answer the burning questions du jour. Of course, the manager is free to drop in on senior management at any time to discuss current corporate priorities, as long as they can ensure that the DW/BI system is done soon.

To relieve this pressure, DW/BI managers take refuge in carving off a little piece of the required solution for a given department and bringing it to completion. Often the DW/BI manager is pleasantly surprised by the success of this effort. As all good managers will, the DW/BI manager replicates a successful process and continues with further point implementations.

Unfortunately, in many cases, building separate point solutions rather than a conformed enterprise data warehouse has become an excuse for ignoring any kind of design framework that might tie these independent systems together into a coherent whole. Isolated, independent stovepipe solutions that cannot usefully be tied together are the bane of DW/BI systems. They are much worse than a simple lost opportunity for analysis. Independent stovepipe systems are dead ends that continue to perpetuate incompatible views of the enterprise. Stovepipe solutions enshrine the reports that cannot be compared with one another. And stovepipe systems become legacy implementations in their own right, where, by their very existence, they block the development of an integrated enterprise data warehouse.

So if building the data warehouse all at once is too daunting and building it as isolated pieces defeats the overall goal, what is to be done?

Bus Architecture

The answer to this dilemma is to start with a quick and succinct effort that defines the overall enterprise DW/BI data architecture. In Chapter 3, we described an initial program-level requirements gathering process that results in the creation of the enterprise data warehouse bus matrix, shown in Figure 3.5. Each row of the matrix corresponds to a business process within the organization. Each column corresponds to a dimension of the business. The matrix cells are shaded to indicate which columns are related to each row.

The enterprise data warehouse bus matrix *is* the overall data architecture for the DW/BI system. The matrix delivers the big picture perspective, regardless of database or technology preferences, while also identifying reasonably manageable development efforts. Each business process implementation incrementally builds out the overall architecture. In this way, the DW/BI manager gets the best of both worlds. Multiple development teams can work on components of the matrix fairly independently and asynchronously, with confidence that they will fit together like the pieces of a puzzle. At some point, enough dimensional schemas are built to make good on the promise of an integrated enterprise data warehouse environment.

Developing the data architecture via the bus matrix is a rational approach to decomposing the daunting task of planning an enterprise data warehouse. It establishes an architectural framework that guides the overall design, but divides the problem into bite-sized implementation chunks. Build out your integrated, enterprise data warehouse iteratively, business process by business process, using a family of shared conformed dimensions to provide the required integration. These conformed dimensions have a uniform interpretation across the enterprise. Finally, you see the overall enterprise data warehouse for what it is: a collection of business processes bound together with a powerful architecture based on conformed dimensions.

Conformed dimensions are the "bus" of the enterprise data warehouse, as illustrated in Figure 6-4. The word *bus* is an old term from electrical power plants that is now used frequently in the computer industry. A bus is a common structure that everything connects to and derives power from. The bus in your computer is a standard interface that allows many different kinds of devices to connect. If all the devices conform to the standard interface definition imposed by the bus, then these devices can usefully coexist.

By defining a standard bus interface for the DW/BI environment, a new business process may be brought into the data warehouse where it can derive power from and usefully coexist with what is already there.

Value Chain Implications

Many businesses monitor a logical flow of internal activities through a series of business process steps. Each process spawns one or more fact tables because each step represents a unique measurement event.

In the manufacturing world, a product moves from the acquisition of raw materials through to finished goods and ultimately to customer delivery. Managing this flow from point-of-origin to point-of-consumption is often referred to as *supply chain management*, with a series of operational systems corresponding to the logical steps in the chain:

- Raw material purchasing
- Raw material delivery
- Raw material inventory

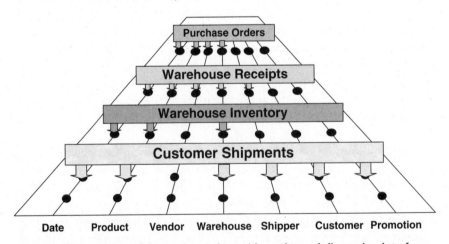

Figure 6-4 Diagram of data warehouse bus with conformed dimension interfaces.

- Bill of materials
- Manufacturing
- Shipping to warehouse
- Finished goods inventory
- Customer orders
- Shipping to customers
- Invoicing
- Payments
- Returns

You can visualize this chain of events in a bus matrix as illustrated in Figure 6-5.

Though there is no physical product built or moved in the same sense as the manufacturing company, insurance companies have a similar value chain:

- Marketing
- Agent/broker sales
- Rating
- Underwriting
- Reinsuring
- Policy issuing
- Claims processing

	Date	Raw Material	Supplier	Plant	Product	Shipper	Warehouse	Customer	Sales Rep	Promotion Deal
Raw Material Purchasing	X	X	X	X		X				
Raw Material Delivery	X	X	X	X		X				
Raw Material Inventory	X	X	X	X						
Bill of Materials	X	X		X	X					
Manufacturing	X	X	X	X	X					
Shipping to Warehouse	X			X	X	X	X			
Finished Goods Inventory	X			X			X			
Customer Orders	X				X	X		X	X	X
Shipping to Customer	X				X	X	X	X	X	X
Invoicing	X				X		X	X	X	X
Payments	X				X			X	X	X
Returns	X				X	X		X	X	X

Figure 6-5 Bus matrix for manufacturing supply chain.

- Claims investigation
- Claims payments
- Salvage
- Subrogation

These examples can be approached in a similar way. A fact table and its associated dimensions are defined for each step in the chain. The conformed dimensions are used as the bus framework for separately implementing each step in the chain. Dimensional models could be implemented in any sequence with the full confidence that the framework of conformed dimensions would always give guidance to the subsequent implementation efforts and guarantee that all the fact tables work together in the future.

Common Matrix Mishaps

When drafting a data warehouse bus matrix, people sometimes struggle with the level of detail expressed by each column or row. Matrix row mishaps commonly fall into the following two categories:

- **Departmental or overly encompassing rows.**   The matrix rows shouldn't correspond to the boxes on your corporate organization chart, which represent functional groups, not business processes. Sure, some departments may be responsible for or acutely interested in a single business process, but the matrix rows shouldn't look like a list of direct reports to your CEO.
- **Report-centric or too narrowly defined rows.**   At the opposite end of the spectrum, your bus matrix should not resemble a laundry list of requested reports. A single business process, such as shipping orders, often supports numerous analyses like customer ranking, sales rep performance, or product movement analysis. The matrix row should reference the business process, not the derivative reports or analytics.

When defining the matrix columns, architects naturally fall into the similar traps of defining columns that are either too broad or narrow:

- **Overly generalized columns.**   A bus matrix "person" column might refer to a wide variety of people, from internal employees to external suppliers and customer contacts. Because there's virtually zero overlap between these populations, it adds confusion to lump them into a single generic dimension.
- **Separate columns for each level of a hierarchy.**   The columns of the bus matrix should refer to dimensions at their most detailed level. Some business process rows may require an aggregated version of the detailed dimension, like sales forecast metrics at the product group level.

Rather than creating separate matrix columns, such as product, product group, and line of business, for each level of the product hierarchy, we advocate a single column for product. As the cell is shaded to show participation with a business process row, you can denote the level of detail in the cell (if it's not at the most granular level). An even more extreme example of this mishap is to list each individual descriptive attribute as a separate column; this defeats the concept of dimensions and results in a completely unruly matrix.

Taking the Pledge

If the DW/BI team succeeds in establishing a set of master conformed dimensions for the enterprise, it is extremely important that the development teams actually use these dimensions. The commitment to use the conformed dimensions is more than a technical decision. It is a business policy decision that is critical to making the enterprise data warehouse function.

NOTE Because the creation of conformed dimensions is as much a political decision as it is a technical decision, the use of the conformed dimensions must be supported from the highest executive levels. This issue should become a sound bite for the enterprise CIO. Fortunately, the hype around master data management has elevated awareness of this issue and opportunity.

More on Dimensions

This section focuses on common patterns and challenges that a designer is likely to confront when modeling dimension tables.

NOTE Chapter 9 contains explicit advice for handling these common design concepts in the ETL system, such as the subsystem for managing slowly changing dimensions. Right now, we're focused on recognizing and modeling the patterns. We'll defer discussion about creating these tables and attributes until Chapter 9.

Date and Time

The date dimension occupies a special place in every data warehouse because virtually every fact table is a time series of observations; fact tables always have one or more date dimensions. Figure 6-6 illustrates a standard date dimension table at a daily grain that contains a number of useful attributes for navigating, filtering, and describing calendars. Only a handful of these attributes can be generated directly from an SQL date format field; holidays, workdays, fiscal periods, last day of month flags, and other groupings or filters must be embedded in the dimension. Remember that the primary reason for this detailed date table is to remove every last vestige of calendar knowledge

Date Dimension
Date Key (PK)
Date
Full Date Description
Day of Week
Day Number in Calendar Month
Day Number in Calendar Year
Day Number in Fiscal Month
Day Number in Fiscal Year
Last Day in Week Indicator
Last Day in Month Indicator
Calendar Week Ending Date
Calendar Week Number in Year
Calendar Month
Calendar Month Number in Year
Calendar YYYY-MM
Calendar Quarter
Calendar Year-Quarter
Calendar Year
Fiscal Week
Fiscal Week Number in Year
Fiscal Month
Fiscal Month Number in Year
Fiscal Year-Month
Fiscal Quarter
Fiscal Year
Holiday Indicator
Weekday Indicator
Workday Indicator
SQL Date Stamp
… and more

Figure 6-6 Example date dimension table.

from the BI applications. Calendar navigation should be driven through the date dimension table, not through hard coded application logic.

Surrogate Date Keys

Earlier in this chapter, we discussed the benefits of using surrogate keys for dimension tables. The mandate to use surrogate keys also applies to date dimensions. It is a mistake to use an SQL date format field as the join key between the date dimension table and fact table. First, a date format key is typically 8 bytes, so you are wasting 4 bytes in the fact table for every date key in every row. Second, a date format field can't easily accommodate special date dimension rows to identify an unknown date or future date. These special cases can be handled gracefully with a surrogate date key.

For most dimensions, the surrogate key should be totally meaningless. However, with the date dimension, we encourage you to assign surrogate sequence number keys in chronological order. Unlike most dimensions, there's no need to worry about new, totally unexpected dates.

Designers sometimes want to use an even more meaningful integer in the form of YYYYMMDD as the primary key of the date dimension table instead of a surrogate sequence number. If the motivation for using a YYYYMMDD key is to bypass the date dimension and filter directly on a recognizable field in the fact table, then this is a bad idea. If the reason behind the YYYYMMDD key is to establish and maintain date-based fact table partitions, as we discuss in Chapter 8 on performance tuning, then we're willing to bend the rules about intelligent keys, as long as you promise that all queries will continue to utilize the date dimension table.

Time of Day

Fine-scale tracking of individual transactions may introduce a meaningful date and timestamp into the data that is accurate to the minute or even the second. In this case, we do not create a combined date/time dimension with one row for every minute or second of every day. Because there are more than 31 million seconds in a year, this combined dimension would be enormous. Date analysis is usually quite distinct from the analysis of time periods within the day, so we separate these into two distinct dimensions in the fact table.

Time of day should be treated as a dimension only if there are meaningful textual descriptions for periods within the day, such as the lunch hour rush or third shift, or hierarchical groupings. This dimension table would have 1,440 rows if time of day was tracked to the minute or 86,400 rows if the grain was one row per second. If the business does not need textual descriptors for time slices within a day, then the time of day may be expressed as a simple non-additive fact or a date/timestamp.

Date/Timestamps

In addition to the date dimension and potential time of day dimension, we sometimes store a full SQL date/timestamp in the fact table to support precise time interval calculations across fact rows.

NOTE If the business needs to calculate and analyze the lag between two specific date/timestamps, then these calculations should be performed in the ETL system and populated as facts for fast and simple direct user access. An example would be the elapsed time in insurance processing between the original claim date and first payment date, which is a key measure of claim processing efficiency.

Figure 6-7 Fact table with multiple time zones.

Multiple Time Zones

For businesses spanning multiple time zones, the date and time of day may need to be expressed both in local time, as well as a global standard time such as Coordinated Universal Time (UTC). This is done with separate date and time dimensions for the local time zone and UTC, as shown in Figure 6-7. Merely providing time zone offsets in either a dimension or fact table isn't effective because of the number of possible time zones, the complexities of switching to and from daylight savings time, and the challenges of applying an offset that translates into the prior or following day on a UTC basis.

Having two explicit time zone interpretations can be quite useful. For example, in analyzing call center behavior for multiple centers in different time zones, calling behavior can be aligned to real time by using the UTC interpretation and aligned on similar local times by using the local time dimensions. Of course, you may opt to standardize on a more familiar time zone, such as the time zone of the organization's headquarters, rather than relying on UTC.

Degenerate Dimensions

Many dimensional designs revolve around a transaction control document, such as an order, invoice, bill of lading, or airline ticket. Usually these control documents correspond to a transaction with one or more line items. Given this perspective, you can quickly visualize the contextual dimensions, but what do you do with the order number, invoice number, bill of lading number, or ticket number itself?

These numbers are the parent header keys used in the design of parent-child transaction systems. The answer is not to discard these header numbers; they should go directly into the fact table. The header ticket number looks like a dimension key (although we don't assign a surrogate key), but by the time you have triaged and decomposed the header record information into separate dimensions, like the transaction date and customer dimensions, the header number is sitting by itself without any remaining attributes. This is called a *degenerate dimension*.

NOTE Degenerate dimensions usually occur in transaction fact table designs where there is a natural parent-child data structure.

Degenerate dimensions are normal and useful. The degenerate dimension key should be the actual transaction number, sitting in the fact without joining to anything. There is no point in creating a corresponding dimension table because it would contain nothing but the transaction number anyway. The degenerate key is the glue that holds the line item rows together. It is required to answer broad questions, like what's the average number of line items on a transaction. The degenerate key can also be used as a link back to the operational systems for compliance, auditing, or researching data quality concerns. Finally, the degenerate dimension often serves as part of the fact table's primary key.

Slowly Changing Dimensions

By definition, dimension table attributes change relatively infrequently. Whereas the values in a fact table potentially change with every measurement event, dimension table attributes are more stable and static. However, many are still subject to change, albeit more slowly and unpredictably than the facts. The dimensional model needs to track time-variant dimension attributes as required by the business requirements. There are three fundamental techniques for handling slowly changing dimensions (SCDs), as well as a myriad of hybrid approaches.

NOTE Within a single dimension table, you may elect to utilize several different methods for tracking attribute changes, depending on the business needs.

Type 1: Overwrite the Dimension Attribute

With a type 1 slowly changing dimension response, when the attribute value changes, the old value is merely updated or overwritten with the most current value. The dimension attribute reflects the latest state, but any historical values are lost. Certainly, this technique is most appropriate for processing corrections. It is also used when the old value has no business significance, understanding that any historically accurate associations are lost with a type 1. In other words, type 1 does not preserve the attribute value that was effective at the time the historical fact row was created.

While the type 1 response appears simple to implement, there's an unexpected complication with type 1 attribute changes. If fact data have been previously *aggregated based on the type 1 attribute*, when the dimension value is overwritten, then any ad hoc summarization based on the new value will no longer tie to the pre-aggregated data. The aggregated data obviously needs to be updated to reflect the new attribute value so that the detail and aggregate data remain in sync.

CAUTION Don't immediately default to type 1 because of the perceived ease of implementation.

Type 2: Add a New Dimension Row

The type 2 slowly changing dimension response is the most popular and powerful technique for accurately tracking changes in attribute values.

With a type 2 change, a new row with a new surrogate primary key is inserted into the dimension table to reflect the new attribute values. Both the prior and new rows include the natural key (or durable identifier) as an attribute, along with a row effective date, row expiration date, and current row indicator, as illustrated in Figure 6-8.

The type 2 response is used when a meaningful change to the dimension has taken place and it is appropriate to perfectly partition history by the changed attribute. Each surrogate key corresponds to a unique version of the dimension row that was true for a span of time. Thus each surrogate key is used in the corresponding fact rows during the time when the particular instance was valid. Obviously, type 2 is necessary if compliance is critical.

NOTE The type 2 approach requires the use of a surrogate key to uniquely identify the new profile. Some designers suggest that you uniquely identify changed dimension rows by concatenating an effective date to the natural key. We strongly discourage this practice. Joining this concatenated dimension key to the fact table would require a double barrel join which is highly inefficient, especially when the join on the effective date is a non-equal join.

Type 3: Add a New Dimension Attribute

The type 3 response to a slowly changing dimension attribute is used relatively infrequently. Type 3 is usually utilized when the change, like the redrawing of sales district boundaries or redefinition of product category boundaries, is a "soft" change. In other words, although the change has occurred, it is still logically possible to act as if the change had not occurred. For example, you may want to track sales performance with either the old or the new sales district definitions. In this case, you cannot partition history disjointly as in a type 2 response, but you simultaneously provide both the old attribute value and new value in the same dimension row. This allows users to choose between the two versions at will.

With a type 3 response, a new column is added to the dimension table. The old attribute value is pushed into a "prior" attribute column and the new

PRODUCT KEY	Product Description	Product Code	Department	Effective Date	Expiration Date	Current Row Ind
12345	IntelliKidz 1.0	ABC999-Z	Education	2/15/2007	5/31/2007	Not current
25984	IntelliKidz 1.0	ABC999-Z	Strategy	6/1/2007	12/31/2007	Not current
34317	IntelliKidz 1.0	ABC999-Z	Critical Thinking	1/1/2008	12/31/9999	Current

Figure 6-8 Sample rows from slowly changing dimension type 2.

attribute value is overwritten in the existing column. This causes all existing BI applications to switch seamlessly to the new attribute assignment, but allows a query or report to return to the old assignments by simply referencing the prior attribute column. With this technique, no new dimension rows are created and no new surrogate keys are created. It should be obvious that this technique works best for a limited number of such soft changes.

If a dimension attribute changes with a predictable rhythm, such as annually, and the business needs to summarize facts based on any historical value of the attribute, not just the historically accurate and current as we've primarily been discussing, you could have a series of type 3 attributes in the dimension. On every dimension row, there would be a "current" attribute that is overwritten, as well as attributes for each annual designation, such as the 2007 assignment, 2006 assignment, and so on. Generalized reporting would likely most often use the current assignment attribute in the dimension.

Mini-Dimensions: Add a New Dimension

The slowly changing dimension workhorse technique, type 2, is inappropriate for tracking attribute changes in large dimension tables with millions of rows. Though relational databases are capable of supporting dimension tables of this size, it is important to adopt a conservative design to keep these dimensions under control.

Unfortunately, huge customer dimensions are even more likely to change than medium-sized product dimensions, which seemingly puts you between a rock and a hard place. You must track the changing nature of the customer dimension, but don't dare use the type 2 technique due to the already imposing size of the table and the frequency of changes.

The solution to this dilemma is to break off the more frequently changing customer attributes into their own separate dimension table, as in Figure 6-9, called a *mini-dimension*. In this example, the new mini-dimension contains customer demographics. The mini-dimension's grain is one row per demographics profile, whereas the grain of the primary customer dimension is one row per customer.

Although the mini-dimension technique allows you to track relatively frequent changes in a large dimension table, it requires a few compromises:

- **Banded values.** The demographic attributes have been clumped into banded ranges of discrete values. This places a limit on the specificity of the data, such as income, and makes it quite impractical to change to a different set of value bands at a later time.

- **Restricted growth.** The mini-dimension itself cannot grow too large; a gross general rule of thumb is that the mini-dimension should have fewer than a couple hundred thousand rows. Surprisingly, a workable

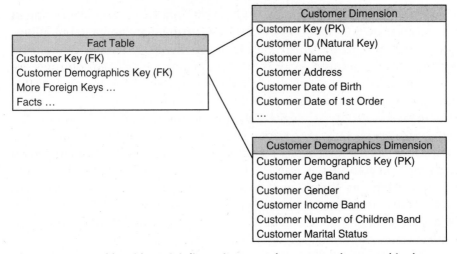

Figure 6-9 Fact table with a mini-dimension to track customer demographic changes.

solution to this challenge is to build a second mini-dimension. It's not uncommon for an organization tracking a very rich set of customer attributes to need separate mini-dimensions for customer demographics, geographic attributes, credit bureau attributes, and market segmentation attributes and scores.

▪ **Separation from core dimension.**   The mini-dimension has been physically separated from the more constant descriptors of the customer, making it harder to browse the data as if it were a single dimension; the demographics data is linked to the core customer data only through the fact table. If desired, you may opt to populate type 1 columns for the current values of the mini-dimension attributes within the customer dimension. This facilitates stand-alone demographic analysis of your customer base without traversing the fact table. It is important to clearly label the type 1 mini-dimension attributes in the core customer dimension as "current."

Finally, a sharp eyed reader may notice that this approach allows you to associate demographics with the customer only when a fact table row occurs, such as a sales event or insurance claim event. If no fact event happens, then no linkage is established. If there is a danger of missing a demographics association, a supplemental factless fact table, as we discuss later in this chapter, can be used to capture the relationship between the customer dimension and mini-dimension over time; a row is loaded when a relationship change occurs. Fortunately, in many industries, there is a natural monthly business process that results in a periodic snapshot fact table that effortlessly captures the relationship of all customers and their applicable mini-dimension values without the need for an additional factless fact table.

Hybrid Slowly Changing Dimension Techniques

These fundamental slowly changing techniques are adequate for most situations. However, sometimes you need hybrid variations that build on these basics to serve more sophisticated analytics. Before using these hybrids, remember the need to balance analytic power against ease of use; strive to maintain equilibrium between flexibility and complexity. These hybrid techniques are not for the faint of heart.

Business folks sometimes want to preserve the historically accurate dimension attribute associated with a fact, but also want the option to roll up historical facts based on current dimension characteristics. None of our fundamental slowly changing dimension techniques addresses this requirement entirely.

One solution is to capture type 2 attribute changes by adding a row to the primary dimension table, but in addition, there's a "current" attribute on each row that is overwritten (type 1) for the current *and* all previous type 2 rows. When a change occurs, the most current dimension row has the same value in the uniquely labeled current and historical ("as was") columns, as illustrated in Figure 6-10.

Instead of having the historical and current attributes reside in the same physical table, the current attributes could sit in an outrigger table joined to the dimension natural key or durable identifier in the dimension table. The outrigger contains just one row of current data for each natural key in the dimension table; the attributes are overwritten whenever change occurs. Alternatively, this outrigger could be a view of the type 2 dimension table, restricted to just the current rows.

Finally, if you have a million-row dimension table with many attributes requiring historical and current tracking, you should consider including the dimension natural key or durable identifier as a fact table foreign key, in addition to the surrogate key for type 2 tracking. This technique essentially associates two dimension tables with the facts, but for good reason. The type 2 dimension has historically accurate attributes for filtering or grouping based on the effective values when the fact row was loaded. The dimension natural key joins to a table with just the current type 1 values. You use the attributes on this dimension table to summarize or filter facts based on the current profile, regardless of the values in effect when the fact row was loaded. Again, the

PRODUCT KEY	Product Description	Product Code	Historical Department	Current Department	Effective Date	Expiration Date	Current Row Ind
12345	IntelliKidz 1.0	ABC999-Z	Education	Critical Thinking	2/15/2007	5/31/2007	Not current
25984	IntelliKidz 1.0	ABC999-Z	Strategy	Critical Thinking	6/1/2007	12/31/2007	Not current
34317	IntelliKidz 1.0	ABC999-Z	Critical Thinking	Critical Thinking	1/1/2008	12/31/9999	Current

Figure 6-10 Hybrid slowly changing dimension with historical and current attributes.

column labels in this table should be prefaced with "current" to reduce the risk of user confusion.

Role-Playing Dimensions

When the same physical dimension table plays distinct logical roles in a dimensional model, we refer to it as *role-playing*. The most common example of role-playing involves the date dimension. Fact tables always have at least one date dimension foreign key, but sometimes there are multiple dates associated with each fact row, such as the transaction date of the event, as well as the effective date. Later in this chapter, we discuss accumulating snapshot fact tables, which often have a handful of dates on each row.

Each date foreign key in the fact table points to a specific date dimension table, as shown in Figure 6-11. You can't join these multiple foreign keys to the same table because SQL would interpret the two-way simultaneous join as requiring the dates to be the same, which isn't very likely.

Instead of a two-way join, you need to fool SQL into believing that there are independent date dimension tables with unique column labels. If you don't uniquely label the columns, users won't be able to tell the attributes apart when several are dragged into a report.

Even though you cannot literally use a single date dimension in Figure 6-11, you want to build and administer a single physical date table behind the scenes. The illusion of independent date dimension tables is created by using views or aliases, depending on the database platform. Now that you have uniquely

Order Date Dimension
Order Date Key (PK)
Order Date
Order Date Day of Week
Order Date Month
… and more

Requested Ship Date Dimension
Requested Ship Date Key (PK)
Requested Ship Date
Requested Ship Date Day of Week
Requested Ship Date Month
… and more

Order Transaction Fact
Order Date Key (FK)
Requested Ship Date Key (FK)
Product Key (FK)
Customer Sold To Key (FK)
Customer Ship To Key (FK)
Customer Bill To Key
Sales Rep Key (FK)
Deal Key (FK)
Order Type Key (FK)
Ship Mode Key (FK)
Payment Terms Key (FK)
Order Number (DD)
Order Line Number (DD)
Order Quantity
Gross Order Dollar Amount
Order Discount Dollar Amount
Net Order Dollar Amount

Figure 6-11 Role-playing date dimensions.

described date dimensions, they can be used as if they were independent with completely unrelated constraints.

Depending on your industry, role playing can occur with a variety of dimensions, in addition to the date, such as:

- Customer (ship to, bill to, and sold to)
- Facility or port (origin, destination)
- Provider (referring, performing)
- Representative (seller, servicer)

NOTE A single dimension may play several simultaneous roles with a fact table. The underlying dimension may exist as a single physical table, but each of the roles must be presented in a separately labeled view.

Junk Dimensions

Especially when modeling a complex transactional business process, after identifying the obvious business dimensions, you are often left with a number of miscellaneous flags and text attributes that can't find an appropriate home in any of the existing dimension tables. This situation leaves the designer with a number of bad alternatives, all of which should be avoided, including:

- **Leave them in the fact table.** Leaving the flags and text attributes in the fact table is bad because it might cause the fact table row length to swell alarmingly. It would be a shame to create a nice tight design and then leave several uncompressed 20-byte text columns in the fact row.

- **Make them into separate dimensions.** Making each flag and attribute into its own separate dimension doesn't work either. This could cause the fact table to swell to an unusually large number of dimension foreign keys. As we mentioned earlier, we strive to have fewer than twenty foreign keys in a fact table for most industries and business processes.

- **Eliminate them.** While tempting, stripping out the flags and indicators could be a mistake if there is demonstrated business relevance to these fields. It is worthwhile, of course, to examine this question. If the flags and text attributes are incomprehensible, inconsistently populated, or only of operational significance, they should be left out.

The key to solving this problem is to study the flags and text attributes carefully and to place them into one or more *junk* dimensions, as illustrated in Figure 6-12, rather than adding more clutter to the fact table.

NOTE *Junk dimension* is a highly technical term; when describing the dimension to business users, you probably want to use different vocabulary, such as the "invoice indicator" dimension.

A simple example of a junk dimension would be taking ten yes/no indicators out of the fact table and putting them into a single dimension. It is okay if there seems to be no correlation among these ten indicators. You simply pack all ten indicators into one dimension with ten attributes; while you're at it, convert the yes/no indicator values to more meaningful, descriptive labels. At the worst, you have $2^{10} = 1,024$ rows in this junk dimension. It probably isn't very interesting to browse among these indicators within the dimension because every indicator occurs with every other indicator. But the junk dimension is a useful holding place for the indicators to support filtering or reporting. And the ten columns in the fact table have been replaced with one small surrogate key.

A subtle issue in the design is whether you create all the combinations in the junk dimension in advance or whether you create junk dimension rows for the combinations of flags as you encounter them in the data. The answer depends on how many possible combinations you expect and what the maximum number could be. Generally, when the number of theoretical combinations is very high and you don't think you will encounter them all, you should build a junk dimension row at extract time whenever you encounter a new combination of fields.

Invoice Indicator Key	Payment Terms	Order Mode	Ship Mode
1	Net 10	Telephone	Freight
2	Net 10	Telephone	Air
3	Net 10	Fax	Freight
4	Net 10	Fax	Air
5	Net 10	Web	Freight
6	Net 10	Web	Air
7	Net 15	Telephone	Freight
8	Net 15	Telephone	Air
9	Net 15	Fax	Freight
10	Net 15	Fax	Air
11	Net 15	Web	Freight
12	Net 15	Web	Air
13	Net 30	Telephone	Freight
14	Net 30	Telephone	Air
15	Net 30	Fax	Freight
16	Net 30	Fax	Air
17	Net 30	Web	Freight
18	Net 30	Web	Air
19	Net 45	Telephone	Freight
20	Net 45	Telephone	Air
21	Net 45	Fax	Freight
22	Net 45	Fax	Air
23	Net 45	Web	Freight
24	Net 45	Web	Air

Figure 6-12 Sample rows from a junk dimension.

NOTE Data profiling can play a role in helping identify appropriate junk dimension opportunities and strategies. Many times what look like independent junk attributes in the fact table turn out to be correlated. At a recent healthcare client, a set of claim transaction attributes theoretically had more than one trillion possible combinations, but when the data was profiled, it was determined that fewer than 80,000 unique combinations were ever observed.

As we mentioned when discussing the mini-dimension, sometimes you may create multiple junk dimensions for a single fact table, depending on the correlations between the miscellaneous flags and indicators.

A final kind of messy attribute that fits well into the junk dimension approach is the open-ended comments field that is often attached to a fact row. If you decide that the contents of the comments field warrant inclusion in the data warehouse, you should proceed by pulling them out of the fact row and into a junk dimension. Often, many of these freeform text comments fields are blank, so you will need a special surrogate key that points to the "no comment" row in the dimension; most of your fact table rows will use this key.

NOTE Text facts are a dimensional modeling oxymoron. Fact tables should consist only of keys, numerical measurements, and degenerate dimensions.

Snowflaking and Outriggers

Dimensions are *snowflaked* when the redundant attributes and decodes are removed to separate tables and linked back into the original table with artificial keys. In other words, a snowflaked dimension is normalized. An example snowflaked product dimension table is shown in Figure 6-13.

Generally, snowflaking is not recommended for your dimensional models because it almost always makes the user presentation more complex and less legible. Database designers who are comfortable with third normal form design disciplines often like this intricacy, but users are typically intimidated by it. Snowflaking also makes most forms of browsing among the dimension attributes slower. Remember that most browses involve selecting the distinct values of a dimension attribute subject to one or more other attributes in the dimension being constrained. Obviously a snowflaked category table will perform extremely well if the user is asking only for the distinct values of category with no ancillary constraints, but if the user is constraining on package type at the same time, then the query needs to join the snowflaked category table back through to the product dimension table and possibly out through another snowflake link to the package type table where the constraint has been placed.

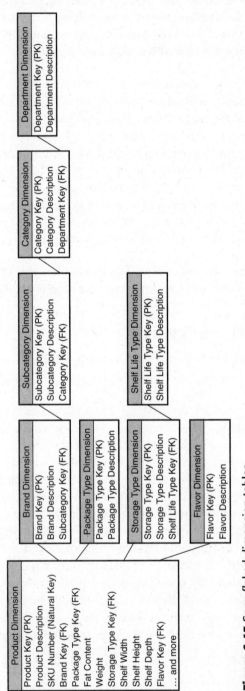

Figure 6-13 Snowflaked dimension tables.

NOTE Any argument that snowflaking of dimensional models assists in their maintenance is specious. Remember, the maintenance work happens in the ETL system before the data is loaded into the dimensional schema in the presentation server.

Some designers snowflake dimensions because they want to save disk space. Surely they can save space by eliminating all those nasty repeating text columns. Granted, if the artificial key required for each snowflaked attribute is shorter than the text string it replaces, some space will be saved. Suppose in a 250,000 row product table, we replaced every 15-byte category name with a 2-byte category key. We have thereby saved approximately 13 bytes on 250,000 rows or 3.25 MB. Our overall product table may well be larger than 100 MB, and the associated sales fact table is potentially hundreds of gigabytes. We have just saved 3 MB on a base of over 100 GB, or 0.003 percent. This negligible savings has been paid for with extra administration in creating and populating the artificial keys, as well as an almost certain performance penalty for cross-attribute browsing.

Despite this general recommendation against snowflaking, there are some situations where we agree it might be advantageous to build an "outrigger" dimension that looks like the beginning of a snowflake, as illustrated in Figure 6-14. In this example, the outrigger is a set of demographic attributes that exist at the county level; all customers in a county share an identical set of attributes. Furthermore, the county demographic data consists of a label, population count, and population percentage for 50 different demographic groupings, so there are 150 attributes. In this case, it makes sense to isolate this demographic data in an outrigger. The demographic data is available at a significantly different grain than the primary dimension and is administered on a different frequency. Also, you might really save space in this case if the underlying dimension is large.

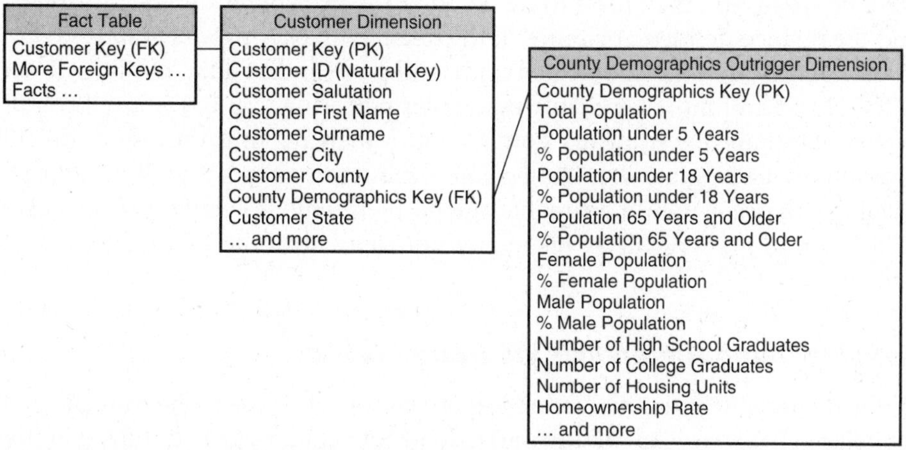

Fact Table	Customer Dimension
Customer Key (FK) More Foreign Keys ... Facts ...	Customer Key (PK) Customer ID (Natural Key) Customer Salutation Customer First Name Customer Surname Customer City Customer County County Demographics Key (FK) Customer State ... and more

County Demographics Outrigger Dimension

County Demographics Key (PK)
Total Population
Population under 5 Years
% Population under 5 Years
Population under 18 Years
% Population under 18 Years
Population 65 Years and Older
% Population 65 Years and Older
Female Population
% Female Population
Male Population
% Male Population
Number of High School Graduates
Number of College Graduates
Number of Housing Units
Homeownership Rate
... and more

Figure 6-14 Example of a permissible snowflaked outrigger.

A more commonly encountered outrigger is a date dimension snowflaked off a primary dimension, such as a customer's date of birth or the product's introduction date. In this scenario, the outrigger date attributes should be descriptively and uniquely labeled to distinguish them from the other dates associated with the business process. It only makes sense to outrigger a primary dimension table's date attribute if the business needs to filter and group the date by non-calendar date attributes, such as the fiscal period or business day indicator. Otherwise, you could just treat the date attribute as a standard date format field. If you do use a date outrigger, be careful that the outrigger dates all fall within the date range stored in the standard date dimension table.

NOTE Though outriggers are a permissible form of snowflaking, your dimensional model should not be littered with outriggers given the potentially negative impact on both legibility and query performance. Outriggers should be the exception rather than the rule.

Handling Hierarchies

Hierarchies are a fact of life in a dimensional model. In this section, we review the common fixed hierarchical relationships, as well as variable depth hierarchies.

Fixed Hierarchies

As a result of dimension table denormalization, simple many-to-one hierarchies within a dimension table are often flattened and presented as a series of attributes in the dimension. In fact, it's not unusual to have more than one well-defined hierarchy in a given dimension. For example, the marketing and finance departments may have incompatible and different views of the product hierarchy. Despite your efforts to define common, conformed dimensions for the enterprise, you may need to retain all of the marketing-defined attributes and the finance-defined attributes in the detailed master product table.

Hierarchies are often associated with drill paths in the data. Drilling down is the oldest and most venerable maneuver performed by users in a DW/BI system. Drilling down means nothing more than delving into more detail, typically by adding another dimension attribute to an existing SQL request. Drilling can occur within a predetermined hierarchy; however, you can also drill down to more detail by using any unrelated attribute that is not part of a hierarchy.

Variable Depth Hierarchies via Bridge Tables

Unfortunately, not all data hierarchies are simple and fixed. The dimensional modeler's challenge is to balance the tradeoff between ease of use and flexibility when representing more complex hierarchies, such as variable depth or ragged hierarchies, because they require a more complex solution than simple denormalization.

Representing a variable depth organization structure or parts hierarchy is a difficult task in a relational environment. Let's assume that you want to report the revenues of a set of commercial customers who have subsidiary relationships with each other. Your organization sells products or services to any of these commercial customers; you may want to look at them individually or as families arranged in a hierarchical structure.

The traditional computer science response to this hierarchy would be to put a recursive pointer in each customer dimension row containing the customer key of its parent. Although this is a compact and effective way to represent an arbitrary hierarchy, this kind of recursive structure cannot be used effectively with standard SQL when you want to both navigate and summarize fact table measurements based on the recursive relationship.

As we further explain in *The Data Warehouse Toolkit, Second Edition*, you can navigate a variable depth hierarchy through the use of a bridge table. Illustrated in Figure 6-15, the bridge sits between the fact table and customer dimension when you want to navigate the hierarchy. If the bridge table is omitted, you can filter and group facts based on the individual customer involved in the transaction, but there's no ability to roll up or drill down through the customer's organization structure.

The organization bridge table contains one row for each pathway from a customer entity to each subsidiary beneath it. There is also a row for the zero-length pathway from a customer to itself. Each pathway row contains the customer key of the rollup parent entity, customer key of the subsidiary entity, number of levels between the parent and the subsidiary, a flag that identifies a subsidiary as being at the bottom-most possible level, and a flag that indicates whether there are any more nodes above the parent.

When you want to descend the organization hierarchy, you join the tables as shown in Figure 6-15. You can now group or constrain on any attribute within

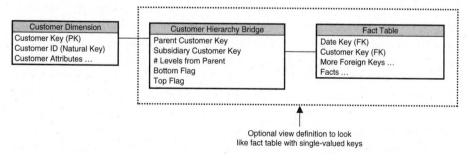
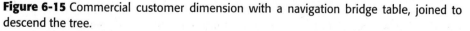

Figure 6-15 Commercial customer dimension with a navigation bridge table, joined to descend the tree.

the customer table, and retrieve facts for all the subsidiaries at or below all the customers implied by the constraint. You can use the number of levels field in the organization bridge table to control the depth of the analysis. A value of 1 would give all the direct subsidiaries of a customer. A value of "greater than zero" would give all subsidiary customers but not the original parent.

Alternatively, when you want to ascend the organization hierarchy, the joins would be altered. The parent customer key would now be joined to the fact table, and the subsidiary customer key would be joined to the customer dimension table.

Although the bridge table allows SQL to navigate and aggregate facts in an unpredictably deep hierarchy, there are downsides to this approach because our twin goals of usability and query performance are both negatively compromised. The bridge table can quickly become huge and unwieldy with the explosion of a complicated organization or bill-of-materials rollup structure. Query performance suffers when the bridge is used. And though the computer scientist may be able to easily navigate the bridge, most users will come to a crashing halt when asked to cross the bridge. Fortunately, some OLAP cube products have built in awareness of recursive parent-child hierarchies to help ease the burden.

Many-Valued Dimensions with Bridge Tables

So far in our designs, there has been a straightforward many-to-one relationship between the fact table and associated dimension tables; many rows in the fact table join to a single row in the dimension table. However, there are some situations in which each fact measurement can be associated with multiple dimension values.

Health care offers a vivid example of a many-valued dimension. Assume we're modeling the hospital billing business process with a row in the fact table for each line item on a bill. The problem for the designer is what to do with the diagnosis dimension. Real patients often have more than one diagnosis. Really sick patients may have ten or more diagnoses. To handle this open-endedness, you cannot add multiple diagnosis dimension foreign keys to the fact table. Not only do you not know what the extreme upper bound is for the potential number of diagnoses, but the resulting schema would be awkward to query. OR joins across dimensions are anathema to relational systems and SQL's GROUP BY logic fails. Likewise, you can't change the grain of the fact table to be one row per diagnosis associated with a hospital bill line item because the billing metrics don't make sense at this granularity.

To resolve the design problem and provide for an arbitrary number of diagnoses, a bridge table is inserted between the fact table and the diagnosis dimension, as in Figure 6-16. Each row in the diagnosis group table contains the diagnosis group key, individual diagnosis key, and weighting factor.

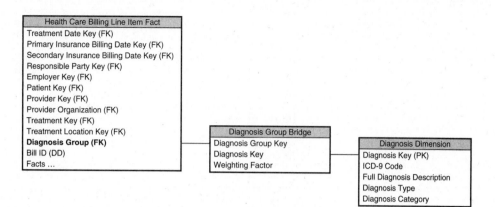

Figure 6-16 Solving the many-valued diagnoses problem with a bridge table.

A patient with three diagnoses would have three rows in their respective diagnosis group. The weighting factor is a fractional value that sums to one for each diagnosis group; the determination of the weighting factor is a business issue. The individual diagnosis key joins to the diagnosis table, which contains a full description of each diagnosis.

With this structure, the user or BI application can perform two types of queries. First, the user can ask for a correctly weighted summary of all billed charges grouped by diagnosis. The join through the bridge table picks up the weighting factor for each diagnosis and multiplies it by the fact amount to allocate the facts according to the contribution of each individual diagnosis in the group. The use of the weighting factor guarantees that the bottom line total is accurate.

Alternatively, the user can request an impact report that performs the same join across the tables, but does not use the weighting factor. In this case, an impact report deliberately double counts the amounts, but correctly determines the impact each diagnosis has in terms of the total fact amounts associated with that diagnosis.

A fact table representing account balances in a bank has an analogous problem. Each account may have one or more individual customers as account holders. To join an individual customer dimension table to an account balances fact table, you need an account-to-customer bridge table that has the same structure as the diagnosis group table in the previous example, as illustrated in Figure 6-17.

Analysis surrounding commercial customers' industry classification codes also faces the many-valued problem. Each commercial customer may be represented by one or more industry classification codes. Again, by building an industry classification group bridge table with the same structure as the last two bridge tables, you can sum up the facts by any attribute found within the individual industry classification dimension table, either correctly weighted

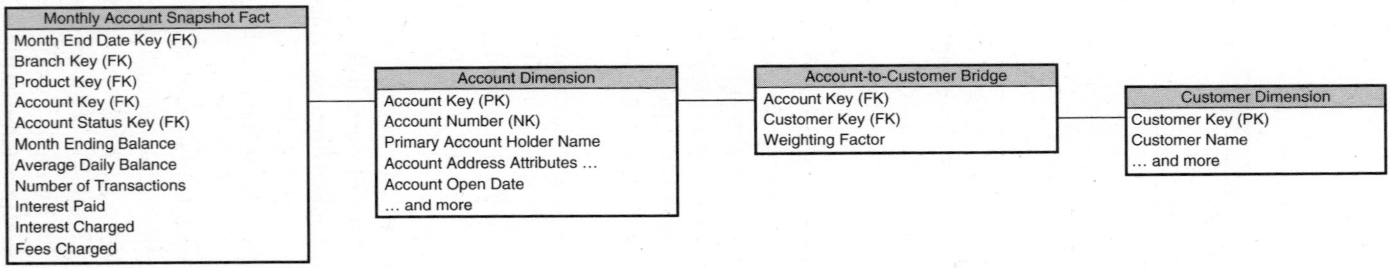

Monthly Account Snapshot Fact

Month End Date Key (FK)
Branch Key (FK)
Product Key (FK)
Account Key (FK)
Account Status Key (FK)
Month Ending Balance
Average Daily Balance
Number of Transactions
Interest Paid
Interest Charged
Fees Charged

Account Dimension

Account Key (PK)
Account Number (NK)
Primary Account Holder Name
Account Address Attributes ...
Account Open Date
... and more

Account-to-Customer Bridge

Account Key (FK)
Customer Key (FK)
Weighting Factor

Customer Dimension

Customer Key (PK)
Customer Name
... and more

Figure 6-17 Solving the multiple customers per account problem with a bridge table.

or as an impact report. You may want to add an attribute on the customer dimension to designate their primary industry classification to simplify some analysis by avoiding the bridge.

Before we leave the topic of bridge tables, we want to reiterate that using bridge tables to resolve many-to-many relationships is the path of last resort due to the implications on usability and performance. Resolving the many-to-many issue directly in the fact table makes for a much simpler solution, however sometimes this just isn't feasible given the natural granularity of the measurement event. In these cases, the bridge comes to the rescue.

More on Facts

Now that we've explored dimension tables in more detail, we turn our attention to fact tables.

Three Fundamental Grains

Regardless of the industry and its associated business processes, all measurement events can be characterized as either transactions, periodic snapshots, or accumulating snapshots. We describe the characteristics of these three fundamental fact table grains in the following sections. The DW/BI environment often pairs complementary fact tables that deliver data at different base granularity for a more complete picture of the business. Though the fact tables share conformed dimensions, the rhythm and associated administration varies by fundamental grain.

Transaction Fact Tables

The most basic and common fact tables are transactional. The grain is specified to be one row per transaction, or one row per line on a transaction. The transaction grain is a point in space and time; the measurements at a transaction grain must be true at that moment.

Transaction data at its lowest level typically has the greatest number of dimensions associated with it. Whenever a transaction event occurs, extensive context about the transaction is also captured, as illustrated back in Figure 6-1.

Rows are inserted into a transactional fact table only when activity occurs. Once a transaction fact row is posted, it is typically not revisited.

As we've described earlier in this chapter, detailed transaction schema are very powerful. The minute measurements allow you to monitor the most granular activities of the business. However, you sometimes need to complement this gory detail with snapshots to more easily visualize behavior or performance trends.

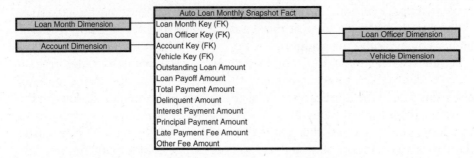

Figure 6-18 Periodic snapshot grained fact table for monthly loans.

Periodic Snapshot Fact Tables

The second most common type of fact table is the periodic snapshot. With periodic snapshots, you take a set of pictures, just as the name implies, capturing the performance of a business process spanning a well defined periodic interval of time and load these pictures into a fact table. At a predetermined interval, such as daily, weekly, or monthly, more pictures are taken at the same level of detail and stacked consecutively in the fact table. Note that this gives the designer a lot of latitude: Any fact that describes activity over the time span is fair game.

Some business processes are naturally represented as periodic snapshots. For example, the value of a bank account is naturally taken as a snapshot on a daily or monthly basis. You can envision inventory balances snapshots on a daily or weekly timeframe. The most familiar financial reports are periodic snapshots. Figure 6-18 illustrates a periodic monthly snapshot of automobile loans.

It should go without saying that the periodic snapshot complements the detailed transaction facts, but is not a replacement. You still need the granular details to ask highly precise questions about performance.

Like the transactional fact tables, periodic snapshot rows are typically not revisited once they've been loaded into the fact table. Periodic snapshots often share many of the same conformed dimensions with the transaction fact tables, however there are typically far fewer dimensions.

Accumulating Snapshot Fact Tables

The third type of fact table is the least frequently encountered, however it serves a very powerful function in certain applications.

Unlike periodic snapshots, which house regularly captured measurements, accumulating snapshots are used to represent activity over an indeterminate time span for processes that have a well defined beginning and end. For example, in Figure 6-19, a row is loaded into the accumulating snapshot fact table for each line on an order when it is originally received. As the order moves through the fulfillment process, the fact table rows are *updated in place*

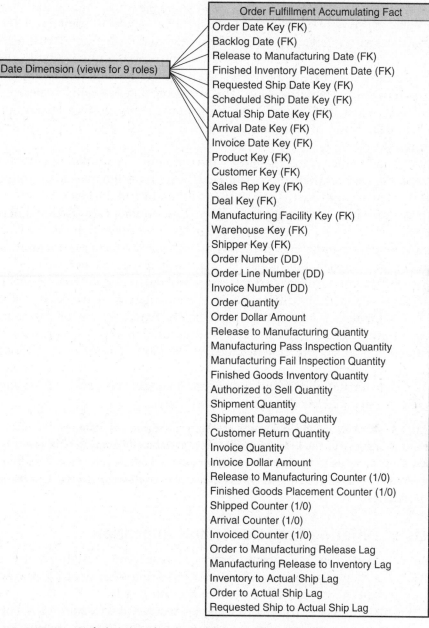

Order Fulfillment Accumulating Fact
Order Date Key (FK)
Backlog Date (FK)
Release to Manufacturing Date (FK)
Finished Inventory Placement Date (FK)
Requested Ship Date Key (FK)
Scheduled Ship Date Key (FK)
Actual Ship Date Key (FK)
Arrival Date Key (FK)
Invoice Date Key (FK)
Product Key (FK)
Customer Key (FK)
Sales Rep Key (FK)
Deal Key (FK)
Manufacturing Facility Key (FK)
Warehouse Key (FK)
Shipper Key (FK)
Order Number (DD)
Order Line Number (DD)
Invoice Number (DD)
Order Quantity
Order Dollar Amount
Release to Manufacturing Quantity
Manufacturing Pass Inspection Quantity
Manufacturing Fail Inspection Quantity
Finished Goods Inventory Quantity
Authorized to Sell Quantity
Shipment Quantity
Shipment Damage Quantity
Customer Return Quantity
Invoice Quantity
Invoice Dollar Amount
Release to Manufacturing Counter (1/0)
Finished Goods Placement Counter (1/0)
Shipped Counter (1/0)
Arrival Counter (1/0)
Invoiced Counter (1/0)
Order to Manufacturing Release Lag
Manufacturing Release to Inventory Lag
Inventory to Actual Ship Lag
Order to Actual Ship Lag
Requested Ship to Actual Ship Lag

Date Dimension (views for 9 roles)

Figure 6-19 Accumulating snapshot fact table for order fulfillment.

to reflect the latest status. Ultimately, the pipeline activity on an order line item is completed when the invoice is generated.

Accumulating snapshot fact tables exhibit several unique characteristics compared to the other two types of fact tables. For starters, accumulating snapshots contain multiple date foreign keys, each corresponding to a major milestone in the workflow. While transactional schemas sometimes have several dates associated with each row, the accumulating fact table is distinctive because many of the date values are unknown when the row is first loaded. As we discussed earlier, you need a special row in the date dimension table to represent unknown future dates. This surrogate date key will be referenced extensively when the accumulating snapshot fact row is first loaded, and then is systematically overwritten as the actual date of the milestone occurrence is captured.

In addition to the typical quantities and amounts, accumulating snapshots often contain two additional types of facts. The first is the milestone counter; there is often a lengthy list of counters corresponding to the key milestones in the pipeline, which take on a 1 or 0 value. These counters are used to quickly determine how many fact rows have progressed to a given point in the workflow. Second, accumulating snapshots often have lag facts representing the length of time between milestones, such as the elapsed time between the first and second milestone, or the first milestone and the final event in the pipeline.

Of course, the primary differentiator of accumulating snapshots is that the fact row is updated. Accumulating snapshots are almost always complemented by one or more transaction fact tables. The accumulation process presents the key transactional activity side-by-side in a single fact table row. Although this delivers query performance and analytic power, it's not an adequate replacement for the underlying transaction fact tables because dimensional details are inevitably lost during the accumulation.

NOTE Transactions and snapshots are the yin and yang of a data warehouse. Transactions give us the fullest possible view of detailed behavior, whereas snapshots allow us to easily and quickly monitor overall performance. We often need them both because there is no simple way to combine these two contrasting perspectives.

Facts of Differing Granularity and Allocation

Sometimes a single business process produces measurements at different levels of detail. For example, metrics are captured for each line on an order, however a single freight charge might be levied for the entire order.

All the measurements in a single fact table must be valid for the table's stated granularity. In other words, you can't have facts with differing granularity in the same fact table; all the measurements must exist at the same level of detail.

So what's a dimensional modeler to do when confronted with measurements that naturally exist at different grains? The first response should be to try to force all of the facts down to the lowest level. This procedure is broadly referred to as *allocating* the higher level facts to a lower granularity to align with the other captured measurements, as illustrated in Figure 6-20.

Order Line Transaction Fact
Order Date Key (FK)
Requested Ship Date Key (FK)
Product Key (FK)
Customer Sold To Key (FK)
Customer Ship To Key (FK)
Customer Bill To Key
Sales Rep Key (FK)
Deal Key (FK)
Order Indicator Key (FK)
Order Number (DD)
Order Line Number (DD)
Order Line Quantity
Gross Order Line Amount
Order Discount Line Amount
Net Order Line Amount
Allocated Freight Amount by Weight
Allocated Freight Amount by Value

Figure 6-20 Header grained facts allocated to the line fact table.

Before allocation can occur, the data stewards need to define the allocation algorithm. Perhaps the header level freight charge is allocated to the line level based on weight, or value, or is merely spread evenly across the order lines. Whatever the rule, it must be defined by the business, possibly entailing some degree of compromise or controversy, which is all the more reason that you'll want the stewards involved. If the business can't agree on a single allocation scheme, you may end up with two uniquely labeled facts: allocated freight charge based on weight for the logistics department and allocated freight charge based on value for finance.

The beauty of allocation is that all the measurements generated by a business process can now live in a single fact table, with every dimension attribute as an equal candidate for filtering or grouping any measurement. Although this is optimal, sometimes it's not achievable. The business may not be able to reach consensus on an allocation rule. We find that discrete "box oriented" businesses, like consumer goods manufacturing, often can reach agreement on allocation rules. Conversely, infrastructure and service oriented businesses, like banks and telecommunications companies, typically have a more difficult time agreeing on allocation rules.

It may be critical that the header fact precisely matches the operational value, which may prohibit allocation and its inevitable rounding errors. In this situation, the modeler has no choice but to present a separate fact table with the granularity of one row per transaction header. This fact table, illustrated in Figure 6-21, would share most of the same dimensions as the lower grained line item fact table, with the notable exception of product. In addition to storing

Order Header Transaction Fact
Order Date Key (FK)
Requested Ship Date Key (FK)
Customer Sold To Key (FK)
Customer Ship To Key (FK)
Customer Bill To Key
Sales Rep Key (FK)
Deal Key (FK)
Order Indicator Key (FK)
Order Number (DD)
Gross Order Header Amount
Order Discount Header Amount
Net Order Header Amount
Order Header Freight Amount

Figure 6-21 Header grain fact table with aggregated line facts.

facts that are naturally captured at the higher level of detail, this fact table could also store aggregated totals from the order line.

Multiple Currencies and Units of Measure

Sometimes fact measurements need to be expressed in multiple currencies or units of measure. In both cases, packaging the measurements and conversion factors in the same fact table row provides the safest guarantee that the factors will be used correctly.

In the case of currency conversion, the most common requirement is to provide the measurements in the local currency in which they were captured, as well as converted to the standardized international currency for the organization. As shown in Figure 6-22, you could store one set of measurements, along with the appropriate conversion rate fact (corresponding to the transaction

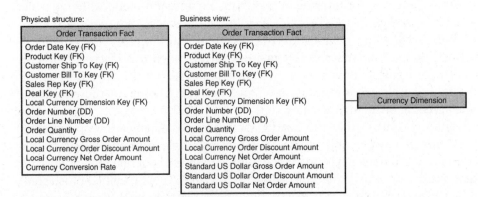

Figure 6-22 Fact table supporting multiple currencies.

date/timestamp rate, or the end of business day close rate, or whatever rate is deemed appropriate per the business rules). You could also supplement the fact table with a dimension foreign key that designates the currency associated with the local currency facts.

You can now deliver this fact table to the users and BI tools through a view that extrapolates using the conversion rate to display both sets of facts. Of course, the local currency facts are semi-additive because they can only be summed correctly when limited to a single currency; the query results would certainly be erroneous if you tried to add up facts captured in Thai bhat, Japanese yen, and euros.

Similarly, in a value chain involving several business processes monitoring the flow of products through a system or multiple measures of inventory at different points, sometimes a conflict arises in presenting the amounts. Different parties along the chain may wish to see the numbers expressed in different units of measure. For instance, manufacturing managers may wish to see the entire product flow in terms of carloads or pallets, whereas store managers may wish to see the amounts in shipping cases, retail cases, scan units (sales packs), or consumer units. Likewise, the same inventory quantity of a product may have several possible economic valuations. You may wish to express the valuation in terms of list price, original selling price, or final selling price. Finally, this situation may be exacerbated by having multiple fundamental quantity facts in each fact row.

Consider an example where you have 13 fundamental quantity facts, 5 unit-of-measure interpretations, and 4 valuation schemes. It would be a mistake to present only the 13 quantity facts in the fact table and then leave it up to the user or BI application developer to seek the correct conversion factors in remote dimension tables. It would be equally bad to present all the combinations of facts expressed in the different units of measure in the fact table because this would require 13×5 quantity facts plus 13×4 valuation facts, or 117 facts in each fact table row! The correct compromise is to build an underlying physical row with 13 quantity facts, 4 unit-of-measure conversion factors, and 4 valuation factors. You need only 4 unit-of-conversion factors rather than 5 because the base facts are already expressed in one of the units of measure. Your physical design now has 21 facts, as shown in Figure 6-23.

Sometimes designers are tempted to store the unit-of-measure conversion factors in the product dimension, however packaging these factors in the fact table reduces the pressure on the product dimension table to issue new product rows to reflect minor changes in these factors. These items, especially if they routinely evolve over time, behave much more like facts than dimension attributes.

You now deliver this fact table to the users through one or more views. The most comprehensive view could actually show all 117 combinations of units of measure and valuations, but obviously you could simplify the presentation

Physical structure:

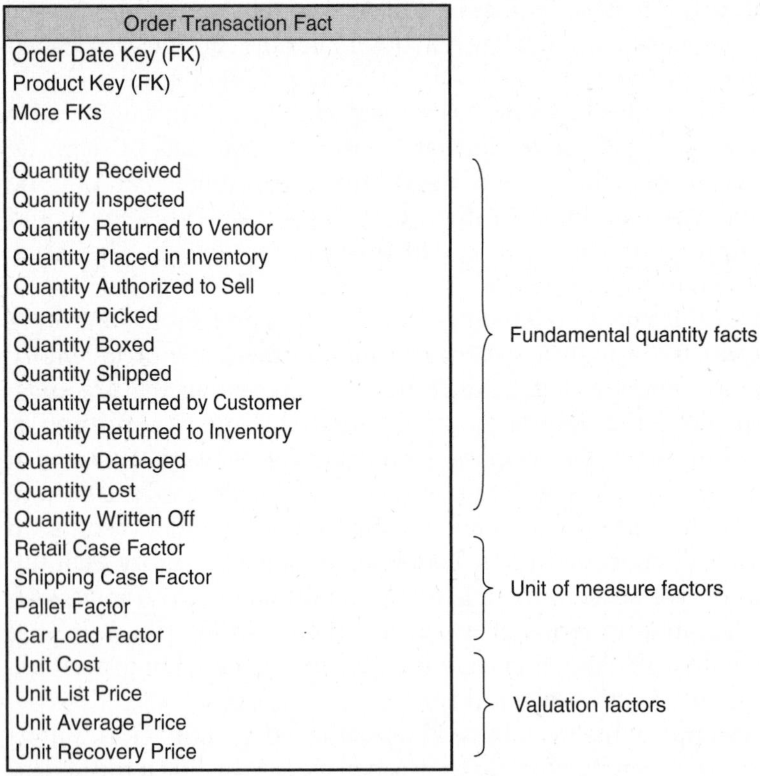

Order Transaction Fact
Order Date Key (FK)
Product Key (FK)
More FKs
Quantity Received
Quantity Inspected
Quantity Returned to Vendor
Quantity Placed in Inventory
Quantity Authorized to Sell
Quantity Picked
Quantity Boxed
Quantity Shipped
Quantity Returned by Customer
Quantity Returned to Inventory
Quantity Damaged
Quantity Lost
Quantity Written Off
Retail Case Factor
Shipping Case Factor
Pallet Factor
Car Load Factor
Unit Cost
Unit List Price
Unit Average Price
Unit Recovery Price

Fundamental quantity facts

Unit of measure factors

Valuation factors

Figure 6-23 Fact table to support multiple units of measure.

for any specific group by only displaying the units of measure and valuation factors that the group wants to see.

Factless Fact Tables

Sometimes organizations have business processes where an event occurs, but no quantifiable measurements are created or generated. These events may be very important to the business because they represent the existence of a relationship between several dimensions, despite the fact that no counts or amounts are generated when the many-to-many collision of dimensions occurs. These factless events result in *factless fact tables*.

You can imagine a factless fact table for capturing student attendance events. You load a row into the fact in Figure 6-24 whenever a student shows up for a class. The grain is one row per class attended by a student each day.

We typically include a dummy counter fact whose value is always 1. You don't even need to physically store this fact; it merely facilitates counting to ask questions such as "how many students attended a class taught by this professor today?"

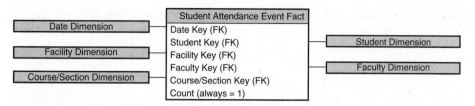

Figure 6-24 Factless fact table for student attendance events.

If the grain of the fact table was one row for each student enrollment (not attendance) in a class each day, then the attendance counter could take on a 1 value if the student attended class or zero otherwise. In this scenario, the fact table is no longer factless because the 1 or 0 valuation is a measurement.

NOTE Factless fact tables are the preferred method for recording events in a data warehouse where there is no natural numeric measurement associated with the event.

Consolidated Fact Tables

Thus far, this chapter has focused on dimensional models that are recognizable images of the operational source system supporting a single business process. In other words, if you have an orders system, you have a corresponding orders dimensional model. We recommend starting with single source dimensional models because they minimize the risk of committing to an impossible, overly ambitious implementation. Most of the risk comes from biting off too much ETL effort.

After several single source dimensional models have been implemented, it is reasonable to potentially combine them into a consolidated dimensional model. Consolidated fact tables merge measurements from multiple processes into a single fact table. Because the measurements physically sit side-by-side in a fact row, they need to be rolled up to a single common level of granularity. As shown in Figure 6-25, the consolidated actual versus forecast schema brings the measurements together for simplified variance analysis. Of course, with conformed dimensions, you could issue separate queries to a forecast fact

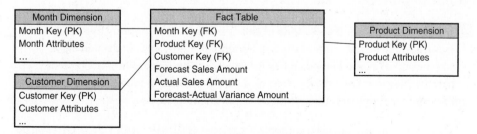

Figure 6-25 Consolidated fact table combining actual and forecast data.

table and a detailed fact table of actuals, and then combine the results on common dimension attributes; however doing this consolidation once in the ETL system rather than at query time will result in faster query response and a less complicated presentation.

Just to reiterate, we suggest consolidated fact tables be built as a complement to existing detailed schema. Because you will invariably aggregate details to reach a common granularity across several processes, it's not appropriate to begin with the consolidated fact table.

Fables and Falsehoods About Dimensional Modeling

Despite the widespread industry acceptance of dimensional modeling, fables and fictitious claims continue to circulate through our industry. These false assertions are a distraction, especially if you're trying to align a team around common best practices. We'll describe the root misunderstandings that perpetuate the misleading myths, followed by specific fables and then the accurate factual response. Hopefully, you'll understand why these fables are as unfounded as fairy tales.

Fables Caused by Focusing on Departmental Reports

The first set of fables result from misunderstandings caused by focusing on departmental reports and analyses, rather than centering the design on measurement processes. Step 1 of the four-step process is to identify the business process; nowhere do we recommend specifying the top ten report layouts or queries.

Requirements analyses that focus exclusively on reports or query templates are vulnerable to modeling data to produce a specific report, rather than capturing the key metrics and related dimensions. Obviously, it's important to consider business usage when designing dimensional models. The dimension attributes must support the BI tool's filtering and labeling requirements. Robust dimension attributes translate into nearly endless slicing-and-dicing combinations. However, don't blindly focus on a top ten list in isolation because priorities and "hot" reports will inevitably evolve over time.

> **NOTE** A caricature-like example of this "report-centric" approach is an organization that built more than one hundred dimensional models, using a combination of star schemas and OLAP cubes, to support order management analysis. They were practically creating a new dimensional model for each slightly different report request. Talk about an unsustainable approach!

Instead of concentrating on specific reports' requirements or departmental needs in a vacuum, we suggest focusing the dimensional design on the physical performance measurement process. In doing so, you can put the following fables to rest.

Fable: Dimensional models are built to address a specific business report or application. When the business needs a new report, another dimensional model is built.

Fact: Dimensional models should be built around physical measurement processes or events. A fact table row is created when a measurement occurs. The associated dimension attributes reflect contextual characteristics and hierarchies. If the business identifies a new report based on the same measurement process, there's absolutely no need to build a new schema. Measurement processes are relatively stable in most organizations; the analytic processes performed against these key metrics are much more fluid.

Fable: Dimensional models are departmental solutions. When a different department needs access to the data, a new dimensional model is built and labeled with the department's vocabulary, necessitating multiple extracts from the same source data repeatedly.

Fact: Dimensional models should not be departmentally bound. A fact table representing a fundamental measurement process need have only one physical instance that's shared across business functions or departments. There is no reason to create multiple extracts from the same source. Metrics resulting from the invoicing process, for example, are made available in a single dimensional model for access across the organization; there's no reason to replicate invoice performance metrics in separate departmental solutions for finance, marketing, and sales. Even if these departmental solutions were sourced from the same repository, they likely use similar, but slightly different naming conventions, definitions, and business rules, defeating the promise of a single version of the truth. The departmental approach is highly vulnerable to inconsistent, non-integrated point solutions.

Fable: You can't incorporate new data sources without rebuilding the original star schema or creating separate fact tables.

Fact: If the new data source is another capture system for an existing measurement process in the presentation server, the new data can be gracefully combined with the original data without altering any existing reporting applications, presuming the granularity is the same. If the new data source is at a different grain representing a new measurement process, a new fact table must be created. This has nothing to do with dimensional modeling; any data representation would create a new entity when a new table with different keys is introduced.

Fable: With dimensional modeling, the fact table is forced to a single grain, which is inflexible.

Fact: Having the discipline to create fact tables with a single level of detail assures that measurements aren't inappropriately double counted. A table with mixed-grain facts can only be queried by a custom application knowledgeable about the varying levels of detail, effectively ruling out ad hoc exploration. If measurements naturally exist at different grains, then the most foolproof design establishes a fact table for each level of detail. Far from being inflexible, this approach protects existing applications from breaking or recoding as changes occur.

Fables Caused by Premature Summarization

The next set of fables result from confusion about the appropriate level of detail in a dimensional model. Some people claim that dimensional models are intended for managerial, strategic analysis and therefore should be populated with summarized data, not operational details. We strongly disagree. Dimensional models should be populated with atomic data so business users can ask very precise questions. Even if users don't care about the details of a single transaction, their questions involve summarizing the details in unpredictable ways. Database administrators may pre-aggregate some information to avoid on-the-fly summarization as we describe in Chapter 8. However, these aggregates are performance-tuning complements to the atomic level, not replacements. If you create dimensional models with atomic details, the following fables are non-issues.

Fable: Dimensional models presuppose the business question and are therefore inflexible. When the requirements change, the model must be modified.

Fact: When you pre-summarize information, you've presupposed the business question. However, dimensional models with atomic data are independent of the business question because users can roll up or drill down ad infinitum. They are able to answer new, previously unspecified questions without database changes.

Fable: Dimensional models are only appropriate when there is a predictable pattern of usage. Dimensional models aren't appropriate for exploratory queries.

Fact: Both normalized and dimensional models contain the same information and data relationships; both are capable of answering exactly the same questions, albeit with varying difficulty. Dimensional models naturally represent the "physics" of a measurement event; fact tables contain the measurements and the dimension tables contain the context. A single dimensional model based on the most atomic data is capable of answering all possible questions against that data.

Fable: Dimensional models are not scalable. If detailed data is stored in a dimensional model, performance will be degraded.

Fact: Dimensional star schemas are extremely scalable. It isn't unusual for modern fact tables to have billions of rows corresponding to the billions of measurement transactions captured. Dimension tables with millions of rows are common. Dimensional models should contain as much history as required to address the business requirements. There's nothing about dimensional modeling that prohibits the storage of substantial history.

Fable: Dimensional models are not extensible and are unable to address future needs of the data warehouse.

Fact: Dimensional models that express data at the lowest level of detail deliver maximum flexibility and extensibility. Users can summarize atomic data any which way. Likewise, atomic data can be extended with additional attributes, measures or dimensions without disrupting existing reports and queries.

Fable: A dimensional model cannot support complex data. It eliminates many-to-many relationships between entities, allowing only many-to-one relationships. A dimensional model can be created from a normalized model; however, a normalized model could not be created from a dimensional model.

Fact: The logical content of dimensional models and normalized models are identical. Every data relationship expressed in one model can be accurately expressed in the other model. Dimension tables express many-to-one relationships, whereas fact tables represent many-to-many relationships.

Fables Caused by Overvaluing Normalization

Some people believe normalization solves the data integration challenge. Normalizing data contributes nothing to integration, except forcing data analysts to confront the inconsistencies across data sources.

Data integration is a process apart from any specific modeling approach. It requires identifying incompatible labels and measures used by the organization, then reaching consensus to establish and administer common labels and measures enterprise wide. In dimensional modeling, these labels and measures reside in conformed dimensions and conformed facts, respectively. As represented in the bus architecture, conformed dimensions are the integration "glue" across measurement business processes. Conformed dimensions are typically built and maintained as centralized persistent master data in the ETL system, then reused across dimensional models to enable data integration and ensure semantic consistency.

Fable: Dimensional modeling concepts like conformed dimensions put an undue burden on the ETL effort.

Fact: Data integration depends on standardized labels, values, and definitions. It's hard work both to reach organizational consensus and then implement the corresponding ETL system rules, but you can't dodge the effort, regardless of whether you're dealing with a normalized or dimensional model.

Fable: Dimensional modeling isn't appropriate when there are more than two unique source systems due to the complexities of integrating data from multiple sources.

Fact: The challenges of data integration have nothing to do with the modeling approach. Paradoxically, dimensional modeling and the bus architecture reveal the labels and measures of a business so clearly that an organization has no choice but to address the integration problem directly.

Fable: Changes to dimension attributes are only an issue for dimensional models.

Fact: Every data warehouse must deal with time variance. When the characteristic of an entity like a customer or product changes, you need a systematic approach for recording the change. Dimensional modeling uses standard techniques known as slowly changing dimensions. When normalized models step up to the issue of time variance, they typically add timestamps to the entities. These timestamps serve to capture every entity change, just like a slowly changing dimension type 2, but without using a surrogate key for each new row the query interface must issue a double-barreled join that constrains both the natural key and timestamp between every pair of joined tables, putting an unnecessary, unfriendly burden on every BI reporting application or query.

Fable: Multiple data marts can't be integrated. They're built bottoms up, catering to the needs of an individual department, not the needs of an enterprise. Chaos is the inevitable outcome.

Fact: It is definitely a struggle to integrate dimensional models built as departmental, stand-alone solutions that haven't been architected with conformed dimensions. That's precisely why we advise against this approach! Chaos won't result if you use the enterprise bus architecture's framework of conformed dimensions, then tackle incremental development based on business measurement processes. Organizational and cultural obstacles are inevitable as consistent definitions, business rules, and practices are adopted across the enterprise.

Conclusion

In this chapter we defined what dimensional modeling is and why it works. We discussed the need for standardized conformed dimensions to tie together all the dimensional models represented in the enterprise data warehouse bus matrix. Finally, we reviewed fundamental dimensional modeling design techniques. With this "what and why" grounding, you're now ready for Chapter 7, where we discuss how the dimensional modeling process and its key activities unfold.

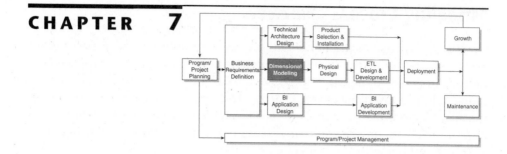

CHAPTER 7

Designing the Dimensional Model

In Chapter 6 we discussed the dimensional modeling approach and outlined common dimensional design patterns. Now it's time to turn our attention to a process for building dimensional models.

We begin with a practical discussion of initial preparation activities that involve organizing the modeling team, reviewing the business requirements, determining naming conventions, setting up the modeling and data research environment, and scheduling facilities. The modeling process itself actually starts during the business requirements activity when the preliminary data warehouse bus matrix is developed. Based on the data architecture established by the bus matrix, the design team engages in initial design sessions that result in a high level model diagram. This is followed by an iterative detailed model development phase, then review and validation.

This chapter should be read by all team members, particularly the data modeler, who leads the effort. The project manager needs to understand the process to ensure that this critical piece of the project is on track. The business analyst must be comfortable with the dimensional modeling activities to help the data modeler translate the business requirements into the database design. Other team members need a basic familiarity with this topic to support the development of the dimensional model and to be prepared to carry the model forward into development of both the ETL system and business intelligence applications.

Modeling Process Overview

Creating a dimensional model is a highly iterative and dynamic process. After a few preparation steps, the design effort begins with an initial graphical model derived from the bus matrix. It identifies the scope of the design and clarifies the grain of the proposed fact tables. The initial design sessions should also identify the major dimensions applicable to each fact table, a proposed list of dimension attributes and fact metrics, and any issues requiring additional investigation.

After completing the high level model, the design team begins to assemble the model table by table and drills down into the definitions, sources, relationships, data quality concerns, and required transformations. The last phase of the modeling process involves reviewing and validating the model with interested parties, especially business representatives. The primary goals of this activity are to create a model that meets the business requirements, verify that data is available to populate the model, and provide the ETL team with a solid starting target.

Dimensional models unfold through a series of design sessions with each pass resulting in a more detailed and robust design that's been repeatedly tested against your understanding of the business needs. The process is complete when the model clearly meets the business requirements. A typical design usually requires three to four weeks for a single business process dimensional model, but the time required will vary depending on the complexity of the business process, opportunity to leverage preexisting conformed dimensions, availability of knowledgeable participants, existence of well documented detailed business requirements, and the difficulty of reaching organizational consensus.

Figure 7-1 shows the dimensional modeling process flow; the modeling process runs down the left side with the deliverables from each task on the right. The key inputs to the dimensional modeling process are the high level bus matrix and the detailed business requirements gathered during the requirements phase. The key deliverables of the modeling process are the detailed bus matrix, high level dimensional model, and detailed dimension and fact table designs.

Although the graphic portrays a linear progression, you should understand that the process is quite iterative. You will make many passes through the dimensional model starting at a high level and drilling into each table and each column, filling in blanks, adding more detail, and changing the design based on new information.

NOTE If your organization is new to dimensional modeling, consider bringing in expert assistance. An experienced dimensional modeler with strong facilitation skills can help you avoid false starts, dead end paths, and endless days spinning on key decision points. This can save weeks of effort and result in a stronger design with crisp deliverables. Insist that the consultant facilitate the modeling process with your team rather than disappearing for a few weeks and returning with a completed design. This will ensure that your entire team has participated in the design process and understands the design tradeoffs. It also leverages the learning opportunity so the team can carry the model forward.

Get Organized

Before beginning to model, it is important to take some time to prepare. This will position the design team for success and assure an effective and efficient design process. Preparation for the dimensional modeling process includes identifying the roles and participants required, reviewing the business requirements documentation, setting up the modeling environment, determining naming conventions, and obtaining appropriate facilities and supplies.

Identify Design Participants

The best dimensional models result from a collaborative team effort. No single individual is likely to have the detailed knowledge of the business

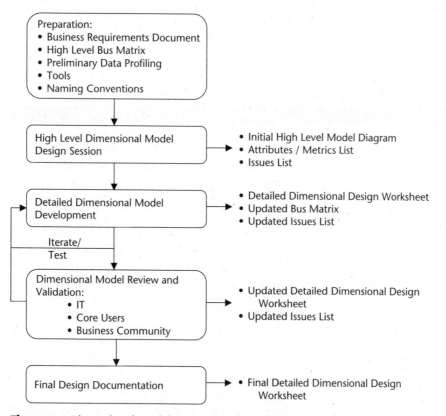

Figure 7-1 Dimensional modeling process flow diagram.

requirements and the idiosyncrasies of the source systems to effectively create the model themselves. Table 7-1 identifies the roles involved in the modeling process. Usually a core modeling team of two or three people does most of the detailed work with help from the extended team. The core modeling team is led by a data modeler with strong dimensional modeling skills and excellent facilitation skills; experience with the source systems is a plus. The core team should also include a business analyst who brings a solid understanding of the business requirements and the types of analysis to be supported, along with an appreciation for making data more useful and accessible. Ideally, the core team will include at least one representative from the ETL team with extensive source systems development experience and an interest in learning. The data modeler has overall responsibility for creating the dimensional model.

We recommend including one or more analytic business users, often called *power users*, as part of the core modeling team. These power users add significant insight, helping speed the design process and improving the richness and completeness of the end result. These are the users who have figured out how to get data out of the source systems and turn it into information. They typically know how to build their own queries, sometimes even creating their own private databases. They are particularly valuable to the modeling process because they understand the source systems from a business point of view, and they've already identified and created the business rules needed to

Table 7-1 Major Participants in the Dimensional Modeling Process

PARTICIPANT	PURPOSE/ROLE IN MODELING PROCESS
Data modeler	Primary design responsibility, facilitator
Power user	Business requirements, source expert, business definitions
Business analyst	Business analysis and source expert, business definitions
Data steward	Drive agreement on enterprise names, definitions, and rules
Source system developers	Source experts, business rules
DBA	Design guidance, early learning
ETL architect and developer	Early learning
BI architect and developer	BI application requirements, early learning
Business driver or governance steering committee	Naming and business definition issue resolution, model validation

convert the data from its form in the source system to something that can be used to support the decision making process.

The core modeling team works closely with source system developers to understand the contents, meaning, business rules, timing, and other intricacies of the source systems that will populate the dimensional model. If you're lucky, the people who actually built or originally designed the source systems are still around. For any given dimensional model, there are usually several source system people you need to pull into the modeling process. There might be a DBA, a developer, and someone who works with the data input process. Each of these folks does things to the data that the other two don't know about. Get to know these folks; develop good relationships with them. Help them understand how the DW/BI system will make their lives better. You will need their full cooperation.

The DBA implementing the physical databases and the ETL architect and developer should also be included in the modeling process. Being actively engaged in the design process will help these individuals better understand the business reasons behind the model and facilitate their buy-in to the final design. Often the DBA comes from a transaction system background and may not understand the rationale for dimensional modeling. The DBA may naturally want to model the data using more familiar design rules and apply third normal form design concepts to normalize the dimensions, physically defeating your dimensional design. ETL designers often have a similar tendency. Without a solid appreciation of the business requirements and justification for the dimensional design, the ETL designer will want to streamline the ETL process by shifting responsibility for calculations to the BI tool, skipping a description lookup step, or using other time saving shortcuts. Though these changes may save ETL development time, the tradeoff may be an increase in effort or decrease in query performance for hundreds of business users compensating and doing the same work countless times in a less efficient manner.

NOTE Expect to repeatedly assign extra computation or data conditioning steps into the ETL process as opposed to burdening the BI application.

Before jumping into the modeling process, take time to consider the ongoing management and stewardship implications of the DW/BI environment. If your organization has an active *data stewardship* initiative, it is time to tap into that function. If there is no stewardship program, it's time to initiate the process. An enterprise DW/BI effort committed to dimensional modeling as an implementation approach must also be committed to a conformed dimension strategy to assure consistency across multiple business processes. An active data stewardship program can help an organization achieve its conformed dimension strategy. Agreeing on conformed dimensions in a large enterprise can be a difficult challenge. The difficulty is usually less a technical challenge and more an organizational communication challenge. Various groups across the enterprise are often committed to their own proprietary business rules and definitions. Data stewards must work closely with all of the interested groups to develop common business rules and definitions, and then cajole the various parts of the organization into embracing the common rules and definitions to develop enterprise consensus. Over the years, some have criticized the concept of conformed dimensions as being "too hard." Yes, it's difficult to get people in different corners of the business to agree on common attribute names, definitions, and values, but that's the crux of unified, integrated data. If everyone demands their own labels and business rules, then there's no chance of delivering the single version of the truth promised by DW/BI systems. Remember, however, that you have a big safety valve that takes pressure off of the enterprise data conforming effort. The separate business units do not have to give up their private attributes and labels, rather they only need to reach agreement with the other business units on an enterprise set of conformed attributes and facts that will be the basis for data integration. If absolutely necessary, this enterprise set can be completely new.

In addition to the roles already discussed, in Chapter 9 we describe two specific ETL team responsibilities required for the ongoing management of the data warehouse environment: the dimension manager and fact provider. The individuals who own these responsibilities are not critical to creating the business process dimensional model. However, they would benefit greatly by participating in the design process. The *dimension manager* is responsible for defining, building, and publishing one or more conformed dimensions. There can be more than one dimension manager in larger organizations; however, a given dimension is the responsibility of a single dimension manager. Dimension managers obviously work closely with the data stewards. Meanwhile, the *fact provider* is responsible for designing, building, and publishing a specific fact table after receiving the dimension handoff from the dimension managers.

Although involving more people in the design process increases the risk of slowing down the process, the improved richness and completeness of the design justifies the additional overhead.

Revisit the Requirements

Before the modeling process can begin, the modeling team must familiarize itself with the business requirements. The first step is to carefully review the detailed requirements documentation. The modeling team must appreciate the challenges and opportunities the business users face as they seek to leverage data and perform analysis in response to business problems. It's the modeling team's responsibility to translate the business requirements into a flexible dimensional model capable of supporting a broad range of analysis, not just specific reports. This can be challenging. Hopefully you've been able to recruit one or two power business users as core modeling team members to help provide this expertise, in addition to the business analyst.

In Chapter 3, we described the detailed project level business requirements document that focuses on the high priority business process and related analyses. It describes the questions and problems management and business analysts are most interested in resolving. The requirements document includes a list of proposed data elements, sample questions, and desired reports that would help answer the questions. All of these are critical inputs to defining the dimensional model. Ultimately, our final dimensional model must be able to easily support these requirements.

The temptation is to move directly into design, skipping the business requirements review. Often the data modeler is an employee of significant longevity with the organization. He may feel that he clearly understands the business and its needs. Please, resist the temptation and do not to skip the business requirements review. It is all too comfortable to develop a source-driven rather than a business-driven data model. An experienced dimensional modeler can easily build a reasonable dimensional model based on the source system data structures. However, this model will inevitably fall short of meeting the business needs in many small but substantive ways. These little shortcomings add up to a weak dimensional model. What's missed is an understanding of how the business derives value from the existing data. Often, the business crafts new categorizations of data based on a combination of attributes and statuses. Uncovering and including these hidden business rules in your dimensional models is the secret sauce for delivering an environment that exceeds, rather than merely meets, business users' expectations.

NOTE You must understand the business requirements in detail before you dive into the task of designing the dimensional model.

Use Modeling Tools

Before jumping into the modeling process, it's helpful to have a few tools in place. Using a spreadsheet as the initial modeling tool is most effective because it allows you to quickly and easily make changes as you iterate through the modeling process. Initially, use the simple spreadsheet model shown in Figure 7-2, which is merely a subset of the more detailed dimensional design worksheet shown in Figure 7-6. As we discuss later, Figure 7-6 captures the key elements of the logical model, plus many of the physical attributes. It also gives you a place to begin capturing ETL information, such as source system table and column(s) and a brief description of the extract and transformation rules. Finally, it includes an initial set of business metadata in the form of names, descriptions, sample values, and comments.

Be sure to extend the attributes and metrics list to include other columns that may be useful in your environment, like physical name (if it will be different

Promotion

Attribute Name	Description	Alternate Names	Sample Values
Special Offer ID	Source system key		
Special Offer Name	Name / description of the Special Offer	Promotion name, Special offer description	Volume Discount 11 to 14; Fall Discount 2006
Discount Percent	Percent item is discounted		
Special Offer Type	Description of the type of promotion, special offer or discount.	Promotion Type	Volume Discount; Discontinued Product
Special Offer Category	Channel to which the Promotion applies	Promotion Category	Reseller; Customer
Start Date	First day the promotion is available		6/15/2008
End Date	Last day the promotion is available		12/31/2008
Minimum Quantity	Minimum quantity required to qualify for the promotion		0
Maximum Quantity	Maximum quantity allowed under the promotion		NULL

Attributes Not Elsewhere Classified

Attribute Name	Description	Alternate Names	Sample Values
SalesReasonID	Sales reason ID from source system		
Sales Reason	Reason the customer bought the product, as reported by the customer (Internet only)		Demo Event; On Promotion; Price; Review; Sponsorship
Sales Reason Type	Grouping for Sales Reason		Marketing; Promotion; Other
Channel	Channel through which the item was sold		Customer; Reseller; Field Sales

Figure 7-2 Example attribute and metrics list.

from the logical), a short description that might easily fit into a tooltip, or a long description that fully captures the definition of the column or table.

Once you reach the later stages of the modeling process and the model begins to firm up, you should convert to whatever modeling tool is used in your organization. Most of the popular modeling tools allow you to lay out the logical model and capture physical and logical names, descriptions, and relationships. Many tools are dimensionally aware with functions to support the creation of a dimensional model. For example, some distinguish between a fact and dimension table, handle role-playing dimensions, and create multiple business process "layers" that correspond to the rows in the bus matrix. They also capture information in their metadata stores and generally have a way to export or exchange that metadata with other systems or a centralized metadata catalog. Once the detailed design is complete, the modeling tools can help the DBA forward engineer the model into the database, including creating the tables, indexes, partitions, views, and other physical elements of the database.

Establish Naming Conventions

The issue of naming conventions will inevitably arise during the creation of the dimensional data model. It's important that the labels you apply to the data are descriptive and consistent in portraying a solid business orientation. Remember, table and column names are key elements of the DW/BI system's user interface, both when users navigate the data model and in the BI applications. Think about what each column name communicates in a report. A column name like "Description" may be perfectly clear in the context of a data model, but communicates nothing in the context of a report.

Part of the process of designing a dimensional model is agreeing on common definitions and common labels. Naming is complex because different business groups have different meanings for the same name, like *revenue,* and different names with the same meaning, like *sales.* The challenge arises because most people are reluctant to change and unwilling to give up the familiar and learn a new way. Spending time on naming conventions is one of those tiresome tasks that seem to have little payback, but is definitely worth it in the long run.

Fortunately, establishing your naming conventions doesn't have to be time consuming. Most large organizations have a function such as data management or data administration that owns responsibility for naming conventions. Leverage their work and, if possible, use the existing naming conventions that your organization has already established. Find the documentation and implement any changes necessary to make them work for the DW/BI system; sometimes existing naming conventions need to be extended to support more user-friendly table and column names.

If your organization doesn't have a set of naming conventions you can adapt to the DW/BI model, you will need to establish them as you develop the dimensional model. To begin, you need to develop an initial strategy for your naming conventions. Even if your organization hasn't established formal naming standards, it may be helpful to study the table and column names in existing systems.

A common approach is to use a column name standard with three parts:

PrimeWord_ZeroOrMoreQualifiers_ClassWord

The prime word is a categorization word that often corresponds to the entity the column is from; in some cases, qualifiers may not be necessary. For example, the field in the sales fact table that represents the amount sold might be sales_dollar_amount.

Next, the core modeling team, in conjunction with the data stewards, should draft an initial set of names and the rationale. During the early design review sessions, set aside time to ensure the names make sense. In addition, spend time with key stakeholders such as the core business users and any senior managers who might have an opinion. If their preferred name for a column is different from your suggested name, ask them to explain what the term means to them. Look for missing qualifiers and class words to clarify the meaning. For example, an analyst might be interested in sales performance, but it turns out that the sales number is really sales_commissionable_amount, which is different from sales_gross_amount or sales_net_amount. The resulting name set should be used to update the data model. Keep track of the alternative names for each field and the reasons people offered for their preferred choices. This will be helpful in explaining any derivations or deviations in the final name set.

During the final model review sessions with key stakeholders, seek final agreement on the naming conventions. Generally, there will have been enough model review iterations and naming discussions so that most issues have already been resolved and the remaining issues are reasonably well understood. The goal is to reach consensus. Often this means someone has to accept the will of the majority and let go of their favorite name for a given column. It is surprising how emotional this can be; people feel pretty strongly about getting the names "right."

Once you have reached agreement on the final name set, document it carefully and work it into the final data model.

Provide for Source Data Research and Profiling

An important preparation task is identifying the resources available to the core modeling team during the design process to improve their understanding of the source data. There are several useful sources for detailed information about an organization's data, including the source system itself, data experts, existing query and reporting systems, and data profiling tools. Be sure to identify these resources prior to beginning the design effort.

Throughout the modeling process, the modeler needs to develop an ever increasing understanding of the source data to learn about its structure, content, relationships, and derivation rules. You need to verify that the data exists, that it is in a usable state, or at least its flaws can be managed, and that you understand what it will take to convert it into the dimensional model.

Data profiling uses query and reporting tools to explore the content and relationships in the system under investigation. Data profiling can be as simple as writing some SQL statements or as sophisticated as a detailed data profiling study. There are tools to make the data profiling task much easier and probably more complete. The major ETL tool vendors include data profiling capabilities in their products; in addition, there are stand-alone profiling tool vendors that provide complex data analysis capabilities well beyond the realm of simple queries.

Obtain Facilities and Supplies

Often overlooked, yet important preparation tasks are the scheduling of appropriate facilities and obtaining a stash of required supplies. Over a several week period, the design team will be scheduling formal design sessions several times each day surrounded by impromptu meetings and discussions. It is best to set aside a dedicated conference room for the duration of the design effort — no easy task in most organizations where meeting room facilities are always in short supply. The meeting room should have enough space to comfortably hold the modeling participants, as well as a couple of flip chart stands. While you're dreaming, big floor-to-ceiling whiteboards on all four walls would be nice, too!

In addition to a meeting facility, the team will need basic supplies, such as flip chart paper. The self-stick variety is very helpful; otherwise a roll of masking tape will suffice for wallpapering the walls with your paper designs. Also, it would be nice if you could bust the budget for a box of new markers. (It's amazing that old, dried up markers are never thrown away; they just find their way to any conference room used by the dimensional designers.) A laptop projector is often useful during the design sessions and is required for the design reviews.

Recall the Four-Step Modeling Process

As briefly described in Chapter 6, we use a four-step process for designing dimensional data models. The process does not occur during a single design session; rather it is the overall strategy that provides context to a series of design sessions over several weeks. Before we discuss the specific design activities, it's important to understand the high level approach. The bus matrix drafted during the requirements gathering identifies the enterprise's business processes and their associated dimensions; this is critical input to the four-step process.

Step 1 – Choose the Business Process

The first step is to choose the business process to be modeled. This choice should already have been made by the business during the prioritization activity discussed in Chapter 3. This business decision normally occurs after the high level business requirements have been gathered. Selecting the initial business process is often no more difficult than picking a row on the bus matrix.

NOTE A good test of whether you have accurately identified a business process is to move to Step 2 and attempt to declare the grain of the fact table for the most detailed data captured by a business process. If you can succinctly state the grain of the fact table for the proposed business process, you are in good shape. However, if you have trouble determining the grain of the fact table or if there is any confusion regarding the level of detail of a single row in a fact table, you are likely mixing more than a single business process. You need to step back and look carefully for additional business processes that may be involved.

Business processes are the fundamental building block of the dimensional data warehouse. We suggest you build your data warehouse iteratively, one business process at a time. Each business process will result in at least one fact table and sometimes a set of related fact tables. Ideally, the core data captured by the initial business process you choose will come from a single source system or module.

Step 2 – Declare the Grain

The second step in creating the high level dimensional model is to declare the grain, or the level of detail in the fact table for the selected business process. Declaring the grain means saying *exactly* what a fact table measurement represents. Example declarations of the grain include:

- An individual line item on a retail sales ticket as measured by a scanner device
- An individual transaction against an insurance policy
- A line item on a bill received from a doctor
- An airline boarding pass
- An inventory measurement taken every week for every product in every store.

Notice that these grain declarations are expressed in business terms. Perhaps you were expecting the grain to be a traditional declaration of the fact table's primary key. Although the grain ultimately is equivalent to the primary key, it's a mistake to list a set of dimensions and then assume that this list is the grain declaration. In a properly executed dimensional design, the grain is first anchored to a clear business measure event. Then, the dimensions that implement that grain become obvious. Every design decision made in Steps 3 and 4 depends on correctly visualizing the grain.

CAUTION The most common design error is not declaring the grain of the fact table at the beginning of the design process. If the grain isn't clearly defined, the whole design rests on quicksand. Discussions about candidate dimensions go around in circles and rogue facts sneak into the design.

Choosing the grain is a combination of what is needed to meet the business requirements and what is possible based on the data collected by the source system. Every fact table design must be rooted in the realities of available physical data sources. In some situations, the business users want data at a lower level of detail than that captured by the source system. In other cases, tremendously more data is available than is required by the business requirements. We strongly recommend starting with the goal of designing the fact tables at the lowest level of detail available, that is, at the most atomic level possible. Building fact tables at the most detailed level possible is one of the cornerstones of dimensional modeling. Atomic data is the most expressive, most dimensional, and most flexible. It is always possible to sum the atomic data to higher levels of summary, but it is impossible to drill down from the summary level if the detailed data is not available.

NOTE While we stress the benefits of atomic data, we are also realists. Atomic data for some processes in some industries represents extreme data volumes; we understand that a less detailed approach may be warranted in isolated cases.

Despite the design team having carefully considered and declared the grain of the fact table, it is reasonable for the design team to change their minds about the grain at some point in the design process. For instance, if the grain was declared to be the daily inventory level of individual stock items in a distribution center, the design team might decide to instead track lot numbers that roll up to stock items because they discovered that the legacy systems were correctly tracking lot numbers. Adding the extra detail of lot numbers might have a significant effect on the choice of dimensions and facts in Steps 3 and 4.

NOTE At any point during the design process, the design team must be able to clearly articulate the grain of the target fact table.

Step 3 – Identify the Dimensions

The third step is to determine the dimensions applicable to the fact table at the stated level of granularity. Most of the major dimensions will fall out naturally once you've determined the grain. One of the powerful effects of a clear fact table grain declaration is that you can very precisely visualize the dimensionality of the fact table. All of the dimensions in the bus matrix should be tested against the grain to see if they fit. Any dimension that takes on a single value in the presence of the grain is a viable candidate.

Sometimes the fact table grain is stated in terms of primary dimensions. "Daily inventory levels of individual stock items in a distribution center" clearly specifies the date, stock item, and the distribution center dimensions. Other dimensions can quickly be tested against the grain to see if they make sense.

The grain declaration lets you think creatively about adding dimensions to a fact table that may not obviously exist in the source data. In retail sales data, marketplace causal factors like promotions and competitive effects may be very important to understanding the data, but this information may not exist in a literal sense in the source system. The grain definition "an individual line item on a retail sales ticket as measured by a scanner device" tells you that you can indeed add a causal "store condition" dimension to the fact table as long as the store condition descriptions vary appropriately by time, product, and store location. Similarly, a weather dimension can be added to the fact table design using the same logic.

NOTE The primary key of the fact table is almost never declared as the complete set of dimension foreign keys.

It is during this step that real world complexities begin to surface in the modeling process. What originally seemed to be a single dimension may end up being two or three dimensions. Often the design team has strong pre-conceived notions about how the data needs to be modeled based on how it's represented in the transaction system. These notions become difficult to change because the source system and all its complexities comprise the only historical window people have had on the data. In banking, for example, the account is a central organizing concept. In the source system, the account is actually a high level entity that contains several other business objects or dimensions. Once you know the account, you know the product, like checking or savings. Once you know the account, you know the customer because the account carries its own customer name and address. Once you know the account, you also know the branch because the account number includes a branch indicator. Yet in the final design, product, customer, and branch are typically their own dimensions. Teasing out these hidden dimensions can be a challenge because they force people to rethink their understanding of the data and its purpose.

Choosing the dimensions may also cause you to rethink the grain declaration. If a proposed dimension doesn't match the grain of the fact table, either the dimension must be left out, the grain of the fact table changed, or a multi-valued design solution needs to be considered. Identification of a useful dimension that participates in the target business process may force the grain down to a lower level of detail. For example, a typical call detail record for a phone company usually includes the originating phone number and the called phone number. A cellular phone company may want to include the cell tower IDs connected to the originating and receiving phones. Because this could change many times during the phone call, what was one call record now becomes several. Adding the tower IDs forces the grain down to a lower level of detail and adds many more rows to the fact table.

Scrutinize the dimensions to make sure they make sense. Consider the impacts on usability and performance of splitting a large dimension into several dimensions or combining dimensions. Look for hidden foreign key relationships and normalized one-to-many relationship hierarchies. Ask hard questions about the assumptions behind each dimension — is it this way because it represents the true nature of the business process, or because it reflects the specific idiosyncrasies of the source system?

Step 4 – Identify the Facts

The final step in the modeling process is to identify the facts or measures from the business process. Declaring the fact table grain establishes the foundation for determining the appropriate dimensions. But declaring the grain also crystallizes the discussion about the measured numeric facts. Simply put, the facts must be true to the grain. Resist the urge to add facts that do not match the fact table grain because they usually introduce complexities and errors in the BI applications.

For many transaction-oriented business processes, there are only a few fundamental facts, like quantity and amount. There are many combinations and calculations derived from these fundamental facts that are used to monitor the business. These calculated measures are important, but are normally not part of the atomic fact table itself. At this early point in the design, you're working to identify the fundamental facts. However, keep track of all the computed facts you come up with as you'll need them soon.

Design the Dimensional Model

As with any data modeling effort, the development of the dimensional model is an iterative process. You will work back and forth between business user requirements and selected source file details to further refine the model. Always be willing to change the model as you learn more. You may identify another dimension or discover that two dimensions are really just one. Adjustments to the grain can also occur.

The process of building dimensional models typically moves through three phases, as illustrated in Figure 7-1. The first is a high level design session that defines the scope of the business process dimensional model. The second phase is detailed model development that involves filling in the attributes and metrics table by table and resolving any issues or uncertainties. The third phase is a series of model reviews, redesign, and validation steps, resulting in the final design documentation.

The entire process typically takes three to four weeks for a single business process, such as sales orders, or a couple of tightly related business processes such as health care claims, which include professional, facility, and drug claims in a set of distinct but closely aligned fact tables. More complex designs involving unrelated fact tables and numerous dimension tables will take longer, which is one reason we don't recommend them as a starting point.

We suggest the core design team schedule a series of design sessions during the model development period. Rather than trying to schedule full day design sessions, it's more beneficial to schedule a morning and afternoon session each day of two to three hour duration for three or four days each week. This approach recognizes that the design team members have other responsibilities and allows them to try to keep up in the hours before, after, and between design sessions. The unscheduled time also provides ample opportunities for the design team members to perform source data research, as well as allows time for the data modeler to iterate through the design documentation, keeping it fresh for each session.

Build the High Level Dimensional Model

The initial task in the design session is to create a high level dimensional model diagram for the target business process. Creating the first draft is straightforward because you start with the bus matrix to kickstart the design. An experienced data warehouse designer could develop the initial high level dimensional model and then present it to the design team for review. Though this is certainly possible, we strongly recommend against it because this approach does not allow the entire design team to observe and participate in the process nor will they learn how to develop a model themselves. Likewise, they will not appreciate the thought process behind the design and inevitable tradeoffs that were made. It is important to keep in mind the dual objective of most DW/BI project tasks: Get the work done and teach the team to become self-sufficient. You'll meet both goals if you work as a team to develop the model.

Conduct the Initial Design Session

The initial design session(s) should bring together the core modeling team, along with any other identified extended team members or interested participants from the source system and ETL team. The focus of this initial session is two-fold. The first is to bring the design team together for the first time to establish a common understanding of the project goals and design process and to establish an esprit de corps. To this end, it may be appropriate to spend much of the initial design meeting discussing the project objectives, scope, and roles and responsibilities. In most situations, a short introduction to dimensional modeling concepts is also appropriate before jumping into the design process itself. Secondly, you want to create the initial high level design. This session should be facilitated by the lead data modeler. It can take two design sessions or more to work through the initial model, so set expectations accordingly.

Your immediate goal is to create the high level dimensional model diagram which is a graphical representation of the dimension and fact tables for the business process. After this initial pass, you will make a quick second pass of the high level design to create an initial list of attributes for each dimension table and proposed metrics for each fact table.

The most effective method to develop the initial model is using flip charts. The lead modeler, acting as the facilitator, should work with the team to walk though the model capturing it on the flip charts. As you work through the model, you will wallpaper the conference room. Keep in mind that much of the initial modeling includes a great deal of brainstorming. Try to capture the ideas, but don't get bogged down. Until the high level graphical model is sketched out, it is difficult to access the design impact of what may seem like a simple request. As you work through the process, it is likely that the team will surface many issues and challenges that may derail the process. The facilitator needs to quickly identify these issues and park them on the issues list. At this point you are trying to very quickly lay out the high level design. There will be plenty of opportunities to talk through the details and issues later.

Document the High Level Model Diagram

The first draft of the design should be graphically summarized in a deliverable called the high level model diagram, shown in Figure 7-3. We often call this graphical representation the *bubble chart* for obvious reasons. This graphical model becomes the initial communications document for the design team. The high level model diagram is a data model at the entity level.

The high level model shows the specific fact and dimension tables applicable to a given business process. It should clearly label each component, state the grain of the fact table, and show all the dimensions connected to the fact table. This graphical representation serves several purposes:

- It is a handy introduction to the design when communicating to interested stakeholders about the project, its scope, and contents.

- It facilitates model discussions between the design team and business partners. It is the jumping off point for communicating the detailed design and for supporting design reviews to ensure the business requirements can be met.

- It is a useful training tool, providing an introduction to the data model that is understandable by even the most casual business users.

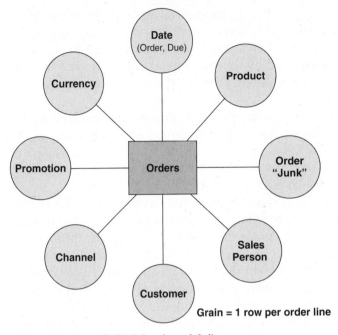

Figure 7-3 Example high level model diagram.

To aid in understanding, it is helpful to retain consistency in the high level model diagrams. Each business process's fact table should be documented on a separate page. Think about the order of the dimensions around the fact table. We recommend that you put the date dimension at the top and work your way around the fact table in order of importance of the dimension. Once you have selected an order for the dimensions, make sure all diagrams are arranged in the same sequence. As you work with the model, people will remember the location of the dimension visually. If you change the location of a dimension from one high level model diagram to the next, they will get confused (and you probably will, too).

Each business process will likely have different dimensionality. We prefer to eliminate a dimension completely when it does not apply to a specific fact table, while leaving the location of the non-applicable dimensions blank for visual continuity.

Identify the Attributes and Metrics

After the high level dimensional model is completed, it's time to focus the design team on the initial set of dimension attributes and fact metrics. Again, keeping the four-step process in mind, the facilitator begins with the dimension tables, walking the design team through each one to identify all the relevant attributes required by the business. Following the initial pass for each dimension table, you then turn to the fact tables to identify the initial set of metrics. The deliverable of this process is called the *initial attribute and metric list*. During this process, utilize a spreadsheet as shown in Figure 7-2, creating one worksheet per table in the model and filling in its attributes or metrics.

At this point, the goal is to brainstorm. Likely, the team will identify a large number of attributes coming from a wide range of sources. That's great; just be sure not to let the team get caught up on sourcing, naming, or derivation concerns at this time. Write down the ideas and make a note of any concerns and controversies on the *issues list*. This document is helpful for remembering all the little details about the model's challenges and how you decided to resolve them.

The deliverables from these initial design sessions are the high level model diagram, the attributes and metrics list by table, and the issues list. At this point, you have identified all the dimension and fact tables, along with a proposed list of attributes and metrics. From here, it's time to jump into the detailed design process.

Develop the Detailed Dimensional Model

After completing the high level design, it's time to focus on the details. From this point forward, the core team should meet on a very regular basis to define a detailed dimensional model, table by table, column by column. It's most effective if you start with the dimension tables, and then work on the fact tables. Focus these sessions on one or two tables at a time — too many and the meeting gets bogged down. We suggest starting the detailed design process with a couple of easy, straightforward dimensions; the date dimension is always a favorite starting point. This will enable the modeling team to achieve early success, develop an understanding of the modeling process, and learn to work together as a team.

The detailed dimensional modeling process is about enriching the high level model with missing information, resolving design issues, and constantly testing the business requirements against the model to confirm completeness. The design team needs to work through each table to identify the interesting and useful attributes for each dimension and appropriate metrics for each fact table. You also need to determine the source locations, definitions, and preliminary business rules that specify how these attributes and metrics are populated.

Identify the Data Sources

An important component of the modeling process is determining the most appropriate data sources to populate the target design. Detailed data analysis is a significant part of the design effort. Several levels of analysis must occur. First, you must understand the data required to support the business requirements to help select the candidate data sources. Second, you must gain an in-depth understanding of each candidate data source, typically through a data profiling process. Part of the challenge of developing the dimensional model is aligning the business requirements with the unfortunate realities of the data available in the enterprise.

From the business requirements, you can identify both formal and informal data sources. The formal sources are supported by IT and will have some level of rigor associated with the maintenance and integrity of the data. You can expect to apply a more thorough data analysis against these formal sources. Informal data comes directly from the business and is often important to the decision making process. Although the informal data is not stored in the corporate data vaults, business users will want and need to integrate the informal data with the formal data sources.

Informal data sources are often included in the data warehouse through the development of a new IT process to capture this data. This may involve simply importing data from a shadow database or developing a user entry system for this data. In both cases, the input data needs to be treated as another data source. This means the data must flow through the rigors of the ETL process to be cleaned and manipulated as you would any other data source.

NOTE Do not simply allow users to input data directly into the data warehouse.

Understand Candidate Data Sources

After you have created the high level design, but before you can progress very far in creating detailed table designs, you need to make decisions about the data source for each table. The first step in this process is to understand all of the sources that are candidates for populating your models. Some candidate data sources may be identified in the business requirements document. Others may be implied based on the business processes and dimensions identified in the bus matrix. Additional candidate sources can be identified by the IT veterans who are familiar with the data lurking in the various nooks and crannies of the organization. They also know about the history and challenges of these sources. Although it may seem very basic to pull together a list of candidate sources with descriptive information about each, this consolidated list does not exist in a single place for most organizations today. Figure 7-4 shows a sample data source definition.

Profile and Select the Data Sources

From this list of candidate data sources, the design team needs to evaluate each and determine the best source. Gather and carefully review whatever documentation is available for the source systems, such as data models, file definitions, record layouts, written documentation, and source system programs. More advanced source systems may have their own metadata repositories with all this information already integrated for your convenience.

Source	Business Owner	IS Owner	Platform	Location	Description
Gemini	Tom Owens	Alison Jones	Unix	HQ - Chicago	Distribution center inventory
Billings	Craig Bennet	Steve Dill	MVS	MF - Dallas	Customer Billings
Plant	Sylvia York	Bob Mitchell	Unix	6 Plants across country	Plant shipments
Sales Forecast	Sandra Phillips	None	Windows	HQ - Sales Dept	Spreadsheet-based consolidated sales forecast
Competitor Sales	Sandra Phillips	None	Windows	HQ - Sales Dept	Access database containing data from external supplier

Figure 7-4 Sample data source definitions.

Perusing the source system data itself usually provides a quick jolt of reality. First, what you see typically does not match the documentation you carefully gathered and reviewed. Second, it is usually more difficult to unravel than you would hope. The older the system, the more time it's had to evolve. It may be advantageous to meet with the source system owners and core business users that have worked with data from the candidate data sources.

Data profiling is the systematic analysis of the source content, from counting the bytes and checking cardinalities to the most thoughtful diagnosis of whether the data can meet the goals of the DW/BI system. Detailed data profiling should be undertaken for every data source that is to be included in this iteration of the data warehouse. Results of the data profiling activities can help in the selection of the best source systems.

Profiling analysis is divided into a series of tests, starting with individual fields and ending with whole suites of tables comprising extended databases. Individual fields are checked to see that their contents agree with their basic data definitions and domain declarations using column screens described in Chapter 9. It is especially valuable to see how many rows have null values or contents that violate the domain definition. For example, if the domain definition is "telephone number," then alphanumeric entries clearly represent a problem. Moving beyond single fields, data profiling then uses structure screens to investigate the relationships between fields in the same table. Fields implementing a key to the data table can be displayed, together with higher level many-to-one relationships that implement hierarchies. Checking for unique key values is especially helpful because the violations (duplicate instances of the key field) are either serious errors, or reflect a business rule that has not been enforced in the source data.

Relationships between tables are also checked in the data profiling step, including assumed foreign key to primary key relationships and the presence of parents without children. Finally, data profiling can check complex business rules unique to the enterprise, such as verifying that all the preconditions have been met for approval of a major funding initiative. These last tests are called *business rule screens*.

The primary outcomes of the data profiling process include the following:

- Basic "go/no go" decision on the candidate data source under consideration. Data profiling may reveal that the data from the source system simply does not contain the information to support the business requirements. In some cases, this knowledge can derail the entire project.

- Source system data quality issues that must be corrected before the project can proceed. These corrections create a huge external dependency that must be well managed for the DW/BI system to succeed.

- Data quality issues that can be corrected in the ETL processing flow after the data has been extracted from the source system. These issues should be captured so the ETL development team can design the transformation logic and exception handling mechanisms required. But don't get your hopes up. Relatively few data quality errors can be decisively corrected by the ETL system.

- Unanticipated business rules, hierarchical structures, and foreign key–primary key relationships. Understanding the data at a detailed level flushes out issues that may need to be incorporated into the dimensional data model.

From this analysis, a decision needs to be made regarding the best source system to populate the dimensional design. The selection of the primary data source is often driven by the business. Suggested criteria to consider include:

- **Data accessibility.**   If two possible feeds exist for the data, one stored in binary files maintained by a set of programs written before the youngest project team member was born and the other from a system that already reads the binary files and provides additional processing, the decision is obvious. Use the second option for your source data.

- **Longevity of the feed.**   Often data for the warehouse could be intercepted at many places throughout a processing stream. If the data coming out of step 5 is the cleanest, but that step is scheduled to be phased out in the next six months, then consider extracting from step 4. Understand the additional processing that is done in step 5 that may clean the data because you may need to include this in the ETL system.

- **Data accuracy.**   As data is passed from system to system, modifications are made. Sometimes data elements from other systems are added; sometimes existing elements are processed to create new elements and other elements are dropped. Each system performs its own function well. However, it may become difficult or impossible to recognize the original data. In some cases, the data no longer represents what the business wants for analysis. If you provide the data from these downstream systems, the users may question the accuracy. In this case, it may be better to go back to the original source to ensure accuracy. However, keep in mind that pulling data from downstream systems is not always bad.

NOTE You will want to document any sources that were considered and not selected. This documentation will be helpful months later when questions may arise about the most appropriate source of the data.

During this period, the core design team is pestering the source system experts with questions and utilizing data profiling capabilities to understand the source data and determine its fitness for inclusion in the model. Your goal is to make sure the data exists to support the dimensional model and identify all of the business rules and relationships that will impact the model.

Establish Conformed Dimensions

During these detailed design sessions, the key conformed dimensions are being defined. Because the DW/BI system is an enterprise resource, these definitions must be acceptable across the enterprise. The data stewards and business analysts are key resources that should reach out to achieve organizational consensus on table and attribute naming, descriptions, and definitions. The design team can take the lead in driving the process, but it is ultimately a business task to agree on standard business definitions and names for the design. This will take some time, but it is an investment that will provide huge returns in terms of users' understanding and willingness to accept the dimensional model. Don't be surprised if folks in the front office, like the business sponsor/driver or governance steering committee, must get involved to resolve conformed dimension definition and naming issues.

Some dimension attribute information may come with the transactional event data, but it is usually minimal and often only in the form of codes. The additional attributes that the users want and need are often fed from other systems or from a master data management (MDM) system. For some dimension tables, there can be multiple sources, especially for the customer dimension. There are often separate non-integrated tables that are used across an organization; the sales, marketing, and finance departments may each have their own customer master data. There are two difficult issues when this happens. First, the customers who are included in these sources may differ and the attributes about each customer may differ. To an extent, this is good because it provides richer information. However, the common information may not match. Assuming you have adequate time and resources, you should work to combine and integrate these sources into a single conformed dimension with clear business rules for populating it with common conformed values.

Identify Base Facts and Derived Facts

The data profiling effort will identify the counts and amounts generated by the measurement event's source system. However, fact tables are not limited to just these base facts. There may be many more metrics that the business wants to analyze that are derived from the base facts, such as year-to-date sales, percentage difference in claims paid versus prior year, and gross profit. You need to document the derived facts, as well as the base facts.

There are two kinds of derived facts. Derived facts that are additive and can be calculated entirely from the other facts in the same fact table row can be shown in a user view as if they existed in the real data. The user will never know the difference.

The second kind of derived fact is a non-additive calculation, such as a ratio or cumulative fact that is typically expressed at a different level of detail than the base facts themselves. A cumulative fact might be a year-to-date or month-to-date fact. In any case, these kinds of derived facts cannot be presented in a simple view at the DBMS level because they violate the grain of the fact table. They need to be calculated at query time by the BI tool. Most BI tools today offer a library capability to develop and maintain derived facts. This is where the official formulas and calculations are defined and then used by everyone.

Defining the full range of metrics can be a challenging political process. You may be defining facts that will become metrics in organizational incentive plan calculations, so managers tend to have strong opinions about their definitions. Also, the broader the audience, the more opinions you need to consider, and the greater the potential divergence among them. Engage the data stewards to help in this process.

Though the derived facts do not need to be completed prior to moving forward with the design of the ETL process, it is important to ensure that all the base facts are accounted for. The dimensional model is not complete until all the base facts required to support the calculation of the necessary derived facts have been identified.

When the business users have specific ideas about what they want and need, the derived facts can be identified during a dedicated design session. In some cases, the users may not have concrete ideas, but you still need to develop a starting set of derived facts. Keep in mind that the initial list of facts is not definitive — once the users get their hands on the DW/BI system, they will want more. You will need to decide who has the authority to add new derived facts to the library.

NOTE Too often, the dimensional design is completed with little thought toward the derived facts required until the team is ready to begin developing the BI applications. Unfortunately, this is late in the process. Often there are dozens and perhaps hundreds of business calculations required that need to be defined and

consensus developed. Likely, this could have been readily accomplished during the initial design process when all of the interested stakeholders were already gathered together working through the preliminary design.

If you have a small number of derived facts, simply use the dimensional design worksheet to capture information regarding the derived facts. For each derived fact, you will need to capture the base facts that are required to support the derived fact and the mathematical formula for deriving the fact. If you have a large number of derived facts, it may be beneficial to capture and document them separately in a document such as the derived fact worksheet shown in Figure 7-5.

Document the Detailed Table Designs

The attribute and metrics list discussed earlier and shown in Figure 7-2 is used as a working deliverable in the early phases of the detail design process. This tool provides an easy place to capture the basic information about each table and column. We prefer this spreadsheet tool because it allows the data modeler to quickly move or copy attributes around the model as needed, so the documentation is efficiently updated between modeling sessions. Providing freshly updated documentation for each design session helps move the process along more quickly because there is less time spent rehashing changes already agreed upon. We usually use the simplified attributes list during the early design discussions.

The key deliverable of the detailed modeling phase is the detailed design worksheet, shown in Figure 7-6. The purpose of this design documentation is to capture the details of the design for communication to other interested stakeholders including the business users, BI application developers, and very importantly, the ETL developers who will be tasked with populating the design. The final dimensional design worksheet is the first step toward creating the source-to-target mapping document. The physical design team will further flesh out the mapping. Once the model is stable, it is appropriate to move the model from the spreadsheet tool into your organization's data modeling tool of choice.

Each dimension and fact table should have a separate detailed table design. At a minimum, the supporting information required includes the attribute/fact name, description, sample values, and a slowly changing dimension type indicator for every dimension attribute. In addition, the detailed fact table design should identify each foreign key relationship, appropriate degenerate dimensions, and rules for each fact to indicate whether it's additive, semi-additive, or non-additive. The detailed table design should also capture attributes and facts that are desired by the users, but are not available or are outside the initial project scope. They should be clearly labeled as not available. Capturing these

Chg Flag	Fact Group	Measure Name	Measure Description	Agg Rule	Formula	Constraints	Transfor-mations
	POS	$ Sales	The dollar amount of the goods sold through the retail channel.	Sum	Sum(Dollar Sales)	None	None
	POS	Total US $ Sales	The dollar amount sold for the total US geography.	Sum	Sum(Dollar Sales)	Geography= Total US	None
	POS	% of Total US $	Dollar sales as a percentage of total US geography.	Recalc	($ Sales/Total US $ Sales) * 100	NA	NA
	POS	Prev. $ Sales	The dollar amount of the goods sold through the retail channel during the previous period.	Sum	Sum(Dollar Sales)	None	Previous period
	POS	Prev. Tot US $ Sales	The dollar amount sold for the total US during the previous period.	Sum	Sum(Dollar Sales)	Geography= Total US	Previous period
	POS	Prev. % of Total US $	The previous period dollars as a percentage of the previous period total US dollars.	Recalc	(Prev $ Sales/Prev Tot US $ Sales) * 100	NA	NA
	POS	$ Chg vs. Prev	The actual change in dollars from previous period.	Sum	$ Sales − Prev $ Sales	NA	NA
	POS	Units	The number of consumer units sold.	Sum	Sum(Units)	None	None
	POS	Avg Retail Price	The average price at the register.	Recalc	$ Sales/Units	None	None
	Inv	Inventory $	The dollar value of units in inventory.	Sum w/Limit	Sum(inv Units) expect across time, then take value from max date.		
	Fcst	Forecast $	The dollar amount of the expected sales through the retail sales channel.	Sum	Sum(Forecast Dollars)	None	None
	Multi Group	% Var to Forecast $	The percentage difference between actual and forecast sales dollars.	Recalc	(Sum(Dollar Sales) − Sum(Forecast Dollars))/ Sum(Dollar Sales)	None	None

Figure 7-5 Example derived fact worksheet.

Table Name: DimOrderInfo
Table Type: Dimension
View Name: OrderInfo
Description: OrderInfo is the "junk" dimension that includes miscellaneous information about the Order transaction
Used in schemas: Orders
Generate script? Y

| Column Name | Target | | | | | | | | | | Source | | | | | | |
	Description	Datatype	Size	Key?	FK To	NULL?	Default Value	Unknown Member	Example Values	SCD Type	Source System	Source Schema	Source Table	Source Field Name	Source Datatype	ETL Rules	Comments
OrderInfoKey	Surrogate primary key	smallint		PK ID		N		-1	1, 2, 3, 4,...		ETL Process					Standard surrogate key	
BKSalesReasonID	Sales reason ID from source system	smallint				N				1	OEI	Sales	SalesReason	SalesReasonID	int	Convert to char; left-pad with zero. R for reseller row.	We need to insert a single row for Reseller
Channel	Sales channel	char	8					Unknown	Reseller, Internet, Field Sales	1	OEI	Sales	SalesReason	Derived		"Internet" for real sales reasons. "Reseller" for reseller row.	
SalesReason	Reason for the sale, as reported by the customer	varchar	30					Unknown		1	OEI	Sales	SalesReason	Name	nvarchar(50)	Convert to varchar; "Reseller" for reseller row.	
SalesReasonType	Type of sales reason	char	10					Unknown	Marketing, Promotion, Other	1	OEI	Sales	SalesReason	ReasonType	nvarchar(50)	Convert to varchar; "Reseller" for reseller row.	
AuditKey	What process loaded this row?	int		FK	Audit Dim	N		-1		1	Derived					Populated by ETL system using standard technique	

Comments
Order_Info is a "junk" dimension with only a handful of rows based on "Channel" and "Sales Reason". We currently have only three channels and sales reasons only for field sales and Internet sales. We can eliminate a dimension by combining these two.

Figure 7-6 Example detailed dimensional design worksheet.

additional requirements in the design allows you to clearly communicate that you understood the requirement, while helping manage the business users' expectations.

Any issues, definitions, transformation rules, and data quality challenges discovered during the detailed design process should be captured. Also, any special design techniques employed such as junk dimensions, mini-dimensions, or bridge tables should be identified.

> **TIP** In addition to the physical database attributes, much of what you learn about the data during the modeling process is not part of the logical model at all, but it is important to the ETL process. Capture this information in the dimensional design worksheet to save the ETL team from reinventing the wheel. Having someone from the ETL team participate in the data modeling sessions can prove valuable in identifying the most pertinent issues.

Update the Bus Matrix

During the detailed modeling process, there is often new learning about the business process being modeled. Frequently, these findings result in the introduction of new fact tables to support the business process, new dimensions, or the splitting or combining of dimensions. It is important to keep the initial bus matrix updated throughout the design process because the bus matrix is a key communication and planning device that will be relied upon by project sponsors and other team members. It also serves as a communication tool for the design team in discussions with other designers, administrators, and business users. The matrix is very useful as a high level introduction to the overall DW/BI system design and implementation roadmap. The matrix shown in Figure 7-7 is an illustration of a more detailed bus matrix that has been updated and extended by the design team to communicate additional information about the associated fact table's granularity and metrics.

Identify and Resolve Modeling Issues

It is important to capture every data related issue as it arises to keep track of the issue and its resolution. It would not be unusual for the high level model to change during the detailed design as additional information is uncovered. Source system analysis may uncover opportunities or constraints not known earlier or design decisions may result in more or fewer dimensions. Deeper analysis may even result in changes to the fact table grain or spawn new fact tables. It's also possible that new business requirements will surface and need to be addressed.

The design session facilitator should reserve adequate time at the end of every design session to review and validate new issue entries and their assignments. Assign someone to track and capture issues for the issue list in

Business Process	Fact Tables	Granularity	Facts	Date	Policyholder	Coverage	Covered Item	Employee	Policy	Claim	Claimant	3rd Party
Policy Transactions	Corporate Policy Transactions	1 row for every policy transaction	Policy Transaction Amount	X Trxn Eff	X	X	X	X	X			
	Auto Policy Transactions	1 row per auto policy transaction	Policy Transaction Amount	X Trxn Eff	X	X Auto	X Auto	X	X			
	Home Policy Transactions	1 row per home policy transaction	Policy Transaction Amount	X Trxn Eff	X	X Home	X Home	X	X			
Policy Premium Snapshot	Corporate Policy Premiums	1 row for every policy, covered item, and coverage each month	Written Premium Revenue Amount, Earned Premium Revenue Amount	X	X	X	X	X Agent	X			
	Auto Policy Premiums	1 row per auto policy, covered item, and coverage each month	Written Premium Revenue Amount, Earned Premium Revenue Amount	X	X	X Auto	X Auto	X Agent	X			
	Home Policy Premiums	1 row per home policy, covered item, and coverage each month	Written Premium Revenue Amount, Earned Premium Revenue Amount	X	X	X Home	X Home	X Agent	X			
Claim Transactions	Claim Transactions	1 row for every claim transaction	Claim Transaction Amount	X Trxn Eff	X	X	X	X	X	X	X	X
	Claim Accumulating Snapshot	1 row per covered item and coverage on a claim	Original Reserve Amount, Assessed Damage Amount, Reserve Adjustment Amount, Current Reserve Amount, Open Reserve Amount, Claim Amount Paid, Payments Received, Salvage Received, Number of Transactions	X	X	X	X	X Agent	X	X	X	
	Accident Event	1 row per loss party and affiliation in an auto claim	Implied Accident Count	X	X	X Auto	X Auto	X	X	X Auto	X	X

Figure 7-7 Example detailed bus matrix.

every meeting. We often see this role become the responsibility of the project manager, who is typically adept at keeping the list updated and encouraging progress on resolving open issues, if they're participating in design sessions. Figure 7-8 is an example issues list that is useful for tracking issue minutia during the process.

Between design sessions, the core design team is typically busy profiling data, seeking clarification and agreement on common definitions, and meeting with source system experts to resolve data challenges. As the design matures, these activities tend to become very focused on the remaining open issues. Some issues may be outside the design team's sphere of influence or responsibility. These issues need to be reviewed closely and escalated to the appropriate person for closure. Do not be afraid to solicit additional assistance from the project manager or even the project sponsor. In many cases, the primary obstacle to getting closure is freeing up enough time to work on the issues. The project manager may need to work with both IT and business management to get the required time allocated. Make sure that management understands what is at stake — if the modeling process is delayed, the entire project will be delayed.

Review and Validate the Model

Once you're confident in the model, the process moves into the review and validation phase identified in Figure 7-1. This phase involves reviewing the model with successive audiences, each with different levels of technical expertise and business understanding to get feedback from interested people across the organization. At a minimum, the design team should plan on talking to three groups:

- Source system developers and DBAs who can often spot errors in the model very quickly
- Core business or power users who were not directly involved in the model development process
- Finally, the broader user community.

The core modeling team will get valuable feedback from the review and validation process. The greater DW/BI team also benefits from these reviews in the form of a more informed and engaged business user community. Feedback from these sessions should be incorporated into the final design documentation.

Of course, throughout the design process, the modeling team should occasionally lift itself from the detailed design activities to step back and review the overall design within the team. This provides a forum for reviewing decisions and exploring alternative ways to model the data.

Chng Flag	Issue #	Task / Topic	Issue	ID Date	Rptd By	Resp	Date Closed	Status	Priority
	27	Employee	Research availability of historical data.	2/18/2008	Team	BH	-	Open	High
	28	Sales Territory	Research relationships and history among Sales Territory, Sales Rep, and Customer tables in the source system.	2/18/2008	Team	RB	-	Open	High
	29	Customer	Assess projected impact of combined Field Sales, Internet and Reseller on data size and growth of Customer table.	2/18/2008	Team	BB	-	Open	High
	30	Customer	Verify understanding of and support for combined Customer table with core users.	2/18/2008	Team	BB	-	Open	High
	31	Promotions	Discuss special offer / promotions with marketing to understand how these might change.	2/18/2008	Team	LB	-	Open	Med
	32	Order_Info	Verify concept of Channel with Marketing and Sales.	2/18/2008	Team	CK	-	Open	High
	33	Order_Info	Verify usability of combined Channel and Sales Reason fields in the same table.	2/18/2008	Team	CK	-	Open	High
	34	Order_Info	Determine list of possible combinations between Channel and Sales Reason.	2/18/2008	Team	CK	-	Open	High

Figure 7-8 Example data model issues list.

Perform IT Data Model Review

Typically the first public design review of the detailed dimensional model is with your peers in the IT organization. This audience is often comprised of reviewers who are intimately familiar with the target business process because they wrote or manage the system that runs it. They are also at least partly familiar with the target data model because you've already been pestering them with source data questions. Good preparation and a carefully orchestrated presentation will help make this a successful session.

> **NOTE** These IT folks know a lot about the transaction system and the business processes it represents. The IT data model review may require more than one session if you have more than 8 or 10 dimensions to cover or if your audience is particularly interactive.

Preparation

The IT review can be challenging because the reviewers often lack an understanding of dimensional modeling. In fact, most of them probably fancy themselves as pretty proficient third normal form modelers. Their tendency will be to apply transaction processing-oriented modeling rules to the dimensional model. Rather than spending the bulk of your time debating the merits of different modeling disciplines, it is best to be prepared to provide some dimensional modeling education as part of the review process.

Session Flow

Start the session with a review of basic dimensional modeling concepts. Don't spend too much time on this, but make sure everyone knows that analytics are different from transactions and therefore need a different type of data model. Make sure they know the differences between fact and dimension tables and that dimensions are denormalized for good reason.

When everyone has the basic concepts down, begin with a review of the bus matrix. This will give everyone a sense for the project scope and overall data architecture, demonstrate the role of conformed dimensions, and show the relative business process priorities. Next, illustrate how the selected row on the matrix translates directly into the high level dimensional model diagram, like the example in Figure 7-3. This gives everyone the entity-level map of the model and serves as the guide for the rest of the discussion.

Most of the review session should be spent going through the dimension and fact tables one by one. This group can handle the spreadsheet version of the detailed data model, so make copies of all the detailed worksheets.

It is also a good idea to review any remaining open issues for each table as you go through the model. Often someone in the group has the answer, or at least knows where to find it. Discuss the availability of dimension change history for all type 2 slowly changing dimension attributes and for the fact table itself — where is this historical data and how can it be extracted?

Several changes to the model will come out of this meeting. Remember to assign the task of capturing the issues and recommendations to someone on the team.

Review with Core Users

In many projects, this review is not required because the core business users are members of the modeling team and are already intimately knowledgeable about the data model. Otherwise, this review meeting is very similar in scope and structure to the IT review meeting. The core business users are more technical than typical business users and can handle more detail about the model. Often, especially in smaller organizations, we combine the IT review and core user review into one session. This works if the participants already know each other well and work together on a regular basis.

Present to the Business Users

This session is as much education as it is design review. You want to educate people without overwhelming them, while at the same time illustrating how the dimensional model supports their business requirements. In addition, you want them to think closely about how they will use the data so they can help highlight any shortcomings in the model.

Create a presentation that follows the same outline as the IT review. Start with basic dimensional concepts and definitions, and then describe the bus matrix as your enterprise DW/BI data roadmap. Review the high level model diagram, and finally, review the important dimensions, like customer and product.

We typically use the high level model diagram to present the individual dimension tables to the users rather than the detailed design worksheets. Certainly the high level model in Figure 7-3 is a great place to start. You will find that the model makes sense to the users once they understand how to interpret the diagrams.

Allocate about a third of the time to illustrate how the model can be used to answer a broad range of questions about the business process. Pull some interesting examples from the requirements document and walk through how they would be answered. The power users will get this immediately. Reassure the rest of your audience that most of this complexity will be hidden behind a set of easy-to-use structured reports. The point is to show you can answer just about every question they might ask about this business process.

There are usually only minor adjustments to the model once you get to this point. After working so hard to develop the model, the users may not show what you consider to be appropriate enthusiasm; they may not ooh and aah. The model seems obvious to the users and makes sense; after all, it is a reflection of their business. This is a good thing; it means you have done your job well! The oohs and aahs will come when the business users see the real data for the first time.

Finalize the Design Documentation

You can consider yourself finished with the dimensional modeling design effort when you have exhausted the issues list or the project team, whichever comes first. Realistically, the project team will be exhausted long before the dimensional model is complete. The most important issues are the model's ability to support the business requirements and the identification of source data that can reasonably populate the model.

As with other data modeling, you could spend months trying to track down every single issue. It is simply not feasible to take that much time. Over the years, it has been proven that the last several issues can take as much time to resolve as the first 50 or 60, and the final result has minimal actual business impact. Once most of the issues have been addressed, the remaining should be prioritized. As time goes on, you will find that more and more of the issues are either resolved or determined to be future enhancements. If you are waiting on input from other people to continue, then you must escalate this to the project manager because it can impact the entire project schedule.

Once the model is in its final form, the design documentation should be compiled. This document typically includes:

- Brief description of the business process(es) included in the design.
- High level discussion of the business requirements to be supported pointing back to the detailed requirements document.
- High level data model diagram.
- Detailed dimensional design worksheet for each fact and dimension table.
- Open issues list highlighting the unresolved issues.
- Discussion of any known limitations of the design to support the project scope and business requirements.
- Other items of interest, such as design compromises or source data concerns.

Because the design team has been capturing source profiling information, data issues, and transformation rules on the detailed dimensional design worksheet (Figure 7-6), it forms the basis for the project's source-to-target mapping document. The source-to-target map describes how each target table and column in the data warehouse will be populated. It's one of the key recipes used by the ETL kitchen developers. The mapping outlines *what* needs to happen, without going into the details of *how*.

The final detailed dimensional design worksheet captures everything the modeling team learned about the data during the design process, along with guidance about valid values, decodes, slowly changing dimension rules, and more complex transformations. Information about the target tables is further embellished during the physical design process, as we describe in Chapter 8, including physical names, data types, and key declarations. Ultimately, the details about the target data structures are completely fleshed out in the final source-to-target map, which is the key hand-off from the project's modeling phase to the ETL design phase detailed in Chapters 9 and 10.

Embrace Data Stewardship

We've been focused on the tactics of the dimensional design process, but we can't leave this topic without getting on our soapbox again about the importance of establishing a data stewardship program in your organization. Achieving data consistency is a critical objective for most DW/BI programs. Establishing responsibility for data quality and integrity can be extremely difficult in many organizations. Most operational systems effectively capture key operational data. A line in the order entry system will typically identify a valid customer, product, and quantity. Optional fields that may be captured at that point, such as user name or customer SIC code, are not usually validated, if they get filled in at all. Operational system owners are not measured on the accuracy or completeness of these fields; they are measured on whether or not the orders get taken, filled, and billed. Unfortunately, many of these operationally optional fields are important analytic attributes. Quality issues or missing values become significantly magnified under the scrutiny of hundreds of analytic business users with high powered query tools.

Identifying and dealing with these issues requires an organizational commitment to a continuous quality improvement process. Establishing an effective data stewardship program is critical to facilitating this effort. The primary goal of a data stewardship program is the creation of corporate knowledge about its data resources to provide legible, consistent, accurate, documented, and timely information to the enterprise. Stewardship is also tasked with ensuring that corporate data asset is used correctly and to its fullest extent, but only by those individuals authorized to leverage the data.

Lack of consistent data across the organization is the bane of many DW/BI system efforts. Data stewardship is a key element in overcoming consistency issues. Unfortunately, you can't purchase a wonder product to create conformed dimensions and miraculously solve your organization's master data management issues. Defining master conformed dimensions to be used across the enterprise is a cultural and geopolitical challenge. Technology can facilitate and enable data integration, but it doesn't fix the problem. Data stewardship must be a key component of your solution.

In our experience, the most effective data stewards come from the business community. As with technology, the DW/BI team facilitates and enables stewardship by identifying problems and opportunities and then implementing the agreed upon decisions to create, maintain, and distribute consistent data. But the subject matter experts in the business are the ones rationalizing the diverse business perspectives and driving to common reference data. To reach a consensus, senior business and IT executives must openly promote and support the stewardship process and its outcomes, including the inevitable compromises.

Conclusion

Dimensional modeling is an iterative design process requiring the cooperative effort of people with a diverse set of skills. The design effort begins with an initial graphical model pulled from the bus matrix and presented at the entity level. This model is created and critically scrutinized in an early set of high level design sessions that also yield an initial list of attributes or metrics for each table and issues requiring additional investigation. At this point, the detailed modeling process takes the model, table by table, and drills down into the definitions, sources, relationships, data quality problems, and required transformations. The primary goals are to create a model that meets the business requirements, verify that the data is available to populate the model, and provide the ETL team with a solid starting point and clear direction.

The task of determining column and table names is interwoven into the design process. The organization as a whole must agree on the names, definitions, and derivations of every column and table in the dimensional model. This is more of a political process than a technical one, and will require the full efforts of your most diplomatic team member.

The detailed modeling process is followed by several reviews. The three most common review sessions involve interested members of the IT organization, the more technically sophisticated business users, and the general business user community. This last session is as much an educational event as it is a review.

The end result is a dimensional model that has been tested against the business needs and the data realities and found capable of meeting the challenge.

Managing the Effort and Reducing Risk

Follow these best practices to keep the dimensional modeling effort and risk in check:

- ◆ Assure the data modeler leading the design process is an expert dimensional modeler. If not, consider supplementing with an outside resource.
- ◆ Every member of the design team must thoroughly and completely understand the business requirements.
- ◆ Be sure to include power users as part of the design team.
- ◆ Continuously probe the proposed source data with your data profiling tools to assure the data required to support the proposed data model is available.

Assuring Quality

Key steps to assure quality include:

- ◆ Adhere to dimensional modeling best practices.
- ◆ Insist on active participation of power users in the design process.
- ◆ Conduct extensive data profiling.
- ◆ Do not skip the IT and user review sessions.

Key Roles

Key roles for designing the dimensional model include:

- ◆ The data modeler leads the dimensional modeling efforts.
- ◆ The business analyst, power users, and BI application developers represent the business users' analytic needs.
- ◆ Data stewards help drive to organizational agreement on the dimensional model's names, definitions, and business rules.
- ◆ Source system experts bring knowledge of the operational systems.
- ◆ The ETL team learns about the sources, targets, and gets a sense of the heavy lifting they'll need to do to convert from one to the other.

(continued)

BLUEPRINT FOR ACTION *(continued)*

- ◆ Interested parties in the IT and broader business communities will review and provide feedback on the design.
- ◆ The database and data access tool vendors provide principles for database design to optimize their products.

Key Deliverables

Key deliverables for designing the dimensional model include:

- ◆ High level model diagram
- ◆ Attribute and metrics list
- ◆ Detailed dimensional design worksheet
- ◆ Issues list

Estimating Considerations

It can take from two weeks to several months to build a model, depending on the complexity of the data and industry, access to key business personnel to make decisions, and their willingness to participate. The scope of the project is also a factor. In general, the logical dimensional data model design typically takes 3–4 weeks for a single fact table and its related dimensions. If the number of dimensions is relatively small, or the dimensions already exist, then the design time can be reduced.

Website Resources

The following templates for designing dimensional models are found on the book's website at www.kimballgroup.com.

- ◆ Example high level model diagram
- ◆ Example detailed dimensional design worksheet

Task List

DIMENSIONAL MODELING

Legend:
- ● Primary responsibility
- ○ Involved
- ◆ Provides input
- □ Informed of results

	Fans	Front Office		Coaches		Regular Line-Up						Special Teams				
	Business Users	Business Sponsor / Business Driver	DW/BI Director / Program Manager	Project Manager	Business Project Lead	Business Analyst	Data Steward / QA Analyst	Data Architect / Data Modeler / DBA	Metadata Manager	ETL Architect / ETL Developer	BI Architect / App Developer / Portal Developer	Technical Architect / Tech Support Specialist	Security Manager	Lead Tester	Data Mining / Stats Specialist	Educator
1 Review business requirements	◆	◆	◆	○	○	●	○	○		○	○					
2 Review/develop data warehouse bus matrix	◆	◆	◆	○	◆	●	◆	●		○	○					
3 Select business process	◆	○	○	○	●	○		●		○	○					
4 Declare fact table grain	◆			○	○	○		●		○	○					
5 Identify dimensions	◆			○	○	○		●		○	○					
6 Identify metrics	◆			○	○	○		●		○	○					
7 Develop high level model diagram	◆			○	○	○		●		○	○					
8 Document attributes list	◆			○	○	○		●		○	○					
9 Identify candidate data sources	◆			○	○	○		●		○	○					
10 Profile data				○		○		●		○	○					
11 Develop base and derived metrics	◆			○	○	○		●		○	○					
12 Design detailed dimensional model	◆			○	○	○		●		○	○					
13 Review data model with IT	○	□	□	○	○	○		●	○	○	○	○	○	□	○	○
14 Review data model with business users		□	□	○		○		●		○	○					
15 Review design recommendations for BI Tool				○		○		●		○	●					
16 Review design recommendations for DBMS				○		○		●		●						
17 Finalize logical design documentation		□	○	○	□	○	□	●	□	□	□	□	□	□	□	□
18 Draft source to target data map				○		○		●	◆	●						
19 User acceptance/project review	○	□	○	●		○	□	○	□	□	□	□	□	□	□	□

CHAPTER 8

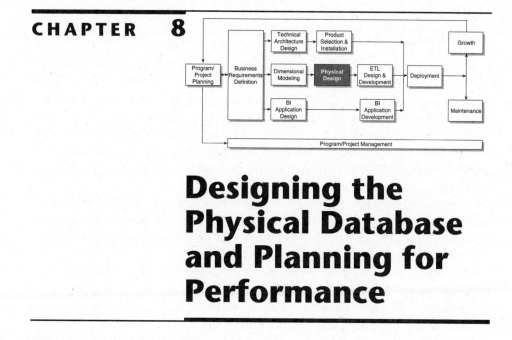

Designing the Physical Database and Planning for Performance

Chapters 6 and 7 showed you the elements of the logical database design. This chapter outlines the steps required to turn a logical design into a physical database. Because the details of implementation vary widely by platform and project and because software, hardware, and tools are evolving rapidly, this chapter offers only a broad introduction to the subject.

The data architect and database administrator are the primary audience for this chapter. The project manager should read the chapter to better understand the requirements of performance tuning on the design of the system, along with the associated project tasks. The technical architect and technical support specialists, especially those involved with defining and maintaining the security strategy, should also become familiar with these physical design concepts.

The details of the physical data model and database implementation are, of course, highly dependent on the individual factors of a project: the logical data model, relational database management system (RDBMS) platform, data volumes, usage patterns, and access tools. Nonetheless, some overarching themes and guidelines appear:

- Make a plan and tie this physical implementation plan to the overall project plan.

- Don't succumb to the temptation to do something the easy (but wrong) way as a temporary measure. It's very likely to stay that way.

- Develop standards and follow them.
- Use tools where available.

Figure 8-1 shows a high level model of the physical design process. Begin by developing naming and database standards, then build the physical model on the development server; the ETL development process will use this database. As the ETL system is being developed and you have some data to work with, the project's architects will clarify the requirements for various additional data structures, including security, auditing, and staging tables, and indexes on database tables. After you have some data loaded into the system, you can design the OLAP database.

Once the ETL system development and OLAP database design are largely completed, you will have better information for the final steps in the physical design process. As we describe in Chapter 13, you should finish the physical design on a test server that is configured similarly to the final production server. Aggregations are an important tool to improve query performance. Whether you're using OLAP or relational aggregations, you'll need to design aggregates. The final step is to plan the physical storage details, including partitioning, tablespaces, and disk layout.

You should expect to iterate over the physical data model during the early weeks of this Lifecycle stage. It's common to add new ETL staging tables throughout the ETL development process. You'll continue to tweak elements such as indexing, aggregations, and security even fairly late in the project in the weeks leading up to deployment. It's very common to adjust tables and columns a little bit too, as your colleagues start working on the ETL system and inevitably learn more hard truths about the data.

Develop Standards

You need to create system-wide standards for various components of your DW/BI system. By consistently applying standards, you'll make it much easier for your business users and developers to navigate the complex system. If your company's IT department has standards, you should use them. However, existing standards were probably developed for OLTP systems, and they may need to be modified for your purposes.

There are system-wide decisions for how you will create tables in the data warehouse database. Like all general decisions, you may run into specific instances where it's practical to violate the decision. Simply document the general decision, and document your decisions each time you create an object in a different way. The following sections offer details to keep in mind as you develop or evaluate your standards.

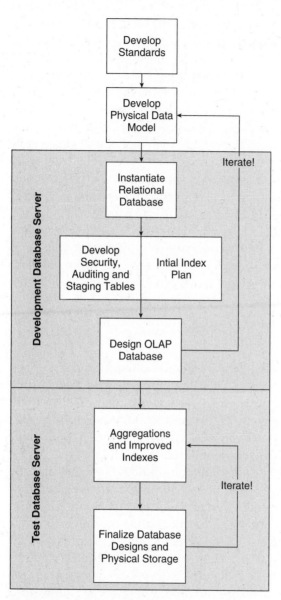

Figure 8-1 High level physical design process.

Follow Naming Conventions

Table and column names in the relational data warehouse should be virtually identical to the names in the logical model. As we discussed in Chapter 7, database object names should be consistent, descriptive, and oriented to the business user. Remember, table and column names are key elements of the user interface, both for navigating the data model and viewing reports and analyses.

Use a consistent table and column naming style. The most appealing column naming style is title case with spaces between the words, such as [Customer Key]. Other styles look more technical and may disconcert business users, and the spaces provide natural break points when the column name wraps in a report header. However, there are two problems with the embedded space style. Not all query and administrative tools handle the spaces correctly. This problem has lessened in recent years — most tools can handle complex column names. We've also found that developers dislike the embedded space style because they hate to use brackets around the column name. The least risky column naming style is to use all lowercase with underscores between words, such as customer_key. These column names look attractive enough in reports. Many organizations prefer to use HiLow case, such as CustomerKey.

If your naming conventions include capitalization, you need to be aware of the setting for the database's case sensitivity. It's important that your development, test, and production servers be set up with the same database case sensitivity mode so that your scripts work consistently throughout the deployment process.

To Null or Not to Null?

You should avoid null strings in the data warehouse dimension tables. They are confusing to business users, especially when they construct queries that filter on an attribute that's sometimes null. Even worse, many DBMSs will generate an error if you try to directly compare a NULL value to a specific string value. If you declare a column to be NOT NULL, specify a default value such as "N/A," "Not known," or a zero-length string.

As we discussed in Chapter 6, null date columns are best handled by surrogate keys to the date dimension. In other words, instead of using columns of type date or datetime, use a foreign key to the date dimension whenever the dates in that column are guaranteed to fall within the range of your calendar date dimension. The date dimension can contain placeholders for unknown dates of various types. If you choose not to map all date columns to a foreign key, you may map the missing date to a specific date, such as the smallest or largest date value the database can hold. Alternatively, allow nulls on the date column attribute. In either case, you'll need to train the business users how to filter on the column; neither solution is ideal.

Place Staging Tables

As we discuss in Chapter 10, most ETL systems need a set of staging tables to support the ETL process. Different ETL systems may use more or fewer staging tables. Create a separate database or schema to hold the staging tables rather than mixing them in with the queryable data warehouse database. Segregating staging tables keeps the data model tidier, and more importantly provides flexibility for moving the staging data to a different server to support a very high ETL load. Also, name staging tables in a way that ties them to the process or purpose they serve. Good examples are customer_key_deduplication_map or newly_encountered_page_keys.

Develop File Location Standards

You need to develop and use standards for the locations of source code, scripts, binaries (if any), and database files. Even if there are only one or a few developers during the initial phase, a successful DW/BI team will require teamwork — in series, if not in parallel. Use a source control system with capabilities like checkout, check-in, differencing, and merge. Before you develop a lot of code, decide how to structure the code and script libraries. One approach is to have the major branches of your code tree based on subject area or table, like billing, customer, and product. Another approach is to have the top branches based on similar functions, such as data definition language, initial loads, and daily loads.

Standards regarding where to locate application documents, such as data models and documents required by your chosen ETL application, also need to be developed.

Use Synonyms or Views for User Accessible Tables

As an exception to the rule that both business users and programmers use the same names, we recommend that access to all tables be granted through synonyms, which most RDBMSs support. A *synonym* is simply another name for a table, analogous to an alias or shortcut to a file on your PC. This sounds like an arbitrary rule, but we have never regretted following it and have always regretted not doing so. The time will come when the data warehouse team needs to physically restructure a large table. The synonym provides an extra layer of indirection that can greatly simplify the deployment of the new version. Trust us now; you'll thank us someday.

An alternative or complementary approach is to provide access through views. A view appears to users of the database like a table. Most often, you define a single table view on the base tables that performs a simple unfiltered SELECT statement to explicitly list the columns that will be available to the business users. You may exclude columns that are used only for processing or auditing. With table synonyms or single table views, the purpose of the view layer is to provide a layer of insulation that can simplify the deployment of changes after the system is in production. A view is more flexible than a synonym; you can rename columns and create simple calculations in a view.

If the physical design calls for a snowflaked dimension — typically because of BI access tool requirements — we usually create a separate, physical denormalized dimension table for those users who occasionally must access the data more directly. We cautiously evaluate the performance consequences of using any view — even a single table view — before incorporating it into the data warehouse. In theory, there should be no noticeable performance degradation for access through a single table view.

> **CAUTION** We recommend only limited — and carefully planned and justified — use of multi-table views in the data warehouse. Realistically, a ten table join is going to process more slowly than a single flat table containing the same data.

Although it is tempting to think that you can create your warehouse by defining simplifying views over a normalized data structure, it works only for the tiniest data stores with the cleanest data. If your users have more than a very infrequent need for data to be structured dimensionally, the physical tables really should be structured dimensionally. If someone important in your organization insists on delivering views on normalized dimensions, run the experiment of materializing one of these views into a single table. Then tune the database correctly for the flat dimension and watch the queries speed up!

Primary Keys

We recommend developing a general policy for how to declare primary and foreign keys in the relational data warehouse. This decision is easy to make for the dimension tables, but it's a bit trickier for fact tables.

As we described in Chapter 6, dimension tables use a single column integer type surrogate key as their primary key: the column that is guaranteed to be unique for each row. A surrogate key is simply a number assigned in sequence to identify the row, and bears no relationship to the keys or identifiers in the source system. As a general policy, declare the dimension table's surrogate key to be the primary key for the table.

> **NOTE** There are several ways to manage the assignment of surrogate keys. Your ETL tool may provide this functionality. In Oracle data warehouses, it's common to use the SEQUENCE operator. Many Sybase and SQL Server systems use the IDENTITY keyword in the table's definition.

Determine the data types for the key columns. For good query performance, it's important that key columns be the most efficient data type for joining. This characteristic varies among databases, but it's usually an integer. At least one major database stores all numbers, integer or float, in the same format, so for relatively low-cardinality keys, a fixed-length CHAR may be more efficient. Your DBAs need to understand the storage characteristics of your RDBMS.

Date keys should also be reduced to efficient surrogate keys, despite the temptation to leave them as dates. Almost all warehouse queries involve a condition on time, so it's especially important that the join to the date table be efficient. A surrogate key for date also allows the existence of non-date entries, like "not applicable" rather than null, or 12/31/9999. However, we recognize that developers are people too, so we don't object to using date surrogate keys in yyyymmdd form, such as 20081231.

For fact tables, you must first understand what the logical primary key is. As we discussed in Chapter 6, the fact table's grain is determined by the realities of the data source. Logically, the fact table's primary key consists of multiple columns, each of which is a foreign key to a dimension table. However, the primary key is typically a subset of the dimension table foreign keys. You don't need every foreign key referenced in the fact table to uniquely identify the row.

Many fact tables also have a logical key that ties back to the source systems. For example, a transaction detail fact table might have a logical key that consists of order number and line item. These are degenerate dimensions in dimensional modeling parlance.

You could create a surrogate key for the fact table, as we've described doing for the dimension table, but in many cases it provides no value. The dimensions tell us what makes a row unique, and the fact table surrogate key is usually of little value for querying. There are a few circumstances when assigning a surrogate key to the rows in a fact table is beneficial:

- Sometimes the business rules of the organization legitimately allow multiple identical fact rows to exist. Normally you'd include a column from the source system, such as a timestamp, that would make the rows unique. Occasionally, that's just not possible.

- Certain ETL techniques for updating fact rows are only feasible if a surrogate key is assigned to the fact rows. Specifically, one technique for loading updates to fact rows is to insert the rows to be updated as new rows, then delete the original rows as a second step in a single transaction. The advantages of this technique from an ETL perspective are improved load performance, recovery capability, and audit capabilities. The surrogate key for the fact table rows is required because multiple identical primary keys will exist for the old and new versions of the updated fact rows between the time of the insert of the updated row and the delete of the old row.

- A sequentially assigned surrogate key makes it easier to determine where a load job was suspended for ETL restart and recovery.

- Surrogate keys make individual fact records easier to identify by DBAs for debugging or special administrative purposes. In other words, "please look at record 1774648" is unambiguous and easy to respond to.

- Certain specially constructed BI applications can rely on a one-to-many relationship between fact tables where the fact table surrogate key from the parent is inserted as a foreign key in the child. Structurally this is similar to a degenerate dimension in an explicit parent-child set of fact tables, but the surrogate key approach is useful when degenerate dimensions are not available.

NOTE As a general rule, define the fact table primary key as a composite key consisting of the set of dimension foreign keys or degenerate dimensions that uniquely define a row in the fact table. Evaluate on a table-by-table basis whether you need to create a surrogate primary key for each fact table.

Foreign Keys

The next question to consider is whether to declare and enforce foreign keys between the fact table and its associated dimensions. Declaring the foreign key relationship will prevent you from getting a referential integrity violation in the database, ensuring that you can't put a row in the fact table that does not have a corresponding row in all its related dimension tables.

There is no doubt that the best practice, and the starting point for your implementation, is to declare the foreign key relationships between facts and dimensions. However, it is common, especially in implementations with large data volumes, to remove those relationships or set them as unenforced. The reason people remove the constraints is to improve ETL data load performance. Dropping these constraints can be a very offensive notion to database administrators. Because you manage the dimensions' surrogate keys in the data warehouse, your ETL process should prevent you from inserting a fact row if its corresponding dimension rows do not exist at the time the data is inserted. The greatest danger, therefore, comes from deleting dimension rows, which is not a common practice in data warehousing.

Many data warehouse teams will drop the constraints during the initial load of historical data, and then reinstate and recheck the constraints, and leave the constraints in place during incremental processing.

If you are seriously considering disabling the foreign key constraints to load data in an acceptable timeframe, there are several issues to consider. You should research and understand how your database's query optimizer behaves if the constraints are not declared or enforced. Most database engines have star schema query paths that the query optimizer can recognize and use only if the constraints are in place. Therefore, it's common practice to reinstate the constraints after each incremental load, but using a keyword like NOCHECK (the syntax varies by database engine). Without checking the constraint after the data is loaded, you're asking the database engine to trust that referential integrity is in place. Not all database engines will trust you; some will not use the star schema optimization unless the constraints are actually checked. Even if your database engine will not use star schema optimization, it's better to reinstate the constraint without checking referential integrity than to leave the constraint off entirely. At least you'll protect the database from unintentional dimension table deletes between loads.

A better approach than declaring but not checking the constraints is to partition the fact table. In most database engines, it's possible to load today's data into an empty table or partition, enforce and check constraints, and then switch that partition into the larger fact table. The advantage of this approach is that you can use fast loading techniques into the new day's partition, and only need to check referential integrity on that day's data (assuming daily loads). Managing a partitioned table adds complexity to your system, and usually requires a certain amount of scripting for automation. We return to a discussion of partitioned tables later in this chapter.

NOTE Declare and enforce foreign key constraints between facts and dimension tables. If and only if you cannot load data during the time allotted, consider dropping the constraints. You can reinstate the constraints after the load, but use the "no check" option. Reinstating and rechecking the constraints after each incremental load is impractical unless the fact table is partitioned.

Develop the Physical Data Model

Now that you've developed some system-wide policies and standards, it's time to develop the physical data model. The starting point for the physical data model is the logical model. The physical model should mirror the logical model as much as possible, although some changes in the structure of tables and columns may be necessary to accommodate the idiosyncrasies of your chosen RDBMS and access tools. In addition, your physical model will include staging and other maintenance tables and columns that are usually not included in the logical model.

The major difference between the physical and logical models is the thorough and detailed specification of the physical database characteristics, starting with the data types and flowing through to table partitioning, table storage parameters, and disk striping.

This book is not intended to be a reference guide for physical database design, nor is it intended to replace a skilled DBA on the project team. The following discussion focuses on how database administration for a data warehouse is different than for an OLTP system, and where, in our experience, the greatest pitfalls lie.

Design the Physical Data Structure

The logical model should be complete before you begin working on the physical model. During the development of the logical model, you performed fairly significant data profiling to ensure the model is feasible. You did a lot of source to target mapping, and have notes about where to source each table and column.

The logical data model and its associated documentation are the starting point for the physical model. Keep the physical model simple and similar to the logical model, although differences are inevitable. You may need to deviate from the logical model to support the specific requirements of your access tool, improve query performance, or keep the maintenance cycle within an acceptable window.

As you move through the data model, table by table, you will collect more information. Some of the information, like data type, is necessary to create the tables. Other information isn't necessary until later, when you develop the ETL system, OLAP databases, or other downstream processes. But this is a great time to collect that information for future use.

Many data modeling tools have places to store all this information, and if your team is comfortable with using a data modeling tool, by all means use it for the development and annotation of the physical model. However, many teams have only a few licenses for data modeling tools. We've found that the low tech approach of collecting information in a spreadsheet usually improves the team's productivity; the data modeling tools sometimes get in the way of collecting and sharing information.

Finalize the Source-to-Target Map

The detailed dimensional design worksheet described in Chapter 7 forms the basis of the source-to-target map, but it will be further embellished by the physical design team with additional metadata at both the table and column level.

For each table, you will need to verify or collect the following information:

- Ensure the table's name conforms to your naming standards.
- Specify a display name and a name for the main view that users access.
- Describe the table for business users. Many data access tools can show this description as a tooltip.
- Optionally, describe the table for team members or other technical users.
- Identify whether the table is fact, dimension, metadata, or staging. You will probably develop additional staging tables as the ETL system is designed and implemented. Make sure you add any new tables to the model.
- Specify the source table or tables, and write a brief description of the data's transformation.

There is also more information to collect and specify for each column:

- Ensure the column's name conforms to your naming standards.

- Specify a display name, business description, and optionally a technical description for the column. These names will show up in the various BI applications including OLAP cubes.

- Optionally specify a grouping name for the column. A grouping name is particularly useful in dimension tables with many columns as a way of grouping together related columns. For example, a customer dimension table may have more than a hundred columns, including a dozen related to addresses, several dozen about customer demographics, and a handful about customer names. A small but growing number of BI tools include the concept of grouping names, though they each refer to this concept differently. As you're developing the physical model, you're thinking deeply about all the columns. This is a good time to specify this information.

- Ensure that each column has the correct data type, length, and precision. Usually, columns will have data types that are based on their storage in the source systems. Because the data warehouse typically integrates data from multiple source systems, you may need to convert some types.

- Be conservative about specifying shorter columns than the source systems use. We've seen source systems that regularly use varchar (2000) for all string columns, even if the largest value in the column has 10 characters. As far as the relational data warehouse is concerned, there's no real downside to leaving the column defined so large. However, you need to consider other components of the system, such as your ETL tool and BI application technologies. Many of these tools get performance gains by allocating fixed memory for strings, even if they're defined in the relational database as varchar. In this case, you could be consuming a lot of memory on strings that are mostly blank. On the other hand, if you do redefine the column to be shorter, you should implement appropriate safeguards in the ETL process to ensure you're not truncating important information.

- Specify how to handle a changed value for each dimension attribute using the slowly changing dimension techniques described in Chapter 6.

- Specify the source system, table, and column for each target column. Include a brief description of any transformations to the column's data. For example "Source ADDRESS.ZIPCODE converted from integer to character."

- Specify whether NULL values are permitted for the column. Specify a default value for the column if NULLs are not permitted.

- Specify whether the column is part of a multi-level hierarchy or drilldown path, such as day to month to quarter to year. Ideally, name that hierarchy, such as "Fiscal Calendar."

- Don't forget to add columns for maintenance and auditing purposes. For example, if any columns in the dimension table are tracked as type 2, you should add effective and expiration columns to the table to track the date range for which the row is active, a flag indicating whether the row is currently active, and optionally a column that indicates what process led to the new type 2 row being created.

- Add additional columns that may be required by your user access tools. For example, you may add a current period indicator to the date dimension table, or you may add sort order columns for various attributes.

Star versus Snowflake

The logical data model is usually structured as a star schema, with each dimension collapsed into a single table, as illustrated in Figure 8-2. We generally prefer this flattened structure to a more normalized set of tables because:

- Users who query the relational database directly are better able to navigate the model.

- Relational queries usually perform better against this structure.

- The flattened table is often easier to manage in the ETL process with fewer tables and associated keys.

Product	
PK	**Product Key**
	Product SKU
	Product Name
	Product Descr
	Product Color
	Product Subcategory Key
	Product Subcategory
	Product Subcategory Descr
	Product Category Key
	Product Category
	Product Category Descr
	other attributes...

Figure 8-2 Example of a denormalized star dimension.

Alternatively, a snowflaked dimension shows each hierarchical level separated into its own table, as illustrated in Figure 8-3. The snowflake structure supports the following:

- The database engine ensures referential integrity between levels of the hierarchy. In this example, each product is associated with one and only one subcategory and category. Keep in mind, however, that checking the integrity of hierarchies is a step that occurs early in the ETL pipeline, not in the presentation server.

- Future fact tables at a higher grain can hook into the appropriate level of the snowflake structure. For example, sales forecasts are usually done at a product category or subcategory level, rather than at the individual SKU level. A fact table containing sales forecast data would point to the product subcategory level of the dimension table structure.

- Each hierarchical level has its own surrogate key, which may otherwise be useful when creating summary dimension tables or for creating OLAP cubes.

If your primary BI access tool has already been chosen, you should modify the schema to address its requirements. Some tools work better when the dimension tables are normalized into a snowflake; others are more flexible. If the tool encourages a snowflake yet hides that complexity from the end user, it's acceptable to deviate from the logical model. However, you should keep the dimensions in a denormalized star structure unless you have an excellent reason for snowflaking.

NOTE In most cases, each dimension table (both logical and physical) should be denormalized or flattened into a single table structure.

If your data access tool requires a snowflake design, consider keeping a flat denormalized version of the dimensions for users of other BI tools. Although you could define a database view that flattens the snowflake structure into a star dimension, it usually makes sense to make a separate physical copy of the dimensions. The cost of maintaining the denormalized dimension table is amply repaid by improved usability and performance.

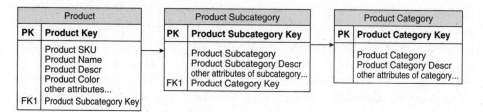

Figure 8-3 Example of a snowflake dimension.

Use a Data Modeling Tool

Plan to use a data modeling tool to develop the physical data model. Information will flow more naturally from the popular data modeling tools through the ETL engine and into the metadata that users will access to learn about the data in the warehouse.

The advantages of using a data modeling tool include:

- It integrates the data warehouse model with other corporate data models.
- It helps assure consistency in naming and definition. A data modeling tool is not a magic bullet, but most tools have features that let the team create a pool of commonly used column names, or permit one column to inherit the characteristics of another, and even to change characteristics when the parent column's definition changes. To take greatest advantage of your data modeling tool, the team must develop and follow a set of standards for its use in your environment.
- It creates good documentation in a variety of useful formats.
- It generates physical object definition scripts for most popular RDBMSs.
- It provides a reasonably intuitive user interface for entering comments about table and column objects.

In the previous section we recommended that you collect a lot of information about tables and columns that may not fit naturally into a data modeling tool. Although you may begin the modeling process in a spreadsheet, your data modeling tool will be able to hold all the information you have collected, perhaps as multiple comments or as table and column extended properties. Once you move from the spreadsheet environment to the data modeling tool, the spreadsheet will have little value. It will document the physical model at a point in time, but will diverge from the real database.

TIP The sample detailed dimensional design worksheet from Chapter 7, available on the book's website at `www.kimballgroup.com` includes columns to hold supplemental information.

Develop Initial Sizing Estimates

In the early stages of the physical design, the data warehouse team is often pressured to estimate the warehouse's size. Whether you need to support platform decisions, order disks, or simply satisfy management's curiosity, it's useful at this point to develop a quick ballpark estimate of the storage requirements for the entire warehouse. Your team's DBA will develop a much more accurate estimate of short- and long-term space requirements when designing the database's physical storage.

Although in theory we would prefer to use the modeling tool to develop sizing estimates, those tools are not convenient at this stage of the project. We usually are forced to use annotations on the data models' printouts combined with a simple spreadsheet to store the calculations, but check out your data modeling tool's capabilities first.

NOTE In almost all data warehouses, the size of the dimension tables is insignificant compared to the size of the fact tables. The second biggest consideration is the size of the indexes on the fact tables.

Tasks to develop the preliminary sizing estimates include:

- Estimate row lengths for fact tables and very large dimension tables. Take into account that varchar and nullable columns are typically much smaller than their maximum length; we usually sample 1000 or so rows from the source to get a reasonable estimate. A very rough rule of thumb, useful early in the process for figuring out what class of hardware to evaluate, is to assume that each fact table row takes 100 bytes.

- For each table, estimate the number of rows for the full historical load (by year of history if the size of the historical load is still under debate), and for incremental rows per load when in production.

- For a standard RDBMS, count on indexes to take up as much room as the base data. You'll do a more precise estimate after you develop the initial indexing plan.

- For temp/sort space, you typically need about twice as much temp space as an index to build that index. You should also think about what kinds of sorting and grouping operations you expect your users to execute or when you need to build aggregations. If someone will be doing a grouping operation on the entirety of your largest table, your temp space must be at least as large as your largest table. By using partitioned tables, as discussed shortly, you may be able to reduce the temp space requirements.

- Aggregate tables can take up considerable space, depending on the degree of aggregates stored in the database, the sparsity of the data, and the depths of the hierarchies. On average, aggregates and their indexes take up as much room as the atomic level fact tables. This is a very general rule of thumb, and it should be smothered with caveats if you need to use it.

- Like aggregate tables, OLAP cubes can take up considerable space. OLAP database technologies vary widely in how efficiently they store the data, ranging from 40–300 percent (or considerably more) of unindexed relational data. Depending on technology and cube structure, the OLAP database can be similar in size to a fact table index, or consume the vast majority of the DW/BI system's disk space.

▪ OLAP databases may need significant additional space to support cube processing. Cube processing consists of extracting data from the relational data warehouse, storing it in proprietary format, and computing and storing aggregations. If your cubes are large, you'll rely primarily on incremental cube processing, so you should allocate space to hold a day of cube data. If you are fully reprocessing your cubes every load cycle, allocate at least as much storage as the cube itself requires. The various OLAP vendors vary widely in how they handle processing; these are just general guidelines during the initial sizing.

▪ In sum, a very general rule of thumb is that the entire data warehouse typically takes up three or four times as much space as the data in your atomic star schema.

There are several other databases that are part of the overall DW/BI system. Most of these are quite small, but several can grow to be significant.

▪ Reserve 20 MB for metadata tables. That should be more than enough.

▪ The staging database and file system storage requirements vary quite widely, depending on how you design your ETL system. At the minimum, you can plan on the staging area holding a day of data for a daily load cycle. It's a good practice to hold onto the extracted data for an extended period, at least a week and often a month or longer. Make sure you plan for the storage required for the one-time historical load, which may be far larger than the space required for ongoing incremental loads.

▪ You will probably develop a logging database where the operations of the DW/BI system are logged. This is kind of like a metadata database, but the metadata you hold in the logging database includes information about how much data was extracted and how long the ETL process took, who is connected to the system, and what they are doing. The size of the logging database will vary depending on the policies you set for what is being monitored, in what detail, and how long the logs are kept. Reserve at least 10 GB for the logging database, and significantly more if you are tracking detailed activity for many users.

▪ Many BI tools require a database as part of their operations. The database holds report definitions, user and usage information; it is used to schedule and distribute reports. Usually this reporting database is fairly small, unless you archive report snapshots — the data and rendering of the report at the time it was run. In the absence of report archival, you can plan on the BI tool databases taking 10 GB or less.

Build the Development Database

You will need to get a development database in place before ETL work can begin. It's common to create the database too early before the design has settled down. Try to hold off until there's at least a day or two between design changes in the model.

At the start, don't worry about the physical details of the development database because the initial development steps deal with relatively small data volumes. By the time you build the development database, many organizations haven't even chosen their final hardware platform.

It helps to have a resource designated as the development database administrator. This person should keep an eye on disk usage and the general health of the shared development database. Early on, it's a small time commitment. You just want someone to check on things every week, so folks aren't surprised by running out of space.

You will need to manage changes to the database structure during the development cycle. As we discuss in Chapter 13, there are tools that can help with the technical bits, but the hard part is making sure everyone is communicating correctly and warning other team members of upcoming changes.

As the development process gets closer to completion, the team will shift to testing and deployment mode. Later in this chapter, we describe the physical decisions, such as indexing and disk layout, that the development database administrator must focus on during testing and deployment.

Design Processing Data Stores

There are several additional sets of tables that you will need to design and deploy as part of the complete BI system. These include:

- **Staging tables to support the ETL system.**   Staging tables are often designed to hold the current day's data for daily processing. Some ETL designs don't use staging tables at all, or simply make a copy of the current extract for archival and auditing purposes. Other ETL system designs make heavy use of staging tables, sometimes with several tables to hold data at different points in the transformation process. For the greatest future flexibility, segregate staging tables into their own database or schema. Even if this schema is located on the same database server as the data warehouse, by separating the data stores from the outset, you can more easily offload the staging database and ETL operations to a different server in the future.

- **Auditing tables for ETL processing and data quality.** As we discuss in Chapter 9, there are many ways to build an ETL auditing system. Most implementations add a column to each data warehouse table that links to one or more audit tables. Once you have designed your auditing system, ensure the physical model is modified to reflect those changes. The auditing tables are usually located in the data warehouse database schema because the fact and dimension tables contain foreign key references to them.

- **Access monitoring tables for business user access.** As we discuss in Chapter 13, you should monitor access to the DW/BI system. Your compliance or business requirements will drive the design of your monitoring system. Your reporting system and BI tools may provide functionality for monitoring usage. Most organizations create a logging or monitoring database or schema that can be separated from the data warehouse contents if necessary.

- **Security tables.** If each business user's information access is filtered to a portion of the data — for example to a specific sales region or set of employees — you will need to define additional data structures in the data warehouse to support that access. For example, in healthcare, the most common solution is to have a set of tables that defines the employee IDs, organization IDs, or patient IDs that each business user is allowed to access. Predefined reports would join the fact table to the appropriate security table to return only the rows appropriate for each user. For ad hoc access, you should create a view that joins the security table to the fact table, filtering on the business user's ID. Ad hoc relational access generally requires granting business users login privileges to the relational data warehouse database. OLAP databases contain security features that make it easier (or even possible) to define complex security roles. But even if you rely on OLAP as your primary presentation server, you will probably find yourself creating the kind of security tables described here.

It is common for the design of these additional tables to evolve during the development cycle, even into the beginning of the deployment phase.

Develop the Initial Index Plan

Get into the habit of thinking of the index plan that you develop at this stage in the project as the *initial* index plan; plan to adjust indexes over the life of the warehouse, as you better understand usage patterns and as usage patterns change. Use an expert for the initial plan if one is available, but you absolutely must develop expertise in-house. You will need to learn how to generate and read the query plans generated by your RDBMS.

CAUTION When hiring or contracting with an expert for indexing, it is particularly important to verify expertise and experience with dimensional warehouses. Do not pay a premium for a consultant — however skilled — whose experience is limited to OLTP and normalized databases.

This section briefly examines the different types of indexes and query strategies that are used by the major RDBMSs, and then discusses the indexing strategies for fact and dimension tables in greater detail.

Indexing and Query Strategy Overview

To develop a useful index plan, it's important to understand how your RDBMS's query optimizer and indexes work and how warehouse requirements differ from OLTP requirements. Remember that most RDBMSs were developed first to support OLTP systems, and only relatively recently have been modified to support the fundamentally different requirements of data warehousing. The following discussion is necessarily general and incomplete, and it is not intended to substitute for expertise in your specific RDBMS.

B-Tree Index

The first kind of index that RDBMSs developed is the classic B-tree, which is particularly valuable for high-cardinality columns like order_number or customer_key. The B-tree index builds a tree of possible values with a list of row IDs that have the leaf value. Finding the rows that contain a given value involves moving up the tree, comparing the value at each branch with the given value. If the given value is higher, you go up one branch; if it is lower, you go down the other branch. If it is the same, you have found your match, and you return the list of row IDs associated with that node or leaf. B-tree indexes may be built on multiple columns. Although some RDBMSs have developed alternative indexing techniques that are useful to data warehousing, others use only B-trees. The B-tree is the default index type for most databases. Some RDBMSs automatically build a unique B-tree index on the declared primary key of a table; it is through this index that the primary key constraint is enforced.

Some database engines will use only one B-tree index on a table to resolve a query. Others can use multiple B-tree indexes in a single query.

Clustered Index

Some database engines have clustered indexes. Clustered indexes sort and store the table's data rows based on their key values. There can only be one clustered index per table. Clustered indexes are appropriate for a high cardinality column or sets of columns. In fact, the clustered index is usually unique or nearly unique; by default a table's primary key index is defined as a clustered index. The clustered index's key values usually become the row identifier for all other indexes, so if the clustered index is built on many columns, all indexes will be large. The clustered index, if it exists, is usually highly favored by the query optimizer.

Bitmapped Index

Many database engines support bitmapped indexes, which are the opposite of B-tree indexes in that they are more appropriate for columns of low cardinality. Bitmapped indexes are extremely useful in the denormalized dimensions of a star schema that contain many low cardinality attributes. The classic examples are indexes on gender codes or yes/no indicators. The bitmapped index is essentially a string of bits for each possible value of the column. Each bit string has one bit for each row. Each bit is set to 1 if the row has the value the bit string represents, or 0 if it doesn't. In the case of a customer table with a gender column, there might be three bit strings in the bitmapped index, one for the "M" values, one for the "F" values, and one for the "?" values. The bitmapped index is usually much smaller than a B-tree index on the same column. Computers are particularly good at the vector manipulations involved in comparing these bit strings.

Usually, bitmapped indexes can be built only on a single column, although the database optimizer can use more than one bitmapped index in a query. Thus while a single bitmapped index on gender provides little benefit, if a query's condition includes limits on gender, age, and income and those three columns are bitmapped, a relatively small subset of rows can be targeted using the bitmapped indexes together. Bitmapped indexes are commonly used on the attributes and hierarchies of dimension tables and are used today by several RDBMSs for the fact tables.

The database engines that offer bitmapped indexes have been investing in the technology so that bitmapped indexes are useful for increasingly higher cardinality columns.

Other Index Types

Some RDBMSs use additional index structures or optimization strategies that are usually proprietary. Many of these are particularly useful to data warehouse applications, as we discuss in greater detail later in this chapter. You should carefully evaluate the index technologies available within your chosen RDBMS. Indeed, the indexing and query optimization technologies available and their applicability to data warehousing applications should be among the most important factors in your RDBMS platform decision process.

Star Schema Optimization

Most relational databases attack the *n*-way join problem inherent in a star query by providing star schema optimization, though the relational databases vary in their effectiveness. We have seen performance improvement of up to *60 times* from using star schema optimization rather than classic sequential joins on systems that are otherwise configured identically.

You want standard queries against a dimensional star schema to start at the dimension tables that have conditions on them, and then assemble a list of composite dimension key combinations that meet those conditions. Typically, this is a relatively small list compared to the total number of keys in the fact table. Next, the optimizer should use this list of partial or complete fact table keys to extract the appropriate rows from the fact table, using an index on the fact table keys.

The strategy effectively requires a Cartesian product between the unrelated dimension tables. In theory, a Cartesian product is a very bad thing, but in the case of star schema queries, it is far more efficient than joining the dimension tables through the fact table one by one.

Some RDBMSs that support star schema optimization require special indexes for that optimization to work. Other RDBMSs determine if a star strategy is appropriate from the structure of the query.

Indexing Dimension Tables

Dimension tables should have a single column primary key and hence one unique index on that key. If bitmapped indexes are available in your RDBMS, add single column bitmapped indexes to the dimension attributes that are most commonly used for applying filters or creating row headers. If your relational engine does not have bitmapped indexes, you should evaluate whether it's useful to create a handful of B-tree indexes on dimension attributes. These indexes will certainly be used when business users are browsing the dimension. You may be surprised to see that secondary indexes on a dimension table might also be used for the main query that joins dimensions and facts. Some relational engine query optimizers will use multiple B-tree indexes in the same query.

Small dimension tables seldom benefit from additional indexing. Large dimension tables, such as a customer dimension, are often used for single table queries in their own right. They support useful questions like "How many customers meet a specific profile?" If your business requirements indicate that these queries will be executed frequently and the dimension table is large, it will be valuable to develop a set of indexes on the dimension attributes that are most frequently used in filters.

As with the fact tables, columnar DBMSs with a wide range of index types have simpler index rules: Index individually every column likely to be used as a join condition, filter, or grouping column.

Indexing Fact Tables

The first fact table index will be a B-tree or clustered index on the primary key. When you declare a primary key constraint on a table, a unique index is built on those columns in the order they were declared. Some optimizers are strongly drawn to the primary key index, especially if the table's data are sorted in the same order as the index. Thus, we strongly recommend that the primary key, and hence its primary key index, be carefully constructed to be of greatest use in querying. Most data warehouse queries are constrained by date, and the date key should be in the first position in the primary key index. Having the date key in first position also speeds the warehouse maintenance process, where incremental loads are keyed by date. Make sure the date key is the event activity date of the fact table record, not the administration date when the record was loaded. The activity date is the one that will be used in query constraints.

The determination of other fact table indexes, outside of the primary key index, is very dependent on the index types and optimization strategies available within your RDBMS. As of this writing, the latest releases of the major RDBMSs permit more than one index on a table be used at the same time in resolving a query. In the old days we had to define multiple composite indexes on the fact table keys to cover the likely query paths. Now, it is more common simply to create a single column index on *each* fact table key and let the optimizer combine those indexes as appropriate to resolve the queries.

If your chosen RDBMS does not permit multiple indexes in a query, then almost certainly you did not choose that RDBMS but rather had the choice thrust upon you. In this situation, you must create multiple composite indexes on the fact table columns. Typically, we do not include all of the key columns in all of the composite indexes, and we alternate the order of columns in a useful way. As the complexity of the schema increases, so does the number of fact table key indexes. A four-dimension schema may have two- or three-key indexes, including the obligatory primary key index; an eight-dimension schema may have six or more.

The initial index plan often includes no fact table indexes other than the single column key indexes. If the business requirements indicate that users will frequently be filtering on fact column values, for example, looking for transactions greater than $1,000,000, the initial index plan will also include an index on those fact columns. Typically, non-key fact table indexes are single column indexes; these are relatively rare and are usually less useful than key indexes.

If your dimensional relational database supports even a modest amount of querying — either predefined reports or ad hoc querying — you should design an aggregation strategy, as we describe later in this chapter. Any summary tables or materialized views that you create in the relational database should be indexed, using similar techniques to those just described for the base level fact table.

Indexing for Loads

Most of the time, we worry about an index's utility for BI queries. However, most successful warehouses are under pressure to keep the system's load and maintenance period as brief as possible. Be sure to analyze any queries used in the maintenance process and build indexes to make those important and time-consuming steps as efficient as possible.

If a load adds more than 10 to 20 percent to the size of a table, it is often more time effective to drop indexes before insertion, add the data, and then rebuild all the indexes. You should perform a simple test in your own environment before deciding how to proceed.

Indexing for OLAP

It's becoming increasingly popular to use an OLAP database as a queryable data store. The standard practice for building an OLAP database is first to create a dimensional relational database, and use it to feed the OLAP database. Once you've started building your OLAP database, capture the queries that it executes against the dimensional relational database for processing of dimensions, full cube processing, and incremental cube processing, and then add indexes to the relational data warehouse as appropriate to support OLAP processing.

In a minority of cases, you will direct all business users to the OLAP database, and source all standard reports from OLAP as well. In such an environment, the relational data warehouse is relegated to the back room. It can be very lightly indexed, generally requiring indexes only to support the ETL and OLAP processing. It is still relatively unusual to have 100 percent of user access going to OLAP cubes, but it will become more common as OLAP technology matures.

OLAP database engines use indexes, and like relational databases, they too have a query optimizer. Unlike relational databases, OLAP technology is opaque to the database administrator; you have little control — usually zero control — over what, where, and how the OLAP engine will index the data. This lack of control disturbs long time relational database administrators, but our view is that indexing a dimensional schema is a problem that technology ought to be able to solve, and we would rather not be bothered.

Analyze Tables and Indexes after the Load

Some database engines do not automatically recompute statistics on tables and indexes after each load process; some aren't recomputed even after a complete index rebuild. This is a very important step to postpend to any load or index creation process, because the query optimizer must have accurate information on the size of tables and indexes to develop effective query plans.

Design the OLAP Database

Your OLAP database design depends strongly on the OLAP technology that you have chosen. Although OLAP technologies share certain characteristics with each other, the OLAP market is relatively immature and there is a lot of variability in functionality and scalability. This is different from the situation for relational databases, which are more similar to each other than they are different.

All the OLAP databases are strongly dimensional; they have dimensions and facts that are directly analogous to the dimension tables and fact tables in the dimensional relational data warehouse. An OLAP dimension is very similar to a relational dimension. The most important difference is the importance placed on hierarchical dimension relationships. These hierarchical dimension relationships exist and are important in the relational database, too. Hierarchical dimensions enable drillup and drilldown within a hierarchy, as from year to month to day. But these hierarchies tend to be much more important for an OLAP implementation than for a relational. If you're building a relational-only DW/BI system, you can probably get away with imperfect hierarchies. By contrast, the first thing a new OLAP practitioner usually notices is how very picky the OLAP server is about clean hierarchies: that a hierarchical attribute on one level roll up to one and only one attribute on a higher level.

The basic OLAP facts are also directly analogous to their dimensional relational sources. Like the relational database, the OLAP database benefits from using efficient (usually integer) keys in storage and index structures. You'll define some basic facts that are sourced directly from the dimensional relational database.

OLAP Data Granularity and Drillthrough

The first key design decision for the OLAP database is the level of data granularity it will contain. It's difficult to offer advice without talking about specific products, because the scalability of OLAP databases still varies widely. Some popular OLAP technologies are appropriate only for small or highly summarized data, corresponding to tens of gigabytes of source data. But OLAP database vendors have been improving scalability for the past decade, and OLAP can currently scale to multiple terabytes.

It's inevitable that as soon as you exclude information from an application such as the OLAP database, business users will want access to that information. That's why people like to build big cubes, but that's not the only way to address the problem. In any major OLAP technology, you can make the cube appear bigger than it is by predefining drillthrough paths that let the business user reach from within the cube to the source database — usually the dimensional relational source — that contains more information or details. Some OLAP technologies support a very flexible drillthrough action structure, but most do an adequate job on the basic drillthrough functionality.

If you implement drillthrough paths in the OLAP cube, you'll need to ensure the relational databases that serve up the drillthrough queries are correctly indexed. Usually, the drillthrough queries are well constrained. Most return a small number of detailed data rows, usually dozens or hundreds. The drillthrough queries are known in advance so they are easily indexed.

Perfecting the OLAP Dimensions

Although the basic structure of the dimensions flows naturally from the relational dimension tables, you will have an opportunity to add more metadata. At the very least you can add business names and descriptive comments, which are almost always revealed to business users as tooltips. You should always annotate the dimensions.

You may be able to define multiple hierarchies within a dimension. For example, many date dimensions include both a calendar and fiscal hierarchy. Usually these can be sourced directly from columns in the relational data warehouse dimension tables.

Sometimes you may want to add attributes in the OLAP database that are computed from attributes stored in the dimension table. For example, a customer dimension might store customer date of birth or age, and in the OLAP database you may want to display an age range. You should have collected this information during requirements gathering. If users will be connecting to both the relational database and the OLAP version, it's a good practice to make these definitions on the relational side, perhaps in the database views. If users are primarily accessing the OLAP database, or the derived attributes are very complicated, it can often be a lot easier to implement them only in OLAP. One of OLAP technology's strengths is its robust and flexible language for defining calculations.

Build the OLAP dimensions one at a time, process them, and examine them closely. The dimensions become a key user interface element for the finished DW/BI system. They should be clean, well formed, correctly named, with nice hierarchies and as much grouping, labeling, and descriptive information as you can include. It's very common to uncover data issues as you're building the dimensions, which may require additional data cleanup.

Some of the OLAP tools require that the dimensional sources be flattened into a star structure; some require that the hierarchical levels be normalized into a snowflake; most are able to accept either structure. This should not be an important criterion for choosing your OLAP technology; it's easy enough to create an additional copy of the dimension tables to support any structural requirements of the OLAP tool, should that be necessary.

Defining OLAP Calculations

We've already talked about creating the basic cube with facts coming directly from a fact table in the dimensional relational data warehouse. This basic cube may include facts at the same grain as the fact table, or it may be built from a simple aggregation such as a sum.

The next major step in designing the OLAP database is to add calculated facts or measures. Most OLAP databases are designed to browse a dimensional model, and often include many calculations found in reports. For example, a report may include measures such as profitability or production contribution to margin. Rather than have these calculations in the definition of a report, a far better design places the definition for complex calculations in the OLAP database engine. Moving calculations to the OLAP database does two things: It makes the definitions consistent so they're available to all OLAP applications and users, and it moves the calculations to a database server platform that is designed for high performance calculation.

The definition of calculations is another advantage of OLAP technology. OLAP databases all use languages that are an order of magnitude more powerful than SQL for defining complex calculations. An example of such a language is MDX (Multi-Dimensional eXpressions), though MDX is by no means the universal query language of OLAP engines. MDX is defined in the XML for Analysis (XML/A) standard; if your OLAP engine implements XML/A, you can use MDX to query it.

In addition to defining new calculated measures such as profitability, the OLAP databases provide a place to define default aggregation rules for measures. Most facts are additive, but some, such as inventory measures, are additive only in certain dimensions. You don't add inventory balances from January, February, and March to arrive at first quarter inventory balance; instead you use a rule such as average or end-of-period.

Build the Test Database

The activities in this chapter have, until now, largely been performed in the development environment. At this point, we are turning our attention to several performance-related topics that you may address later in the project. In order to design aggregations, finalize indexes, and configure the physical storage, you need significant data volumes, production quality hardware, and good information on usage patterns.

As we describe in Chapter 13, there comes a point in the project when it's time to build out the test server, load and test the historic data, and begin testing the incremental load process against live data. The test server should be as similar to the production server, in all respects, as you can afford.

Design Aggregations

The single most dramatic way to improve performance in a large data warehouse database is to provide a proper set of aggregate or summary records that coexist with the atomic grain facts. The benefits of a comprehensive aggregation plan are realized with every DW/BI hardware and software configuration, including both relational and OLAP databases. A properly designed DW/BI system includes multiple sets of aggregations, representing common grouping levels within the key dimensions of the data. As discussed in Chapter 4, an aggregation navigator is required, because we cannot expect business users to find the correct version of the fact table to answer their queries. This aggregation navigator is generally part of the database engine, though some BI tools also include this functionality.

At its simplest, aggregations are simply summary tables that can be derived by executing an SQL query that performs a GROUP BY. Some aggregations will aggregate past an entire dimension — for example, dropping the product dimension. Other aggregations will aggregate past levels of a dimension — for example, moving from daily to monthly data.

Deciding How to Aggregate

We've briefly described aggregations as summary tables that can be populated by an SQL query performing a GROUP BY. This is the simplest way to think of aggregations, but there are many technologies that you can use to implement and manage the aggregations. The choice of technology is largely dependent on the database engine that you're using for most of your business user access.

Oracle implementations often rely on materialized views. *Materialized views* are aptly named; they are view definitions that actually materialize, or physically store, their result set. Oracle materialized views are simply summary tables. The definition of the materialized view includes the view or summarization definition, storage parameters, and population and data refresh parameters. In the definition of the materialized view, include the optional clause to enable query rewrite. The query rewrite clause will let the materialized view leverage Oracle's built-in aggregation navigation technology. As with normal tables, Oracle's materialized views can be indexed, partitioned, and secured. You can use one materialized view in the definition of another materialized view, for example to build a quarterly aggregation from a monthly one.

You can improve the effectiveness of Oracle's built-in aggregation navigation by defining dimension structures within the relational database. The CREATE DIMENSION SQL syntax lets you define hierarchies, such as the calendar and fiscal date hierarchies that we have already mentioned. The more you use the CREATE DIMENSION statement to declare hierarchical relationships in your dimensions, the better Oracle's query rewrite technology is able to use an appropriate mid-level aggregation. This makes sense. If you don't explicitly tell the engine that days roll up to months, and from there to quarters and years, there's no way for the query optimizer to infer that relationship without a very expensive scan. Declare this information as metadata, and the optimizer can use the knowledge at query time.

An alternative approach to implementing relational aggregations is to use an OLAP engine. Aggregation management and navigation are core competencies of OLAP — they were among the first features that led to the development of OLAP engines decades ago. The principles are exactly the same for OLAP aggregations as for relational summary tables or materialized views. The OLAP engine will create summary tables, but in this case they're stored in the proprietary OLAP storage mode rather than in the relational database. Storage mode aside, they're entirely analogous to a relational summary table or materialized view. The OLAP database administrator generally has less control over how the OLAP aggregations are stored or indexed than with summary tables or materialized views. The OLAP engine manages those details, hopefully as well or better than most DBAs would do.

The other database engines each have a preferred mechanism for managing aggregations. The technical details differ, but the fundamental principles are exactly the same.

An alternative approach to using the database engine's built-in aggregation management and navigation is to purchase a BI query and reporting tool that has aggregation navigation functionality. We are always somewhat uncomfortable with this architecture, because even though the performance gains can be wonderful, the benefit is restricted to a single front end BI tool. Thus, this is seldom the best choice with the most up-to-date versions of the database engines. We would prefer to rely on the relational or OLAP database engine for this functionality. However, if your database engine doesn't provide built-in aggregation management functionality, it's better to use application-level aggregation navigation than none at all.

NOTE We consider aggregation management and navigation functionality a valuable selection criterion for the presentation server's database platform.

Deciding What to Aggregate

The art of good aggregation design is to aggregate neither too much nor too little. In the past, OLAP engines were justly criticized for aggregating too much. First generation OLAP engines created and stored every possible aggregation, which led to the widely noted explosion of data volumes in OLAP databases. The more scalable OLAP engines available today do not make this mistake.

On the other end of the scale is the system that creates too few aggregations: perhaps a monthly aggregation and a handful of others. In an ideal world, we'd like most queries to be answered from an aggregation rather than from the most atomic data.

The best way to decide which aggregations to build is to monitor queries and design aggregations to match query patterns. We've seen organizations take this approach to the extreme by creating what amounts to a summary table for each major predefined report. In most cases, instantiating a report-specific summary table is very inefficient and impractical.

One of the subtleties of aggregation design is to balance the size of a potential aggregation (smaller is better) against its use, both directly and in second order queries that might use the aggregation indirectly. Many DBAs will build a monthly aggregation. Monthly is appealing because we get a 30-fold decrease in data volume for a level of aggregation that's usually popular with business users. (Note that it's probably not really a 30-fold decrease in data volume, because the data will be unevenly distributed throughout the month.) In most cases a monthly aggregation is appealing where a quarterly one is not, because there are only three months in a quarter. The actual size of aggregation tables is dependent on the dimension hierarchy levels that are included in the aggregation, combined with the sparsity of the data. It's extremely difficult to predict aggregation table size in advance. Most people create a sample table to extrapolate summary data volumes.

Even with a query log and crystal ball-like understanding of business users' query patterns, determining the optimal set of aggregations is a very difficult problem. In this area, OLAP databases provide substantially more assistance than relational technologies.

Maintaining Aggregations

In addition to building aggregations when you first create them, you must maintain them over time. To a large extent this is an ETL task. The task is usually handled by the aggregation management functionality, unless you create summary relational tables from scratch. Nonetheless it's important that you understand what's going on beneath the covers.

When new daily data is loaded into the atomic fact table, the aggregations must be updated too. You never want a query that uses an aggregation to return a different result than the same query against the atomic table. With a simple addition of new facts, aggregations are updated by summarizing the new day of data to the grain of each aggregation, and adding it to the existing summarization.

If you're maintaining summary tables by hand, your ETL process must include a step to keep the summary tables up to date. In most cases, aggregations managed by the database — such as materialized views or OLAP aggregations — do this for you. The data structure should remain consistent during processing. Either keep the entire data warehouse offline until the aggregations have finished their incremental processing, or bind the entire process into a single transaction. It's important for the reliability and auditability of the system that queries always provide 100 percent consistent results, whether the query is executed against the base table or an aggregation.

As we discussed in Chapter 6, a problem arises if the dimension table processes a type 1 attribute overwrite for an attribute that is used in an aggregation. Imagine that you have a very simple fact table with daily data at the product SKU level, and you've defined an aggregation by month and product subcategory, as illustrated in Figure 8-4.

We'll walk through two scenarios, starting with the more simplistic. Say one of the product subcategory descriptions is changed from Men's Shoes to Men's Footwear. Tracking this change is unimportant to the business; they just want to see the most current description on their reports, but don't care about the old description, so you've opted to treat it as a type 1 overwrite attribute. In this case, the ETL system would need to update the product subcategory description in both the base product dimension table, as well as the conformed shrunken product subcategory dimension. The change can be handled by dimension table updates alone; no need to touch the atomic fact tables or aggregates. The users get the same results if they query the atomic data, grouping by product subcategory, as they would from a query against the aggregated data.

But consider a different situation. What happens if an existing SKU is reassigned to a different product subcategory, say Men's Accessories? Again, the business users and data stewards want to report product SKU results based on their current subcategory assignment; they don't care that the product used to roll up into Men's Shoes. Based on these business rules, the subcategory description is again handled as a type 1 attribute. When this reassignment occurs, the ETL system needs to update the base dimension with

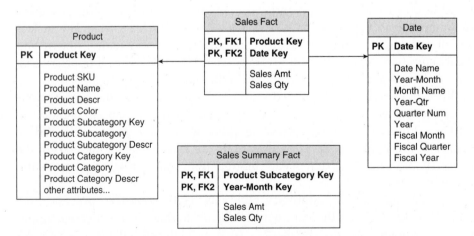

Figure 8-4 Summary table at the granularity of product subcategory by month.

the new subcategory description value. No problem at the detailed level, but you've now created an inconsistency between the atomic and aggregated data because all the historical rows in the aggregated fact table have summarized the SKU's sales into the old subcategory. This detail-to-aggregate inconsistency is unacceptable! The task of maintaining aggregations just grew more complex because now the change is no longer confined to the dimension table; you need to also recalculate and update the historical aggregated fact rows so they're consistent with any on-the-fly summarization of the detailed fact records by product subcategory.

The most obvious solution to minimize this disruption is to avoid creating aggregations on type 1 attributes. This addresses the problem of managing the aggregations when the attribute changes, but may lead to suboptimal query performance. Some argue that snowflaking or normalizing the product dimension would solve this dilemma, but that's a fallacy. Of course, you'll need shrunken conformed dimensions corresponding to the aggregate fact table's granularity. But the challenge we've illustrated is not a dimension table issue. The problem is that you have historical rows in your aggregate fact table that are no longer accurate. Differently structured dimension tables won't get you out of this.

> **NOTE** Type 1 dimension attribute changes cause substantial disruption to any aggregations that are built on that attribute. This is true whether the aggregation exists as a summary table, materialized view, or OLAP aggregation. But the reverse is true; aggregations that are not built on the changed attribute are not affected by the change.

Finalizing Indexes

Once you are working on the test server to test performance and design aggregations, it's inevitable that you will revisit your index plan. If you're using relational aggregations rather than OLAP, you will want to extend the index plan to include the aggregate tables or materialized views. Read Chapter 13 for a discussion of how to conduct performance tests and some of the issues you should watch out for as your index plans evolve.

Design and Build the Database Instance

Your data warehouse's presentation layer should exist in its own instance of the RDBMS on its own hardware server so that system wide parameters, such as memory, can be optimized to your warehouse's requirements. Although the specific settings vary by RDBMS and project, a few parameters are absolutely vital to data warehouse database performance. As usual, document exactly what you are setting each parameter to, why, and which parameters are most likely to require adjustment as the database grows and evolves.

Examples of the kinds of database parameters to worry about include memory settings and database recovery models. Make sure your database is not unduly memory constrained. Ensure that the database uses a recovery model that works well with your backup strategy. If your data volumes are significant, ensure that the database is set up to support bulk loading.

Memory

Data warehouse query performance benefits from significant memory because most queries involve multistep processing. If the results of the first step of a complex query can be held in memory, the subsequent processing is much faster than if the temporary results must be written to disk.

Some warehouse applications are able to keep a working set of data in memory, to be accessed at memory speeds by multiple users. Even very large data warehouse databases tend to use a subset of data most often, perhaps dimension tables or measurement data from the most recent week. If most users of the system are querying the same data and that dataset is small enough to fit in memory, the queries will benefit from the memory cache. The benefits can be significant, with performance improvements of up to 30 times resulting from accessing data in memory rather than from disk.

Block Size

Some RDBMSs permit the DBA to select the database's block size, typically ranging from 2 K to 32 K. Many data warehouse operations are performed much faster in a database with large blocks: Data loads and table scans are examples. Other operations, notably queries that retrieve data scattered throughout the fact table, are less efficient with large blocks. This may seem counterintuitive, but remember that any read operation will bring the entire block into memory. This is great if the target data is contiguous, but if they are not, then relatively little of the result set will fit in cache, because each block consists mostly of data that is of little interest.

The answer then, as with so many data warehouse configuration problems, depends on the unique circumstances of your system. If your load window is a real problem or you know the key query access patterns and can efficiently sort the data accordingly, you should choose large blocks and structure the data so that frequently accessed data are contiguous. If loading is less of a problem and access patterns are unpredictable, small blocks are a better bet.

Save the Database Build Scripts and Parameter Files

Most RDBMSs permit the DBA to configure and build the database using a point-and-click graphical user interface (GUI). Although such GUIs are convenient, they typically do not self-document well. We recommend the use of a GUI interface only if the DBA uses a process or tool to capture the resulting information. At the minimum, you should have a script scheduled to run every night against the data dictionary tables to generate and archive the table definition script from the actual schema.

Any team member who changes the layout of a physical table in the presentation server should model that change first in the data modeling tool and preferably generate the changes from the tool rather than by retyping (or pointing and clicking) at the database console. However, we have found that data modeling tools do not always generate the complete table definition script in the way it needs to be run, especially when the change is to an existing table. (You typically do not want to drop and re-create a very large table in order to add a new column.) In this case, start with the data model, generate the table definition script from the model, and edit and save it according to your group's code management standards.

Changes to physical tables earlier in the ETL processing pipeline trigger more complex tracking responsibilities. Occasionally your source system will notify you of a change that needs to propagate all the way through your DW/BI system and into the final BI applications. For this you need a serious impact analysis tool, which we discuss under subsystem 29 in Chapter 9 on ETL.

Once again we want to emphasize the benefits of using a code management tool for the DW/BI environment. The best tools ease the coordination problems associated with large teams working on the same code base. You can generate reports or post web pages of the changed code, and permit reverting to earlier code should you — unlikely as it sounds — mess things up.

Develop the Physical Storage Structure

There is a level to the physical model that lies below the data structures we've already discussed: the storage structures of blocks, files, disks, partitions, and table spaces or databases. Your DW/BI project will greatly benefit from the services of a physical DBA who has extensive experience with your hardware and RDBMS platform and, just as important, is knowledgeable about the requirements of data warehouses. If such a resource is not available within your company, consider bringing in a consultant either to do the work outlined next or perhaps to conduct a review of the physical design.

Compute Table and Index Sizes

As discussed earlier in this chapter, we recommend that a rough estimate of disk requirements be made at the beginning of the physical design process. The main goal of the preliminary sizing estimates was to support platform decision making.

Now that the logical and physical design has been finalized, it's time to put data to disk. Accurate computations are necessary; use an expert. If you need to go it alone, thoroughly read and follow the documentation provided by your RDBMS vendor and use vendor-supplied sizing tools where available.

Determine the timeframe for which you are planning your storage requirements, but document and understand the growth requirements beyond that timeframe. Typically, we plan for an initial data load of fixed size, plus at least six months of growth during ongoing loads. Plan for success, and understand how and when to add new drives should your team be pressured to move swiftly into production or add more historical data.

Develop the Partitioning Plan

If your RDBMS supports partitioning tables, and your data volumes are significant, you should partition your fact tables. The best way to partition tables is by activity date, with data segmented by month, quarter, or year into separate storage partitions. Typically, only fact tables and their indexes are partitioned. The partitioned table looks like a single table, but it is managed in separate pieces.

There are several advantages to partitioning the fact table. At query time, a query will access only the partitions necessary to resolve the query. This sounds like a huge advantage, but it turns out that it's often only a very modest improvement over the query performance of a properly indexed table. The greatest advantages to partitioning come during table loading and maintenance operations.

Table partitions can make it possible to perform a fast load during incremental processing. In most database engines, a table can be loaded in fast mode only if the table is empty or the table has no indexes or constraints enabled. You should check your database engine's documentation in this area to ensure you understand these conditions in your environment. The performance difference between fast loads and "not fast" loads can be 100 times or more.

The advantage that partitions offer at load time is that you can fast load a single partition. For example, if you load your data warehouse daily, and you partition by day, you can fast load each day's data into its own partition.

Partitioned fact tables offer significant advantages at maintenance time too. Some data warehouse databases keep a rolling window of data online, such as three or five years of data. Every so often — usually monthly or daily — a process deletes the oldest data from the table. If your table is not partitioned, this delete process is very expensive and time consuming. With partitions, you can easily and quickly delete the oldest partition. Again, exactly how you perform this operation differs between the RDBMSs, but the concepts are very similar.

Finally, most database engines offer the option to declare that some partitions are read-only, which is important for performing fast incremental backups.

You may be able to set up your partitioned table so that only the current partition or partitions are backed up. This makes a huge difference for the maintainability of very large tables.

To take full advantage of table partitioning, you typically have to declare the criteria that uniquely determine into which partition a row will be placed and similarly partition your indexes. The second condition can certainly be eased, but at the cost of some performance both during queries and maintenance.

There are several kinds of partitioning available today in the different RDBMSs. Most offer at least range partitioning, and some offer hash partitioning or a combination of range and hash partitioning. Most fact tables use range partitioning by date, in order to take advantage of the maintenance advantages of partitioning. Typically, if you use hash partitioning, you'll do so in addition to range partitioning rather than in place of range partitioning. The value of hash partitioning is to create partitions of approximately equal size and avoid data hot spots. Some RDBMSs let you create partitions on multiple columns such as date and product; other database engines support only single column partitioning. Multi-column partitioning can substantially improve query performance, but it's more complex to manage than single column partitioning.

In order to take advantage of partitioning for incremental loads, you will need to develop some scripts that will automatically create new partitions as time marches forward, and place those partitions in the appropriate file or table spaces. Partitioning helps address many thorny problems, but it greatly increases the complexity of your system. If you have a single fact table that's of moderate size (several hundred gigabytes or more), you should almost certainly be partitioning it. If your entire data warehouse database is fairly small, partitioning may not be worth the additional development, testing, and licensing cost.

NOTE Partitioning can significantly improve your warehouse's performance and maintainability, and implementing partitions from the outset is not tremendously difficult. If your RDBMS supports partitioning, and your data warehouse contains one or more large fact tables, you will almost certainly benefit from partitioning.

Set up Storage

Where and how you store your data will also have a large impact on system performance and manageability. Most organizations have system administrators or consultants who specialize in storage systems, so we will not go into great detail here on these topics but will instead focus on what's most important for data warehouse systems.

DW/BI systems are obviously data intensive, so you will need a lot of storage. We've already provided the rule of thumb that you'll need 3 to 4 times (or more) as much disk space as you have unindexed data in the relational data warehouse. The indexes, aggregate tables, OLAP cubes, staging areas, and work space combined all use as much space as the data itself. Luckily, disk space is cheap.

In order to maximize performance of your system, your data should be spread across as many disks as possible. Those disks should be managed by as many hardware controllers as possible. In other words, you should opt for a system with many small disks and many hardware controllers, rather than a system with a few controllers that manage a few large disks.

Fault Tolerance

You are strongly advised to use fault tolerance in your storage system. Fully redundant storage is best, though if your project is strongly price sensitive, you can get away with RAID5 for the majority of the database. The system tables and transaction logs should be fully mirrored. RAID5 provides redundancy at a lower monetary cost than full mirroring, but does so by reducing performance. Full mirroring gives you full and instant recovery from a disk failure with no degradation in performance.

> **CAUTION** Remember that no fault-tolerant configuration is a substitute for regular backups. Even with a fully mirrored configuration, someone could login under the system account and delete a fact table or inadvertently corrupt data by running the wrong script.

Storage Area Networks

Organizations increasingly are using a storage area network (SAN) architecture for enterprise storage. With a SAN, you can attach remote computer storage devices such as disk array controllers to servers. To the server's operating system the devices appear to be locally attached devices. SANs improve storage efficiency because multiple applications share the same pool of storage. It's possible to configure the SAN so that applications are isolated from each other, and of course you would generally want to do that.

Some organizations are reluctant to use SANs because of concerns about performance. Although it is probably true that the best managed direct disk system will perform slightly better than a SAN, the manageability advantages of the SAN make it a compelling choice for many organizations. It is, however, very important that you obtain expert assistance in setting up your SAN. A poorly configured SAN can have a huge negative impact on the performance of your system.

Configuration of Volumes and Drives

The easiest configuration to manage, regardless of the level of fault tolerance, is one that defines a single array volume to hold all the database's tables and indexes. The RAID controller balances the application's I/O by performing low-level data striping of files across all the disks in the volume, without further intervention required by the DBA. This configuration delivers very good query performance and is easy to manage. It is appropriate for small data warehouses.

If you are not using RAID technology, the DBA and system administrator need to understand access patterns well enough to predict which tables and indexes will be accessed simultaneously and segment the data so each drive receives approximately the same number of data requests. This is particularly difficult to do in a data warehousing environment where usage patterns are constantly evolving.

When the amount of data and indexes exceeds the capacity of a single controller, you will have a multiple volume system. When your warehouse is managing a medium-to-large amount of data, requiring multiple volumes, the length of the load window is often a significant problem. A good way to segment data on a multiple volume system is to do it in such a way as to improve load performance. If you are loading from a flat file into the database, you want the source data on one volume, the tables and indexes on a second and third, and the transaction log (if you have one) segmented on a fourth volume.

Be careful to avoid creating a query bottleneck. For best query performance, you should segment storage so that data accessed together, such as the customer dimension and fact table, are on different disks. Although large warehouses are more difficult to manage, at least they use enough disk space that you can usually segment data so that it meets *both* the easier-to-load and the faster-to-query requirements.

NOTE Remember that the best way to avoid I/O bottlenecks is to have as many disk controllers as possible. You are better off with many smaller drives controlled by multiple controllers, than a few large drives and a few controllers. Clearly, the large-drives-and-few-controllers option is less costly. You need to find the best balance among cost, performance, and reliability for your system.

Conclusion

The details of physical implementation vary dramatically from project to project and platform to platform. The data volumes of the project are one of the key drivers, because it is significantly harder to complete the physical design for a multi-terabyte warehouse than it is for a 50 GB database, although their business requirements and logical designs may be identical.

The hardware, software, and tools available to the team can make the physical implementation tasks run smoothly, or much more difficult than they need to be. With the help of good tools, the team can spend less time managing file layouts, partitions, and indexes, and more time designing new implementations and meeting the users' data access requirements in a successful DW/BI environment.

Managing the Effort and Reducing Risk

The greatest risk surrounding the physical database design is the tendency for teams to assume that the design is fixed at the outset. The physical design will evolve during the development cycle; performance related design elements, such as indexes and aggregation strategies, will continue to evolve even after you're in production.

The task of initially creating the database design, especially in the development environment, is straightforward and low risk. The physical table and column names are derived almost exactly from the logical model as described in Chapters 6 and 7. You will add some processing metadata and staging tables for the ETL application. The exact structure of these additional columns and tables may not be apparent until the ETL system design is under way.

To minimize changes to the data model after the ETL system begins development, be sure to fully investigate data contents before creating the physical database and tables. Ensure in advance that you're declaring a character column that's sufficiently wide.

Your strategies for indexing and aggregating the data will change once the system has been tested for performance characteristics. Once the DW/BI system is in production, you should still expect that indexing and aggregation table design will change over time. You can simplify the process of managing future changes by planning in advance for the inevitable.

Assuring Quality

To deliver a high performance system, you must develop procedures to modify the indexing and aggregation strategies once the ETL system is built and the data is loaded. The initial plans, developed when you first create the database, should be modified over time as you gain more information about how business users will actually use the database.

OLAP technology, and other front room BI tools, may contain features to help you build better indexes and aggregations. If you are using server-based tools on top of your relational data warehouse, make sure you use

(continued)

performance-enhancing recommendations that are based on system usage, not just theoretical considerations such as data volumes.

Key Roles

Key roles for completing the physical design include:

◆ The database administrator should act as the primary driver for this portion of the project.

◆ The business analyst, data modeler, project manager, and business project lead must support the database administrator by offering recommendations and answering any questions that may arise.

◆ The security manager should be involved with the project from early in its lifecycle; don't think of security as something you tack on at the end.

◆ The OLAP database administrator may be a different person than the relational database administrator.

Key Deliverables

Key deliverables for completing the physical design include:

◆ Physical data model on the development server
◆ Final source-to-target map
◆ Initial index plan
◆ OLAP database design
◆ Aggregation plan
◆ Partition plan

Estimating Considerations

The effort required to design and implement the physical database depends on the complexity of the project. For the development environment, the task can take a day or two. For the test and production environments, you will need to develop and test strategies for partitioning, data file placement, indexing, and aggregation strategies.

(continued)

BLUEPRINT FOR ACTION *(continued)*

◆ The physical design process effort can vary significantly. At one end of the spectrum, it could be a one week effort in the case where a DBA is implementing a well designed logical model for a single, relatively small collection of data. At the other end of the spectrum, the physical design effort can take months.

◆ Planning for physical design can be a more time consuming process if naming conventions aren't already in place. An even greater degree of uncertainty stems from a lack of clarity around the logical or business names for the data elements. Vague, conflicting definitions at this point are a sure sign of trouble. These problems should have been addressed during the dimensional modeling. Worse case, they must be resolved at this point or they will haunt the warehouse for a long time.

◆ The size of the database and complexity of the technical environment have a major impact on the effort. The process is multiplicative rather than additive as complexity increases. Multiple platforms and multiple instances bring the added difficulty of inter-operation.

◆ The level of DBA skill and experience with the target platform can also affect the timeline. Relying on an inexperienced DBA can more than double the length of the physical design process, and in most cases, will produce an inferior implementation.

◆ A complex security model will increase the time required to complete the physical design.

Website Resources

The following template for designing the physical database is found on the book's website at www.kimballgroup.com:

◆ Example spreadsheet (PhysicalModelTemplate.xls) to collect table names, descriptions, and technical information for the early design of the physical model.

Task List

PHYSICAL DESIGN

Task	Business Users	Business Sponsor / Business Driver	DW/BI Director / Program Manager	Project Manager	Business Project Lead	Business Analyst	Data Steward / QA Analyst	Data Architect / Data Modeler / DBA	Metadata Manager	ETL Architect / ETL Developer	BI Architect / App Developer / Portal Developer	Technical Architect / Tech Support Specialist	Security Manager	Lead Tester	Data Mining / Stats Specialist	Educator
PHYSICAL DATABASE DESIGN																
1 Define standards for physical objects								●		●						
2 Design physical tables & columns				○		○	○	●		○						
3 Finalize the source to target map				○		○		●		○						
4 Estimate database size								●		○						
5 Design development database								●		●						
6 Design auditing, staging and security tables								○	◆	◆	◆	◆	○	☐		
7 Develop initial index plan						◆		●		◆	○					
8 Design the OLAP database						○		●		◆	◆					
9 Develop initial aggregation plan						○	◆	●	◆	◆		◆		☐		
10 Develop initial partitioning plan								●				◆		☐		
11 User acceptance/project review		☐	☐	●	☐	○	○	○	☐	○	○	○	○	☐	☐	☐
PHYSICAL DATABASE IMPLEMENTATION																
1 Install and setup the RDBMS								●				○				
2 Build physical storage structure								●				○				
3 Implement table partitioning								●								
4 Complete table and index sizing								●		○						
5 Create tables and indexes								●								
6 Create OLAP database								●								
7 User acceptance/project review		☐	☐	●	☐	○		○	☐	○	○	○	○			☐

Column groups: **Fans** (Business Users) · **Front Office** (Business Sponsor / Business Driver, DW/BI Director / Program Manager) · **Coaches** (Project Manager, Business Project Lead) · **Regular Line-Up** (Business Analyst, Data Steward / QA Analyst, Data Architect / Data Modeler / DBA, Metadata Manager, ETL Architect / ETL Developer, BI Architect / App Developer / Portal Developer, Technical Architect / Tech Support Specialist) · **Special Teams** (Security Manager, Lead Tester, Data Mining / Stats Specialist, Educator)

LEGEND:
- ● Primary responsibility
- ○ Involved
- ◆ Provides input
- ☐ Informed of results

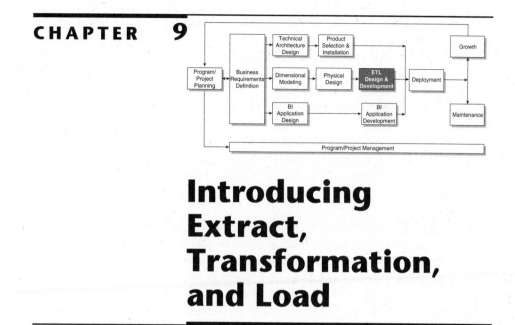

CHAPTER 9

Introducing Extract, Transformation, and Load

The back room's extract, transformation, and load (ETL) system is often estimated to consume 70 percent of the time and effort of building a DW/BI environment. Building an ETL system is unusually challenging because so many outside constraints put pressure on the ETL design: the business requirements, source data systems, budget, processing windows, and skill sets of the available staff. It can be hard to appreciate just why the ETL system is so complex and resource intensive. Everyone understands the three letters: You get the data out of its original source location (E), you do something to it (T), and then you load it (L) into a final set of tables for the users to query.

When asked about the best way to design and build the ETL system, many designers say, "Well, that depends." It depends on the source, it depends on limitations of the data, it depends on the scripting languages and ETL tools available, it depends on the staff's skills, and it depends on the BI tools.

The "it depends" response is dangerous because it becomes an excuse to take an unstructured approach to developing your ETL system, which in the worst case scenario results in an undifferentiated spaghetti-mess of tables, modules, processes, scripts, triggers, alerts, and job schedules. This kind of "creative" design approach should not be tolerated. With the wisdom of hindsight from thousands of successful data warehouses, a set of ETL best practices have emerged. There is no reason to tolerate an unstructured approach.

Careful consideration of these best practices has revealed 34 subsystems that are required in almost every dimensional data warehouse back room. No wonder the ETL system takes such a large percentage of the Lifecycle resources! But the good news is that if you study the 34 subsystems, you'll recognize almost all of them and be on the way to leveraging your experience as you build each of these subsystems.

The ETL system is the foundation of the DW/BI project; its success makes or breaks the data warehouse. This chapter describes the key components of the ETL system architecture. It sets the stage for Chapter 10, which outlines the process of building the ETL system based on the architectural foundation established here.

REFERENCE The ETL architecture topics described in this chapter are examined in more detail in *The Data Warehouse ETL Toolkit* (Wiley Publishing, 2004). We strongly suggest that the ETL team have access to this book as a reference when designing and developing your ETL system.

This chapter should be thoroughly read by the ETL team. The data architect, data modelers, and DBAs should also be familiar with the content. The project manager should use this chapter as the foundation for educating the rest of the organization about the complexity of the ETL environment. The rest of the project team can simply skim the chapter to become familiar with the basic steps, but do not need in-depth knowledge of these concepts.

Round Up the Requirements

Establishing the architecture of your ETL system begins with one of the toughest challenges: rounding up the requirements. By this we mean gathering and understanding all the known requirements, realities, and constraints affecting the ETL system. The list of requirements can be pretty overwhelming, but it's essential to lay them on the table before launching into the development of your ETL system.

The ETL system requirements are mostly constraints you must live with and adapt your system to. Within the framework of these requirements, there are opportunities to make your own decisions, exercise your judgment, and leverage your creativity, but the requirements dictate the core elements that your ETL system must deliver. The following ten sections describe the major requirements areas that impact the design and development of the ETL system.

Business Needs

From an ETL designer's view, the business needs are the DW/BI system users' information requirements. We use the term *business needs* somewhat narrowly here to mean the information content that business users need to make informed business decisions. Because the business needs directly drive the choice of data sources and their subsequent transformation in the ETL system, the ETL team must understand and carefully examine the business needs.

In many cases, the original business user interviews (described in Chapter 3) and data source investigation that occurred during dimensional modeling (described in Chapter 7) don't fully reveal the data's complexities and limitations. The ETL team sometimes makes significant discoveries that affect whether the business needs can be addressed as originally hoped for. Of course, they may also discover unexpected "nuggets" in the data sources that enhance users' decision making capabilities. Even during the technical back room development of the ETL system, you must maintain a dialog among the ETL team, data architects and modelers, business analysts, and business users. In a larger sense, the business needs and content of the data sources are both moving targets that constantly need to be reexamined and discussed.

Compliance

Changing legal and reporting requirements have forced many organizations to seriously tighten their reporting and provide proof that the reported numbers are accurate, complete, and have not been tampered with. Of course, data warehouses in regulated businesses, such as pharmaceuticals and telecommunications, have complied with regulatory reporting requirements for years. But certainly the whole tenor of financial reporting has become much more rigorous for everyone.

Some compliance issues will be outside the scope of the DW/BI system, but many others will land squarely within its boundaries. Typical due diligence requirements for the data warehouse include the following:

- Saving archived copies of data sources and subsequent data staging.
- Providing proof of the complete transaction flow that changed any data results.
- Fully documenting algorithms for allocations, adjustments, and derivations.
- Supplying proof of security of the data copies over time, both online and offline.

Data Quality

Three powerful forces have converged to put data quality concerns near the top of the list for executives. First, the long term cultural trend that says "if only I could see the data, then I could manage my business better" continues to grow; today every knowledge worker believes instinctively that data is a crucial requirement for them to function in their jobs. Second, most organizations understand that their data sources are profoundly distributed, typically around the world, and that effectively integrating myriad disparate data sources is required. And third, the sharply increased demands for compliance mean that careless handling of data will not be overlooked or excused.

These powerful converging forces illuminate data quality problems in a harsh light. Fortunately, the big pressures are coming from the business users, not just from IT. Business users are aware that data quality is a serious and expensive problem. Thus the organization is more likely to support initiatives to improve data quality. But most users probably have no idea where data quality problems originate or what should be done to improve data quality. They may think that data quality is a simple execution problem for the ETL team. In this environment, the ETL team needs to be agile and proactive; data quality cannot be improved by ETL alone.

Security

Security awareness has increased significantly in the past few years across IT, but often remains an afterthought and an unwelcome burden to most DW/BI teams. The basic rhythms of the data warehouse are at odds with the security mentality; the data warehouse seeks to publish data widely to decision makers, whereas the security interests assume that data should be restricted to those with a need to know. Additionally, security must be extended to physical back-ups. If media can easily be removed from the backup vault, then security has been compromised as effectively as if the online passwords were compromised.

During the requirements roundup, the DW/BI team should seek clear guidance from senior management as to what aspects of the data warehouse carry extra security sensitivity. If these issues have never been examined, it is likely that the question will be tossed back to the data warehouse team. That is the moment when an experienced security manager should be invited to join the design team. Compliance requirements are likely to overlap security requirements; it may be wise to combine these two topics during the requirements roundup.

Data Integration

Data integration is a huge topic for IT because, ultimately, it aims to make all systems work together seamlessly. The "360 degree view of the enterprise" is a familiar name for data integration. In many cases, serious data integration must take place among the organization's primary transaction systems before data arrives at the data warehouse. But rarely is that data integration complete, unless the organization has settled on a single enterprise resource planning (ERP) system, and even then it's likely that other important operational systems exist outside the primary ERP system.

Data integration usually takes the form of conforming dimensions and conforming facts in the data warehouse. *Conforming dimensions* means establishing common dimensional attributes across business processes so that "drill across" reports can be generated using these attributes. *Conforming facts* means making agreements on common business metrics such as key performance indicators (KPIs) across separated databases so that these numbers can be compared mathematically by calculating differences and ratios.

Data Latency

Data latency describes how quickly source system data must be delivered to the business users via the DW/BI system. Data latency obviously has a huge effect on the ETL architecture. Clever processing algorithms, parallelization, and potent hardware can speed up traditional batch-oriented data flows. But at some point, if the data latency requirement is sufficiently urgent, the ETL system's architecture must convert from batch to streaming oriented. This switch isn't a gradual or evolutionary change; it's a major paradigm shift in which almost every step of the data delivery pipeline must be re-implemented.

Archiving and Lineage

Archiving and lineage requirements were hinted at in the previous compliance and security sections. Even without the legal requirements for saving data, every data warehouse needs various copies of old data, either for comparisons with new data to generate change capture records or reprocessing. We recommend staging the data (writing it to disk) after each major activity of the ETL pipeline: after it's been extracted, cleaned and conformed, and delivered.

So when does staging turn into archiving where the data is kept indefinitely on some form of permanent media? Our simple answer is a conservative one: All staged data should be archived unless a conscious decision is made that specific datasets will never be recovered in the future. It's almost always less problematic to read the data from permanent media than it is to reprocess the data through the ETL system at a later time. And, of course, it may be impossible to reprocess the data according to the old processing algorithms if enough time has passed.

And while you are at it, each staged/archived dataset should have accompanying metadata describing the origins and processing steps that produced the data. Again, the tracking of this lineage is explicitly required by certain compliance requirements, but should be part of every archiving scenario.

User Delivery Interfaces

The final step for the ETL system is the handoff to the BI applications. We take a strong and disciplined position on this handoff. We believe the ETL team, working closely with the modeling team, must take responsibility for the content and structure of the data that makes the BI applications simple and fast. This attitude is more than a vague motherhood statement. We believe it's irresponsible to hand off data to the BI application in such a way as to increase the complexity of the application, slow down the query or report creation, or make the data seem unnecessarily complex to the business users. The most elementary and serious error is to hand across a full blown normalized physical model and walk away from the job. This is why we go to such lengths to build dimensional structures that comprise the final handoff.

The ETL team and data modelers need to work closely with the BI application developers to determine the exact requirements for the data handoff. Each BI tool has certain sensitivities that should be avoided and certain features that can be exploited if the physical data is in the right format. The same considerations apply to data prepared for OLAP cubes.

Available Skills

Some ETL system design decisions must be made on the basis of available resources to build and manage the system. You shouldn't build a system that depends on critical C++ processing modules if those programming skills aren't in house or can't be reasonably acquired. Likewise, you may be much more confident in building your ETL system around a major vendor's ETL tool if you already have those skills in house and know how to manage such a project.

You need to consider the big decision of whether to hand code your ETL system or use a vendor's package. Technical issues and license costs aside, you shouldn't go off in a direction that your employees and managers find unfamiliar without seriously considering the decision's long term implications.

Legacy Licenses

Finally, in many cases, major design decisions will be made implicitly by senior management's insistence that you use existing legacy licenses. In many cases, this requirement is one you can live with since the environmental advantages are pretty clear to everyone. But in a few cases, the use of a legacy license for ETL development is a mistake. This is a difficult position to be in, and if you feel strongly enough, you may need to bet your job. If you must approach senior management and challenge the use of an existing legacy license, be well prepared in making your case; and be willing to accept the final decision or possibly seek employment elsewhere.

The 34 Subsystems of ETL

With an understanding of the existing requirements, realities, and constraints, we're ready to introduce the 34 critical subsystems that form the architecture for every ETL system. Although we have adopted the industry ETL acronym to describe these steps, the process really has four major components:

- **Extracting.** Gathering raw data from the source systems and usually writing it to disk in the ETL environment before any significant restructuring of the data takes place. Subsystems 1 through 3 support the extracting process.

- **Cleaning and Conforming.** Sending source data through a series of processing steps in the ETL system to improve the quality of the data received from the source, and merging data from two or more sources to create and enforce conformed dimensions and conformed metrics. Subsystems 4 through 8 describe the architecture required to support the cleaning and conforming processes.

- **Delivering.** Physically structuring and loading the data into the presentation server's target dimensional models. Subsystems 9 through 21 provide the capabilities for delivering the data to the presentation server.

- **Managing.** Managing the related systems and processes of the ETL environment in a coherent manner. Subsystems 22 through 34 describe the components needed to support the ongoing management of the ETL system.

Extracting Data

To no surprise, the initial subsystems of the ETL architecture address the issues of understanding your source data, extracting the data, and transferring it to the data warehouse environment where the ETL system can operate on it independent of the operational systems. While the remaining subsystems focus on the transforming, loading, and system management within the ETL environment, the initial subsystems interface to the source systems for access to the required data.

Subsystem 1 – Data Profiling

Data profiling is the technical analysis of data to describe its content, consistency, and structure. In some sense, any time you perform a SELECT DISTINCT investigative query on a database field, you are doing data profiling. There are a variety of tools specifically designed to do powerful profiling. It probably pays to invest in a tool rather than roll your own because the tools allow many data relationships to be explored easily with simple user interface gestures. You will be much more productive in the data profiling stages of your project using a tool rather than hand coding all your data content questions.

Data profiling plays two distinct roles: strategic and tactical. As soon as a candidate data source is identified, a light profiling assessment should be made to determine its suitability for inclusion in the data warehouse and provide an early go/no go decision. As we discussed in Chapter 3, ideally this strategic assessment should occur immediately after identifying a candidate data source during the business requirements analysis. Early disqualification of a data source is a responsible step that will earn you respect from the rest of the team, even if it is bad news. A late revelation that the data source doesn't support the mission can knock the DW/BI initiative off its tracks (and be a potentially fatal career outcome for you), especially if this revelation occurs months into a project.

Once the basic strategic decision is made to include a data source in the project, a lengthy tactical data profiling effort should occur to identify as many problems as possible. Usually this task begins during the data modeling process as described in Chapter 7 and extends into the ETL system design process. Sometimes the ETL team is expected to include a source with content that hasn't been thoroughly evaluated. Systems may support the needs of the production process, yet present ETL challenges because fields that aren't central to production processing may be unreliable and incomplete for analysis purposes. Issues that show up in this subsystem result in detailed specifications that are either 1) sent back to the originator of the data source as requests for improvement, or 2) form requirements for your data quality subsystem.

The profiling step provides the ETL team with guidance as to how much data cleaning machinery to invoke and protects them from missing major project milestones due to the unexpected diversion of building systems to deal with dirty data. Do the data profiling up front! Use the data profiling results to set the business sponsors' expectations regarding realistic development schedules, limitations in the source data, and the need to invest in better source data capture practices.

Subsystem 2 – Change Data Capture System

During the data warehouse's initial historic load, capturing source data content changes is not important because you are loading all data from a point in time forward. However, many data warehouse tables are so large that they cannot be refreshed during every ETL cycle. You must have a capability to transfer only the relevant changes to the source data since the last update. Isolating the latest source data is called *change data capture* (CDC). The idea behind change data capture is simple enough: Just transfer the data that has been changed since the last load. But building a good change data capture system is not as easy as it sounds. The key goals for the change data capture subsystem are:

- Isolate the changed source data to allow selective processing rather than a complete refresh.

- Capture all changes (deletions, edits, and insertions) made to the source data, including changes made through non-standard interfaces.

- Tag changed data with reason codes to distinguish error corrections from true updates.

- Support compliance tracking with additional metadata.

- Perform the change data capture step as early as possible, preferably before bulk data transfer to data warehouse.

Capturing data changes is far from a trivial task. You must carefully evaluate your strategy for each data source. Determining the appropriate strategy to identify changed data may take some detective work. The data profiling tasks described earlier will help the ETL team determine the most appropriate strategy. There are several ways to capture source data changes, each effective in the appropriate situation:

- **Audit columns.**   In some cases, the source system has appended audit columns that store the date and time a record was added or modified. These columns are usually populated via database triggers that are fired off automatically as records are inserted or updated. Sometimes, for performance reasons, the columns are populated by the source application instead of database triggers. When these fields are loaded by any means other than database triggers, you must pay special attention to their integrity, analyzing and testing each column to ensure that it's a reliable source to indicate change. If you uncover any NULL values, you must find an alternative approach for detecting change. The most common situation that prevents the ETL system from using audit columns is when the fields are populated by the source application and the DBA team allows back end scripts to modify data. If this occurs in your environment, you face a high risk of missing changed data during your incremental loads.

- **Timed extracts.**   With a timed extract, you typically select all rows where the date in the create or modified date fields equal SYSDATE-1, meaning all of yesterday's records. Sounds perfect, right? Wrong. Loading records based purely on time is a common mistake made by most beginning ETL developers. This process is horribly unreliable. Time-based data selection loads duplicate rows when it is restarted from mid-process failures. This means that manual intervention and data cleanup is required if the process fails for any reason. Meanwhile, if the nightly load process fails to run and skips a day, there's a risk that the missed data will never make it into the data warehouse.

- **Full "diff compare."** A full diff compare keeps a full snapshot of yesterday's data, and compares it, record by record against today's data to find what changed. The good news is that this technique is thorough: you are guaranteed to find every change. The obvious bad news is that, in many cases, this technique is very resource intensive. If you must do a full diff compare, try to do the comparison on the source machine so you don't have to transfer the entire table or database into the ETL environment. Of course, the source support folks may have an opinion about this. Also, investigate using cyclic redundancy checksum (CRC) algorithms to quickly tell if a complex record has changed.

- **Database log scraping.** Log scraping effectively takes a snapshot of the database redo log at a scheduled point in time (usually midnight) and scours it for transactions that affect the tables of interest for your ETL load. A variant of scraping is "sniffing" which involves monitoring the redo log process, capturing transactions on-the-fly. In any case, scraping the log for transactions is probably the messiest of all techniques. It's not uncommon for transaction logs to get full and prevent new transactions from processing. When this happens in a production transaction environment, the knee-jerk reaction from the responsible DBA may be to empty the log so business operations can resume, but when a log is emptied, all transactions within it are lost. If you've exhausted all other techniques and find log scraping is your last resort for finding new or changed records, persuade the DBA to create a special log to meet your specific needs.

- **Message queue monitoring.** In a message-based transaction system, the queue is monitored for all transactions against the tables of interest. The contents of the stream are similar to what you get with log sniffing. One benefit is this process is relatively low overhead, assuming you already have the message queue in place.

Subsystem 3 – Extract System

Obviously, extracting data from the source systems is a fundamental component of the ETL architecture. If you are extremely lucky, all your source data will be in a single system that can be readily extracted using your ETL tool. In the more common situation, each source might be in a different system, environment, and/or DBMS.

Your ETL system might be expected to extract data from a wide variety of systems involving many different types of data and inherent challenges. Organizations that need to extract data from mainframe environments often run into issues involving COBOL copybooks, EBCDIC to ASCII conversions, packed decimals, redefines, OCCURS fields, and multiple and variable record types. Other organizations might need to extract from sources in relational DBMS, flat files, XML sources, web logs, or a complex ERP system. Each presents a variety of possible challenges. Some sources, especially older legacy systems, may require the use of different procedural languages than your ETL tool can support or your team is experienced with. In this situation, request that the owner of the source system extract the data for you into a flat file format.

NOTE Although XML-formatted data has many advantages because it is self-describing, you may not want it for large, frequent data transfers. The payload portion of a typical XML formatted file can be less than 10 percent of the total file.

There are two primary methods for getting data from a source system: as a file or a stream. If the source is an aging mainframe system, it is often easier to extract into files and then move those files to the ETL server.

If you are using an ETL tool and your data is in a database (not necessarily an RDBMS), you may be able to set up the extract as a stream. Note that we're not necessarily talking about an ongoing trickle stream, but rather that the extract can be constructed so that data flows out of the source system, through the transformation engine, and into the staging database as a single process. By contrast, an extract to file approach consists of three or four discrete steps: extract to file, move file to ETL server, transform file contents, and load transformed data into the staging database.

NOTE Although the stream extract is more appealing, extracts to file have some advantages. They are easy to restart at various points. As long as you save the extract file, you can rerun the load without impacting the source system. You can easily encrypt and compress the data before transferring across the network. Finally, it is easy to verify that all data has moved correctly by comparing file row counts before and after the transfer. Generally, we use a data transfer utility such as FTP to move the extracted file.

Data compression is important if you need to transfer large amounts of data over a significant distance or through a public network. In this case, the communications link is often the bottleneck. If too much time is spent transmitting the data, compression can reduce the transmission time by 30 to 50 percent or more, depending on the nature of the original data file.

Data encryption is important if you are transferring data through a public network, or even internally in some situations. If this is the case, it is best to send everything through an encrypted link and not worry about what needs to be secure and what doesn't. Remember to compress before encrypting.

Cleaning and Conforming Data

Cleaning and conforming data are critical ETL system tasks. These are the steps where the ETL system adds value to the data. The other activities, extracting and delivering data, are obviously necessary, but they simply move and load the data. The cleaning and conforming subsystems actually change data and enhance its value to the organization. In addition, these subsystems can be architected to create metadata used to diagnosis what's wrong with the source systems. Such diagnoses can eventually lead to business process reengineering initiatives to address the root causes of dirty data and improve data quality over time.

Improving Your Data Quality Culture and Processes

It is tempting to blame the original data source for any and all errors that appear downstream. If only the data entry clerks were more careful! We are only slightly more forgiving of keyboard-challenged salespeople who enter customer and product information into their order forms. Perhaps we can fix data quality problems by imposing constraints on the data entry user interfaces? This approach provides a hint about how to think about fixing data quality because a technical solution often avoids the real problem. Suppose Social Security number fields for customers were often blank or filled with garbage on an input screen. Someone comes up with the brilliant idea to require input in the 999-99-9999 format, and to cleverly disallow nonsensical entries such as all 9's. What happens? The data entry clerks are forced to supply valid Social Security numbers to progress to the next screen, so when they don't have the customer's number, they type in their own.

Michael Hammer, in his book, *Reengineering the Corporation* (Collins, revised 2003) struck to the heart of the data quality problem with a brilliant observation. Paraphrasing Hammer: "Seemingly small data quality issues are, in reality, important indications of broken business processes." Not only does this insight correctly focus our attention on the source of data quality problems, but it also shows us the way to the solution.

Technical attempts to address data quality will not prevail unless they are part of an overall quality culture that must come from the top of an organization. The famous Japanese car manufacturing quality attitude permeates every level of those organizations; quality is embraced enthusiastically by all levels, from the CEO to the assembly line worker. To cast this in a data context, imagine a company like a large drug store chain, where a team of buyers contracts with thousands of suppliers to provide the inventory. The buyers have assistants, whose job it is to enter the detailed descriptions of everything purchased by the buyers. These descriptions contain dozens of attributes. But the problem is that the assistants have a deadly dull job and are judged on how many items they enter per hour. The assistants have almost no awareness of who uses their data. Occasionally the assistants are scolded for obvious errors. But more insidiously, the data given to the assistants is itself incomplete and unreliable. For example, there are no formal standards for toxicity ratings, so there is significant variation over time and across product categories for this attribute. How does the drug store improve data quality? Here is a nine-step template, not only for the drug store, but for any organization addressing data quality:

- Declare a high level commitment to a data quality culture.
- Drive process reengineering at the executive level.
- Spend money to improve the data entry environment.
- Spend money to improve application integration.
- Spend money to change how processes work.
- Promote end-to-end team awareness.
- Promote interdepartmental cooperation.
- Publicly celebrate data quality excellence.
- Continuously measure and improve data quality.

At the drug store, money needs to be spent to improve the data entry system so it provides the content and choices needed by the buyers' assistants. The company's executives need to assure the assistants that their work is important and affects many decision makers in a positive way. Diligent efforts by the assistants should be publicly praised and rewarded. And end-to-end team awareness and appreciation of the business value derived from quality data is the final goal.

Subsystem 4 – Data Cleansing System

The ETL data cleansing process is often expected to fix dirty data, yet at the same time the data warehouse is expected to provide an accurate picture of the data as it was captured by the organization's production systems. Striking the proper balance between these conflicting goals is essential. The key is to develop an ETL system capable of correcting, rejecting, or loading data as is, and then highlighting with easy-to-use structures, the modifications, standardizations, rules, and assumptions of the underlying cleaning apparatus so that the system is self-documenting. We're not asking for much, are we?

One of our goals in describing the cleansing system is to offer a comprehensive architecture for cleansing data, capturing data quality events, as well as measuring and ultimately controlling data quality in the data warehouse. Some organizations may find this architecture challenging to implement, but we are convinced it is important for the ETL team to make a serious effort to incorporate as many of these capabilities as possible. If you are new to ETL and find this a daunting challenge, you might well wonder, "What's the minimum I should focus on?" The answer is to start by undertaking the best data profiling analysis possible. The results of that effort will help you understand the risks of moving forward with potentially dirty or unreliable data and help you determine how sophisticated your data cleansing system needs to be.

The purpose of the cleansing subsystems is to marshal technology to support data quality. Your goals for the subsystem should include:

- Early diagnosis and triage of data quality issues.
- Requirement for source systems and integration efforts to supply better data.
- Ability to provide specific descriptions of data errors expected to be encountered in ETL.
- Framework for capturing all data quality errors and precisely measuring data quality metrics over time.
- Attachment of quality confidence metrics to final data.

Quality Screens

The heart of the ETL architecture is a set of *quality screens* that act as diagnostic filters in the data flow pipelines. Each quality screen is a test. If the test against the data is successful, nothing happens and the screen has no side effects. But if the test fails, then it must drop an error event record into the error event schema, and choose to halt the process, send the offending data into suspension, or merely tag the data.

Although all quality screens are architecturally similar, it is convenient to divide them into three types, in ascending order of scope. Jack Olson, in his seminal book, *Data Quality: The Accuracy Dimension* (Morgan Kaufmann, 2002) classified data quality screens into three categories: column screens, structure screens, and business rule screens.

Column screens test the data within a single column. These are usually simple, somewhat obvious tests, such as testing whether a column contains unexpected null values, if a value falls outside of a prescribed range, or if a value fails to adhere to a required format.

Structure screens test the relationship of data across columns. Two or more fields may be tested to verify that they implement a hierarchy, such as a series of many-to-one relationships. Structure screens also test foreign key/primary key relationships between fields in two tables, and also include testing whole blocks of fields to verify that they implement valid postal addresses.

Business rule screens implement more complex tests that do not fit the simpler column or structure screen categories. For example, a customer profile may be tested for a complex time-dependent business rule, such as requiring that a lifetime platinum frequent flyer has been a member for at least five years and has flown more than two million miles. Business rule screens also include *aggregate threshold* data quality checks, such as checking to see if a statistically improbable number of MRI examinations have been ordered for minor diagnoses like a sprained elbow. In this case, the screen only throws an error after a threshold of such MRI exams is reached.

Responding to Quality Events

We have already remarked that each quality screen has to decide what happens when an error is thrown. The choices are: 1) halting the process; 2) sending the offending record(s) to a suspense file for later processing; and 3) merely tagging the data and passing it through to the next step in the pipeline. The third choice is by far the best choice, whenever possible. Halting the process is obviously problematic because it requires manual intervention to diagnose the problem, restart or resume the job, or abort completely. Sending records to a suspense file is often a poor solution because it is not clear when or if these records will be fixed and re-introduced to the pipeline. Until the records are restored to the data flow, the overall integrity of the database is questionable because records are missing. We recommend not using the suspense file for minor data transgressions. The third option of tagging the data with the error condition often works well. Bad fact table data can be tagged with the audit dimension, as we describe in subsystem 6. Bad dimension data can also be tagged using an audit dimension, or in the case of missing or garbage data, can be tagged with unique error values in the field itself.

Subsystem 5 – Error Event Schema

The error event schema is a centralized dimensional schema whose purpose is to record every error event thrown by a quality screen anywhere in the ETL pipeline. Although we are focusing on data warehouse processing, this approach can be used in generic data integration (DI) applications where data is being transferred between legacy applications. The error event schema is shown in Figure 9-1.

The main table is the error event fact table. Its grain is every error thrown (produced) by a quality screen anywhere in the ETL system. Remember that the grain of a fact table is the physical description of why a fact table record exists. Thus every quality screen error produces exactly one record in this table, and every record in the table corresponds to an observed error.

The dimensions of the error event fact table include the calendar date of the error, the batch job in which the error occurred, and the screen that produced the error. The calendar date is not a minute and second timestamp of the error, but rather provides a way to constrain and summarize error events by the usual attributes of the calendar, such as a weekday or the last day of a

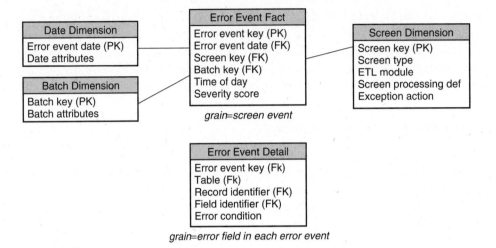

Figure 9-1 Error event schema.

fiscal period. The time-of-day fact is a full relational date/timestamp that specifies precisely when the error occurred. This format is useful for calculating the time interval between error events because you can take the difference between two date/timestamps to get the number of seconds separating events.

The batch dimension can be generalized to be a processing step in cases where data is streamed, rather than batched. The screen dimension identifies precisely what the screen criterion is and where the code for the screen resides. It also defines what to do (halt the process, send the record to a suspense file, or merely tag the data) when the screen throws an error.

The error event fact table also has a single column primary key, shown as the error event key. This surrogate key, like dimension table primary keys, is a simple integer assigned sequentially as records are added to the fact table. This key field is necessary in those situations where an enormous burst of error records is added to the error event fact table all at once. Hopefully this won't happen to you.

The error event schema includes a second error event detail fact table at a lower grain. Each record in this table identifies an individual field in a specific data record that participated in an error. Thus a complex structure or business rule error that triggers a single error event record in the higher level error event fact table may generate many records in this error event detail fact table. The two tables are tied together by the error event key, which is a foreign key in this lower grain table. The error event detail table identifies the table, record, field, and precise error condition, and likewise could optionally inherit the date, batch, and screen dimensions from the higher grain error event fact table. Thus a complete description of complex multi-field, multi-record errors is preserved by these tables.

The error event detail table could also contain a precise date/timestamp to provide a full description of aggregate threshold error events where many records generate an error condition over a period of time. You now appreciate that each quality screen has the responsibility for populating these tables at the time of an error.

Subsystem 6 – Audit Dimension Assembler

The audit dimension is a special dimension that is assembled in the back room by the ETL system for each fact table. The audit dimension in Figure 9-2 contains the metadata context at the moment when a specific fact table record is created. You might say that we have elevated metadata to real data! To visualize how audit dimension records are created, imagine that this shipments fact table is updated once per day from a batch file. Suppose that today we have a perfect run with no errors flagged. In this case, we would generate only one audit dimension record and it would be attached to every fact record loaded today. All of the categories, scores, and version numbers would be the same.

Now let's relax the strong assumption of a perfect run. If we had some fact records whose discount dollars triggered an out-of-bounds error, then one more audit dimension record would be needed to handle this condition.

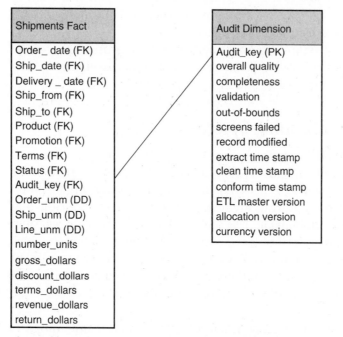

Figure 9-2 Sample audit dimension attached to a fact table.

Subsystem 7 – Deduplication System

Often dimensions are derived from several sources. This is a common situation for organizations that have many customer facing source systems that create and manage separate customer master tables. Customer information may need to be merged from several lines of business and outside sources. Sometimes the data can be matched through identical values in some key column. However, even when a definitive match occurs, other columns in the data might contradict one another, requiring a decision on which data should survive.

Unfortunately, there is seldom a universal column that makes the merge operation easy. Sometimes the only clues available are the similarity of several columns. The different sets of data being integrated and the existing dimension table data may need to be evaluated on different fields to attempt a match. Sometimes a match may be based on fuzzy criteria, such as names and addresses that may nearly match except for minor spelling differences.

Survivorship is the process of combining a set of matched records into a unified image that combines the highest quality columns from the matched records into a conformed row. Survivorship involves establishing clear business rules that define the priority sequence for column values from all possible source systems to enable the creation of a single row with the best-survived attributes. If your dimension is fed from multiple systems, you will want to maintain separate columns with back references, such as natural keys, to all participating source systems used to construct the row.

There are a variety of data integration and data standardization tools to consider if you have difficult deduplicating, matching, and survivorship data issues. These tools are quite mature and in widespread use.

Subsystem 8 – Conforming System

Conforming consists of all the steps required to align the content of some or all of the columns in a dimension with columns in similar or identical dimensions in other parts of the data warehouse. For instance, in a large organization you may have fact tables capturing invoices and customer service calls that both utilize the customer dimension. It is highly likely that the source system for invoices and customer service have separate customer databases. It is likely there will be little guaranteed consistency between the two sources of customer information. The data from these two customer sources needs to be conformed to make some or all of the columns describing customer share the same domains.

The conforming subsystem is responsible for creating and maintaining the conformed dimensions and conformed facts described in Chapter 6. To accomplish this, incoming data from multiple systems needs to be combined and integrated so that it is structurally identical, deduplicated, filtered of invalid data, and standardized in terms of content rows in a conformed image. A large part of the conforming process is the deduplicating, matching, and survivorship processes described previously. The conforming process flow combining the deduplicating and survivorship processing is shown in Figure 9-3.

To implement conformed dimensions and facts, the conforming subsystem needs domain mappings that are the reference metadata for capturing the relationship between explicitly valid values from source systems to the conformed dimension and conformed fact values. Most ETL tools support this capability.

Delivering Data for Presentation

The primary mission of the ETL system is the handoff of the dimension and fact tables in the delivery step. For this reason, the delivery subsystems are the most pivotal subsystems in your ETL architecture. Though there is considerable variation in source data structures and cleaning and conforming logic, the delivery processing techniques for preparing the dimensional table structures are more defined and disciplined. Use of these techniques is critical to building a successful dimensional data warehouse that is reliable, scalable, and maintainable.

Many of these subsystems focus on dimension table processing. Dimension tables are the heart of the data warehouse. They provide the context for the fact tables and hence for all the measurements. Although dimension tables are usually smaller than the fact tables, they are critical to the success of the data warehouse because they provide the entry points into the fact tables. The delivering process begins with the cleaned and conformed data resulting from the subsystems just described. For many dimensions, the basic load plan is relatively simple: Perform basic transformations to the data to build dimension rows for loading into the target presentation table. This typically includes surrogate key assignment, code lookups to provide appropriate descriptions, splitting or combining columns to present the appropriate data values, or joining underlying third normal form table structures into denormalized flat dimensions.

Preparing fact tables is certainly important because fact tables hold the key measurements of the business that the users want to see. Fact tables can be very large and time consuming to load. However, preparing fact tables for presentation is typically more straightforward.

Subsystem 9 – Slowly Changing Dimension Manager

One of the more important elements of the ETL architecture is the capability to implement slowly changing dimension (SCD) logic. The ETL system must determine how to handle a dimension attribute value that has changed from the value already stored in the data warehouse. If the revised description is determined to be a legitimate and reliable update to previous information, the appropriate slowly changing dimension technique must be applied.

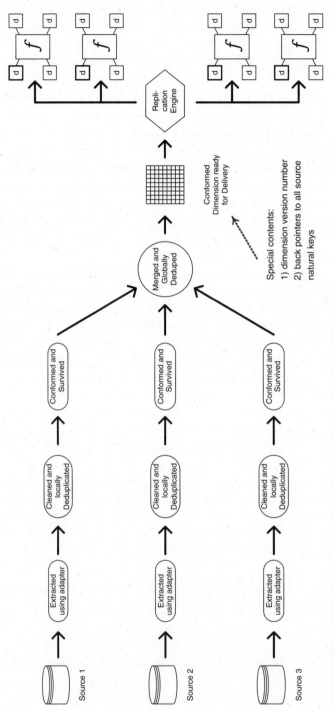

Figure 9-3 Deduplicating and survivorship processing for conformed dimensions.

As described in Chapter 6, when the data warehouse receives notification that an existing row in a dimension has changed, there are three basic SCD responses — type 1 overwrite, type 2 add a new row, and type 3 add a new column. The SCD manager should systematically handle the time variance in the dimensions using these three techniques as well as the hybrid technique, which is simply the combination of types. In addition, the SCD manager should maintain appropriate housekeeping columns for type 2 changes. Figure 9-4 shows the overall processing flow for handling SCD surrogate key management.

The change data capture process described in subsystem 2 obviously plays an important role in presenting the changed data to the SCD process. Assuming the change data capture process has effectively delivered appropriate changes, your SCD process can take the appropriate actions.

Type 1: Overwrite

The type 1 technique is a simple overwrite of one or more attributes in an existing dimension row. You take the revised data from the change data capture system and overwrite the dimension table contents. Type 1 is appropriate when correcting data or when there is no business need to keep the history of

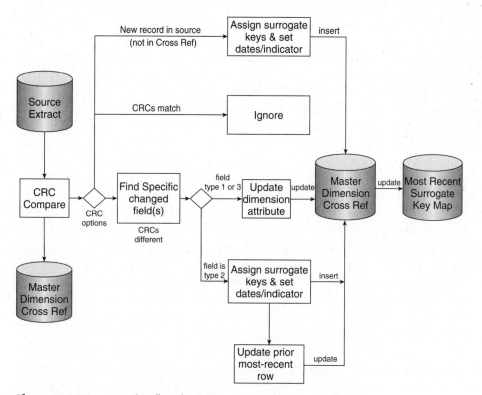

Figure 9-4 ETL processing flow for SCD surrogate key management.

previous values. For instance, you may receive a corrected customer address. In this case, overwriting is the right choice. Note that if the dimension table includes type 2 change tracking, you should overwrite all existing rows for that particular customer. Type 1 updates must be propagated forward from the earliest permanently stored staging tables to all affected staging tables so that if any of them are used to re-create the final load tables, the effect of the overwrite is preserved.

Some ETL tools contain UPDATE else INSERT functionality. This functionality may be convenient for the developer, but can be a performance killer. For maximum performance existing row UPDATEs should be segregated from new row INSERTs. If type 1 updates cause performance problems, consider disabling database logging or use of the DBMS bulk loader.

Type 1 updates will invalidate any aggregates built upon the changed column, so the dimension manager (subsystem 17) must notify the affected fact providers (subsystem 18) to drop and rebuild the affected aggregates.

Type 2: Create a New Row

The type 2 SCD is the standard technique for accurately tracking changes in dimensions and associating them correctly with fact records. Supporting type 2 changes requires a strong change data capture system to detect changes as soon as they occur. For type 2 updates, copy the previous version of the dimension row and create a new dimension row with a new surrogate key. If there is not a previous version of the dimension row, create a new one from scratch. You then update this row with the columns that have changed. This is the main workhorse technique for handling dimension attribute changes that need to be tracked over time.

The type 2 ETL process must also update the most recent surrogate key map table, assuming your ETL tool doesn't handle this automatically. These little two-column tables are of immense importance when loading fact table data. Subsystem 14, the surrogate key pipeline, supports this process.

The lookup and key assignment logic for handling a changed dimension row during the extract process is shown in Figure 9-4. In this example, your change data capture process (subsystem 2) is using a CRC compare to determine which rows have changed in the source data since the last update. If you are lucky, you already know which dimension records have changed and can omit this CRC compare step. Once you have identified rows that have changes in type 2 attributes, you need to generate a new surrogate key from the key sequence and update the surrogate key map table.

When a new type 2 row is created, you need at least a pair of timestamps, as well as an optional change description field. The pair of timestamps defines a span of time from the begin effective time to the end effective time when the complete set of dimension attributes is valid. A more sophisticated treatment of a type 2 SCD row involves adding five additional ETL housekeeping columns. As shown in Figure 9-4, this also requires the type 2 ETL process to find the prior effective row and make appropriate updates to these housekeeping columns:

- Calendar Date (date of change)
- Row Effective DateTime (exact date/timestamp of change)
- Row End DateTime (exact date/timestamp of next change, defaults to 12/31/9999 for most current dimension row)
- Reason for Change column or text column to capture columns changed codes
- Current Flag (current/expired)

CAUTION Sometimes back-end scripts are run within the transaction database to modify data without updating the respective metadata fields such as the last_modified_date. Using these fields for the dimension timestamps will cause inconsistent results in the data warehouse. Always use the system or "as of" date to derive the type 2 effective timestamps.

The type 2 process does not change history as the type 1 process does, thus type 2 changes don't require rebuilding affected aggregate tables as long as the change was made "today" and not backward in time.

Type 3: Add a New Column

The type 3 technique is designed to support attribute "soft" changes that require a user to refer either to the old value of the attribute or the new value. For example, if a sales team is assigned to a newly named sales region, there may be a need to track the old region assignment, as well as the new one. The type 3 technique requires the ETL system to be able to alter the dimension table to add a new column to the schema, if this situation was not anticipated. Of course, the DBA assigned to work with the ETL team will in all likelihood be responsible for this change. You then need to push the existing column values into the newly created column and populate the original column with the new values provided to the data warehouse. Figure 9-5 shows how a type 3 SCD is implemented.

Similar to the type 1 process, type 3 changes invalidate any aggregates built upon the changed column so the dimension manager must notify the affected fact providers so that they drop and rebuild the affected aggregates.

Hybrid: Combination of Types

Each dimension table will use one, two, or all three of these techniques to manage data changes. In some cases, the techniques will be used in *hybrid*

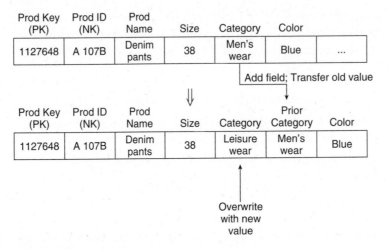

Figure 9-5 Type 3 SCD process.

combinations, as described in Chapter 6. In this situation, you use two columns in a dimension to present both a current (type 1) view of an attribute, as well as an historical (type 2) version of the same attribute. This technique can be quite powerful from a modeling and business perspective. From an ETL perspective, you simply look at the first column as a type 1 column and the second column as a type 2 column, both columns being sourced from the same source field. Normal type 1 and type 2 processing applies.

Subsystem 10 – Surrogate Key Generator

As you recall from Chapter 6, we strongly recommend the use of surrogate keys for all dimension tables. This implies that you need a robust mechanism for producing surrogate keys in your ETL system. The surrogate key generator should create surrogate keys independently for every dimension; it should be independent of database instance and able to serve distributed clients. The goal of the surrogate key generator is to generate a meaningless key, typically an integer, to serve as the primary key for a dimension row.

Although it is very common to create surrogate keys via database triggers, this technique creates performance bottlenecks. If the DBMS is used to assign surrogate keys, it is preferable for the ETL process to directly call the database sequence generator. For improved efficiency, consider having the ETL tool generate and maintain the surrogate keys. Avoid the temptation of concatenating the operational key of the source system and a date/timestamp. Though this approach seems simple, it is fraught with problems and ultimately will not scale. In Chapter 10 we describe how to incorporate the surrogate key generator into the ETL process.

Subsystem 11 – Hierarchy Manager

It is normal for a dimension to have multiple, simultaneous, embedded hierarchical structures. These multiple hierarchies simply coexist in the same dimension as dimension attributes. All that is necessary is that every attribute be single valued in the presence of the dimension's primary key. Hierarchies are either fixed or ragged. A fixed hierarchy has a consistent number of levels and is simply modeled and populated as a separate dimension attribute for each of the levels. Slightly ragged hierarchies like postal addresses are most often modeled as a fixed hierarchy. Profoundly ragged hierarchies are typically found with organization structures that are unbalanced and of indeterminate depth. The data model design and ETL solution required to support ragged hierarchies require the use of a bridge table containing the organization map.

Snowflakes or normalized data structures are not recommended for the presentation level. However, the use of a normalized design may be appropriate in the ETL staging area to assist in the maintenance of the ETL data flow for populating and maintaining the hierarchy attributes. The ETL system is responsible for enforcing the business rules to assure the hierarchy is populated appropriately in the dimension table.

Subsystem 12 – Special Dimensions Manager

The special dimensions manager is a catch-all subsystem: a placeholder in the ETL architecture for supporting an organization's specific dimensional design characteristics. Many of these design techniques were introduced in Chapter 6 and all are described in *The Data Warehouse Toolkit, 2nd Edition* (Wiley, 2002). Some organizations' ETL systems will require all of the capabilities discussed here, whereas others will be concerned with few of these design techniques:

- **Date/Time dimensions.** The date and time dimensions are unique in that they are completely specified at the beginning of the data warehouse project and they don't have a conventional source. This is okay! Typically these dimensions are built in an afternoon with a spreadsheet. But in a global enterprise environment, even this dimension can be challenging when taking into account multiple financial reporting periods or multiple cultural calendars.

- **Junk dimensions.** Junk dimensions are made up from text and miscellaneous flags left over in the fact table after you have removed all the critical fields. There are two approaches for creating junk dimensions in the ETL system. If the theoretical number of rows in the dimension is fixed and known, the junk dimension can be created in advance. In other cases, it may be necessary to create newly observed junk dimension rows on the fly while processing fact row input. As illustrated in

Figure 9-6, this process requires assembling the junk dimension attributes and comparing them to the existing junk dimension rows to see if the row already exists. If not, a new dimension row must be assembled, a surrogate key created, and the row loaded into the junk dimension on the fly during the fact table load process.

- **Mini-dimensions.** Mini-dimensions are a technique used to track dimension attribute changes in a large dimension when the type 2 technique is infeasible. This technique is most typically used for large customer dimensions. From an ETL perspective, creation of the mini-dimension is similar to the junk dimension process just described. There are two alternatives: building all valid combinations in advance or recognizing and creating new combinations on the fly. Whereas junk dimensions are usually built from the fact table input, mini-dimensions are built from dimension table inputs. The ETL system is responsible for maintaining a multi-column surrogate key lookup table to identify the base dimension member and appropriate mini-dimension row to support the surrogate pipeline process described later. Keep in mind that very large, complex customer dimensions may require several mini-dimensions.

- **Shrunken dimensions.** Shrunken dimensions are conformed dimensions that are a subset of rows and/or columns of one of your

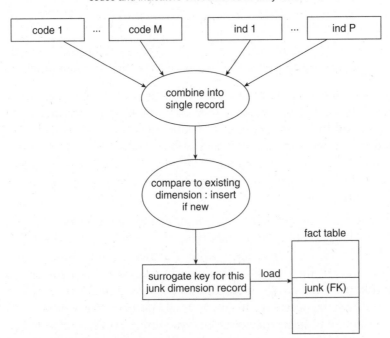

Figure 9-6 Architecture for building junk dimension rows.

base dimensions. The ETL data flow should build conformed shrunken dimensions from the base dimension rather than independently to assure consistency.

- **Small static dimensions.**   A few dimensions are created entirely by the ETL system without a real outside source. These are usually small lookup dimensions where an operational code is translated into words. In these cases, there is no real ETL processing. The lookup dimension is simply created directly by the ETL team as a relational table in its final form.

- **User maintained dimensions.**   Often the warehouse requires that totally new "master" dimension tables be created. These dimensions have no formal system of record; rather they are custom descriptions, groupings, and hierarchies created by the business for reporting and analysis purposes. The ETL team often ends up with stewardship responsibility for these dimensions, but this is typically not successful because the ETL team is not aware of changes that occur to these custom groupings, so the dimensions fall into disrepair and become ineffective. The best case scenario is to have the appropriate user department agree to own the maintenance of these attributes. The warehouse team needs to provide a user interface for this maintenance. Typically this takes the form of a simple application built using the company's standard visual programming tool. The ETL system should add default attribute values for new rows that the user owner needs to update. If these rows are loaded into the warehouse before they are changed, they still appear in reports with whatever default description is supplied.

NOTE The ETL process should create a unique default dimension attribute description that shows that someone hasn't done their data stewardship job yet. We favor a label that concatenates the phrase "Not yet assigned" with the surrogate key value, as in "Not yet assigned 157." That way, multiple "Not yet assigned" values do not inadvertently get lumped together in reports and aggregate tables. This also helps identify the rows for correction.

Subsystem 13 – Fact Table Builders

Fact tables hold the measurements of an organization. Dimensional models are deliberately built around these numerical measurements. The fact table builder subsystem focuses on the ETL architectural requirements to effectively build the three primary types of fact tables: transaction grain, periodic snapshot, and accumulating snapshot fact tables. An important requirement for loading your fact tables is maintaining referential integrity with the associated dimension tables. The surrogate key pipeline (subsystem 14) is designed to help support this need.

Transaction Grain Fact Table Loader

The transaction grain represents a measurement event defined at a particular instant. A line item on an invoice is an example of a transaction event. A scanner event at a cash register is another. In these cases, the timestamp in the fact table is very simple. It's either a single daily grain foreign key or a pair consisting of a daily grain foreign key together with a time-of-day foreign key, depending on what the source system provides and the analyses require. The facts in this transaction grain table must be true to the grain and should describe only what took place in that instant.

Transaction grain fact tables are the largest and most detailed of the three types of fact tables. The transaction grain fact table loader receives data from the changed data capture system and loads it with the proper dimensional foreign keys. The pure addition of most current records is the easiest case, simply bulk loading new rows into the fact table. In most cases, the target fact table should be partitioned by date to ease the administration and speed the performance of the table. An audit key, sequential ID, or date/timestamp field should be included to allow backup or restart of the load job.

The addition of late arriving records is more difficult, requiring additional processing capabilities described in subsystem 16.

Finally, in the event it is necessary to update existing records, the processing should be handled in two steps. The first step is to insert the corrected rows without overwriting or deleting the original rows, and then delete the old rows in a second step. Using a sequentially assigned single surrogate key for the fact table makes it possible to perform these two steps separately.

Periodic Snapshot Fact Table Loader

The periodic snapshot grain represents a regular repeating measurement or set of measurements, such as a bank account monthly statement. This fact table also has a single date field, representing the overall snapshot period. The facts in this periodic snapshot grain table must be true to the grain and should describe only measures appropriate to the time span defined by the period. Periodic snapshots are a common fact table type and are frequently found in the financial industry for monthly account balances, for standard financial reporting, and for inventory balances. The periodicity of a periodic snapshot is typically daily, weekly, or monthly.

Periodic snapshots have similar loading characteristics to those of the transaction grain fact tables. The same processing applies for inserts and updates. Assuming data is promptly delivered to the ETL system, all records for each periodic load will cluster in the most recent time partition. Traditionally, periodic snapshots have been loaded en masse at the end of the appropriate period. For example, a credit card company might load a monthly account snapshot table with the balances in effect at the end of the month. The traditional end-of-period load is being modified, with some organizations populating a hot rolling periodic snapshot. In the rolling snapshot, special rows are loaded with the most current balances in effect as of the previous day, or possibly even updated more frequently. As the month progresses, the current month rows are continually updated with this most current information. A caveat to be aware of is that the hot rolling snapshot can be difficult to implement if the business rules for calculating the balances at the period end are complex. In some cases, these complex calculations are dependent on other periodic processing outside the data warehouse and there is not enough information available to the ETL system to perform these complex calculations on a more frequent basis.

Accumulating Snapshot Fact Table Loader

The accumulating snapshot grain represents the current evolving status of a process that has a finite beginning and end. Usually these processes are of short duration and therefore don't lend themselves to the periodic snapshot. Order processing is the classic example of an accumulating snapshot. The order is placed, shipped, and paid for within one reporting period. The transaction grain provides too much detail separated into individual fact table records, and the periodic snapshot is just the wrong way to report this data.

The design and administration of the accumulating snapshot is quite different from the first two fact table types. All accumulating snapshot fact tables have a set of dates, usually four to eight, which describe the typical process workflow. For instance, an order might have an order date, actual ship date, delivery date, final payment date, and return date. In this example, these five dates appear as five separate date-valued foreign surrogate keys. When the order row is first created, the first of these dates is well defined, but perhaps none of the others have yet happened. This same fact row is subsequently revisited as the order winds its way through the order pipeline. Each time something happens, the accumulating snapshot fact row is destructively modified. The date foreign keys are overwritten, and various facts are updated. Often the first date remains inviolate because that describes when the row was created, but all the other dates may well be overwritten, sometimes more than once.

Many RDBMSs utilize variable row lengths. Repeated updates to accumulating snapshot fact rows may cause the rows to grow due to these variable row lengths, affecting the residency of disk blocks. It may be worthwhile to occasionally drop and reload rows after the update activity to improve performance.

An accumulating snapshot fact table is an effective way to represent finite processes with well defined beginnings and endings. However, the accumulating snapshot by definition is the most recent view. Often it makes sense to utilize all three fact table types to meet various needs. Periodic history can be captured with periodic extracts, and all the infinite details involved in the process can be captured in an associated transaction grain fact table. The presence of many situations that violate standard scenarios or involve repeated looping though the process would prohibit the use of an accumulating snapshot.

Subsystem 14 – Surrogate Key Pipeline

Every ETL system must include a step for replacing the operational natural keys in the incoming fact table record with the appropriate dimension surrogate keys. Referential integrity (RI) means that for each foreign key in the fact table, an entry exists in the corresponding dimension table. If you have a sales record in a sales fact table for product surrogate key 323442, you need to have a row in the product dimension table with the same key, or you won't know what you've sold. You have a sale for what appears to be a nonexistent product. Even worse, without the product key in the dimension, a user can easily construct a query that will omit this sale without even realizing it.

The key lookup process should result in a match for every incoming natural key or a default value. In the event there is an unresolved referential integrity failure during the lookup process, you will need to feed these failures back to the responsible ETL process for resolution as shown in Figure 9-7. Likewise, the ETL process will need to resolve any key collisions that might be encountered during the key lookup process.

After the fact table data has been processed and just before loading into the presentation layer, a surrogate key lookup needs to occur to substitute the operational natural keys in the incoming fact table record with the proper current surrogate key. To preserve referential integrity, we always complete our updating of the dimension tables first. In that way, the dimension tables are always the legitimate source of primary keys we must replace in the fact table. This processing is depicted in Figure 9-7.

One approach is to use the actual dimension table as the source for the most current value of the surrogate key corresponding to each natural key. Each time you need the current surrogate key, you would look up all the records in the dimension with the natural key equal to the desired value and then select the surrogate key that aligns with the historical context of the fact row using the current row indicator or begin and end effect dates.

Although this is logically correct, this approach is clearly inefficient. It is much faster to maintain a surrogate key mapping lookup table that has exactly one record for each natural key. These records contain the single *current* value of the surrogate key corresponding to the operational natural key. If the fact records are sorted by the particular natural key, this lookup between the incoming fact record and the surrogate key lookup table can be accomplished with a single pass sort merge operation. During processing, each natural key

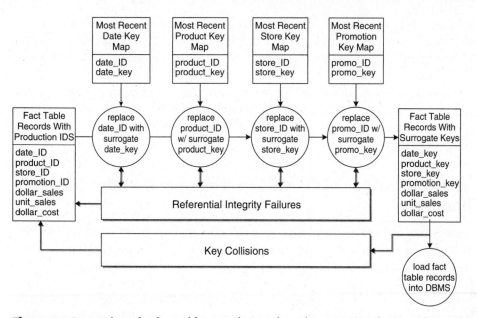

Figure 9-7 Processing of a fact table record to replace the operational natural keys with dimension surrogate keys.

in the incoming fact record is replaced with the correct current surrogate key. Don't keep the natural key in the fact record — the fact table only needs to contain the surrogate key. Do not write the input data to disk until all fact rows have passed all the processing steps. If possible, all required lookup tables should be pinned in memory so that they can be randomly accessed as each incoming record presents its natural keys. This is one reason for using the key map tables rather than relying on the dimension table itself. Some ETL tools offer a high speed, in-memory cache capability that can be utilized in lieu of the key map tables. This can eliminate the need to create and maintain the key map tables, but the overhead of this process may prove to be a performance bottleneck. Small dimensions don't need a highly tuned, complex architecture.

As illustrated at the bottom of Figure 9-7, the surrogate key pipeline will need to handle key collisions in the event you attempt to load a duplicate row. This is an example of a data quality problem appropriate for a traditional structure data quality screen as discussed in subsystem 4. In the event a key collision is recognized, the surrogate key pipeline process will need to choose to halt the process, send the offending data into suspension, or apply appropriate business rules to determine if it is possible to correct the problem, load the row, and write a row into the error event schema.

Note that you will need a slightly different process to perform surrogate key lookups if you ever need to reload history or if you have a lot of late arriving fact rows because you don't want to map the most current value to a historical event. In this case, you need to create logic to find the surrogate key that applied at the time the fact record was generated. This means finding the surrogate key where the fact transaction date is between the key's effective start date and end date.

When the fact table natural keys have been replaced with surrogate keys, the fact record is ready to load. The keys in the fact table record have been chosen to be proper foreign keys, and the fact table is guaranteed to have referential integrity with respect to the dimension tables.

Subsystem 15 – Multi-Valued Dimension Bridge Table Builder

Sometimes a fact table must support a dimension that takes on multiple values at the lowest granularity of the fact table, as described in Chapter 6. If the grain of the fact table cannot be changed to directly support this dimension, then the multi-valued dimension must be linked to the fact table via a bridge table. Bridge tables are common in the healthcare industry, in sales commission environments, and for supporting variable depth hierarchies (see subsystem 11).

The challenge for the ETL team is building and maintaining the bridge table. As multi-valued relationships to the fact row are encountered, the ETL system has the choice of either making each set of observations a unique group, or reusing groups when an identical set of observations occurs. Unfortunately, there is no simple answer for the right choice. In the event the multi-valued dimension has type 2 attributes, the bridge table must also be time varying, such as a patient's time variant set of diagnoses.

One of the bridge table constructs presented in Chapter 6 was the inclusion of a weighting factor to support properly weighted reporting from the bridge table. In many cases, the weighting factor is a familiar allocation factor, but in other cases, the identification of the appropriate weighting factor can be problematic because there may be no rational basis for assigning the weighting factor.

Subsystem 16 – Late Arriving Data Handler

Data warehouses are usually built around the ideal assumption that measured activity (fact records) arrive in the data warehouse at the same time as the context of the activity (dimension records). When you have both the fact records and the correct contemporary dimension rows, you have the luxury of maintaining the dimension keys first, and then using these up-to-date keys in the accompanying fact rows. However, for a variety of reasons, your ETL system may need to process late arriving fact or dimension data.

In some environments, you may need to modify the standard processing procedures to deal with late arriving facts, namely fact records that come into the warehouse very much delayed. This is a messy situation because you have to search back in history within the warehouse to decide which dimension keys were in effect when the activity occurred. In addition, you may need to adjust any semi-additive balances in subsequent fact rows. In a heavily compliant environment, it will also be necessary to interface with the compliance subsystem.

Late arriving dimensions occur when fact measurements arrive at the data warehouse without its full context. In other words, the statuses of the dimensions attached to the activity measurement are ambiguous or unknown for some period of time. If you are living in the conventional batch update cycle of one or more days' latency, you can usually just wait for the dimensions to be reported. For example, the identification of the new customer may come in a separate feed delayed by several hours; you may just be able to wait until the dependency is resolved.

But in many situations, especially real time environments, this delay is not acceptable. You cannot suspend the rows and wait for the dimension updates to occur; the business requirements demand that you make the fact row visible before you know the dimensional context. Your ETL system needs additional capabilities to support this requirement. Using customer as the problem dimension, your ETL system will need to support two situations. The first is to support late arriving type 2 dimension updates. In this situation, you need to add the revised customer record to the dimension with a new surrogate key and then go in and destructively modify any subsequent fact rows' foreign key to the customer table. You also need to reset the effective dates for the affected dimension rows. In addition, you will need to scan forward in the dimension to see if there have been any subsequent type 2 rows for this customer and change this column in any affected rows.

The second situation occurs when you receive a fact row with what appears to be a valid customer natural key, but you have not yet loaded this customer in the customer dimension. It would be possible to load this row pointing to a default row in the dimension table. This approach has the same unpleasant side effect discussed earlier of requiring destructive updates to the fact rows' foreign keys when the dimension updates are finally processed. Alternatively, if you believe that the customer is a valid new, but not yet processed customer, you assign a new customer surrogate key with a set of dummy attribute values in a new customer dimension record. You then return to this dummy dimension record at a later time and make type 1 overwrite changes to its attributes when you get more complete information on the new customer. At least this step avoids destructively changing any fact table keys.

There may be no way to avoid a brief provisional period where the dimensions are "not quite right." But these maintenance steps can minimize the impact of the unavoidable updates to the keys and other fields.

Subsystem 17 – Dimension Manager System

The dimension manager is a centralized authority who prepares and publishes conformed dimensions to the data warehouse community. A conformed dimension is by necessity a centrally managed resource; each conformed dimension must have a single, consistent source. It is the dimension manager's responsibility to administer and publish the conformed dimension(s) for which he has responsibility. There may be multiple dimension managers in an organization, each responsible for a dimension. The dimension manager's responsibilities include the following ETL processing:

- Implement the common descriptive labels agreed to by the data stewards and stakeholders during the dimension design.
- Add new rows to the conformed dimension for new source data, generating new surrogate keys.
- Add new rows for type 2 changes to existing dimension entries, generating new surrogate keys.
- Modify rows in place for type 1 changes and type 3 changes, without changing the surrogate keys.
- Update the version number of the dimension if any type 1 or type 3 changes are made.
- Replicate the revised dimension simultaneously to all fact table providers.

It is easier to manage conformed dimensions in a single tablespace DBMS on a single machine because there is only one copy of the dimension table. However, managing conformed dimensions becomes more difficult in multiple tablespace, multiple DMBS, or multi-machine distributed environments. In these situations, the dimension manager must carefully manage the simultaneous release of new versions of the dimension to every fact provider. Each conformed dimension should have a version number column in each row that is overwritten in every row whenever the dimension manager releases the dimension. This version number should be utilized to support any drill-across queries to assure that the same release of the dimension is being utilized by any user or BI application that is integrating data from multiple presentation servers.

Subsystem 18 – Fact Provider System

The fact provider owns the administration of one or more fact tables and is responsible for their creation, maintenance, and use. If fact tables are used in any drill-across applications, then by definition the fact provider must be using conformed dimensions provided by the dimension manager. The fact provider's responsibilities include:

- Receive or download replicated dimensions from the dimension manager.

- In an environment where the dimension cannot simply be replicated but must be updated locally, the fact provider must process dimension records marked as new and current to update current key maps in the surrogate key pipeline and also process any dimension records marked as new but postdated.

- Add all new records to fact tables after replacing their natural keys with correct surrogate keys.

- Modify records in all fact tables for error correction, accumulating snapshots, and late arriving dimension changes.

- Remove aggregates that have become invalidated.

- Recalculate affected aggregates. If the new release of a dimension does not change the version number, aggregates have to be extended to handle only newly loaded fact data. If the version number of the dimension has changed, the entire historical aggregate may have to be recalculated.

- Quality assure all base and aggregate fact tables. Be satisfied that the aggregate tables are correctly calculated.

- Bring updated fact and dimension tables online.

- Inform users that the database has been updated. Tell them if major changes have been made, including dimension version changes, postdated records being added, and changes to historical aggregates.

Subsystem 19 – Aggregate Builder

Aggregates are the single most dramatic way to affect performance in a large data warehouse environment. Aggregations are like indexes; they are specific data structures created to improve performance. Your ETL system will need to effectively build and use aggregates without causing significant distraction or consuming extraordinary resources and processing cycles.

Chapter 4 describes aggregate navigation, query rewrite, and related architectural components required to support your aggregation strategy. From an ETL viewpoint, your aggregation builder will need to populate and maintain aggregate fact table rows and shrunken dimension tables where needed by aggregate fact tables. The fastest update strategy is incremental, but a major change to a dimension attribute may require dropping and rebuilding the aggregate. In some environments, it may be faster to dump data out of your DBMS and build aggregates with a sort utility rather than building the aggregates inside the DBMS. Additive numeric facts can be aggregated easily at extract time by calculating break rows in one of the sort packages. Aggregates must always be consistent with base data. The fact provider (subsystem 18) is responsible for taking aggregates offline when they are not consistent with the base data.

User feedback on the queries that run slowly is critical input to designing aggregations. Though you can depend on informal feedback to some extent, you will need to capture a log of frequently attempted slow running queries. You should also try to identify the non-existent slow running queries that never made it into the log because they never run to completion, or aren't even attempted due to known performance challenges.

Subsystem 20 – OLAP Cube Builder

OLAP cubes present dimensional data in an intuitive way, enabling analytic users to slice and dice data. OLAP is a sibling of dimensional models in the relational database, with intelligence about relationships and calculations defined on the server that enable faster query performance and more interesting analytics from a broad range of query tools. You shouldn't think of an OLAP server as a competitor to a relational data warehouse, but rather an extension. Let the relational database do what it does best: provide storage and management.

You should consider your relational dimensional schema as the foundation for your OLAP cubes if you elect to include them in your architecture; the relational schemas are the preferred source for OLAP cubes. Because many OLAP systems do not directly address referential integrity or data cleaning, it is best to load OLAP cubes at the end of the conventional ETL process.

You should recognize that some OLAP tools are more sensitive to hierarchies than relational schemas. It is important to strongly enforce the integrity of hierarchies within dimensions before loading an OLAP cube. Type 2 SCDs fit an OLAP system well because a new surrogate key is just treated as a new member. Type 1 and type 3 SCDs that restate history do not fit OLAP well. Overwrites to an attribute value can cause all the cubes that use that dimension to be rebuilt in the background, become corrupted, or be dropped. Read that last sentence again.

Subsystem 21 – Data Propagation Manager

The data propagation manager is responsible for the ETL processes required to transfer conformed, integrated enterprise data from the data warehouse presentation server to other environments for special purposes. Many organizations need to extract data from the presentation layer to share with business partners, customers, and/or vendors. Similarly, some organizations are required to submit data to various government organizations for reimbursement purposes, such as healthcare organizations that participate in the Medicare program. Many organizations have acquired packaged analytic applications. Typically these applications cannot be pointed directly against the existing data warehouse tables, so data needs to be extracted from the presentation layer and loaded into proprietary data structures required by the analytic applications. Finally, most data mining tools do not run directly against the presentation server. They need data extracted from the data warehouse and fed to the data mining tool in a specific format. Data mining is described in more detail in Chapter 11.

All the situations described here require extraction from the data warehouse presentation server, possibly some light transformation and loading into a target format — in other words ETL. You should consider data propagation to be a part of your ETL system and leverage your ETL tools to provide this capability. What is different in this situation from conventional data warehouse ETL processing is that the requirements of the target are not negotiable; you MUST provide the data as specified by the target.

Managing the ETL Environment

A DW/BI system can have a great dimensional model, well deployed BI applications, and strong management sponsorship. But it will not be a success until it can be relied upon as a dependable source for business decision making. One of the goals for the data warehouse is to build a reputation for providing timely, consistent, and reliable data to empower the business. To achieve this goal, the ETL system must constantly work toward fulfilling three criteria:

- **Reliability.**   The ETL processes must run consistently to completion to provide data on a timely basis that is trustworthy at any level of detail.

- **Availability.**   The data warehouse must meet its service level agreements. The warehouse should be up and available as promised.

- **Manageability.**   A successful data warehouse is never done. It constantly grows and changes along with the business. In order to do this, the ETL processes need to evolve gracefully as well.

The ETL management subsystems help achieve the goals of reliability, availability, and manageability. Operating and maintaining a data warehouse in a professional manner is not much different than any other systems operations: Follow standard best practices, plan for disaster, and practice. Most of the requisite management subsystems that follow will be very familiar to many of you.

Subsystem 22 – Job Scheduler

Every enterprise data warehouse should have a robust ETL scheduler. The entire ETL process should be managed, to the extent possible, through a single, metadata-driven job control environment. Major ETL tool vendors package scheduling capabilities into their environments. If you elect not to use the scheduler included with your ETL tool, or are not using an ETL tool, you will want to utilize your existing production scheduling or perhaps manually code your ETL jobs to execute.

Scheduling is much more than just launching jobs on a schedule. Of course, you need a reliable mechanism to manage the ETL execution strategy. In addition, the scheduler needs to be aware of and control the relationships and dependencies between ETL jobs. It needs to recognize when a file or table is ready to be processed. If your organization is processing real time into the data warehouse, you need a scheduler that supports your selected real time architecture. The job control process must also capture metadata regarding the progress and statistics of the ETL process during its execution. Finally, the scheduler should support a fully automated process, including notifying your problem escalation system in the event of any situation that requires resolution.

The infrastructure to manage this can be as basic (and labor-intensive) as a set of SQL stored procedures, or as sophisticated as an integrated tool designed to manage and orchestrate multi-platform data extract and loading processes. If you are using an ETL tool, you should expect your tool to provide this capability. In any case, you need to set up an environment for creating, managing, and monitoring the ETL job stream.

The job control services needed include:

- **Job definition.** The first step in creating an operations process is to have some way to define a series of steps as a job and to specify some relationship among jobs. This is where the execution flow of the ETL process is written. In many cases, if the load of a given table fails, it will impact your ability to load tables that depend on it. For example, if the customer table is not properly updated, loading sales facts for new customers that did not make it into the customer table is risky. In some databases, it is impossible.

- **Job scheduling.** At a minimum, the environment needs to provide standard capabilities, like time- and event-based scheduling. ETL processes are often based on an upstream system event, like the successful completion of the general ledger close or the successful application of sales adjustments to yesterday's sales figures. This includes the ability to monitor database flags, check for the existence of files, and compare creation dates.

- **Metadata capture.**   No self-respecting IT person would tolerate a black box scheduling system. The folks responsible for running the loads will demand a monitoring system (subsystem 27) to understand what is going on. The job scheduler needs to capture information about what step the load is on, what time it started, and how long it took. In a hand-crafted warehouse, this can be accomplished by having each step write to a log file. Your ETL tool should capture this data every time an ETL process executes.

- **Logging.**   This means collecting information about the entire ETL process, not just what is happening at the moment. Log information supports the recovery and restarting of a process in case of errors during the job execution. Logging to text files is the minimum acceptable level. We prefer a system that logs to a database because the structure makes it easier to create graphs and reports. It also makes it possible to create time series studies to help analyze and optimize the load process.

- **Notification.**   Once your ETL process has been developed and deployed, it should execute in a hands-off manner. It should run without human intervention, without fail. If a problem does occur, the control system needs to interface to the problem escalation system (subsystem 30).

NOTE Somebody needs to know if anything unforeseen happened during the load, especially if a response is critical to continuing the process.

Subsystem 23 – Backup System

The data warehouse is subject to the same risks as any other computer system. Disk drives will fail, power supplies will go out, and sprinkler systems will turn on accidentally. In addition to these risks, the warehouse also needs to keep more data for longer periods of time than operational systems. Though typically not managed by the ETL team, the backup and recovery process is often designed as part of the ETL system. Its goal is to allow the data warehouse to get back to work after a failure. This includes backing up intermediate staging data necessary to restart failed ETL jobs. The archive and retrieval process is designed to allow business users access to older data that has been moved out of the main warehouse onto a less costly, usually lower-performing media.

Backup

Even if you have a fully redundant system with a universal power supply, fully RAIDed disks, and parallel processors with failover, some system crisis will eventually occur. Even with perfect hardware, someone can always drop the wrong table (or database). At the risk of stating the obvious, it is better to prepare for this than to handle it on the fly. A full scale backup system needs to provide the following capabilities:

- **High performance.** The backup needs to fit into the allotted time-frame. This may include online backups that don't impact performance significantly, including real time partitions.

- **Simple administration.** The administration interface should provide tools that easily allow you to identify objects to back up (including tables, table spaces, and redo logs), create schedules, and maintain backup verification and logs for subsequent restore.

- **Automated, lights out operations.** The backup facility must provide storage management services, automated scheduling, media and device handling, reporting, and notification.

The backup for the warehouse is usually a physical backup. This is an image of the database at a point in time, including indexes and physical layout information.

Archive and Retrieval

Deciding what to move out of the warehouse is a cost-benefit issue. It costs money to keep the data around — it takes up disk space and slows the load and query times. On the other hand, the business users just might need this data to do some critical historical analyses. Likewise an auditor may request archived data as part of a compliance procedure. The solution is not to throw the data away, but to put it some place that costs less, but is still accessible. Archiving is the data security blanket for the warehouse.

As of this writing, the cost of online disk storage is dropping so rapidly that it makes sense to plan many of your archiving tasks to simply write to disk. Especially if disk storage is being handled by a separate IT resource, your requirement to "migrate and refresh" is replaced by "refresh." You only need to make sure that you can interpret the data at various points in the future.

How long it takes the data to get stale depends on the industry, the business, and the particular data in question. In some cases, it is fairly obvious when older data has little value. For example, in an industry with rapid evolution of new products and competitors, history doesn't necessarily help you understand today or predict tomorrow.

Once a determination has been made to archive certain data, the issue becomes what are the long term implications of archiving data? Obviously, you need to leverage existing mechanisms to physically move the data from its current media to another media and assure that it can be recovered, along with an audit trail that accounts for the accesses and alterations to the data. But, what does it mean to "keep" old data? Given increasing audit and compliance concerns, you may face archival requirements to preserve this data for five, ten, or perhaps even 50 years. There are many complications to consider in this scenario, as we further explore in Chapter 13. What media should you utilize? Will you be able to read that media in future years? Ultimately, you may find yourself implementing a library system capable of archiving the data, and regularly refreshing the data and migrating it to more current structures and media.

Subsystem 24 – Recovery and Restart System

After your ETL system is in production, failures can occur for countless reasons beyond the control of your ETL process. Common causes of ETL production failures include:

- Network failure
- Database failure
- Disk failure
- Memory failure
- Data quality failure
- Unannounced system upgrade

To protect yourself from these failures, you need a solid backup system (subsystem 23) and a companion recovery and restart system. You must plan for unrecoverable errors during the load because they will happen. Your system should anticipate this and provide crash recovery, stop, and restart capability. First, look for appropriate tools and design your processes to minimize the impact of a crash. For example, a load process should commit relatively small sets of records at a time and keep track of what has been committed. The size of the set should be adjustable, because the transaction size has performance implications on different DBMSs.

The recovery and restart system is used, of course, for either resuming a job that has halted or for backing out the whole job and restarting it. This system is significantly dependent on the capabilities of your backup system. When a failure occurs, the initial knee-jerk reaction is to attempt to salvage whatever has processed and restart the process from that point. This requires an ETL tool with a solid and reliable checkpoint functionality so that it is able to perfectly determine what has processed and what has not to restart the job at exactly the right point. In many cases, it may be best to back out any rows that have been loaded as part of the process and restart from the beginning.

The longer an ETL process runs, the more you must be aware of vulnerabilities due to failure. Designing a modular ETL system made up of efficient processes that are resilient against crashes and unexpected terminations will reduce your risk of a failure resulting in a massive recovery effort. Careful consideration of when to physically stage data by writing it to disk, along with carefully crafted points of recovery and load date/timestamps or sequential fact table surrogate keys will enable you to build in appropriate restart logic.

Subsystem 25 – Version Control System

The version control system is a "snapshotting" capability for archiving and recovering all the logic and metadata of the ETL pipeline. It controls check-out and check-in processing for all ETL modules and jobs. It should support source comparisons to reveal differences between versions. This system provides a librarian function for saving and restoring the complete ETL context of a single version. In certain highly compliant environments, it will be equally important to archive the complete ETL system context alongside the relevant archived and backup data. Note that master version numbers need to be assigned for the overall ETL system, just like software release version numbers.

> **NOTE** You do have a master version number for each part of your ETL system as well as one for the system as a whole, don't you? And, you can restore yesterday's complete ETL metadata context if it turns out that there is a big mistake in the current release? Thank you for reassuring us.

Subsystem 26 – Version Migration System

After the ETL team gets past the difficult process of designing and developing the ETL process and manages to complete the creation of the jobs required to load the data warehouse, the jobs must be bundled and migrated to the next environment — from development to test and on to production — according to the lifecycle adopted by your organization. The version migration system needs to interface to the version control system to control the process and back out a migration if needed. It should provide a single interface for setting connection information for the entire version.

Most organizations isolate the development, testing, and production environments. You need to be able to migrate a complete version of the ETL pipeline from development, into test, and finally into production. Ideally, the test system is configured identically to its corresponding production system. Everything that you do to the production system should have been designed in development and the deployment script tested on the test environment. Every back room operation should go through rigorous scripting and testing, whether deploying a new schema, adding a column, changing indexes, changing your aggregate design, modifying a database parameter, backing up, or restoring. Centrally managed front room operations like deploying new BI tools, deploying new corporate reports, and changing security plans should be equally rigorously tested, and scripted if your front end tools allow it. More on this in Chapter 13.

Subsystem 27 – Workflow Monitor

Successful data warehouses are consistently and reliably available, as agreed to with the business community. To achieve this goal, the ETL system must be constantly monitored to ensure that the ETL processes are operating efficiently and that the warehouse is being loaded on a consistently timely basis. Your job scheduler (subsystem 22) should capture performance data every time an ETL process is initiated. This data is part of the process metadata captured in your ETL system. The workflow monitor leverages the metadata captured by the job scheduler to provide a dashboard and reporting system taking many aspects of the ETL system into consideration. You will want to monitor job status for all job runs initiated by the job scheduler including pending, running, completed, and suspended jobs, capturing the historical data to support trending performance over time. Key performance measures include the number of records processed, summaries of errors, and actions taken. Most ETL tools capture the metrics for measuring ETL performance. Be sure to trigger alerts whenever an ETL job takes significantly more or less time to complete than indicated by the historical record.

In combination with the job scheduler, the workflow monitor should also track performance and capture measurements of the performance of infrastructure components, including CPU usage, memory allocation and contention, disk utilization and contention, database performance and server utilization and contention. Much of this information is process metadata about the ETL system and should be considered as part of the overall metadata strategy (subsystem 34).

The workflow monitor has a more significant strategic role than one might suspect. It is the starting point for the analysis of performance problems across the ETL pipeline. ETL performance bottlenecks can occur in many places; a good workflow monitor will show you where the bottlenecks are occurring. In the next chapter, we discuss ways to improve performance in the ETL pipeline, but here is a list, more or less ordered starting with the most important bottlenecks:

- Poorly indexed queries against a source system or intermediate table
- SQL syntax causing wrong optimizer choice
- Insufficient random access memory (RAM) causing thrashing
- Sorting in the RDBMS
- Slow transformation steps
- Excessive I/O
- Unnecessary writes followed by reads
- Dropping and rebuilding aggregates from scratch rather than incrementally

- Filtering (change data capture) applied too late in the pipeline
- Untapped opportunities for parallelizing and pipelining
- Unnecessary transaction logging, especially if doing updates
- Network traffic and file transfer overhead

Subsystem 28 – Sorting System

Certain common ETL processes call for data to be sorted in a particular order, such as aggregating and joining flat file sources. Because sorting is such a fundamental ETL processing capability, it is called out as a separate subsystem to assure it receives proper attention as a component of the ETL architecture. There are a variety of technologies available to provide sorting capabilities. Your ETL tool will undoubtedly provide a sort function, your DBMS can provide sorting via the SQL SORT clause, and there are a number of sort utilities available.

The key is to choose the most efficient sort resource to support your requirements. The easy answer for most organizations is to simply utilize their ETL tools' sort function. However, in some situations it may be more efficient to use a dedicated sort package, although ETL and DBMS vendors claim to have made up much of the performance differences.

Subsystem 29 – Lineage and Dependency Analyzer

Two increasingly important elements being requested from your ETL system are the ability to track both the lineage and dependencies of data in the warehouse:

- **Lineage.**   Beginning with a specific data element in an intermediate table or user report, identify the source of that data element, other upstream intermediate tables containing that data element and its sources, and all transformations that data element and its sources have undergone.
- **Dependency.**   Beginning with a specific data element in a source table or intermediate table, identify all downstream intermediate tables and user reports containing that data element or its derivations and all transformations applied to that data element and its derivations.

Lineage analysis is often an important component in a highly compliant environment where you must be able to explain the complete processing flow that changed any data result. This means that your ETL system must be able to display the ultimate physical sources and all subsequent transformations of any selected data element, chosen either from the middle of the ETL pipeline or on a final delivered report. Dependency analysis is important when assessing changes to a source system and the downstream impacts on the data warehouse and ETL system. This implies the ability to display all affected downstream data elements and final report fields affected by a potential change in any selected data element, chosen either in the middle of the ETL pipeline or an original source (dependency).

Providing these capabilities requires being on top of your ETL documentation and metadata. ETL tools are frequently described as self-documenting. Certainly, you should leverage the documentation capabilities of your ETL tool, but be sure to carefully evaluate these capabilities before you decide to forego your own documentation and metadata management process. Whether you use an ETL tool or hand code your ETL system, it's a piece of software like any other and needs to be documented. As your data warehouse and ETL system evolve, the ETL team needs to be able to quickly understand and describe the details of the system. When compliance knocks and asks for information on tracking changes to a particular set of data, you will need to respond. Solid documentation and metadata are your support mechanism at these times.

The ETL team should establish a design template and group like activities together. The template should clearly identify the specific ETL elements associated with extracts, transformations, lookups, conformation, dimension change management, and final delivery of the target table. Document the template flow in painstaking detail. Use the templates to build out the flow for each dimension and fact table. The table-specific documentation should focus on what's different from the standard template. Don't repeat the details; highlight what's important. Pepper your ETL system with annotations, if your ETL tool supports them.

Subsystem 30 – Problem Escalation System

Typically, the ETL team develops the ETL processes and the quality assurance team tests them thoroughly before they are turned over to the group responsible for day-to-day systems operations. To make this work, your ETL architecture needs to include a proactively designed problem escalation system similar to what you may have in place for other production systems.

Once the ETL processes have been developed and tested, the first level of operational support for the ETL system should be a group dedicated to monitoring production applications. The ETL development team becomes involved only if the operational support team cannot resolve a production problem.

Ideally, you have developed ETL processes, wrapped them into an automated scheduler, and have robust workflow monitoring capabilities peering into the ETL processes as they execute. The execution of the ETL system should be a hands-off operation. It should run like clockwork without human intervention and without fail. If a problem does occur, the ETL process should automatically notify the problem escalation system of any situation that needs attention or resolution. This automatic feed may take the form of simple error logs, operator notification messages, supervisor notification messages, and system developer messages. The ETL system may notify an individual or a group depending on the severity of the situation or the processes involved. ETL tools can support a variety of messaging capabilities including email alerts, operator messages, and notification to a PDA device, phone call, or page.

Each notification event should be written to a database to understand the types of problems that arise, their status, and resolution. This data forms part of the process metadata captured by your ETL system (subsystem 34). You will need to assure you have organizational procedures in place for proper escalation so that every problem is resolved appropriately.

In general, support for your ETL system should follow a fairly standard support structure. First level support is typically a help desk that is the first point of contact when a user notices an error. The help desk is responsible for resolution whenever feasible. If the help desk cannot resolve the issue, the second level support is notified. This is typically a systems administrator or DBA on the production control technical staff capable of supporting general infrastructure type failures. The ETL manager is the third level support and should be knowledgeable to support most issues that arise in the ETL production process. Finally, when all else fails, the ETL developer should be called in to analyze the situation and assist with resolution.

Subsystem 31 – Parallelizing/Pipelining System

The goal of the ETL system, in addition to providing high quality data, is to load the data warehouse within the allocated processing window. In large organizations with huge data volumes and a large portfolio of dimensions and facts, loading the data within these constraints can be a challenge. The paralleling/pipelining system provides capabilities to enable the ETL system to deliver within these time constraints. The goal of this system is to take advantage of multiple processors or grid computing resources commonly available. It is highly desirable, and in many cases necessary, that parallelizing and pipelining be invoked automatically for every ETL process unless specific conditions preclude it from processing in such a manner, such as waiting on a condition in the middle of the process.

Parallelizing is a powerful performance technique at every stage of the ETL pipeline. For example, the extraction process can be parallelized by logically partitioning on ranges of an attribute. Verify that the source DBMS handles parallelism correctly and doesn't spawn conflicting processes. If possible, choose an ETL tool that handles parallelizing of intermediate transformation processes automatically. In some tools, it is necessary to hand create parallel processes. This is fine until you add additional processors, and your ETL system then can't take advantage of the greater parallelization opportunities unless you manually modify the ETL modules to increase the number of parallel flows.

Subsystem 32 – Security System

Security is an important consideration for the ETL system. A serious security breach is much more likely to come from within the organization than from someone hacking in from the outside. Although we don't like to think it, the folks on the ETL team present as much a potential threat as any group inside the organization. We recommend you administer role-based security on all data and metadata in the ETL system. To support compliance requirements, you may need to prove that a version of an ETL module hasn't been changed or show who made changes to a module. You should enforce comprehensive authorized access to all ETL data and metadata by individual and role. In addition, you will want to maintain an historical record of all accesses to ETL data and metadata by individual and role. Another issue to be careful of is the bulk data movement process. If you are moving data across the network, even if it is within the company firewall, it pays to be careful. Make sure you use a file transfer utility that uses a secure transfer protocol.

Another back room security issue to consider is administrator access to the production warehouse server and software. We've seen situations where no one on the team had security privileges; in other cases, everyone had access to everything. Obviously, many members of the team should have privileged access to the development environment, but the production warehouse should be fairly strictly controlled. However, someone from the warehouse team needs to be able to reset the warehouse machine if something goes wrong. Finally, we urge you to guard your backup media. The backup media should have as much security surrounding them as the online systems. Chapters 4 and 5 provide a more detailed discussion on security. We reiterate our earlier recommendation about a dedicated security manager on the DW/BI team.

Subsystem 33 – Compliance Manager

In highly compliant environments, supporting compliance requirements is a significant new requirement for the ETL team. Compliance in the data warehouse boils down to "maintaining the chain of custody" of the data. In the same way a police department must carefully maintain the chain of custody of evidence to argue that the evidence has not been changed or tampered with, the data warehouse must also carefully guard the compliance-sensitive data entrusted to it from the moment it arrives. Furthermore, the data warehouse must always be able to show the exact condition and content of such data at any point in time that it may have been under the control of the data warehouse. The data warehouse must also track who had authorized access to the data. Finally, when the suspicious auditor is looking over your shoulder, you need to link back to an archived and time stamped version of the data as it was originally received, which you have stored remotely with a trusted third party. If the data warehouse is prepared to meet all these compliance requirements, then the stress of being audited by a hostile government agency or lawyer armed with a subpoena should be greatly reduced.

The compliance requirements may mean that you cannot actually change any data, for any reason. If data must be altered, then a new version of the altered records must be inserted into the database. Each record in each table therefore must have a begin timestamp and end timestamp that accurately represents the span of time when that record was the "current truth." The big impact of these compliance requirements on the data warehouse can be expressed in simple dimensional modeling terms. Type 1 and type 3 changes are dead. In other words, all changes become inserts. No more deletes or overwrites.

But for heaven's sake, don't assume that all data is now subject to draconian compliance restrictions. It is essential that you receive firm guidelines from your chief compliance officer before taking any drastic steps.

The foundation of your compliance system is the interaction of several subsystems already described, married to a few key technologies and capabilities:

- **Lineage analysis.** Show where a final piece of data came from to prove the original source data plus the transformations including stored procedures and manual changes. This requires full documentation of all the transforms and the technical ability to re-run the transforms against the original data.

- **Dependency analysis.** Show wherever an original source data element was used.

- **Version control.** It may be necessary to re-run the source data through the ETL system in effect at the time, requiring identifying the exact version of the ETL system for any given data source.

- **Backup and restore.** Of course the requested data may have been archived years ago and need to be restored for audit purposes. Hopefully, you archived the proper version of the ETL system alongside the data so that both the data and the system can be restored. It may be necessary to prove that the archived data hasn't been altered. During the archival process, the data can be hash coded and the hash and data separated. Have the hash codes archived separately by a trusted third party. Then, when demanded, restore the original data, hash code it again, and then compare to the hash codes retrieved from the trusted third party to prove the authenticity of the data.

- **Security.** Show who has accessed or modified the data and transforms. Be prepared to show roles and privileges for users. Guarantee the security log can't be altered by using a write once media.

- **Audit dimension.** The audit dimension ties runtime metadata context directly with the data to capture quality events at the time of the load.

Subsystem 34 – Metadata Repository Manager

The ETL system is responsible for the use and creation of much of the metadata describing your DW/BI environment. Part of your overall metadata strategy (discussed in Chapter 4) should be to specifically capture ETL metadata, including the process metadata, technical metadata, and business metadata. You need to develop a balanced strategy between doing nothing and doing too much. Make sure there's time in your ETL development tasks to capture and manage metadata. And finally, make sure someone on the DW/BI team is assigned the role of metadata manager and owns the responsibility for creating and implementing the metadata strategy.

Real Time Implications

Real time processing is an increasingly common requirement in data warehousing. There is a strong possibility that your DW/BI system will have a real time requirement. More and more business users expect the data warehouse to be continuously updated throughout the day and grow impatient with stale data. Building a real time DW/BI system requires gathering a very precise understanding of the true business requirements for real time data and identifying an appropriate ETL architecture incorporating a variety of technologies married with a solid platform.

Real Time Triage

Asking business users if they want "real time" delivery of data is a frustrating exercise for the data warehouse team. Faced with no constraints, most users will say, "that sounds good, go for it!" This kind of response is almost worthless.

To avoid this situation, we recommend dividing the real time design challenge into three categories, which we call *instantaneous, frequently*, and *daily*. We use these terms when we talk to business users about their needs, and we design our data delivery pipelines differently for each of these choices.

Instantaneous means that the data visible on the screen represents the true state of the source transaction system at every instant. When the source system status changes, the screen responds instantly and synchronously. An instantaneous real time system is usually implemented as an enterprise information integration (EII) solution, where the source system itself is responsible for supporting the update of remote users' screens and servicing query requests. Obviously such a system must limit the complexity of the query requests because all the processing is done on the source system. EII solutions typically involve no caching of data in the ETL pipeline because EII solutions by definition have no delays between the source systems and the users' screens.

EII technologies offer reasonable lightweight data cleaning and transformation services, but all these capabilities must be executed in software because the data is being continuously piped to the users' screens. Most EII solutions also allow for a transaction protected write-back capability from the users' screens to the transactional data. In the business requirements interviews with users, you should carefully assess the need for an instantaneous real time solution, keeping in mind the significant load that such a solution places on the source application and the inherent volatility of instantaneously updated data. Some situations are ideal candidates for an instantaneous real time solution. Inventory status tracking may be a good example, where the decision maker has the right to commit available inventory to a customer in real time.

Frequently means that the data visible on the screen is updated many times per day but is not guaranteed to be the absolute current truth. Most of us are familiar with stock market quote data that is current to within 15 minutes but is not instantaneous. The technology for delivering frequent real time data (as well as the slower daily real time data) is distinctly different from instantaneous real time delivery. Frequently delivered data is usually processed as micro-batches in a conventional ETL architecture. This means that the data undergoes the full gamut of change data capture, extract, staging to file storage in the ETL back room, cleaning and error checking, conforming to enterprise data standards, assigning of surrogate keys, and possibly a host of other transformations to make the data ready to load into the presentation server. Almost all of these steps must be omitted or drastically reduced in an EII solution. The big difference between frequently and daily delivered data is in the first two steps: change data capture and extract. In order to capture data many times per day from the source system, the data warehouse usually must tap into a high bandwidth communications channel such as message queue traffic between legacy applications, or an accumulating transaction log file, or low level database triggers coming from the transaction system every time something happens. If the rest of the ETL system can be run many times per day, then perhaps the design of the following stages can remain batch oriented.

Daily means that the data visible on the users' screen is valid as of a batch file download or reconciliation from the source system at the end of the previous working day. A few years ago, a daily update of the data warehouse was considered aggressive, but today daily data would be a conservative choice. There is a lot to recommend daily data. Quite often processes are run on the source system at the end of the working day that correct the raw data. When this reconciliation becomes available, that is the signal that the data warehouse can perform a reliable and stable download of the data. If you have this situation, you should explain to the business users what compromises they will experience if they demand instantaneous or frequently updated data. Daily updated data usually involves reading a batch file prepared by the source system or performing an extract query when a source system readiness flag is set. This, of course, is the simplest extract scenario because you take your time waiting for the source system to be ready and available. Once you have the data, the downstream ETL batch processing is similar to that of the frequently updated real time systems, but it only needs to run once per day.

The business requirements gathering step is crucial to the real time ETL design process. The big decision is whether to go instantaneous, or live with frequent or daily updates. The instantaneous solutions are quite separate from the other two, and you would not want to change strategy midstream. On the other hand, you may be able to gracefully convert a daily ETL pipeline to frequently, mostly by altering the first two steps of change data capture and extract.

Real Time Tradeoffs

Responding to real time requirements means you'll need to change your DW/BI architecture to get data to the business users' screens faster. The architectural choices you make will involve tradeoffs that affect data quality and administration.

We assume that your overall goals as ETL system owners are not changed or compromised by moving to real time delivery. We assume that you remain just as committed to data quality, integration, security, compliance, backup, recovery, and archiving as you were before you started designing a real time system. If you agree with this statement, then read the following very carefully! Here are typical tradeoffs that occur as you implement a real time architecture:

- **Replacing a batch file extract with reading from a message queue or transaction log file.**   A batch file delivered from the source system may represent a clean and consistent view of the source data. The batch file may contain only those records resulting from completed trans-actions. Foreign keys in the batch files are probably resolved, such as when the file contains an order from a new customer whose complete identity may be delivered with the batch file. Message queue and log file data, on the other hand, is raw instantaneous data that may not be subject to any corrective process or business rule enforcement in the source system. In the worst case, this raw data may 1) be incorrect or incomplete because additional transactions may arrive later; 2) contain unresolved foreign keys that the DW/BI system has not yet processed; 3) require a parallel batch oriented ETL data flow to correct or even replace the hot real time data each 24 hours. And if the source system applies complex business rules to the input transactions seen in the message queues or the log files, then you really don't want to recapitulate these business rules in the ETL system!

- **Restricting data quality screening only to column screens and simple decode lookups.**   As the time to process data moving through the ETL pipeline is reduced, it may be necessary to eliminate more costly data quality screening, especially structure screens and business rule screens. Remember that column screens involve single field tests and/or simple lookups to replace or expand known values. Even in the most aggressive real time applications, most column screens should survive. But structure screens and business rule screens by definition require multiple fields, multiple records, and possibly multiple tables. You may not have time to pass an address block of fields to an address analyzer. You may not be able to check referential integrity between tables. You may not be able to perform a remote credit check through a web service. All of this may require that you inform the users of the provisional and potentially unreliable state of the raw real time data, and may require that you implement a parallel, batch oriented ETL pipeline that overwrites the real time data periodically with properly checked data.

- **Allowing early arriving facts to be posted with old copies of dimensions.**   In the real time world, it is common to receive transaction events before the context (such as the identity of the customer) of those transactions is updated. In other words, the facts arrive before the dimensions. If the real time system cannot wait for the dimensions to be resolved, then old copies of the dimensions must be used if they are available or generic empty versions of the dimensions must be used otherwise. If and when revised versions of the dimensions are received, the data warehouse may decide to post those into the hot partition, or delay updating the dimension until a batch process takes over, possibly at the end of the day. In any case, the users need to understand that there may be an ephemeral window of time where the dimensions don't exactly describe the facts.

- **Eliminating data staging.**   Some real time architectures, especially EII systems, stream data directly from the production source system to the users' screens without writing the data to permanent storage in the ETL pipeline. If this kind of system is part of the DW/BI team's responsibility, the team should have a serious talk with senior management about whether backup, recovery, archiving, and compliance responsibilities can be met, or whether those responsibilities are now the sole concern of the production source system. At the very least, the data stream going through the DW/BI system should be captured in its entirety, although this is a band-aid solution because it may be very difficult to process such a data stream at a later point in time.

Real Time Partitions in the Presentation Server

To support real time requirements, the data warehouse must seamlessly extend its existing historical time series right up to the current instant. If the customer has placed an order in the last hour, you need to see this order in the context of the entire customer relationship. Furthermore, you need to track the hourly status of this most current order as it changes during the day. Even though the gap between the production transaction processing systems and the data warehouse has shrunk in most cases to 24 hours, the insatiable needs of our users require the data warehouse to fill this gap with real time data.

The design solution for responding to this crunch is building a real time partition as an extension of the conventional, static data warehouse. To achieve real time reporting, you build a special partition that is physically and administratively separated from the conventional data warehouse tables. Ideally, the real time partition is a true database partition where the fact table in question is partitioned by activity date. If such partitioning is not feasible, then the real time partition must be a separate table subject to special rules for update and query.

In either case, the real time partition ideally should meet the following tough set of requirements. It must:

- Contain all the activity that has occurred since the last update of the static data warehouse. Assume for now that the static tables are updated each night at midnight.

- Link as seamlessly as possible to the grain and content of the static data warehouse fact tables, ideally as a true physical partition of the fact table.

- Be indexed so lightly that incoming data can continuously be "dribbled in." Ideally, the real time partition is completely un-indexed, although this may not be possible in certain RDBMSs where indexes have been built that are not partitionable.

- Support highly responsive queries even in the absence of indexes by pinning the real time partition in memory.

The real time partition can be used effectively with both the transaction grain and periodic snapshot grain fact tables. We have not found this approach to be needed with accumulating snapshot fact tables.

Transaction Grain Real Time Partition

If the static data warehouse fact table has a transaction grain, it contains exactly one record for each individual transaction in the source system from the beginning of "recorded history." The real time partition has exactly the same dimensional structure as its underlying static fact table. It contains only the transactions that have occurred since midnight when you last loaded the conventional data warehouse tables. The real time partition may be completely un-indexed, both because you need to maintain a continuously open window for loading and because there is no time series as you keep only today's data in this table. Finally, if the real time partition is a separate physical table, you can avoid building aggregates on this table because you want a minimalist administrative scenario during the day.

If the real time partition is a true table partition, then all applications will gracefully bridge between the static portion of the fact table and the real time partition. If the real time partition is a separate physical table, then you must attach the real time partition to your existing applications by drilling across from the static fact table to the real time partition. Time series aggregations (for example, all sales for the current month) in this case would need to send identical queries to the two fact tables and add them together.

In a relatively large retail environment experiencing 10 million transactions per day, the static fact table would be pretty big. Assuming that each transaction grain record is 40 bytes wide (seven dimensions plus three facts, all packed into four byte fields), you accumulate 400 MB of data each day. Over a year, this would amount to about 150GB of raw data. Such a fact table would be heavily indexed and supported by aggregates. But the daily real time slice of 400 MB should be pinned in memory. Your real time partition can remain biased toward very fast loading performance, but at the same time provide speedy query performance.

Because you send identical queries to the static fact table and the real time partition, you can relax and let the aggregate navigator sort out whether either of the tables has supporting aggregates. In the case just described, only the big static fact table needs them.

Periodic Snapshot Real Time Partition

If the static data warehouse fact table has a periodic grain (say, monthly), then the real time partition can be viewed as the current hot rolling month as described earlier in this chapter. Suppose you are a big retail bank with 15 million accounts. The static fact table has the grain of account by month. A 36-month time series would result in 540 million fact table records. Again, this table would be extensively indexed and supported by aggregates to provide good query performance. The real time partition, on the other hand, is just an image of the current developing month, updated continuously as the month progresses. Semi-additive balances and fully additive facts are adjusted as frequently as they are reported. In a retail bank, the "core" fact table spanning all account types is likely to be quite narrow, with perhaps four dimensions and four facts, resulting in a real time partition of 480 MB. The real time partition again can be pinned in memory.

Query applications drilling across from the static fact table to the real time partition have slightly different logic compared to the transaction grain. Although account balances and other measures of intensity can be trended directly across the tables, additive totals accumulated during the current rolling period may need to be scaled upward to the equivalent of a full month to keep the results from looking anomalous.

Finally, on the last day of the month, the periodic real time partition can, with luck, just be merged onto the static data warehouse as the most current month, and the process can start again with an empty real time partition.

Conclusion

In this chapter we have introduced the key building blocks of the ETL system. Chapter 10 shows you how to use these building blocks to assemble your ETL system.

As you may now better appreciate, building an ETL system is unusually challenging; the ETL system must address a number of demanding requirements. In this chapter we identified and reviewed the 34 subsystems of ETL, and gathered these subsystems into four key areas that represent the ETL process: extracting, cleaning and conforming, delivering, and managing. Careful consideration of all the elements of your ETL architecture is the key to success. You must understand the full breadth of requirements and then set an appropriate and effective architecture in place. ETL is more than simply extract, transform, and load; it's a host of complex and important tasks.

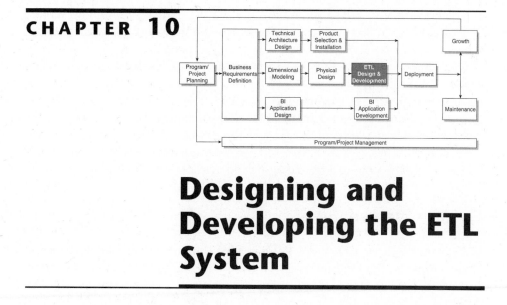

CHAPTER 10

Designing and Developing the ETL System

The process of developing the extract, transformation, and load (ETL) system is the iceberg of the DW/BI project. So many challenges are buried in the data sources that developing the ETL application invariably takes more time than you expect. This chapter is structured as a ten-step plan for creating the data warehouse's ETL system. The concepts and approach described in this chapter apply to systems based on an ETL tool, as well as hand coded systems.

This chapter should be studied in detail by everyone on the ETL team. Data architects, modelers, and DBAs should also read this chapter. Project managers should peruse this chapter to better appreciate the complexity of ETL system design and development. The chapter is optional reading for the rest of the project team.

ETL Process Overview

How do you think we will advise you to begin the process of building the ETL application? For once we will skip our primary mantra of *focus on the business requirements* and present our second favorite aphorism: *Make a plan*. It's rare to see an ETL system that is planned in a concrete and documented way. This is understandable because so much of the work to this point has been planning and designing; now everyone is anxious to see some real data.

Nonetheless, you need a plan. Like anything else, if you don't have a plan, you cannot explain to others where you are going or how you expect to get there.

This chapter follows the flow of planning and implementing the ETL system. We implicitly discuss the 34 ETL subsystems presented in Chapter 9, broadly categorized as extracting data, cleaning and conforming, delivering for presentation, and managing the ETL environment. Table 10.1 describes the structure of this chapter and maps these topics to the 34 subsystems.

Several of these topics are addressed further in Chapter 13 where we describe the process of deploying and managing the overall DW/BI system.

Getting Started

Before you begin the ETL system design for a dimensional model, you should have completed the logical design, drafted your high level architecture plan, and drafted the source-to-target mapping for all data elements. The physical design and implementation work described in Chapter 8 should be well under way.

The ETL system design process is critical. Gather all the relevant information, including the processing burden your extracts will be allowed to place on the transaction systems and test some key alternatives. Does it make sense to host the transformation process on the source system, target system, or its own platform? What tools are available on each, and how effective are they? You're likely to write some code from scratch, including SQL queries and automation scripts. Use a source code control system from the outset. Again, what you actually need to do depends on the scope of your project and the tools available to you.

IMPORTANCE OF GOOD SYSTEM DEVELOPMENT PRACTICES

ETL development may follow an iterative, interactive process, but the fundamental systems development practices still apply:

- Set up a header format and comment fields for your code.
- Hold structured design reviews early enough to allow changes.
- Write clean, well-commented code.
- Stick to the naming standards.
- Use the code library and management system.
- Test everything — both unit testing and system testing.
- Document everything.

Table 10-1 Map of Process Flow to ETL Subsystems

ETL PROCESS STEP	EXTRACTING DATA	CLEANING AND CONFORMING	DELIVERING FOR PRESENTATION	MANAGING THE ETL ENVIRONMENT
Plan				
Create a high level, one-page schematic of the source-to-target flow.	1			
Test, choose, and implement an ETL tool (Chapter 5).				
Develop default strategies for dimension management, error handling, and other processes.	3	4, 5, 6	10	
Drill down by target table, graphically sketching any complex data restructuring or transformations, and develop preliminary job sequencing.		4, 5, 6	11	22
Develop One-Time Historic Load Process				
Build and test the historic dimension table loads.	3	4, 7, 8	9, 10, 11, 12, 15	
Build and test the historic fact table loads, including surrogate key lookup and substitution.	3	4, 5, 8	13, 14	
Develop Incremental Load Process				
Build and test the dimension table incremental load processes.	2, 3	4, 7, 8	9, 10, 11, 12, 15, 16, 17	
Build and test the fact table incremental load processes	2, 3	4, 5, 8	13, 14, 16, 18	
Build and test aggregate table loads and/or OLAP processing.			19, 20	
Design, build, and test the ETL system automation.		6	17, 18, 21	22, 23, 24, 30

Develop the ETL Plan

ETL development starts with the high level plan, which is independent of any specific technology or approach. However, it's a good idea to decide on an ETL tool before you do any detailed planning; this will save you redesign and rework later in the process.

Step 1 – Draw the High Level Plan

Start the design process with a simple schematic of the pieces of the plan that you know: sources and targets. Keep it very high level, highlighting in one or two pages the data sources and annotating the major challenges that you already know about. Figure 10-1 illustrates what we mean. This schematic is for a fictitious utility company's data warehouse, which is primarily sourced from a 30-year-old COBOL system. If most or all of the data come from a modern relational transaction processing system, the boxes often represent a logical grouping of tables in the transaction system model.

This one-pager is a good way to communicate some of the project's complexity to management. It's probably as deep as they — indeed, most people — will want to delve into the ETL system.

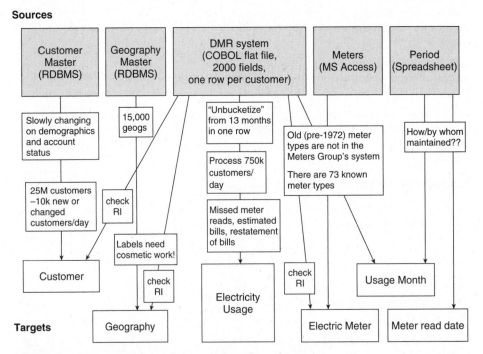

Figure 10-1 Example high level data staging plan schematic.

As you develop the detailed ETL system specification, this high level view will gather additional details. Figure 10-1 deliberately highlights contemporary questions and unresolved issues; this plan should be updated and released frequently. You may want to keep two versions of the diagram: a simple one for communicating with people outside the team and a detailed version for internal documentation.

Step 2 – Choose an ETL Tool

There are a multitude of ETL tools available in the data warehouse marketplace. Most of the major database vendors offer an ETL tool, usually at additional licensing cost. There are also excellent ETL tools available from third party vendors.

ETL tools serve a variety of functions. Some are particularly good at extracting information from specific source systems, especially the older mainframe systems built in COBOL and other non-relational data structures. The value of these tools is particularly large if your cadre of COBOL developers has already retired.

ETL tools read data from a range of sources, including flat files, ODBC, OLE DB, and native database drivers for most relational databases. The tools contain functionality for defining transformations on that data, including lookups and other kinds of joins. They can write data into a variety of target formats. And they all contain some functionality for managing the overall flow of logic in the ETL system.

If your source systems are relational, your transformation requirements are straightforward, and you have good developers on staff, the value of an ETL tool may not be immediately obvious. It seems a simple matter to write some SQL, tie it together with scripts, and use the expensive and powerful relational engine to do the heavy lifting of the ETL system. Indeed, hand coded (usually SQL based) systems are still quite common. However there are several reasons that using an ETL tool is an industry standard best practice:

- **Self-documentation that comes from using a graphical tool.** A hand coded system is usually an impenetrable mass of staging tables, SQL scripts, stored procedures, and operating system scripts. When a new developer joins the project — or even if the original developer reviews the code a year later — it is extraordinarily difficult to figure out what is going on and why. Because ETL tools are graphical, it's much easier to see the basic flow of the system and understand where important transformations are taking place. Ironically, many ETL tools generate very poor documentation; some offer no palatable way to print the control flow other than screenshots.

- **ETL tools offer advanced transformation logic,** such as fuzzy matching algorithms, integrated access to name and address deduplication routines, and data mining algorithms.

- **Improved system performance at a lower level of expertise.** Relatively few SQL developers are truly expert on how to use the relational database to manipulate extremely large data volumes with excellent performance. If you have those skills, you might be able to hand code an ETL system that outperforms one that you could implement in your chosen ETL tool. But what about the next person who is expected to maintain or extend the system?

You should not expect to recoup your investment in the ETL tool on the first phase of your data warehouse project. The learning curve is steep enough that you may feel your project could have been implemented faster by hand. The big advantages come with future phases, and particularly with future modifications to existing systems.

The ETL tool market continues to mature, and products offer substantial features, performance, and manageability at decreasing prices. We recommend selecting an ETL tool early on and using it right from the start. In a production system, the long-term improvements in manageability, productivity, and training are significant.

Step 3 – Develop Default Strategies

Once you have an overall idea of what needs to happen and what your ETL tool's infrastructure requires, you should develop a set of default strategies for the common activities in the ETL system. These activities include:

- **Extract from each major source system.**   We described the basic strategies for extracting data from source systems in Chapter 9. At this point in the ETL system design process, determine the default method for extracting data from each source system. Will you normally push from the source system to a flat file, extract in a stream, use a tool to read the database logs, or another method? You can modify this decision on a table by table basis. If you are using SQL to access source system data, make sure you are using native data extractors rather than ODBC, if you have the choice.

- **Archive extracted data.**   You should archive extracted data, before it's been transformed, for at least a month. Some organizations archive extracted data permanently. The purpose of the archive is system auditability and recoverability. Work with your internal audit organization to determine how long to archive extracted data. It's common to store the archived data in files rather than database tables.

- **Police data quality for dimensions and facts.** As we described in Chapter 9, you should measure data quality during the ETL process rather than wait for your business users to find data problems. Develop a general, standardized process for how you will check data quality, and what you will do if the data does not pass quality control. There is a policy component to this step: How should data quality problems be handled for facts and dimensions? In addition, there's a technical decision: How will you implement data quality checks, and how will you stop the load or page an operator? The technical decision, of course, depends on your ETL architecture. We described a comprehensive architecture for measuring and responding to data quality issues in ETL subsystems 4 through 8.

- **Manage changes to dimension attributes.** In Chapter 9, we described the logic required to manage changes in dimension attributes, notably type 1 (overwrite history) and type 2 (track history). You will need to implement type 1 row updates and add new rows for type 2 changes. Most ETL tools have wizards or design patterns for managing attribute changes; choose and document the method that works best for the majority of your dimensions. You might need an alternate strategy for a handful of dimensions, especially very large dimensions.

- **Ensure the data warehouse and ETL system meet the requirements for system availability.** The first step to meeting system availability requirements is to document them. You should also document when each data source becomes available, and block out high level job sequencing. If you suspect that system availability will be a problem in your environment, you must evaluate architectural alternatives, such as background processing on an alternative server.

- **Design the data auditing subsystem.** You should tag each row in the data warehouse with auditing information that describes how the data entered the system. We describe the auditing subsystem in greater detail later in this chapter.

- **Organize the ETL staging area.** Most ETL systems will stage the data at least once or twice during the ETL process. By staging, we mean the data will be written to disk for a later ETL step to use. We already discussed the practice of archiving the extracted data; this is akin to staging, but you may not actually use the archived data in any subsequent process. As you design the ETL system, you will develop a clearer understanding of how large the staging area must be and whether you will depend primarily on the file system or database to hold the staged data. These decisions are dependent on your choice of ETL tool. Some tools and architectures make heavy use of staging tables or files; others operate on data in a pipeline and seldom write it to disk until it's time to insert it into the data warehouse presentation server.

The default strategies described here will become part of the table-specific modules for the ETL system. As you go on to write the detailed specification, you can refer to this general policies section. When it comes time to actually develop the ETL system, you'll find that the modules for each table are structured similarly, which makes for a more maintainable system.

Step 4 – Drill Down by Target Table

Once you've developed overall strategies for common ETL tasks, start drilling into the detailed transformations needed to populate each target table in the data warehouse. Begin by completing the source-to-target mappings we described in Chapter 7. In an ideal world, you finished the source-to-target mappings as you finalized the physical model, but now is the time to ensure that you know where the data is coming from for each column in each target table.

At the same time you're finalizing the source-to-target mappings, you must complete the data profiling. This task occurred earlier in the Lifecycle at a high level during the requirements definition and then a more detailed pass during the dimensional modeling. However, the ETL team will inevitably want to do more data profiling and investigation to thoroughly understand the necessary data transformations for each table and column.

Ensure Clean Hierarchies

It's particularly important to investigate whether hierarchical relationships in the dimension data are perfectly clean. Consider a product dimension that includes a hierarchical rollup from product SKU to product category, as illustrated in Figure 10-2. For this hierarchy to be of greatest value, each product SKU must roll up to one and only one model, and so on up the tree.

Clean many-to-one hierarchies are important for several reasons. If you plan to create precomputed aggregations — which are important for query performance in either relational or OLAP implementations — or if you will be adding data at a higher level of granularity, it is important that your hierarchies be clean. If you have large data volumes, you will need intermediate aggregations to achieve excellent query performance; intermediate aggregations are most useful only when they are defined on clean hierarchies.

Another common design in an enterprise DW/BI system is to have data at different levels of granularity. For example, the business users probably develop sales forecasts at the subcategory or model level, not for each SKU.

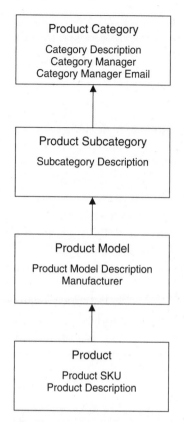

Figure 10-2 Example product hierarchy.

A sales forecast fact table would use a conformed shrunken subset of the product dimension, but in order to join smoothly with the actual sales data, you need clean hierarchies.

In our experience, you are unlikely to have reliable hierarchies unless the hierarchical data is well managed in the source system. The best source system will normalize the hierarchical levels into multiple tables, with foreign key constraints between the levels. In this case, you can be confident that the hierarchies are clean. If your source system is not normalized — especially if the source for the hierarchies is an Excel spreadsheet on a business user's desktop — then you must either clean it up or plan not to use that hierarchy for aggregate data.

Cleaning up hierarchies, especially those developed by business users, is a great role for a master data management (MDM) system. Relatively few organizations have strong MDM tools in place, which means that it falls on the DW/BI team to do this work. Sometimes DW/BI teams that are wrestling with this problem build a normalized version of the dimension: a *snowflake* as it's commonly called. There's nothing wrong with implementing a normalized version of the dimension for ETL purposes, though of course you should not present that complexity to the users in the presentation server.

Develop Detailed Table Schematics

You should also be planning which tables to work on and in which order, as well as sequencing the transformations within each table. Graphically diagram the complex restructurings. Where the high level plan fits a set of fact tables onto a single page (more or less), the detailed plan graphics can devote a page or more to each complex target table. Sometimes it makes more sense to structure the diagrams around the source tables instead of the target tables. The schematic is backed up with a few pages of pseudo-code detailing complex transformations. Figure 10-3 illustrates the level of detail that we've found useful for the table-specific drilldown; it's for one of the tables in the utility company example illustrated previously.

All of the dimension tables must be processed before the key lookup steps for the fact table. The dimension tables are usually fairly independent from each other, but sometimes they have processing dependencies too. It's important to clarify these dependencies because they become fixed points around which the job control will flow.

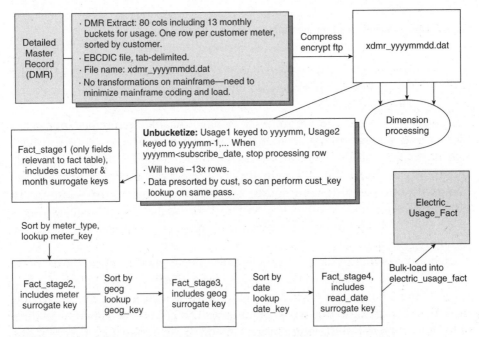

Figure 10-3 Example first draft of detailed load schematic for the fact table.

Develop the ETL Specification Document

We've walked through some general strategies for high level planning and the physical design of your ETL system. Now it's time to pull everything together and develop a detailed specification for the entire ETL system.

All the documents you have developed so far — the source-to-target mappings, data profiling reports, physical design decisions — should be rolled into the first sections of the ETL specification. Then document all the decisions we have discussed in this chapter, including:

- Default strategy for extracting from each major source system.
- Archival strategy.
- Data quality tracking and metadata.
- Default strategy for managing changes to dimension attributes.
- System availability requirements and strategy.
- Design of the data auditing subsystem.
- Locations of staging areas.

The next section of the ETL specification describes the historic and incremental load strategies for each table. A good specification will include between two and ten pages of detail for each table, and document the following information and decisions:

- Table design, including column names, data types, keys, and constraints.
- Historic data load parameters (number of months) and volumes (row counts).
- Incremental data volumes, measured as new and updated rows/ load cycle.
- Handling of late arriving data for facts and dimensions.
- Load frequency.
- Handling of changes in each dimension attribute (types 1, 2, or 3).
- Table partitioning, such as monthly.
- Overview of data sources, including a discussion of any unusual source characteristics such as an unusually brief access window.
- Detailed source-to-target mapping.
- Source data profiling, including at least the minimum and maximum values for each numeric column, count of distinct values in each column, and incidence of nulls. Also, a negotiated list of data quality enhancements that must be made in the source system before the data is usable.

- Extract strategy for the source data, such as source system APIs, direct query from database, or dump to flat files.
- Change data capture logic for each source table detailing how agreement between the source system and the data warehouse is to be accomplished.
- Dependencies, including which other tables must be loaded before this table is processed.
- Transformation logic, documented as pseudo-code or a diagram.
- Preconditions to avoid error conditions. For example, the ETL system must check for file or database space before proceeding.
- Recovery and restart assumptions for each major step of the ETL pipeline.
- Archiving assumptions for each table, including length of data retention and metadata describing the table contents.
- Cleanup steps, such as deleting working files.
- Estimate of whether this portion of the ETL system will be easy, medium, or difficult to implement.

The final section of the ETL specification describes the overall work flow and provides a first cut at job sequencing. Create a dependency tree that specifies which tables must be processed before others. Whether or not you choose to parallelize your processing, it's important to know the logical dependencies that cannot be broken.

NOTE Although most people would agree that all of the items we've described in the ETL system specification document are necessary, it's a lot of work to pull this document together, and even more work to keep it current as changes occur. A detailed ETL system specification for a business process dimensional model can easily be 70–100 pages long and take weeks to develop. Realistically, if you pull together the "one-pager" high level flow diagram, data model and source-to-target maps, and a five-page description of what you plan to do, you'll get a better start than most teams. Still the more thoroughly you plan and document, the better.

Develop a Sandbox Source System

During the ETL development process, you'll need to investigate the source system data at great depth. If your source system is heavily loaded, and you don't already have some kind of reporting instance for operational queries, the DBAs may be willing to set up a static snapshot of the database for the ETL development team. Early in the development process, it's convenient to poke around the source systems without worrying about launching the kind of killer query that, presumably, your project is supposed to prevent.

NOTE Some source systems require data to be extracted through their programming interfaces. In this situation, you need to check with the vendor to ensure your sandbox system is not in violation of their license.

The simplest way to build the sandbox source is to restore the source databases from a consistent point-in-time backup. If your source data is very large, consider using your ETL tool to grab a random set of fact data. Many people pull only the most recent few months of data into the sandbox, but this approach omits the inevitable problems you'll encounter with older data.

A better approach is to identify a random set of members from the largest dimension (usually customers); make sure you've chosen a random set of customers, not just the first 10,000 in the table. Then pull over the complete set of tables to source the other dimensions. Finally, extract a set of fact transactions that correspond to that random subset of customers.

It's easy to build a sandbox source system that simply copies the original; build a sandbox with a subset of data only if you have very large data volumes. On the plus side, this sandbox could become the basis of training materials and tutorials once the system is deployed into production.

You don't have to build a sandbox system. If your source system doesn't have major performance problems, and you coordinate with its DBAs about when and how to run queries, you don't need this extra step. In small companies, the source system DBAs are intimately involved with the DW/BI project and can easily facilitate careful use of their operational databases.

Develop One-Time Historic Load Processing

Once the ETL specification has been created, we typically focus on developing the ETL process for the one-time load of historic data. Occasionally you can make the same ETL code perform both the initial historic load and the ongoing incremental loads, but more often you build separate ETL processes for each. The historic and incremental load processes have a lot in common, and depending on your ETL tool, you may be able to reuse significant functionality from one to the other. As we'll describe, the two processes are sufficiently different that it's usually not worth the trouble to build a single ETL system component that serves both functions.

In general, start building the ETL system with the simplest dimension table. Usually at least one dimension table is managed completely as a type 1 dimension: a dimension for which you are not tracking history. The primary goal of this step is to work out the infrastructure kinks, including connectivity, security, and file transfer problems that always seem to exist.

Once you've successfully built the simple dimension tables, tackle the historic loads for dimensions with one or more columns managed as type 2.

Typically, the techniques or code that you develop for one slowly changing dimension are reusable for all. Your second and subsequent slowly changing dimensions will be much easier than your first, even if they are larger tables.

After you have successfully loaded the dimension tables, you can design and implement the historic load of the fact data. The ETL process for dimension tables is characterized by complex transformations on relatively small data volumes. The ETL process for the fact table historic load usually involves fairly simple transformations, but on very large data volumes.

> **TIP** Strive to isolate the ETL process for each table in its own file, module, package, or script. Some ETL tools will allow you to create one file or module that contains all of the logic for populating the entire data warehouse. That's usually not a good idea because it reduces the flexibility and maintainability of your system. For one thing, multiple developers will find it much more difficult to work on the system without stepping on each others' work. This is true even with excellent source control software. But even with a single developer, modularizing the ETL system leads to a more maintainable application in the long run. As you develop, test, and deploy the inevitable changes to a system already in production, you will benefit from modularized coding techniques.

With this understanding of the general ETL process flow for the one-time historic load, we'll delve into the details, starting with the dimension tables.

Step 5 – Populate Dimension Tables with Historic Data

In this section, we discuss ETL dimension processing, starting with the simplest scenario.

Populate Type 1 Dimension Tables

The easiest type of table to populate is a dimension table for which all attributes are managed as type 1 or update in place. With a type 1 dimension, you extract the current value for each dimension attribute from the source system. The primary source is often a lookup table or file that can be pulled in its entirety to the ETL tool. Work closely with the data owners and source system team so that you understand the characteristics of the source. Is the file you've been directed to the authoritative source for the dimension information? How is it updated? Is there a time of day when you should not access it? When are transactions against it complete for the target load period? Is there a reliable timestamp for changed records?

Sometimes the data, although logically simple, is stored in an inaccessible way. The source system owners can most efficiently convert the data into a useful structure. More often than not, they will use their standard reporting tools to generate an extract report. A report, as long as it is correctly defined and can be scheduled, is a perfectly acceptable extract mechanism.

As you define the report or query that extracts the dimension's source data, confirm that you are getting one row per entity: that the column or columns you've identified as the source system natural key do indeed uniquely identify a dimension member. If the source report or query joins multiple tables, it's easy to mistakenly specify a query that generates duplicate rows. An easy way to confirm uniqueness is to verify that the row count equals the count of distinct members in the extract stream.

Dimension Transformations

Even the simplest dimension table may require substantial data cleanup and will certainly require surrogate key assignment.

Simple Data Transformations

The most common, and easiest, form of data transformation is data type conversion. At the most basic level, data that comes from a mainframe has to be converted from the EBCDIC character set to ASCII. In addition, your logical and physical models often specify that values be stored in a different data type than the source: date, number, or character. All ETL tools have rich functions for data type conversion. This task can be tedious, but it is seldom onerous.

Within dimension tables, we recommend that you replace null values with either a default value or an empty string, as discussed in Chapter 8. The primary reason for this replacement is usability; business users are perplexed by the behavior of database NULLs. All ETL tools allow you to write an expression to replace null values.

Combine from Separate Sources

Often dimensions are derived from several sources. Customer information may need to be merged from several lines of business and from outside sources. There is seldom a universal key that makes this merge operation easy. The raw data and the existing dimension table data may need to be sorted at different times on different fields to attempt a match. Sometimes a match may be based on fuzzy criteria; names and addresses may match except for minor spelling differences.

Most consolidation and deduplicating tools and processes for the important customer dimension work best if you begin by parsing names and addresses into their component pieces. For example, an address in the United States can consist of several dozen components, beginning with street number, street name, and street type (avenue or boulevard). This parsing is important when you consider that punctuation can cause an exact match to fail. Corporations' and individuals' names should be parsed in a similar way. Some data consolidation tools have country- and language-specific intelligence for parsing names and addresses.

After the data parsing and cleansing step, data from multiple sources is compared. For best performance, again using customer as an example, it's customary to do an exact match pass first, looking for equity in a handful of fields such as name, national ID number, and postal code. Once a pair of records is determined to be a match, place an entry in a mapping table with the warehouse surrogate key, and the matching keys from all the various source systems.

Next, you will need to design a set of passes using fuzzy logic that accounts for misspellings, typos, and alternative spellings such as I.B.M., IBM, and International Business Machines. Some ETL tools include fuzzy lookup technology that you can use to implement imperfect matching, but you'll get better results if you use a tool that's targeted for name and address matching. For best results, especially for consumer name consolidation, you can send your data to a data matching service that keeps track of all known spellings of names and addresses in a country (a creepy concept, but a useful service.)

All of the fuzzy matching algorithms return answers that are not guaranteed to be precise matches. That's why they're called fuzzy. You need to analyze the results of the customer consolidation routines, whether you've written them in-house or are using a service. Your business users must provide direction on the acceptable level of imprecision in the matching algorithm. In some cases, your organization may need to launch a project to obtain affirmation from customers that accounts can be merged. In other cases, such as marketing mail lists to potential customers, tolerances are greater.

In most organizations, there is a large one-time project to consolidate existing customers. This project is as much analysis as it is data manipulation. Ideally, the organization will leverage this investment by implementing new business and transaction processes to prevent new bad data from creeping in. This is a tremendously valuable role for master data management systems.

Decode Production Codes

A common merging task in data preparation is looking up text equivalents for production codes. In some cases, the text equivalents are sourced informally from a nonproduction source such as a spreadsheet. The code lookups are usually stored in a table in the staging database. Use your ETL tool's lookup or merge functionality to perform the lookups in stream or define a SQL query that joins to the staging table.

Make sure that your ETL system includes logic for creating a default decoded text equivalent for the case where the production code is missing from the lookup table. This is likely to occur if the decodes are "managed" in a spreadsheet. During the historic load, you can easily find these missing values, and enter them into the lookup staging table manually. But think ahead to the incremental loading process; it often makes sense to create a rule to generate a dummy label that can easily be updated later. For example, you can create a dummy label: "Production Code ABC: No description available." When the description does eventually flow into the system, it is easy to update the string.

Validate Many-to-One and One-to-One Relationships

Your most important dimensions will probably have one or more rollup paths, such as product to product model, subcategory and category, as illustrated in Figure 10-4. As we've already discussed, in most cases you want these hierarchical rollups to be perfectly clean.

You can verify a many-to-one relationship between two attributes such as product to product model, by sorting on the "many" attribute and verifying that each value has a unique value on the "one" attribute. A sequential scan of the data will show whether there are any violations. Each attribute value in the sorted column must have exactly one value in the other column. Alternatively, use the SQL HAVING clause to find violations. You could execute a query to return the set of products that have more than one product model:

```
SELECT product_sku,
count[*] as row_count,
count(distinct product_model) as model_count
FROM staging_database.product
GROUP BY product_sku
HAVING count(distinct product_model) > 1 ;
```

Check your ETL tool's capabilities to see what features are available for this common test. Data profiling tools should be able to perform this test with simple commands.

Product Dimension

Product Key (primary key)
Product SKU (natural key)
Product Name
Product Descr
Product Model ID
Product Model
Product Model Descr
Manufacturer
Product Subcategory ID
Product Subcategory
Product Subcategory Descr
Product Category ID
Product Category
Product Category Descr
Product Category Manager
Category Manager Email

Figure 10-4 Product dimension table that includes a hierarchical relationship.

Many database administrators want to validate this kind of relationship by loading into a normalized version of the dimension table in the staging database. This normalized dimension table would look like a snowflake dimension as illustrated in Figure 10-5. The snowflake structure has some value in the staging area: It prevents you from loading data that violates the many-to-one relationship. However, in general you should pre-verify the relationships as we have just described, so that you never attempt to load bad data into the dimension table. Once the data is pre-verified, it's not tremendously important whether you make the database engine reconfirm the relationship at the moment you load the table or tables.

If the source system for a dimensional hierarchy is a normalized database, it's usually unnecessary to repeat the normalized structure in the ETL staging area. However, if the hierarchical information comes from an informal source such as a spreadsheet managed by the marketing department, you may benefit from normalizing the hierarchy in the staging area.

A similar but stricter problem exists for confirming a one-to-one relationship between two attributes, such as product SKU and product name. The business requirements that led to the dimensional model should clarify whether there

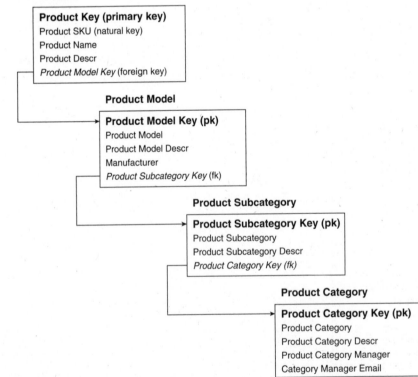

Product

| Product Key (primary key) |
| Product SKU (natural key) |
| Product Name |
| Product Descr |
| *Product Model Key* (foreign key) |

Product Model

| Product Model Key (pk) |
| Product Model |
| Product Model Descr |
| Manufacturer |
| *Product Subcategory Key* (fk) |

Product Subcategory

| Product Subcategory Key (pk) |
| Product Subcategory |
| Product Subcategory Descr |
| *Product Category Key (fk)* |

Product Category

| Product Category Key (pk) |
| Product Category |
| Product Category Descr |
| Product Category Manager |
| Category Manager Email |

Figure 10-5 Snowflaked hierarchical relationship in the product dimension.

should be a unique product name for each product SKU. If this is a requirement of the design, you must confirm the relationship in both directions. You can use the same techniques we've already described for the many-to-one relationship, applying the test to both attributes. It's seldom useful to fully normalize the staging table by placing the second attribute such as Product Name in its own table. Certainly you'd never want to take that level of normalization to the version of the dimension in the presentation server database. Even the simplest user queries would be joining an absurd number of tables and query performance would suffer tremendously.

Dimension Surrogate Key Assignment

Once you are confident that you have a version of your dimension table with one row for each true unique dimension value, you can assign the surrogate keys. Maintain a table in the ETL staging database that matches production keys to surrogate keys. This key map will be used later during fact table processing.

Surrogate keys are typically assigned as integers, increasing by one for each new key. If your staging area is in an RDBMS, surrogate key assignment is elegantly accomplished by creating a sequence. Although syntax varies among the relational engines, the process is first to create a sequence, and then to populate the key map table.

One-time creation of the sequence:

```
create sequence dim1_seq cache=1000; — choose appropriate cache level
```

Populate the key map table:

```
insert into dim1_key_map (production_key_id, dim1_key)
select production_key_id, dim1_seq.NEXT
from dim1_extract_table;
```

Not all major relational engines use the sequence construct. The other common technique is to specify a table column as an IDENTITY column. The IDENTITY keyword in the CREATE TABLE command means that when rows are inserted, the relational engine will automatically populate the key column. The SEQUENCE and IDENTITY approaches work a bit differently, but they achieve the same result and both are common techniques.

As an alternative, most ETL tools have their own surrogate key generator that works outside the database. Or it would be simple to write your own surrogate key generator, but there's seldom a compelling reason to do so.

Dimension Table Loading

Once the data is properly prepared, the load process is fairly straightforward. This is particularly true for the process we've described because the transformations have been performed in the ETL process. All you have to do now is load the prepared data into the target tables. Even though the first dimension table is usually small, use your database's bulk or fast loading utility or interface. You should use fast loading techniques for most table inserts, and so should develop expertise with that technology from the outset.

Every major relational database engine has technology to load data into the database quickly. Each has a stand-alone utility that you can call from the operating system. This bulk loading utility was originally designed to load data into a table from a flat file. Most require a control file that's separate from the data file. The control file describes the content and format of the data file including the character you're using to delimit columns.

Most databases also have an interface that works in a similar way. Some have extended the SQL syntax to include a BULK INSERT statement. Others have published an API to load data into the table from a stream. This API isn't something you should learn about directly; your ETL tool should implement that API as a data loading option.

Bulk loading is important to the data warehousing scenario because it inserts data fast; we have seen inserts perform ten or even a hundred times faster using fast bulk load techniques than using the more familiar row-by-row logged inserts.

The bulk load utilities and APIs come with a range of parameters and transformation capabilities. Some of the primary suggestions for using these technologies are:

- **Turn off logging.** Transaction-oriented databases keep track of all changes to the database in a log file. Logging allows the database to recover its current state if it runs into a fatal error; it is vital for a transaction database. However, the log adds significant overhead and is not valuable when loading data warehouse tables. You should design your ETL system with one or more recoverability points where you can restart processing should something go wrong.

- **Bulk load in fast mode.** Most of the database engines' bulk load utilities or APIs require several stringent conditions on the target table to bulk load in fast mode. These conditions vary, but a common set of conditions is that either the table must be unindexed or it must be empty (in which case it can have indexes in place). If these conditions are not met, the load should not fail; it simply will not use the "fast" path.

- **Pre-sort the file.** Sorting the file in the order of the primary index speeds up indexing significantly. In some cases, this is a parameter in the bulk loader or index command. Of course, you should always evaluate the entire process. Compare the time required to pre-sort, load the data, and index the table to the timing without the pre-sort step.

- **Transform with caution.** In some cases, the loader will let you do data conversions, calculations, and string and date/time manipulation.

Use these features carefully and test performance. In some cases, these transformations cause the loader to switch out of high speed mode into a line-by-line evaluation of the load file. We recommend using your ETL tool to perform most transformations.

- **Rely on the ETL tool.** Most ETL tools contain features that leverage database engines' bulk loaders. Make sure you understand the way these features work with your relational database.

- **Truncate table before full refresh.** The TRUNCATE TABLE statement is the most efficient way to delete all the rows in the table. It's commonly used to clean out a table from the staging database at the beginning of the day's ETL processing.

NOTE Most relational engines have a TRUNCATE TABLE command that is logically equivalent to a DELETE command. Physically, a truncate table is much more efficient because it does not log the deletions and frees up all table space without needing to reorganize or restructure the table. Be warned, however, that there is often no way to undo a TRUNCATE TABLE command.

Load Type 2 Dimension Table History

Recall that each attribute in each dimension table is typically managed as type 1 (update in place) or type 2 (track history by adding new rows to the dimension table). Most dimension tables contain a mixture of type 1 and type 2 attributes. In Chapter 9, we described the logical steps necessary to manage a dimension that contains type 2 attributes, and how to extend the dimension table's design to include a row effective and row end date/timestamp.

Most of the work associated with a dimension that includes type 2 attributes takes place in the incremental processing ETL system, which we describe later in this chapter. However, this is a task that you also need to consider now as you're designing the system to populate the dimension tables with the initial historic data.

You should recreate history for dimension attributes that are managed as type 2. If business users have identified an attribute as important for tracking history, they want that history going back in time, not just from the date the data warehouse is implemented. It's usually difficult to recreate dimension attribute history, and sometimes it's completely impossible. Operationally, the historic dimension attributes, such as old customer addresses, are often moved to a separate history table or archived offline. You will need to do some detective work to evaluate which attributes' history can be reconstructed and how difficult it will be to do so. Even if it seems to you like too much work to reconstruct history, the business community should evaluate the costs and benefits, and make that call.

Once you've identified the sources of the attributes' history, you need to construct the image of the full dimension row at each point in the past.

You know the current values for each dimension attribute, so start with the present. Working backward in time, make a new copy of the dimension row each time an attribute change occurs. Be sure to set the row effective date/timestamp column correctly. Don't write the constructed rows into the dimension table at this point; instead write them to a staging table or file, or keep them as a structure in memory.

You may need to make multiple passes over the dimension table, always moving from the present to the past, in order to process changes in different sets of type 2 attributes. Make sure you keep the rows for each dimension member (such as customer) in reverse chronological order; re-sort the data between passes if you need to.

This process is not well suited for standard SQL processing. It's better to use a database cursor construct or, even better, a procedural language such as Visual Basic, C, or Java to perform this work. Most ETL tools enable script processing on the data as it flows through the ETL system.

When you've completely reconstructed history, make a final pass through the data to set the row end date/timestamp column. It's important to ensure there are no gaps in the series. We prefer to have the row end date/timestamp for the older version of the dimension member be one time increment (usually one day) before the row effective date/timestamp for the new row. Again, it's easiest to accomplish this task by using a procedural script, starting from the present and working backward. The output of this task should be assigned surrogate keys and written to the target dimension table.

> **NOTE** You may be bothered by the fact that the rows for each dimension member such as customer are sorted in reverse chronological order for the historic load, but then in normal order for the ongoing incremental loads. The surrogate key should be meaningless, but if the ordering troubles you, re-sort before the final load.

Populate Date and Other Static Dimensions

Every data warehouse database should have a date dimension, usually at the granularity of one row for each day. The date dimension should span the history of the data, starting with the oldest fact transaction in the data warehouse.

It's easy to set up the date dimension for the historic data because you know the date range of the historic fact data you'll be loading. Most projects build the date dimension by hand, typically in a spreadsheet. The spreadsheet program's date and string functions are sufficient to automatically create the image of the rows that you're planning to load. Your date dimension may include attributes for identifying holidays or meaningful corporate dates, such as year-end closing period or peak period. If so, you will probably have to populate those attributes manually.

Once you've built the date dimension, you can load it into the data warehouse by first saving it as text, and then use standard data loading techniques to load the flat file.

NOTE You can find a sample Date dimension spreadsheet on the book's website at www.kimballgroup.com.

You will create a handful of other dimensions in a similar way. For example, you may create a budget scenario dimension that holds the values "Actual" and "Budget." You should get business user signoff on all constructed dimension tables, and you'll probably find that you're using a spreadsheet to develop these tables too. Alternatively, you could simply write INSERT statements because these tables often have very few rows.

Step 6 – Perform the Fact Table Historic Load

The one-time historic load of the fact table data differs fairly significantly from the ongoing incremental processing. The biggest worry during the historic load is the sheer volume of data, often thousands of times bigger than the daily incremental load. On the other hand, you have the luxury of loading into a table that's not in production. If it takes several days to load the historic data, that's usually tolerable. As we describe later in this chapter, the incremental fact table ETL system developer worries as much about automating and bullet-proofing the application as about processing performance.

The historic load is more like a data integration project than an application. It needs to be repeatable, but you don't need to implement the same kind of automation as for the ongoing incremental process.

Historic Fact Table Extracts

As you are identifying records that fall within the basic parameters of your extract, you need to make sure these records are useful for the data warehouse. Many transaction systems keep operational information in the source system that may not be interesting from a business point of view. These include entries to track intercompany transactions, accounting adjustments, and amortized transactions. The business rules created during the design phase will help determine how each of these events is to be represented in the warehouse and which filters and sums should be applied during the extract as a result.

Determining and validating these rules can get unpleasant. Your extract has little chance of being right the first time. Business rules that were overlooked or forgotten during data analysis surface during the extract process. Tracking down these subtle differences requires skillful detective work and endless patience.

It's also a good idea to accumulate audit statistics during this step. As the extract creates the results set, it is often possible to capture various subtotals, totals, and row counts.

Audit Statistics

During the planning phase for the ETL system, you should have identified various measures of data quality. These are usually calculations, such as counts and sums, that you compare between the data warehouse and source systems to cross-check the integrity of the data. If these data quality statistics haven't been captured yet, this step will make a pass through the data to compute them. These numbers should tie backward to operational reports and forward to the results of the load process in the warehouse. They should be stored in the metadata catalog in a table created for this information.

The tie back to the operational system is important because it is what establishes the credibility of the warehouse. Pick a report from the operational system that is agreed on as the official definition of what is right: the authoritative source. If the result set doesn't tie back to the source, it's likely that something has changed in the business rule that has not been reflected in the extract. It is better to stop the process and check it out now. This is a good argument for including the extract as part of the source system's responsibilities. If they make substantive changes in the source, they may forget to pass that information on. On the other hand, if they own the extract process, they are more likely to roll any changes all the way through.

NOTE There are scenarios where it's difficult or impossible for the warehouse to tie back to the source system perfectly. In many cases, the data warehouse extract includes business rules that have not been applied to the source systems. Also, differences in timing make it even more difficult to cross-check the data. If it's not possible to tie the data back exactly, you need to be able to explain the differences.

Fact Table Transformations

In most projects, the fact data is relatively clean. The ETL system developer spends a lot of time improving the dimension table content, but the facts usually require fairly modest transformation. This makes sense, because in most cases the facts come from transaction systems that are used to operate the organization from day to day.

The most common transformations to fact data include transformation of null values, pivoting or unpivoting the data, and precomputing derived calculations. Then all fact data must enter the surrogate key pipeline to exchange the natural keys for the dimension surrogate keys that are managed in the data warehouse.

Null Fact Table Values

All major database engines support a null value explicitly. In many source systems, however, the null value is represented by a special value of what should be a legitimate fact. Perhaps the special value of −1 is understood to represent null. In most cases, you should replace the "−1" in this scenario with NULL. A null value for a numeric measure is reasonable and common in the fact table. Nulls do the "right thing" in calculations of sums and averages across fact table records. It's only in the dimension tables that we strive to remove all the nulls. You do not, however, want to have any null values in the fact table foreign key columns that reference the dimension table keys. These should always be defined as NOT NULL.

Null values in data are tricky because philosophically there are at least two kinds of nulls. A null value in the data may mean that at the time of the measurement, the value literally did not exist and could not exist. In other words, any data value at all is wrong. Conversely, a null value in the data may mean that the measurement process failed to deliver the data, but the value certainly existed at some point. In this second case, you might argue that to use an estimate value would be better than to disqualify the fact record from analysis. This distinction is particularly important in data mining applications.

If you have ignored our repeated advice about surrogate keys and have designed a fact table that uses dates as foreign keys to the date dimension table, null dates will present a particular problem. There is not a good way to represent null dates in your fact table record. You cannot use a null-valued foreign key in the fact table because null in SQL is never equal to itself. In other words, you cannot use a null value in a join between a fact table and dimension table. You should implement the join with an anonymous integer key and then have a special record in the dimension table to represent the null date.

Improve Fact Table Content

As we discussed in Chapter 6, all of the facts in the final fact table row must be expressed in the same grain. This means that there must be no facts representing totals for the year in a daily fact table or totals for some geography larger than the fact table grain. If your extract includes an interleaving of facts at different grains, the transformation process must eliminate these aggregations, or move them into the appropriate aggregate tables.

The fact record may contain derived facts, although in many cases it is more efficient to calculate derived facts in a view or OLAP database rather than in the physical table. For instance, a fact record that contains revenues and costs may want a fact representing net profit. It is very important that the net profit value be calculated correctly every time a user accesses it. If the data warehouse forces all users to access the data through a view, it would be fine to calculate the net profit in that view. If users are allowed to see the physical table, or if they often filter on net profit and thus you'd want to index it, precomputing it and storing it physically is preferable.

Similarly, if some facts need to be presented simultaneously with multiple units of measure, the same logic applies. If users access the data through a view or OLAP database, then the various versions of the facts can efficiently be calculated at access time.

Restructure Fact Data

Improving the content of the data isn't the only fact table transformation that takes place in the ETL system. Sometimes the structure also needs work — either denormalizing or renormalizing the database to make it more useful from a business point of view. A common example of fact denormalization is a financial schema that has an amount type field in the source for the fact table, indicating whether the associated number is a budget, actual, or forecast amount. In the warehouse, it usually is better to pivot those entries into separate columns, simplifying the calculation of variances.

Your ETL tool probably includes a pivot and unpivot transform that you can use to perform this task. Alternatively, you could use SQL syntax. This syntax varies slightly in the various relational engines, but the following SQL provides an example:

```
SELECT
account_number,
sum(case when amt_type='actual' then trxn_amt else 0) as actual_amt,
sum(case when amt_type='budget' then trxn_amt else 0) as budget_amt
FROM source_trxn_table
group by account_number;
```

In some scenarios, you may reverse this process to normalize the fact data by unpivoting. In many legacy systems, the main data source is a large flat file that is used for report generation. For example, the utility system described in Figure 10-1 has thirteen months of data in thirteen columns of a single row. These numbers are the "right" numbers, so this is the source to draw from. The transformation task here is to take that information and "unpivot" it from a single row into a date column and the associated amounts with a row for each month.

Pipeline the Dimension Surrogate Key Lookup

It is tremendously important that you maintain referential integrity (RI) between the fact table and dimension tables; you must never have a fact row that references a dimension member that doesn't exist. You should not have a null value for any foreign key nor should any fact row violate referential integrity to any dimension.

The surrogate key pipeline is the name for the final fact processing before you load the data into the target fact table. All other data cleaning, transformation, and processing should be complete. The fact data should look just like the target fact table in the data warehouse, except it still contains the natural keys from the source system rather than the warehouse's surrogate keys. The surrogate key pipeline is the process that exchanges the natural keys for the surrogate keys, and handles any referential integrity errors.

Dimension table processing must complete before the fact data enters the surrogate key pipeline. You must already have processed any new dimension members or type 2 changes to existing dimension members, so their keys are available to the surrogate key pipeline.

In the surrogate key pipeline for the historic load, you must associate each fact with the type 2 dimension row that was in effect when the transaction occurred. This is more complex than the standard case for incremental processing, where you're usually processing the facts that arrived yesterday. You must handle referential integrity violations too, but this can be a simpler problem for the historic load.

First let's discuss the referential integrity problem. It's easy to ensure referential integrity during the historic load because you don't need to fully automate the process so that it runs lights out. Instead, a good approach is to stage the clean fact data before it enters the surrogate key pipeline. Then, create a list of the natural keys for each dimension that are used in the historic data. You could do this by issuing a SELECT DISTINCT query on the staged fact data for each natural key. Alternatively, your ETL tool may provide a high performance method for generating these sets.

Next, it's a simple matter to confirm that each natural key found in the historic fact data is represented in the dimension tables. Investigate any problems and either fix the dimension table or redesign the fact table extract to filter out spurious rows, as appropriate. This is a manual step; pause the historic load at this point so that you can investigate and fix any referential integrity problems before you proceed.

Now that you're confident that there will be no referential integrity violations, you can design the historic surrogate key pipeline without any RI error handling, as illustrated in Figure 10-6.

The historic surrogate key pipeline differs from the incremental surrogate key pipeline described in Chapter 9. The historic load is a one-time process, and it's often easier to just stop and fix problems by hand before continuing. You don't need the kind of bulletproof automated system that you need for incremental processing.

There are several approaches for designing the historic load's surrogate key pipeline for best performance, and your design will depend on the features available in your ETL tool, the data volumes you're processing, and your dimensional design. In theory, you could define a query that joins the fact staging table and each dimension table on the natural keys, returning the facts and the surrogate keys from each dimension table. If the historic data volumes are not huge, this will actually work quite well, assuming you've staged the

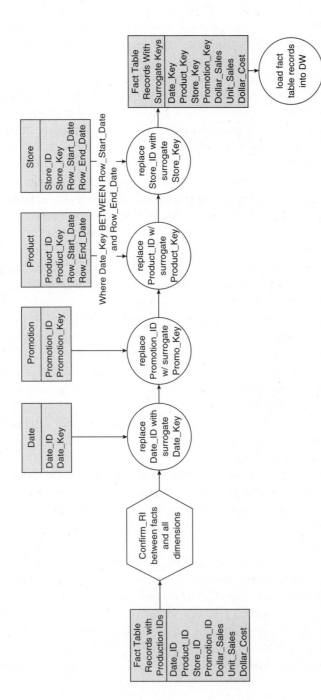

Figure 10-6 Historic surrogate key pipeline.

fact data in the relational database, and have indexed the dimension tables to support this big query. This approach has several benefits:

- It leverages the power of the relational database.

- It performs the surrogate key lookups on all dimensions in parallel.

- It simplifies the problem of picking up the correct dimension key for type 2 dimensions. As illustrated in Figure 10-6, the join to the type 2 dimensions must include a clause that specifies that the transaction date fall between the row effective date and row end date for that image of the dimension member in the table.

No one would be eager to try this approach if the historic fact data volumes were large, in the hundreds of gigabytes to terabyte range. The more dimensions you have, the less appealing this approach. However, recall from Chapter 8 that most large fact tables will be partitioned by date, often by month. It may be perfectly reasonable to use this approach on a month of data at a time.

The complex join to the type 2 dimension tables will create the greatest demands on the system. Many dimensional designs include a fairly large number of (usually small) dimension tables that are fully type 1, and a smaller number of dimensions managed as type 2. You could use this relational technique to perform the surrogate key lookups for all the type 1 dimensions in one pass, and then handle the type 2 dimensions separately. Make sure the effective date and end date columns are indexed properly.

An alternative to the database join technique we've been describing here is to use your ETL tool's lookup operator. Depending on your ETL tool, it may be easy, difficult, or impossible to implement these lookups in parallel. Again, depending on your ETL tool's performance characteristics, consider a design that loops over each day of data in the fact table; in this way you can use a simple equijoin technology on the lookups for the type 2 dimensions. The looping will be expensive because the tool's lookup operator will need to cache the appropriate subset of the dimension for each day of data. But in some cases, the looping will still perform better than the expensive complex join condition in the lookup operator.

When all the fact table production keys have been replaced with surrogate keys, the fact record is ready to load. The keys in the fact table record have been chosen to be proper foreign keys to the respective dimension tables, and the fact table is guaranteed to have referential integrity with respect to the dimension tables.

Assign Audit Dimension Key

As we describe in Chapter 9, an enterprise class data warehouse should include an audit key on each fact row. The audit key points to an audit dimension that describes the characteristics of the load, including timings and measures of data quality.

The audit dimension and auditing subsystem can be complex, consist of multiple tables, and contain many measures of data quality. At its simplest, the audit subsystem should contain at least one audit dimension table that captures the most basic information. That simple auditing system design would insert one row into the audit dimension each time an ETL job is run. The surrogate key to that audit dimension row must be added to the fact table stream so it can be stored in the fact table.

In your ETL tool, the first thing you should do in a job, package, or module, is set up the logic to add a new row to the audit dimension. Do this step before you start the extraction and transformation process. Grab the key for the audit dimension row you just inserted. ETL tools support variables, so you can store this simple scalar value in an ETL variable.

Either immediately after or immediately before the surrogate key pipeline, add the audit dimension key to the fact data. Then insert the fact data in the data warehouse fact table, as described in the next section. Finally, at the end of the job or module that loads the historic facts, go back to the audit dimension to update information about how long the job took and how many rows were loaded during processing.

Fact Table Loading

Your main concern when loading the fact table will be load performance. If you have followed our recommendations, you should have a perfectly clean set of data to load into the fact table. As you're developing the ETL system, you're likely to find errors the first time you try to insert data into the target table. There always seem to be data type mismatches, primary key violations, and other troubles. You should, of course, use a small dataset to test the ETL process before throwing the full set of historic data at it.

No matter how well you test the historic ETL load process, it's likely that you will still run into a problem when you're running the complete load. Some ETL tools will let you set up an error flow that siphons off the rows that fail the table insert process. During the historic load, you would probably direct that error flow to a file, and deal with problem rows by hand later.

Some database technologies support fast loading with a batch size that you specify. Look at the documentation for your fast loading technology to see how to set this parameter. You probably do not want to set the batch size to 0, which usually means infinity. This means that all rows will be committed in a single transaction. This setting may theoretically provide great load performance, but will place substantial burden on the memory of the data warehouse relational database. Nor do you want to set the batch size to 1, which would mean that each row is committed one at a time. You can experiment to find the ideal batch size for the size of your rows and your server's memory configuration. Most people don't bother to get so precise, and simply choose a number like 10,000 or 100,000 or 1 million.

Aside from using the bulk loader and a reasonable batch size (if appropriate for your database engine), the best way to improve the performance of the historic load is to load into a partitioned table, ideally loading multiple partitions in parallel. The steps to loading into a partitioned table include:

1. **Disable foreign key (referential integrity) constraints between the fact table and each dimension table before loading data.** When foreign key constraints are enabled, the database engine compares the data in each row's foreign key columns to the primary key values in the parent table. Load performance can improve by one or two orders of magnitude by disabling the foreign key constraints on the fact tables.

2. **Drop or disable indexes on the fact table.** It's usually faster to load data and then rebuild all indexes, compared to loading data with the indexes in place. But this is not always true and performance characteristics differ from one relational engine to another. Confirm with your database's documentation; it's even better to test on a reasonably sized subset of data in your environment.

3. **Load the data using fast loading techniques,** as we described earlier in this chapter for dimensions. The fast loading techniques are tremendously important for the historic load of fact data. If the fact table is partitioned, loading multiple partitions in parallel may substantially improve loading performance.

4. **Create or enable fact table indexes.**

5. **If necessary, perform steps to stitch together the table's partitions.** These steps vary from one database engine to another, but are generally quite simple and fast metadata operations. You should also check with your database engine's documentation to confirm whether you should build indexes before or after stitching together the partitions.

6. **Confirm each dimension table has a unique index on the surrogate key column.**

7. **Enable foreign key constraints between the fact table and dimension tables.** The database engine will validate the foreign key relationships for every row in the fact table when you re-enable the constraints after the load.

Test, Test, and Test Again

You will no doubt feel like celebrating when the historic fact data finally finishes its loading process. This is a huge milestone, but you cannot declare victory until you've confirmed that the data is accurate. We discuss the testing process at length in Chapter 13.

Make sure you budget enough time to thoroughly test the validity of the historic data before moving on to tackle the incremental load process. Make a complete backup of the database once it's been verified. As we describe in Chapter 13, it's very important that your business users, data stewards, and quality analysts are involved in the data quality assurance process.

Develop Incremental ETL Processing

One of the biggest challenges with the incremental ETL process is identifying new, changed, and deleted rows. Hopefully your source systems can easily provide a stream with the rows that have been inserted or updated since the previous load. If not, you should really try to get the source system administrators to assume responsibility for identifying inserts, updates, and deletes. If the data warehouse assumes this burden, the solution will almost certainly be more costly than if the problem is addressed on the source system where the data is created.

Once you have a stream of inserts, modifications, and deletions, the ETL system will apply transformations following virtually identical business rules as for the historic data loads. Depending on the features of your ETL tool, you may be able to re-use components from the historic load programs.

The historic load for dimensions and facts consisted largely or entirely of inserts. In incremental processing, you'll primarily be performing inserts, but updates for dimensions and some kinds of fact tables are inevitable. Updates and deletes are expensive operations in the data warehouse environment, so we'll describe techniques to improve the performance of these tasks.

It's a good idea to design your incremental load process to handle one day at a time and to have that day set by a parameter. You can use this process to load data for several days in a row, as long as you are able to feed in each day's datasets.

Step 7 – Dimension Table Incremental Processing

As you might expect, the incremental ETL system development begins with the dimension tables. Dimension incremental processing is a lot like the historic processing we described previously.

Dimension Table Extracts

In many cases, there is a customer master file or product master file that can serve as the single source for a dimension. In other cases, the raw data is a mixture of dimensional and fact data. For example, customer orders may include customer information, product information, and numeric facts from the detailed line items of the order.

Often it's easiest to pull the current snapshots of the dimension tables in their entirety and let the transformation step determine what has changed and how to handle it. If the dimension tables are large, you must use the fact table technique, described later in this chapter, for identifying the changed record set. It can take a long time to look up each entry in a large dimension table, even if it hasn't changed from the existing entry.

If possible, construct the extract to pull only rows that have changed. This is particularly easy and valuable if the source system maintains an indicator of the type of change. With such an indicator you can put new records in one file to be added to the dimension table without lookups. Updated records are placed in a second file that will undergo the slowly changing dimension process. If you don't know the change type, the entire results set of changed records goes through the slowly changing dimension process.

Identify New and Changed Dimension Rows

The DW/BI team may not be successful in pushing the responsibility for identifying new, updated, and deleted rows to the source system owners. In this case, the ETL process needs to perform an expensive comparison operation to identify new and changed rows.

The dimension data should be cleaned and transformed before it undergoes the identification process. Make sure you follow the same rules for the incremental data transformation as for the initial historic load, including such difficult-to-diagnose transformations as string padding with spaces.

Once the incoming data is clean, it's easy to find new dimension rows. The raw data has an operational natural key, which must be matched to the same column in the current dimension row. Remember, the natural key in the data warehouse dimension is an ordinary dimensional attribute and is not the dimension's surrogate key.

First, look at your ETL tool to see if there is a transform or wizard that will perform this task for you. In some tools, this task is fully integrated with logic to manage dimension changes; in other tools, they are separate tasks or wizards; and other tools do not have any wizards to support this functionality. Even if there is no wizard, you can certainly use your ETL tool to perform the comparison to identify new and changed rows.

Find new dimension members by performing a lookup from the incoming stream to the master dimension, comparing on the natural key. Any rows that fail the lookup are new dimension members and should be inserted into the dimension table. An alternative method for identifying new rows is to use an outer join between the incoming data and the existing dimension table. This technique requires that the incoming data be staged in the relational database.

If the dimension contains any type 2 attributes, set the row effective date/timestamp column to the date the dimension member appeared in the system; this is usually yesterday if you are processing the data every night. Set the row end date/timestamp column to your default value for the current row. This should be the largest date supported by the system.

The next step is to determine if the incoming dimension row has changed at all. The simplest technique is to compare column by column between the incoming data and the current corresponding member stored in the master dimension table. This comparison can be accomplished in SQL or in some kind of conditional operator in your ETL tool. Throw away the incoming rows that have not changed at all.

If the dimension is large, with more than a million rows, the simple technique of column-wise comparison may be too slow. This is particularly true if there are many columns in the dimension table. A popular alternative method is to use a hash or checksum function to speed the comparison process. Add to your dimension table two new housekeeping columns: HashType1 and HashType2. Into the HashType1 column place a hash of a concatenation of the type 1 attributes; similarly for HashType2. Hashing algorithms are commonly used for encryption. The algorithms convert a very long string into a much shorter string that is close to unique. (Computer scientists, please forgive this description.) This is a common technique for high performance dimension change management. Compute the hashes and store them in the dimension table. Then compute the hashes on the incoming rowset in exactly the same way, and compare to the stored values. The comparison on a single, relatively short string column is far more efficient than the pair-wise comparison on dozens of separate columns.

Alternatively, your relational database engine may have syntax such as EXCEPT that enables a high performance query to find the changed rows.

As a general rule, you should not delete dimension rows that have been deleted in the source system. These dimension members probably have fact data associated with them. This is especially possible with conformed dimensions that are replicated to multiple remote fact tables by the dimension manager. Instead, manage an attribute in the dimension table that keeps track of that status. Many source systems perform a similar "soft delete" that updates a flag on the row or moves the row to a history or deleted table. If your source system actually deletes the row, you'll need to use the same kind of comparison techniques we've already described. You would be well served to push back this problem to the source system owners, if that's at all possible.

Process Changes to Dimension Attributes

The ETL application must contain business rules to determine how to handle an attribute value that has changed from the value already stored in the data warehouse. If the revised description is determined to be a legitimate and reliable update to previous information, then the techniques of slowly changing dimensions must be used.

The first step in preparing a dimension record is to decide if you already have that record. The raw data has a natural key that must be matched to the same attribute in the current dimension row.

If all the incoming dimensional information matches the corresponding row in the dimension table, no further action is required. If the dimensional information has changed, apply a type 1 or type 2 change to the dimension.

NOTE You may recall from Chapter 6 that there are three primary methods for tracking changes in attribute values. Type 3 requires a change in the structure of the dimension table, creating a new set of columns to hold the "previous" versus "current" versions of the attributes. This type of structural change is seldom automated in the ETL system; it's more likely to be handled as a one-time change in the data model.

The lookup and key assignment logic for handling a changed dimension record during the extract process is shown in 10-7. In this case, the logic flow does not assume that the incoming data stream is limited only to new or changed rows.

Many ETL tools contain transforms or wizards for handling changes to dimension attributes during the incremental processing. This is certainly a desirable feature in an ETL tool, but it is not necessary. As you can see by examining Figure 10-7, the logic is quite straightforward. The only challenging step is the comparison to identify changed rows.

Step 8 – Fact Table Incremental Processing

Most data warehouse databases are too large to replace their central fact tables in a single load window. Instead, new and updated fact rows are processed incrementally.

NOTE It is much more efficient to incrementally load only the records that have been added or updated since the previous load. This is especially true in a journal-style system where history is never changed and only adjustments in the current period are allowed.

The ETL process for fact table incremental processing differs from the historic load. The historic ETL process doesn't need to be fully automated; we can stop the process to examine the data and prepare for the next step. The incremental processing, by contrast, must be fully automated. You certainly don't want to plan for human intervention during each load cycle. Your system should

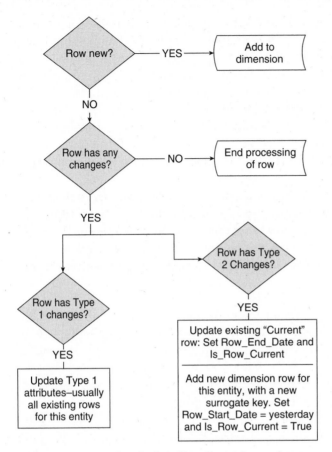

Figure 10-7 Logic flow for handling dimension updates.

include data quality checkpoints at which you can programmatically decide whether to stop, pause and page an operator, or continue to load the data.

Fact Table Extract and Data Quality Checkpoint

As soon as you extract the new and changed fact rows from the source system, write a copy of the untransformed data to the staging area. At the same time, compute measures of data quality on the raw extracted data. The staged data serves three purposes:

- **Archive for auditability.** Most organizations will archive this staged data for some time, usually several months or more. Your internal audit organization will be pleased with this feature of the ETL system.

- **Provide a starting point after data quality verification.** After you compute the measures of data quality, you need to determine whether the extract meets the minimum requirements necessary to continue. The data should be stored on disk while you make that determination.

- **Provide a starting point for restarting the process.** Design your system to enable restart after a catastrophic error during processing. In most cases, it's much better to restart from a static dataset that's part of the ETL system than to begin at the extract from the source system. Most ETL tools contain functionality for restarting jobs, but they all require that you design the system with this scenario in mind — it's a lot more complicated than just marking a checkbox labeled "Enable Restartability."

The design of the next step in your ETL system will drive whether the extracted data should be staged to a table or file. Writing to a file provides higher performance, but if the next step takes advantage of features of the relational database, you can write the extracted data into a table in the staging database. If the source system extract pushes data directly to a file, as many mainframe-based extracts do, that file serves the purposes described here.

Fact Table Transformations and Surrogate Key Pipeline

The transformations for the incremental fact data are very closely related to the transformations that you built for the historic load. You should be able to take advantage of the earlier code or transformations built in your ETL tool, though some tools enable re-use better than others do.

The surrogate key pipeline for the incremental fact data is similar to that for the historic data. The key difference is that the error handling for referential integrity violations must be automated. There are several methods for handling referential integrity violations:

- **Halt the load.** This is seldom a useful solution, though it's often the default in many ETL tools.

- **Throw away error rows.** There are situations where a missing dimension value is a signal that the data is irrelevant to the business requirements underlying the data warehouse. You should place this filter condition earlier in the ETL process, preferably in the extract logic, but there may be situational design reasons for implementing the logic in the surrogate key pipeline.

- **Write error rows to a file or table for later analysis.** Design a mechanism for moving corrected rows into the data warehouse. The ETL system should send a message to the appropriate resource. This technique is a reasonable failsafe approach for a relationship where you are confident that referential integrity violations will not occur. This approach is not a good choice for a financial system, where it is vital that all rows be loaded so that assets equal liabilities.

- **Fix error rows by creating a dummy row in the dimension, and returning its surrogate key to the pipeline.** The most attractive error handling for referential integrity violations in the incremental surrogate key pipeline is to create a dummy dimension row for the unknown natural key. The natural key is the only piece of information that you may have about the dimension member; set all other attributes to default values. Query and return the new dimension member's surrogate key to the error row, and merge that error row back into the surrogate key pipeline.

▪ **Not recommended: "Fix" error rows by mapping them to a single unknown member in each dimension.**   As we described in Chapter 8, it's common to insert a single dummy row in each dimension table, called the "unknown member" row. You may assign a specific surrogate key value, such as −1. The problem with this approach is that all error rows are mapped to the same dimension member, for any value of the natural key in the fact table extract. Because you don't keep the natural key in the fact table, you're throwing away the information needed to fix the error row in the future. This approach is not recommended.

For most systems, you can perform the surrogate key lookups against a query, view, or physical table that subsets the dimension table. Filter the dimension table rows so the lookup works against only the current version of each dimension member.

If the dimension table is very large, you may be able to gain significant performance improvements by making a preliminary processing pass on the fact data. The first pass identifies the natural keys for the very large dimension that are actually used in the incremental facts, and builds a lookup table only for those keys. This technique will be most beneficial if the incremental transactions occur for a relatively small subset of dimension members. For example, in a retail sales or Internet business process, the customer dimension could be quite large. But perhaps less than five percent of all possible customers actually have transactions during any one day. The relatively small set of keys in use today may fit into the ETL tool's lookup cache, where the entire customer key map would not.

Late Arriving Facts and the Surrogate Key Pipeline

In most data warehouses, the incremental load process begins soon after midnight and processes all the transactions that occurred the previous day. However, there are scenarios where some facts arrive late. This is most likely to happen when the data sources are distributed across multiple machines or even worldwide, and connectivity or latency problems prevent timely data collection.

If all your dimensions are managed completely as type 1 overwrites, late arriving facts present no special challenges. But most systems have a mixture of type 1 and type 2 attributes. The late arriving facts must be associated with the version of the dimension member that was in effect when the fact occurred. The lookup for the late arriving facts should use a join condition that identifies the correct surrogate key.

This complex join condition will perform substantially slower than the equijoin condition of the standard case. In cases where late arriving facts occur, it's usually true that the vast majority of data is for "yesterday," a second notable subset for the day before, and then a trickle of data over a range of dates. You should separate out the normal facts from the late arriving ones, and use the equijoin technique on that largest volume of data. You may do the same for the facts that are one day late, and then process all the later facts by using a lookup with a complex join condition.

Incremental Fact Table Load

The physical process of loading the incremental fact table rows is the same as we have previously discussed. As with the historic fact load, you should use your database's bulk load technology to perform the inserts into the fact table. Your ETL tools should handle this for you.

In the historic fact load, it's very important to ensure that data loads use fast load techniques. In most data warehouses, these fast load techniques may not be available for the incremental load. The fast load technologies often require stringent conditions on the target table, such as that it be empty or unindexed. For the incremental load, it's usually faster to use non-fast load techniques than to fully populate or index the table. For small to medium systems, insert performance is usually adequate.

If your fact table is very large, you should already have partitioned the fact table for manageability reasons. If you are always loading incremental data into an empty partition, you should be able to use fast load techniques. With daily loads, you'd be creating 365 new fact table partitions each year. This is probably too many partitions for a fact table with long history. Consider implementing a process to consolidate daily partitions into weekly or monthly partitions.

The largest fact tables are usually transactional. Transaction level fact tables are loaded through inserts; updates of fact data are unusual or even forbidden. A periodic snapshot fact table, as described in Chapter 6, usually has month end snapshots. Data for the current month is sometimes updated each day for current-month-to-date. In this scenario, monthly partitioning of the fact table makes it easy to reload the current month with excellent performance.

The accumulating snapshot fact table keeps track of a relatively short-lived process, such as filling an order. The accumulating snapshot fact table is characterized by many updates for each row over the life of the process. This table is expensive to maintain, especially if your database engine does not support bulk updating analogous to the bulk insert techniques. In order to apply many updates with best performance, stage the new image of the target row into a staging table. Then use SQL set operations to update many rows in a single transaction.

Speed Up the Load Cycle

Processing only changed increments is one way to speed up the data staging cycle. This section lists several additional techniques you may find valuable.

More Frequent Loading

Although it is a huge leap to move from a monthly or weekly process to a nightly one, it is an effective way to shorten the load time. Every nightly process involves 1/30 the data volume of a monthly one. Most data warehouses are on a nightly load cycle.

If your nightly processing is too expensive, consider performing some pre-processing on the data during the day. During the day, move data into a staging database or operational data store. Perform data cleansing tasks throughout the day. After midnight, you can consolidate multiple changes to dimension members, perform final data quality checks, assign surrogate keys, and move the data into the data warehouse.

Parallel Processing

One way to shorten the load time is to parallelize the ETL process. This can happen in two ways: multiple steps running in parallel and a single step running in parallel.

CAUTION There are good ways and bad ways to break processing into parallel steps. One very simple way to parallelize is to extract all source data together, then load and transform the dimensions, and then check referential integrity between the fact table and all dimensions simultaneously. Unfortunately, such an approach is likely to be no faster — and possibly much slower — than the even simpler sequential approach because each step launches parallel processes that compete for the same system resources such as network bandwidth, I/O, and memory. To structure parallel jobs well, you need to account not just for logically sequential steps but for system resources.

▪ **Multiple load steps.** Divide the ETL job stream into several independent jobs submitted together. Think carefully about what goes into each job. The primary goal is to create jobs that are independent. If one load requires the results of another load before it can run successfully, the two loads should be sequential in the same job. An obvious example is the referential integrity check from the fact table to the dimensions; the dimension processing must complete first.

- ■ **Parallel execution.**   The database itself can also identify certain tasks it can execute in parallel. For example, creating an index can typically be parallelized across as many processors as are available on the machine. Each processor works on a chunk of the data, and the results are merged together at the end. Parallel indexing is especially easy if the table and index are partitioned. In this case, each index is independent of the others; no merging is required. This capability is a standard part of most mainstream databases today. Make sure your database can parallelize activities and that this feature is enabled. Monitor your jobs and see what happens.

Parallel Structures

You can set up a three-way mirror or clustered configuration on two servers to maintain a continuous load data warehouse, with one server managing the loads and the second handling the queries. The maintenance window is reduced to a few minutes daily to swap the disks attached to each server. This is a great way to provide high availability on your system.

Depending on your requirements and budget, there are several similar techniques that you can implement for tables, partitions, and databases. For example, you can load into an offline partition or table, and swap it into active duty with minimum downtime. Other systems have two versions of the data warehouse database, one for loading and one for querying. These are less effective, but less expensive, versions of the functionality provided by clustered servers.

Step 9 – Aggregate Table and OLAP Loads

An aggregate table is *logically* easy to build. It's simply the results of a really big aggregate query, stored as a table. Not surprisingly, it's usually more difficult than that, but luckily, aggregate tables are often fairly easy to maintain.

The problem with building aggregate tables from a query on the fact table, of course, occurs when the fact table is just too big to process within the load window. Thus we see aggregate tables facing the same incremental versus full refresh choice as the base tables for the same reason. Luckily, the incremental load file for the fact table is a good source for the aggregate table incremental load. An aggregate table that still includes daily data can easily be appended to, if the incremental fact load includes only the latest day's data.

If the aggregate table includes an aggregation along the date dimension, perhaps to monthly grain, the aggregate maintenance process is more complex. The current month of data must be updated, or dropped and recreated, to incorporate the current day's data.

A similar problem occurs if the aggregate table is defined on a dimension attribute that is managed as type 1 overwrite. Any type 1 change in a dimension attribute affects all fact table aggregates that are defined on that attribute. A process must "back out" the facts from the old aggregate level, and move them to the new one, as we discussed in Chapter 8.

It is very important that the aggregate management system keep aggregations in synch with the underlying fact data. You do not want to create a system that can return a different result set to the querying user if the query is directed to the underlying detail facts or to a pre-computed aggregation.

Most data warehouses do not manage aggregate tables directly. Instead, they use technology such as relational database indexed or materialized views, an OLAP data store, or perhaps third party software to manage the process. The aggregate management technology should handle the updates that we have described here. We've described the issues so that you can understand the conditions that will force the aggregate table update process to take an unusually long time.

Most aggregate management technologies do a good job of handling the simple problem: adding new fact rows into existing aggregate tables. They perform the aggregations accurately with good or even excellent performance. In our experience, they perform substantially less well on the harder problems associated with backing out data from one part of the aggregation and adding it to another. The hardest of these problems are those associated with fact table updates or changes in a type 1 dimension attribute.

The aggregate management technologies are risk-averse, meaning they are inclined to recompute a significant portion (or all) of the aggregate table in order to handle a complex update. At the time of this writing, this criticism applies to both relational and OLAP technologies' aggregate management. There's not much you can do about this problem, unless you want to build a custom application to manage the aggregates yourself. This is not an appealing solution.

The aggregate management technologies let you control which aggregates are built. A wise data warehouse manager will use caution in defining an aggregate on a type 1 dimension attribute and will probably limit the number of aggregates associated with a fact table that receives many updates.

Step 10 – ETL System Operation and Automation

The ideal ETL operation runs the regular load processes in a lights out manner, without human intervention. Although this is a difficult outcome to attain, it is possible to get close. Of course, you identified the operational functions you need for your warehouse in your architecture plans, didn't you? As a reminder, we'll list the typical operational functions again here, and then offer a brief description of a few approaches to implementing them.

Schedule Jobs

Scheduling jobs is usually straightforward. Your ETL tool should contain functionality to schedule a job to kick off at a certain time. Most ETL tools also contain functionality to conditionally execute a second task if the first task completed successfully. It's common to set up an ETL job stream to launch at a certain time, then query a database or file system to see if an event has occurred. You may start processing at 2 am, and then pause until the ETL job sees that files have landed in a specific directory.

If your ETL tool doesn't have this functionality, or if you don't like the way it works, it's a simple matter to write a script to perform this kind of job control. Every ETL tool has a way to invoke a job from the operating system command line. Many organizations are very comfortable using scripting languages, such as Perl, to manage their job schedules.

Some organizations have a corporate standard job control management tool. You probably wouldn't purchase job control software exclusively for the DW/BI system, but it's a simple matter to use it to start the ETL jobs. Use the job control tool's functionality to make an operating system call to launch the ETL tool.

Handle Predictable Exceptions and Errors Automatically

Although it's easy enough to launch jobs, it's a harder task to make sure they run to completion, gracefully handling data errors and exceptions. Elegant error handling is something that needs to be built into your ETL jobs from the outset. Previously in this chapter we've described several techniques for assuring data quality; at the very least, confirm that row counts are reasonable. The automated ETL system will be designed with one or more data quality checks, and you will build in the methods for handling problems. Will you halt processing and notify an operator? Will you fix data rows as well as you can, and load them into the database — properly flagged so they can be audited later? Or will you stage bad data into error tables for manual intervention in the morning? A high quality ETL automation system will use all of these techniques and more, depending on the situation. You must understand that the most you can expect from your ETL tool is a set of features you can use to identify and process errors and notify operators. The burden is on your ETL designer to use those features to develop a highly automated ETL system.

Handle Unpredictable Errors Gracefully

Some errors are predictable, such as receiving an early arriving fact or a NULL value in a field that's supposed to be populated. For these errors, as we just described, you're generally able to design your ETL system to fix the data and continue processing. Other errors are unforeseen, and range from receiving data that's completely garbled to experiencing a power outage during processing.

You want to look for ETL tool features and system design practices that will help you recover from the unexpected. Some ETL tools let you combine multiple steps, including database manipulation steps, into a single transaction. If the job crashes in the midst of processing, the entire transaction rolls back. A solid, flexible system design will stage data during processing to provide a midpoint for restarting the system. In general, these data staging steps correspond to the points at which you check data quality.

Once again, though, it is up to your ETL designer to craft a system that can be restarted after a crash or other significant error. You must decide which data operations to combine into a transaction, and build the capability to restart gracefully into your system. Many ETL products provide tools and features to enable you to build a solid system, but doing so is a lot more complicated than checking a checkbox or running through a configuration wizard.

Maintain Database Objects

There are many database management tasks that fit smoothly into the ETL cycle. These tasks include database backups, periodic index maintenance, table partition management, and tablespace growth. We describe these activities in greater detail in Chapter 13. As an example, it's a good practice to back up the relational data warehouse after every nightly load. It is logical to integrate the backup script into the ETL job sequence. Many ETL tools will contain tools to launch a backup directly from within the ETL environment. At the very least, you can launch the backup script as the final step in your job sequence after the data loads have finished.

For the warehouse to truly be a production system, you need to provide these capabilities in some form. They can be rudimentary at first, but you should plan to retrofit with more robust tools fairly soon. Nothing slows down warehouse progress faster than a creaky, failure-prone production process. The whole team can end up being diverted to monitor and patch the process, so new data sources are put on hold. Also, management begins to lose confidence because the problems are fairly public — they inevitably cause the data to be unavailable at the least opportune time.

Develop and Test ETL Automation

The design of automated ETL operations for incremental processing must begin early in the project and be woven into the fabric of the ETL system. In this chapter we've described many techniques for error handling and automated recovery. You should also take the time to evaluate data quality throughout the ETL process, and perhaps automatically halt the load if the data does not pass the quality benchmark.

We return to the subject of developing and testing the ETL application in Chapter 13 in the context of deploying and maintaining the complete DW/BI system.

Conclusion

Developing the ETL system is one of the greatest challenges of the DW/BI project. No matter how thorough your interviews and analyses are, you will uncover data quality problems when you start building the ETL system. Some of these data quality problems may be bad enough to force a redesign of the schema.

The extract logic is a challenging step. You need to work closely with the source system programmers to develop an extract process that generates quality data, does not place an unbearable burden on the transaction system, and can be incorporated into the flow of your automated ETL system.

The ETL system seems mysterious, but hopefully at this point you realize that it's fairly straightforward. We have tried to demystify the jargon around implementing dimensional designs, emphasizing the importance of using surrogate keys and describing in detail how to handle key assignments.

We hope that the many ideas presented in this chapter have sparked your creativity for designing your ETL system. More than anything else, we want to leave you with the notion that there are many ways to solve any problem. The most difficult problems require patience and perseverance — a willingness to keep bashing your head against the wall — but an elegant and efficient solution is its own reward.

BLUEPRINT FOR ACTION

Managing the Effort and Reducing Risk

The greatest risk surrounding the ETL system development is to skip the planning step. The team is always eager to start moving data into the data warehouse. But remember that the ETL system *will* have an architecture, whether that architecture is planned or merely evolves.

The second greatest risk is that some unexpected landmine in the data will make the ETL system much more expensive to build, or perhaps even infeasible. The process of evaluating and profiling data should begin at the very earliest stages of the overall project lifecycle, long before the ETL system development begins.

One of the best ways to reduce the risk of the ETL system development project is to convince the source system application owners to assume responsibility for delivering the data to the ETL system, that is, to own the extract step. By far the most efficient method for extracting clean data is to place some kind of process on the source system itself. If the DW/BI team identifies new and changed rows, and cleans the data no matter how poor

(continued)

quality it is, the source system owners will not be motivated to address their data quality issues.

We've outlined many best practices for effectively developing the crucial steps in the ETL system. The performance of the extraction, transformation, and loading steps is always critical, and creative thinking may be required to overcome an obstacle.

We strongly recommend using an ETL tool. The ETL tool will probably not provide productivity benefits on the first iteration of your ETL system development, but will pay for itself in reduced cost of maintenance, revision, and extension over time.

Assuring Quality

The ETL system must ensure the accuracy of the data in the data warehouse. This focus on quality begins at the outset when data is extracted from the source systems. That data should be tested for data quality measures and archived so it can be audited. If the extracted data fails the data quality tests, the load should be halted or otherwise flagged.

As data flows through the ETL system, you may be improving its quality. Often those improvements are simple, like decoding cryptic transaction system codes or parsing names into multiple columns. Sometimes the improvements are more difficult, like consolidating multiple customer accounts into a single view of the customer. In the most complex cases involving system consolidation, you may have to make fuzzy or imprecise decisions; those decisions and the criteria that underlie them must be documented. At all points in the process, business users must sign off on the quality of the data.

Key Roles

Key roles for ETL system development include:

◆ The ETL team is on the front line for this entire part of the project. The ETL team must communicate clearly and often to the rest of the team. This not only keeps everyone informed about progress, but makes it easy to solicit assistance when appropriate.

◆ The project manager must take a proactive role to partner closely with the ETL team. Often the ETL team gets overwhelmed and buried in the details. The project manager must keep an eye on the big picture and intercede on their behalf.

(continued)

BLUEPRINT FOR ACTION *(continued)*

◆ The quality assurance analysts and data stewards begin to take an active role during ETL development. The quality assurance processes need to be designed with their guidance. Also, as the data is loaded, it must be validated.

◆ The database administrator continues active involvement by setting up appropriate backup, recovery, and archival processes.

Key Deliverables

Key deliverables for ETL system development include:

◆ ETL system specifications, including the high level ETL process, default strategies for common processes, and detailed ETL plan for each table.

◆ ETL system to handle historic dimension and fact loads, incremental dimension and fact loads, aggregate and OLAP processing, and automation.

Estimating Considerations

The overall estimate of the effort required to build the ETL system is the single largest source of uncertainty and risk in planning a DW/BI system. It is impossible to know how complex the system needs to be until the programmer faces the actual data sources in microscopic detail. If a single data field is discovered to have been used for two purposes, the complexity of the data extract routines can double. An off-the-shelf tool may need to be augmented with custom hand-written code. Although many people tend to wince at the following guideline, we have found over the years that allocating six work months of development labor for each major data source turns out to be wise in the long run.

Website Resources

The following resource for developing the ETL system is available on the book's website at www.kimballgroup.com:

◆ Date dimension spreadsheet

Task List

ETL SYSTEM DESIGN & DEVELOPMENT

Legend: ● Primary responsibility ○ Involved ◆ Provides input □ Informed of results

	Fans	Front Office		Coaches		Regular Line-Up							Special Teams			
	Business Users	Business Sponsor / Business Driver	DW/BI Director / Program Manager	Project Manager	Business Project Lead	Business Analyst	Data Steward / QA Analyst	Data Architect / Data Modeler / DBA	Metadata Manager	ETL Architect / ETL Developer	BI Architect / App Developer / Portal Developer	Technical Architect / Tech Support Specialist	Security Manager	Lead Tester	Data Mining / Stats Specialist	Educator
ETL SYSTEM DESIGN																
1 Design high level ETL process				○				◆		●		◆				
2 Test, choose and implement an ETL tool				○				○		●	○	○	○			
3 Develop default strategies for extracting data				○				○		●		◆				
4 Develop default strategies for archiving extracted data				○				○		●		○				
5 Develop default strategies for policing data quality				○			○			●		○				
6 Develop default strategies for dimension change mgmt				○				○		●		○				
7 Design strategy to meet availability requirements				○			○	○		●		○				
8 Design data auditing subsystem				○			○	○		●		○				
9 Design the structure of the ETL staging area				○				○		●		◆				
10 Develop plan for maintaining dimension hierarchies				○				○		●		◆				
11 Design detailed ETL plans for each table				○				○		●		◆				
12 Set up initial job sequencing				○				○		●		◆				
13 Document the ETL system specification			□	○			○	○	□	●		◆	□		□	
14 User acceptance/project review		□	□	●	○	○	○	○	□	○	○	○	□	○	□	○
ETL SYSTEM DEVELOPMENT																
1 Build dimension table surrogate key mgmt system				○				○		●		◆				
2 Build the audit system or template				○				○		●		◆				
3 Load the date table and other static dimensions				○				○		●						
4 Build historic loads for type 1 dimension tables; test				○			○	○		●				◆		
5 Build historic loads for type 2 dimension tables; test				○			○	○		●				◆		
6 Build fact table surrogate key pipeline				○			○	○		●		◆		◆		
7 Build historic fact table loads; test				○				○		●						
8 Build dimension attrib incremental change mgmt sys				○			○	○		●		◆		◆		
9 Build dimension table incremental loads; test				○			○	○		●						
10 Build fact table incremental loads; test				○			○	○		●				○		
11 Build agg table load/OLAP cube processing; test				○			○	○		●				○		
12 Design, build and test ETL system automation				○				○		●				○		
13 User acceptance/project review		□	□	●	○	○	○	○	□	○	○	○	□	○	□	○

LEGEND:
- ● Primary responsibility
- ○ Involved
- ◆ Provides input
- □ Informed of results

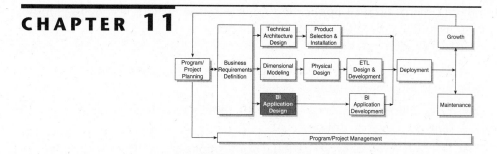

CHAPTER 11

Introducing Business Intelligence Applications

At this point in the Lifecycle, we climb out of the detailed back room issues of architecture, database design and development and move into the front room. The main front room development activities involve designing and building the initial set of reports and analyses called *business intelligence (BI) applications*. BI applications range from simple parameter-driven standard reports on one end of the spectrum to complex analytic systems or operational-level applications at the other end.

In this chapter, we begin with a brief description about the need for BI applications. We then present the analytic cycle, which is the generalized process business users follow for analytic decision making. The analytic cycle provides a framework for understanding how BI applications are used and the resulting implications on their design and development. With this framework in mind, we then describe the broad spectrum of potential applications that fit under the BI applications umbrella in greater detail. In the next chapter, we describe the process of creating these applications.

The entire team should read this chapter and the next. Understanding how business users will access the information in the DW/BI system helps the data modeler, DBA, and ETL developer make more informed decisions about design trade-offs. This shared understanding and common terminology also helps the team communicate better. Because technical details are specific to individual products, this chapter is not technical in nature. The task of relating the general BI application approach to a specific technology is the responsibility of the BI application developer.

In this chapter you learn:

- ▪ The analytic cycle and its implications for designing business intelligence applications.

- ▪ Basic concepts about the types of BI applications, their value, and delivery platform options.

- ▪ Descriptions and organizational implications of common BI applications, including standard reports, analytic applications, dashboards and scorecards, data mining, and operational BI.

- ▪ Role of the BI portal as the business users' primary access point for BI applications.

Importance of Business Intelligence Applications

Most knowledge workers in your organization will not build their own reports, so you must provide these people with an appropriate way to gain access to the information in the data warehouse. This is the primary role of BI applications. Think about the implications of this statement: For this majority of business users, the BI applications are the only view of the DW/BI system they will have. If the applications are confusing, perform poorly, are unappealing or inaccurate, they will taint the entire DW/BI system. Many of these users will turn to alternative sources for the information, or worse, start projects to build their own data warehouses or marts. Bottom line: the BI applications must be great. They must meet a demanding list of design requirements, including:

- ▪ **Be correct.** BI applications must provide accurate audit reports and document differences compared to other systems.

- ▪ **Perform well.** A response time of less than five seconds for the average query is a good goal.

- ▪ **Be easy to use.** Users who have enough skill to order a book online should be able to use at least the standard reports. Getting customized results with less than ten mouse clicks is a good goal.

- ▪ **Look good.** Tools and reports should be clear and attractive.

- ▪ **Be a long-term investment.** Applications must be properly documented, maintained, enhanced, and extended.

BI applications fill a critical gap in meeting the organization's range of data access needs. Figure 11-1 shows the range of reporting needs from strategic to operational. At the top end of the information access spectrum, some users will build their own queries against the data warehouse from scratch; this is

Types of BI Applications and Consumer Modes

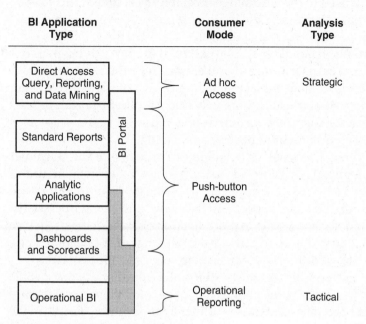

Figure 11-1 Types of BI applications.

what we mean by *ad hoc access*. These business analysts, or power users, are usually charged with creating more complex analyses in an effort to address a pressing problem or opportunity. You can identify a power user with a simple test: Ask if they use functions or macros in Excel. At the other end of the spectrum, operational BI occurs at the tactical level; each execution is usually low value, has short-term impact, and is predefined. Operational BI is usually leveraged over all transactions in an operational system, or across a large set of users, like all the agents in a call center. The gap between these two endpoints is wide. In our experience, a large percentage of the DW/BI system user base, perhaps as high as 80 to 90 percent, will fall in the middle or toward the lower end of this spectrum. These users will need prebuilt, parameterized reports. As BI matures, organizations are finding even more ways to meet the information needs of these groups in the middle and at the lower end.

NOTE To many business professionals, *ad hoc* is simply the ability to change the parameters on a report to create their own personalized version of that report. This need shows itself through statements like "I want this report, but by month rather than quarter," or "Can we see this report at the district level instead of region?" For many users, this is as ad hoc as they ever want to get. The standard report set of BI applications needs to be the primary access tool for most of these business users.

There are usually dozens or even hundreds of BI applications in a mature DW/BI system, too many for the users to find what they need in a simple list. This means you need to provide a high level interface, called the *BI portal*, which imposes a rational order on the list of applications. The BI portal must meet the same strict design requirements as the BI applications. Although the design of a BI portal is yet another responsibility of the DW/BI team, in our opinion, it is welcome because it means you are dealing with the "problems" of success. We talk more about the planning and design of the BI portal later in this chapter. Most BI applications are accessed via the BI portal, at least initially. Once the user identifies an interesting report, they may access it directly via the tool environment or hosting application.

It is difficult to categorize users as belonging to only one of the consumer modes shown in Figure 11-1. Most ad hoc users also make regular use of standard reports and other analytic applications. Some push-button users will build their own simple ad hoc reports on occasion, and some operational level users will do ad hoc analysis to explore an odd behavior or event they've noticed in the data. You will need to provide the full range of application types; users will gravitate toward the ones they need to solve specific problems.

One of the driving forces behind the need for BI applications is that people vary significantly in terms of the depth and quality of their technological capabilities. You may be surprised by how difficult it is for many people in the business community to understand what you thought was simple technology. If your plan is to provide a tool and let the users build all their own reports, we encourage you to reconsider. The warehouse needs to support a range of technical skill levels and degrees of analytical sophistication.

Analytic Cycle for Business Intelligence

Business analysis follows a common process from monitoring activity to identifying a problem or opportunity and determining an action to take, and finally back to monitoring the results of that action. The analytic cycle breaks the process into five distinct stages as shown in Figure 11-2. This section walks through each of these stages in detail to understand their objectives and impact on the architecture and design of the BI applications provided to your business users.

Stage 1: Monitor Activity

Standard reports are the starting point for the analytic cycle. Users work with these reports to examine current results versus previous periods or plan in order to provide a report card on the state of the business. BI application requirements in the monitor activity stage focus on the presentation layer and include technologies such as dashboards, portals, and scorecards. Many data warehouse implementations stop at this stage and declare success.

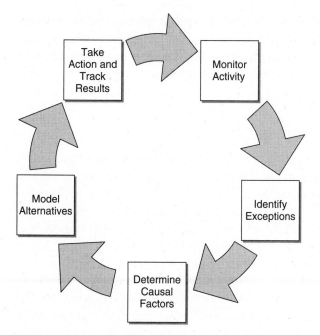

Figure 11-2 Analytic cycle for BI analysis.

Stage 2: Identify Exceptions

This stage focuses on the identification of "what's the matter?" or "where are the problems?" The emphasis in this stage is to identify the exceptions to normal performance, as well as the opportunities. Most business managers have asked the DW/BI team to replicate a stack of reports in the data warehouse, when in reality, they really only want the parts of the reports marked with highlighters and yellow stickies. The exceptions stage is essential in helping users wade through the deluge of data to focus on the opportunities that deserve the most attention.

The identify exceptions stage requires additional capabilities, such as distribution servers that distribute alerts to users' devices of choice based upon exception triggers and visualization tools to view the data in different more creative ways, including trend lines, spark lines, geographical maps, or clusters.

Stage 3: Determine Causal Factors

This stage tries to understand the "why" or root causes of the identified exceptions. Identifying reliable relationships and interactions between variables that drive exceptional performance is the key. Successfully supporting users' efforts in this stage will require your DW/BI system architecture to include additional software including statistical tools and/or data mining algorithms, such as association, sequencing, classification, and segmentation, to quantify cause-and-effect. This step frequently requires new data to investigate causal factors. For instance, if you are trying to understand a broad sales downturn in West Virginia during a particular month, you might want to include a weather data source for that area and time.

Stage 4: Model Alternatives

In this stage, you build on cause-and-effect relationships to develop models for evaluating decision alternatives. The data warehouse is a treasure trove of historical insight; many times, you can predict the effect of a potential decision by finding a similar situation in the warehouse's historical data. The ability to perform what-if analysis and simulations on a range of potential decisions is considered the final goal when following a typical analytic cycle. You hope to successfully answer strategic questions such as: What happens to my market share, revenue, and units sold if I achieve a greater than 10 percent price differential versus my top two competitors? Or, what are the impacts on my inventory costs if I can achieve 95 percent sales forecast accuracy instead of my usual 90 percent? Your data warehouse architecture may also need to accommodate additional technologies in the model alternatives stage, including statistical tools and data mining algorithms for model evaluation, such as sensitivity analysis, Monte Carlo simulations, and goal seeking optimizations.

Stage 5: Take Action and Track Results

Ideally, you can enable a closed loop process in your BI applications and feed the recommended actions back to the operational system. The take action/track results stage places additional demands on your data warehouse architecture. You need to access operational systems from the data warehouse via APIs or SOA calls. You may need to enhance existing dimensional models or build performance management tracking databases to record the results of specific business decisions and determine which decisions worked and which ones didn't. Technologies applicable in this area include distribution services that enable users to respond with recommended actions from email, PDAs, pagers, or cell phones, not just deliver alerts.

The results of the action should be captured and analyzed in order to continuously fine tune the analysis process, business rules, and analytic models. This brings you right back to the monitor activity stage to start the cycle all over again. As Figure 11-2 shows, these stages occur in a circular process. The result of each analytic cycle becomes input to the next cycle. The results of one decision must be monitored, analyzed for exceptions, and so on through the five stages.

More Implications of the Analytic Cycle

The analytic cycle helps us understand how business users will use the DW/BI system and what tools we must provide to make their experience as simple and seamless as possible. It provides a framework for analysis that underlies all analytic activity from the five minute quick query to the five week marketing program review.

The analytic cycle is implicit in the quick query, with most of the cycle processing occurring in the analyst's head. But the cycle must be explicitly applied to any analytic applications you build. A comprehensive BI application environment needs to moves users beyond standard reports. The environment needs to proactively "guide" users through the analysis of a business situation, ultimately helping them make an insightful and thoughtful decision. The goals are to:

- Proactively guide business users beyond basic reporting.
- Identify and understand exceptional performance situations.
- Capture decision-making "best practices" for each exceptional performance situation.
- Share the resulting "best practices" or intellectual capital across the organization.

Understanding the analytic cycle helps ensure that you provide a complete solution to each analytic opportunity identified in the business requirements definition process. Keep the analytic cycle in mind as the different types of BI applications are reviewed in the next section.

Types of Business Intelligence Applications

Referring back to Figure 11-1, we see that BI applications break down into several major subsets. These include:

- **Direct access query and reporting tools** allow users to query the dimensional model directly and define a results set. Simple ad hoc tools only deliver tabular results sets, whereas more advanced tools allow the creation of fully realized, complex reports. In these cases, the ad hoc tools also serve as the development tools for standard reports that other users run themselves.
- **Data mining** is included in the direct access box because often a small set of statistical analysts use data mining tools to explore the data in the warehouse for useful patterns and relationships. The resulting models are often embedded in other BI applications. Because data mining is

rarely seen by most users, we will hold off on its description until later in this section.

- **Standard reports** are predefined, preformatted reports that generally provide some level of user interaction, like the ability to enter a parameter, drill down to a lower level of detail, and link to related reports.

- **Analytic applications** are managed sets of reports that usually embed domain expertise regarding the analysis of a particular business process. Most analytic applications require an interface layer for user access. Analytic applications often take advantage of data mining models.

- **Dashboards and scorecards** generally involve a combination of reports and charts that use exception highlighting and drilldown capabilities to analyze data from multiple business processes.

- **Operational BI and closed loop applications** include the use of applications that are more sophisticated than typical operational reports. These applications leverage the rich historical context across multiple business processes available in the data warehouse to guide operational decision making. Operational BI applications often include data mining models to help identify patterns and opportunities at the operational level. These applications also frequently include transactional interfaces back to the source systems.

We describe each of these BI application types in the following sections; the primary organizing framework for the BI applications, the BI portal, is discussed in a separate section of this chapter.

Direct Access Query and Reporting Tools

Ad hoc query and reporting tools provide the user with direct access to the dimensional model, usually through a metadata layer that provides additional column sub-groups, business descriptions, and join definitions. Because of the complexity of the tool and the need to understand the details of the data, ad hoc tools are mostly used by expert power users who have both technical and business savvy. Typically, the user can drag-and-drop columns into the report area, set constraints, define calculations, and add formatting. The end result in most ad hoc query tools is a report. The analyst often takes the resulting report or dataset into another environment, usually Excel, for further manipulation. This is why there are dozens of Excel add-ins for query and report generation. This is also why Microsoft has invested heavily in its own query and reporting capabilities for Excel.

One reason ad hoc tools are complex is that SQL was not meant to be a report writer language. The OLAP languages are more sophisticated, but the queries are harder to formulate. In both cases, the query tools must overcome the underlying difficulty of translating a business question into the syntax of a query language. As a result, these tools can be challenging to use for anything beyond the simplest query. They demo well, but the real world is usually not as easy. Their use is typically limited to business analysts and power users because they require a fairly significant investment in learning, not just for the tool but for the data as well.

In general, ad hoc query tools should include functionality in at least four areas: query formulation, analysis and presentation, user experience, and technical features. The following list includes functionality that is critical to defining reports and analyses, regardless of whether they are used in an ad hoc fashion or to build standard reports and more advanced analytic applications. This list is not meant to be exhaustive; we left out many basic ad hoc capabilities because they are found in almost all products.

Query Formulation

As its name suggests, the query tool's primary job is to formulate queries. This is a challenging task made more difficult by the evolution of SQL standards and the emergence of OLAP languages that allow the creation of increasingly complex queries. The kinds of query formulation capabilities you may need include:

- **Multipass or multiset queries.**   To calculate comparisons or correctly calculate nonadditive measures in report break rows, the query tool must break the report down into a number of simple queries that are processed separately by the RDBMS. Some tools formulate these queries as separate queries and combine the results based on a local join of the separate sets. Other tools create SELECT statements in the FROM clause for each separate query and combine the results as part of the query using an outer join. Multipass queries also allow drilling across to different fact tables in several conformed business process dimensional models, potentially in different databases. For example, sales and costs might be in different databases, but as long as they share the same dimensions, like organization and date, you can create a simple contribution report by querying the two sources and combining the results in the query tool. Finally, multipass queries give the database optimizer and aggregate navigator a chance to speed up the report because each atomic query is simple and easily analyzed.

  Note that the analytic language used by OLAP engines can do the equivalent of multipass queries more easily in a single statement. Not that the syntax is easy, but the multiset logic can be more easily expressed if you have a front end tool that allows you to formulate these queries.

- **Alerts.**   As data volumes grow exponentially, the query tool needs to help the user identify records that stand out from the others, usually based on a comparative rule, such as "show me districts that had a sales drop or increase of more than 10 percent over last month." Alerts are often used on dashboards and scorecards to measure performance. They highlight exceptional entries that are too high or too low when compared to an expected value, like sales plan or budget.

▪ **Successive constraints.** The results of one query are used as a limit or filter on subsequent queries. This is a particularly important capability for creating behavioral study groups where you identify a cohort and examine its behavior as a unit. For example, doctors and researchers might be interested in identifying a group of patients with specific characteristics and then tracking their progress over time. They might want to identify the heavy smokers in a clinical trial group to see if the drug being tested reduces the risk of getting lung cancer. Any database with customer information will need successive constraints at some point. The value of this capability is not limited to people, however. A semiconductor company may want to identify a set of silicon chip wafers and follow them through the production process to examine failure rates. These constraint lists may be too large to store in the tool and thus may need to be passed back to the database so the join can be performed remotely. In some cases, it's important to track the original participants in a long term historical study, instead of the participants that currently meet the criteria. In this situation, you'd save the study group participant list by creating temporary tables or view definitions in the database, although talk of writing lists or views to the database will make the DBAs nervous. This is a standard capability in some BI tools.

▪ **Semi-additive summations.** There is an important class of numeric measures in common business fact tables that are not completely additive. Anything that is a measure of intensity is usually not additive across all dimensions, especially the date dimension. For example, inventory levels and account balances are not additive across time. Everyone is familiar with taking the semi-additive fact, such as a bank balance, and creating a useful summary at the end of the month by averaging across time. Unfortunately, you cannot use the basic SQL AVG function to calculate this kind of average across time; AVG averages across all of the dimensions, not just time. If you fetch five accounts and four time periods from the RDBMS, AVG will divide the total account balance by 20 (five times four) rather than doing what you want, which is to divide by four. It isn't difficult to divide by four, but it is a distraction for the user or application developer, who must stop and store the number four in the application explicitly. What is needed is a generalization of the SUM operator to become AVGTIMESUM . This function automatically performs a sum, but it also automatically divides by the cardinality of the time constraint in the surrounding query. This feature makes all applications involving inventory levels, account balances, and other measures of intensity significantly simpler. Note that semi-additive sums are a standard capability of OLAP engines.

- **ANSI SQL 99 support.** SQL 99 added basic OLAP capabilities to SQL, including a WINDOW construct that allows you to aggregate across a defined subset of a query to generate rolling averages, for example. Lots of interesting SQL92 capabilities, such as UNION, MINUS, and nested SELECT statements in various locations of a SELECT statement (including the FROM clause, which enables the multiset query previously described), are supported by the database vendors, but are not fully supported by many BI tool vendors. Nested selects can be used to address many of the preceding challenges and they also offer another alternative to the successive constraint problem without writing to the database.

- **Direct query string entry.** As a last resort, you will probably need to be able to view and alter the SQL or OLAP language generated by the tool. This includes creating complex queries and adding optimizer hints. If you find yourself doing this very often, something is wrong with either your tool or data model design.

Analysis and Presentation Capabilities

In most cases, your query tool must do more than get the data and bring it back to the desktop in a tabular form. The tool must also support the business requirements for manipulating data and putting it into a presentation quality format.

- **Basic calculations on the results set.** This should include a range of math, statistical, string, sequential processing, conditional, and reporting functions. These calculations are often used to overcome other deficiencies in the tool. For example, it is possible to create a computed column using an IF or CASE statement that copies the description column if the rank ≤ 25 or the value "All Other" if it's greater. This new column can then be used as the description in the pivot step to show a top 25 report that includes a total for All Other and the grand total for the company; and it can even calculate the percentage of total for each of the top 25. How much of your business do your top 25 customers represent, anyway?

- **Pivot the results.** Pivoting is the basis of multidimensional or cross tabulation analysis. The row-based results set that SQL generates almost always ends up being presented in a format with one or more dimensions displayed across the top of the report and one or more down the side. The report title usually gives it away (e.g., monthly sales report by region or monthly sales by sales rep by product). Many people assume pivot functionality is tied to OLAP tools. This is not true. The pivot feature should be independent of the data source. It is true that the OLAP database provides metadata to automatically display hierarchies, but the major BI tools support this in the relational database as well.

- **Drill down.** This function allows users to add more detail to a results set by including additional columns. These columns may be limited to a specific hierarchy, such as region to district to office, or they may simply be attributes that support the analytic hypothesis under investigation, such as drilling down to gender may reveal differences in color preferences.

- **Column calculations on pivot results.** These calculations create a computed column that is a function of two or more of the pivoted columns. For example, if a query returned two months of data, say, July and August of the current year, you should be able to calculate a change or percentage change between the two columns. Note that you may not want to display one or more of the source columns for the calculation. Single-column calculations, like percentage of column, cumulative, and *n*-tiles, fall into this category as well.

- **Column and row calculations.** Some calculations, like showing one row value as a percentage of another row value, are useful. Share calculations and ratios rely on this capability.

- **Sorting.** Sorting, especially by a non-displaying element, is important. For example, a financial report might show line items in a particular order that has nothing to do with the information displayed. It is not alphabetical. In such cases, a sort order column in the dimension specifies the appropriate display order. You don't necessarily want to see that element on the report, but you do want to use it in the sort. Some tools allow you to physically specify the display order by dragging and dropping rows or columns. But what happens when new values show up in the results set?

- **Complex formatting.** Formatting is often more important than it probably should be. Whatever productivity gains we may have reaped from the personal computer have been diluted by the print-tweak-repeat cycle. Of course, formatting can be critical, especially if senior management is the audience. You need to have a full range of graphic design tools, including lines, boxes, shading, images, fonts, and sizes, and you need to have pixel level control of the placement of report elements.

- **Charting and graphs.** These elements are the sizzle of the analytical steak. Almost every report ends up as a graph, if only to do some eyeball correlation analysis or forecasting. If the data has to leave the tool to go elsewhere for this capability, the transfer had better be truly seamless. It should be push-button simple, and the data source query should be linked to the charting tool to make it possible to automatically update the chart the next time the query is run.

- **Compound documents.**   The dashboard interface is essentially a compound document made up of several individual reports, graphs, and highlighters. These all may be connected together by a shared parameter, like date, so changing the parameter will change the contents of all the sub-reports connected to it. In some cases, this linked set of sub-reports can be created in the portal tool.

- **User-changeable variables.**   User-changeable variables or parameters can be included anywhere in the query document, from the query filter to the report headings. For example, if you limit a sales rep report to a single region, you'd like that region name to be accessible to the report header in the final report: sales by rep for the last 12 months for the Southeast Region. Variables should also be used to prompt users for input. When this happens, they should have access to the appropriate pick lists. Finally, the tool should be able to iteratively set variables based on a list or query result set. The region sales report just mentioned could be run for a list of regions, dynamically created by a query stored in the region name variable.

User Experience

The road to success in high tech is littered with the remains of superior technology. This applies to BI tools as well. It doesn't matter that the tool meets all of your technical requirements if the users can't use it or don't like it. The following capabilities help improve the users' experience of the analytical environment:

- **Ease of use.**   The tool should feel natural and have an intuitive interface. This is a matter of opinion. Often it means the tool works like a Microsoft tool. You must involve your users in assessing this. Let them participate in the BI tool evaluation and get a sense of how they rate the usability of the tool.

- **Metadata access.**   The tool should provide the user with context-sensitive help, not only about the tool, but about the data as well. This means the tool must provide a flexible way to draw from the descriptive data in the metadata catalog.

- **Pick lists.**   The tool should provide a way to look up the list of values that can be used as constraints or filters in a query. Ideally, this list should be done in a way that supports the cross-browsing of dimension attributes. For larger dimensions, a simple SELECT DISTINCT isn't helpful if thousands of rows are returned. A direct pick list request against a high cardinality attribute in a 75 million row dimension table can never return to the desktop, so there must be a hierarchy in the dimension that allows the user to constrain the query at a higher level, thus limiting the results of subsequent pick lists. It's possible to get down to a short list pretty quickly. A smart tool will allow you to protect the user from asking for a SELECT DISTINCT on 75 million rows.

- **Seamless integration with other applications.**   Integration includes the ability to make the reports available in another application. Most tools have portal integration components that let them display directly in the BI portal. They also have APIs that let the BI developers embed reports in virtually any application.

- **Export to multiple file types.**   Ideally, this includes a full publishing capability of the final report and/or chart to a file directory, email, or directly to the web.

- **Embedded queries.**   Users should be able to initiate queries from other applications. It should be possible, for example, to call a query from a spreadsheet and have it return rows into a specific region, which then feeds a complex financial model. The formulas in the spreadsheet may need to adjust to a variable length results set.

Technical Features

The following technical issues are not sexy demo features, and the need for them may not be immediately obvious. Some, like the ability to multitask and cancel queries, are so fundamental to the tool's usability that your users will get angry if they are missing.

- **Multitasking.**   Users must be able to run other programs and create and run other queries while a query is running.

- **Cancel query.**   Users should be able to kill a single query they initiated while it is in process without killing all of them. This cancel should manage a clean break from the database server, and should not require rebooting the desktop machine.

- **Scripting.**   A scripting language and command line interface is critical for automating report execution.

- **Connectivity.**   Make sure you can get to all the database platforms desired. Connectivity includes connecting to other data sources — text, spreadsheets, XML files, other relational databases, and OLAP engines.

- **Scheduling.**   The tool needs to provide or take advantage of some kind of scheduling system. Users will want to defer queries for overnight processing or set them up for processing on a regular basis.

- **Metadata driven.**   The administrator should be able to define simple subsets of the warehouse, such as only those tables involved in a single business process dimensional model. This may include predefined join paths, column groupings, business descriptions, calculated columns, and pick list sources. This setup process should be simple and fast.

- **Software administration.**   This is a disappearing problem with the adoption of the web as an application platform. Until the transition is complete, make sure the vendor includes administration utilities that allow you to update any software, data models, local pick lists, and connectivity software from a central location.

- **Security.**   Ideally, the tool will participate in whatever user authentication system is available. Tool-based security is not that valuable in the DW/BI environment unless it participates with the network security service and the database. The BI tool may need to provide authorization functions, limiting users to only those reports or data subsets they are allowed to see.

- **Querying.**   Direct querying of the database should be supported without an administrative layer or with minimal work (i.e., initial setup of less than 10 minutes). This is especially valuable for the warehouse team because they are constantly examining new data sources, often on different platforms.

This section described many features that are commonly required of ad hoc query and reporting tools. You need to understand and document the types of users your system will serve, the kinds of problems they need to solve, and which of the features described in this chapter are going to be most valuable.

Standard Reports

Standard reports are at the basic end of the BI application spectrum. They are typically parameter-driven reports with a predefined, preformatted output. Standard reports provide users with a core set of information about what's going on in a particular area of the business. Standard reports are the reports the majority of the non-technical business users, the push-button users, look at every day. Most of what people asked for during the requirements definition process would be classified as standard reports. They may sound dull, but they're often the workhorse BI applications for the business.

The value to the push-button user is clear: the standard reports represent an easy-to-use means to get the information needed with a very short learning curve. The reports offer some flexibility through parameter selection and potentially content specification. The organization gets value from the reports as well, because they are usually part of the initial project deployment and provide immediate access to the information in the warehouse.

These reports serve as the official source for enterprise metrics, and provide a quality-assured reference point for these metrics. These reports must either tie back to existing points of reference, or the differences must be clearly documented. By the same token, if an ad hoc user can tie her own query results back to results from the standard reports, she can be reasonably certain that she is using the appropriate query logic.

Some typical examples of standard report titles might be:

- YTD Sales vs. Forecast by Sales Rep
- Monthly Churn Rate by Service Plan
- Five-Year Drop Out Rate Time Series by School
- Direct Mail Response Rates by Promotion by Product
- Audience Counts and Percent of Total Audience by Network by Day of Week and Time of Day
- YTD Claims vs. Forecast by Vehicle Type
- Call Volume by Product as a Percent of Total Product Sales

We described the key functional requirements for standard reports in the data access services section in Chapter 4.

Analytic Applications

Analytic applications are more complex than standard reports. They are usually targeted at a specific business process and encapsulate a certain amount of domain expertise about how to analyze and interpret that business process. Because analytic applications are designed to solve a specific problem, they are usually meant for the users who are responsible for that problem: the promotions managers, sales managers, cost center managers, or brand managers who will use the tools on a regular basis. They may go so far as to include complex, code-based algorithms or data mining models that help identify underlying issues or opportunities. Another advanced feature in some analytic applications is the ability for the user to feed changes back into the transaction systems based on insights gained from using the application. At the far end of the spectrum, analytic applications are sold as black-box, stand-alone applications in part to protect the intellectual capital that went into their creation. Common analytic applications include:

- Promotion effectiveness
- Web path analysis
- Affinity program analysis
- Shelf space planning
- Fraud detection

- Sales force management

- Category management

A promotion effectiveness analytic application might allow the user to investigate the impact of several variables on the response rate to a credit card promotion. The promotion analysis screen would include several panes, each one containing a graph or report. The main pane might show overall response rates to a campaign with several related panes showing response rates associated with the major variables of the campaign, including the five different creative pieces that were used, the offers, such as extra loyalty points versus 0 percent rollover rate, and the channels used, such as direct mail, email, and web. Related panes would allow the user to see response rates by customer attribute, such as gender or date of birth ranges. The real power of this kind of application comes from the user's ability to interact with the variables and look for combinations that generate the greatest response rate. The promotion analysis screen ties in with the other components of the application, such as campaign planning.

Take caution: The more targeted an analytic application is, the more tempting it is to implement it as a stand-alone system. In other words, you can do promotion analysis without having to spend all that time and energy building the DW/BI system. This has a grain of truth in it, but that's because the justification applies the entire cost of building the DW/BI system against the value of the specific BI application. What this argument misses is that much of the data transformation has to take place in either case. In other words, it's much more efficient to do the data cleansing once in the DW/BI system and make it available to all users and applications that can use it, including the analytic application in question. If the analytic application has enough business value, it should be one of the top priority DW/BI system projects. The work it takes to support the analytic application will generate much greater long-term value if the underlying data is available to all who need it across the organization.

Pre-Built Analytic Applications

There is a broad range of pre-built applications available from the major BI tool vendors and from companies with hands-on industry and functional experience. Pre-built analytic applications that focus on specific opportunity areas can incorporate domain expertise that would take years to develop in-house. Where your requirements line up with these offerings, it makes great sense to purchase and implement these pre-built apps. Other pre-built applications that focus more on basic reporting can be a good starting point, but in many cases are more work than you might expect.

These pre-built applications often come with ETL components and under-lying data structures (usually dimensional models) that make it easier to get them installed and running. In some cases, if a business is working from standard source systems and has not customized them, these applications can be up and running in a matter of days. There is still customization on the front end, and of course, these applications are not free.

Read/Write Analytic Applications

There is a separate class of analytic application that requires both read and write access. These applications include planning, budgeting, forecasting, and what-if modeling. These applications are essentially transaction systems, but often end up connected to the DW/BI system because the base level input data for these applications is fed from the data warehouse.

For example, the forecasting process takes historical sales information and projects it into the future. This can be as simple as increasing prior sales by three percent, or it may involve intense statistical modeling. The forecasting process often involves multiple iterations of multiple versions with input from various parts of the organization. These forecast versions can be included in the data warehouse. You'll need to set up a separate fact table, typically at a much coarser grain than the actual sales data. After the forecast is stored back in the warehouse, the versions can be compared. Once the final forecast is approved, you will need standard reports that compare actual sales to forecast.

If the DW/BI team ends up owning the forecasting system, it will introduce another layer of complexity. The forecasting system is essentially a transaction process, which comes with the requisite needs for managed database updating, security, and transaction monitoring. However, keep in mind that the volume of activity is generally much lower than most production operational systems.

Because most data access tools are designed for read access, building this kind of system requires more traditional application development skills and tools. Though it is possible to develop a simple planning and forecasting tool, given the complexity in creating and managing multiple versions of multiple forecasts and applying complex allocations rules that require input from across the organization, it's worth investigating packaged planning and forecasting applications.

These planning and forecasting applications are a key component of performance management applications described in the next section. Planning and forecasting applications provide the targets that can then be compared to actuals as the starting point for assessing performance. If you don't know the goal, you can't tell if you've reached it.

Dashboards and Scorecards

Dashboard and scorecard applications cover a range of reporting interfaces and applications. Although these applications originated as executive interfaces, they have migrated out across organizational ranks. The common themes across these reporting applications are information consolidation, exception highlighting, and ease of use.

Dashboards provide the interface tools that support status reporting and alerts across multiple data sources at a high level, and also allow drilldown to more detailed data. The alerts can be generated by comparing the actual number, like sales, to a fixed number, a percentage, or, in many cases, to a separate target or goal number. A dashboard is usually aimed at a specific user type, such as a sales manager. The sales management dashboard might include a sales by region vs. plan report with a drilldown to district and sales rep and highlights for those entities below 90 percent of plan. It might also have pipeline information including deal counts by sales cycle stage and projections of dollar sales compared to plan. Applications based on dashboard tools are particularly appealing to management because they offer the possibility of quickly identifying a problem anywhere in the business and drilling down into the detail to identify its causes.

Figure 11-3 provides an example of a sales dashboard. This one is based on some of the ideas and examples in *Information Dashboard Design: The Effective Visual Communication of Data* (O'Reilly, 2006) by Stephen Few, which takes many of Edward Tufte's recommendations for communicating data and

Sales Overview Dashboard

Sales Summary
as of 11/01/2008

Total US	Actual to Date	Year End Forecast
Revenue	$ 130,626	$ 168,822
Plan	$ 122,992	$ 159,889
% Plan	106%	106%

Current vs. Prior Year Revenue

Key Performance Indicators

Measure	10/31	Target
Sales plan attainment %	106 ⇧	100
Close rate (Leads/Deals %)	5.3 ⇩	7.5
Rebuy rate (3+ orders/Total)	56 ⇧	65
Customer satisfaction score	85 ⇩	92
Ontime shipments %	99 ⇧	97

Revenue YTD
Last 12 Months   Region   YTD Actual vs. Plan (Actual Plan) ($ 000) % Plan

Region	($ 000)	% Plan
Northeast	15,239	92
Southeast	12,150	103
Central	13,459	105
Southwest	35,075	102
West	23,417	118
Northwest	31,287	114

Revenue Forecast
Forecast vs. Plan (Forecast Plan) ($ 000) % Plan

($ 000)	% Plan
18,286	84.7
14,822	96.7
17,631	106.1
46,650	104.4
28,569	110.4
42,863	119.8

Product Sales YTD
Last 12 Months   Category   YTD Actual vs. Plan (Actual Plan) ($ 000) % Plan

Category	($ 000)	% Plan
Accessories	35,112	98
Components	23,422	90
Hard Drives	3,497	94
Jump Drives	24,257	135
Music Players	35,421	107
Video	1,283	105

Regional Pipeline   Northeast ▼

Customer	Opp Size	Probability	Exp. Rev	Age
1 Ajax Chemical	2.30	0.7	1.61	104
2 Ambro Works	1.15	0.9	1.04	93
3 Jefferson Mfg.	1.20	0.8	0.96	83
4 Custom Mix	0.95	0.7	0.67	98
5 Trotter Plastics	1.30	0.5	0.65	110
6 Planex, Inc	0.80	0.8	0.64	108
7 Tyler Systems	0.75	0.6	0.45	117
8 Metro Mfg.	0.50	0.8	0.40	67
All others	4.1	0.5	2.05	56
Total Verbal	13.05		8.46	92.89

Data as of: 01-Oct-2008
All revenue amounts in US dollars

Figure 11-3 Example dashboard application.

applies them to dashboards. It is high density, information rich, but still easy to view and understand. The round dots indicate areas of particular concern. In the main bar graphs, the gray horizontal bars are actual sales numbers and the short, vertical bars are sales plan numbers. The lines on the left of each metric or region are called spark lines. They show a full year's worth of activity in a small space and are intended to communicate general trends and unusual patterns. It's usually pretty easy to pick out exceptional performance using spark lines, whether it's good or bad.

A related application known as a *scorecard* can be the means to manage performance across the organization. This category of applications works to tie corporate objectives to specific measures. These measures can then be used to track performance against the objectives, thus leading to another name for this category: corporate performance management (CPM) or just *performance management*. The objectives typically come from a planning system, which is a necessary component of a performance management application.

THE BALANCED SCORECARD One example of the scorecard approach is the *balanced scorecard*, as defined by Drs. Robert Kaplan and David Norton. In the balanced scorecard approach, management must first determine the organization's goals and strategy. These are used to define metrics that measure the organization's performance against its strategy from four perspectives: internal business processes, learning and growth, customer, and financial. These measures, also known as key performance indicators (KPIs) in other approaches, are then made available via the scorecard where they are tracked and trended. Everyone in the organization who has the ability to impact one or more of these measures must be able to monitor their performance. In the balanced scorecard, Kaplan and Norton have defined a strategy-driven process for determining measures that will guide the organization to do the right thing. The first challenge here is that management must first determine what needs to be measured in order to manage it.

Although there is huge value in a well-designed and implemented dashboard or performance scorecard application, there are a couple of significant implications for the DW/BI program. Primarily, these applications are almost always *consolidated applications* because they require data from several business processes before they can be properly implemented. We've seen several examples of DW/BI teams who took on a dashboard application as their first deliverable and ended up creating a rat's nest of interconnected spreadsheets and ETL programs that had to be manually operated on a weekly or daily basis. Dashboards and scorecards usually don't work well if you try to implement them before most of the key business process dimensional models are in place.

One class of requirements addressed by dashboards and scorecards was originally called executive information systems (EIS) back in the 1980s. These applications have made a strong resurgence in recent years, in large part because many larger organizations have their core data warehouse in place, and have built out an effective set of standard reports. With this basic foundation to build on, it is much easier to address the executives' cross-system, cross-organizational requirements.

Operational Business Intelligence

For most operational processes, the operational systems provide the information needed for employees to accomplish their basic job responsibilities. Operational BI is targeted at the same people who are running the business at the transaction level, but it recognizes that many jobs could be done more effectively if they were performed with the benefit of a broader information context.

For example, a service rep who handles customer billing problems can answer inquiries with historical billing and payment data from the transaction system. However, the same rep can potentially increase revenue and improve customer satisfaction if he can provide the customer with a "special offer" to upgrade her account, add a service, provide free shipping on the next order, or any number of other appealing options. The key to making this happen is to enable the service rep to make custom offers to each customer based on the customer's individual history. The underlying rules engine may take into account information from across the data warehouse. For example, the specific service or upgrade offer may be based on what customers with similar purchasing behaviors have demonstrated an interest in. A higher level rule might restrict such offers if the customer has called customer service more than two times in the past 30 days where the resolution was categorized as "customer problem" — we don't want to encourage bad behavior.

The local impact of each use of an operational BI application is relatively small, maybe on the order of a few dollars or less. However, the broad use of such a system means the overall impact could be substantial. In certain cases, your primary goal of adding business value might be best met by a carefully chosen operational BI application.

Careful is a good watchword when you are dealing with operational level reporting. Many operational reporting requirements sneak in the back door of the DW/BI system, when they really should be handled by the transaction systems. This is often because the DW/BI team has better reporting tools and a reputation for doing reports well. Any time a reporting requirement includes a need for instantaneous or near-instantaneous data, it is a hint that the requirement may be better served in the transaction system environment.

Part of this difficulty comes from the fact that the boundary between operational BI and operational systems is rapidly blurring. Systems like sales force automation systems have components that are clearly operational, such as tracking customers and sales contacts. They also have components that have a BI flavor, such as ranking prospects based on the output of a data mining model or identifying potential churn candidates based on customer service calls or usage behaviors. Simply providing a list of the top ten customers as part of the sales rep's primary dashboard is more likely to be a data warehouse query than a transaction system query. Having both of these requirements in one application means either the BI team will have to build or support operational systems, or the operational folks will need to learn BI tools. In either case, the service level implications for the DW/BI system are more users, shorter data load cycles, and greater system availability. It may help to revisit the real time section in Chapter 9 for a reminder on the implications.

> **CAUTION** Just as we mentioned with analytic applications, it is possible to create operational BI applications without the overhead of a data warehouse in the middle. In this case, your operational BI application must have specific, narrow data requirements that can be queried directly from the source systems without the need for much cleansing, integration, or historical context and without overtaxing the source systems. In many cases, this is the best approach; however, stand-alone operational BI applications can be a slippery slope. Make sure your operational BI applications don't take on more and more ETL-like tasks and that you don't end up building a lot of stand-alone data stores to support each separate operational BI application. You may end up with multiple, redundant, disparate stovepipe systems — exactly what you were trying to avoid in the first place.

Data Mining

Although data mining generally does not function as a stand-alone BI application, data mining models are often embedded in BI applications to improve their effectiveness and accuracy. Moving forward, data mining will become a more important component of most DW/BI systems for three reasons. First, it is more easily available than in the past. Most of the database vendors are including data mining as part of their core database products. Second, the current generation of data mining tools is easier to use. The user interfaces are better, and the tools automatically do much of the data preparation required by the data mining algorithms. Third, data mining works. Including data mining models in your BI applications as part of the data preparation process and even as part of the transaction system can help increase sales, reduce fraud and churn, and more accurately forecast revenue streams.

Data Mining Overview

Data mining is *a process of data exploration with the intent to find patterns or relationships that can be made useful to the organization.* Data mining takes advantage of a range of technologies and techniques for exploration and execution. From a business perspective, data mining helps you understand and predict behavior, identify relationships, or group items, such as customers or products, into coherent sets. The resulting models can take the form of rules or equations that you apply to new customers, products, or transactions to better understand how you should respond to them. These models can then be accessed from analytic applications or operational BI applications to provide guidance, alerts, or indicators to the user.

The field of data mining is known more broadly as *knowledge discovery and data mining*, or more specifically, knowledge discovery in databases (KDD). Both terms shed light on the purpose and process of data mining. The word "mining" is meant to evoke a specific image. Traditional mining involves digging through vast quantities of dirt to unearth a relatively small vein of valuable metallic ore, precious stones, or other substances. Data mining is the digital equivalent of this analog process. You use automated tools to dig through vast quantities of data to identify or discover valuable patterns or relationships that you can leverage in your business.

Our brains are good examples of data mining tools. Throughout the course of our lives, we accumulate a large set of experiences. In some cases we're able to identify patterns within these experiences and generate models we can use to predict the future. Those who commute to work have an easy example. Over the weeks and months, you begin to develop a sense for the traffic patterns and adjust your behavior accordingly. The freeway will be jammed at 5:00 pm, so you might leave at 4:30, or wait until 6:00, unless it's Friday or a holiday. Going to the movies is another example of altering behavior based on experience. Deciding what time to arrive at the theater is a complex equation that includes variables like when the movie opened, whether it's a big budget film, whether it got good reviews, and what showing you want to see. These are personal examples of building a data mining model using the original neural network tool.

Data mining has finally grown up and has taken on a central role in many businesses. All of us are the subject of data mining dozens of times every day — from the junk mail in our mail boxes, to the affinity cards we use in the grocery store, to the fraud detection algorithms that scrutinize our every credit card purchase. Data mining has become so widespread because these techniques can measurably and significantly increase an organization's ability to reach its goals. Data mining is used for many purposes across the organization, from increasing revenue with more targeted direct market-ing programs, and cross-sell and up-sell efforts, to cutting costs with fraud detection and churn/attrition reduction, to improving service with customer affinity recommendations. A charitable organization might use data mining to increase donations by directing its campaign efforts toward people who are more likely to give.

A full discussion of data mining is beyond the scope of this book. When it comes time to include data mining in your DW/BI system, the following list will help you think about the kinds of functionality your organization might need. Data mining breaks out into five major categories: clustering, classifying, estimating and predicting, affinity grouping, and anomaly detection. We describe these in more detail in the following sections.

Clustering

Clustering is a pure example of undirected data mining, where the user has no specific agenda and hopes that the data mining tool will reveal some meaningful structure. An example of clustering is looking through a large number of initially undifferentiated customers and trying to see if they fall into natural groupings. The input records to this clustering exercise ideally should be high-quality verbose descriptions of each customer with both demographic and behavioral indicators attached to each record. Clustering algorithms work well with all kinds of data, including categorical, numerical, and textual data. It is not even necessary to identify inputs and outputs at the start of the job run. Usually the only decision the user must make is to ask for a specific number of candidate clusters. The clustering algorithm will find the best partitioning of all the customer records and will provide descriptions of the *centroid* of each cluster in terms of the user's original data. In many cases, these clusters have an obvious interpretation that provides insight into the customer base. Once the clustering model has been trained, you can use it to classify new cases by matching the new case to the "nearest" centroid. It often helps to first cluster customers based on their buying patterns and demographics, and then run predictive models on each cluster separately. This allows the unique behaviors of each cluster to show through rather than be overwhelmed by the overall average behaviors.

Specific techniques that can be used for clustering include statistics, memory-based reasoning, neural networks, and decision trees.

THE POWER OF NAMING When Claritas originally created its customer segmentation system called PRIZM, they likely used clustering techniques to identify about 60 different groups of consumers. The resulting clusters, called lifestyle types, were numbered 1 through 60+. It's clear that someone at Claritas realized that numbers were not descriptive and would not make good marketing. So, they came up with a clever name for each cluster; a shorthand way to communicate its unique characteristics. A few of the names are: 02. Blue Blood Estates (old money, big mansions), 51. Shotguns and Pickups (working class, large families, mobile homes), and 60. Park Bench Seniors (modest income, sedentary, daytime TV watchers).

Classifying

An example of classifying is to examine a candidate customer and assign that customer to a predetermined cluster or classification; for example, assigning each customer to an interest level with discrete values of disinterested, casual, moderate, active, or eager might be part of a sales force automation application. Another example of classifying is medical diagnosis. In both cases, a verbose description of the customer or patient is fed into the classification algorithm. The classifier determines to which cluster centroid the candidate customer or patient is nearest or most similar. Viewed in this way, clustering may well be a natural first step that is followed by classifying. Classifying in the most general sense is immensely useful in many data warehouse environments. A classification is a decision. You may be classifying customers as credit worthy or credit unworthy, or you may be classifying patients as either needing or not needing treatment.

Techniques that can be used for classifying include standard statistics, memory-based reasoning, genetic algorithms, link analysis, decision trees, and neural networks.

Estimating and Predicting

Estimating and predicting are two similar activities that normally yield a numerical measure as the result. For example, you may find a set of existing customers who have the same profile as a candidate customer. From the set of existing customers, you may estimate the overall indebtedness of the candidate customer. Prediction is the same as estimation, except that you are trying to determine a result that will occur in the future. Numerical estimates have the additional advantage that the candidates can be rank ordered. You may have enough money in an advertising budget to send promotion offers to the top 10,000 customers ranked by an estimate of their future value to the company. In this case, an estimate is more useful than a simple binary classification.

Specific techniques that can be used for estimating and predicting include standard statistics and neural networks for numerical variables, as well as the techniques described for classifying when predicting only a discrete outcome.

Affinity Grouping

Affinity grouping is a special kind of clustering that identifies events or transactions that occur simultaneously. A well known example of affinity grouping is market basket analysis. Market basket analysis attempts to understand what items are sold together at the same time. This is a hard problem from a data processing point of view because there are thousands of different products in a typical retail environment. It is pointless to enumerate all the combinations of items sold together because the list quickly reaches astronomical proportions. The art of market basket analysis is to find the meaningful combinations of different levels in the item hierarchy that are sold together. For instance, it may be meaningful to discover that the individual item Super Cola 12 oz. is very frequently sold with the category of Frozen Pasta Dinners. Companies, like Amazon, mine the vast quantities of data generated by millions of customers browsing their web sites and making purchase selections, popularizing the phrase: "Customers who bought this item also bought these items:"

Specific techniques that can be used for affinity grouping include standard statistics, memory-based reasoning, link analysis, and special-purpose market basket analysis tools.

Anomaly Detection

Several business processes rely on the identification of cases that deviate from the norm in a significant way. Fraud detection in consumer credit is a common example of anomaly detection. Anomaly detection can take advantage of any of the data mining algorithms. Clustering algorithms can be tuned to create a cluster that contains data outliers, separate from the rest of the clusters in the model. Anomaly detection involves a few extra twists in the data mining process. Often it's necessary to bias the training set in favor of the exceptional events. Otherwise, there may be too few of them in the historical data for the algorithm to detect. After all, they are anomalies.

Data Mining in the Applications Architecture

Data mining, like standard reporting, is typically a separate system (or systems) with separate tools designed to apply various forms of statistical analysis. It should be viewed as another client to the warehouse, but without the daily demands a reporting system might have. The services a data mining application might need from the warehouse are more like the ETL services, as described in the subsystem 21 for data propagation in Chapter 9.

From the BI application perspective, the data mining tools will be called on to act as service providers themselves. That is, they could be considered an application layer between the front end tools and the database. In this scenario, a front end tool will use the APIs of the data mining tool to pass it a set of parameters and instructions. The front end tool would then incorporate the results directly into a report or model. This scenario becomes easier to implement given that the database vendors have incorporated data mining capabilities directly into the database engine, and in many cases, have exposed these engines via SOAP protocols.

The DW/BI team should be sensitive to a possible mismatch between the data warehouse and the data mining tools. An enterprise data warehouse offering a 360 degree view of all customer facing business processes is a spectacular resource for the data miner. The good news is that a comprehensive drill across "observation set" can be prepared for data mining analysis that associates dozens of interesting attributes, facts, and key performance indicators with each customer. The bad news is that this drill across report is probably an expensive, slow running report. Most data mining tools would like this report as a flat file, which they are capable of analyzing at the rate of dozens or hundreds of observations per second. Even more alarming, some of the data mining tools (such as clustering algorithms and case based reasoning tools) want to process this answer set over and over. The solution to this mismatch is to run the drill across report as a batch file and then hand this batch file off to the data mining team for their analysis, offline from the presentation server.

NOTE Although data mining tools are improving, successful data mining is not easy. It involves a complex set of tools and requires a solid understanding of statistical analysis. Get help if you don't know what you're doing.

If your organization is early in its experience with DW/BI systems, data mining will not likely be part of your first BI application. However, as soon as data mining looks useful, we encourage you to get a copy of Michael Berry and Gordon Linoff's book, *Data Mining Techniques for Marketing, Sales, and Customer Support, 2nd Edition* (Wiley 2004). The categorization described in this chapter comes from this book; it will give you a wealth of information about specific tools and techniques.

Navigating Applications via the BI Portal

If the BI applications are the primary access vehicle for most of the business user community, the BI portal is the primary access interface for those BI applications. The public reason for building the BI portal is to give your users a well organized, useful, easily understood place to find the tools and information they need. Like the BI applications themselves, the BI portal is the first impression most business users have of the DW/BI system.

NOTE Some of the material in this section was originally published in the *Microsoft Data Warehouse Toolkit* (Wiley Publishing, 2006). We include it here because the portal concept is completely platform independent and critical to all DW/BI systems.

Because business users' first impressions are important, a successful BI portal must be:

- **Usable.** People have to be able to find what they need.
- **Content rich.** The portal should include a great deal more than just the reports. It should include as much support information, documentation, help, examples, and advice as possible.
- **Clean.** The portal should be nicely laid out so people are not confused or overwhelmed by it.

- **Current.**   It should be someone's job to keep the content up-to-date. No broken links or 12-month-old items labeled "New!" are allowed.

- **Interactive.**   The portal should include functions that engage the users and encourage them to return. A good search tool, metadata browser, or support oriented newsgroup are ways for people to interact with the portal. A capability for users to personalize their report home page, and save reports or report links to it, makes it directly relevant to them. It also helps to have new items appear every so often. Surveys, class notices, and even data problem warnings all help keep it fresh.

- **Value oriented.**   This is the organizational change goal. You want everyone who comes to the BI portal to end up with the feeling that the DW/BI system is a valuable resource, something that helps them do a better job. In a way, the BI portal is one of the strongest marketing tools the DW/BI team has and you need to make every impression count.

The process of creating the BI portal requires a careful balancing of two basic design principles: density and structure.

- **Density.**   Our minds can process an incredible amount of information. The human eye is able to resolve images at a resolution of well over 300 pixels per inch at a distance of 20 inches. Compare this with the paltry 93 pixels per inch resolution of the typical computer screen. Our brains have evolved to rapidly process all this information looking for the relevant elements. The browser gives us such a low resolution platform that we have to use it as carefully and efficiently as possible. Every pixel must contribute.

- **Structure.**   Although we need to fill the BI portal home page with information, it doesn't work if we jam it full of hundreds of unordered descriptions and links. Your brain can handle all this information only if it's well organized. For example, a typical major daily newspaper has an incredible amount of information, but you can handle it because it's structured in a way that helps you find what you need. At the top level, the paper is broken up into sections. If you're looking for certain kinds of information, you know which section to start with. Some readers look at every section, but most skip a few that they deem irrelevant to their lives. The next level down within each section may be divided into subsections, but the most common organizing structure is the headline. Headlines (at least non-tabloid headlines) attempt to communicate the content of the article in as few words as possible. These headlines are the "relevant elements" that allow readers to quickly parse through the newspaper to find information that is interesting to them.

REFERENCE Edward Tufte's books provide a good general reference for structure and information display, including *Visual Explanations: Images and Quantities, Evidence and Narrative* (Graphics Press, 1990).

Density Considerations

The idea of density translates to the BI portal in a couple of ways. Primarily, it means we flatten the information hierarchy. Categories are often represented as hierarchies in the browser. You see a list of choices, each representing a topic. Click on a topic, and you're taken to a page with another list of choices, and so on until you finally reach some content. Flattening the hierarchies means bringing as much information to the top level pages as possible. Information that was captured in the hierarchy of pages is now collapsed down to an indented list of category and subcategory headings on a single page.

Figure 11-4 translates these concepts into the world of a fictitious manufacturer called BigCo. The BI portal shown here demonstrates how two levels of report categories have been collapsed into one page. The portal is easy to navigate because you can identify major categories of information based on the headings and ignore them if they don't apply to your current needs, or examine them more closely if they seem relevant. Having the two levels

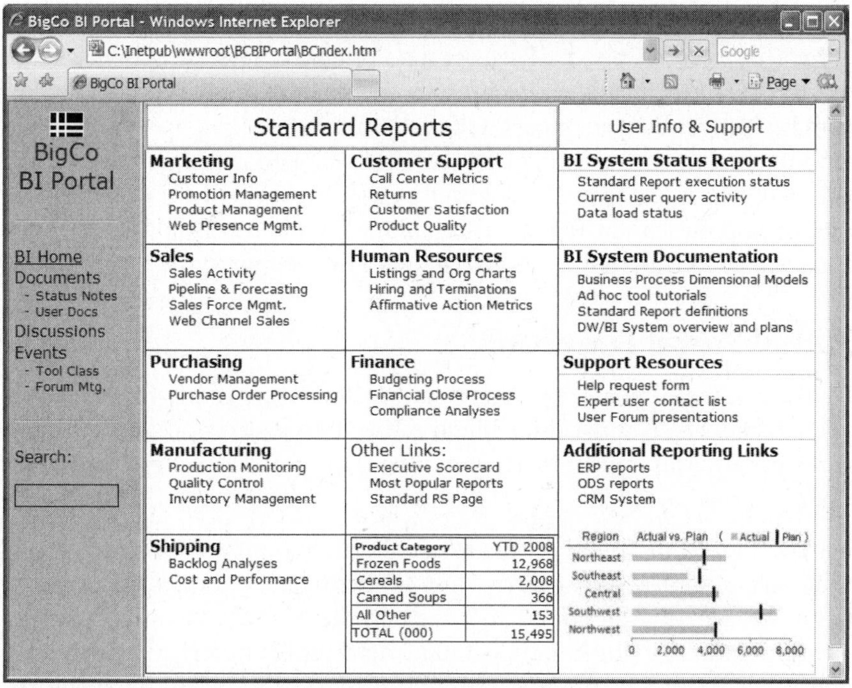

Figure 11-4 Example BI portal home page.

on the same page actually gives the user more information because the two levels help define each other. For example, Sales helps group the sales-related subcategories together, but at the same time, each subcategory helps the user understand what activities are included in Sales.

Navigation Structure Based on Business Processes

The BI portal's first responsibility is to provide a navigation framework for the BI applications. The navigation framework is the approach you take to organizing the BI applications so people can find them when they need them. This is not as simple as it might sound. Every word you include on the portal — every header, description, function, and link — all need to communicate what content people will find behind it.

Generally, the best way to organize the portal is to use the organization's business processes as the main outline. Look at Figure 11-4 from a business process perspective. The left column under Standard Reports includes the organization's major business processes; this structure essentially follows the organization's value chain as depicted in the data warehouse bus matrix. In the example shown, marketing and sales business processes come early in the value chain, working to bring in new customers and new orders. Once the company has orders, they purchase materials from their suppliers, manufacture goods, and ship them out to the customers. Customer support may interact with the customers at any point along the way, and even after the product has been shipped. There are also internal business processes that generate information that is useful across the organization, like headcount data from human resources, or cost data from finance.

Beyond business process categories, the BI portal needs to have a standard layout so people can easily find what they're looking for. If your organization has a standard page layout that you can adapt for the BI portal, use it. Your users won't have to learn a new interface when they come to the BI portal.

Additional Portal Functions

Although one of the BI portal's primary responsibilities is to provide access to the standard reports, it must offer much more than just reports. In addition to the categories and report lists, you need to provide several common functions:

- **Search.** The search tool serves as an alternative report locator if the business process categories aren't adequate. A good search tool that indexes every document and page on the BI web site and all the report metadata, including report name and report description, can dramatically shorten the amount of time it takes a user to find what she wants.

- **Metadata browser.**   A metadata browser can be as simple as a few active web pages or reports that allow the user to browse through the metadata's descriptions of the databases, schemas, tables, columns, business rules, load statistics, report usage, and report content. In short, interested users can learn a lot about the DW/BI system through the metadata browser.

- **User forum.**   It may make sense to host a support-oriented discussion forum on the BI portal. This can be a good way for users to find help when they need it. It can also create a record of problems and their solutions for future reference. It takes a fairly large user community to generate the critical mass of activity needed to make a newsgroup successful. It also takes time and energy to moderate a user forum.

- **Personalization.**   Users should be able to save reports or report links to their personal pages, along with any parameter settings they've chosen. This personalization can be a powerful incentive for people to return to the portal every day.

- **Information center.**   It helps keep things interesting to have new items appear on a regular basis. Offer a survey, have people register for tool training, or post a notice of an upcoming user forum meeting.

There is also a whole set of support and administration content the BI portal needs to provide. This includes online training/tutorials, help pages, metadata browser, example reports, data cheat sheets, help request forms, and contact information for the DW/BI team. In Figure 11-4, this information goes in the lower right corner, the least valuable real estate on the screen (at least for languages that read from left to right and top to bottom). We discuss this supporting content again in Chapter 13 on deployment.

Creating and maintaining the BI portal is much more work than most DW/BI teams ever expect. The effort is worth it because the BI portal is the farthest-reaching tool the DW/BI team has for delivering value to the organization. It is also one of your best tools for marketing the DW/BI system.

Application Interface Alternatives

As we've described, portal-based interfaces to the BI applications are popular due to their rich toolset for managing the user experience; however there are alternatives. Like many front room architecture issues, this is another soft topic because most BI tools use the web as their primary delivery vehicle, most tool suites include multiple delivery mechanism options, and most tools can be included in other tools via their service oriented architecture (SOA) design.

In addition to portal interfaces, alternative delivery mechanisms include:

- **Direct tool-based interface.**   You can simply develop a set of reports and provide them to the users directly using the standard data access tool interface. If your tool does not have a built-in, shared report repository capability, it is possible to create a simple file structure on the network to match the navigation path. This is not very flexible, but it is fast, and might be a good place to start while you experiment with other options.

- **Custom-coded interface.**   Many data access tools provide APIs, and in some cases full software development kits (SDKs), to allow you to develop your own interface which then invokes the core tool functionality and displays the resulting report elements. This is typically a programming development effort using one of the web-based development tools. This approach is harder to maintain, but more powerful in its ability to programmatically provide any function needed. Most operational BI applications are built with custom code, which allows them to more easily integrate with the operational systems. Again, the interface provides the structured navigation to the appropriate report components.

Finally, an interesting variation of the custom-coded theme is the application intended for a handheld device. These applications have unique user interfaces, communications capabilities, and security issues, along with aggressive real time and alerting requirements.

Conclusion

BI applications are the bridge that enables a large majority of the organization to take advantage of the information in the DW/BI system. They are a mandatory component of every successful DW/BI system. BI applications come in a range of flavors, including standard reports, analytic applications, dashboards and scorecards, and operational business intelligence. Data mining plays a significant role in identifying the patterns or relationships that can be used in the analytic applications or operational BI applications.

Almost all of the BI applications are delivered to the users via the BI portal. This portal must meet the same stringent design requirements as the BI applications in order to provide the best user experience possible.

Now that you have this understanding of what we mean by BI applications under your belt, the next chapter offers techniques for defining and building your BI applications.

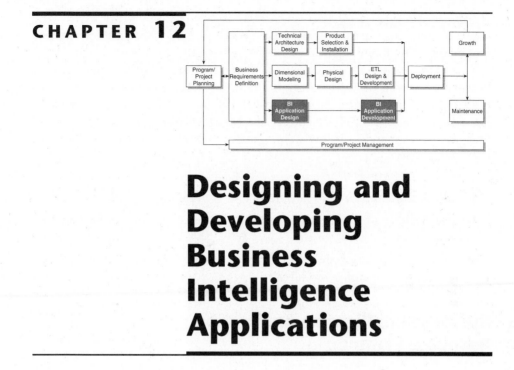

CHAPTER 12

Designing and Developing Business Intelligence Applications

his chapter guides you through the process of designing and developing the business intelligence (BI) applications. In any given iteration of the Lifecycle, designing the BI applications starts immediately after the requirements definition step is completed and senior management has agreed on the top priority. With this boundary in place to narrow your focus, the BI application track begins with a specification step that involves designing a report template, identifying and specifying the applications themselves, and designing a navigation framework to organize the applications so users can find them.

In most cases, you will not be able to do much with the BI application specifications until the Lifecycle's data track is close to completion and you have selected and installed a BI tool. At that point, you can pull the specification documents off the shelf and get to work on the development step, creating and testing the target BI applications. If your applications list includes more sophisticated analytic applications, you may need additional programming expertise and/or tools to help.

Before you roll out the BI applications during deployment, you need to carefully test them for accuracy and performance. Finally, dedicated resources are required to maintain and enhance the BI applications. This job only gets bigger with each Lifecycle iteration and the expanded acceptance and success of the DW/BI system. In fact, as BI applications grow in use and sophistication, the time and energy the DW/BI team must dedicate to creating and maintaining them will also increase dramatically.

This chapter is most applicable to the BI application architect and developer; however, everyone on the team should read it. The data modeler can leverage the BI application specifications to test the data model prior to its physical instantiation, and the ETL developer can see the benefits that result from all that extra work managing slowly changing dimensions and cleansing the data in the back room.

In this chapter you learn:

- A structured approach to designing and developing BI applications
- Specific tips and techniques for specifying, building, and deploying the applications
- Additional guidance on creating more advanced analytical applications, including data mining models and operational BI applications.

Business Intelligence Application Resource Planning

If it's not clear by now, the BI applications are a critical part of the overall DW/BI system. You must have a significant set of resources dedicated to the production and maintenance of all flavors of BI applications. There are two primary resource issues every team will face: What is the role of the BI application developer and who should fill that role.

Role of the BI Application Developer

Obviously, the BI application developer must develop, maintain, enhance, and extend the core set of BI applications. Note that this puts the BI application developer in the position of being a consumer software provider. This person must provide usable, working, documented, and supported solutions for a technically unsophisticated user community.

Beyond the basic development role, someone must also be available to respond to business requests for additional reports or applications. Regardless of how well you execute the application specification process, someone will show up the day after the applications are rolled out and ask for something different. That's just the nature of business intelligence.

Who Does the BI Applications Job?

We recommend a central group of BI developers as part of the overall DW/BI team, with additional BI developers located in the business. This central group is part of the core project team and is involved in the requirements definition process and dimensional model design. Along with the business analysts, they are usually the best representatives of the business users (other than the business users themselves, of course). The central group is charged with creating and maintaining the official BI applications.

We also usually find BI application developers at the local or departmental level. These folks are engaged in supporting business people with more specific, focused analyses that are relevant to their local programs or opportunities. We also try to involve these key power users in the initial BI applications development process. It may not make things go faster, but it gives these folks an opportunity to learn the data and tools so they can be immediately productive in their business areas when this iteration is deployed. Make this a special event. Reserve a conference or training room for a week or two and have the whole group meet and work together every morning for several hours. You can all learn from each other, and working together helps in building positive working relationships. Bring donuts.

Clearly, building and supporting BI applications is a big job. A good guideline is to plan for as many people on the user-facing front room of the DW/BI system as you have in the back room. In addition to the application development task, the user-facing team also provides new reports, enhancements, maintenance, documentation, user support, and business metadata.

Lifecycle Timing

This chapter reflects a discontinuous timeframe because the BI application process occurs in two places in the Lifecycle. The report templates should be specified just after the requirements are completed. Even with a detailed requirement findings document, much information related to applications remains stored in the brains of the interview participants. It is important to capture this information immediately so that it is not lost. If you wait until you are ready to develop the BI applications, the people who were involved in the requirements gathering process may be off on another project. Even if the same team is in place, a several month time lag between the completion of the requirements and application specification will mean a significant rediscovery effort.

Once the specifications are captured, you do not need to return to the BI application development process until much later in the project's lifecycle. You can't begin BI application development until after the data access tool is selected, the initial database design is in place, and some of the initial data loads have been run.

Because of this difference in timing, we have split this chapter into two sections: specification and development.

Business Intelligence Application Specification

The BI application specification step involves several tasks: designing the report template, identifying and specifying the applications themselves, and designing the navigation framework and portal. This must happen as soon after the requirements definition process as possible, while the application related requirements are still fresh in your mind.

Creating BI applications is a true software product development effort. You must get your customers involved in the specification process if you want to help solve their business problems. Before you dive into the specification process, take the time to identify and recruit a core set of key business users who have domain expertise around the target business process and who understand the analytic opportunities. You should get these users involved in creating and prioritizing the report list, specifying individual applications, and evaluating different navigation strategies. If the business folks don't think the reports are useful, or they can't find the one they want, they will not use the BI system.

The specification of BI applications breaks down into five major activities that we explore in the following sections.

Create Application Standards and Templates

Develop a set of naming standards and a template that captures the general look and feel of your reports and applications before you start to create individual report specs.

Determine Naming Standards

It's not unusual for the DW/BI team to spend hours debating the name of each data element and table, but most organizations completely overlook the need to develop standards for the data access environment. These standards cover areas like naming, formatting, and common fields. They are particularly important in helping users quickly understand the nature of a report — its contents, sources, and timing. Putting some thought into standards now will help you create a consistent set of specifications. These will then be easier to develop and roll out across many user groups. Of course, your standards will evolve. The tool you choose may not be able to implement the standards you have defined; this isn't necessarily bad — there may be a better way to accomplish the same thing. Be prepared to modify your standards as needed when you get to the development phase.

Naming reports is perhaps the most obvious area where you need standards. You should consider including the type of report and type of data in the report name. For example, the name Regional Claim Amount Paid Exceptions denotes that the report identifies exceptions based upon paid claim amounts by region. Depending on your data access tool, you may need to name multiple kinds of objects such as business measures, filters or constraints, and templates. Develop a consistent naming strategy for each object within the data access environment.

> **TIP** Although full names are great, they can become unmanageable within the confined space of a computer screen or sheet of paper, so abbreviations can be helpful. Work with the business users to develop a glossary of acceptable abbreviations. Typical abbreviations include YA for year ago and YTD for year to date. We recommend having fields in your metadata to hold both short name and long name. The short name is useful on reports and the long name is useful when describing the content and meaning of the report. Finally, you might be able to leverage some naming standards from the dimensional modeling activity.

Create the Application Templates

Once you have a set of naming standards, you can turn your attention to creating a standard template for the physical layout of your BI applications.

> **NOTE** Much of the discussion in this section is taken from material found in the *Microsoft Data Warehouse Toolkit* (Wiley, 2006). However, our recommendations in this area are relevant to all tools and platforms.

Creating templates is important because people can find information more quickly if it is presented to them in a consistent fashion. If you read the newspaper regularly, you are familiar with this phenomenon. The information is grouped in categories: sports, business, lifestyle, and world news. Even though different newspapers generally carry much of the same information, each has its own format standards. You may even have had first hand experience with the importance of standards and consistency; if your favorite magazine or newspaper ever changed its format, it probably caused you some level of discomfort.

The BI application team is effectively in the publishing business. You need to have your own format and content standards and use them consistently. You'll need standards at the portal level and at the individual document level. We deal with the portal issues in the section about the navigation structure later in this chapter.

At the individual report level, you should create a template to identify the standard elements that will appear in every report, including their locations and styles. You can prototype this in whatever tool works, but eventually, you will create this template in your BI tool and save it to the tool's template library. It's helpful to define standard templates before you begin specifying the individual applications because the templates will give you a common structure and context for each application.

The following standard elements need to be defined and in most cases included on every BI report or application that comes out of the DW/BI system:

- **Report name.**   Create a clear, descriptive name for the report that communicates the contents of the report to the viewer. You should also create a short name for report list displays in the BI portal.

- **Report title.**   Develop standards for the information that appears at the top of the page and how it's displayed. This could include the title and any subtitles. All parameter selections and filters should be displayed in the title, row or column headers, or in the report header or footer.

- **Report body.**   Column/row layout of data, including:

  - Data justification: Right justified for numbers, left justified for row headers, right justified or centered for column headers.

  - Display precision: Dependent on data, so you must figure it out for all your numeric fields.

  - Column and row heading format: Often bold, underlined, or colored to distinguish them from report data (and test this in print form).

  - Background fills and colors.

  - Formatting of totals or subtotal breakout rows.

- **Header and footer.**   The following items should be found somewhere in the header or footer. Create a standard layout, font, and justification scheme, and stick to it.

  - Report name.

  - Parameters and filters used. Users must understand how the report contents are defined. For example, knowing that a report excludes intracompany sales can reduce confusion.

  - Navigation category.

  - Report notes regarding any unusual definitions or content.

  - Page numbering.

  - Report run time and date.

  - Data source(s): Which dimensional model(s) sourced the data in the report, and was it the relational or OLAP database.

  - Confidentiality statement.

  - DW/BI reference: Name and logo.

- **Report file name.**   The report definition file name is based on your standard file naming convention. The file itself and any associated code should be under source control.

Figure 12-1 shows one way to lay these elements out on a page. The angle bracket signs (<>) and curly brackets ({}) indicate elements that are context sensitive; they may be system variables or parameters specific to the report that is being run.

Not all report information is displayed on the report itself. You will also need to create the following information for each report:

- User variables and other user interactions, like drilldown paths and links.

- Report metadata, including description, calculations, derivations, author, and date created.

- Security requirements, including a list or description of the security groups who can see the report.

- Execution cycle, if the report is to run automatically on a periodic basis.

- Execution trigger event, if the report is to be executed in response to a system event like the completion of the nightly data load.

- Delivery mechanisms, such as email, web site, file directory, or printer.

- Delivery list, which is generally the name of an email distribution list.

- Standard output format, such as text, html, PDF, Excel, or Word.

- Page orientation, size, and margin settings.

These elements are essentially *report metadata*. Therefore, this information should be kept in a metadata repository that is accessible from within the BI tool so it can be used during report creation. This same metadata repository should also be accessible by the users on demand from outside the BI tool when

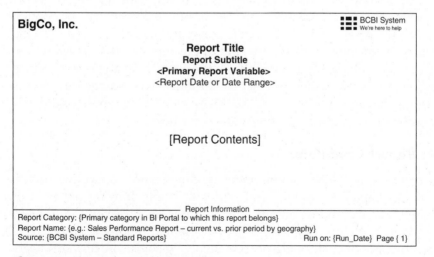

Figure 12-1 Example standard template.

they need to understand more about a given report. The major BI tools include this type of metadata repository. Meanwhile, you can use a spreadsheet or text document to capture your report metadata while you are creating the BI application specs.

Create Dashboard and Analytic Application Templates

Dashboards and analytic applications are generally more complex than simple standard reports. When your project includes dashboards or analytic applications, you should create a standard template for these as well. It will include the same basic elements found in Figure 12-1, but you will need to think a bit more about the graphical layout of the sub-components on the dashboard or application page. A typical dashboard or analytic application incorporates several different elements, including reports, charts, and special dashboard controls such as alert indicators.

The dashboard's visual nature reminds us to offer a suggestion. It's often beneficial to involve someone who has graphic design and user interface design skills in creating the templates. The BI applications must look good because they are the sole representative of the DW/BI system to most of the organization. You are creating a brand and your branding starts here; include your DW/BI system logo in the same spot of every official report and application you produce.

Determine the Initial Application Set

Once you have your standards and templates in place, the next step in the BI specification process is to develop the target list of reports. The goal is to end up with a small set of high value reports that provide a range of report types. *Small* is of course a relative term. Ten or fifteen reports may be enough to start with for some organizations; others may feel a need for, and have the resources to build, dozens of reports and applications in the first iteration. Recall that some of these reports might be more complex analytic applications or might be grouped together for delivery through a dashboard. The process of generating the target list involves three tasks: identifying report candidates, consolidating the candidate list, and setting priorities.

Identify Report Candidates

The project's consolidated requirement findings and supporting notes, described in Chapter 3, are the ideal places to begin drawing up a list of potential reports. Depending on how well you documented your interviews, each interview write-up may have a list of potential reports to draw from. Approach this as a brainstorming process involving some core business users who are intimately familiar with the initial business process. Use a spreadsheet like the one shown in Figure 12-2 to make a list of individual report requests,

Doc Title: Candidate Report List		Project: BBC-BI System: Orders business process				Prepared By: Warren Thornthwaite			Date Prepared: 07/09/2008
#	Report Name	Short Description	Report Category	Primary Owner	Bus. Value	Level of Effort	Report Type	Data Elements	Comments
1	Sales Rep Performance Ranking	Total orders by Sales Rep for target year and prior year, with rank for each year and the change in rank.	Sales Performance	Warren	9	3	Table	Year, Emp. Name, Order Dollars.	Add a drill down to order details for a selected Rep.
2	Product Performance	Product Orders and Market Share by Current Period vs. Prior for a specific geography.	Marketing Results	Joy	8	4	Matrix & Pie Chart	Product hierarchy, Date, Geography hierarchy, Order Dollars.	This may be part of Prod Mgmt dashboard.
3	Territory Orders Time Series	Last 13 months Actual Orders vs. Forecast by Territory.	Orders Analysis	Bob	7	3	Table & Line Chart	Month, Sales Territory, Order Dollars, Forecast Dollars.	NOTE: Forecast may not be in initial release.
4	Product Orders Time Series	Last 13 months Actual Orders vs. Forecast by Product level.	Marketing Results / Orders Analysis	Joy	8	3	Table & Line Chart	Product Description, Order Quantity, Forecast Order Quantity.	NOTE: Forecast may not be in initial release.

Figure 12-2 Candidate report list.

one request per line. Include a name, type of report, row data elements, column data elements, measures, and additional attributes that might help in the consolidation process, such as listing the groups or departments that are interested in the report.

You will likely find reports that require data from business processes other than the one chosen for the current project. You should put those on a separate list for later consideration during the appropriate Lifecycle iteration. Once you have a first pass of the candidate report list, get additional users involved in a design session to review it. They will likely add several more report candidates, and their questions will help clarify some of the existing candidates.

Consolidate the Candidate List

Once the list is reasonably complete, refocus the group on consolidating the list. The point here is to identify those reports on the list that are essentially different versions of the same report. Categorize according to the items in the spreadsheet — which data elements does each report contain in each section? Sometimes, categories quickly become apparent because of the way the business views the world. It may be helpful to think about the types of analysis typically performed. In some cases, this is a quick step because you've already filtered out similar reports while you were creating the list.

Prioritize the Report List

Once you have the list of candidate reports, work with the users to assign a priority to each one. Some of the factors to consider include business value, data availability, degree of development difficulty, scope of use, and user importance. Sometimes the CEO's report comes first, regardless of its true business value. Remember, your goal is to identify a small number of reports and applications that will serve as the starting point. The underlying business goal is to identify a set of templates that will help address the issues that are keeping the executives awake at night. Keep in mind that the initial reports are not intended to provide a total solution for your users, but to use your limited resources to deliver the greatest value to the most users possible (or at least to the most important users).

> **NOTE** Keep in mind that as the business people begin to use the system, they will find that some reports they thought were needed are not as useful as expected. They will also begin to identify new reports that would be useful across the organization. Through use of the DW/BI system, the report requirements will change. In fact, if there have been no requests to change or extend the initial application set within the first week or two, it is likely that no one is using the DW/BI system.

If you can't actually rank the reports, at least try to split them up into three groups: the As, Bs, and Cs. The axes from the prioritization process described in Chapter 3 can help here. Rank each report in terms of its business value and level of effort. Reports that provide high business value and are relatively easy to create make the A list. Limit the A list to 15 reports or less, keep the B list handy if you have extra time, or for the next iteration, and encourage your users to work on the C list if they feel strongly about it. The A list is what you plan to implement. You should review this final list with key DW/BI stakeholders to make sure everyone understands and agrees to it.

WHAT TO DO WITH EXISTING REPORTS Many organizations already have some kind of reporting system in place. This can cause problems for the BI team because the new versions rarely match the old versions, so lots of time and energy is wasted trying to reconcile the two report sets, causing lost confidence in the warehouse. Here are a few strategies for dealing with existing report sets:

- Set expectations early on that the new reports won't match the old ones, including detailed documentation as to why they will be different, such as better business rules or improved data cleansing in the data warehouse's ETL process.

- Rather than recreate the existing report set, see if you can simply redirect its data feeds to pull from the DW/BI system. In many cases, existing reporting systems start with their own extracted tables. It may be easier to replace the data source than rebuild the reports.

- If you need to convert the reports to the DW/BI system, include key business users in your data validation step and then pull the plug on the old system. Conversion does have some benefits by providing all reports in a consistent environment and reducing the maintenance costs for multiple systems.

- Make sure you have enough resources to handle both converting the existing reports and building new ones. Converting existing reports adds little value to the business. Most business users and sponsors want to see something new and interesting out of the warehouse, not the same old, boring stuff.

Develop Detailed Application Specifications

Now that you have determined the overall look and feel and created the target list, you are ready to define the initial BI applications.

You must continue to involve the business users in this process. They will know more about the subtle nuances of creating many of these reports than you do. They also know what kinds of applications and reports are needed to deliver the business value identified during the requirements definition. In the case of more advanced dashboards or analytic applications, they have the domain expertise you are trying to capture or validate in the application itself. You can't do this alone. If you are creating operational BI applications or closed loop applications, you will also need to enlist the help of operational system developers who know the APIs that will allow your applications to interact with the operational systems as needed.

The specification process is relatively straightforward and has two underlying purposes. The first is to capture enough information so you can faithfully create the applications some months down the road. The second is to ensure that the DW/BI system is delivering something of value to the business community. In addition to the reports themselves, you also reap a host of other benefits from creating the detailed application specifications, including data model validation and identification of enhancements, user engagement, a performance tuning query suite, and a BI tool selection test set.

One of the best ways to specify the individual report/applications is to divide and conquer. Split the target list of reports up among the available business and technical folks who are capable of developing reports. Have each person work through the following for their subset of the target list, and bring the results back for group review and discussion. Each report/application should have the following set of documentation:

- **Mock up.** The mock up is the primary communications vehicle about the report. It is a physical example of the report, including all the visual components. To create a mock up, start with your standard template and fill in the report-specific elements: rows, columns, calculations, and formatting.

- **User interactions.** List all the points where the user can interact with the report, including variables, parameters, lists, limits, drilldown paths, and links. If the user interactions occur separate from the report layout, create a mock up of the user interaction interface as well.

- **Datasets.** Describe the datasets that fill the various sections and components of the report, including the report body and selection lists that support user interactions. Note any sources that are external to the warehouse, and indicate the sources for metadata elements as well. If you know SQL, it can be helpful to create simple SQL queries to define the datasets.

- **Algorithms, advanced calculations, and business rules.** Include descriptions of any advanced analytics or data mining models that will be needed in the application. For example, this might include an algorithm to determine the baseline response rate to a promotion to determine the increase or lift gained by target marketing.

- **Interactions with other reports/systems.** If the report links to other reports, or is intended to allow the user to feed results back to the operational systems or elsewhere, describe those interactions and include links to API documentation.

If you are designing a dashboard, break down the interface into each component section and use these steps to document each section. Then include an overall mock up and documentation for the dashboard itself that refers to the component section documents.

Specify Application Content

Each standard report mock up provides the layout of a report that is most often driven by a set of parameters. The user sets the parameters from pick lists or by accepting the defaults when they run the report. This parameter-driven approach allows users to generate dozens or potentially hundreds of variations on the basic standard report. Figure 12-3 shows a sample report mock up.

The <(Geography Name)> parameter in Figure 12-3 is a combination of constraints that will be used to select the desired geographic areas and then combine them for the purposes of this report. For example, this template could

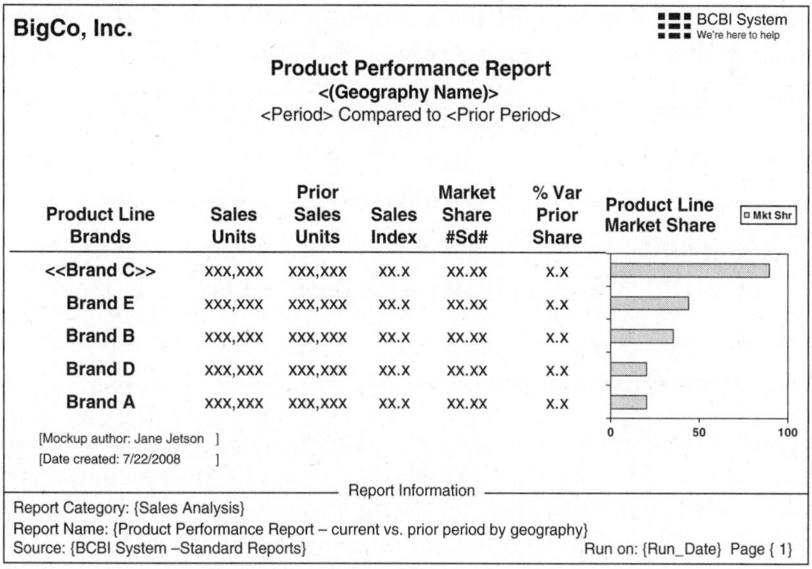
BigCo, Inc.

BCBI System
We're here to help

Product Performance Report
<(Geography Name)>
<Period> Compared to <Prior Period>

Product Line Brands	Sales Units	Prior Sales Units	Sales Index	Market Share #Sd#	% Var Prior Share
<<Brand C>>	xxx,xxx	xxx,xxx	xx.x	xx.xx	x.x
Brand E	xxx,xxx	xxx,xxx	xx.x	xx.xx	x.x
Brand B	xxx,xxx	xxx,xxx	xx.x	xx.xx	x.x
Brand D	xxx,xxx	xxx,xxx	xx.x	xx.xx	x.x
Brand A	xxx,xxx	xxx,xxx	xx.x	xx.xx	x.x

[Mockup author: Jane Jetson]
[Date created: 7/22/2008]

Report Information
Report Category: {Sales Analysis}
Report Name: {Product Performance Report – current vs. prior period by geography}
Source: {BCBI System –Standard Reports} Run on: {Run_Date} Page { 1}

Figure 12-3 Sample report mock up.

produce reports at the level of the Total Company, Eastern Region, Southeast District, South Florida Branch, and sales rep — from the top of the hierarchy all the way down to the lowest level of detail. These different report results can be produced simply by changing the constraints on the geography dimension with no changes to the structure of the report itself. Likewise, this could be a daily, monthly, or quarterly report by changing the <Period> parameter. A user can also flexibly define the previous period, perhaps as Year Ago or Yesterday. The parentheses around Geography Name indicate that it is also a page break variable, meaning the report will generate a new page for each geographic entity selected.

> **NOTE** If you are comfortable with SQL or your OLAP language, it might be easier to write the SQL queries you would use to generate the report contents. If you base these queries on the business process dimensional model, it will be clear where the data comes from when it's time to build the applications. Of course, this presumes the model has already been finalized.

In addition to user-entered parameters, there are several user interaction functions that are helpful to indicate on the mock up. For example, the double angle bracket signs (<<>>) indicate drilldown capabilities; a user could click on an entry in this column or row header and drill down to the next level of detail.

We've found it useful to indicate the following functions on the mock up. You may have additional needs, or prefer to use other indicators.

<>	User entered parameter, typically selected from list
<<>>	Drillable field
#Sd#	Sort order indicator, (a)scending or (d)escending
{}	Application entered variable, either from the system or metadata
\\ \\	Link/URL to another report or documentation source
( )	Page or section break field
[ ]	Report template comments

The Product Performance report shown in Figure 12-3 could be a central component in the brand manager's dashboard. Some of the dashboard-type features like conditional formatting or trend indicators can help quickly communicate areas that might be problems or opportunities.

There are two parts to each BI application specification: a mock up and a definition. The definition provides basic information about the report or application, and the mock up provides a visual representation of how the content will look on the page.

The BI application definition includes the name, description or purpose, frequency, parameters and their associated pick lists, user interactions, and default constraints. Unusual processing requirements should also be noted here. Figure 12-4 shows the start of a sample BI application definition for the standard report shown in Figure 12-3.

Design the Navigation Framework and Portal

Although you are starting with only 15 or so templates, this will soon change. As people gain experience with the initial data, they will come up with modifications to existing reports or requests for new reports. This does not mean the business users don't know what they want — you are not allowed to say that! It does mean they are learning about the power and flexibility of the DW/BI system and are exploring information needs they were afraid to ask for in the past. Of course, each Lifecycle iteration will add data from additional business processes with BI applications to go along with the new data. Also, users will develop new reports that you will want to make available to other users. If users create as many reports as the warehouse team, you can easily end up with 100 standard reports or more before you know it. Even with meaningful naming standards, it would be difficult to navigate a list of 100 reports.

You need to devise a method for grouping and organizing these BI application objects. We've found the organization's business processes to be a good starting point for structuring this navigation framework and associated BI portal. Figure 12-5 shows a simple navigation framework with sales related business processes like sales activity and sales pipeline at the top level of the

Doc Title: BI application definition	Project: BCBI System -- Orders business process					Prepared by: Warren Thornthwaite	Date Prepared: 7/9/2008		
Report Num: 2 Report Name: Product Performance									
Report Description: The Product Performance report shows unit volume and market share by brand for a specific geography. This provides a snapshot of the volume movement.									
#	Report Element / Attribute	Page Location	Function Type	Default value(s)	Source	Generated In:	Query	Comments	
1	Geography Name	Initial prompt screen	Page/ Section break	N/A	Initial prompt screen	Reporting tool	SELECT DISTINCT Geography_Name FROM Employee	Sales wants this at the region level, but it may be helpful to have a version that allows user selection of the geography level.	
2	Product Line	Row header title	Pull down menu	Top Product Line	Initial prompt screen	Reporting tool			
3	Period	Initial prompt screen	Pull down menu	Current month	Initial prompt screen	Reporting tool		User can determine granularity of period (e.g., week, month, quarter, year).	
4	Prior Period	Initial prompt screen	Pull down menu	Year ago month	Initial prompt screen	Reporting tool		Note: Prior period must be before current period and must be at same grain as Period.	
5	Report Category	Footer	Application generated	N/A	Report metadata	Hard coded		See if the tool can read this from the metadata at execution time, otherwise, hard code.	
6	Brand	Row headers	Report content / Drill down	Product Line Based	Data query	Reporting tool	See separate query doc for syntax	Note drill down on standard product hierarchy.	
7	Sales Units	Column	Report content	N/A	Data query	Reporting tool	See separate query doc for syntax	Sum of Sales Units from Sales Fact table.	

Figure 12-4 Example BI application definition.

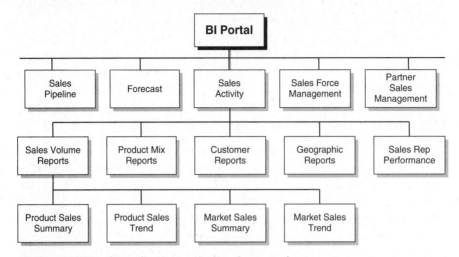

Figure 12-5 Simple application navigation framework.

BI portal. If a business user knows how the organization works, they should be able to quickly find the information they are looking for.

Portal tools help with this grouping and organizing process by allowing multiple organizational frameworks on top of a single report set. Portals also allow users to create their own personal report lists. We talk more about this in the BI portal development section later in this chapter.

> **NOTE** You must develop a strategy that will help your users find what they need quickly. Note that the BI application metadata can be extremely useful in supporting this navigation. Make sure you capture it now so you can put it to work in the development process.

At this stage, you are creating a preliminary design for the navigation framework. This basic business view of the reports and how they group together should be tool independent. However, because so much of the navigation's implementation depends on the chosen tool set, detailed navigation design will take place during the development phase, as we describe later in this chapter.

Review and Validate the Applications and Model

The BI application specs provide a good way to logically test the dimensional model once it begins to take shape. Take each report specification and verify that the attributes, constraints, hierarchies, measures, and appropriate grain all exist in the model. This is a simple eyeball comparison. Look at each report, compare it to the model and think about how you would write the SQL or

OLAP queries for the report. This process often surfaces problems in both the dimensional model and report design, which are much easier to deal with at this early point in the design phase rather than after all the database and ETL work is done.

If you have resources and data available, and you have selected and installed your front end BI tool, you can do some prototyping. This will give you, and your users, more confidence in the correctness of your application specs. In some cases, this will also allow you to begin making progress on the development step. In the best case, when it actually comes time to implement, all you need to do is redirect your prototype reports to run against the production database. Be careful, however. Some BI tools tie the data and report together very tightly, so migrating to a new data model might be a challenge.

Even if you don't have your front end tool in place, you can query data sources directly from Excel if you have SQL skills (and permission). Or you can build a simple relational dimensional model or cube to test the reports against the design.

NOTE If you haven't selected a BI tool yet, your BI applications specs can also be used as a test case to make sure the tool you select can do the job you need it to do. Ask the vendor to have a consultant show you exactly what it takes to create every report on your list using their tool set. Better yet, get a trial version and build them yourself using test data in your environment once the dimensional model is complete.

Review with the Business

Once you are comfortable that the application specifications are complete and that the dimensional model will support them, the next step is to hold an official review session with the core users and all other interested stakeholders. Their feedback and buy-in will make a big difference in their support later when the BI applications roll out. Step through the documentation and any prototypes you put together that will help communicate the nature and content of the applications.

These specifications will inevitably change when you get to the application development phase of the project, so set expectations appropriately. Also, remind the users that these represent a starter set, not the final and complete list of reports that will be developed.

Once you get through the review and incorporate any feedback, you can't do much more until the dimensional model has been built and populated with at least test data, and you have selected and installed your BI tool(s). Put your BI application specification set on the shelf and come back when it's time.

Business Intelligence Application Development

Is it that time already? Well, pull those specs off the shelf and let's get to work. The specific BI application development tasks vary according to your BI tools and the applications you are building. This section describes a high level process and offers recommendations. The application development process follows a standard software development flow: prepare, build, test, and then deploy. Let's examine each of these steps in a bit more detail.

Prepare for Application Development

Sorry, but you don't get to start building applications quite yet. Because it may have been a while, the first thing to do is to review the BI application specifications that you developed earlier in the project. Update them to reflect any changes in the data, data model, or business requirements that have occurred since the specs were created.

You have additional prep and set-up work to do before application development can begin. In particular, you need to install and test the BI tools and set up user security, as well as usage and performance tracking.

Install and Test the BI Tools

This can be more work than you'd think. Some of the larger BI tools have many components, each of which operates as a separate service. You may need to install infrastructure components required by the BI tool, like a web server. Once the basic components are in place, you usually need to define metadata to access the database.

Populate BI Tool Metadata

Most BI tools require that some metadata be defined before you can start development. The richness and complexity of defining the metadata is highly tool dependent. At the low end, definition may simply be selecting tables to be used right out of the DBMS system tables and setting up default joins, or reading directly from the OLAP database. At the high end, full business definitions, default drill paths, and shared metrics must be predefined.

Create Business Metadata

Recall from Chapter 4 that business metadata is data that describes the contents of the DW/BI system. We believe business metadata is the most important metadata in your DW/BI system because its sole purpose is to help users understand what's in the DW/BI system and how to use it. Most BI tools have business metadata elements that help the users understand and navigate the dimensional model. The ability to group dimension and fact tables together into business process dimensional models, and to group attributes into categories are good examples of this kind of business metadata. Make sure you fill in all the business metadata elements available in your BI tool. Study these features carefully to see how you can leverage them to help simplify your users' experience. If your BI tools don't support all the business metadata you've decided is important, you will need to create additional metadata structures to house these elements.

If your BI tool stores its report metadata in a metadata repository, it is usually possible to set up a few simple queries to allow users to search for reports by category, data element, and report type, for example. You should set up the search so that once they find the report they want, the final link will invoke that report. Ultimately, your entire report navigation framework could be built into the metadata. Reports could easily belong to multiple categories; changing the navigation structure would be simply a matter of editing the metadata.

Test the BI Tools

Once the BI tool metadata has been populated, the basic functions of the data access tool should be working. Build some simple queries or reports to test each attribute within each dimension to see if everything has been defined properly. If strange and unusual things happen, it may be because of the metadata definitions, but may also be the result of errors in the data or data model. You should also try out the tool's full functionality as part of this initial test. Create a report, put it in a dashboard, publish it to the portal, schedule it for daily execution, and email the results to yourself.

Debugging the tool's metadata definitions requires a deep understanding of the tool metadata and the ability to look directly at the data in the tables. The data access tools perform many functions on your behalf based upon the metadata and the values in the tables.

Validate Your BI Application Interface Strategy

Now that you have your BI tools in place, you can make some final decisions about your approach to provide user access to the BI applications. As we described in Chapter 11, you may decide to use a web based portal tool, the navigation components of your BI tool, dashboard tools, or code-based interfaces. You will probably use some combination of these options depending on the types of applications you are building and the nature of the targeted user communities.

Set Up User Security

In many cases, you may elect to use the BI application environment to manage data access security for your users. The major reporting tools offer fairly robust security capabilities, including ways to limit the reports users can see or execute, and even limit users to subsets of the data. Refer to the security sections in Chapter 5 and Chapter 13 on deployment for more details.

Set Up the Report Process Metadata System

As we discussed in Chapter 4, process metadata is data that tracks the ongoing operation of a given activity. In the BI applications case, this is data about the use and performance of the BI applications. The major BI tools record this metadata in their own log files or metadata structures; you can usually draw most of the tracking data you need from these structures. It's a good idea to get this logging system set up early on in the development process. You can use the information to measure performance and troubleshoot scheduling and execution problems. You will need the information later to monitor usage and performance. You may also need it for security and compliance purposes. Best to set up this system sooner rather than later.

If your BI tools do not provide a way to record process metadata, you will need to figure out how to record it yourself. Most database products have a mechanism to log usage. In some cases, there is a specific audit system to capture user access information. In other cases, you may need to query the system tables directly. It's a good idea to build multiple levels of usage and performance tracking because keeping usage and performance metadata at the individual user and query level can generate a lot of data. You should have a summary level table that tracks daily access by user with measures like total query count, total rows returned, total bytes returned, average CPU seconds per query, disk reads, and disk writes. It's also a good idea to have a detailed logging routine that you can turn on and off. This allows you to capture individual queries and their performance for tuning purposes. Depending on the number of users you have and how active they are, you probably don't want this running all the time. You can usually cut the number of rows in this detail table down by filtering out some of the background queries that are generated by your BI tools, the enterprise reporting server, or any other applications that access the data warehouse on a regular, routine basis.

It's also a great idea to create a set of BI applications that run against the report process metadata. These can help you identify exceptional behavior or performance issues before they become serious problems. They also give the DW/BI system DBAs a good reason to learn how to use the BI tools; cross training is always a good thing.

Build the Applications

At this point you have the specs, your tools and approach are in place, and you have completed all the necessary preparations. Finally, you can sit down at the keyboard and get started with the actual development. It may seem that we encourage you to spend too much time on upfront planning, but a little effort up front can save you days, or even weeks, of work later.

In this section, we describe the basic steps for building BI applications. We then present application development guidelines, along with discussion about the inclusion of data mining models. Finally, we describe moving your BI applications into the report scheduling system for automated execution and distribution.

Follow the Core Process

Developing BI applications in most tools generally involves three major activities: 1) defining the user interactions, 2) creating the queries, and 3) formatting the results.

The nature of the application, the tools you are using, and the application approach you've chosen will determine how much work each of these three areas will need. For example, if you are creating a report that will be used by senior management, often in a printed form, the formatting will take more time. On the other hand, if you are delivering a dataset to advanced users via an Excel pivot table, you generally don't have to spend a lot of time on the formatting. They are going to change it anyway.

Define the User Interactions

At the simple end of the applications spectrum, there may be no user interaction at all. The set of official reports might be completely static; they are scheduled to run when the ETL process is complete and made available via the BI portal. At the other end of the spectrum, some reports not only allow users to specify parameters, but also allow them to interact directly with the report itself, adding or removing attributes and restructuring the report format. In the middle ground, most BI applications allow users to specify parameters and view the results.

Your task at this point is to review the application specs and identify the user interactions. Determine the most appropriate interaction tool, like a drop-down selection list with single or multiple choices, or a fixed list with check boxes or radio buttons. You need to think through how you are going to populate each selection list, including the default value and sort order.

You also need to figure out how you will present these selections to the user. Much of this depends on the tool you are working with, but you may have options. Some tools allow you to present a parameter selection window before the report is executed. Others run the report with the defaults and let the user change the parameters as part of the actual report interface.

NOTE A good BI application developer is sympathetic to the needs of business users and accepts the reality that most of these users will not read a manual. A good BI application developer also will constantly strive to make the user interfaces easier to use. A basic measure of ease of use is the number of mouse clicks it takes to get to a desired result. Three clicks or less is great. More than ten clicks should automatically put the application on a need-to-redesign list.

Create the Queries

Most BI tools have a report design interface that allows you to graphically build the needed queries. The main query incorporates the various parameters found in the report design specs. Each parameter usually has its own query that generates the associated selection list. This is usually created as part of defining the parameter. In some cases, this parameter definition can be stored in the central metadata repository and reused in other applications.

Keep in mind that your main query might actually require access to multiple dimensional models, potentially on multiple servers. The BI tools are getting much better at handling this drill across query. In other cases, you may have to build it on your own. When this happens, you will need some way to temporarily assemble multiple small results sets and do a sort-merge on the row headers.

As sophisticated as most BI tools are today, it's not unusual to have to enhance the SQL or OLAP language that the tool generates. This is especially true if you are building analytic applications or operational BI applications. In these cases, you are typically working in a software development environment where the query generation tools are rudimentary at best; expect to write and test at least some of your own queries.

Format the Results

If you've ever created a report in Excel, you know how much format twiddling can go on. The more exacting the results have to be, the longer it takes to work through the formatting. This is made more difficult by the fact that you actually have to format for multiple targets. The initial report viewing will be on the monitor, so this clearly needs to be readable and look good. However, you also need to make sure the report looks good when it is printed. You should also verify that it is appropriately formatted when exported to Excel and PDF files and whatever other target formats are important in your organization. This formatting process can be frustrating. In fact, some BI tools don't even try to support exact formatting. Some vendors offer a tool that is meant for user interaction and simple reporting, and another tool meant for "pixel-perfect" formatting. Make sure you understand what your tools are capable of doing before you drive yourself crazy.

NOTE You must have at least some data to adequately develop the BI applications, even if it is only test data. The data access tools are driven by the data itself, and it is difficult, if not impossible, to determine if you are on the right track unless you are able to see data. Ideally, you will be developing the applications during the test phase of the database, which will allow you to develop against a full presentation server environment that is close to its production form.

Design and Develop Analytic Applications

In Chapter 11 we described analytic applications as more complex than standard reports. Typically targeted at a specific business process and encapsulating domain expertise, they may also provide a means for the user to feed changes back into the transaction system based on guidance from the analytic application. You may or may not have any full scale analytic applications in your initial report set.

Although it is possible to build this kind of application in the standard front end tool report building environment, it is more common to use a standard programming tool to weave the components together into a coherent application. In other words, an analytic application may be a program that paints the user interface (UI), manages the user interactions, displays report and graph components from your BI tool via the tool's API, and directs certain user selections to an operational system. The sales dashboard application shown in Chapter 11's Figure 11.3 could be built using one of the more advanced dashboard tools, but the Regional Pipeline report in the lower right corner adds an analytic twist. This report calls on a data mining model that forecasts the probability of a deal closing between the report date and the end of the year. This probability is used to calculate an expected revenue number for the region and highlight major deals that are at risk.

The process of developing an analytic application is similar to the general process for building other BI applications. The business requirements and specification steps are essentially the same, and the major BI tools support the development of more complex analytic applications within their toolsets. Depending on the complexity of the application and your system environment, it may make more sense to develop the core of your application in a more standard programming environment, typically a web-based tool, like ASP.NET or JSP. More complex applications might benefit from the local execution of JavaScript via an AJAX architecture. In any case, the major BI tools provide APIs and software development kits (SDKs) for their toolsets that allow you to build the reports and chart elements using their tools, and then generate and display the report elements from within your custom application.

As we described in Chapter 11, this kind of analytic application is often embedded in an overall product designed to address a specific business process. If the opportunity you are addressing is a common one, it often makes sense to buy an analytic application rather than try and build it. Products are available from the major BI tool vendors and many other third parties that specialize in certain business processes.

Design and Develop Operational BI Applications

Operational BI applications are usually custom developed to query the data warehouse and the operational systems, and then enable the user to invoke transaction processes from within the BI application. These applications provide operations workers with a richer context for decision making and more directed guidance on which decisions might be best. These are often called closed-loop systems because they provide the user with the ability to act on that guidance immediately, usually by directly initiating an event in the transaction system.

Be careful about including operational BI in your DW/BI system. The service levels required for keeping strictly analytic systems available are often not quite as high as those needed for operational systems. People in operations positions cannot do their jobs if the applications that support them are not running. Therefore, operational BI puts the DW/BI system, or at least part of it, at a 24/7 service level for availability. Also, there are often more people in operations roles, so operational BI applications can stress the performance service levels of the DW/BI system as well.

As if that isn't enough, operational BI usually pushes the DW/BI system in terms of data latency. These applications often require data that is closer to real time. Handling customer questions about orders is difficult if you aren't loading the order information until the next day.

Service levels and data latency tend to push operational BI applications into their own section of the DW/BI system architecture. The real time layer and operational system monitors are both components designed specifically to meet these operational BI requirements, as we described in Chapter 9. It takes a lot of work to deliver this, so make sure you clearly understand the business value and the level of effort required.

One example of a high value operational BI application is a complex sales incentive system where each sales rep's performance is based on his sales and the sales of other sales reps further down the sales organizational hierarchy. The incentive plan has several tiers, like gold, silver, or platinum, at each organizational level. When a rep at a given level attained the next tier, it could impact the incentive bonus at all levels above that rep. The organization has hundreds of thousands of independent reps working worldwide. Making these reps aware of where they and those who report to them stand and what they need to reach the next tier was enough incentive to generate a significant increase in sales. This required data from three major sources: the incentive system, actual sales to date (within the last 15 minutes), and the sales organization hierarchy. But simply making this data available wasn't enough. The closed loop portion of this application meant allowing the sales people to act on the opportunities identified by contacting lower level reps who were close to the next level of performance and offer them assistance in closing deals. It also meant tying back into the operational system to allow push-button contact through emails, online alerts, or phone calls.

Though the operational and low latency requirements add to the excitement, the process of developing operational BI applications is quite similar to developing the analytic applications described earlier.

Include Data Mining Models

We have referred to data mining several times as a potential component in your BI applications. From the application perspective, this typically takes the form of making calls to a pre-defined data mining model with specific parameters, such as customer attributes or purchase history. The model returns the appropriate values, such as product recommendations or a fraud alert.

Creating the underlying data mining model used in an analytic application is usually a separate activity. Data mining is more of a process than an application, as shown in Figure 12-6. It starts with a business phase, exploring opportunities for applying data mining with business folks and verifying the existence of appropriate data to support those opportunities. Once an opportunity has been identified, the second phase is where the data mining actually takes place. In a highly iterative process, the data miner requests descriptive datasets called observation sets or case sets. These sets are fed into the data mining tool where the data miner selects different combinations of algorithms, parameters, and input variables. These combinations are called *models*, and the goal is to create models that appear to be most correlated or predictive. The best model (at least within the time allowed) is then moved into the operations phase.

Moving a model into operation can be as simple as calling it from the ETL process where it calculates a customer lifetime value score during the nightly load process. Or it can be as complex as incorporating the model into the organization's production online e-commerce system to make live product recommendations. These models are also embedded in analytic applications and operation BI applications.

Other analytic applications include planning and forecasting tools that use data mining time series algorithms to account for seasonality and find best-fit curves for sales forecasts. Even operational BI systems often embed data mining models as part of their rules engine to identify opportunities or problems in the transaction flow and bring those to the attention of the right operations people, or in some cases initiate a direct response from within the system. For example, systems that detect fraud or make product recommendations at the transaction level use models that are built from the historical attributes and behaviors captured in the transaction events in the data warehouse.

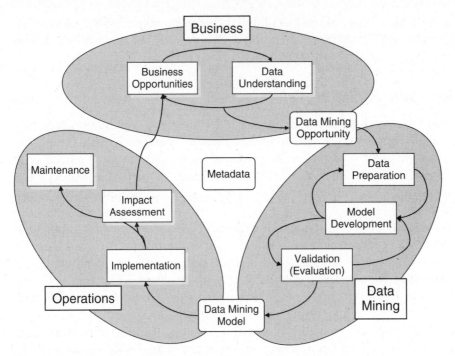

Figure 12-6 Data mining model development and implementation process.

Validate the Data and Data Model

Just as the BI applications specs were used to validate the data model earlier, you can now use the BI applications to validate the data model and the data itself. Problems with the tools, data model, or data will show up at this point. Leave time in your project plan to track down these problems and take corrective action. It's a bit late in the game for major changes, but better late than never. The more rigorous you are in designing your dimensional model and building the ETL process, the fewer problems you will run into at this point.

Create the Navigational BI Portal

Once you have more than a couple of reports, you have to provide a navigation framework or BI portal that allows people to find the information they need. Refer back to Figure 11.4 for a basic example of the top level of a BI portal.

The overall BI portal will have multiple levels, each with its own purpose and design. At the top level, the portal is primarily a navigation tool. Most of the real estate of the top level of a BI portal is devoted to a framework for organizing the standard BI applications and dashboards to help people find what they are looking for. Usually, each entry at the top level is a group or category of reports. The least ambiguous way to organize the top level is to have the categories follow business processes, much like the bus matrix.

This top level will change over time as new rows from the bus matrix work their way into the DW/BI system.

Portal pages at the second level usually focus on reports based on data from the selected business process. For example, Figure 12-7 shows a sample sales business process portal page with several reports that look at sales data from different aspects. Figuring out what goes where gets more complicated at this level because most users need data from multiple business processes to get their job done. This means they will need to go up and down the portal hierarchy finding specific reports. This is also why dashboards came into being. If you have a group of people with similar needs, it makes sense to create a dashboard to bring the various reports together into a single interface rather than make those users go report hunting every time they sit down to work. You will also cross-link some reports and dashboards in multiple areas of the BI portal.

The indented items in Figure 12-7 are links to the actual reports. Use the report descriptions from the metadata repository to generate a mouse-over message about each report. You may also want to have a thumbnail of each report or dashboard that can give people a visual memory guide.

Obviously, a new DW/BI system will only have data from one or two business processes, so the top level of the BI portal will be a bit sparse. As a result, your initial navigation framework may start at the second level, and you can add on the top level later.

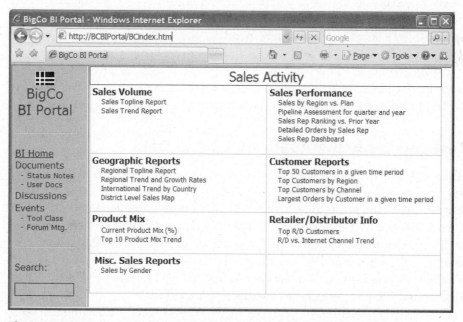

Figure 12-7 Sample second level portal page for the sales business process.

Developing the BI portal is tied directly to your chosen software. In general, portal tools are fairly easy to work with, but they want to control the screen layout. This can be a problem if you want to build an information-rich BI portal like we described in Chapter 11, but it is usually possible to find a work-around.

Set Up Report Scheduling

Often there's a subset of BI applications you need to execute automatically on a scheduled basis, either for performance or timing reasons. If there are five standard reports that take a few minutes to run, and a thousand business users look at them first thing every morning, it makes sense to run these reports once as soon as the ETL process is finished and save the completed reports. When users request the report, the system will simply select the completed report rather than rerun it 1,000 times. And the users will be impressed by the excellent performance of the DW/BI system.

Most BI tool vendors provide a reporting service that allows you to schedule standard reports to run with predefined parameters. These reports may run at a regularly scheduled time, or they may run as the result of an event, such as completion of the data load process. The report's results may be stored centrally and retrieved as requested by the users or automatically distributed to specified users via email, file system, or even printed.

The specifics of report distribution and management are highly dependent on your data access tool. Many data access tools support report caching where users simply retrieve the final report from a report repository. If you have a large user community, you will need to agree on which reports will be included in the scheduler and who is allowed to schedule them.

This is another area that will evolve over time in your environment. As the users learn more about what they want and need from a business perspective, you will also learn about how you can respond from a systems perspective.

Test and Verify the Applications and Data

As in any successful software development effort, testing is a required step in creating BI applications. First, for each report, check your logic. Create a simple query and copy the data for a report into a spreadsheet and recreate the calculations by hand. Verify that your percentages and variances are based on the correct numbers. Change the parameters and run it again. Run it on another computer, in another building. Try it on a different browser or version. If you have freeform entry fields, enter garbage numbers for the parameters. Once you think it is perfect, have someone else test it.

Once you have confirmed the report is working correctly, it is time to look at the data itself. It is surprising how quickly data issues can be identified using today's data access tools. Some of the most common issues you are likely to find include:

- **Meaningless descriptions.** Often the names and descriptions that are supplied by the source systems were not designed for browsing and report labels. Though it may seem like a good idea to use the existing names, once you see them in a pick list or as row and column headers, you may change your mind.

- **Duplicate dimension information.** The ETL process should include checks to make sure that there are no duplicate keys. However, two different keys from the source data may represent the same thing. This may not surface during the ETL process, but it will become glaringly obvious when you look at the data via the BI tool.

- **Incorrect dimensional relationships.** Check to make sure that the correct information is pulled when drilling. Sometimes the attributes within a dimension are not properly assigned, which causes unusual results.

- **Data not balancing.** Another data issue that comes up during application development is the inability to balance the data to another existing system. There can be several causes. One could be that the BI application is calculating a business measure differently. Another is that the facts themselves may be created using different business rules than in the legacy system. Finally, the facts should represent the same thing, but the values do not match. Though this is often perceived as a data warehouse problem, in many cases the data warehouse is correct, which means the existing system is wrong or not accurate. This can be unsettling to users. Set the expectation during the dimensional design process that the reports won't match if you implement new and improved business rules. Even if you manage expectations early, be prepared to conduct detailed sessions to describe why the data warehouse is correct, but different.

- **Performance tuning.** It's common for the initial set of BI applications to not perform well right out of the gate. These are generally very complex reports or analyses. They often represent a range of business needs across the initial dataset or multiple datasets in subsequent iterations. The good news is you are developing these prior to making the system generally available and you have an opportunity to tune the database based on these real world report requirements.

The BI application developer must work closely with the ETL and database teams to work through these issues.

Complete the Documentation

Beyond the business level documentation that should already be securely stored in the metadata catalog, it is vital to document the application template infrastructure information as well. This includes the naming standards, information about where the master templates are kept, and who the system owner is. The training materials described in Chapter 13 are also part of this documentation.

Plan for Deployment

In general, BI application deployment is not as rigorous as database or transaction application deployment because it's not as dangerous. Deployment can be as simple as creating a link to the new reports in the BI portal, granting access permission, and sending out an email. This flexibility allows you to deploy new BI applications as you create them based on business priorities.

If your BI tool doesn't offer code management capabilities like version tracking and roll back, figure out how to include the BI applications in your development environment code management system.

Business Intelligence Application Maintenance

BI applications are not a one-time project. The initial set, and all subsequent additions, will need to be maintained and enhanced. This means someone will need to revisit the reports on a regular basis to verify their continued correctness and relevance in the organization. The team will also need resources to respond to requests for additional reports and analyses. Invariably, soon after the initial report set is released, someone will say something like "these reports are great, but what I really would like is..." and then offer up a new report description. Over time, you will need to keep the templates up-to-date. This includes the following kinds of activities:

- Adding new BI applications built by both business users and the DW/BI team.
- Updating BI applications to include new data sources or changes to existing sources.
- Monitoring BI application performance.
- Removing unused BI applications based on the monitoring system, which should capture usage by report name in the process metadata.

Conclusion

Business intelligence applications are the primary means for delivering value from the DW/BI system to the organization. They show value quickly and lower the barrier to entry for most of the business user community. Design and development happen in two separate steps in the Lifecycle. You capture the specifications for the BI applications soon after the completion of the requirement definition. Once the specs are in place, there is usually a significant waiting period before you can begin development because it's difficult to develop the BI applications before the dimensional model is in place and contains at least a subset of data.

Building robust, usable, correct BI applications is a big task. The central DW/BI team should have resources dedicated to this task, who also participate in the requirements gathering and dimensional model design process. Their understanding of the business is a critical component of getting things right early on in the process. The development process itself is fairly standard, except that it is typically based on the BI tool of choice and therefore subject to its idiosyncrasies.

BLUEPRINT FOR ACTION

Managing the Effort and Reducing Risk

The greatest risks for BI application specification and development are to not focus on delivering business value, and to underestimate the effort involved.

Go back to the business requirements document and make sure you are providing applications that address the high value opportunities.

Include core business users and their management in both the design and development steps, and set expectations about their involvement early on.

Refer back to the analytic cycle to make sure you are providing users with a complete environment that guides them through the full analytic process.

Allow time for tool selection if you are getting a new BI tool.

Schedule a few days of consulting time with an expert in your BI tool, especially if this is your first time working with the tool. Hire them for a day or two to help you get set up and headed in the right direction, then bring them back after a week or two when you've had some experience and created a long list of questions. This can significantly accelerate your learning curve.

(continued)

BLUEPRINT FOR ACTION *(continued)*

Assuring Quality

Testing is the primary quality assurance tool in applications development. You need to test as much as you can to make sure the application works as expected. This includes:

◆ Test calculations — add it up, do the division, and calculate the ratios. Make sure the report itself is internally consistent and correct.

◆ Test at different levels in the hierarchies. What adds up correctly at the summary level may not be right when you start to drill down to the details.

◆ Test edge parameters. For example, what happens to a report that compares data from a requested year to a prior year when the selected year is the earliest year in the database and there is no prior year?

◆ Compare to existing sources. If some elements of the report are available elsewhere, and if the results should match, make sure they do. If you expect the results to be different because of improvements in data quality or business rule definition, see if you can match the existing source by applying these improvements by hand. Review these differences with key business users and document them in the BI portal.

Key Roles

Key roles for designing and developing BI applications include:

◆ The BI application architect and developer are the primary drivers of the application development.

◆ The business analyst works closely with the BI application developer to develop the specifications and test the applications, and may play a role in developing the applications as well. In some cases, the business analyst is the BI application developer.

◆ Business users with advanced reporting and analysis skills may also be involved in designing and developing the BI applications, especially the standard report set.

◆ The DW/BI quality assurance analyst examines the data via the applications and verifies the data and application accuracy.

(continued)

Key Deliverables

Key deliverables for designing and developing BI applications include:

- Application development and naming standards document
- Application templates
- Prioritized candidate application list
- Detailed application specs for target applications
- Navigation framework and BI portal design
- Completed initial applications including documentation
- Completed BI portal for initial applications

Estimating Considerations

BI application specification and navigation design can take several weeks. It should start immediately following the requirements definition and be completed at about the same time as the dimensional model.

BI application development may begin as soon as the database structures are in place and at least some test data is available. In general, you should allow four to six weeks for the development of the templates, because some time will invariably be spent debugging the ETL process. There can be wide variations on the development time, depending on the BI data access tool, internal skill sets, application complexity, and resource availability.

Development of the navigation framework and BI portal varies too widely for general guidelines. Work with people who have experience using the software you have selected to develop a realistic timeline for development.

The following estimates reflect a basic set of 10 to 20 reports developed by one person. Of course, your mileage will vary depending on the available tools and experience level.

BI Application Specification

- Identify and prioritize list: 5 to 10 days of research and discussion with core business users.
- Document individual applications: 2 hours per report (5 to 10 days). More time for more complex analytic applications, data mining, and dashboards.

(continued)

BLUEPRINT FOR ACTION *(continued)*

- ◆ User review and discussion: half-day meeting.
- ◆ Incorporate feedback: $1\frac{1}{2}$ days.

Development

- ◆ Tool setup and testing, including metadata layer: 5 days.
- ◆ Report development: count on a half-day per report including formatting, distribution setup, and functional testing.
- ◆ Documentation and metadata: a quarter-day per report.
- ◆ Testing and validation: could take as long as development (or longer if things don't match as expected).

Website Resources

The following templates for designing and developing BI applications are available on the book's website at www.kimballgroup.com:

- ◆ Report mock up template
- ◆ Report description template

Task List

Legend symbols: ● Primary responsibility · ○ Involved · ◆ Provides input · ☐ Informed of results

BI APPLICATION DESIGN & DEVELOPMENT

	Fans	Front Office		Coaches		Regular Line-Up						Special Teams				
	Business Users	Business Sponsor / Business Driver	DW/BI Director / Program Manager	Project Manager	Business Project Lead	Business Analyst	Data Steward / QA Analyst	Data Architect / DBA	Data Modeler / Metadata Manager	ETL Architect / ETL Developer	BI Architect / App Developer / Portal Developer	Technical Architect / Tech Support Specialist	Security Manager	Lead Tester	Data Mining / Stats Specialist	Educator

BI APPLICATION DESIGN

#	Task	BU	BSp	DW/BI	PM	BPL	BA	DS	DA	MM	ETL	BI	TA	SM	LT	DM	Ed
1	Create BI application standards and templates	◆			○	○	○					●			○	◆	
2	Identify and prioritize candidate applications	◆			○	●	○					○			☐	○	
3	Document detailed BI application specifications						○		○			●				○	
4	Design navigation framework						○					●					
5	Validate the applications and data model	○			○	○	○	○	○			●					
6	Review BI application specs with business users				○	●	○					●					
7	Revise BI application specs						○					○					
8	Develop BI application test plans				○	○	○	○		☐	☐	○	☐	☐	●	☐	☐
9	User acceptance/project review	○	○	○	●	○	○	○				○					

BI APPLICATION DEVELOPMENT

#	Task	BU	BSp	DW/BI	PM	BPL	BA	DS	DA	MM	ETL	BI	TA	SM	LT	DM	Ed
1	Review application specifications and standards	◆			○	○	○	○		●		○					
2	Populate BI tool metadata	◆					○			○		○					
3	Create business metadata					◆	◆	○		○		●				○	
4	Test BI tools						○					●					
5	Set up user security	○					○		◆	●		○	○	○			
6	Set up report process metadata system						○	◆	○	●		○				○	
7	Develop BI applications				○	○	○	●			○	●				○	
8	Validate data model and data						○	●	◆	●	○	●				◆	
9	Provide data accuracy & cleanliness feedback				○	○	○	●				●					
10	Develop BI portal						○					●					
11	Set up report execution scheduling				○	○	○					●			○		
12	Test BI applications and verify data				○	○	○	○				●					
13	Document BI applications			☐	○	○	○		○	○	○	●					
14	Develop BI application maintenance procedures				○	○	○	○		○	○	●					
15	Develop BI application deployment procedures		☐	☐	○	○	○	○	○	○	○	●					
16	User review/project acceptance	○			●	○	○	○	○	○	○	○	☐		☐	☐	☐

LEGEND:
- ● Primary responsibility
- ○ Involved
- ◆ Provides input
- ☐ Informed of results

CHAPTER 13

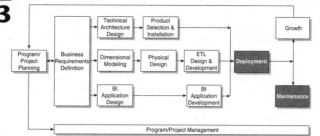

Deploying and Supporting the DW/BI System

The deployment step is the most exciting phase of the Lifecycle when we finally present the data warehouse and its BI front end to the business community. The quality of this first impression drives the acceptance of the DW/BI solution — and you only get one shot at it. Like any big event, there are a lot of details that must fall into place for the show to be successful. Deployment includes all the pieces needed to give the business users access to the information in a form that works for them. Much of this starts early in the Lifecycle; at the same time that you are creating the architecture and building the data warehouse and the BI applications, you also need to be creating documentation, preparing training, and organizing the user support processes. All these operational services need to be in place before the curtain goes up for the first time.

The technical tasks of testing and deploying the system are not as much fun as the user-facing rollout tasks. It's detail-oriented work to move code from the development environment to the test system, fully test both functionality and performance, and then deploy the system into production. These technical deployment tasks are particularly challenging as you deploy incremental changes to an existing production system.

Once you're in production, there are many operational tasks necessary to keep the system performing well. These include ongoing monitoring to understand what business users are doing, performance tuning, index maintenance, system backup, and other equally exciting topics. A system that operates solidly, with as little human intervention as possible, requires that you think about these issues early on. Some of these issues are interwoven into the design of the ETL system and deployment process.

This chapter is split into three parts: The first concentrates on the system deployment process, and the second spotlights all the other critical but less technical activities needed to ensure a successful deployment. The third section describes operational and maintenance tasks.

Project managers should read this chapter closely. Team members who interact directly with business users, including desktop administrators, educators, and user support representatives, will also find the material useful. Database administrators and ETL system operators should read the sections on operations and maintenance. Finally, project sponsors and drivers should be familiar with the overall coordination effort, as well as the deployment readiness checklist.

System Deployment

The DW/BI system is a complex software project that needs to be tested extensively before you deploy. Throughout the development process, you should have been conducting unit tests to confirm that components have been written properly. As we discuss in the next section, you need to perform extensive end-to-end system testing, too.

Most people find testing to be tedious and boring, so it's easy to under invest in these tasks. Be warned: The less time you spend on testing, the harder the deployment process will be. If you don't perform end-to-end testing before you deploy to production, you're guaranteed to find problems in production. If you don't rigorously check data quality, your business users will do it for you, and lose confidence in the DW/BI system at the same time. If you don't check performance and tune the system in advance, you'll have to do it while trying to avoid disrupting business users.

If you test, tune, and adjust the system before deployment, the move to production will be fairly straightforward. This is especially true if this is a new system. As we discuss later in this chapter, moving incremental changes into production while minimizing user impact can be a delicate dance.

Pre-Deployment Testing

To successfully deploy a new DW/BI system, or changes to an existing system, plan ahead and test repeatedly until you have verified:

- **Testing procedures:** Your system testing procedures are sufficiently rigorous that you can prove to users or auditors that the system has been thoroughly tested.

- **Data quality assurance testing:** The data is accurate and complete, both for the historical load and ongoing incremental loads.

- **Operations process testing:** The databases load and process correctly.

- **Performance testing:** The system performs well both for loads and queries and reports.

- **Usability testing:** Business users can find what they need and accomplish necessary tasks.

- **Deployment testing:** Deployment scripts are solid and have been rehearsed.

- **User desktop readiness:** Business users' desktop machines have sufficient power to use the new tools, and those tools are installed.

System Testing Procedures

Your data warehouse system is a software project, in addition to being an exercise in business politics. As part of deployment, you must test that the system works, in whole and in part. The testing discussed in this section should be formalized to the greatest extent you and your organization can tolerate. The *exact* methodology used to keep track of tests and results is much less important than having *some* methodology. If your organization already uses a testing methodology, you should be able to make that system work for your BI project. If you don't already use a testing methodology, adopt or develop one for this project.

Any testing methodology will contain at least four major steps: Define your tests; develop a primary test dataset; develop datasets to test unusual conditions; and, finally, run these tests and log the results.

If your organization does software development, you may have a test team in-house already. If so, you should talk to this team to get information about which tools and procedures they use. Try to have an internal testing expert assigned to your project for the deployment phase. It's tempting to have the developers also assume the testing role, but it's almost always better to have a different set of eyes perform tests. In a smaller or more resource-constrained team, we've seen front room team members make effective testers for the back room processes.

Think Like a Software Development Manager

Throughout the system development, testing, and rollout, it is very helpful to pretend to be a professional software development manager. Actually, it's not pretending. Real software development managers go through the same steps. The best software development managers have learned the same lessons:

- The project is 25 percent done when your developer gives you the first demo of the working application. The first demo from a proud developer is an important milestone that you should look forward to, but seasoned software development managers know that the developer has only passed the first *unit test*. The second 25 percent is making the application pass the complete *system test*, where all the units are working. The third 25 percent is validating and debugging the completed system in a *simulated production* environment. The final 25 percent is documenting and *delivering the system* into production.

- Don't believe developers who say their code is so beautiful that it is self-documenting. Every developer must stay on the project long enough to deliver complete, readable, high-quality documentation. A rough rule of thumb is one line of documentation for each line of code (or setting).

- Use a bug tracking system. Set up a branch in your bug tracking or problem reporting system to capture every system crash, every incorrect result, and every suggestion. A manager should scan this system every day, assigning priorities to the various problems. An application cannot be released to the user community if there are any open high priority bug reports.

- Be proactive if you collect bug reports from users and testers. Be fanatical about acknowledging receipt of every reported bug, allowing the users and testers to see what priority you have assigned to their reports and what the resolution status of their reports is, and then fixing all the bugs that can be replicated and have high enough priority.

- Place a very high professional premium on testing and bug reporting. Establish bug-finding awards. Have senior management praise these efforts. Make sure that the application developers are patient with the users and testers.

Define Tests

Begin the testing process by making a list of the tests you plan to run and expected outcomes. Define tests to be small; keep breaking down the tests to smaller tasks until you have something simple that is easily verified. Use a test tracking tool that you already have in-house, or purchase an inexpensive one. You can use a spreadsheet such as Excel to track tests and results, but there are many specialized tools available that are not very expensive.

Document each test to describe the exact steps for running the test and verifying the results. The best test sets are automated: Write scripts to run tests and check results. It's often as easy to automate a test as it is to document the steps you want a person to follow, and it's far easier to run the second or third (or twentieth) time. At the very least, stick the query script used to verify a result into the test matrix so the tester can easily find it and copy/paste.

Develop Test Datasets

Begin the test process for the incremental loads by defining tests that work against a known set of data. You can test most of the system's functionality by using a dataset that you've cooked up. The advantage of a predefined, static dataset is that you can easily check results. Follow this test dataset all the way through the process, from ETL to the relational and OLAP databases, and into the predefined reports. More than half of the system's tests are usually performed by one normal run through the basic test dataset.

It's common to include imperfect data in the primary test dataset, as long as your processes have been designed to identify and handle that data during normal operations. For example, perhaps you expect one fact table to have early-arriving facts and you've automated the process of creating a dummy dimension member to ensure referential integrity. You'd want to include test data for this normal (but imperfect) data condition within your primary test dataset.

You should expect to run tests over and over, so automate the process of restoring the test databases to the pre-test state. Build an application that compares the end results of all your tests against known correct results. Then after each run of your test suite, find all the test results that deviate from the correct answers. This style of repetitive checking is called *regression testing*, and it is invaluable for uncovering errors that you introduced with "one last change."

Make absolutely sure that you run the regression test suite against the very last and final release of your ETL and BI systems. Even if all you changed is the date on the copyright notice, run the regression test suite again. It is so easy to omit something in the final release packaging.

During operations testing, as we discuss later in this chapter, you're checking that the control flow of the system operates as expected. It's as important to test with bad data as it is to test with good data, especially if you've defined data quality conditions that will cause processing to stop. Plan to create alternative datasets to test error conditions that affect the control flow.

Elsewhere in the testing process, as you get closer to deploying the system, you'll need to test with live data. For now, isolate the control flow error condition testing from the tests of connectivity and integration across multiple systems.

Run Tests and Log Results

When you're actually running tests, you must keep track of which systems and data you used, and what the test results were. There's nothing particularly unusual about this part of testing a DW/BI system. As with any other software and system testing, the important thing is to run the tests and log the results. The key information to collect is the status of the test and any specific comments from the tester's observations.

Data Quality Assurance Testing

Do not skimp on data quality testing. We have seen many projects lose vital goodwill with business users because the initial deployment wasn't well tested. The data needs to be checked very carefully before the system goes live. You should develop subsystems and procedures for continuing to check data accuracy during operations. Delivering bad data is much worse than delivering no data at all.

Data quality testing, at its heart, consists of running a query or report from the source system or systems, running the corresponding query or report from the data warehouse, and comparing results. The magic comes in knowing the corresponding query or report. You may need significant business knowledge to match up the multiple systems. For this reason, and more importantly, for buy-in from the business community, you must include the business users and quality analysts in the data quality assurance process.

Make sure you can reproduce existing reports to the penny. Sometimes we find that existing reports have long been in error. This makes it harder to verify the new reports, but you absolutely must audit them and document any discrepancies. If you have an internal audit group, enlist their assistance in this process.

We've often been asked to recommend tools to help test data quality. We don't know of any tools that help with the hard part of testing: determining what data needs to be tested and how to do so. At the very least, the data quality testing reports should include row counts, grand totals and subtotals along major dimensions and hierarchies, including time.

Your BI applications may include some complex calculations. These are also difficult to validate. You should have someone test the calculations externally — usually in Excel — to confirm that they're correct. Report definitions sometimes include calculations as well. Check everything. In a budget variance report that displays budget, actual, and variance figures, confirm that the variance is truly the difference between the other columns. Even in this trivial case you may see a penny difference due to rounding. Discuss that rounding with your business users and get a decision from them on how to handle it.

As with other kinds of tests, it's useful to automate data quality tests as much as possible. During testing and deployment, you'll typically run the data quality tests at least three times:

- **Test the historical load:** Historical load testing is primarily a data quality assurance process.

- **Test the outcome of running the primary test dataset:** This static dataset is usually small and easiest to check thoroughly.

- **Test the real data:** Once you start running live data through your test system, you should test the validity of that data, as we describe in the next section.

Any automated data quality tests that you developed for the deployment phase should eventually be folded into the ETL process. Develop processes for logging the results of the ongoing data quality tests, and publish data quality reports to the business community.

Operations Process Testing

Developers have been focusing on one component of the DW/BI system at a time. Even if your team is small, you usually isolate subsystems during development. Experienced teams begin small-scale operations and end-to-end testing from the outset. As soon as two components are ready, check how they fit together. Every time you develop another piece of the puzzle, step back and make sure everything still works.

Now it's time to pull everything together and confirm that the entire system operates as designed. First, verify end-to-end operations using the primary set of static data that we described earlier in this chapter. The primary testing dataset should run from start (extracting from source systems) to finish (running and delivering reports) without triggering any errors that stop processing.

NOTE As we described previously in this chapter, it's common for your primary test dataset to contain examples of the kind of errors expected in normal operations. These errors should be handled within your ETL modules, and should not halt processing.

The operations process testing should verify that ETL jobs start when they should and run correctly under normal operation. Confirm that OLAP cubes are processed as expected. Verify that standard reports are built on schedule, only after the underlying data has been correctly updated. Use team members' email addresses to confirm that report distribution via email works as expected.

Check all the branches in your incremental ETL processing. Perhaps your scheduling system kicks off the master job at 1:30 a.m., and the process first checks if the transaction system has finished its nightly processing. Verify that the communication between the transaction and ETL systems works as expected.

As discussed in Chapter 10, your ETL system should check row counts and checksums. Ideally, you've built processes for handling unusual events, such as an unbelievably low or high row count. Test these procedures, using alternative datasets and configurations.

Although there are potentially dozens of infrastructure-related problems that surface during operations testing, you will almost inevitably stumble over security issues. The warehouse is generally run using system accounts that are independent of any individual user ID. But systems are often developed using the developer's personal account.

We've experienced what seem to us incredibly long delays at client sites, waiting to get system accounts set up and authorized. Depending on your organization, it can take a long time just to get a system account set up, not to mention getting the necessary authorizations into the various source systems, warehouse servers, and other resources. In a large organization, you should plan on it taking a few weeks or more to iron this out (depending on whom you know).

Live Testing

Once you're confident that your historical data is accurate and the operational processes are clean, you can begin testing with real data. Before you begin live testing, back up the database after the historical load's data has been tested. Hope for smooth sailing, but plan for rocky seas.

Set up the test system so that it points to the same operational sources that you'll use in production. You need to run the live testing for long enough to see real world patterns in the data and operational environment. Nightly loads need at least a week, perhaps several weeks, of exercising with live data before the system launches. If there's an operational cycle that may affect your system, such as a monthly closing process, you should ensure your tests span a complete cycle. If you load data on a monthly cycle, it's not realistic to leave the data in live testing for very many load cycles. Two iterations is a lot better than one, if you can manage it.

There are several reasons to perform live testing:

- **System integration:** No matter how thorough and realistic your test datasets and test systems have been, you probably haven't been connecting to the production systems on a regular basis. All sorts of things can go wrong, beginning with the permissions on the test system's account and server. Your test system should be as similar to your production system as possible, especially with respect to which services, such as ETL and the RDBMS, run on which machine.

- **Data quality testing:**   You need to run your data quality tests against the data after incremental processing.

- **Performance testing:**   Performance testing works best against a live load, at least as a final confirmation that performance tuning has been effective.

Performance Testing

Everyone should do some performance testing before deploying their system into production. The larger and more complex your system is, and the more users — especially ad hoc users — you have, the more important it is for you to conduct rigorous performance testing. You want to launch your system with the best performance possible, and you certainly want to be confident that you can perform all processing within the necessary load windows.

You may have several goals for conducting performance tests. The most common are:

- **System tuning.**   How can you tweak the system to deliver the best possible performance?

- **Confirmation of service levels:** Will you meet your downtime and query performance requirements?

- **Headroom analysis:** How long will today's system and hardware meet your requirements, as the data warehouse continues to grow?

As with everything else associated with systems, the performance testing process is best begun with some planning. Specify the goals from your testing process, and develop tests to address those goals.

System Tuning

The first question to ask before you begin system tuning is what will you measure? You need the obvious measure of timing, but if you want to improve performance, you need more information than that. Later in this chapter we discuss the kinds of information that should be logged during system operation. These counters and event traces are invaluable to diagnose performance problems, both during the testing period and operations.

Start by running a baseline test that measures system performance based on your best guess of optimal system configuration. Imagine that you were going to go into production without doing any performance testing at all. This baseline test should measure the performance and operating characteristics of that best guess system.

Next, test one change at a time. Change an index. Test. Change a parameter. Test. If you change more than one thing at a time, you'll never know which change was helpful. Use a spreadsheet to track tests and results. If you're trying to wring the last ounce of performance from the system, you may need several iterations. Use the one-change-at-a-time technique to develop an improved optimal configuration. Try a second set of one-at-a-time changes against that new configuration until you're satisfied with the performance.

It's vital to conduct system tuning performance tests on the nearly completed system as a whole. You can and should unit test individual components of the system, such as cube processing. But unless the production system will run each unit in isolation, this testing is far from conclusive. The biggest problems you'll encounter arise from competition for scarce resources — usually memory — across multiple units of the system.

Service Level Confirmation

Increasingly, DW/BI teams are entering into service level agreements (SLAs) with the user community. These agreements cover data latency, user downtime, and often user query performance.

If you have an SLA in place, then you surely must test that your system is likely to conform to the agreement. This is often a first step that leads to more extensive performance testing for tuning work, or even alternative system sizing and configuration efforts. But if you've cleverly made an agreement with pretty low minimum standards, you may simply need to confirm you're above those standards.

> **TIP** Service level agreements (SLAs) are a valuable tool for focusing management attention on important issues. But don't let your SLA drive you to deliver mediocrity by striving only to meet the stated requirements. Under promise and over deliver. Never promise more than your clients are requesting, but always try to deliver more than they've imagined possible.
>
> Be very careful in negotiating service level agreements that include ad hoc query performance metrics. Don't let yourself agree to an absolute ceiling for ad hoc query times, such as all queries complete in less than ten seconds. You'd be much better off agreeing that 90 percent of queries would complete in less than five seconds. In a system of any size and complexity, it's always possible to write an ad hoc query that exceeds any reasonable maximum.
>
> Clearly specify in the SLA what you mean by important terms, such as query completion. Does this mean on the server side, or does it also include the transport (over a potentially low bandwidth network) to the client? The SLA is a contract between you and your users. You probably don't need to include the legal department on this contract, but you should take it seriously. Your management will take it seriously if you don't maintain service levels.

ETL Processing Performance: Getting Data In

It is straightforward to conduct high level performance testing for the ETL system. The live testing described earlier in this chapter is the basis for the processing performance tests. It's easy to confirm that a certain data volume loads in a certain amount of time. It can be more difficult to identify exactly where in the ETL process you have bottlenecks and opportunities for improvement.

The simplest approach to building a processing system is to serialize the major components. With this approach, all ETL work to the relational database finishes before you begin cube processing, and that completes before you start generating reports. Such a serialized system is easy to performance test and diagnose because the units of work are isolated. You can test and tune each unit separately. Unless your load window is very small or your latency requirements approach real time, you'll probably start off with serialized processing.

It may be possible to design your processing system so that work is parallelized. You need to process shared dimensions before you load facts, but you should be able to load multiple dimensions at the same time. You can make significant improvements in the overall loading time by parallelizing some activities, but this is a much harder system to design and tune. Your performance tests must run on the integrated processing system. All parts of the DW/BI system compete for resources: ETL, the relational database for building indexes and serving queries, the OLAP database for dimension and cube processing, and BI tools for rendering reports. Because of resource contention, you cannot simply test each component separately and sum their processing times. This is true even if the different components are distributed across multiple servers because there's always some burden placed on the upstream servers.

Another issue to consider is confirming that changes made to improve the performance of one part of the system don't negatively impact another part of the system. The classic problem is index and aggregation design. You may want lots of indexes and aggregations for queries to run quickly. But these structures must be maintained, which can place an intolerable burden on the processing performance. Every time a change is considered, evaluate the effects on a complete test system before deploying to production.

Query Performance: Getting Data Out

It's much harder to test query performance, especially ad hoc query performance, than processing performance. The fundamental problem is that you don't know what your users are going to query. You can ask them and get some ideas, but those ideas will be imprecise.

Standard reports are either pre-run and cached, or run on demand. Typically pre-run reports are executed at the end of the ETL processing. The work is more like a processing workload than a query and reporting workload. You may be able to set up your reporting tool to email the results of a pre-run report to the users; doing so shifts the entire burden of report generation to a scheduled time. Alternatively, users might access the pre-run report from the BI portal, in which case there's a modest on-demand element associated with displaying the report. A thorough performance test of pre-run standard reports should simulate the predicted pre-run report usage patterns, such as 500 people accessing the report at random times between 8 a.m. and 9:30 a.m.

A standard report that's executed on demand involves more work. The first demand is on the relational data warehouse or OLAP database to serve up the basic data for the report. Then the BI tool works on that result set to render the report. Finally, the report is distributed, usually across the web to the user's browser window. On-demand reports are often used for parameterized reports, for infrequently accessed reports that don't warrant pre-executing and storing the results, and for reports with low latency. A good performance test for on-demand reports includes a realistic estimate of who is running the reports, when, and with what parameters. In the absence of real world data about how users are running reports, it's difficult to accurately estimate the use of the report cache.

Finally, laboratory tests of ad hoc query performance are fiendishly difficult. The first problem is to know what users are going to want to do. You know your predefined reports and other BI applications, but ad hoc is, well, ad hoc. You have to return to your business requirements document to extract information about analyses. By collecting query text, watch what the early business users and testers are doing with the system. Of course, if you're testing a system that's already in production, you should collect a broad range of queries from the system logs.

One of the biggest challenges in performance testing ad hoc query loads is how to capture the typical analytic experience. The business user issues a query — either an ad hoc query or a standard report — then explores around that data by drilling up, drilling down, and launching new related lines of inquiry. The user will look at a screen of information for a while before deciding where next to go. A good ad hoc query performance and scalability test will consist of sets of related queries separated by user think times. No one said this was going to be easy.

The OLAP database engines, BI tools, and relational database engines all have caches from which similar queries can be served. These caches are valuable because they greatly improve the performance for the common behavior we just discussed: a chain of queries on a related topic. It's really difficult to design query performance and scale tests that take appropriate advantage of caches, without going too far and unrealistically assuming all queries will be resolved from cache.

We have not seen a query testing tool on the market that adequately addresses these behavior patterns.

Usability Testing

Unless you have developed custom user-oriented software as part of your BI solution, usability testing will not be a huge burden. With shrink-wrapped front end BI tools, there are relatively few things you can change. You can typically change the names of things (columns, tables, and reports) and the way they are organized. It's very important that the database structures, reports, and dimension contents are clean and make sense to business users. You often do a lot of usability-oriented testing and cleaning during the process of building the BI applications and reports, as we described in Chapter 12.

You should perform some usability testing with actual business users. As with all usability tests, you need to find fresh minds: people who have not been intimately associated with the project. Walk a few people through the BI portal and the reports, and see what trips them up.

Before your new system goes live, you must have implemented security at the user, role, report, and database levels. If users don't have the correct security permissions set, the system is — from their point of view — completely unusable.

Desktop Readiness and Configuration

The final task in the technical deployment process is to ensure that the business users' desktop machines are ready for the tools and analyses. In our experience, most desktop PCs can handle the rigors of querying, reporting, and analysis. They already support large spreadsheets and desktop databases. In some ways, the BI system actually should reduce the strain on the user's PC by moving most of the data management back to the warehouse servers.

Create a minimum configuration based on the front end tools, the amount of data typically returned, and the complexity of the BI applications. This minimum configuration includes CPU speed, memory, disk space, and maybe monitor size. It should also indicate the base computer type and operating system supported. We've been in organizations that insist on supporting multiple operating systems on users' desktops: Windows, Apple, Linux, and UNIX. Obviously, this diversity has a big impact on the architecture and tool selection long before you get to deployment.

When you go out into the user community, consider the following issues:

- **Connectivity:** Connectivity is not usually an issue in today's highly networked organizations, but there could be a problem getting from one part of the organization to another. For example, a remote field office may not have the appropriate network configuration to get to the data warehouse server. Bandwidth to the desktop is usually not an issue either, but it's worth verifying. You may have some sales reps who work from the road with poor connections. If they are working with large datasets, their user experience may be disappointing. If you know about the problem, you can at least set expectations, even if you can't fix it.

- **Installation:** Some front end BI tools are desktop based and need software installed on the user's machine. Most are now browser-based and do not need local software installed. Be careful, however, because some of the browser-based tools actually download a "plug-in" that runs on the local PC. This can lead to version problems with the client software. Test the installation process from a selection of user machines and document any problems. If the installation process is anything more than clicking a button on the DW/BI website, make sure you document it clearly in a set of installation instructions.

Speaking of version problems, even the completely browser-based clients can have significant problems with older versions of Internet browsers, and may only support a few browser products. The required products and versions should be part of the minimum configuration document.

Deployment

Your first deployment of a new system on new hardware is effectively free. Most organizations use the production system for testing and even user training before the new system goes live. You can think of the deployment process in this simple case as nothing more than an email — sending a message when the system has passed all tests and is ready to go live.

After that first deployment, it gets a lot harder. Any modifications to the system — and there are always modifications — should be accomplished with minimal disruption to the business user community. The only way to do this is to:

- Perform testing on a test system that's as similar to the production system as possible.

- Where possible, use scripts rather than clicking through a user interface. Any time you need to open a tool and click through a wizard, you open the possibility of doing the wrong thing.

- Develop a deployment process playbook that describes exactly what to do and in what order. This is especially vital if you can't simply run a script but instead must do something within a tool.

- Test the playbook on the test system before trying it on production.

Relational Database Deployment

There are several ways to deploy a relational database from test to production. The easiest, of course, is to declare the test system to be production (email deployment).

If you want to deploy the entire database for a brand new system, you could use backup and restore. You'd need to modify the restore script to move the data files to the correct location on the production server, if your test server is configured differently.

If you are modifying an existing relational data warehouse by adding a new subject area, the process is much the same. Generate CREATE scripts for the new tables and associated objects, such as indexes and views. If these are truly additions, the impact of creating new empty objects in the production system should be zero (but test it first!).

Over time, you'll surely modify existing tables somewhat. This is a trickier proposition, because if you ALTER a table you run a risk of breaking the existing ETL processes. Certainly you can mitigate this risk by thorough testing on your test system.

During the development process for a significant change, your developers may be creating multiple ALTER scripts for a table. For example, they may alter the table to add a new column, then later change the datatype for that new column, and finally create some additional new columns. There are some excellent tools available to help you manage changes to database structures. If you don't use a tool, you need to develop procedures to track and consolidate these multiple ALTER scripts.

TIP You can find tools to help manage database structure changes by searching the web for *SQL Compare*.

After you generate the CREATE or ALTER scripts, you may need to modify the location of data files. Ideally, your test system is configured like your production system, so running the scripts on the test system is an excellent test. If the systems are configured differently, test the scripts as much as possible, and document what is different and what to verify during the production run.

TIP Recall from Chapter 8 that we recommended you always build a layer of views to abstract access to the relational tables. This view layer can provide valuable flexibility for modifying the production system in steps, keeping the old table and view around until you're confident that you can safely switch over to the new structure.

You may want to bring data from test to production, without taking the draconian step of using a full database restore. In this case, you can build a simple ETL module to copy the data from test to production for the subset of tables.

TIP The deployment playbook for deploying a new relational database, or modifications to an existing database, should include the following:

- Any edits to SQL scripts, such as editing file locations or database names. It's far safer to parameterize these changes, but writing the scripts is a lot more complicated if you do so.

- Create any static data in the new database, including a new small dimension or some metadata.

- If edits are made directly in scripts, provide some mechanism for verifying that the edits were done correctly. At the very least, advise the operator to search for specific phrases that should have been changed during the editing process.

- Run command for any scripts, such as SQL scripts, including any parameters used in the script execution.

- ETL programs that will load data into some or all tables.

- Scripts or instructions to verify that all completed correctly.

ETL Deployment

The ETL system sits in the middle of the DW/BI system. It's particularly important to test the ETL system deployment process: in other words, the steps that you will take to deploy the ETL system from test to production. You'll need to test that all necessary components were copied to the target server and that all connections are set up correctly.

TIP The deployment playbook for deploying an ETL module should include the following:

- Location of the ETL system files to be copied to the production server.

- Where to copy the ETL files to.

- Instructions, if any, for installing the ETL program files, including all dialog box choices.

- Instructions for creating any operating system global variables that the ETL module uses.

- Scripts or instructions to verify that all completed correctly.

OLAP Database Deployment

The specific techniques for deploying an OLAP database depend on your chosen OLAP technology. You can always deploy a new OLAP database by copying over the metadata files that define that database, and then fully processing the database on the production server. You can probably process the database on the test server, and use some kind of backup/restore mechanism to move the metadata and data to the production server, but check your OLAP tool's documentation for details.

As ever, the process of deploying incremental changes in the structure of an OLAP database is a much greater challenge. An unfortunate characteristic of

OLAP is that modifications in cube structure are relatively likely to result in a significant reprocessing effort. For example, it's possible that a change in the structure of a dimension might require full processing of all portions of the OLAP database that subscribe to that dimension. If significant reprocessing is necessary to deploy a structural change, you may consider processing the database on one server and then copying it to the production server, assuming your OLAP tool will let you do that.

Report Deployment

Deploying a new report is easy compared to changing a database or ETL module. With a new DW/BI project, you will likely develop the initial suite of reports on a test server, ideally against a complete set of data. As soon as the production server is populated, migrate any existing reports, and continue report development on the production server.

You will modify and create reports far more often than you'll modify the underlying databases. All reports should be tested before they're released to the user community. The most important tests are to ensure the report definitions are accurate. Complex reports that access a lot of data should be tested for performance. You may need to write a stored procedure to generate the report's dataset as efficiently as possible.

Most companies develop and test new reports in a private area of the production report server, rather than set up a completely separate test instance of the BI tool. Standard reports don't change data, so you don't need to worry about damaging the databases.

As you may expect, the hardest part of deploying reports isn't technical but political. The greatest challenge is to create policies and procedures that enable your business community to contribute new reports and analyses, while maintaining the appropriate level of control over published reports. You should develop a quality assurance process and procedures for publishing reports to a broad audience. This is particularly important for highly regulated companies.

NOTE Sometimes changes to the underlying databases will require that existing reports be modified. Earlier in this chapter we stressed the importance of end-to-end testing for any significant modifications to the DW/BI system. It's important that the standard report suite be tested before database changes are moved into production. It's usually easy to fix reports in response to a schema change, but if you forget this step, the user experience is the same as if you messed up the underlying data. From their point of view, the DW/BI system is broken. Also, any change that breaks a standard report will likely break user reports as well. If you are implementing these kinds of changes, notify your users early and discuss what they will need to do to deal with the changes. You may want to set up a user report migration project to help rewrite the key user reports.

Documentation and Training

One would hope that business users are able to use the new system without a lot of documentation and training. After all, you spent a lot of time and trouble organizing and naming things in a sensible way. In our experience, the business users do need some guidance about the new features and resources. But developing good user-oriented system documentation isn't difficult; most of the documentation is metadata dressed up in presentable clothes. If you've been capturing metadata all along, much of this effort is to create a nice front end for users to access that metadata.

As we detailed in Chapters 11 and 12, the BI portal is the organization's single source for reporting and analysis and associated information. The main content of the BI portal will be the navigation hierarchy and standard reports. Around the edges of the main BI portal page, users should find links to the documentation and tools described here.

Core Documentation

The data is the first thing to document. Describe the business process subject areas including facts and dimensions, and the tables, columns, calculations, and other rules that make up those subject areas. Document the standard reports and other BI applications, though their documentation is often integrated with the reports themselves.

Business Process Dimensional Model Descriptions

The starting point for most BI documentation is the business process dimensional model. Write a clear, succinct description of each dimensional model in the system. For example, if order processing was the initial row selected on the bus matrix, you need a document that describes the orders subject area by answering questions such as:

- What is the nature of the business process captured in this data?
- What are the salient business rules?
- What is the grain of the fact table?
- What date range of data is included in the fact table?
- What data has been left out (and why)?
- What dimensions participate in this business process? Many of the dimensions will need their own descriptive documents that this document can link to.

This document should have a few screen captures that show the target schema in a graphical form (like the high level model diagram described in

Chapter 7), some example values, and a few reports to demonstrate the kinds of business questions it can address.

Table and Column Descriptions

Once people have a general understanding of a particular schema, they need to be able to drill down into the details, table by table and column by column. This is where the descriptive metadata captured when you were building the initial target model comes back into service. The table name, column names, descriptions, sample values, and even the overall comments will be helpful to a user trying to understand the contents of the table in question.

If you have a rich set of table and column metadata stored in a queryable database, write several reports for users to browse that information. A table-level report with drilldown to information about columns may be all the documentation that users need.

OLAP databases are largely self-documenting, especially if you've gone to the trouble of populating all descriptive fields. The front end query tools display the structures of dimensions, hierarchies, and facts as part of the user interface for constructing a query. In addition to that interface, see if your OLAP tool vendor can provide a web-based interface to browse the structure of the OLAP cube.

Report Descriptions

Each report must have a base set of descriptive information as part of the standard template described in Chapter 12. You can include some of this information, like the report title and description, in the report definition. Other information will need to be captured in the metadata repository. In particular, the navigation framework for the BI portal and assignment of individual reports to categories and groups are critical parts of helping people understand the information available. These category assignments should follow the same organizing framework used to present the reports in the BI portal. In fact, this metadata could be used to dynamically create the portal interface.

Additional Documentation

Data and report documentation are certainly the most commonly used, but other documentation is also important. The most valuable additional documentation comes in the form of online tutorials, support guides, and a list of colleagues who use the system and may be able to help.

As we discuss later in this chapter, you should develop and deliver training to the business users. Consider posting an annotated version of the classroom materials on the BI portal.

A support guide will help your business users know whom to call when they have a problem. You should list the escalation hierarchy with contact names, email addresses, and phone numbers. Knowing who else is trained can guide users to people close by who may be able to help them. Keep a current list of users available on the BI portal with an indicator showing which users are designated analytic support power users and which users have at least had ad hoc tool training.

User Training

One of the main purposes of the BI applications is to provide access to the data in the warehouse to the 80 to 90 percent of the organization who will never learn to query the data directly. Unfortunately, the remaining business users will never learn either, unless you teach them. Offer classes that will help users climb the learning curve to master both the ad hoc tool and underlying data. While you're at it, even though the BI applications should be self-guiding, offer a short class to everyone who will be using the BI applications, even if they never touch the ad hoc tool.

Teaching advanced users to directly query the warehouse breaks down into two phases: development and delivery. Development is all of the work it takes to design the curriculum and create the training materials. Delivery is the actual classroom presentation of the materials and exercises, and the web-based delivery of the materials.

You'll have to develop most of the training materials because the most important thing to teach the users is the unique characteristics of your data and environment. No tool vendor can supply you with this kind of material. You can probably find an external expert to develop and deliver the curriculum, but we favor assigning the task to someone on the front room BI team. A front room team member should have the necessary expertise with the data and systems. The same characteristics that make someone an effective front room team member — empathy for the business users' point of view — make them a good choice as a trainer. Finally, the training class itself is a good opportunity to develop critical business relationships.

You need to start developing the business user training after the database is stable and front end tools have been selected, but long enough before the actual rollout begins to be able to create and test a solid set of course materials. The DW/BI educator might also need to create supporting materials and a training database.

Design and Approach

Before you actually sit down to write the training materials, spend a few minutes thinking at a high level about who your audiences are, what skill levels they have, and how much they will be using the tools. This will help you determine your overall curriculum: What classes will you offer and how they relate to each other. The initial system rollout usually requires two classes: an introductory ad hoc query class that might last a day or two and a short BI applications class that may only last an hour or two. After the system has been in use for a few months, offer an advanced techniques class for ad hoc users. It may also be useful to provide a separate, data-centric class for each new business process subject area added to the data warehouse.

Part of the design process includes outlining each class, as shown in Figure 13-1 for an ad hoc query class. The outline will evolve during development, testing, and delivery of the class based on the reality of what it takes to teach people, and how long it takes them to learn.

Develop Training Materials

It's surprisingly difficult to create high quality course materials for hands-on training. Many of the classic communications principles apply. Each module

Time	Content
	Introduction
15	DW / BI system overview
10	Goals of the class
5	Student expectations
	Tool overview
5	Demo basic elements and user interface
10	Demo the query building process
20	Exercise 1—Simple query
15	Break
	Querying multiple tables
10	Demo: Constructing a query from multiple tables
25	Exercise 2—Simple multi-table query
10	Review and questions
	Calculations and formatting
15	Demo: Creating a calculated column with conditional formatting
30	Exercise 3—Report formatting and calculations
10	Review and questions
60	Lunch
	Working with query templates
15	Demo: Using, modifying, and saving query templates
60	Exercise 4—Sales over time
15	Review and questions
15	Break
	Working with reports
15	Demo: Saving, scheduling and sharing reports
30	Exercise 5—Saving and scheduling reports
15	Review and questions
75	*Exercise 6—Self-paced problem set*

Figure 13-1 Introductory one-day ad hoc query course outline.

should be short enough to finish within the average adult attention span of 45 minutes to an hour. Each module should follow the same structure, beginning with a summary of the lesson and the key points the student should learn from the module. The body of the module should use a relevant business problem as the motivation for working through the material. For example, learning how to count the number of customers who responded to a new promotion would be more interesting than learning how to count the number of rows in a system table, even if the two exercises teach exactly the same concept. The exercises should be well illustrated with screen captures that look exactly like what the students will see on their computers.

The modules should become progressively more complex, with the early ones providing step-by-step instructions and the later ones offering higher-level guidance. This gives the students the opportunity to memorize the basic steps so they can create a report without having to be prompted. Near the end of the class, students should be able to handle an instruction like "set up the following query:" followed by a screen capture of a completed query. Include bonus exercises at the end of each module to keep the quick learners occupied.

Create a Training Database

It's nice to design the courses to work directly against the production data warehouse database. When users return to their desks, they can see exactly the same environment they used in class. However, it's equally common to create a training database. A small, static training database means that screenshots in exercises will always match what people see when they do the exercise. A training database can mask confidential data and ensure consistent query performance.

Create the training database as early in the course development process as possible with a representative dataset that reflects the world people will be returning to when they leave class.

Make sure to teach the content of the training database as part of the first module. If the training is highly specific to an in-house business process, add a complete data content module at the beginning of the class. In the long run, successful use of a BI tool is 50 percent data knowledge and 50 percent tool knowledge.

Plan for the Level of Effort

Creating a good training class takes a lot of work. You should count on at least eight hours of work to create an hour of class materials. A one-day class will take about a week and a half to two weeks of hard work for someone with experience developing course materials. If this is your first time, you should expand the estimate to give you more time to research other examples of good materials and test the materials you create.

Maintenance and Support

The tasks required to keep your DW/BI system operating in great shape are not difficult, but you need to plan and build for a maintainable system from the outset. If you've waited until the testing and deployment phase to start thinking about backups, ongoing performance tuning, and user support, it's too late. Your system is at great risk for hitting a snag and taking a lot of user goodwill and trust with it. When deadlines are looming and users are clamoring for data and reports, it's too late to start designing your operating procedures.

Both the front room and back room have maintenance activities that you must plan for. In the front room, develop procedures and mechanisms for communicating with the users, handling users' questions, and managing security. The back room team should set in place their plans for running the ETL jobs, monitoring resources, conducting ongoing performance tuning, and backing up and recovering vital data.

Unfortunately, many CIOs presume that the size of their DW/BI team will halve when the new system goes into production. This is an unrealistic expectation for two reasons. First, a successful data warehouse is always undergoing change, so there will always be some development effort. Secondly, even in the absence of change, you should expect to see resources shift from back room development to front room support. As much as we want the data warehouse to be self-servicing, you realistically need to plan for ongoing user-oriented support. In our experience, the data warehouse team remains the same size — or even grows — once the program moves into production.

Manage the Front Room

We detail the primary tasks of the front room operations team in the following sections.

Provide User Support

A well designed and implemented DW/BI system is much easier to use than a poorly designed one, but it's still not easy. The DW/BI team will need to provide ongoing support to its user community. We recommend a three-tiered support approach. The first tier is the website and self-service support; the second tier is your power users in the business groups; the third tier is front end people on the DW/BI team.

NOTE You can't rely on the existing IT help desk to provide much support for the DW/BI users. At best, we've found that help desk personnel can help solve connectivity problems. For real help, you need to have business users talk to someone who understands the business problems, data content, and BI tool and applications. Having your users reinstall the software is not going to cut it.

■ **Tier One: Website.** Having great content and the tools to find it (navigation, search, and metadata browser) are fundamental to providing support through the website. It helps to have a brief demo of the website in every class to show people where to go for help. You will still get calls from people who could have easily found the answer themselves, but decided it was easier to call you. If the answer is on the website, walk them through the steps to find it. Once they become aware of the help that's available and comfortable with how to find it, they will be more likely to help themselves first next time.

■ **Tier Two: Power Users.** If a user needs help creating an ad hoc query, or needs a specific report that doesn't already exist, they need to talk to someone with the skills to help. Set the expectation that this initial contact should be with someone who is based in the business, hopefully in the person's department. We call this support contact the *power user*. The power user has strong ad hoc query skills, a deep knowledge of the contents of the data warehouse, and a sense for the business issues that can only come from working in the business. The key to creating this support structure is setting expectations with senior management and the power users early on. This role should become part of the power user's job description and performance reviews. They should view themselves as the local pros and should encourage people to ask for help. You need to foster this sense of association with the DW/BI system by treating the power users well. We've talked about the various points throughout the process where the experts provide input and guidance. All of this involvement serves to emphasize the importance of their role. You must take seriously the task of nurturing these relationships.

■ **Tier Three: DW/BI Team.** When the website and local experts are unable to solve the problem, the DW/BI team should offer a support resource of last resort. The front end team actually has responsibilities across all support tiers. They own the DW/BI website and must maintain and enhance its content. They own the relationships with and the training of the power users. And they must provide direct support to the users when needed. This list of responsibilities represents a significant amount of work. Plan on having as many DW/BI team members dedicated to these front room tasks as you had focused on the back room — in an eight person DW/BI team, for example, at least four people will be dedicated to front room responsibilities.

NOTE In some larger organizations, the BI portion of the DW/BI team is split off from the data warehouse resources to become its own entity. We believe the DW/BI system is so closely tied to the business that splitting the two is like what happens when a cartoon character gets cut in half: The bottom half can't see where it's going, and the top half has lost its mobility. It's important to dedicate

people to the front end responsibilities, but separating them out into their own organization is generally not productive in the long run.

As we described in Chapter 12, the BI applications should be self-supporting, with pull-down menus, pick lists, and help screens. However, the BI team will need to monitor their usage, maintain them as the data and data structures change, and extend and enhance them as additional data becomes available. The BI team will also need to provide a means for users to give feedback on existing BI applications and request new ones.

Many IT organizations began building their DW/BI systems with the goal of letting users create their own reports. The real goal was more self-serving — the IT folks wanted to get off the report generation treadmill. Unfortunately, while this treadmill may slow down a bit, it never goes away. Even though accessing data is easier, the majority of knowledge workers do not have the time or interest to learn how to meet all their own information needs from scratch. The BI team will need to include creating custom reports in its responsibilities list, and make sure there are resources available to meet the most important requests. The good news is that these custom reports can almost always be turned into parameterized standard reports and integrated into the existing BI application set.

Maintain the BI Portal

The BI portal described in Chapters 11 and 12 is a useful place to publish information about the BI system. Here's an additional set of operations and maintenance information that should go on the portal:

- Data warehouse status: what is the most recent day of data for each business process.
- Schedules of planned outages.
- Honest and complete status of any unplanned outages.
- Clear warnings to users about problems in the system, such as data quality issues. Include an honest and complete assessment of when the problems will be fixed. Users should have access to the audit dimension, described in Chapter 9, to judge the quality and reliability of their data.
- The system's current operational status, including:
  - How many queries have been answered in the last hour.
  - How many reports have been generated.
  - Current number of active users.
  - On demand report of active queries, including how long they've been running and who's running them.

- Proof points about the system's capacity to foster user confidence in the system:
  - How long the last data load took.
  - How big was the largest data load and how long it took.
  - Maximum count of simultaneous users.

As we discuss in Chapter 14, every twelve to eighteen months, you should review the entire DW/BI system. Evaluate what's working well for the users and what should change. Remember, change is inevitable; it's a sign of a healthy DW/BI system. As part of this periodic evaluation, consider refreshing the look, layout, and content of the BI portal.

Manage Security

Security should be implemented at the database level, both relational and OLAP, as well as in the BI application. Most user access will come through structured BI applications, including the reporting system. Part of the security manager's ongoing responsibilities is to ensure that reports and other BI applications are correctly secured. You may want to review the security discussion in Chapter 5 for alternatives and recommendations.

Most reporting tools have a reasonably intuitive user interface for managing roles and privileges. It may even be possible for you to distribute a piece of the security management to the business units. A power user in a business unit could be granted privileges to manage security for reports developed for and by that business unit.

Security that's implemented in the database itself is usually handled by the DW/BI security manager. Although the database engines include basic tools for defining security, some organizations write a custom application to help the security manager synchronize roles across the operating system, relational database, and OLAP database. A relatively simple custom tool can greatly reduce the burden, and potential errors, in managing security.

Monitor Usage

The usage of your DW/BI system has a huge impact on its performance. You should always be collecting counts of queries run and rows returned by type of application. You will need to develop a monitoring system that combines measures that are output by the operating system, as well as those output by the database and BI application software.

You also should collect sample queries. Sample queries will help you tune system performance with new indexes or aggregations. You may also be able to identify training opportunities by seeing what strange queries your users are putting together.

Some organizations collect the text of all queries submitted to the system, or at least all ad hoc queries. This is actually a lot of data, and is probably overkill unless you have a compliance mandate for collecting such information. By collecting all queries, all the time, you're placing a non-trivial performance burden on the system. And your logging database will grow to be quite large. A reasonable alternative is to turn on query text logging only occasionally, for example from 1 p.m. to 3 p.m. daily or even weekly.

At the very least, you should log information about which users are logging in to the system, including the BI portal, any BI applications, and user-authenticated logins to the databases. It's also a good practice to log query execution — who is issuing a query and how long the query takes. As we've described, the text of the query is extraordinarily valuable, but it may be too expensive in terms of storage to collect it all.

Report on Usage

Your BI portal website should devote a small amount of screen real estate to reporting on system usage. VPs and directors are often very interested in how much their staff is using your system. They tend to be competitive people; simply seeing another department using the DW/BI system has been known to spur a VP to encourage his or her staff to use the system more. So a time series of reporting and ad hoc use by department is a good report to publish.

The BI team should also know who is doing what with the system, how much, and when. This information is imperative for performance tuning, as well as identifying problem areas and users whose skills may be leveraged more broadly. If you're monitoring the text of ad hoc queries, you should communicate with business users what, how often, and why you're monitoring their use, what you plan to do with the information, and who has access to that information. This isn't a big deal; just put a few sentences in the informational document for new users.

Manage the Back Room

Back room system management encompasses several components, including data reconciliation support, ETL system execution and monitoring, resource monitoring, data growth and disk space management, performance tuning, and backup and recovery.

The more automated you can make your DW/BI systems management, the better. At the very least, you should automate backups and the execution of the ETL system to populate the data warehouse and OLAP databases. Your relational database provides management tools; many third party database management tools are also available. There's no excuse for not implementing some system automation.

Unlike other issues where we've mentioned how small teams might cut corners, organizations of any size benefit from system automation. Indeed, the smallest organizations are perhaps least equipped to apply human resources to a problem that can be automated. It's hard to imagine how a DW/BI team of one to three people could possibly operate without significant automation.

The ideal management system requires no human intervention except for the occasional troubleshooting. Such a system automatically adds and drops partitions, checks for disk space, reports on performance problems or unusual usage, and corrects the vast majority of data oddities during the ETL process.

No matter how automated your operations are, you must have a plan. Like all plans, your operations plan should be written down.

Support Data Reconciliation

Data quality verification and reconciliation must occur prior to any user access. However, some data errors might slip through the net. As you define your support strategy, be sure to earmark resources for data reconciliation shortly after deployment.

Especially when previously reported information is found to be incorrect, it may require some digging to help the users fully comprehend the inaccuracies surrounding information that they had been using for years to run their business. For example, it's quite possible that historical reporting was based on a series of flags tied to the customer, product, or account file. The logic behind the flag setting has probably become convoluted over time. We've worked on many projects where the historical reporting was incorrect due to error-prone data entry or misinterpretation of the flags within a report. Over the years, bonuses have been paid, product strategies implemented, and customer retention plans initiated on the basis of this erroneously reported information. It may take some doing to convince your users that they've been using faulty information to support management decisions in the past.

The quality assurance analysts assigned to data reconciliation require a broad set of skills. They will need access to the data warehouse, as well as to the source systems or production reports. It is also helpful to have a solid understanding of the data transformation process.

Execute and Monitor the ETL System

The ETL system, as we described in Chapters 9 and 10, should be designed to operate each night without human intervention. In general, the ETL system should be bullet-proof and fix foreseeable errors automatically. This is particularly true in systems that reduce latency by loading data intraday. There just isn't time for someone to step in and do something on an ongoing basis.

Not all data errors are foreseeable. You may have designed your ETL system to log all error conditions to an error event table as described in Chapter 9.

If your ETL system includes a path to identify data rows in an error table, it's imperative that you develop and follow procedures to research and fix those error rows as soon as possible. Ideally, the ETL system will send an alert to a DW team member at the same time as it places rows in an error table.

A quick glance at a time series of error rates can provide valuable insight about data or process problems. Because you have a reporting infrastructure in place, send a data quality report in a daily or weekly email to the back room team members.

Monitor Resources

You need to implement and understand two types of monitoring. First, what's going on in your system? What system resources such as memory are being used, when, and by what processes? If you don't monitor system events and resource usage, you'll never be able to troubleshoot and tune your system. The other kind of monitoring focuses on the users: Who's accessing the system, and when? What queries are they running and how much time are those queries taking? If you don't know what your users are doing, you'll never be able to satisfy them.

Currently, the DW/BI vendors do an adequate job of providing tools to monitor resource usage for each component of the DW/BI system, including the databases, ETL system, and BI applications. Unless you purchase all of your technology from a single vendor, you're unlikely to have great, consistent, and integrated monitoring tools that combine information from the multiple components.

In addition to integrating information from the different DW/BI components, you may need to combine information even within a component. Often, there is some information that you monitor at the operating system level, and other information that you extract from each tool's profile or logging system. A large organization will end up building a monitoring database that combines all this information so it can easily be consumed and analyzed.

Part of your operations plan should be to establish a baseline performance profile for your system. It is orders of magnitude easier to fix a performance problem in the future if you've kept track of how the system performed over time.

The most important measures to track in your performance baseline are pretty obvious: the usage of memory, processors, and disk. Plan to monitor your production servers all the time, perhaps at 15 minute intervals. Store the monitored information in a database.

In addition to the ongoing monitoring, it's really useful to create a fine-grained baseline on a monthly basis. This baseline will differ from the ongoing monitoring by sampling performance more frequently, say at 5 second intervals.

You should ramp up the logging frequency just before kicking off ETL processing and return to normal levels as soon as the ETL job completes. The standard baseline of 10–15 minute logging frequency is entirely inadequate for diagnosing performance problems within the ETL system.

Manage Disk Space

One of the most common reasons for ETL job failure is one of the easiest to prevent: running out of disk space.

At the very minimum, set up an alert in the operating system to warn when free space on each disk falls below a certain threshold. Set up two alerts: one to warn when you're within a month of running out of disk space, and one to blare stridently when you're about a week away.

How do you know what level of free space to check for? Focus on the big files that you accumulate:

- **Staging files for fact table extracts.** Some organizations keep the fact table extract files online forever, for restartability, recoverability, or regulatory reasons. Others keep less than 30 days online, and back up the rest. If you keep a set number of extracts on disk, consider the growth in monthly data volumes. Make a conservative guess and then make an entry in your operations plan to re-check this guess periodically.

- **Relational database filegroups, including temp space.** You should monitor the logical disks on which your database files are located.

- **OLAP databases, including temp space.** Make sure you understand the disk space requirements for OLAP processing. Sometimes you need significantly more disk space to support processing than the data consumes once the processing is complete.

It's almost universally true that the incremental disk space you'll be using each month goes to fact data storage, whether in the file system, relational database, or OLAP database. Most dimensions are relatively small and static in size, at least compared to fact tables.

Tune for Performance

You should have done performance tuning as part of the deployment and testing process when you initially moved your system into production. It's inevitable that system usage will evolve over time, as business users grow more experienced with the system, and of course as the business itself evolves.

Develop a plan, and assign resources, to conduct ongoing performance tuning on a regular schedule, be it quarterly, semi-annually, or annually. You must collect enough system and database statistics to understand how system usage and performance is changing over time. A simple report on key statistics, including query counts and average execution time, will help you evaluate if your system's performance is deteriorating. Ideally, you will identify and fix problems before your business users notice.

Backup and Recovery

No matter the availability requirements for your system, you need a backup and recovery plan. This seems like an intuitively obvious statement, but we've seen DW/BI systems that purported to be in production, but had no backup plan.

It's as important to have a recovery plan as it is to have a backup plan. And it's equally important to test these procedures. When the inevitable emergency happens, you want to be ready, practiced, and calm. Go through the drill of recovering the database at least once. Take extensive notes about what information you need to have and where to find it. Database recovery is like public speaking; most people hate it, but if you have to do it, you'll be much more capable if you practice first. Your test system is an ideal platform for testing these procedures. If you haven't fully tested your recovery procedures, you're lying to yourself and your management that you have a real backup and recovery plan.

In the DW/BI world, you can experience the same kinds of emergencies as transaction systems, from server outages and disk failures to earthquakes and floods. You also need to plan for your daily or monthly load cycle to break down occasionally. You may hope this will never happen, and you will develop your ETL system so that it's fairly unlikely. But let's face it: the data warehouse is at the end of a long train of data flows over which you have no control. Only a foolish DW/BI manager would neglect to plan for backing out a bad load. The auditing system described in Chapter 9 lays the foundation for identifying the rows that were changed during a specific load process.

The relational databases are usually the most vital sets of information to back up regularly. Ideally, back up the following databases after each load:

- Relational data warehouse databases
- Staging databases
- Staging data in the file system
- Metadata databases

You also need to set up a regular schedule to back up the data warehouse logging databases.

Your backup and recovery strategies are intertwined with the database technology you're using. Most systems use the standard database backup facilities for relational backup and recovery. The relational database is usually quite large, and so it's often challenging to run a backup at the end of each nightly load cycle. There are several alternatives:

- Store the data warehouse data on a storage area network (SAN) and use the SAN software to perform the backup. The SAN backup techniques are high performance. This approach has been a common practice for very large data warehouses.

- Partition the large fact tables, and set aged partitions to be read-only. Perform occasional full backups, but rely primarily on a strategy of partial and partial differential backups.

The logging database is written to constantly; it's more like a transactional database than a data warehouse database. Some DW/BI teams think the logging data is vitally important, and implement a very strong backup strategy. Other teams are sanguine about the notion of losing a week's worth of logging data, and manage the database far more loosely. Obviously, if your logging data contains usage data necessary for regulatory compliance, you need to develop a serious backup and recovery strategy.

Approaches differ on backup and recovery strategies for the staging databases. Many teams think of the data in the staging tables as ephemeral, and back up only the table CREATE scripts. On the other hand, most staging databases contain only data for the most recent loads — for example, the last seven days — so a full database backup is really fast.

You may have built a simple application for business users to manipulate custom hierarchies or other dimension attributes. This application is a transaction system, however small scale. Typically you want the application to write directly to a different database than the data warehouse, one with full recovery mode and log backups. Similarly, the metadata database should also be treated more like a transactional database than the large data warehouse database.

Understand how your BI components leverage the relational database. Your ETL tool, OLAP database, reporting tool, or job scheduler may each store information in the relational database. These should all be backed up consistently. If your ETL tool doesn't store all its information in the relational database, make sure you have a system in place to back up the definitions of the modules.

If you are using an OLAP database as part of your DW/BI system, you need to carefully evaluate your backup and recovery options. In our experience, OLAP databases have been weaker in this area than relational databases. Most offer a mechanism to back up the OLAP database, but that mechanism may not be practical for very large data volumes; you may need to implement a file-based backup mechanism or use a SAN-based strategy. You should treat the definition of the OLAP database — the database metadata — as a key corporate asset. Worst case, you could always reprocess the OLAP database, even if that takes several days. It's important to always keep up-to-date backups of the OLAP metadata.

Long Term Archiving

Most enterprises have some data that for legal or compliance reasons must be archived for very long periods, perhaps many years. The challenge, of course, is how to choose an archive strategy that will last that long. Most physical media, including tape storage, CDs, and DVDs, are not assured of being viable after many years of storage. Even if the media are readable, very few data formats are guaranteed to be readable twenty or fifty years from now. And finally, if an application is required to interpret the data, what system does it run on?

Although complete answers to these questions are beyond the scope of this book, we recommend a two part strategy for very long term archiving:

1. Instead of betting on any single physical media technology, you should plan on a periodic program of migrating and refreshing. Every three years, for instance, make sure that the data can be read and that it is stored on the most current media of the day. In today's environment, it makes sense to leave much archived data on disk drives.

2. Encapsulate your current application run time environment on a virtual machine. Archive that virtual machine image, and subject it to the migrate and refresh cycle. Although the ability to run a virtual machine is itself subject to obsolescence, this approach has the best chance of avoiding ancient applications, operating systems, and hardware.

Conclusion

Successful deployment and operation of the DW/BI system requires thoughtful planning and coordination prior to the completion of development efforts. The first area to focus on is technical: testing the application and moving components from development to test to production.

A solid testing process includes different kinds of tests, including data quality assurance, operations process, performance, usability, and deployment testing. Only after you've completely tested the system are you ready to deploy. Deployment is usually straightforward for a new system, but can be a very delicate dance for modifications to an existing system in production.

Testing and deploying the technical bits are only half the story. You also need to focus on desktop installation, integrated user education, and support. Once the system is in production, you'll need ongoing support teams. The front room team will provide user support, including answering questions and delivering ongoing training, maintaining the BI portal, managing security, and monitoring usage. Meanwhile, the back room team will support data reconciliation, execute and monitor the ETL system, monitor resources including disk space, conduct performance tuning, and manage ongoing backups.

BLUEPRINT FOR ACTION

Managing the Effort and Reducing Risk

The greatest risk associated with deploying and supporting the DW/BI system is to under invest in the effort, or start worrying about the issues too late in the process. The issues that surround a solid deployment and ongoing operations aren't very exciting, especially compared to gathering business requirements and developing the dimensional model. Most CIOs are reluctant to believe that the team required for ongoing operations is about the same size as the team that developed the system in the first place.

The initial deployment of a new DW/BI system is usually low risk. You have plenty of time to test functionality and performance before notifying the users that the new system is open for business. The greatest deployment risk for a new DW/BI system is failing to honestly assess your readiness to deploy. Don't allow a pre-determined deployment date to blindly override the realities of your readiness.

But change is inevitable for a healthy system, and deploying a significant change requires expert management with a commitment to quality control. Get professional testing help, and supplement those testers with people in other roles on the team, including the front room team. Don't rely on the developers to design and execute the system tests for the components they developed. Most importantly, plan for, document, and test the process of deploying a change in advance of the actual event. Leave nothing to chance!

The user-oriented pieces of the deployment puzzle are generally low risk, assuming you make the investment in creating documentation and training materials. You can improve the quality of the training materials by using resources from outside the team, perhaps a corporate training unit or training consultant. The best role for these experts is to advise on the format and structure of the materials; the best training and documentation will be developed by the front room team members themselves.

Once the DW/BI system is in production, it needs considerable care and support. The front room operations, including support, communication, portal enhancements, and security management, require a larger team than many organizations anticipate. Make sure the CIO and business sponsor are prepared for the staffing requirements. The back room maintenance should be as automated as possible. You will need some staff to pursue and correct data quality problems, monitor the system, and conduct ongoing performance testing.

(continued)

Assuring Quality

The deployment and support efforts are all about assuring quality. The development and quality assurance teams must be committed to a smooth deployment, especially of changes to a system already in production. Even if your DW/BI system doesn't have requirements for high availability, users' confidence is damaged by extensive downtime. High quality training and documentation materials present a professional image of the DW/BI system. Senior business people will be using these materials; don't misspell words or make grammatical errors. One of the best ways to ensure quality of automated system operations is to have the developers on call when things go wrong.

Key Roles

Keys roles for deployment and ongoing operations include:

- The lead tester is responsible for developing and overseeing the testing plan, developing the testing methodology, choosing testing tools, and coordinating the activities of all the testers.

- The quality assurance analyst is in charge of most pre-deployment testing, including functional tests, tests of the deployment process, and the vital data quality tests.

- The database administrator is responsible for performance testing and tuning, both before deployment and during ongoing operations.

- The data warehouse educator's responsibilities are front and center now with the development and delivery of business user education courses.

- The project manager and business project lead determine the structure and staffing of the user support organization, based on direction and feedback from management and the project sponsors.

Key Deliverables

Key deliverables for deployment and ongoing support include:

- Test plan: test methodology, testing tools, test scripts, and test datasets.

- System deployment playbook: detailed instructions on exactly how to move the new system from the test to the production environment. The deployment playbook is especially vital when you're making changes to a system that's already in production.

(continued)

BLUEPRINT FOR ACTION *(continued)*

◆ Business user documentation, leveraging documentation and/or metadata that was developed throughout the Lifecycle.

◆ Training materials and database.

◆ Operations plan: database maintenance activities and schedule, backup and restore strategy.

◆ Front room support plan: staffing plan for a help desk (if any), user-facing BI analysts on the DW/BI team, and power users in the business user community. The front room support team is usually responsible for maintaining the BI portal as well.

Estimating Considerations

Planning for pre-deployment testing should begin with the ETL developers, who develop unit tests for the functionality of the code they're writing. Identify a lead tester early in the project, so that a rigorous suite of tests can be developed as the ETL code is being written. The lead tester's role is usually part-time until the ETL development is almost finished. The lead tester and QA analyst will work full-time on the project during the testing phase. The pre-deployment testing phase usually lasts four to eight weeks. Other team members can supplement the primary QA analyst as testers during the crunch period.

Appropriate lead times for desktop upgrades, installations, and associated security must be considered during deployment planning.

Developing documentation can be a simple task. If the team has been good about collecting metadata in a usable format, the detailed documentation can be provided by reports on the metadata tables. Supplement that detailed documentation with a business-oriented summary of each dimensional model. With good metadata in place, it can take a few days to write the summaries, develop the metadata reports, and integrate them into the BI portal. If you haven't yet written a single description of a table, column, or predefined report, your task will take weeks.

It typically takes one day to develop one hour of educational material. In other words, count on eight days to develop a one-day training session. Course development requires access to complete and stable data and BI applications.

Ongoing front room support requires a surprisingly large team. A rule of thumb is that this team will be as large as the initial DW/BI development team. The ongoing back room support should require fewer people. If the hardware and operating system issues are managed as part of a data center, most organizations need about the same number of DBAs as a similar-sized transaction system. You will also need to identify resources to address data quality issues as they arise.

Task List

DEPLOYMENT & MAINTENANCE

	Fans	Front Office		Coaches		Regular Line-Up						Special Teams				
	Business Users	Business Sponsor / Business Driver	DW/BI Director / Program Manager	Project Manager	Business Project Lead	Business Analyst	Data Steward / QA Analyst	Data Architect / Data Modeler / DBA	Metadata Manager	ETL Architect / ETL Developer	BI Architect / App Developer / Portal Developer	Technical Architect / Tech Support Specialist	Security Manager	Lead Tester	Data Mining / Stats Specialist	Educator
Pre-Deployment Testing																
1 Develop a plan for implementing testing		◆		○			○	○		○	○			●		
2 Purchase and implement test management tools							○	○		○	○			●		
3 Develop test datasets	□						●	○		○	○			○		
4 Define tests				●			●	○		○	○			●		
5 User acceptance/project review	□	□	□	●	○	○	○	○	□	○	□	○	□	○	□	○
Data and Process Testing																
1 Test historic load	○			○	○		●	○		○				○		
2 Test primary dataset for incremental load				○	○		●	○		○				○		
3 Conduct live tests with real data	○			○	○		●	○		○				○		
4 Test overall process and system integration	○			○	○		○	○		○				●		
5 Test month-end or other unusual conditions	□			●	○		●	○		○				○		
6 User acceptance/project review		○	□	○	○	○	○	○	□	○	○	○		○		○
Performance Tuning																
1 Test conformance to service level agreements				●	○	○	○	○		○	○	○		○		
2 Test performance of data loads				○				○		●		○		○		
3 Improve performance of data loads				○				○		●		○				
4 Test query performance	○				○	○	○	●			●	○		○		
5 Improve query performance via new indexes and/or aggregations				○				●		○	○	○				
6 End-to-end testing of system after performance-related changes				●	○			●		○	○	○		○		
7 User acceptance/project review	□	○	□	●	○	○	○	○	□	○	○	○		○	□	□
Other Testing																
1 Usability testing of BI applications and portal	○	○		○	○	○	○				●					
2 Confirm desktop readiness	○			○	○						○	●				
3 User acceptance/project review	□	□	□	●	○	○	○			○	○	○		○	□	○

(Continued)

	Fans	Front Office		Coaches			Regular Line-Up						Special Teams				
DEPLOYMENT & MAINTENANCE	Business Users	Business Sponsor / Business Driver	DW/BI Director / Program Manager	Project Manager	Business Project Lead	Business Analyst	Data Steward / QA Analyst	Data Architect / DBA	Data Modeler / DBA	Metadata Manager	ETL Architect / ETL Developer	BI Architect / App Developer / Portal Developer	Technical Architect / Tech Support Specialist	Security Manager	Lead Tester	Data Mining / Stats Specialist	Educator
System Deployment																	
1 Develop playbook for relational DW deployment				○	○		○	●	○	○			○	○			
2 Develop playbook for ETL system deployment				○	○		○	○		○	●		○	○			
3 Develop playbook for OLAP database deployment				○	○		○	●	○	○		●	○	○		○	
4 Develop playbook for BI application deployment				●	○		○	○		○		●	○	○			
5 Deploy new or changed system	☐	○		●	○	○	○	○			○	○	○				○
6 User acceptance/project review			☐	●	○		○	○					○				
User Facing Deployment																	
1 Develop documentation				○	○	○	○	◆		○		○	○	◆		○	●
2 Develop training	○	○		○	○	○	○	◆		○		○	○	◆		○	●
3 Deliver training	○ ☐		☐	○	○	○	◆	◆		◆	◆	◆	○	◆		◆	●
4 User acceptance/project review		○		●	○	○	○	○		◆	○	○	○	○		◆	○
Back Room Operations																	
1 Develop back room operations plan				○				●									
2 Maintain physical database and disks								●									
3 Maintain indexes and partitions								●									
4 Perform regular backups and test recovery								●									
Front Room Operations																	
1 Develop support plan	◆			○		◆						●	●				
2 Ongoing BI portal maintenance												○	◆				
3 Ongoing user guidance for developing queries and reports	◆ ◆					○						○	●				
4 Ongoing standard report development						○						●	◆				

LEGEND:

- ● Primary responsibility
- ○ Involved
- ◆ Provides input
- ☐ Informed of results

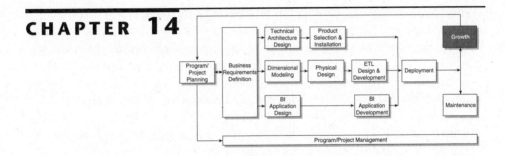

CHAPTER 14

Expanding the DW/BI System

You have successfully deployed the initial phase of your DW/BI system. You have cause to celebrate, but you can't rest on your laurels. As soon as possible, you will launch projects to add new content to the data warehouse, and reach out to new segments of the business user community. You need to balance these new development efforts with the ongoing maintenance and support that's so vital to an effective and vibrant user community.

Project managers should read this chapter very closely. Business and IT management and sponsors should also read it to understand the effort required to fully reap the benefits of your DW/BI initiative. Finally, other team members involved in the ongoing support of the warehouse should become familiar with the recommendations presented in this chapter.

Manage the Existing Environment

In a traditional systems development effort, deployment signals a hand-off from the development team to the maintenance organization. You'd expect to free development resources for other projects. However, a DW/BI system is never really finished. Ongoing care and nurturing of the warehouse simply can't be turned over to a separate maintenance organization while the DW/BI team moves on to tackle the next implementation.

There are several reasons why it works best to keep the DW/BI maintenance and development teams together. Chapter 13 described a set of activities to manage the front room: user support, training, and communication. The front room team works closely with the business users, and gathers valuable information for the design and success of new content. The next round of development should benefit from their knowledge of the business users' requirements, and the successes and challenges of the existing implementation. You may be able to use some of these front room support staff to pitch in during the testing and application development for the next phase.

Ideally, you have automated and bullet-proofed the ETL system, so that it can operate with very little human intervention. In most cases, standard operations can be handled by data center operations staff. But any staff that is focused on overcoming ETL system challenges — either technical or data-centric — should be part of the core data warehouse team. They will have significant insight into how to improve the systems or data for the next round.

Ironically, most of the development resources are spent in the back room: designing and developing the data warehouse databases and ETL system. As you go forward, those resources are shifted to the front room. Even without adding new data into the DW/BI system, you should expect to see the data warehouse team remain approximately constant in size as resources shift to the front room. This is a significant change from most system development projects. The DW/BI manager must ensure management understands this point and provides enough funding for both ongoing support and new development.

Reach the Business Users

Your DW/BI system will fail if business users aren't using it. Make sure your front room team is continuing to support and educate the business users. Offer the basic training courses every quarter to reach new hires and new user communities.

You can learn a lot about how well the current system is working by observing users in their natural habitat. Spend a few hours in a department that should be using the DW/BI system, and see how people are interacting with the BI portal, ad hoc tools, and data. You will surely be able to teach them something, and you'll undoubtedly learn something about how easy the system is to use.

Manage Up

As your system matures, you should establish an ongoing executive steering committee or advisory board. The steering committee should be composed of executives from across the organization; it should meet regularly to set goals, establish priorities, and allocate funds. If you can, be proactive about suggesting committee membership. As discussed in Chapter 2, you should look for a committee that has:

- **Visionary leadership.**   Members of the steering committee need to "get it": they must be able to visualize the potential impacts of information and analyses on the organization's ability to meet its goals. You want committee members who are passionate about the value of informed decision-making.

- **Enterprise focus.**   Members of the steering committee must be able to think about the good of the enterprise as a whole, rather than just their own piece of the puzzle. Look for committee members who participate in annual planning meetings and processes.

- **Budget authority or the ability to affect funding decisions.**   The DW/BI system isn't cheap, as the recently completed project has probably convinced you. It doesn't really get any cheaper in the long run as you start tackling more difficult problems. The ideal steering committee will include the people who make major funding decisions and can ensure your future system development — and maintenance! — has the needed resources. At the very least you need committee members with significant influence over these decisions.

- **Committee membership from both IT and business.**   IT should be represented on the steering committee, but the focus of the committee is the same as that for the DW/BI system: the business.

Look to the executive steering committee to provide guidance for the next areas of development of the system. You can use this committee to raise the visibility of enterprise-wide issues such as data stewardship. Of course, the committee should also be advised of technical projects, such as migration to new hardware or software.

Measure and Market Your Success

Measure the performance of your DW/BI system against the system's success criteria that you negotiated at the project's outset. Publicize success within your organization, and perhaps externally as well. If the system is not performing well, figure out why and take corrective action before you tackle a new development project.

Evaluate ROI

You probably predicted the return on investment for the DW/BI system before the project began. You should retroactively assess the return on investment (ROI) after the solution is implemented. Evaluating ROI is an ongoing process because you shouldn't expect to see all the rewards from the new system as soon as it's deployed.

However, immediately after deployment is a good time to summarize and analyze the system's development costs. The largest costs, of course, are the people costs for the core DW/BI team, as well as hardware and software purchases. An honest assessment of cost will also account for the time "donated" by the business users, especially those you relied on heavily during requirements, testing, and application development. In addition, quantify the cost of ongoing maintenance. The maintenance costs can be tricky: As you start new DW/BI development projects, some team members will play multiple roles.

The fun part of evaluating ROI is assessing the return. It's certainly easier to do this once the system is in production than when you first predicted ROI at the project's inception. Benefits may include:

- **Improved business user productivity.** We have seen DW/BI systems free up significant resources in the user community. In a few extreme cases, highly skilled people used to spend nearly half their work time pulling data together, a task now accomplished for them by the DW/BI system. You can conservatively estimate this benefit based on hours saved per month. Ideally you'd like to capture the business value of their improved productivity, but that would be very difficult to quantify.

- **Reduced burden and cost on transaction systems.** In cases where all reporting and analysis used to be done on a transaction system and is now offloaded to the data warehouse, you can see a tremendous boost in the performance and manageability of the transaction system. Often, transaction systems are able to reach a higher level of service once the DW/BI system is in place. Sometimes, that higher level of service can be attained on less expensive hardware than previously. This benefit can be difficult to quantify. The biggest win will be the business value gained from having the transaction systems operate more smoothly.

- **Improved business decisions.** The real return from the DW/BI system comes from better decisions. Improved business decisions cannot be 100 percent ascribed to the new system because they depend on many factors. However, as decisions are made based on information and analyses from the new system, the DW/BI project should take credit for some portion of the financial impact. If a bank uses the DW/BI system to price instruments and evaluate risk, some portion of the financial benefit should be claimed. If effective marketing plans or targeted sales efforts are built from DW/BI data, claim a percentage of the results. As you're developing your ROI, make sure you clearly indicate the overall benefits and what percentage you're claiming. It helps to include quotes from business people to the effect that "they couldn't have done it without the new system." In the majority of projects we've worked on, there has been a single insight or decision that more than pays for the cost of the system. You never know in advance what it's going to be, but it almost always happens. The DW/BI manager needs to keep plugged into the business users, so she can identify decisions that legitimately can be claimed as resulting from the system.

- **Improved operations.**   As your DW/BI system matures and you build more closed loop applications and operational BI into your systems, you'll be in a great position to claim credit. For example, the DW/BI system may serve as the foundation for a fraud detection system. With this type of application, you can claim most of the benefits as resulting from the DW/BI system.

Keep a written log of all business impact success stories. You'll want to note who, what, when, how, and how much was associated with each example so you can provide complete details when asked. You'll be surprised by the usefulness of this log, especially if your business sponsor is promoted or leaves the organization and the new person questions whether the ongoing investment is worthwhile.

Monitor Success and Service Metrics

About a month after deployment, conduct a thorough post-deployment assessment. This task is different from the analysis of ROI; it focuses instead on softer measures of project and system success.

First, evaluate the development cycle of the project. Look back at your initial project plan and understand how and why the schedule deviated from that initial plan. It's almost inevitable that the data was dirtier, and the ETL tasks more difficult, than originally expected. Develop a plan for doing better on the next round.

Evaluate the deployment phase, too. Poor testing and deployment procedures are a common cause of last minute delays and bad data. If the deployment process wasn't smooth, and especially if you put bad data in front of business users or disrupted their work day, you should plan to have a more structured release process next time.

Most importantly, evaluate the system's usefulness and performance from the business users' point of view. During the requirements gathering phase, we directed you to collect quantifiable measures of project success from business users. Measure performance against these criteria, and interview business users to gauge the general level of satisfaction with the DW/BI system. Solicit feedback concerning the user education, deployment, and support processes. You need user input about what worked and what didn't, in order to improve the processes for the next round of development and deployment.

If you have a service level agreement for the DW/BI systems' uptime and query performance, confirm that you are meeting those service levels.

NOTE It's important that you track performance against success and service metrics on a regular basis, not just immediately following the deployment. It is also useful to capture this information over time to support success and service performance trending. Don't assume that no news is good news. No news usually means that no one is using the data warehouse.

Data for many of the metrics can be captured routinely by system utilities, but less operationally oriented metrics must be gathered directly from the business users. You'll need to talk with your business users to continually assess their satisfaction level and gauge the fit of the DW/BI system with current business requirements. You can't rely on written surveys to gather this type of feedback.

Proactively Market the Data Warehouse

When you develop a new order entry system, the system's users don't have much choice about whether they use it or not; if the new system doesn't get used, orders don't get processed. By contrast, using the data warehouse is often completely optional. Business users have been making decisions without access to information for years, and some will prefer to continue doing so.

Marketing of the data warehouse is important to support both funding for ongoing maintenance as well as growth initiatives. Someone on the team should be assigned responsibility for public relations. This individual, often the DW/BI program manager, becomes the spokesperson. A spokesperson is more important for a data warehouse project than for typical systems development projects due to the potential impact it may have on every department within an organization. The spokesperson should develop a standard DW/BI presentation to discuss the system's mission, accomplishments to date (with examples and dollar impacts), available data, current users and usage trends, and future plans.

Your log of DW/BI business impact examples will be relevant material for your marketing plan. These successes should be broadcast throughout the organization, and the industry, if appropriate. You can employ a variety of media, including the BI portal, IT and corporate newsletters, industry publications, and vendor success stories. Solicit management's help to broadcast the wins. Users will be motivated to use the data warehouse and perhaps be part of the next success story, if management's support is highly visible.

Communicate Constantly

We've stressed the importance of communication throughout the planning, development, and deployment stages of your project. We hope it's a habit now, because your communication job is never done. Frequent communications with your important constituents will make the future phases of your DW/BI system much easier to get off the ground.

- **Business sponsors and drivers.**   Maintain regular, predictable reporting to sustain their sponsorship. Communicate successes as well as problems and your plans for addressing them. Communication will help address ongoing funding and resource allocation requirements.

- **Business users.**   The users need detailed tactical information about the DW/BI system. Communicate openly about problems, and keep users informed about upcoming design and development efforts.

- **General business community.**   You should broadcast general updates to the rest of the business community to keep them informed of current status and future plans. These may take the form of a quarterly one-page update or a column in your corporate newsletter.

- **IT management.**   IT management should also receive the general broadcast updates. In addition, inform them of more detailed plans for the data warehouse to ensure that they're considering implications on their areas of responsibility, such as network capacity planning or operational system application development.

- **Data warehouse team updates.**   It's critical that you maintain communication within the data warehouse team. Unfortunately, status meetings are often dropped as the schedule tightens around deployment and then not resumed following deployment. Make team communications a priority.

Prepare for Growth and Evolution

A successful DW/BI system will evolve and grow. If anything, you should constantly be forced to throttle back the requests for new data sources, faster delivery of data, new data mining scores and labels, and new key performance indicators. A changing system is a sign of success, not failure. It indicates your existing business users are asking for more data and BI applications. At the same time, they're spreading the news about the DW/BI system at the grass roots level, so new users will be clamoring for data, tools, and applications. Everyone involved with the DW/BI system from both the business and IT communities should anticipate and appreciate the evolution of the system as it matures.

The factors that influenced the early design of your data warehouse — including business sponsorship, users and their requirements, technical architecture, and available source data — are evolving rapidly. The Kimball Lifecycle approach is designed to help the data warehouse respond gracefully to change.

Before you think about growth opportunities, you should assess your current environment. If your current system is not successful, we recommend you make adjustments before building anew on the same foundation. Next, develop procedures for prioritizing the many growth opportunities you'll receive. Finally, follow the Kimball Lifecycle from the beginning, adding new content and applications to the DW/BI system.

Assess Your Current Environment

If you've followed this book's advice from the outset, we expect that your DW/BI system is heavily used and warrants the investment in additional resources to maintain it. But what if that's not the case? What do you do if your users aren't jumping on the bandwagon? This symptom often points to more serious underlying problems. Take the following self-check test. If you can't answer yes to these questions, refer to the appropriate Lifecycle chapter and perform resuscitative measures.

- Do you have an effective steering committee?
- Does the DW/BI team understand the business user requirements? Do the business users believe the team understands their needs?
- Is the data organized dimensionally for query performance, or is it structured to support operational performance?
- Do the business users like the tools they use every day? Is it easy for them to move data into Excel?
- Is the data accurate? Does it match current operational reporting? If not, does the data warehouse team thoroughly understand the data inconsistencies and have they informed the business users?
- Is the data refreshed in a timely manner?
- Are the users happy with query performance? Is query performance consistent and predictable?
- Has the data warehouse team built BI applications? Is it easy for users to move away from pre-built reports and applications, and start creating their own analyses?
- Have the business users received basic training on the data, application templates, and data access tools?
- Do the users know what the data means and where it comes from? Do they have access to table and column definitions and what typical values should be?
- Do the business users know whom to call if they're having problems with the DW/BI system? Does anyone respond to their calls in a timely manner?
- Is there continuing education available beyond the deployment?

If you fail this test — if you can't answer yes to most of these questions — you should address these existing issues before you launch a new development project. Once your users are happy, you'll have a solid foundation upon which to build your expanded system.

Prioritize Opportunities for Growth

One of the steering committee's responsibilities is to prioritize growth and evolution opportunities. The effort required to add another attribute to an existing dimension table differs significantly from that required to add a new business process to the data warehouse. Typically, we see two organizational processes put into place to handle prioritization of growth and evolution opportunities, one for relatively minor projects and another for major data warehouse initiatives.

Prioritize Minor Enhancements

A minor enhancement to the DW/BI system might consist of additional dimension attributes or calculated facts, additional BI applications based on existing data, or changes to existing applications. Minor enhancements typically require days or a few weeks to complete, rather than measuring the effort in work months.

Your organization probably has a process in place for change service requests. The prioritization of minor DW/BI enhancements is typically handled in a similar fashion. The data warehouse support team receives and reviews user feedback, possibly submitted via email to a change request mailbox. The team researches and scopes the effort required to implement the enhancement.

In most organizations, minor enhancements are handled by the DW/BI team, with quarterly notification to the steering committee of recent changes. The support team presents a preliminary prioritization recommendation to the steering committee. Make sure you tell the user who submitted the request what its priority is, and when the enhancement is in place.

NOTE Don't fall prey to the simplistic reasoning that because a requested change is small, it's not worth doing. This argument can be extended to not doing anything at all. Remember that the competitive advantage established by Japanese auto manufacturers was largely based on the strategy of a thousand little improvements.

Prioritize Major Initiatives

A major enhancement to the DW/BI system might involve data from a business process that is not yet represented in the warehouse. Major enhancements typically represent a relatively large investment in incremental design, development, and maintenance resources measured in work months rather than days of effort.

In these cases, the project's business sponsor or DW/BI program manager typically presents the opportunity to the steering committee. The opportunity's feasibility and business justification should be analyzed before going to the steering committee. New projects should meet the same criteria we described in Chapter 2. Each project should be meaningful to the business as determined by your prioritization process, manageable in terms of the number of users and amount of data, and doable in a reasonable time frame. The steering committee employs their agreed upon prioritization criteria to establish the sequencing of major initiatives.

Manage Iterative Growth

At this point, you're ready to tackle your next DW/BI project. Don't forget to remain focused on the business. We've seen organizations that use this business-oriented approach for their first warehouse project fall back into old habits as the next project queues up.

As you embark on subsequent projects, you'll be leveraging the foundation already put in place, while preparing for new variables. You may be delivering existing information to new users or new information to existing users. In either case, you should continue to use the Kimball Lifecycle described throughout this book. The knowledge and experience gained during your initial project should be leveraged on subsequent projects. As illustrated on the overall Lifecycle diagram, you should now loop back to the beginning of the Lifecycle.

The following section reviews each major step of the project lifecycle and highlights changes or extensions as it is applied to subsequent phases.

- **Project planning and management.** Each new initiative should be established as a defined project. Projects should be clearly scoped, with defined start and stop dates, a scope document, project plan, and management techniques as recommended in Chapter 2. Assign a project manager to each initiative. You will need new resources to support both ongoing maintenance of the first phase and new development for future projects. For the same reasons you should start small with the initial phase, keep additional projects at a reasonable scope. Depending on your resource levels, it is possible to stagger several concurrent initiatives with multiple separate project teams. This approach allows for concurrent design and development, rather than relying on a serial timeline, but it also requires additional program coordination and communication.

- **Business requirements definition.** Users' business requirements should be the driver at all times. Use the requirements gathering techniques described in Chapter 3 to direct your next project.

- **Technical architecture strategy and infrastructure.** Leverage the existing technical architecture, but make adjustments as required and document any changes to the technical architecture strategy.

- **Dimensional modeling.** As discussed in Chapters 6 and 7, embracing the enterprise data warehouse bus architecture and conforming your business dimensions is the key to supporting integration within your data warehouse over time. Even if your first project had a departmental focus, follow enterprise-class design techniques; push for future projects that standardize dimensions and information across the enterprise. Conformed dimensions deliver integration, as well as reduced time to market because subsequent projects can leverage the existing dimensions.

- **ETL.** The ETL system described in Chapters 9 and 10 and constructed for your first deliverable should be a strong foundation for future development. It's common for second phase projects to have more complex ETL than the initial project. But as an offset, now your ETL developers have tool expertise, and have built the techniques and infrastructure for running the ETL system in your environment. The design we described for data quality tracking is intended to be expanded incrementally. Once the error event schema is in place, then data quality screens can be added one at a time indefinitely. A data quality team should constantly be improving quality by proposing and implementing new and better screens

- **Application design and development.** BI applications are an invaluable component of the DW/BI system. It often works well for the initial phase to focus on data, predefined reports, and ad hoc analyses. Once you have that basic system in place, you have a great platform to build more complex BI applications, such as customer relationship management, fraud detection, product pricing and placement, and various data mining applications. You should be able to leverage the application design and development infrastructure described in Chapters 11 and 12. A DW/BI system must not only expose data to business users, but it should be a platform for asking "why" and "what if" questions. The users can bring their intellectual capital to bear only if they are given useful choices when trying to explore these questions. After initial deployment, the DW/BI team should return and examine these critical decision making points to ask what additional data sources would be helpful to the business users.

- **Deployment planning, education, and support.** Once again, you'll want to leverage existing deployment, education, and support processes described in Chapter 13. Business user education needs to accompany every release of new data content or application templates to a user population, not just the first deployment. Additional training is also warranted if there are major changes to the BI tool environment.

Conclusion

Congratulations! Your hard work has paid off. The first business process of your DW/BI system is in full production and beginning to generate real business value. In this chapter, we highlighted recommendations to ensure your system remains vital, healthy, and poised for growth. Remember to always put the business users first, without sacrificing attention to the technical environment. You should measure, track, and communicate program successes on an ongoing basis.

Last but not least, remember that success breeds success. Be prepared for the onslaught of requests for more data, reports, and users; those are problems you would like to have. Continue to rely on the Kimball Lifecycle as your system grows and evolves.

BLUEPRINT FOR ACTION

Managing the Effort and Reducing Risk

Growth risks are reduced by first assessing whether your initial, just-completed DW/BI system has a positive financial return on investment, meets business users' needs, and satisfies the definitions of success as defined at the outset of the project. Establish or re-establish an executive steering committee to help prioritize new efforts in response to the changing demands of the business world.

Regular, frequent monitoring of progress and proactive communication and involvement with the business will boost both the actual and perceived quality of your system and processes.

As you iterate through the Lifecycle to incorporate data from additional business processes, you may be tackling harder problems than in the initial phases. Develop a plan for increasing the skills of existing staff, or hiring new skills, to meet these more challenging development projects.

Assuring Quality

Prepare your management to increase the size of the DW/BI team to support both ongoing operations and new growth. Make sure you have an effective executive steering committee in place. If you can affect the composition of that group, make sure they'll be on your side and keep an enterprise approach.

(continued)

BLUEPRINT FOR ACTION *(continued)*

Expanding the DW/BI system to support new users and create new BI applications is really fun. It usually gets easier as you're building from a collection of best practices. Make sure you document the approaches that have been successful, so future teams can leverage what you've learned.

Key Roles

Key roles for expanding the DW/BI system include:

◆ The DW/BI director or program manager is responsible for ongoing strategy, success evaluation, marketing, and communicating about the DW/BI program up, down, and across the organization.

◆ The project manager and business project lead drive the project definition activities for future growth, with heavy involvement from both business and IT sponsors.

◆ The executive steering committee guides prioritization for new major efforts.

◆ The entire development team is involved in new projects.

◆ Make sure the business-facing support folks remain involved, too. They will be very knowledgeable about what is working — and not working — in the existing system.

Key Deliverables

Key deliverables for expanding the DW/BI system include:

◆ Ongoing marketing and communications plans, including periodic assessment of ROI

◆ Steering committee charter, including roles and responsibilities

◆ Steering committee periodic update presentations

◆ Opportunity prioritization plan

◆ Program charter, scope, and timelines

Estimating Considerations

Unlike most systems development projects, the DW/BI system is never done. There's no end in sight regarding data warehouse growth activities and associated timeframes. Subsequent projects should be staffed, planned, and managed as described in Chapter 2. Now it's time to go back to the beginning and do it all over again!

Glossary

This glossary is a quick reference guide to DW/BI terms used repeatedly in this book or that may not be defined as carefully as we would like in other sources. We have not tried to define every industry acronym and term you may encounter, such as RAID, SOAP, and UDDI. For these, please go to the Internet!

24/7   Operational availability 24 hours a day, 7 days a week.

3NF   See *Third normal form*.

Accumulating snapshot fact table   Type of fact table with multiple dates representing the major milestones of a process or workflow that has a well defined beginning and end. A record is placed in an accumulating snapshot fact table just once, when the activity it represents first occurs, then the fact record is revisited and updated with subsequent workflow activities. Contrast with *periodic snapshot fact table* and *transaction fact table*.

Additive (facts)   Measurements in a fact table that can be added across all the dimensions. Amounts and simple counts are usually additive. Ratios, unit prices, percentages, and distinct counts are generally *non-additive*. Account balances and inventory levels are generally *semi-additive*.

Ad hoc queries   Queries that are formulated by the user on the spur of the moment. Although some business users are interested in and capable of formulating ad hoc queries, the majority of the business community will be more satisfied with the ability to execute predefined applications that query, analyze, and present information from a dimensional model.

Aggregate navigator   Layer of software between the client and data that intercepts the client's query and effectively rewrites that query to use the appropriate predefined aggregate. The aggregate navigator shields the user application from needing to know if an aggregate is present. In this sense, an aggregate behaves like an index. Most relational database suppliers and OLAP vendors have incorporated aggregate navigation capabilities into their database management systems.

Aggregates   Physical rows in a database, created by aggregating (usually by summing) other records in the database for the purpose of improving query performance. Sometimes referred to as pre-calculated summary data. In DB2, aggregates are known as automatic summary tables; in Oracle, aggregates are delivered as materialized views. See *Aggregate navigator*.

Algorithm   Standard method for computing something; essentially a mathematical recipe.

Alias (SQL)   An alphanumeric identifier in an SQL expression that stands for a physical table name. Some database engines also offer *synonyms* which are similar.

Allocations   Assignment or proration of measured values (usually costs) to several accounts, customers, products, or transactions. For instance, the overhead costs in a manufacturing plant might be allocated to the various product lines made in the plant. The allocation process is a politically sensitive one that is best left to the business community or finance department. Allocations are often less contentious in discrete manufacturing businesses and more contentious in businesses with significant infrastructure, such as telecommunications and financial services companies.

Analytic application   Prebuilt data access application that contains powerful analysis algorithms based on domain expertise, in addition to normal database queries. An analytic application sometimes uses data mining algorithms. Prebuilt analytic applications packages include promotion analysis, budgeting, forecasting, and business activity monitoring (BAM).

ANSI   American National Standards Institute, the recognized standards publishing body for a range of businesses, professions, and industries.

ASCII   American Standard Code for Information Interchange. An 8-bit character set encoding. ASCII can only support 127 characters, which is not enough for international usage. See *Extended ASCII* and *UNICODE*.

Atomic data The most detailed granular data captured by a business process and stored in a fact table. Atomic data delivers maximum flexibility and extensibility.

Attribute A descriptive column (field) in a dimension table. The only column in a dimension table that isn't an attribute is the primary key.

Audit dimension A special dimension that tracks operational metadata for each fact row, and potentially each dimension row. The operational metadata in the audit dimension might include an identifier for the process that created or updated the row, data quality, lineage, and confidence.

Authentication Verification that you are who you say you are. There are several levels of authentication; a static password is the first level, followed by a system-enforced password pattern and periodically required changes. Beyond the password, authentication may require some physical or biometric evidence of identity, such as a magnetic card or thumbprint. This is described as a two-factor authorization scheme. There are hardware- and network-based schemes that work from a pre-assigned IP address, particularly on dial-in connections. Authentication is an enterprise infrastructure service that the DW/BI system should be able to leverage.

Authorization Determining what specific content a user is allowed to access. Once you've identified someone to your satisfaction, you need to determine what they are authorized to see. Authorization is a much more complex problem in the DW/BI system than *authentication* because limiting access can have a significant maintenance and computational overhead.

B-tree index A relational index that is particularly useful for high cardinality columns. The B-tree index builds a tree of values with a list of row IDs that have the leaf value. Contrast with *bitmap index*.

Behavior study group A group of customers or products used in an analysis or report that cannot be defined by constraining on dimensional attributes or is too large to be enumerated by an SQL IN clause. The behavioral study group often is defined from an original analysis that isolates interesting purchase behavior or credit behavior. We suggest building study groups as simple one-column tables of natural keys. These simple tables are joined to their respective dimensions to effectively act as a global constraint, restricting the application to the members of the study group.

BI See *Business intelligence*.

BI applications   The value-add analytics within the DW/BI system. BI applications include the entire range of data access methods from ad hoc queries to standard reports to analytic applications. See *Business intelligence*.

BI portal   The business users' interface to access standard reports and other BI applications, along with metadata reports, documentation, tutorials, and other supporting information.

Bitmap index   A relational indexing technique most appropriate for columns with a limited number of potential values relative to the total number of rows in the table (low cardinality). Bitmapped indexes gain their power because they can be combined to allow several weak, low cardinality constraints to create a single powerful constraint. Contrast with *B-tree index*.

Bridge table   A table with a multipart key capturing a many-to-many relationship that can't be accommodated by the natural granularity of a single fact or dimension table. Serves to bridge between the fact and dimension tables to support many-valued dimension attributes or ragged hierarchies. Sometimes historically referred to as a helper or associative table.

Bubble chart   A high level graphical representation of a business process dimensional data model. Useful for communicating data models to a non-technical audience.

Bus architecture   The data architecture for the DW/BI system's presentation area based on *conformed* dimensions and facts. Without adherence to the bus architecture, a business process dimensional model is a stand-alone stovepipe application. See *Bus matrix*.

Bus matrix   A graphical representation of the bus architecture where the matrix rows correspond to an organization's business processes and the matrix columns map to the *conformed dimensions*. Shaded cells in the matrix show the association between business processes and relevant dimensions.

Business dimensional lifecycle   See *Kimball Lifecycle*.

Business intelligence (BI)   A generic term to describe leveraging the organization's internal and external information assets to support improved business decision making. Some commentators use the term *business intelligence* to refer only to the reporting and analysis of data stored in the data warehouse. Because the industry has not reached agreement, we consistently use the phrase *data warehouse/business intelligence (DW/BI)* to mean the complete end-to-end system. Though some would argue that you can theoretically deliver BI without a data warehouse, and vice versa, that is ill-advised from our perspective. Linking the two together in the DW/BI acronym further reinforces their dependency.

Business measure   Business performance metric captured by an operational system and represented as a physical or computed fact in a dimensional model.

Business metadata   Metadata that describes the contents of the data warehouse in user accessible terms. It tells you what data you have, where it comes from, what it means, and what its relationship is to other data in the warehouse. Most of the metadata that business users access is business metadata. See *Metadata*, *Process metadata*, and *Technical metadata*.

Business process   Major operational activity or event, such as the orders process, supported by a source system that collects the associated performance measurements. Thus a business process can be thought of as a fundamental data source. Business processes make up the rows of the bus matrix. Choosing the business process is the first of four key steps in the design of a *dimensional model*.

Business process dimensional model   See *Dimensional model*.

Cache   A temporary storage space for objects or data expected to be used in the near future.

Cardinality   The number of unique values for a given column in a table. Low cardinality refers to a limited number of values relative to the overall number of rows in the table.

Cartesian product   A set comprised of all the possible combinations from multiple constraints.

CDC   See *Change data capture*.

Change data capture (CDC)   An ETL capability utilized to extract and transfer only the relevant changes to source data since the last update.

Checksum   See *Cyclic redundancy checksum*.

Churn   A business concept that measures the turnover rate among the customer base.

CIO   Chief information officer within an organization.

Composite key   Key in a database table made up of several columns. Same as *concatenated key*. The overall key in a typical fact table is a subset of the foreign keys in the fact table. In other words, it usually does not require every foreign key to guarantee uniqueness of a fact table row.

Concatenated key   See *Composite key*.

Conformed dimensions   Dimensions are conformed when they are either exactly the same (including the keys) or one is a perfect subset of the other. Most important, the row headers produced in answer sets from two conformed dimensions must match perfectly.

Conformed facts   Facts from multiple fact tables are conformed when the technical definitions of the facts are equivalent. Conformed facts are allowed to have the same name in separate tables and can be combined and compared mathematically. If facts do not conform, then the different interpretations must be given different names.

Consolidated fact table   Fact table that combines business measurements from multiple business processes.

Constraint   Phrase in the SQL FROM or WHERE clause. A constraint is either a join constraint or application constraint.

Continuously valued (facts)   Numeric measurement that can take on virtually any value within a broad range. Continuously valued measurements should be facts in the fact table as opposed to discrete attributes in a dimension table.

Copybook   Traditional COBOL header file that describes all the columns in an underlying data file.

Cost based optimizer   Software in a relational database that tries to determine how to process the query by assigning estimated costs to various table lookup alternatives.

CRC   See *Cyclic redundancy checksum*.

CRM   See *Customer relationship management*.

Cross-selling   The technique of increasing sales by selling a new product to existing customers. See also *Up-selling*.

Cube   Name for a dimensional structure on a multidimensional or online analytical processing (OLAP) database platform. See *Multidimensional database*.

Customer relationship management (CRM)   Operational and analytic processes that focus on better understanding and servicing customers to maximize mutually beneficial relationships with each customer. Full scale CRM systems include all the major customer touch points, like promotions, email solicitations, sales force interactions, and customer support.

Cyclic redundancy checksum (CRC)   An algorithm used to map an input value to a smaller value that is useful for comparing two complex items, such as customer records, to see if anything has changed. The CRC can be stored with an existing record, and then compared with the CRC computed on an incoming record. If there are any differences between the records, the CRCs will be different. This eliminates the requirement to check each constituent field in the record. Also known as a *hash function* or *hash code*.

Dashboards and scorecards   Multi-subject user interfaces showing reports and graphs of key performance indicators (KPIs), sometimes in near real time. A type of *BI application*.

Data access tool   A client tool that queries, fetches, or manipulates data stored in a database, preferably a dimensional model located in the data presentation area.

Data extract   Process of copying data from an operational system in order to load it into a data warehouse. The initial step in the ETL process.

Data mart   In the first edition of *The Data Warehouse Lifecycle Toolkit* (Wiley 1998), the term data mart was used extensively instead of business process dimensional models. However, the term has been marginalized by others to mean summarized departmental, independent non-architected datasets. See *Dimensional model*.

Data mining and models   A process of identifying patterns and relationships in the data. Exploratory data mining involves analysis of large "observation sets" usually downloaded from the data warehouse to data mining software. Data mining is also used to create the underlying models used by some analytic and operational BI applications.

Data profiling   The use of query and reporting tools to explore the content and relationships of source system data. Data profiling can be as simple as writing SQL statements or as sophisticated as a detailed data profiling study. There are tools to make the data profiling task much easier and probably more complete.

Data quality assurance   The step during the deployment process where the data is tested for consistency, completeness, and fitness to publish to the business user community.

Data staging area   Physical workspace for data during the ETL process. The staging area is usually a combination of relational database tables and operating system files.

Data stewardship   An organizational function to address data definitions, consistency, integration, quality, and knowledge in an enterprise.

Data warehouse (DW)   See *Enterprise data warehouse*.

Database management system (DBMS)   A computer application whose sole purpose is to store, retrieve, and modify data in a highly structured way. Data in a DBMS usually is shared by a variety of applications. Relational databases (RDBMSs) and OLAP databases are both examples of database management systems.

DBA   Database administrator.

DD   See *Degenerate dimension*.

Decision support system (DSS)   The original name for data warehousing. See also *DW/BI system*.

Decode   The textual description associated with an operational code, flag, or indicator.

Degenerate dimension   A dimension key, such as a transaction number, invoice number, ticket number, or bill-of-lading number that has no attributes and hence does not join to an actual dimension table.

Denormalize   Allowing redundancy in a table so that the table can remain flat, rather than *snowflaked* or normalized, in order to optimize analytic query performance and ease-of-use. Contrast with *normalize* or *third normal form*.

Dependency   Beginning with a specific data element in a source table or an intermediate table, identify all downstream intermediate tables and user reports containing that data element or its derivations and all transformations applied to that data element and its derivations. Also called *impact*. Contrast with *lineage*.

Derived facts   Facts that are derived from the base metrics in a business process dimensional model. There are two kinds of derived facts: derived facts that are additive and can be calculated entirely from the other facts in the same fact table row and non-additive calculations, such as a ratio or cumulative facts that are typically expressed at a different level of detail than the base facts themselves.

Detailed bus matrix   A more detailed version of the data warehouse bus matrix where fact tables are identified for each business process, as well as the fact table granularity and measurements. See *Bus matrix*.

Dimension manager   The individual responsible for defining, building, and publishing one or more conformed dimensions.

Dimension table   A table in a dimensional model with a single part primary key and descriptive attribute columns. Serves as an entry point or mechanism for slicing the additive measures located in the fact table of the dimensional model.

Dimensional data warehouse   Set of queryable tables in the DW/BI system that are designed using dimensional modeling and align to the bus matrix.

Dimensional model   A data model structured to deliver maximum query performance and ease of use. In the relational DBMS environment, a fact table is based on a measurement event, generally with one record for each discrete measurement. The fact table is then surrounded by a set of dimension tables describing precisely what is known in the context of each measurement record. Because of the characteristic structure of a dimensional model, it is often called a *star schema*. Dimensional models have proved to be understandable, predictable, extendable, and highly responsive to ad hoc demands because of their predictable symmetric nature. Dimensional models are the basis of many DBMS performance enhancements, including powerful indexing approaches and aggregations. Dimensional models are the basis for the incremental and distributed development of data warehouses through the use of conformed dimensions and conformed facts. Dimensional models are also the logical foundation for all OLAP systems.

Dimensional modeling   A methodology for logically modeling data to maximize analytic query performance and ease of use.

Direct access queries   The classic ad hoc requests initiated by business users from data access tools.

Directory server   A server that keeps track of all the users of a system, as well as all resources available on the system, such as database servers, file servers, printers, and communications resources. The industry standard way to communicate with a directory server is the Lightweight Directory Access Protocol (LDAP).

Double-barreled joins   Multiple parallel joins between a single dimension table and a fact table. Double-barreled joins should be avoided.

Drill across   The act of requesting identically labeled data from two or more fact tables in a single report. Drilling across only works if the dimension values used as row labels are conformed.

Drill down   The act of adding more detail to a report or data view, often by moving down to a lower level of a hierarchy, as from year to month, or alternatively by including any additional non-hierarchical attributes in the SELECT list of a query.

Drill up   The act of summarizing information in a report or data view, usually by removing attributes or moving up to a higher level of a hierarchy, as from month to year.

DSS   See *Decision support system*.

DW/BI system   The complete end-to-end data warehouse and business intelligence system. Although some would argue that you can theoretically deliver business intelligence without a data warehouse, and vice versa, that is ill-advised from our perspective. Linking the two together in the DW/BI acronym reinforces their dependency. Independently, we refer to the queryable data in your DW/BI system as the *enterprise data warehouse*, and value-add analytics as *BI applications*. We disagree with others who insist that the data warehouse is a highly normalized data store whose primary purpose is to serve as a source for the transformation and loading of data into summarized dimensional structures.

Enterprise data warehouse (EDW)   The queryable data in your DW/BI system. Others in the industry refer to the EDW as a centralized, atomic, and normalized layer of the data warehouse, used as a source for dimensional data marts that are created and published to the user community on demand. We discourage this interpretation of the EDW, preferring to think of the EDW as the largest possible union of presentation server data. See *DW/BI system*.

Enterprise resource planning (ERP) application A class of operational applications aimed at spanning some or all of the business functions of a complete enterprise. ERP applications are sources for data that's moved into the DW/BI system.

Entity-relationship (ER) diagram (ERD) Drawings of boxes and lines to communicate the relationship between tables. Both third normal form (3NF) and dimensional models can be represented as ER diagrams because both consist of joined relational tables. The key difference between the models is the degree of dimension normalization. Properly constructed 3NF and dimensional models express the same data relationships and generate the same query results.

Error event schema A component of the ETL system that captures every error event encountered by a data quality screen.

ETL system Extract, transformation, and load system consisting of a set of processes by which the operational source data is prepared for the data warehouse. Consists of extracting operational data from source applications, cleaning and conforming the data, and delivering the data to the presentation servers, along with the ongoing management and support functions.

ETL tool A software application used to develop and deliver the ETL system.

Extended ASCII The extension of the American Standard Code for Information Interchange to include European accented characters and other special characters. This encoding uses the high 128 characters in the 8-bit ASCII format to allow a total of 255 possible characters. Extended ASCII serves most European applications, but is insufficient for Asian character sets, which require UNICODE. See *ASCII* and *UNICODE*.

Extensible Markup Language (XML) A cousin of HTML that provides structured data exchange between parties. XML contains data and metadata but no formatting information, as contrasted with HTML, which contains data and formatting information but no metadata. When XML is used together with XML schema declarations, target relational tables can be defined and loaded. XML is a flexible, strongly hierarchical framework for assigning tags to fields within a document. XML does not specify what the tags should be. It is up to various organizations or industry groups to define and use consistent sets of tags, and this effort is the main gating factor slowing the widespread use of XML. XML is usually used as the format for the payloads of *service oriented architecture* (SOA) communications.

Extract, transform(ation), and load   See *ETL system.*

Fact   A business performance measurement, typically numeric and additive, that is stored in a fact table.

Fact provider   The individual responsible for designing, building, and publishing a specific fact table after receiving dimension data from the relevant dimension managers.

Fact table   In a dimensional model, the central table with numeric performance measurements characterized by a composite key, each of whose elements is a foreign key drawn from a dimension table.

Factless fact table   A fact table that has no facts but captures the many-to-many relationships between the dimension keys. Most often used to represent events or coverage information that does not appear in other fact tables.

File Transfer Protocol (FTP)   TCP/IP protocol that is used for transferring files between computers.

FK   See *Foreign key.*

Flat file   A simple denormalized data structure stored in the file system, usually either delimited (as with a comma) or formatted with fixed width fields.

Foreign key (FK)   A column in a relational database table whose values are drawn from the values of a primary key in another table. In a dimensional model, the components of a composite fact table key are foreign keys with respect to each of the dimension tables.

Grain   The business meaning of a single row in a fact table. The declaration of the grain of a fact table is the second of four key steps in the design of a dimensional model.

Granularity   The level of detail captured in a fact table. See *Grain*.

Greenwich Mean Time (GMT)   The local standard time at zero degrees longitude, which runs through the Royal Navy Observatory near London. Greenwich Mean Time has been superseded by Coordinated Universal Time (UTC), which means effectively the same thing.

Hash code or hash function   See *Cyclic redundancy checksum*.

Hierarchy   A relationship where data rolls up into higher levels of summarization in a series of strict many-to-one relationships. Hierarchies are reflected by additional columns in a dimension table.

Housekeeping columns   Additional columns appended to a dimension table to facilitate the ETL process. Often not accessible by business users.

Impact or impact analysis   See *Dependency*. Contrast with *lineage*.

Impact report   When reporting with a bridge table, the weighting factor assigned to the multi-valued dimension is ignored. The resulting totals provide a summarization for any case in which the multi-valued dimension was involved, regardless of the extent of the involvement. Contrast with *weighted report*.

Index   A data structure associated with a table that is logically ordered by the values of a key and used to improve database performance and query access speed.

IP address   The numeric address of a particular host or subnet on the Internet.

Julian day number   A representation of a calendar date as the simple count of days from the beginning of an epoch, such as January 1, 1900. True Julian dates are numbered in the millions and are not used often as the literal basis of date values.

Junk dimension   An artificial dimension with low-cardinality flags, indicators, and decodes thereby removing these items from the fact table.

Key performance indicator (KPI)   Financial and non-financial metrics used to assess the strategic performance of an organization.

Kimball Lifecycle   A methodology for planning, designing, implementing, and maintaining DW/BI systems as described in *The Data Warehouse Lifecycle Toolkit, Second Edition* (Wiley 2008). Originally called the *Business Dimensional Lifecycle*.

KPI   See *Key performance indicator*.

LDAP   Lightweight Directory Access Protocol, a standard currently agreed to by most of the major systems vendors for describing the users of a network and the resources available on a network. See *Directory server*.

Lineage   Beginning with a specific data element in an intermediate table or user report, identifying the source of that data element, other upstream intermediate tables containing that data element and its sources, and all transformations that data element and its sources have undergone. Contrast with *dependency* and *impact*.

Logical design   The phase of a database design concerned with identifying the relationships among the data elements. Contrast with *physical design*.

Many-to-many relationship   A logical data relationship in which the value of one data element can exist in combination with many values of another data element and vice versa.

Many-valued dimensions   Normally a fact table record is joined to a single dimension record, such as a single date or product. But occasionally, it is valid to connect a fact table record to a dimension representing an open-ended number of values, such as the number of simultaneous diagnoses a patient may have at the moment of a single treatment. Also referred to as *multi-valued dimensions*. Typically handled using a *bridge table*.

Master data management (MDM)   Centralized facilities designed to hold master copies of shared entities, such as customers or products. MDM systems are meant to support transaction systems and usually have some means to reconcile different sources for the same attribute. They provide a bridging mechanism to move from the old transaction silos to a single source for customer or product information. Having an MDM capability in place removes a huge data cleansing and integration burden from the ETL system.

Metadata   All the information that defines and describes the structures, operations, and contents of the DW/BI system. We identify three types of metadata in the DW/BI system: technical, business, and process. See *Technical metadata*, *Business metadata*, and *Process metadata*.

MDM   See *Master data management*.

MDX   A query language for several OLAP databases. At the time of this writing, MDX is as close to a standard OLAP query language as exists. MDX is analogous to the SELECT statement in SQL, but is a richer analytic language. MDX is fully described in the XML/A (XML for Analysis) specification standard.

Mini-dimensions   Subsets of a large dimension, such as customer, that are broken off into separate, smaller artificial dimensions to control the explosive growth of a large, rapidly changing dimension. The continuously changing demographic attributes of a customer are often modeled as a separate minidimension.

Mirrored database   A physical organization of data where the entire database is duplicated on separate disk drives. Mirrored databases offer a number of performance and administrative advantages.

Modeling applications   A sophisticated BI application with analytic capabilities that transform or digest the output from the data warehouse. Modeling applications include forecasting models, behavior scoring models that cluster and classify customer purchase behavior or customer credit behavior, allocation models that take cost data from the data warehouse and spread the costs across product groupings or customer groupings, and most data mining tools.

Most recent indicator   A housekeeping column on a dimension table, typically used in conjunction with type 2 slowly changing dimensions, that indicates the most current profile record.

Multidimensional database   Database in which the data is managed in a predefined dimensional structure, including precalculated aggregates, as opposed to tables in a relational database platform. Although multidimensional databases do not scale to the sizes that relational database systems can, they typically offer better query performance and a more advanced analytic language than their relational counterparts. Also known as a *multidimensional online analytic processing system* or *MOLAP*.

Multipass SQL   Query capability supported by some data access tools in which the results of separate queries against separate dimensional models are combined column by column via the conformed dimensions. Not the same thing as a union, which is a row-by-row combination of separate queries.

Multi-valued dimensions   See *Many-valued dimensions*.

Natural key   The identifier used by the operational systems. Natural keys often have embedded meaning. They may appear as dimension attributes in dimensional models but should not serve as the dimension table primary key, which always should be a surrogate key. Also known as business key, source key, production key, transaction key, or operational key.

Non-additive (facts)   A fact that cannot logically be added across rows. May be numeric and therefore usually must be combined in a computation with other facts before being added across rows. Examples of non-additive numeric facts include ratios, unit prices, temperatures, and distinct counts.

Normalize   A logical modeling technique that removes data redundancy by separating the data into many discrete entities, each of which becomes a table in a relational DBMS.

Null   A data field or record for which no value exists. We avoid null fact table foreign keys by assigning a dimension surrogate key to identify "Not Applicable" or "To Be Determined" conditions.

ODS   See *Operational data store*.

OLAP database or engine   See *Multidimensional database*.

One-to-many relationship   A logical data relationship in which the value of one data element can exist in combination with many values of another data element, but not vice versa.

Online analytical processing (OLAP)   OLAP is a loosely defined set of principles that provide a dimensional framework for business intelligence. The term *OLAP* also is used to define a confederation of vendors who offer nonrelational, multidimensional database products aimed at business intelligence. Contrast with *online transaction processing*.

Online transaction processing (OLTP)   The original description for all the activities and systems associated with entering data reliably into a database. Most frequently used with reference to relational databases, although OLTP can be used generically to describe any transaction processing environment. Contrast with *online analytical processing*.

Operational BI   Real time or near real time queries of operational status, often embedded in an application interface and accompanied by transaction write-back interfaces.

Operational data store (ODS)   A physical set of tables sitting between the operational systems and the data warehouse, or a specially administered hot partition of the data warehouse itself. The main reason for an ODS is to provide immediate reporting of operational results if neither the operational system nor the conventional data warehouse can provide satisfactory access. Because an ODS is necessarily an extract of the operational data, it also may play the role of source for the data warehouse. The term ODS has been used by many experts to mean many different things; as a result, the term is not very useful.

Outrigger table   A secondary dimension table attached to a dimension table. Contrast with *snowflake* which fully normalizes the dimension attributes.

Parent-child hierarchy   The use of a recursive, or self-referencing, mechanism to track the relationships in a hierarchy. An employee dimension may have a field that points to the manager's record in the employee dimension. Parent-child hierarchies are efficient, but difficult to query.

Parent-child transaction system   Hierarchical organization of data typically involving a header and set of line items, such as an order header and line item detail. The dimensional modeling approach strips all the information out of the header (parent) into separate dimensions and leaves the original parent natural key as a degenerate dimension.

Parsing   Decomposing operational fields, such as a name or address, into standard elemental parts.

Partitioned tables   Tables (and their associated indices) that are managed as physically separate tables but appear logically as a single table. Large fact tables are candidates for partitioning, often by date. Partitioning can improve both query and maintenance performance.

Periodic snapshot fact table   A type of fact table that represents business performance at the end of each regular, predictable time period. Daily snapshots and monthly snapshots are common. Snapshots are required in a number of businesses, such as insurance, where the transaction history is too complicated to be used as the basis for computing snapshots on the fly. A separate record is placed in a periodic snapshot fact table each period regardless of whether any activity has taken place in the underlying account. Contrast with *accumulating snapshot fact table* and *transaction fact table*.

Physical design   The phase of a database design following the logical design that identifies the actual database tables, columns, and index structures used to implement the logical design.

PK   See *Primary key*.

Portal   A website designed to be the first point of entry for visitors to the Web. Portal sites usually feature a wide variety of contents and search capabilities in order to entice visitors to use them. The BI portal is the business user entry point to the DW/BI system. See *BI portal*.

Power users   Highly capable analytic business users.

Presentation server   The database platforms where the data is stored for direct querying by business users, reporting systems, and other BI applications. The enterprise data warehouse includes one or more presentation servers which provide access to data from all major business processes at both the summary and atomic level, and serves as the single source for analytic data.

Primary key (PK)   A column or columns in a database table that uniquely identify each row in the table.

Process metadata   Metadata that describes the results of various operations in the warehouse. In the ETL process, each task logs key data about its execution, such as start time, end time, CPU seconds used, disk reads, disk writes, and rows processed. Similar process metadata is generated when users query the warehouse. Process metadata is accessed primarily by the DW/BI team. See *Metadata*, *Business metadata*, and *Technical metadata*.

Program   Ongoing coordination of resources, infrastructure, timelines, and communication across multiple projects; a program is an overall umbrella encompassing more than one project.

Quality screen   A component of the ETL system that acts as a diagnostic feature in the data flow to recognize and respond to data quality problems. See *Error event schema*.

Ragged hierarchy   A hierarchy with an unbalanced and arbitrarily deep structure that usually cannot be described in advance of loading the data. Sometimes referred to as a *variable depth hierarchy*. Organization charts often are ragged hierarchies. See *Bridge table*.

RDBMS   See *Relational database management system*.

Real time partitions   A physically separate and specially administered set of tables, apart from the conventional data warehouse, to support more real-time access requirements. See also *Operational data store*.

Referential integrity (RI)   Mandatory condition in a data warehouse where all the keys in the fact tables are legitimate foreign keys relative to the dimension tables. In other words, all the fact key components are subsets of the primary keys found in the dimension tables at all times.

Relational database management system (RDBMS)   Database management system based on the relational model that supports the full range of standard SQL. Uses a series of joined tables with rows and columns to organize and store data.

RI   See *Referential integrity*.

ROI   Return on investment, usually expressed as a rate describing the net growth of an investment during its lifetime.

Role-playing dimensions   Situation where a single physical dimension table appears several times in a single fact table. Each of the dimension roles is represented as a separate logical table with unique column names, usually implemented through views.

Roll up   To present higher levels of summarization. See *Drill up*.

SCD   See *Slowly changing dimensions*.

Schema   The logical or physical design of a set of database tables, indicating the relationship among the tables.

Semantic layer   An interface layer placed between the user's BI tool and the physical database structure.

Semi-additive (fact)   Numeric fact that can be added along some dimensions in a fact table but not others. Inventory levels and balances cannot be added along the date dimension but can be added along other dimensions.

Service oriented architecture (SOA)   An architecture that relies on service orientation as its fundamental design principle. In an SOA environment, independent services can be accessed without knowledge of their underlying platform implementation. As of this writing, significant issues such as providing acceptable security have not been solved in general SOA environments. Thus we regard SOA architecture as a promising but immature approach that bears watching over the next several years.

Six Sigma   Practices to systematically improve business processes by eliminating defects. It is widely accepted that a Six Sigma process produces fewer than 3.4 defective parts per million opportunities (DPMO). The Six Sigma methodology was originally formulated by Motorola in the 1980s based on the quality management and improvement work from W. Edwards Deming and others.

Slice and dice   Ability to access a data warehouse through any of its dimensions equally. Slicing and dicing is the process of separating and combining warehouse data in seemingly endless combinations.

Slowly changing dimensions (SCD)   The tendency of dimension attributes to change gradually or occasionally over time. There are three standard techniques for tracking attribute changes in a dimension. Type 1 overwrites the old value of the attribute with the new value. Type 2 creates a new row when the attribute changes. Type 3 adds an alternate column to the dimension to maintain the old value when the attribute changes.

Snapshot   See *Accumulating snapshot fact table* or *Periodic snapshot fact table*.

Snowflake   A normalized dimension where a flat, single table dimension is decomposed into a tree structure with potentially many nesting levels. In dimensional modeling, the fact tables in both a snowflake and star schema would be identical, but the dimensions in a snowflake are presented in third normal form. Although snowflaking can be regarded as an embellishment to the dimensional model, snowflaking generally compromises user understandability and browsing performance. Space savings typically are insignificant relative to the overall size of the data warehouse. Snowflaked normalized dimension tables may exist in the staging area to facilitate dimension maintenance.

SOA   See *Service oriented architecture*.

Source system   An operational system of record whose function it is to capture the transactions or other performance metrics from a business's processes. Alternatively, the source system may be external to the organization but is still capturing information that is needed in the data warehouse.

Sparse   A fact table that has relatively few of all the possible combinations of key values.

SQL   Structured Query Language, the standard language for accessing relational databases.

Standard reports   Regularly scheduled reports typically delivered as web-based reports, spreadsheets, or PDFs to an online library. The most common type of BI application.

Star schema   The generic representation of a dimensional model in a relational database in which a fact table with a composite key is joined to a number of single level dimension tables, each with a single primary key. Also called star join schema. See *Dimensional model*.

Stock keeping unit (SKU)   A standard term in manufacturing and retail environments to describe an individual product.

Surrogate key   Integer keys that are sequentially assigned as needed in the ETL system. In the dimension table, the surrogate key is the primary key. A surrogate key cannot be interpreted by itself; it is not a smart key. Surrogate keys are required in many data warehouse situations to handle slowly changing dimensions, as well as missing or inapplicable data. Also known as artificial keys, integer keys, meaningless keys, nonnatural keys, and synthetic keys.

System of record   The official operational source for a given data element or dataset. May not necessarily be a transaction system.

TCP/IP   Transmission Control Protocol/Internet Protocol, the basic communication protocol of the Internet, consisting of a transport layer (IP) and an application layer (TCP).

Technical metadata   The definitions of the objects and processes that make up the DW/BI system from a technical perspective. This includes the system metadata that defines the data structures themselves, such as tables, fields, data types, indexes, and partitions. Business users are interested in some technical metadata, but not all. See *Metadata*, *Business metadata*, and *Process metadata*.

Temporal inconsistency   Tendency of an OLTP database to change its primary data relationships from moment to moment as transactions are processed. The database is changing constantly and historical values are not necessarily preserved.

Third normal form (3NF)   Database design approach that eliminates redundancy and therefore facilitates updates and insertion of new rows into tables in an OLTP application without introducing excessive data locking problems. Sometimes referred to as normalized. See *Normalize.*

Time stamping   Tagging each record with the time the data was processed or stored.

Topology   The organization of physical devices and connections in a system.

Transaction fact table   A type of fact table in which the fact table granularity is one row for the lowest level of detail captured by a transaction. A record in a transaction fact table is present only if a transaction event actually occurs. The transaction fact table is the most common type of fact table in a DW/BI system. Contrast with *periodic snapshot fact table* and *accumulating snapshot fact table.*

Type 1 SCD   A slowly changing dimension (SCD) technique where the changed attribute is overwritten. History is lost.

Type 2 SCD   A slowly changing dimension (SCD) technique where a new dimension record with a new surrogate key is created to reflect the change. History is preserved.

Type 3 SCD   A slowly changing dimension (SCD) technique where a new column is added to the dimension table to capture the change. An "alternate reality" is created. History may be lost.

UNICODE   The UNICODE worldwide character standard is a character coding system designed to support the interchange, processing, and display of the written texts of the diverse languages of the modern world, including Japanese, Chinese, Arabic, Hebrew, Cyrillic, and many others. UNICODE is a 16-bit implementation, which means that database columns defined using UNICODE will be twice as wide as their corresponding ASCII columns.

Up-selling   Selling a product or service to an existing customer, where the goal is to get the customer to purchase a more expensive or higher value version than previously purchased or requested. See *Cross-selling.*

UTC   Coordinated Universal Time, an international standard for time. For practical DW/BI purposes, UTC is analogous to GMT, but it's based on the atomic clock.

Value banding (facts)   Grouping facts into flexible value bands as specified in a band definition table.

Value chain   Sequence of business processes that describe the movement of products or services through a pipeline from original creation to final sales.

Variable depth hierarchy   See *Ragged hierarchy*.

VIEW (SQL)   SQL statement that creates logical copies of a table or a complete query that can be used separately in a SELECT statement. Views are semantically independent, so the separate roles of a role-playing dimension usually are implemented as views.

Weighted report   When using a bridge table, the facts in the fact table are multiplied by the bridge table's weighting factor to appropriately allocate the facts to the many-valued dimension. Contrast with *impact report*.

XML   See *Extensible Markup Language*.

XML/A   XML for Analysis, a standard specification of querying and some management activities for OLAP databases. Several OLAP vendors, but not all, support XML/A in their products. The XML/A specification includes the query language MDX.

Index

C